C# Design and Development E… One-on-One™

Part V: Resources and Tools

Expert One-on-One™

C# Design and Development

Expert One-on-One™

C# Design and Development

John Paul Mueller

WILEY

Wiley Publishing, Inc.

C# Design and Development Expert One-on-One™

Published by
Wiley Publishing, Inc.
10475 Crosspoint Boulevard
Indianapolis, IN 46256
www.wiley.com

Published simultaneously in Canada
ISBN: 978-0-470-41596-2
Manufactured in the United States of America

10 9 8 7 6 5 4 3 2 1

Library of Congress Cataloging-in-Publication Data

Mueller, John, 1958-
C# design and development : expert one-on-one / John P. Mueller.
p. cm.
Includes index.
ISBN 978-0-470-41596-2 (paper/website)
1. C# (Computer program language) I. Title.
QA76.73.C154M83 2009
005.13'3--dc22
2009000840

This book is dedicated to my wife Rebecca: a gift from God, regiven as I complete this book.

About the Author

John Mueller is a freelance author and technical editor. He has writing in his blood, having produced 82 books and more than 300 articles to date. The topics range from networking to artificial intelligence and from database management to heads-down programming. Some of his current books include a Windows power optimization book, books on both Windows Server 2008 GUI and Windows Server 2008 Server Core (*Administering Windows Server 2008 Server Core*), and a programmer's guide that discusses the new Office Fluent User Interface (RibbonX). His technical editing skills have helped more than 58 authors refine the content of their manuscripts. John has provided technical editing services to both *DataBased Advisor* and *Coast Compute* magazines. He's also contributed articles to the following magazines: *CIO.com, DevSource, InformIT, Informant, DevX, SQL Server Professional, Visual C++ Developer, Hard Core Visual Basic, asp.netPRO, Software Test and Performance,* and *Visual Basic Developer.*

When John isn't working at the computer, he enjoys spending time in his workshop crafting wood projects or making candles. On any given afternoon, you can find him working at a lathe or putting the finishing touches on a bookcase. He also likes making glycerin soap, which comes in handy for gift baskets. You can reach John on the Internet at `JMueller@mwt.net`. He is also setting up a Web site and blog at `http://www.johnmuellerbooks.com/`; feel free to look and make suggestions on how he can improve it.

About the Technical Editors

Russ Mullen has been consulting and programming for more years than he cares to remember. He has tech edited more than 70 books, ghost-written chapters, and coauthored several books.

Robert Fayman has been developing and maintaining applications for the past 10 years. Although his programming language of choice is C#, he often spends more time maintaining code written in Classic ASP and PHP, to name two. He also spends many hours researching the newest technologies, trying to find more tools for his toolbox. When not behind the computer, he enjoys spending time with his wife, two sons, dog, and cat.

Credits

Acquisitions Editor
Katie Mohr

Development Editor
William Bridges

Technical Editors
Russ Mullen and Robert Fayman

Production Editors
Tim Tate and Amy Weintraub

Copy Editor
Cheryl Hauser

Editorial Manager
Mary Beth Wakefield

Production Manager
Tim Tate

Vice President and Executive Group Publisher
Richard Swadley

Vice President and Executive Publisher
Barry Pruett

Associate Publisher
Jim Minatel

Project Coordinator, Cover
Lynsey Stanford

Compositor
Craig Johnson, Happenstance Type-O-Rama

Proofreader
Publication Services, Inc.

Indexer
Jack Lewis

Acknowledgments

Thanks to my wife, Rebecca, for working with me to get this book completed. I really don't know what I would have done without her help in researching and compiling some of the information that appears in this book. She also did a fine job of proofreading most of my rough draft.

Russ Mullen and Robert Fayman deserve thanks for their technical edit of this book. Both technical editors added greatly to the accuracy and depth of the material that you see here, each in his own way. I appreciated the time the technical editors devoted to checking my text, especially the code, for accuracy. As I wrote this book, I also spent a good deal of time bouncing ideas off the two technical editors, which is a valuable aid to any author.

Matt Wagner, my agent, deserves credit for helping me get the contract in the first place and taking care of all the details that most authors don't consider. I always appreciate his assistance. It's good to know that someone wants to help.

A number of people read all or part of this book to help me refine the approach, test the examples, and generally provide input that all readers wish they could have. These unpaid volunteers helped in ways too numerous to mention here. I especially appreciate the efforts of Eva Beattie, Osvaldo Téllez Almirall, and all of the others who provided input on this book. I'd like to thank each person by name who wrote me with an idea, but there are simply too many.

Finally, I would like to thank Katie Mohr, William Bridges, Amy Weintraub, Cheryl Hauser, and the rest of the editorial and production staff for their assistance in bringing this book to print. It's always nice to work with such a great group of professionals.

Contents

Introduction

Anyone can write code given enough training, but very few developers can use code to write a great application. In fact, it's highly likely that many developers don't even know what constitutes a great application. Over the years, developers have bought into the idea that great applications contain many features and users are very aware of all the flexibility the application provides. It's like a really bright light that no one can ignore and it actually detracts from the user experience because it distracts the user from doing something useful. My idea of a great application is one that's like a light switch. Anyone can figure out a light switch and most of us don't think twice about turning it on. In fact, many of us use light switches without even realizing we're using them — the thought of the light switch doesn't even exist.

Imagine the user experience of an application that is so simple, so elemental, that anyone can figure it out. Yet, the application does everything the user needs to accomplish a given task and has the speed to perform the task quickly. You may think that such an application is a myth, but *C# Design and Development* tells you how to create it. This book is all about practical design. Sure, I've gone completely against the grain of some academic books out there, but the fact that users are still confused by applications tells me that we need a new book — this is that book. Solidly constructed applications help users perform tasks in light switch mode — they don't have more than a passing thought about the entire experience.

The practical information provided in this book helps you, the developer, too, especially if you're working in a team environment. Imagine experiencing fewer development problems, getting tasks done on time, and maintaining your sanity during the application process. *C# Design and Development* tells you how to accomplish all of these tasks and many more. For example, you'll discover that there are many ways to design applications, not just the technique you may have learned in school. In addition, you'll discover the best techniques for specific application types, making it easier for you to create good designs from the outset.

The reason you need *C# Design and Development* is that you can use it to create better applications, faster, and with less turmoil. The applications you create will require less maintenance and will actually deliver what they promise. You'll get all this just by reading this tome. It's hard to imagine getting such value in any other book. (Of course, I'm assuming you'll actually follow the book's advice to obtain all of the benefits it can provide.)

Whom This Book Is For

This book is for anyone who writes applications. Even though there are many references to team development, most of the information in this book also applies to consultants or lone developers in an organization. Everyone who writes applications, even as a hobby, will want this book because it speaks to all developers. Although some of the examples are quite advanced, even beginning and intermediate developers will be able to understand the concepts in Parts I through III (the advanced examples in Part IV really are for the expert).

What This Book Covers

C# Design and Development discusses a number of design issues. You'll find all the expected topics covered, such as determining which design strategy to use in a given situation. This book also discusses your application's lifecycle and how to ensure your application has proper support throughout the lifecycle. Some topics are specific to teams, such as how to choose team members and approaches you can use to keep team members happy and working together.

Part of the book discusses the unexpected or perhaps simply the new. For example, you'll discover a new concept called the performance triangle, which consists of speed, reliability, and security. No other book that I know of uses this concept to consider how to create balanced applications that actually do meet user expectations. Speaking of the user, you'll likely find that this book has more than a few new ideas on how to deal with users as well. Much of this new material is the result of in-depth research, surveys, and other information gathered over a relatively long time. It's interesting to know how things work in the real world versus the theories expressed in the classroom.

Part IV of this book is special. This part of the book examines some techniques you can use to create better applications using less code. In some cases, the techniques also help you work around potential limitations in the .NET Framework. This section isn't for everyone, and you probably won't use the techniques in every project. These techniques address specific issues that you'll face with particular projects. I based the choices in this part of the book on reader surveys collected over the last several years. If you don't find the technique you wanted, feel free to contact me at `JMueller@mwt.net` and ask for a survey — I really do use them to create better books.

One of the most asked questions is how to find decent tools. Everyone knows that there are more tools out there than any developer could test in a lifetime (and by that time, the information collected would prove useless). Part V of the book addresses the tool needs that every developer has and helps you locate that perfect tool.

How This Book Is Structured

I wanted to make this book approachable and easy. Many design and development books make the whole process seem difficult, and many of them stick to academic principles that don't work in a real-world environment. This book is designed so that you can either read it cover-to-cover or use it as a reference. I broke the book into parts that consider particular development issues. In addition, the parts follow the basic development process, from design to release. Here are the parts and an explanation what they'll do for you:

- **Part I: Design Strategies:** This part focuses on the problem of designing the application. However, it goes far beyond simple design. This part of the book also considers how to build a good development team — how to locate just the right people for your particular application. In addition, this part of the book spends considerable time reviewing the needs of all of the stakeholders in an application — everyone from the developers who build it, to management, to users, to clients who require the output of the application. Finally, this part of the book helps you create a balanced design — one that won't disappoint by being unreliable or not providing enough security.

- **Part II: Coding Strategies:** This part focuses on the implementation process. Now that you have a great design, it's time to create an application based on that design. This part actually begins by exploring your work environment. Many developers don't optimize their work environment and therefore find their work difficult. Once you have a great work environment, you can begin coding. This part also explores the debugging, testing, and Quality Assurance (QA) processes. Finally, you discover the ins and outs of deploying your completed applications. Unfortunately, deployment is where many other books end — this book also includes a chapter on maintaining your application after you put it into production.
- **Part III: Speed, Reliability, and Security:** This part of the book focuses on the requirements for building and maintaining a balanced application. The performance triangle, which consists of speed, reliability, and security, is an essential part of the application development and maintenance process. If you don't maintain a balance, you'll find that your application performs poorly and that people won't like using it. Maintaining balance is part art and part science — this part of the book helps you understand both.
- **Part IV: Special Coding Methodologies:** I've written many applications since I graduated from college 22 years ago. In addition, I've kept records of hundreds of reader surveys and researched a host of material online. This part of the book reflects the most common special coding techniques that developers require. As previously mentioned, you may not ever need these techniques or you may even feel that you don't want to use them. This part of the book isn't for everyone, but it does have practical advice on how to accomplish seemingly impossible tasks when you need to do them.
- **Part V: Resources and Tools:** Everyone needs resources and tools to accomplish their programming goals — the Visual Studio environment simply doesn't provide enough resources and tools for you to get the job done in many cases. This last part of the book answers the question of how to find a good resource or tool. It examines both Microsoft products and the products you can obtain from third parties. You'll also find reviews of some tools that I personally find useful. I encourage you to do as this part of the book says — have a bit of fun filling your toolbox with the resources and tools you like best.

What You Need to Use This Book

You have to have a copy of Visual Studio 2008 with C# installed to use this book. I'm assuming that you're using either Windows XP or Vista to use the book, but it should also work with older versions of Windows. (I haven't tested anything with older versions, however.)

I used the Visual Studio 2008 Team System edition to write the book. If you have a different edition of the product, you can expect to see some differences in your screenshots and may find a few minor menu differences. Don't worry; your version of Visual Studio 2008 will work just fine. Each of the book's technical editors used a different edition of the product and verified that the examples worked as intended. In addition, I received edition difference information from a number of the beta readers, so even though I used the Visual Studio 2008 Team System edition and the chapters reflect this fact, the information will work with other editions as well.

You also need to know how to write C# code. This isn't a book about writing code — it's a book about designing and developing applications that really work. If you don't have some experience writing C#

code, then this book is going to prove confusing for you and you should probably look for a language book before you begin using this one.

Conventions

To help you get the most from the text and keep track of what's happening, we've used some conventions throughout the book. A typical example follows:

Notes, tips, hints, tricks, and asides to the current discussion are offset and placed in italics like this.

As for styles in the text:

- We *highlight* new terms and important words when we introduce them.
- We show keyboard strokes like this: Ctrl+A.
- We show file names, URLs, and code within the text like so: `persistence.properties`.
- We present code in the following way

```
We use a monofont type with no highlighting for most code examples.
```

Source Code

As you work through the examples in this book, you may choose either to type in all the code manually or to use the source code files that accompany the book. All of the source code used in this book is available for download at `http://www.wrox.com`. Once at the site, simply locate the book's title (either by using the Search box or by using one of the title lists) and click the Download Code link on the book's detail page to obtain all the source code for the book.

Because many books have similar titles, you may find it easiest to search by ISBN; this book's ISBN is 978-0-470-41596-2.

Once you download the code, just decompress it with your favorite compression tool. Alternately, you can go to the main Wrox code download page at `http://www.wrox.com/dynamic/books/download.aspx` to see the code available for this book and all other Wrox books.

Errata

We make every effort to ensure that there are no errors in the text or in the code. However, no one is perfect, and mistakes do occur. If you find an error in one of our books, like a spelling mistake or faulty piece of code, we would be very grateful for your feedback. By sending in errata you may save another reader hours of frustration and at the same time you will be helping us provide even higher quality information.

To find the errata page for this book, go to `http://www.wrox.com` and locate the title using the Search box or one of the title lists. Then, on the Book Search Results page, click the Errata link. On this page you can view all errata that has been submitted for this book and posted by Wrox editors.

A complete book list including links to each book's errata is also available at `www.wrox.com/misc-pages/booklist.shtml`.

If you don't spot "your" error on the Errata page, click the Errata Form link and complete the form to send us the error you have found. We'll check the information and, if appropriate, post a message to the book's errata page and fix the problem in subsequent editions of the book.

p2p.wrox.com

For author and peer discussion, join the P2P forums at `p2p.wrox.com`. The forums are a Web-based system for you to post messages relating to Wrox books and related technologies and interact with other readers and technology users. The forums offer a subscription feature to e-mail you topics of interest of your choosing when new posts are made to the forums. Wrox authors, editors, other industry experts, and your fellow readers are present on these forums.

At `http://p2p.wrox.com` you will find a number of different forums that will help you not only as you read this book, but also as you develop your own applications. To join the forums, just follow these steps:

1. Go to `p2p.wrox.com` and click the Register link.
2. Read the terms of use and click Agree.
3. Complete the required information to join as well as any optional information you wish to provide and click Submit.
4. You will receive an e-mail with information describing how to verify your account and complete the joining process.

You can read messages in the forums without joining P2P but in order to post your own messages, you must join.

Once you join, you can post new messages and respond to messages other users post. You can read messages at any time on the Web. If you would like to have new messages from a particular forum e-mailed to you, click the Subscribe to this Forum icon by the forum name in the forum listing.

For more information about how to use the Wrox P2P, be sure to read the P2P FAQs for answers to questions about how the forum software works as well as many common questions specific to P2P and Wrox books. To read the FAQs, click the FAQ link on any P2P page.

Part I: Design Strategies

1

Defining the Language Environment

Most professional programmers use more than one programming language. A programmer who relies on a single language for every task is like a carpenter who treats everything as a nail. Just as carpenters use a particular fastener for a specific need, programmers rely on programming languages that suit an individual development need. This chapter approaches the use of a particular programming language to meet a specific need in a development environment. Throughout the chapter, you discover how the language environment determines not only which language will work best but also how you interact with the language you select.

In some cases, you use multiple languages in a single application. Although the use of multiple languages tends to increase complexity, using the right tool for the job also tends to make the work easier. Just as a carpenter relies on both hammers and screwdrivers to build a bookcase, a programmer may use multiple languages to make creating a particular application easier. Just as the carpenter could use nails for every need on the bookcase, but will obtain a poorer result by doing so, the developer often achieves poor results by using just one programming language. This chapter views the use of multiple languages in the context of the language environment and as a prerequisite for application design.

Understanding the language environment means that you can take the next step in designing your application, which is to determine what resources you have available. Even if you're working by yourself, you must consider the language resources you have, because most developers aren't completely fluent in every aspect of all the languages they use. You may decide to learn a new development technique in order to use a particular language or live with a less than optimal language environment in order to rely on a language you use well. Defining available resources is critical in the team environment because you need to know what individual team members can do to advance the project before you design it. This chapter describes a process of inventorying the tools at your disposal and then gathering them for use in the application design and development process.

Defining the Design Strategy Elements

It's natural to say at the outset of a project that you want to accomplish a particular task. You don't know how you'll accomplish it at this point, but simply that you plan to accomplish it. Before you can define a language environment, you have to have some idea of what you want to accomplish. In many cases, you need to consider some rudimentary steps to accomplish your goal as well. For example, you may want to write an application that retrieves data from a Web service, performs some analysis on that data, and presents it to the user. Each of these tasks forms a design strategy element for your application.

Developers can become stuck in a rut when it comes to programming languages. When you talk to someone who's used Visual Basic exclusively, that person can normally tell you about all the inadequacies of C# in detail without too much thought. Likewise, developers who use C# exclusively often see the warts found in Visual Basic quite easily. A developer who takes time to learn both C# and Visual Basic will tell you that each has some distinct advantages and disadvantages, but that you can develop most applications using either language.

However, some languages do provide a specific set of features that differ from common programming languages. For example, you can use F# (I'll describe this new Microsoft language later in the chapter) to perform list processing, pattern matching, and other forms of analysis. Microsoft even makes it easy to combine C# or Visual Basic with F# so that you can obtain the best of both languages in a single application. When you consider the sample application described earlier in this section, you could use:

- C# to obtain the data from the Web service
- F# to process that data
- C# to display the data to the user

This second case points out a scenario where using multiple languages is more than a political statement; it's a necessity to make application development as easy as possible. The advanced features of a language can easily offset the added complexity of using multiple languages in many cases.

Don't assume that a developer on your team has experience in only one or two languages. The use of a particular language by the developer may simply indicate that the company hired the developer to use the language. Many developers have experience in multiple languages. For example, even though I mainly work with Visual Basic and C#, I have also worked with everything from Assembler and ROM BASIC to LISP and Prolog. I've worked relatively often with PHP, Java, and C++ as well. However, unless someone asks me about my skill set, they may simply assume my language knowledge includes mainly Visual Basic and C#.

Of course, you need someone on your development team with F# experience to write an application that uses F# for analysis purposes. Depending on the inventory you conduct, you may find that all your developers know C# or Visual Basic. In this case, the optimal language environment doesn't use F#, but you should still consider using the best language for the job at the outset of the planning process.

Your strategy has to consider the developers in your team, even if you have a team of one. You don't want to create an application where half the team twiddles its collective thumbs waiting for the other half of the team to complete a process. An application development effort may require that you write the low-level code using C# and the user display elements in Visual Basic. With proper planning, you can move the development process along rapidly by letting each team complete the part of the application most suited to its particular language.

Considering the C# Language

This book is about using the C# language to develop applications of various types. You'll work through the particulars of designing an application that relies on C# as its main language. C# is a great language for many uses. For example, it's possibly the best language that Microsoft makes available for developing applications that use a combination of native code and managed libraries. The Platform Invoke (P/Invoke) capability of C# is significantly better than other Microsoft languages. However, C# isn't a perfect language, so you need to understand its deficiencies and consider how you can use other languages to overcome these deficiencies. The following sections discuss these issues.

Understanding the Benefits

In many respects, C# and Visual Basic.NET are very much alike. Both contain all the common coding elements you might expect. It's possible to create conditional statements, loops, structures, classes, and all the other common elements found in applications using either language. The fact that the syntax differs slightly between languages isn't a major concern. However, C# does possess certain benefits not found in Visual Basic.NET that may affect your decision to use C# as your main programming language. The following sections discuss each of these benefits and define why you should consider them when defining your language environment.

C/C++-Like Syntax

The future of development for most organizations is some type of managed code. Using the .NET Framework provides a considerable number of benefits when compared to native code languages such as C++. For example, working with a managed application means that the developer no longer needs to worry about memory allocated for managed needs because garbage collection handles that requirement for the developer. The vast number of viruses and other nasty software on the market that rely on memory errors to do their dirty work attests to the need for this kind of automated memory allocation arrangement.

Unfortunately, most organizations can't simply drop all their native code in favor of a managed alternative. Consequently, you may find that you need to maintain that C++ code sitting in your library for quite some time. Because C# and C/C++ share so many syntax features, it's easy for C/C++ developers to move between C# and C/C++ as needed. The transition isn't without some learning curve, but the curve is significantly smaller than moving to some other language. It really is relatively easy to write code using C# one day and C/C++ the next.

While it's possible to create managed code using C++, most developers consider the process extremely difficult. Unlike other .NET languages, C++ requires that you follow some absurd coding practices. Most developers prefer to use C# when needed to create managed applications.

It's important to note that the brace construction used to delimit blocks of code in C# also appears in a number of other languages such as Java and JavaScript. In fact, there are enough similarities with these other languages that a C# developer can probably learn Java or JavaScript with relative ease when compared to learning a language that relies on other construction techniques such as Visual Basic.

The designers of C# and Java both wanted to improve on some primary problems with C++. Here's a list of some of the features that C# and Java share that help you create a better language environment than using C++ as your language of choice (you can find some other interesting comparisons at `http://www.softsteel.co.uk/tutorials/cSharp/lesson2.html` and `http://blogs.msdn.com/ericgu/archive/2005/01/26/360879.aspx`):

- Both languages compile into machine-independent byte code that runs in a managed environment. Although the .NET Framework runs exclusively on Windows today, you can run the C# Intermediate Language (IL) code on other platforms such as Linux using alternative environments such as Mono (`http://www.mono-project.com/Main_Page`).
- Memory errors occur less often because both languages rely on garbage collection to manage memory.
- You can view the internal workings of applications created with either language using reflection.
- Applications have less code because neither language requires that you use header files.
- Using classes is less cumbersome because classes are scoped to packages or assemblies. In addition, you don't have to worry about the order in which classes appear in the application. Classes also descend from objects and you allocate them from the heap using the `new` keyword.
- It's possible to lock threads with ease, providing superior thread synchronization.
- A class can contain another class to provide inner classes.
- Some potential runtime errors are avoided by eliminating global variables — every variable is part of a class. In addition, both languages provide bounds checking for arrays and strings, making some types of application bugs exploitable by virus writers a thing of the past.
- Both languages rely on the `.` operator to separate object elements. You no longer need to worry about whether to use the `::` or `->` operators.
- Both languages provide full support for the `null` and `boolean`/`bool` keywords.
- The managed environment automatically initializes all values before use, so you won't have any of those mystery values from C++ pop up.
- All conditional statements rely on a Boolean comparison, rather than using `integer` values directly.
- `Try` blocks provide support for a `Finally` clause that lets you perform cleanup even if a code sequence fails, which should help eliminate memory and state problems.

This list isn't meant to provide you with a complete comparison between C#, Java, and C++, but it does illustrate that there are important issues to consider as part of defining the language environment for your application. You may find situations where C++, despite its deficiencies, is still the language of choice for a particular situation. Knowing the deficiencies of each language in your arsenal is important because this knowledge helps you make the right language choice.

Unsafe Code Capability

The Common Language Runtime (CLR) constantly monitors everything your managed application does, which makes the code more reliable. CLR considers managed code safe because you can't do things like add pointers together or perform other kinds of pointer arithmetic found in older languages such as C/C++. In the past, using pointers led to all kinds of problems, including memory corruption, so modern applications generally don't perform direct pointer manipulation. In fact, direct pointer manipulation doesn't work with .NET applications because the garbage collector constantly changes the pointer addresses (which is the reason you must pin and unpin `IntPtr` managed pointers when making P/Invoke calls).

Unfortunately, you still have the vast array of native-code applications to consider when designing your applications. You may need to access Windows directly to perform some tasks or work with an older DLL where pointer manipulation is required. When you encounter this situation, you have two choices. You could wrap the code you need in a C++ DLL and make it available to your applications using P/Invoke in a manner that doesn't require the use of unsafe code. The second choice is to work with the older code directly and place the pointer code within an unsafe code block. C# is one of the few managed languages that let you use unsafe code blocks. You can find a useful tutorial on using unsafe code blocks at `http://www.csharp-tutorials.com/unsafe-code-execution/`.

In-Depth Debugging

Generally, you'll find that the C# debugger provides more information than the Visual Basic debugger, provided you're working with the same application in both debuggers. This section also bases its appraisal of C# on the use of the Microsoft debugger. If you use a third-party product, you may find that it provides more or less capability than the Microsoft product.

Some things work the same between Visual Basic and C# — a loop is still a loop. However, you'll notice a difference when working with some complex development problems. For example, a Language Integrated Query (LINQ) call in C# always shows every step of the process used to create the query results. In some cases, Visual Basic shortcuts the process and shows only a few of the steps, making it harder to diagnose problems with your LINQ statement.

Of course, the question is whether you always need the complete attention that C# provides. The answer depends on your application. As application complexity increases and you use more advanced language features, the requirement for a debugger that provides in-depth information also increases.

The debugging differences with other languages extend to other needs. C# usually makes it easy to drill down into an object to any level. This accessibility means that you spend less time trying to figure out what an object actually contains. In some cases, you have to work hard with other languages to determine what an object contains, especially when an object resides within another object.

Additional IntelliSense Functionality

When you create your own applications, you can use the triple comment `///` symbol in C# to create a documentation block where you fill out information for various application elements such as classes and functions. Visual Basic.NET 2008 adds this feature as the `'''` symbol. After you add these special code blocks, you can set the compiler to create an eXtensible Markup Language (XML) file containing detailed information about your application. However, C# still provides superior IntelliSense support for these special XML files, which means that C# provides better IntelliSense support for the code you write.

C# also provides multiline comments, a feature it shares with C++. If you want to create a multiline comment for Visual Basic, you must start each comment line individually.

Coding Additions

C# supports a number of coding additions — features that you won't necessarily find in other managed development languages. One of the more useful is the availability of strong iterator support, including the `yield` keyword. When an application iterates a collection, the `yield` keyword helps the developer control how the iteration occurs and can stop the iteration as needed.

Anonymous methods make it possible to create applications that run faster and require less code as well. An anonymous method is literally a method that has no name. The method appears in-line in place of the usual method reference. Using anonymous methods can also make it easier to debug the code because the code appears in-line where the developer can easily see it during a debugging session.

In some cases, you want to place an interface definition in multiple files. Unlike other .NET languages, C# lets you use the `partial` keyword with:

- `class`
- `struct`
- `interface`
- Method names

Sometimes you want to make class code available without requiring the developer to create an instance of the class. C# supports a static class for this purpose. For example, a math class may not have any properties or state information to maintain, so a static class works just fine. In this case, all members of the class are also static, which means you can access them directly. (A Visual Basic module is a close cousin of this feature.)

You'll also find a few coding niceties in C#. For example, C# uses the = operator for assignment and the == operator for comparison. Using different symbols for each purpose makes their use clearer in your code and helps avoid potential misinterpretations.

Exploding Developer Mind Share

At one time, most developers acknowledged that Visual Basic held a surprising lead in languages that most developers would know. However, C# seems to be gathering an increasing level of developer mind share and has possibly overtaken Visual Basic as the modern favorite. According to a *Visual Studio* magazine survey (`http://visualstudiomagazine.com/columns/article.aspx?editorialsid=2333`), 41 percent of the developers polled now use C#, contrasted to 34 percent for Visual Basic. Of course, this is only one survey, but other hints abound. For example, Microsoft often makes examples available for new technologies in C#, rather than Visual Basic as it did in the past.

For the purposes of this book, it doesn't matter whether C# or Visual Basic is the new developer mind-share king. What does matter is that using C# means you can find the developers you need for a project with greater ease when using either C# or Visual Basic than when using other languages. In short, using C# provides a big advantage in locating the specific skills your project requires. Given that many of the new C# developers on the market are converts from Visual Basic, you may very well find that the C# developer you hire to help with a project also has Visual Basic knowledge, giving you essentially two developers for the price of one.

Understanding the Deficiencies

Every programming language has a deficiency or two. The very act of addressing one need necessarily means that the language isn't addressing another requirement. C# tends to provide lower level functionality than Visual Basic, but it isn't quite as low level as C++. Consequently, C# tends to cover the middle ground of programming well, but you may find areas where you really need another language to get the desired result. The following sections describe some C# deficiencies you should consider when you begin developing your language environment.

Code Reliability Concerns

When you add the power to work with unsafe code to any language, you also make it possible for the developer to create unreliable code. The low-level functionality that makes C# attractive also makes it a dangerous tool in the wrong hands. A developer needs to know how pointers work before using them in a production environment. The detailed level of debugging that C# provides is only useful when the developer understands what the debugging displays are showing. It's possible for a well-meaning developer to create a terrifying time bomb using the wrong techniques in C#.

C# also assumes developer proficiency in other areas. For example, Visual Basic checks math operations and provides the developer with feedback about errors that result in overflows or underflows. By default, C# doesn't check numeric operations. The result is an application that can execute faster than a comparable Visual Basic application, but this feature is only useful in experienced hands. You can overcome this C# deficiency by using the `checked` and `unchecked` contexts within your application.

Another potential code reliability concern is that C# doesn't automatically correct variable name punctuation. If you use the wrong case for a variable name in Visual Basic, the Integrated Development Environment (IDE) automatically corrects the name to use the correct case. Consequently, you could write a C# application that contains `myVariable`, `Myvariable`, and `MyVariable`, all three of which are different variables.

Visual Basic has its own code reliability concern in that strong typing is optional. Without strong typing, an application can handle data incorrectly and corrupt them. Fortunately, the default in Visual Basic is to rely on strong typing. In addition, converting `True` *to a numeric value could yield* `1` *or* `-1` *depending on the conversion used.*

Too Much Information

A Visual Basic developer doesn't see anything other than essential information. Although the Visual Basic developer can optionally reveal this information, the default is to keep the programming environment simple. Consequently, while a C# developer spends time looking through unneeded entries, the Visual Basic developer can locate a needed item quickly. For example, Visual Basic hides certain project files from Solution Explorer and hides namespace information from the editing area.

Microsoft has embraced information hiding as a means of simplifying interfaces. The information hiding appears more often in user applications such as Office (where, as an example, unused menu options disappear from view), but it's interesting to see how the same approach can help developers. Of course, information hiding also means that a developer has to search for a particular item on the few occasions the item is necessary for development. Consequently, information hiding is a two-edged sword that normally works for the developer, but on rare occasions can turn against the developer as well.

Coding Complexities

Anyone will tell you that C# isn't as complex as C++ when it comes to creating programming constructs, but you'll also discover that languages such as Visual Basic make coding even easier. For example, creating delegates is considerably simpler in Visual Basic than in C# because Visual Basic lets you use `AddressOf MyObject.MyFunction` to access the delegate function.

One of the major missing elements in C# is optional parameters. Both Visual Basic and C++ support optional parameters. The lack of this feature makes it considerably harder to create Office applications using C#. In addition, C# lacks support for variables in property methods, which may make it harder to create certain classes of application.

Visual Basic provides a convenience item not found in C#. You receive automatic wire-up of events with event handlers using the handlers construct. Although this is a small feature, it does improve developer efficiency and makes it possible to see the wire-up in the same place that the event handler appears.

Developing with Multiple Languages

Most applications you create use a single language because this tends to reduce the cost of updates later, and using a single language makes the code significantly more manageable. However, your team may consist of a mix of developers, in which case, using the languages that each developer knows will make the development process faster. In addition, some languages do provide capabilities that are not robust enough. For example, even though C# does provide great P/Invoke functionality, you may still find an occasion to use C++ for native code modules. The three languages commonly used with C# are:

- Visual Basic.NET
- Visual C++
- F#

Of course, you can use any language you want with C#. Some developers use IronPython (see `http://www.codeplex.com/Wiki/View.aspx?ProjectName=IronPython` for details) with C# when they need Python flexibility matched with .NET capability. The following sections describe some of the benefits of using additional languages.

Using Visual Basic.NET

Some organizations view Visual Basic.NET with disdain due to its naming similarity with the ancient BASIC language. The two languages couldn't be more different. Visual Basic.NET provides significant capability and exceptional development performance. The fact that Visual Basic.NET often hides complexity that C# developers must deal with as part of their development environment means that you can use it to create code fast. Visual Basic.NET also tends to protect the programmer more from accidents that C# developers must keep in mind, such as numeric overflows. It isn't a bad idea to require less-proficient developers to use Visual Basic.NET until they gain experience.

Using C++

It's easy to think that C++ has seen better days and then relegate it to the dustbin alongside COBOL and FORTRAN. Interesting as it may seem, companies today are actually looking for a few COBOL and FORTRAN programmers to maintain the huge mass of code written in an earlier time for mainframes that still work today. In fact, you can read an article about the need for COBOL programmers in California at `http://weblog.infoworld.com/tech-bottom-line/archives/2008/08/calling_all_cob.html?source=NLC-DAILY&cgd=2008-08-07`. C++ is an older language, but it's also a capable language that can help you bridge the gap between the managed programming environment and Windows.

Using C++ is almost mandatory in some cases. For example, if you have a real-time application that works with specialized equipment, such as factory automation, C++ is almost a required part of your application development plans. C# does provide better capabilities than most .NET languages for working with low-level code, but it can't fulfill every low-level need easily. The coding becomes quite messy at some point with a host of unsafe code sections. You may as well use C++, a language designed to get the low-level programming task done.

Using F#

In many cases, you need to work with data in new ways in today's applications. For example, most systems today come with multiple processors, but most programming languages don't use this capability very well. F# is a new language that joins other functional languages such as ML (`http://en.wikipedia.org/wiki/ML_programming_language`), OCaml (`http://caml.inria.fr/`), and Haskell (`http://www.haskell.org/`). A functional language differs from an imperative language such as C# or Visual Basic.NET in that it works with equations. You can't assign values to F# identifiers — the value of an identifier always remains the same. However, you can interact with that identifier in a number of ways to analyze the identifier and deduce new results from existing data.

The reason you want to add F# to your repertoire is that it lets you use those multiple processors in your system with extreme efficiency. Because an F# identifier never changes value, it doesn't matter which processor works with it. You don't have to worry about state information either. The lack of tracking baggage means that F# applications are quite fast, too. In short, F# adds a new dimension to your application development environment that differs from many other languages you use. You can find a good overview of F# at `http://www.devsource.com/c/a/Languages/Exploring-the-New-F-Language/`.

Multiple Platform Scenarios

Multiple platform scenarios are becoming more common as companies merge and developers see a need to explore open source. Fortunately, you can still use C# for your project while also working with Java and back-end servers such as IBM WebSphere. Although the tools are a bit hard to find, vendors such as Mainsoft (makers of Visual MainWin, `http://www.mainsoft.com/products/index.aspx`) can make things work in a multi-platform environment. You can read a review about Visual MainWin at `http://www.devsource.com/c/a/Add-Ons/Mainsoft-ASPNET-AJAX-Linux/`.

Fortunately, you have a number of options in a multiple platform environment. Although Visual MainWin allows complete sharing of code between platforms, you could also rely on Web services or other techniques when the need for code sharing is minimal and you don't require the ultimate in application speed. Vendors also provide a number of bridging tools, such as JNBridge (`http://www.jnbridge.com/`) that offer a middle bound between the full cross-compiler solutions and Web services.

No matter what kind of multiple platform solution you use, it does affect the language environment to some extent, which means you must include this requirement in your decision. Even a full solution, such as Visual MainWin, does require some changes on the part of the developers in your organization to accommodate the tool. When working with a Web service, the developers on your team will have to create a completely different kind of application.

Many multiple platform solutions are available, so don't accept the first solution you see. For example, many developers are unaware that you can turn a COM+ application into a Web service. In this situation, you could gain a speed advantage by accessing the COM+ application locally and using the Web service for remote access. You can even turn your C# application directly into a COM+ application and then make the resulting COM+ application accessible as a Web service (see the technique at `http://www.devsource.com/c/a/Using-VS/Designing-COM-Applications-with-a-Web-Service-Appeal/`*).*

Inventorying Your Tools

You've probably collected a host of tools while working on various applications. The problem for most developers isn't a lack of tools — it's more likely too many tools. In fact, you may not even know which tools you have available. Because the tools you use affect the language environment, it's important to choose the right tools. For example, you may have two design tools, but one is geared more toward database applications and the other is geared more toward Web services. If you're creating a database application, then you want to use the first tool.

A tool inventory should include all your available tools. You should categorize them at time of purchase to keep application tasks in mind. However, when you begin a new project, you should also categorize them with your development team in mind. When you have two tools that will perform equally well in creating a particular application, then you need to choose the tool that works best with the capabilities and skills of your development team. Of course, you'll want to ask the team members about experiences they've had with the various tools in your arsenal.

It's easy to overlook some important issues when creating a tool inventory. The following list details some issues you should consider while creating your inventory:

- Do you have enough licenses for the tool?
- Are the members of your team skilled in the use of this tool?
- Does the tool provide everything needed for this application, or do you need to purchase add-ons for it?
- Are there potential alternatives for this tool that your company can acquire?
- Will the tool integrate successfully with the development environment?
- Are any of the team members reluctant to use the tool due to a bad previous experience with it?
- Will it be difficult to find replacements for a particular tool if the team member who knows how to use it leaves?
- Is the tool completely up to date with patches and service packs?

Gathering Your Resources

The vast majority of your programming resources come in human form. Even if you're using an article on the Internet as a source of information, a human wrote the article. The people on your team represent the largest potential source of change when it comes to the language environment. In fact, you should consider three potential levels of change to the language environment:

- Language resources
- Skills
- Experiences

The human resources for your project are further affected by biases, preference for particular tools, and the desire to make their mark on the project. The following sections provide an overview of the resources you need to consider as part of the language environment. The remainder of the book provides additional details on this topic as appropriate.

Inventorying Team Language Resources

Anyone with a four-year computer science degree will have experience in more than one language. The experience may not be enough to write an application, but the fact that users have experienced the language means that they have learned something about it. The experience reduces the learning curve for the language and makes it possible that the team member could potentially use that language as part of your project. The only problem with colleges and universities is that they seem to have differing language plans — one school may emphasize Java while another emphasizes Visual Basic.NET. You can't determine that someone has a certain set of skills based solely on the person's degree.

Self-taught individuals also have a wealth of experience with languages. Someone who starts with Visual Basic for Applications (VBA) as part of working with Office may move on to Visual Basic, and from there on to Transact Structured Query Language (T-SQL). After spending a lot of time on the Web, this team member may have also learned JavaScript and other languages in order to set up a personal Web site.

Unfortunately, you won't discover any of these skills until you conduct an inventory. Just because a team member is currently working with C# doesn't mean this person lacks other programming language skills. In order to create the best design for your application, you must also know that a particular team member worked extensively with C++ at one time and specialized in creating DLLs for another organization.

Considering Team Skills

It's nice that you know a particular team member knows C#, C++, and Visual Basic with a smattering of T-SQL thrown in for good measure. However, most languages are extremely complex, so it's possible for someone to become proficient in one aspect of a language, such as database design, and not in others. Consequently, knowing that the team member wrote code that accessed SQL Server databases is better than simply knowing that this member knows how to write in C#. Every application development experience that team members have improves their skill. However, skills always focus on a particular need, so you also need to know about the need that the application answered.

Skills are also transient. A team member's skill fades as time passes without exercising that skill. In addition to determining that the team member has written code to access SQL Server, you also need to know how much time has passed since the team member engaged in that activity. A team member who wrote SQL Server code eight years ago will offer far less proficiency than someone who performed the same task two weeks ago. It's important to remember, though, that people can polish their skills quickly. Even eight-year-old experience is better than no experience at all.

The final skill consideration is learning environment. A VBA programming skill developed using Office 95 is less useful for today's application needs than a skill developed using Office 2007. The same concern holds true for any skill. The skill is usually matched to a particular product version, which means you must consider what has changed since the team member developed the skill. For example, in the case of Office 2007, the Microsoft Office Fluent User Interface (RibbonX) significantly reduces the usefulness of a skill developed using Office 95 because many of the older techniques no longer work.

Understanding the Significance of Experience

Unless your team members are joined at the hip, they've had different development experiences. A development experience helps shape the way the team member views a particular application development requirement and may help you achieve a better result. The developer experience includes these aspects:

- Language
- Project type
- Project size
- Individual project task
- Tools used to write the application
- Individual or team effort
- Manager personality and management style
- Developer personality and management style
- Skills of other developers on the team
- Success or failure of the project

All these project aspects affect the members of your team in some way. The more positive experiences with projects of the same type that you plan to create, the better suited that member is for the project. However, even negative experiences are helpful. A team member who has had a negative experience and taken time to analyze what went wrong knows at least one technique that won't work for your project. Often, these team members can spot potholes in the road before they become a problem and can even warn you about them.

Some managers have a hard time accepting input from the members of their team. It's important to accept such input without necessarily implementing it. Any input can help you create a better project, but not all input is useful for your particular project. Likewise, it's hard for some team members to share experiences, especially negative experiences. A good manager can draw out these experiences in a positive manner and use them in a constructive way to improve the project. Of course, as with any skill, it takes time to develop this skill and practice is the best way to build the skill.

Defining External Resource Requirements

You may not know whether you need help from outside sources today. However, it's a good idea to begin looking for potential holes even at this early stage of the application development process in your team's language resources, skills, and experiences. The earlier you can identify the need for additional resources, the better your chances of finding precisely the right resource. In some cases, you may find that you can't hire the resource you need, which means that you'll have to set up a consulting contract with the individual as soon as possible. Otherwise, you may get to the point of needing help today only to find that the resource won't be available anytime soon.

It isn't uncommon to find that a top-notch consultant is booked for a year or more in advance. The more specialized your need, the further ahead you need to schedule time from a consultant. If you wait until the last minute, you may obtain the consultant services you need, but at an incredibly high price. In addition, because the consultant didn't have time to schedule your project, you'll find that the consultant's time is divided, so you won't get the full benefit of the consultant's experience for your project.

Of course, resources come in a number of forms. It's possible for a project to move along fine until it requires something special. You may need special graphics files to test your application. Unless you schedule the artist's time well in advance, the images may not be ready when you need them. The same holds true for any specialized need. Many projects today require developers with unique talents, such as the ability to mix sight, sound, and code into a cohesive whole. Often, you know about these needs even before you begin much planning because the basic tasks require some level of specialized interaction.

Developing Your Design Strategy

The purpose of this chapter is to acquaint you with the language environment. Many projects fail because the designer didn't start with the right language. Sure, the language the designer chose could work, but it didn't because it wasn't the optimal choice. Of course, designers have to work in the real world, so this chapter discusses real-world language environment concerns, such as the availability of staff with the correct language skills. The most important idea that you can take away from this chapter is that there isn't a silver bullet language that works in every situation. Sometimes, you even have to mix languages in order to achieve optimum results in a minimum of time.

It's important to get started with your project as quickly as possible, but it's also important to perform the right steps at the right time. The essential step described in this chapter is to create a language environment — to consider how the use of a particular language will affect the development of your application. Take time now to consider the basic tasks your application performs. You don't have to provide a sequence or anything complex, just the simple ideas of retrieving data, processing it somehow, and presenting it to the user. Inventory the languages that your team knows and then assign those languages to the various application tasks. This simple step helps you understand why you're using a particular language in a particular place. While you work on that language inventory, you may also want to create an inventory of skills and experiences.

Applications have a lifecycle. You design, write, maintain, and finally retire them. It's important to consider the entire application lifecycle before you write the first line of code. Chapter 2 presents the application lifecycle and the different strategies you can use to implement the lifecycle. Of course, you perform this thought process before you begin designing the application. Mulling the application in your mind and writing some basic ideas down on paper are the steps you take after you consider the language environment.

2

Understanding the Application Lifecycle

Just about anything that you can think of has a lifecycle. For example, a car begins in an assembly plant, goes to the dealer, and is bought by someone who drives it a few years, before it goes to a used car lot where someone else buys it, before it eventually ends up in the junkyard. You can track the life of an individual car with online services now, such as AutoTrader (`http://www.autotrader.com/`) or CARFAX (`http://www.carfax.com/`). Like cars, software has a lifecycle. Someone develops an idea, creates a design around that idea, builds the application, places it in a production environment, maintains the software, and eventually retires the software when it's no longer needed. Buying a used car without researching it can end up in a bad purchase that will cost you considerable money in maintenance and other costs. Likewise, understanding the software lifecycle is crucial if you want to avoid unnecessary costs and delays. Software, like cars, can become an albatross around your neck.

Unlike cars, studying the lifecycle of software isn't a straightforward process. In fact, the Machiavellian threads of some software designs prove quite impossible to untie, making any kind of analysis impossible. Fortunately, choosing a sticking-to-a-lifecycle model helps you keep your sanity and makes the software development process easier. This chapter also reviews a number of lifecycle models — those in common use by industry today. You can probably find other models online, and it's important that you find the right model for your particular need, so choosing the right model is time well spent.

This chapter also considers agile programming techniques. An *agile* programming technique is a special programming methodology. This technique promotes:

- Development iterations
- Open collaboration
- Process adaptability

In short, using an agile programming technique tends to ensure project completion through constant review and intense participation by all stakeholders in a project. Of course, it would be simple if there were just one agile programming technique, but like many software development issues, there are many ways to approach the problem. Consequently, this chapter reviews the most popular approaches and helps you understand why they're popular. You need to choose an agile programming technique that works best for your organization and the project you want to complete.

Understanding the Lifecycle Stages

A lifecycle begins at some definite point and ends at a different definite point. In between these two points are a number of stages. You know when you're in the middle of a particular stage, but you may not realize when you've entered or left that stage. Yes, each stage has a specific time frame, but it's hard to see the boundaries when you're in the midst of designing, writing, and maintaining that application. Even though the stages are a series of gray states with some specific middle point, you must still plan for the lifecycle in an attempt to gain an understanding of the application. You can't perform useful work on an application you don't understand. Consequently, many designers muddle about for a while, decide the application is too hard to write, and ultimately fail because they didn't take the necessary first step in application design, which is to understand the application lifecycle completely.

In addition to the liquidity of the lifecycle concept, the stages you encounter while building your application depend on a number of factors. For example, the environment in which you build your application partly determines its lifecycle. The other sections of this chapter begin the discussion of environment, so don't worry about it for now. You must also consider the skills of your team and the organization's management style as described in Chapter 1. No matter how all these factors affect the lifecycle, however, every application encounters the stages described in the following sections.

Developing an Application Concept

Every application begins as someone's idea. In most cases, a single person comes up with the idea and then shares it with other people. Ideas come from a number of sources including:

- Organizational need
- Governmental requirement
- User request
- Another organization
- Article or other professional information source
- Nontechnical source such as television
- Creative flash

The application idea may not even work at the outset. Often an application idea starts as a nonverbal concept — a creative insight into a problem of some type. A developer may sit down with another developer to begin discussing the idea. Many applications start out as rough drawings on a napkin somewhere. The undeveloped application concept always requires some level of verbalization before you can do anything with it at all. In fact, you must define the problem that the application will solve before the application is more than an unusable idea that could end up in the circular file.

In some cases, the developer receives a request for an application from a user. The user presents a requirement and the developer creates an application to meet this requirement. Even in this situation, you must define the problem fully before you can create the solution. The user request often lacks details the developer needs to define a solution.

In some cases, defining the problem is relatively easy. For example, if the government mandates that your organization must adhere to the requirements of Sarbanes-Oxley (see `http://www.soxlaw.com/` for details on the Sarbanes-Oxley Act of 2002), then you already have a good idea about the source of the problem. Of course, just knowing you must adhere to the requirements of the Sarbanes-Oxley Act isn't enough — you must further define the problem as it applies to your organization and the level of compliance that the government requires.

Problem definition can be difficult in other cases. You may discover that another organization outputs its checks faster than your organization, with fewer errors, and at a significantly lower cost. Investigation shows that the other organization is using a technique that you could possibly use in your organization. The trap, here, is that you must determine whether your organization even requires the upgrade. The payback of investment costs for your organization might be 20 years — far too long for a software project. At this point, you have to consider whether you can implement only part of the other organization's solution at a significantly lower cost, or whether your organization needs the solution at all.

The application concept isn't complete as simply an idea. As part of developing an application concept, you must consider a number of organization-specific needs. The following list considers each of the questions you must ask yourself before you go to the next step. (Remember that this is a preliminary stage, so you won't be able to answer most questions completely — you merely think about them at this stage and answer the questions that you can to the fullest extent possible.)

- ❑ Have you defined the problem completely?
- ❑ Does this solution actually solve that problem?
- ❑ Does the organization actually require this solution?
- ❑ Is the payoff period short enough to make the solution worthwhile?
- ❑ Does the organization have the resources required to implement the solution?
- ❑ When is the best time to present the application concept to management?
- ❑ Does the solution break any existing solutions or conflict with laws or other organization requirements?

Some people get stuck in a mode where they think that every idea must be a success — that the organization must implement every idea no matter how absurd. Creative people usually have far more failed ideas than successes. There are days where I have 15 or 20 failed ideas for every good idea that passes critical review. The failed ideas often help the creative person define the problem and its solution better, so don't worry when an idea fails to work out. Make sure you spend time thinking each idea over before you present it to others to determine whether the idea has any chance at all of passing that critical review.

Building an Application Development Team

It may seem a bit early to start talking about a development team. After all, you don't even have a specification put together yet or any idea of whether management will approve your idea. The development team-building process takes time. You don't want to begin pulling people off priority work at the outset, but you do want to know their status. Build a team on paper and discover the status of every person on that list to ensure you have the resources required to build the application once you have it approved. Some projects fail because managers don't take time to start thinking about the people who will work on the project at the outset. Chapter 1 provides you with a number of ideas on how to view the people that you'll potentially use for the project.

You have an application concept at this point. Part of your team-building process is to ask several of your peers to review the application concept as you have it written down and provide a critical (and it's hoped a constructive) review of it. We all have a tendency to think our ideas are the best ever created. It's impossible for you to provide an objective, critical review of your own work. So, besides creating that list of developers you'd like to work with when writing the application you've defined, you also need some peers to review the application concept to ensure you're on firm footing and not creating the next Frankenstein monster of application development.

Don't give people the impression that they'll start working with you tomorrow (or at all for that matter). Most application ideas require far more time than their originators think necessary to get off the ground. In fact, the larger your organization, the more time you should consider setting aside to sell your idea. An entrepreneurial organization requires even more time because the entrepreneur owner often has a hands-on management style that will cost you a lot of time.

This stage covers a lot of ground in the application lifecycle. In fact, it starts when you present your application concept to your peers and ends only when the organization finally retires the application. In a few cases, you may find that people receive requests for application help and information long after the application has supposedly gone the way of the dinosaur. It wasn't long ago that I received a request for help with a Disk Operating System (DOS) application I built about 20 years ago. The request came all the way from Brazil, but it was a request nonetheless. Some applications never go away. However, for most organizations, you can plan on these phases of the development team stage:

1. Peer review of the application concept
2. Initial application specification
3. Application presentation
4. Application design
5. Design implementation
6. Testing and quality assurance
7. Initial application rollout
8. User training and support
9. Application maintenance
10. Application shutdown and transition

That's a lot of different phases for a single application. In most cases, you won't have to worry about supplying staff for more than one or two of these phases (some phases do overlap). However, it's important to realize that you or your successor will eventually supply staff for every one of these phases. Consequently, this stage is the longest running stage of the entire application lifecycle. It pays to begin preparing for as many phases as you can, because someone is going to ask about personnel requirements when you present your application to management. Someone who has answers (even incomplete answers) has a higher chance of getting a project approved than someone who hasn't thought the concept through.

Although you could probably make a case against using developers for some steps, such as user training and support, the fact of the matter is that the developer has to train the support staff at a minimum. Someone who knows how the application works has to tell everyone else how to use it. Because the developer is in the position to know such information, the developer usually ends up providing user training and support of some type.

Defining a Specification

The application concept is a written document that defines the problem and solution in terms that you understand. When you ask other developers in your organization to provide a peer review, you'll probably have to explain many of the application concept issues to them because you don't have any formal document. In fact, you may not even know what to put into a formal document without the peer review. The questions that your peers ask should definitely receive an answer in the next stage of the process, which is defining a specification. A *specification*, for the purposes of this book, is a document you use to sell your idea to management.

The specification contains a number of useful bits of information. In most cases, you'll also provide a presentation, complete with PowerPoint slides, to sell your idea. However, the specification is the document that actually sells that idea. It contains the ideas that management is most interested in seeing. The specification should use language that everyone can understand, provide a good overview of the project (management really doesn't need the gory details), and include as many honest and thorough answers as possible. The following list details the kinds of information you should include:

- Short synopsis of the problem
- Description of why the problem requires a fix
- Potential outcomes of not fixing the problem
- References to any pertinent problem sources (such as government documentation)
- Details of the solution you suggest
- Alternative solutions (when available)
- Approximately how long the project will require
- Personnel needed to implement the design over its lifecycle
- Potential costs of your solution
- Analysis of the trade-offs of alternative solutions
- Anticipated design solution overview
- Potential problems in implementing, rolling out, and maintaining the application

Obviously, you need a great deal of help to put such a document together. Brainstorming with your peers is a good starting point. However, someone is going to use that application. Most modern development techniques call for user interaction from the outset. Otherwise, you can end up with an application that looks nice, but doesn't accomplish anything. Consequently, as you put your specification together, take time to interview the users of your organization — those who actually need the solution you plan to develop.

Most organizations also heavily encumber development with politics. The best ideas sometimes end up nowhere because the originator doesn't have the political clout required to get the idea approved. The specification doesn't make someone in management look good, so management turns up its collective nose at the idea. Try getting as many members of management on board as early as possible in the specification process. If possible, get management involved in writing the specification and give them credit in the document (if for no other reason, you won't be blamed later for the poor wording).

At this point, you have all the stakeholders for a particular project on board and you don't even have it approved yet. Everyone is so excited about your project (you hope) that the approval process may seem like a mere formality. A *stakeholder* is anyone involved in the project and normally includes users, developers, and management. However, depending on the application, a stakeholder could also include third-party vendors, partners, external users, or any number of other people. The cardinal rule to remember when creating your specification is to involve as many people as possible so that everyone has a say and everyone knows about the project.

Determining Whether the Concept Will Work

The specification you write gives everyone a basis for discussion. Depending on the amount of input you get to put the specification together, it can become an extremely useful document. However, you really don't know yet that your application concept will work. At some point, you make a presentation where everyone will consider the viability of your project. It's at this point that your project lives or dies depending on how much work you put into the specification at the outset.

As unfair as it may sound, you gain a reputation for the presentations you provide. It's important to do your homework and not present application ideas that have no chance of approval. Otherwise, people will get used to your presenting half-baked ideas and not listen when you do have a good idea to present. In sum, you need to have a good idea that the concept will work before you present it to management.

When you make your presentation, make sure you have plenty of backup data and experts to help you present the application. Telling management that the users interviewed like your application idea is one thing; having user representatives tell management in person that they like the idea is another. Expect to receive what amounts to terrifyingly unexpected questions. Someone's going to ask a question that you would never think to ask yourself. These difficult questions are often the acid test for your specification. If you do a good job, you should be able to field most of the questions that management asks. When someone does ask a question that you can't answer, say so and promise to provide an answer as soon as possible.

This process is truly political in nature. However, it can also provide you with good ideas for your application. Make sure that someone records the questions and answers provided during the presentation. All this information should appear as part of the design you eventually create for your application. Adding the questions and answers will demonstrate an attention to detail on your part and make it easier to create an application that truly meets everyone's expectations.

One error developers commonly make during a presentation of this sort is to sit on the hot seat all by themselves. It's often possible to place a few people on the hot seat with you and garner some additional resources for your project as well. Always ask questions during the presentation. The questions shouldn't be of the type that elicit yes/no answers, but should instead draw out the information that people keep hidden. If you truly don't understand a management concern, ask the person who has made the request for help. Do whatever you can to get management on your side.

Understanding the Hostile Manager or User

There's a tendency to think of the hostile manager as a pain and respond accordingly. In some cases, the person in question really is a pain and there isn't much you can do about it except try to answer the questions as best you can. However, in some cases, the hostile manager or user has a legitimate concern and feels you won't answer it. These individuals have probably met more than a few developers who nodded their heads yes during a presentation and then promptly forgot to address the concern in code. In other cases, the individual is simply starved for attention of any type.

Someone with a legitimate gripe or simply a need for some attention is an asset, not a pain. Put that person to work as soon as possible. As you present your idea, make sure you get the names and contact information for these individuals. Set up face-to-face conferences with them and work out the details of their participation. Sometimes, the individual will begin making excuses not to meet with you — a fact you should record for your next meeting with that person. The point is to provide individuals with the access to your project that they want.

What happens, though, when the individual does meet with you? In this case, you can begin asking for input. Obtain the full benefit of the person's experiences with similar software and use this as a resource for selling your ideas to others. Most importantly, implement the person's ideas whenever possible to gain acceptance for your application and to ensure the application truly does work as you anticipated.

It's important to remember that the process of presenting your application concept using a specification begins to build a certain level of expectation on the part of management. No, the expectations aren't set in stone at this moment, but management will question you if your design ends up providing something completely different from your presentation. In other words, you can't offer management an application that automatically counts widgets on the assembly line and later present a design for a new type of electronic toothbrush. Consequently, you need to ensure that the specification is as accurate as possible and that it actually marks holes as holes, so management knows that there's more information to come. Never say that time, money, or personnel requirements are exact at this point.

It usually isn't possible to include every stakeholder in the application design process. For example, if a company has 1,000 employees, you don't want to have all 1,000 employees involved in the decision-making process. Consequently, you need to choose representatives from each stakeholder group. It's essential to choose representatives who have a clear understanding of the entire group's needs. In many cases, the most popular person isn't the right choice. The employee who's worked at every level of the organization without saying too much may be the better choice, because that employee has probably heard many discussions over the years and will know the current software problems better than anyone else in the group will. The same holds true for managers and all other stakeholders. Make sure you choose the person most likely to provide good input for your application. When your project allows, make sure you include room for people of all skill levels — novice to expert — to ensure that the application works for everyone.

Creating a Design

Your application concept is approved based on the merits of your specification and your sparkling presentation skills. It's at this point that the real work begins. Before you can write any code, you need a design. The amount of design work you do depends on the lifecycle model you choose and the programming technique you employ (see the "Considering a Lifecycle Model" section of this chapter for details). In general, you must perform enough design work to obtain working software as an output, but the initial design may not include details of every aspect of the application. For example, the agile programming techniques described in the "Using Agile Programming Techniques" section of this chapter require less design work at the outset than the waterfall lifecycle model.

Some developers feel that at this point the initial work with the user and management is over. A good developer will involve the user and management during the design stage. It's far easier to correct misconceptions before you write any code than later, when you have to make changes to existing code to meet user expectations. The design process should end with an application plan that everyone understands and approves. Otherwise, you're just asking for trouble later, after you write code and spend more money on a project that could fail.

The technique you use to start your design depends on your personal preferences. Some developers begin by making sketches of the user interface, some a flowchart showing how the application will work, and still others some type of logic chart. No matter how you start your design, you must consider the audience that will view the result.

Users and managers don't care about the code you write — all they care about is the user interface. Users want to know that the application is easy to use and meets all of their input requirements. Managers want to know that the application outputs all the required reports and that those reports are flexible. The combination of the user and manager design needs is the high-level design.

The developers on your team also care about the high-level design, but let's face it: the high-level design doesn't require as much time as the low-level code. The code that retrieves data from a Web service the user needs and outputs it as a report will require considerably more time than adding a Print button to the user interface. Consequently, the developers on your team must also understand the low-level design. The following sections discuss both high-level and low-level design.

Understanding High-Level Design

There's a tendency to attempt to define every aspect of the high-level design during the initial design phase. Unfortunately, users and managers typically don't know what they want at this point. They haven't used your software, and they don't understand how it will work or what they'll need once they do understand how it works. Remember that the idea is to create a piece of usable software during the initial design phase. Consequently, if you're creating a database application of some sort, you'll probably create the user interface for working with records during the initial design phase and leave the reports for the next design phase. Always ask yourself the question: "What do I need to provide a working application — something the user can interact with today?"

Of course, the moment you decide to work with one piece of the application at a time, the users and managers will create an uproar, "What about my piece of the application?" Part of your design should provide an overview that tells the users and managers when a particular piece of the application will come online. Avoid providing specific dates for these additional design phases. There isn't a good reason to build up user or manager hopes that you'll meet specific dates. Instead, you should work on the first piece of the application until it works completely, and then move on to the next piece — no matter how long it takes to achieve complete functionality.

You'll encounter a certain amount of pressure until you get that first piece of the application completed, because users and managers alike will anticipate the new software now that you've presented it as part of your specification. Consequently, make the first piece small, but completely functional. For example, using the database entry example again, you might want to create the piece of the application that interacts with employee records. Make sure the user can add, delete, and edit employee records — the users will rightfully complain if you present them with a piece of software that can only add records. The next phase may work with customer records or another piece of the input or reporting puzzle, but the point is to meet reasonable goals so that the user and manager can play with the new software.

Make sure you listen to complaints of users and managers as they test the software. One company (which shall remain nameless) designed and implemented a database application that relied heavily on the mouse and didn't use any speed keys. Unfortunately, the employees at this company were all touch typists and never used the mouse. The resulting loss of productivity after the application rollout was monumental (and the application rollout occurred during the company's peak ordering season). The company not only lost employee efficiency and some valuable employees but also lost orders, resulting in lower profitability and customers who didn't feel like waiting all day for the computer. Eventually, the company had to pull the new software, reinstall all the old software, make fixes, and then try to roll out the new software again. All this happened due to a lack of speed keys — a five-minute fix during the initial software trials, but an expensive mistake later. Chapter 4 discusses the user interface requirements in greater detail.

Understanding Low-Level Design

Once you have the working piece of the high-level design in place, begin focusing on the low-level code required to implement it. You have several concerns at this level of the design that might not be apparent at first.

- All of the controls should have some code attached to them, even if it's to display a message box saying, "Not Implemented Yet."
- Consider modularity as part of the design process. Create your design such that you can reuse as much code as possible.
- Get input from your design team. It may make sense to you to display the employee name in the order of last name, first name, middle initial, but a programming restraint may make a first name, middle initial, last name order better.
- Create the application with the entire application in mind, rather than the single working piece that you want to implement initially. Otherwise, you may find that your design works today, but doesn't work at all with additions you must create later.
- Always ask whether a particular low-level addition really addresses a high-level design need completely and appropriately.

The biggest mistake that many developers make during this stage is not maintaining good notes on various design decisions. If someone on your team makes a suggestion, make sure you record the team member's name with the suggestion so you can ask for clarification later. Remember the six words that a good journalist uses when writing a story: who, what, where, when, why, and how. You can't record too much information about your design decisions, but not recording enough information can be deadly. Many projects fail because the team eventually starts pointing fingers when things don't work out right or the team lacks clarification on a critical application feature.

It's also important to remember that individual developers have differing coding styles. One developer may use copious notes, while another relies on white space and clever variable naming to document an application. Part of your low-level design should spell out the group coding style. It shouldn't leave much in the way of individuality. The more individuality that your team can express, the harder the code is to maintain later. Of course, you'll probably want to obtain input from your team on the code style issues. You may find a few new coding tricks along the way. Giving the team members a say also tends to reduce tension later.

Although they aren't a silver bullet solution, you should also consider relying on coding conventions and coding standards used throughout the industry whenever possible. Doing so makes it possible for newer employees to learn how to work with the code faster. In addition, you don't end up reinventing the wheel — you can employ best practices developed and tested by the developers who have come before you.

Low-level code can also suffer from a variety of external issues. For example, one company created an application that retrieved data from a third-party Web service, rather than recreating that information locally. The use of the Web service cut the cost of the application significantly and meant that the developers could create the application significantly faster. The only problem is that no one thought to check with the legal department about any potential contract issues. The company was only allowed to make so many calls to the Web service per minute. Unfortunately, without local data caching, the company made far more than the contracted calls and the Web service simply ignored the extra calls. The result was an application that performed very slowly for no apparent reason. After spending nearly a month troubleshooting the performance problem, someone thought to check the contract. A simple design change brought the application within performance specifications, but the cost was high. Make sure you include all of the stakeholders for an application design — unexpected low-level programming issues can cause significant problems for you and your organization. Chapter 3 discusses the low-level programming interface in greater detail.

Testing the Design

Many organizations go directly from creating the design to implementing it. However, it's always a good idea to test the design. The design testing process doesn't involve any code. Rather, you go through the entire design with the stakeholders involved to ensure that you haven't forgotten anything or need to change something due to a misunderstanding.

Sometimes it's helpful to break the stakeholders into smaller groups when there are many stakeholder needs to consider. Having a large meeting with 40 people all shouting at each other isn't particularly helpful. Breaking the stakeholders into small groups also means that people who are shy are more likely to say something. The design test stage is your last chance in most cases to get the design correct before you implement it. Sure, you can fix any problems later, but that's always expensive when compared to getting the design right in the first place.

You may have to present your design in several forms to get the point across. For example, the high-level design should include some mock-ups that the users can actually test. Where you can't provide a mock-up, you might want to create a PowerPoint presentation that shows the sequence of events that users will see. An application design test may require that you present the data in several forms and include printouts as well so the users can report any significant problems later. Set a deadline for comments or you may find yourself accepting comments for months for a relatively simple part of the design. However, you should encourage users to talk with other employees about the design and get their input as well.

When you create an application mock-up, make sure you also have the software required to make changes to the application interface. Users may have suggestions immediately and it's better to make the required changes while the idea is fresh in the user's mind. Have the users actually try out your functional mock-up and provide them with simulated results. The act of testing out the design before you actually code it will make the user feel more comfortable and provide you with significantly better results.

Managers may have special needs when it comes to the application design. For example, the managers may want to make it possible to add new users from within the application. You don't want the users to know about this feature and test it out. Consequently, you might want to set up a separate testing session to review manager-only features in the application. The manager-only features should rely on security to prevent accidental access by users and you should hide these design elements from view unless a manager logs into the application.

Don't provide just one test iteration for complex user interface features. Make any required changes and then set up another session to test them out. Keep testing the features until the users are sure the interface will work as required. In addition, don't perform all your testing on one day. Users will become desensitized to essential features after a couple of tests. Take time to test the user interface over several days.

Test the expected and unexpected. For example, your application should have a complete set of accessibility features. Most users with special needs will expect you to include speed keys and tooltips as a minimum. You also need to avoid confusing color combinations and situations where sound (or sight) is the only indicator of an error. If possible, have users with special needs test your mock-up before you begin the design implementation.

Implementing the Design

By the time you reach this stage, you should have both a high-level and low-level design for your application, or at least the part that you plan to implement during this particular phase. You should also have copious notes on why you made certain design decisions and whom to ask if you need clarification. The notes may not be in very good order, however, and you need to clean them up at this point. Implementing the design stage means coming up with the final plan you want to pursue for this phase of the software. As previously mentioned, the goal is a fully functional piece of software that you can roll out to specific users for testing. The user should be able to use the software to perform the basic tests that you've planned to implement.

Implementing the design is simply a matter of formalizing everything so that there aren't any questions about the design when you're done. The following list provides some ideas on how you can ensure your application is ready to write:

- Break the development team into groups and assign each group a particular modular task for the application.
- Create the formalized design document with notes about features you plan to implement later.
- Assign users particular testing tasks.

- ❑ Assign testing tasks to any special groups such as managers.
- ❑ Put procedures in place to ensure code safety.
- ❑ Devise a complaint process to ensure you can handle complaints quickly, before they become a problem.
- ❑ Ensure that all developers understand the coding style document.
- ❑ Create a process to ensure all stakeholders remain active with the application while the development team writes, debugs, tests, and rolls out the application.

Every design implementation must consider three elements: speed, reliability, and security. These three elements play off each other and form a triangle of sorts. Increasing speed normally results in a loss of both reliability and security because the software usually performs fewer checks or relies on technologies that require more work on the part of the developer. When you increase reliability through the use of additional checks and proven technologies, you normally see a significant speed decrease and a partial security decrease (in part, because security often inhibits the access required for reliable operation). You can read more about speed in Chapter 5, reliability in Chapter 6, and security in Chapter 7.

Writing the Application

If you've performed all the previous application design stages properly, writing the application should be relatively painless. At this point, all parties should know what to do and how the application should look when the developers finish writing the code. The users should be in place to test the application functionality and you should have additional stakeholders lined up to test special features. If your application includes management features, then you should have one or more managers on the list to test that part of the application.

Part of the application writing process involves code reviews. You should make it a practice to look at the code the developers are putting together. Make sure the code adheres to all the coding style requirements. If necessary, bring the developers together to explain coding style issues. The bottom line is that you shouldn't be able to tell who wrote a particular piece of code based solely on the coding style.

The code your developers put together has significant value. Part of the code writing process is to ensure that the system backs up code each day. In fact, you may want to set the system up to provide multiple backups each day.

> *Some people have a problem sharing with the group. You'll find that they don't check their code back into the system, which means that the code they write is not only inaccessible to the rest of the group, but that it isn't backed up either. Make those team members understand that the code belongs to the team and not to individual members. It's possible that you may have to make the point strongly to gain their attention.*

It's tempting to allow previews of the application. Nonprogrammer stakeholders may drop by and want to see the progress you're making. Unfortunately, letting people preview the application starts up the gossip mill and you may hear all kinds of rumors that aren't true about your application. For some reason, people either tend to talk the application down (it's so full of bugs that it will never get completed), or they seem to need special features that aren't actually there (yes, it does include a spelling checker that works with ancient Klingon). The result is that people are ready to say the application is terrible before they even see it for the first time or they have unrealistic expectations. Keep the application writing process private. If someone asks about the application process, let them know that you're making progress and they'll see the application soon (without giving a specific date). Of course, you'll want to ensure that all the team members follow this process as well.

Meeting the needs of the application developers is also important. You can't perform a backup of the code when Joe decides that he really must work until 2 A.M. and then restart the day at 6 A.M. , so the code suffers when someone doesn't follow normal working hours. (If you must deal with the issue of workers in other time zones, you'll need to agree upon a time when those workers aren't actively engaged in making code changes.) However, the problem is more significant than that. If Joe is only getting 4 hours of sleep every night, there isn't any way for him to perform well. The code he writes is suspect and possibly full of bugs. When you shut the door each night, make sure all the developers on your team shut the door as well. That's one of the benefits of agile programming strategies — you develop the application at a pace your developers can actually support.

Some of you are probably wondering about developer productivity at this point. There are certainly measures of developer productivity, such as lines of code. Of course, basing developer productivity solely on lines of code is foolish because it's easier to write bad code than good code. A developer could write pure gibberish that has no potential for performing the task properly and meet the lines-of-code measurement. Although this book doesn't provide specific developer productivity guidelines, you should use a measure that accounts for error-free lines of code. In other words, the developer who produces the most error-free lines of code each day is your best developer, the one that you can count on most.

The whole topic of writing the application is relatively complex. Part II of the book discusses the many elements of writing an application with greater ease. Chapters 8, 9, and 10 discuss various aspects of the Integrated Development Environment (IDE). Chapter 11 helps you understand how to work effectively with controls and components. Chapter 12 describes the actual act of writing the application and Chapter 13 details the requirements for writing application documentation. Chapter 14 provides information about the very necessary task of handling errors gracefully and successfully.

Debugging and Testing the Application

Every application on the planet has bugs. Software is complex and humans make errors — it's an unpleasant fact. Of course, you don't want to send software out to the public with a huge number of bugs either. Most users won't accept the "I'm only human" excuse for very long. However, software has bugs for far more reasons than the inactivity of lazy, flawed humans. Some developers do want their software entirely bug-free and are willing to do whatever it takes to get to that point (no matter how many years it might require). There's also the constant push of both customers and company marketing staff to get software out the door. At some point, software reaches a good enough stage where users complain only a little and it's possible to continue fixing bugs using patches. The fact remains that it's unlikely you'll ever see software that lacks bugs — at least, software with enough functionality to do something useful.

Fortunately, as the engineering aspects of software have become better defined and developers have started to use best practices in putting software together, the number of bugs encountered in software has decreased. You still have to debug and test the application, but the amount of work required to accomplish the task has decreased. In addition, unit testing and other disciplines have made it possible to perform the debugging a little at a time, reducing the load on any particular group of developers. Users generally want certain things from their software at the outset. The following list provides an overview of the common elements:

- The controls must react as anticipated — a button labeled Print should actually print something.
- The application must handle data without error.
- An application should provide consistent and useful help at several levels, including preventing the user from performing tasks incorrectly.
- Whenever possible, applications should recover from errors, rather than fail gracefully. The user always wants to continue working without restarting the application.
- If absolutely necessary, the application should fail gracefully, rather than simply crash. An automatic restart after a graceful failure is always welcome.
- Error messages should convey information in a form the user understands and provide details to the developer to help improve the patching process.
- The application should provide a relatively high level of both reliability and security, but not prevent the user from performing useful work.
- The developer should never expect the user to remember anything about an error — that's the service the logs provide.

Users tend not to notice that a visual element glitches or that a presentation isn't perfect. The placement of a button a little left of center, rather than directly in the middle of the display, probably isn't a big concern either. Developers who take pride in their work will fix these issues, but they aren't a priority in most cases. However, the bug that causes the program to crash every time the user clicks Print is a big concern because it prevents the user from performing useful work. In short, when debugging your application, think like a user. Remember that the user isn't concerned about your application at all — the only concern users have is that the application performs useful work that lets them make a paycheck and then go home at the appropriate time. All the elegant code in the world doesn't impress the user one iota, but a successful report output does.

The testing and debugging process tends to follow a pattern. Modern tools have made the process go faster and require less effort on the part of the developer, but they haven't interrupted the pattern most developers can recite in their sleep:

1. Compile the application.
2. Run the test suite. If the test suite succeeds, go to Step 7.
3. Accumulate a list of bugs.
4. Prioritize the bugs.
5. Fix the high-priority bugs immediately, work on lower-priority bugs as time permits.
6. Go back to Step 1.
7. Perform user testing. If user testing is successful, go to Step 11.
8. Accumulate a list of bugs.

9. Fix the high-priority bugs immediately, work on lower-priority bugs as time permits.
10. Go back to Step 1.
11. Deploy the application to verify it actually performs as expected. Prepare for more debugging and testing as a result of this step.

Of course, the actual process is a little more complicated than this procedure illustrates. For one thing, you have to create a test suite for your application, and the quality of your test suite will affect how easily you find bugs. If you've ever made a bug report, you know that the report usually asks you to provide a list of steps that replicate the bug. In many cases, this procedure becomes part of the test suite simply because the vendor didn't think to test the application in the way that you've used it. Chapter 15 provides more details about testing and debugging your application.

Testing User Requirements

At this point, you have a shiny new application that has passed all the test suites. You feel pretty good about the application and are ready for user testing. The only problem is that the user is almost certainly going to dash your hopes for an easy deployment. Users do the unexpected — they press key combinations simply to see what will happen, possibly because they're bored to tears and have nothing better to do with their time. (I say this tongue in cheek because most users are extremely busy and tend to do odd things simply because they haven't taken time to read the instructions.)

Developers can't perform user testing — only users can perform user testing. This may seem like an obvious statement at first, but it may surprise you to discover that more than a few organizations leave user testing in the hands of developers or the good folks in quality assurance (QA). If you really want to test the user interface and other user requirements, then you must rely on the users who will actually use the software to perform the task. This is the reason that large vendors, such as Microsoft, commonly engage in beta tests and Community Technology Previews (CTPs). Without user testing, you don't know that your application works as anticipated, despite any level of testing you want to perform otherwise.

Unfortunately, trying to get the user to test the software properly is difficult to say the least. Test results are often affected by the very idea that the user is testing the software. The user tends not to perform tasks using the same set of steps as usual. The "bored factor" doesn't set in and the user's harried schedule doesn't intrude. You don't receive good testing results because the testing environment doesn't reflect the environment in which the user will work with the software. Often, you have to resort to releasing the software as some type of preproduction application, rather than tell the users that they're using beta software (or other testing terms).

Even if the user tests the software using the same techniques as usual, there's a problem with getting good reports. After all, the user has no clue as to how your application works and, more importantly, doesn't care. Consequently, you have to include some type of reporting functionality as part of the software. Many vendors now include an option to send reports automatically for each application error as a general practice. Because the software you're testing is for your organization, you can simply add code to gather the information you need in the background and send it off quietly to maintain the integrity of the test environment.

It's important to remember that user testing isn't the same as lab testing. The user's machine is unlikely to have the same processing power as your development machine. In addition, the user will have all kinds of third-party software running and will likely sneak in a few applications from home. All these factors conspire to place your software in an environment that you can't possibly test using a test suite. User testing is a frustrating but necessary process that every developer must perform at some point during application testing, always before application deployment. Chapter 15 provides additional information about user testing as part of a complete testing and debugging scenario.

Enhancing Reliability and Security

The application is essentially complete. You've debugged it and fixed all the most frightening problems. The users have finally approved of your work and even the managers think you have something worthwhile. The application has basic security and you've even tuned it to ensure it runs relatively fast. Unbelievably, your application still isn't quite finished. It's time to put that final tuning in place. What you have now is a great application, but you want to ensure that it's both reliable and secure. You can't really perform this stage of application development until immediately before deployment because it relies on a frozen design. At this stage, you don't add any new features or do anything else that would tend to modify this version of the program.

You often hear the media talking about application performance and its importance to the world as a whole, but what is performance? Everyone has misused the term performance for so long that it means something different for every person you talk to and sometimes it means several things at the same time. This book uses three terms to discuss performance:

- **Speed:** How fast the application correctly performs the tasks for which you designed it.
- **Reliability:** The amount of time the application runs without crashing, causing damage to the data it manipulates, or confusing the user.
- **Security:** The ability of the application to perform its assigned tasks without divulging any data to unauthorized entities.

An application that performs well has a balanced mix of speed, reliability, and security. Achieving this balance is perhaps the hardest part of application design because people view this requirement in different ways. You probably have users working with your application right now who could care less about security — all they want is for the application to work as fast as possible so they can get done with their work. Some managers may want the application locked down so hard that no one will ever accomplish any useful work with it. Because you're the developer, you have the unenviable task of creating a balanced application that somehow meets everyone's needs — a very difficult task indeed.

When tuning the reliability features of your application, you're looking beyond the basics. You should have already answered the question of what happens when the user types an unexpected entry in a field on a form. The application should already handle unanticipated keystrokes as well. No, tuning at this point becomes a matter of testing and fixing things outside user control. For example, you might want to ask what will happen when the Web service that acts as the locus of information for your application fails. You need to think about the impossible and test for it. Even if you think something can't possibly happen, this is the phase at which you test for that very problem.

Your application also has basic security in place before you get to this point. The application knows to ask the user for name and password (or other identification) as needed. The lines of communication are secure and you know that the application encrypts data transferred on the network. All these basic features are already in place. At this point, you're hardening your application. You may even hire a security company to attempt to get into your application from the outside if you have Internet exposure. It's important to think about what will happen if the user's machine has a virus — will that machine send all your valuable data to someone with ill intent?

Always keep the balanced application scenario in mind. You can't build a wall high enough to keep out every intruder. The application you create will never provide 100 percent reliability either. This stage of application helps you create balance so that the application performs well when you deploy it on the server and user systems. It also enlightens you about potential issues. Security and reliability are as much about knowing the source of problems as they are about writing your application in a specific way. Applications always require monitoring because they will always present some problem you didn't anticipate. Part III of the book helps you achieve this balance. Chapter 18 describes the performance triangle in detail. Chapters 19, 20, and 21 discuss speed, reliability, and security enhancements you can make to your application.

Deploying the Application

You know your application isn't perfect, but it works as anticipated and performs well. It's time to let the user try the application in a production environment. Even if you haven't written the entire application yet, you have enough in place that the user can perform useful work, so it's essential to get the application out into a real-world environment while you work on the next application piece. Of course, there are a number of deployment levels. You may choose to deploy the application locally until you complete it so that you have better control over how users interact with it. Likewise, you might make an enterprise-wide deployment after the application is cast in stone and provides a complete feature set. Chapter 16 discusses these levels of deployment so that you have a better idea of the options you have.

Once you decide where to deploy your application, you also need to consider how to deploy it. In the past, Windows applications often included complex installation programs. In fact, all shrink-wrapped software still includes these installation programs. However, you do have other options that may actually provide installations that are more reliable. For example, you can create an XCopy installation (a reference to the DOS utility of the same name) where the simple act of copying the application to a specific folder on the host system is enough. Applications still require some method of storing settings. One of the most popular methods today for making an XCopy installation work is to program the application to use serialized eXtensible Markup Language (XML) for data storage. Chapter 22 tells you all about serialized XML and shows how your application can benefit from it.

Choosing the right media for your application deployment is also a requirement. The first option that many organizations choose is to download the application through a network connection. Right after the organization restarts its servers because the deployment took them offline, these organizations consider another route. A second valuable option is to use the network locally and DVDs to distribute the application to remote locations. Using this option comes with hidden costs for the DVDs, but it's also very reliable. You may even choose to perform a phased rollout where you install pieces of the application one at a time until the entire application is in place. Even though this option requires more time, it also stresses organization infrastructure less. The technique you use to distribute an application is important because it's one of the issues you can't really test very well — in this case, expect the worst and you probably won't be disappointed.

Many organizations have older machines that don't include newer options such as DVDs. If your application is small enough, you can always use a CD to distribute it. You may choose to use a flash drive to distribute the application, because most computers today have a Universal Serial Bus (USB) port — even older computers. The point is to choose a medium that works well for all the computers in your organization.

After you decide on the deployment method, you need to test it. Make sure you perform tests in every environment in which you plan to deploy the application. Just because an application installation works fine locally doesn't mean that a remote installation will work equally well. It's important to check for issues such as firewalls. Some remote systems may have virus protection that won't work with your installation program, especially if you rely on an Internet connection to perform the installation.

Supporting and Maintaining the Application

For some developers, the application lifecycle ends when they deliver the completed application. The orphaned application ends by not performing as expected for very long. As with anything, applications require support and maintenance.

A developer supports an application by accepting user input about it and researching solutions as needed. In many cases, the developer must provide information to support personnel so that they know how to resolve application issues. In addition, the developer often trains support staff in application usage so that the support staff can help end users. The developer really must do more than simply write code to support the application adequately.

Maintenance occurs when a developer must make a change to an application to prolong its useful life span. Some applications, such as virus protection, require frequent maintenance, while other applications, such as a name and address database, require less maintenance. All applications require maintenance at some point in their lifecycle. Here are some reasons that you'll need to perform maintenance on the applications you write:

- ❑ Users find bugs in the application.
- ❑ The organization's needs change enough to warrant a small change in your application, but not enough to require an entirely new application version.
- ❑ Someone finds a vulnerability in your application that you must fix to ensure the application remains reliable and secure.
- ❑ Organization growth or other changes require that you make changes to the application to support the new environment.
- ❑ Someone makes a suggested change that will greatly improve usability, flexibility, speed, reliability, or security.
- ❑ Users require additional reports or other output.
- ❑ A change in the data source requires that you make a change to the application in order to retrieve data successfully.

It often happens that the developer who writes an application isn't the one who maintains the application. Perhaps you wrote the application and then moved to another city. All the documentation discussed so far in the chapter is the lifeblood of those who follow behind to support and maintain an application. Consequently, you always want to provide the best documentation that you can to those who follow. After all, you may find yourself in the position of maintaining an application, and it's certain that you'll want the best documentation available for your maintenance tasks. Chapter 17 provides additional information about supporting and maintaining applications.

Retiring the Application

At some point, your application will likely near the end of its useful life and you'll have to retire it. In most cases, applications have a definite end of life. However, some applications seem to go on and on (witness some of the COBOL applications still running from the 1960s out there — yes, they're still active, see the article at `http://weblog.infoworld.com/tech-bottom-line/archives/2008/08/calling_all_cob.html`). Consequently, this stage of the lifecycle doesn't necessarily have a distinct starting point.

Despite an inability to see the future, you should plan the retirement of your application. What you need to think about is asking, given a specific set of circumstances, "When will the application fail to serve the users in my organization?" You can usually base the retirement strategy for your application on one of the following events:

- The organization grows in size and the application no longer provides complete access to organization resources.
- The state of software and hardware changes so that the application no longer runs reliably on newer systems.
- The needs of your organization change through mergers, consolidations, or spin-offs.
- The problem the software solves is no longer around — perhaps a new technology solves the problem completely.
- The problem the software solves has changed so that you need a new solution.
- Vendors no longer support the technology used to create the solution.

By planning ahead for any of these (or other) retirement scenarios, you can avoid the situation in which many organizations today find themselves — namely, supporting software so old and fragile that most of the developers have no idea of when it will break next. Organizations typically have to weigh the retirement of software against the cost of creating new software, the inconvenience and costs of transition, and the availability of developers with enough knowledge of the software to retire it. This last requirement is where you come into play. Part of your lifecycle planning must include getting the information required to retire the application into the right hands.

Considering a Lifecycle Model

The lifecycle is a process of a sort. It's not an actual procedure that you follow step by step, but more of a series of application events that occur. In sum, the discussion of the events in a lifecycle is a theoretical view of how things work in general. Of course, you're building a real application and require a real process to complete it. A *lifecycle model* is a method of creating a lifecycle for your application based on real-world goals and requirements. Using a lifecycle model helps you create a sequence of events for your application based on best practices that have evolved through years of trial and error by other developers.

Just as there are different kinds of applications, there are a number of lifecycle models. There isn't any such thing as a right or a wrong lifecycle model. You must choose a lifecycle model that matches the requirements for the:

- Application
- Organization
- Individual developers on your team
- Management expectations
- Expected application lifetime
- Anticipated application goals and output

In many cases, more than one model could help you achieve specific results, so it becomes a matter of choosing the model that best fits all the requirements. You may have to mix and match model elements to create a perfect lifecycle model for your application. However, it's important to remember that this is a model, not a blueprint. Models represent an ideal condition. It's expected that the application will deviate a little from the model — flexibility is the keyword when creating a lifecycle model. With this in mind, the following sections present a few of the common lifecycle models that organizations use to define the events in the life of their applications.

Using the Spiral Model

The spiral model relies on incremental evolutionary prototyping to produce an application. According to a number of sources, Barry Boehm defined this model in his 1988 article entitled, "A Spiral Model of Software Development and Enhancement" (see the Web site at `http://portal.acm.org/citation.cfm?id=45797.45801` for details). Each spiral builds on the previous spiral to define a completed application. The spirals represent a complete development cycle. In short, the customer sees a completed application at the end of each cycle and then evaluates the application for usability and completeness. This is a risk-based process where each cycle analyzes the risk of a particular design to ensure the application will eventually end up as a cohesive and usable product. You typically use the spiral model when:

- The project requirements are hard to define due to project complexity.
- The customer isn't completely sure about the kind of application required to meet a need.
- The technologies used to answer a specific need are new or not completely tested.

The spiral constantly builds the application and encourages customer participation by showing the results of each development cycle. Figure 2-1 shows the basics of the spiral model.

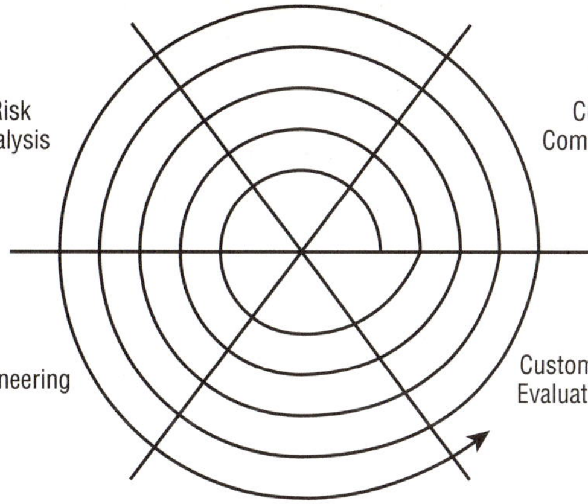

Figure 2-1: The spiral model relies on an evolutionary development process to achieve results.

As shown in the figure, every cycle begins with customer communication and ends with customer evaluation. Here is a description of each of the steps in the spiral model.

- **Customer communication:** The customer communicates needs or requirements for the application to the developer. The first time the customer discusses the project is the hardest because you don't have any application to discuss. Subsequent discussions become easier because the customer can view the application and make requests based on the current application state.
- **Planning:** The developer creates a specification based on the customer's requirements. You begin defining resources for the project and look for potential team members. In most cases, this is the step where you determine whether a particular application concept will even work and may have meetings with the customer to discuss application specification issues.
- **Risk analysis:** The development team performs a critical review of the technical and management risks of the project. The team also begins implementing the design.
- **Engineering:** The engineering step begins the design process in earnest. The design team creates both high-level and low-level design elements. In all cases, the customer sees mock-ups of user interface, report, and other user elements. This is also the point at which you test the design to ensure you've considered all aspects of the application requirements.
- **Construction and release:** Combining a wealth of elements from the standard lifecycle model, developers write, debug, and test the code. The development team also installs the application on the user's system, provides any required documentation, and supports the application as needed.
- **Customer evaluation:** The customer reviews the application and tests all the functions it provides. This step usually requires that the customer provide written feedback on the application. It can also include automated bug reports to the development team. The purpose of this step is to determine whether the application is ready for use or requires another cycle.

Using the Waterfall Model

The waterfall model actually evokes a picture of a waterfall (some developers also call it the sequential software development model). The application planning, design, and implementation flow from one level to the next, until you finally end up with a finished application. A number of versions of the waterfall model exist because many developers started using this model back in 1970. In fact, according to a number of sources, the originator of the model, Winston W. Royce, actually used the model as an example of a flawed development process. However, some developers saw promise in the model and modified it to overcome the flaws Royce specified.

Most developers today see the waterfall model as noniterative and inflexible. In most cases, the waterfall model isn't suitable for large development projects because it's nearly impossible to complete one phase of the development process before you start another. Completing each phase completely is a necessity if you want to obtain optimal results using this model. Another issue is that any bug or design flaw found late in the development process increases the time and effort required to complete the application substantially.

Despite these limitations, large government installations such as the Department of Defense (DOD) and National Aeronautics and Space Administration (NASA) frequently use the waterfall model. Developers who like the waterfall model say that time spent with the design up front can save significant time later and that it's possible to create an application significantly faster using the waterfall model than with other models. In addition, supporters point out that the waterfall model is probably the easiest model to use and understand. You typically use the waterfall model when:

- The software design is relatively simple.
- The technologies used to create the application are all tested and well known.
- The application is an update of existing software.

This book doesn't explore all of the permutations of the waterfall model (see `http://codecourse.sourceforge.net/materials/The-Waterfall-Lifecycle-Model.html` for a description of many of the waterfall model derivatives). Instead, it uses the version commonly called waterfall with feedback as shown in Figure 2-2. This particular model does fix some of the problems with other versions of the waterfall model because it includes a measure of iteration in the process. Even so, use the waterfall model with care on large projects.

When working with the waterfall model, you move up and down the model elements as indicated by the arrows in Figure 2-2. For example, if you run into a problem during integration testing, you might go back to the implementation phase to discover what went wrong. Here's a description of each of the steps in the waterfall model:

- **Requirements:** The development team discusses the specifics of the application with the customer. The development team creates a list of requirements based on this discussion and obtains customer approval for them. The point of this phase is to obtain a list of problems that the application should solve. The customer needs to know what the application should do up front. Otherwise, this phase will lead to flaws later in the process.
- **Specification:** The development team creates a document that describes the application fully. This document includes everything from the design of the user interface to the reports that the application will output. In addition, the development team must consider some of the

low-level issues, such as data access and security. The specification need not include implementation details; it simply states that the application will perform certain tasks in a specific manner. When the customer approves this document, the requirements for the application are set in stone and can't change. However, if the customer sees that the specification doesn't meet the anticipated requirements, this version of the waterfall model sends everyone back to the requirements phase to work out the requirements in more detail.

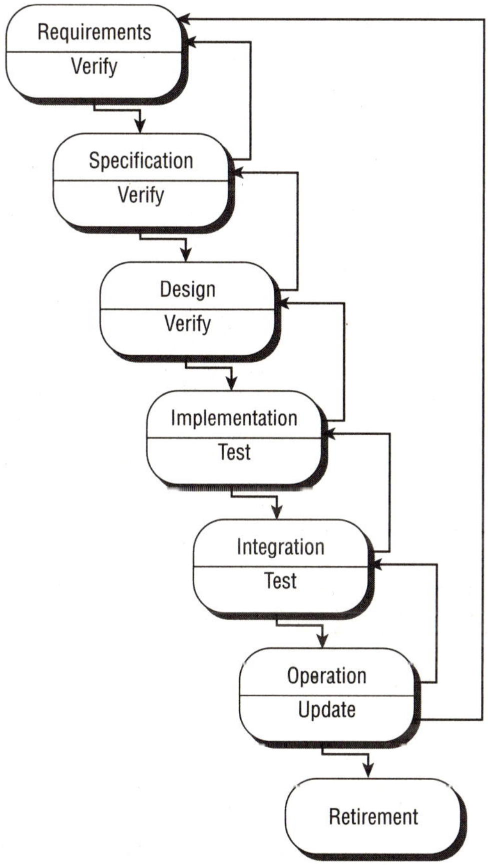

Figure 2-2: The waterfall model is what most developers used before agile and other lifecycle programming technologies became popular.

- **Design:** The development team creates a document that specifies precisely how the application will work. The document specifies precisely how the developers will code each model and may include pseudo-code. In many cases, the details in this document are well beyond the technical capabilities of the customer. However, the customer must still sign off on the document. If the customer doesn't understand how the design works, the development team must explain it. In some cases, the development team must go back to the specification phase to help the customer understand how the application will work.

- **Implementation:** At this point, the development team finally starts writing code. The standard practice is to write one module at a time and test that module completely. Each module is a standalone product. Consequently, the module can appear multiple times in the final application or serve a single purpose as needed. In most cases, the customer sees only the user interface modules without the accompanying low-level modules. The customer doesn't have a working application to test at this point. If one or more modules consistently fail testing, the development team may go back to the design phase to implement changes in the application design. These changes can become costly from a time perspective.
- **Integration:** When the development team completes all of the modules used to create the application, the process of integrating the modules begins. The standard practice is to add the modules required to attain a specific level of application functionality and then perform integration testing on the application as a whole. In some cases, the modules will fail to work together properly. When this situation occurs, the development team may have to go back to the implementation phase to rewrite and test the modules. Most importantly, this is the phase where the customer can lose confidence in the development team and cancel the application development contract. Often, a poorly designed application leaves no other alternative.
- **Operation:** After the application passes integration testing, the development team installs the software on the customer's system and tests it in a production environment. Problems on the customer system usually require a move back to the integration phase and possibly to the implementation phase to make corrections. After a period of successful operation, when the application fails to provide the functionality that the customer desires, the application goes into an update cycle.
- **Retirement:** As with any other application, you eventually retire the application designed using the waterfall model.

Using the Throwaway Model

The throwaway model (also known as the code-and-fix or build-and-fix model) is essentially a placeholder for applications you design and build for yourself. You don't intend to keep the resulting application. You can use this model for a number of tasks including:

- Discovering how a new technology works.
- Prototyping a solution for an existing application.
- Creating a short-term tool for a specific need.
- Prototyping an application feature for other stakeholders to show an output.
- Testing several options to determine which solution will work best.

The throwaway model eschews formal plans and review processes for speed. The application is usually short and not fully functional. In fact, the application may not even have a user interface of any sort. A throwaway application is one in which you worry most about writing the code to discover something unique.

There isn't anything wrong with creating throwaway code, as long as you actually throw it away. One of the problems with throwaway applications is that they can end up on a friend's machine. In many cases, the application then spreads further — sometimes even outside your company. The poorly designed code in a throwaway application has no place in a full-fledged serious application in your company. In fact, you'll generally want to delete the application immediately after seeing what it can do for you.

When using the throwaway model for prototyping, you focus on the application output, rather than the method used to achieve that output. In most cases, the code used for the prototype looks nothing like the code used within the actual application. You may simply set values to a particular value to demonstrate an output, not a particular output. It's important to make others realize that the code you're using is a prototype, rather than the final code. Otherwise, users might have unrealistic expectations about delivery dates and the appearance of the output.

Always label throwaway code as such. Make sure you include comments in the code that make it apparent that the code is not for production use. Some developers are tempted to incorporate throwaway code in the final application. Avoid this potential pitfall because using throwaway code in a production application always has negative results.

Using the Evolutionary Model

The evolutionary model relies on software prototyping as the means for creating an application. In other words, you work intensely with the client by creating the forms and reports required for the application and then adding the glue code required to make those forms and reports functional as you go. This model typically uses the following steps to create an application:

1. Define the basic application (actually a module in this case) requirements.
2. Create a working prototype of the functional unit.
3. Verify the prototype with the customer.
4. Change or elaborate the application requirements as necessary.
5. Repeat Steps 1 through 4 until the customer approves the module.
6. Repeat Steps 1 through 5 for the next module.

As you can see, this is the least structured of all the models discussed so far. Many consultants try to avoid this approach because a simple application can quickly become a huge project. You typically use the evolutionary model when:

- The customer doesn't understand the software requirements at the outset of the project.
- The project involves developing an entirely new type of software that lacks any best practices derived from similar projects.
- The customer is developing experimental products of some type (think inventor here).
- The development team has little or no confidence in the software architecture and algorithms.

The biggest advantage of this particular model is that the development team constantly interacts with the customer, making it less likely that a major design issue will go unnoticed. In addition, the constant customer input tends to ensure that the application will work as desired in the end — as long as you don't encounter counterproductive political forces within the customer organization.

Using the evolutionary model requires strong management because this model can quickly spiral out of control and result in failure. The evolutionary model is a high-risk model, so you don't want to make many (if any) promises about delivery dates or functionality. In fact, this highly experimental model doesn't guarantee any results at all. Of course, this method also promotes sloppy documentation techniques, even if the development team understands the underlying principles well.

Using the Incremental/Iterative Model

The incremental/iterative model creates an application by building it a small piece at a time. The design team breaks the application into functional pieces (called builds) at the outset of the project. The idea is to build each piece separately, test it, and then add it to the whole. If this process sounds a bit like the waterfall model, the incremental/iterative model does build on the waterfall model. However, it also overcomes a considerable number of problems with the waterfall model.

The main problem with this model is the process of breaking the application into components. If the development team creates too few components, the application development process can begin to look like the code-and-fix (throwaway) model where the development team spends most of its time debugging the application. However, creating too many components can result in a loss of the main benefit of this model — creating the software quickly while giving the customer something to test. For example, if you created a word processor using this model, the first component might include the functionality required to type and save documents. The next build might contain print functionality. After that, you might add a spelling checker or some other application functionality.

A secondary problem is that the development team can lose perspective on the overall application picture. This model tends to focus development team attention on one component at a time, which is why there's a speed increase, but managers will need to review the overall application picture constantly. You typically use the incremental/iterative model when:

- The development team has a good understanding of the software requirements.
- The customer requires software as soon as possible with frequent updates.
- The application is easy to divide into components.
- Management wants to maintain firm control over the development of each component.

The incremental/iterative model does promote customer participation and produces software fast, as long as the customer really does know what the software should do. Figure 2-3 shows the basics of the incremental/iterative model.

As you can see from Figure 2-3, each build of the incremental/iterative model consists of four steps required to create that module. The results of the previous build feed into the next build.

The incremental/iterative model has several advantages. Of course, the customer obtains constant updates of working software, so there are fewer surprises. This model is also extremely flexible, making it possible to add or remove application features simply by adding or removing builds (components). The costs of changes to a particular build are also relatively small. From a manager perspective, the incremental/iterative model is relatively easy to manage, because you only need to consider one piece of the application at a time. Here's a description of each of the steps in the incremental/iterative model:

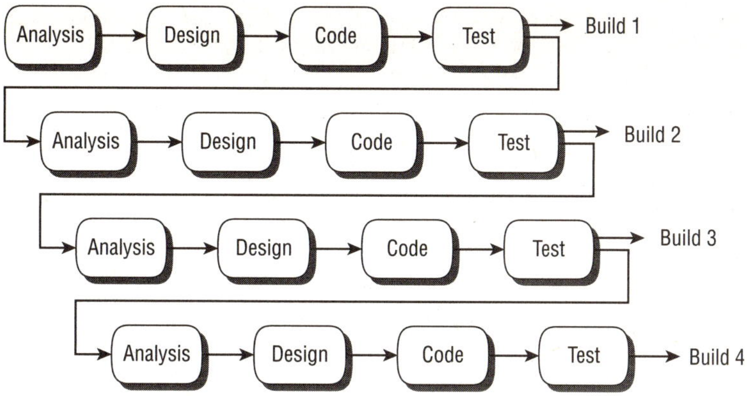

Figure 2-3: The incremental/iterative model is an improved form of the waterfall model.

- **Analysis:** During the first build, the development team creates an overall view of the application by working with the client. The development team then breaks the application down into components that provide specific functionality for each build. During subsequent builds, the development team works with the customer to define the characteristics of the current build. These characteristics include improvements to the previously released build as well as the expectations for the component for the current build. The customer continues to work with the software produced by the previous build to provide input to the development team.
- **Design:** The development team creates a specification and design for the current component. The rest of the application remains a sketch that the development team won't work with until the specified build. Consequently, the development team is forced to focus attention on one aspect of the application at a time, making the development team more efficient. The customer also receives mock-ups of reports and the new user interface elements during this step.
- **Code:** After the customer approves of the design for the current component, the development team writes the code for it. This model requires that the development team pay particular attention to interfaces. In order for this model to work properly, the interfaces must remain the same during each build. Otherwise, the components can't talk with each other.
- **Test:** During this phase, the development team performs debugging and testing. Debugging and testing are relatively easy because of the use of modular programming techniques. The customer becomes involved in user-level testing. After the testing is complete, the development team loads the new build onto the customer equipment and begins the next development cycle.

Using the Rapid Application Development (RAD) Model

James Martin originally introduced the term *RAD* in 1991. In this original form, RAD emphasizes the rapid construction of prototypes to model various processes and the use of iterative development to keep all stakeholders involved and constantly updated on changes to the application. Because RAD emphasizes the use of frameworks and automation, the resulting application generally performs less well than a hand-coded application and the user may see a slight loss of functionality. However, in exchange, the RAD model does provide faster application development and easier application maintenance. Most developers today use some form of RAD for their development, and Microsoft has based Visual Studio on RAD concepts. You typically use the RAD model when:

- The application requires access to complex data sources, such as in a business environment.
- The customer requires constant updates and needs the application quickly.
- Performance and precise functionality aren't a concern.
- Easy maintenance requirements are a concern.
- The customer wants to use as much automation as possible to reduce costs.

There are some negative aspects of using RAD. Unless you use robust tools and manage the development process carefully, a RAD application can end up producing an endless array of prototypes without delivering a completed application. In addition, this model only works on applications that you can modularize, which means that while it does work for the majority of business applications, it wouldn't be a good choice for real-time or factory automation systems for the most part.

This model does provide for quick initial reviews. In fact, using some setups, you could conceivably design the user interface during your initial meeting with the customer. (The code that you use to activate the controls would have to wait until later.) The prototyping nature of this model also promotes constant customer feedback and makes major communication errors less likely than when using other models listed in this chapter. Figure 2-4 shows the basics of the RAD model.

As shown in Figure 2-4, the RAD model relies on a number of modeling or prototyping phases. In each case, the development team spends a lot of time with the customer discussing each aspect of the application design process. Each prototyping phase is a refinement of the phase before it, until you get to the application generation phase in which the development team adds code required to make the prototypes come to life. Here's a description of each of the steps in the RAD model:

- **Business modeling:** The development team focuses on data flow. In fact, RAD specializes in prototyping data flows and making complex environments easier to model. The development team asks the customer questions such as the following:
    - What information drives the business process?
    - What information does the business process generate?
    - Who generates the information used within the business process?
    - Where does the information go once it leaves the business process?
    - How does the business process transform the data?
- **Data modeling:** The development team takes the information derived from the business-modeling phase and uses it to create a series of data objects. Each of these objects represents a particular aspect of the business model. The development team then assigns attributes to each of the objects. Finally, the development team defines the relationships between each of the objects. The output of this phase is the database used to support the application and the various structures within the application used to access the data.

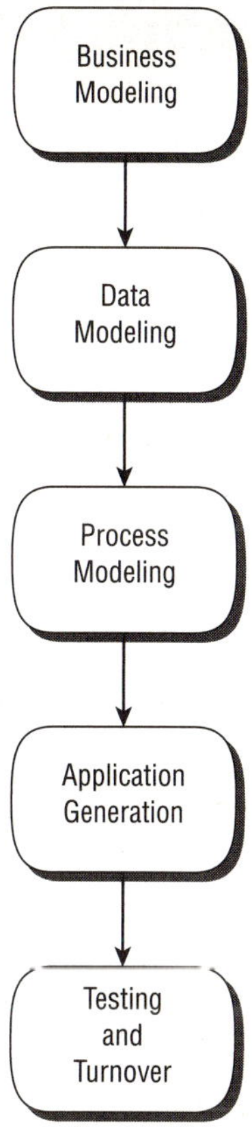

Figure 2-4: Use the RAD model to develop applications faster and make maintenance easier.

- **Process modeling:** The development team transforms the data model into a series of application objects that can retrieve, add, delete, edit, or update the data model objects. As part of this process, the development team defines the flow of data between the various application objects.
- **Application generation:** At this point, the automated tools help the development team generate the user interface used to manipulate the application objects. In addition, the development team uses these tools to create reports and other output the customer requires.
- **Testing and turnover:** The development team performs localized testing and then distributes the application for user-level testing. Because most of this process relies on pretested code, the debugging and testing cycle is shorter than when using other models. However, the development team must still exercise all custom objects and interfaces to ensure the application works as anticipated.

Using Agile Programming Techniques

After you decide on a lifecycle model, you need to consider the programming techniques to use for your application. You make this decision before you begin designing the application because the programming technique helps define the design strategy. This section of the chapter provides insights into a programming technique called agile programming.

Agile doesn't come in just one form — you find many agile programming techniques discussed on the Internet. In fact, agile didn't arrive as a single technology. Many developers contributed toward making agile the programming technology you see today. Consequently, the following sections begin by describing agile programming in a little more detail. The subsections then provide an overview of some of the agile programming techniques.

> **Don't Fall for Fad Development Techniques**
>
> To hear some people talk, you'd think that agile is the next best thing to commercial space travel when it comes to application development. Yes, most developers agree that agile really does meet many of its high-sounding goals. However, as with any other programming technique, agile can fall short when the development team and other stakeholders normally use a different technique and don't understand the agile programming process. If your organization is happy with the results of the waterfall model, then by all means continue to use the waterfall model. Don't fall for the hubbub generated by the latest fad technique to hit the market; use what works for you. Of course, it also doesn't hurt to try new techniques on small projects, which is why you should at least consider agile when time and resources permit. You may very well join the many developers who ask why they didn't start using agile sooner.

Understanding Agile Programming

Developers originally began using agile programming techniques in the mid-1990s as a reaction to the heavily managed waterfall model described in the "Using the Waterfall Model" section of this chapter. Using the waterfall model often resulted in applications that didn't meet the original design goals, applications that arrived late, and an application environment in which changes happened slowly or not at all. Agile programming technologies tend to focus on speed of development and stakeholder interaction.

Not every project is agile programming friendly. The speed of development that agile promotes can result in a loss of application speed, which is an important factor in real-time and embedded application development. In addition, because agile tends to focus on code reuse and the use of off-the-shelf modules, you may find it difficult to customize an application as fully as the customer wants. The greater the level of customization, the more likely it is that your application doesn't fit the agile model.

Most developers today view agile as the best programming technique to apply to the vast majority of applications. The reasons for this viewpoint are many. You can read the details at `http://agilemanifesto.org/`. From an overview perspective, agile provides these benefits over other lifecycle models:

- Customer needs are placed before the application specification, so that the resulting software better meets customer needs. (The term *customer* is used loosely in this case to include any software user, even a user who is part of your organization.)
- The customer receives frequent updates of working software so that it's possible to see changes before they become permanent and the customer can engage in constant testing.
- A developer measures progress using working software, rather than by meeting milestone requirements.
- This programming technique welcomes changes throughout the process, even late in the development cycle
- The development process relies on input from all stakeholders — developers, users, and management.
- Stakeholders engage in face-to-face communication, rather than relying on written documentation.
- Tasks focus on the trusted individual, rather than teams, so that responsibility is easier to assess.
- In many cases, agile provides a simpler programming environment by breaking the task into smaller pieces.
- Theoretically, the use of agile helps break larger groups into smaller, self-organizing teams.
- Agile does as its name implies, by making software development react to changes quickly and efficiently.
- Theoretically, all these features result in higher-quality software based on good design principles.

Agile programming techniques tend not to work well with government and other projects with a high number of written deliverables. The agile developer tends to focus more on a working product than on application documentation. In fact, stakeholders for agile projects often prioritize a working product far higher than any paperwork deliverables.

Benefits of Agile Programming

Agile programming generally works best for small projects with a group of elite programmers. When you get the right group of developers together, they can produce significant application results in an incredibly short amount of time. Comparing agile to other iterative models, you often get results in weeks, rather than months.

One of the best uses of agile programming is when you have a project that lacks precise specifications. The customer doesn't really know what's needed or wanted. The constant interaction with the development team helps the customer derive a workable specification over time. The nearly constant small releases help the customer refine the application requirements without costing the project a significant amount of time and money.

It's important not to confuse agile with what's typically termed as cowboy programming, where the developer shoots from the hip by doing whatever he or she feels is correct. The members of the development team in an agile project face constant scrutiny of their development plans. In addition, agile promotes rigorous and disciplined processes. Consequently, with agile you get all the structure without all the bloat of a normal programming experience.

Unlike most other models (except RAD), agile has a built-in philosophy for handling data. Consequently, database management doesn't have the bolted-on feel that it sometimes has when working with other models. You can read about the six philosophies of agile database management at `http://www.agiledata.org/essays/philosophies.html`.

Deficiencies of Agile Programming

The waterfall lifecycle model may seem like old hat, but as of this writing it's alive and quite well because there really isn't a suitable replacement. The contrast between the waterfall model and agile programming is so huge as to be nearly impossible to comprehend — it's as if the two programming strategies were created in different worlds. Yet, viewing the differences between the two strategies can help you understand some of the criticisms leveled at agile programming. The most important of these is the lack of documentation that commonly occurs when participating in an agile project. Written documentation is a necessity for large projects that commonly have some novice- and intermediate-level developers.

Because agile depends heavily on face-to-face communication, it often falls short when a project spans several sites. The developers and stakeholders require constant communication, so a single site development works best. It's possible to augment the single-site requirement using video conferencing and other techniques, but at some point, the cost for doing so may become prohibitive. If you plan to provide a distributed agile environment, it pays to read articles such as "Bridging the Distance" (`http://www.ddj.com/architect/184414899`) and "Using an Agile Software Process with Offshore Development" (`http://www.martinfowler.com/articles/agileOffshore.html`).

Most organizations view agile as a small-project-only strategy, and unless you're willing to jump through some serious hoops, anything more than 20 developers may not work. Consider the issue of face-to-face contact. When you have a team of five developers, then there's a possibility of 25 contact pairs on any given day, which is quite manageable. However, when you start talking about 40 developers on a team, the number of contacts rises to 1,600 per day, which leaves time for a quick hello to each team member before you go home for the day. Some authors have bridged the small-project gap partially — view articles such as "Supersize Me" (`http://www.ddj.com/architect/184415491`) for ideas.

Common Agile Programming Strategies

As mentioned earlier, agile isn't a single programming strategy. In fact, agile encompasses a number of strategies, each with its particular strength. This chapter doesn't provide a detailed description of each of the agile programming strategies. However, the following sections provide a good overview of each so that you can decide which strategies to review in detail.

Scrum

The Scrum concept of agile programming originally appeared as part of a 1986 article entitled, "The New New Product Development Game" (see `http://harvardbusinessonline.hbsp.harvard.edu/b01/en/common/item_detail.jhtml?id=86116` for details) by Hirotaka Takeuchi and Ikujiro Nonaka. Other people added more to the original concept until Scrum came out as part of *Agile Software Development with SCRUM* by Ken Schwaber and Mike Beedle in 2001. The original intent of this programming strategy is software development project management. However, many developers have adapted Scrum for other uses.

Scrum takes its name from rugby. The individual members of a Scrum include the ScrumMaster who acts as the project manager, Product Owner who represents the stakeholders, and the team (the developers working on the project). The ScrumMaster and Product Owner work together to break an application into components called the product backlog, which is prioritized so the team addresses the most-needed items first. The development process occurs over a period of 15 to 30 days called a sprint. Before the sprint begins, the Product Owner tells the team which items are most important for the current sprint. The team decides which items it can deliver in that time. At this point, the sprint begins and no one can make any changes to the product backlog, which means the requirements are frozen.

You'll find that the Scrum development process is actually divided into two groups called pigs and chickens. The designations come from the following joke:

> *A pig and a chicken are walking down a road. The chicken looks at the pig and says, "Hey, why don't we open a restaurant?" The pig looks back at the chicken and says, "Good idea, what do you want to call it?" The chicken thinks about it and says, "Why don't we call it 'Ham and Eggs'?" "I don't think so," says the pig. "I'd be committed, but you'd only be involved."*

The ScrumMaster, Product Owner, and team are all pigs. They're allowed to speak at meetings and participate actively because they're committed to the application. The users, stakeholders, and managers are all chickens. They provide feedback through recognized channels and can come to meetings to see how the application is progressing. There are actually rules regarding pigs and chickens for meetings, but you'll want to review the resources in this section to discover them. In addition, the pigs are responsible for creating three pieces of documentation: product backlog (the items that haven't been addressed), sprint backlog (describing the items the team will address during the current sprint), and the burn down (the status of tasks for the current sprint).

The advantage of using Scrum is that it's very easy to learn and use — especially if you already have a background in rugby. The breakneck pace of development, however, means that the team may be tempted to take shortcuts in order to meet the requirements of the current sprint. In short, Scrum emphasizes pure speed on the part of the team due to the precise sprint interval. The best place to learn additional information about Scrum is from the ScrumAlliance at `http://www.scrumalliance.org/`.

Crystal Clear

Crystal Clear is all about the people. It focuses on efficiency and habitability, rather than on processes and artifacts. Alistair Cockburn originally proposed Crystal Clear in 2004 as part of his book, *Crystal Clear, A Human-Powered Methodology for Small Teams*. This agile programming technique espouses the following concepts or properties:

- Frequent delivery of usable code to users
- Reflective improvement
- Osmotic communication (preferably by being collocated)
- Personal safety
- Focus
- Easy access to expert users
- Automated tests, configuration management, and frequent integration

Of these concepts, only the first three are required — the rest are optional. The typical Crystal Clear team has no more than eight people because larger groups require more management to perform well. You can discover more about these seven properties in the article entitled, "Crystal Clear Applied: The Seven Properties of Running an Agile Project," by Alistair Cockburn at `http://www.informit.com/articles/article.aspx?p=345009`. You'll also want to read the material on Crystal Clear methods at `http://alistair.cockburn.us/index.php/Crystal_light_methods`.

The concept of osmotic communication is interesting. The group sits in the same room. Someone asks a question and other developers answer or continue to work on their project. Devoting time to the topic at hand is optional, but listening isn't. The idea is that all the developers in the room absorb the communication taking place, as through osmosis. This part of Crystal Clear probably doesn't work well in groups larger than five or six people because larger groups would tend to need some type of managed conversation.

Extreme Programming (XP)

Extreme Programming (XP) is very much like its name says — it relies on programming methodologies taken to an extreme level in order to respond to stakeholder needs more reliably and promptly. In some respects, there's nothing new about XP because it relies on the same software engineering practices used for older development models. What's new is the extreme part of the equation. XP embodies five special goals as shown in the following list:

- Reconcile humanity and productivity.
- Act as a mechanism for social change.
- Provide a path to improvement.
- Define a style of development.
- Create a software development discipline.

Although these are all high-sounding goals, the basic premise behind XP is to introduce flexibility into the development process. XP seeks to introduce the flexibility, while maintaining the deliberate and disciplined approach used by earlier software models. In short, it's attempting to provide you with the best of both the waterfall model and agile programming techniques. You can obtain a better view of XP at `http://www.extremeprogramming.org/`.

Using XP makes it possible to add new requirements as needed to a software development project by introducing a high level of stakeholder interaction. The stakeholders are part of the entire process, making it possible to better gauge the usability of the software before major mistakes occur. However, these merits of XP also have drawbacks. Many XP projects suffer from unstable requirements, a lack of documentation of the interaction between developer and user, and an overall lack of an up-to-date design specification. The lack of documentation of interaction between developer and user is especially troublesome because no one records the compromises that take place during meetings, so a lot of finger pointing takes place at some point because no one can remember precisely what compromise everyone agreed to follow.

Kent Beck created the original form of XP during the Chrysler Comprehensive Compensation System (C3) payroll project in 1996. (You can read about this project in the *Computerworld* article at `http://www.computerworld.com/softwaretopics/software/appdev/story/0,10801,66192,00.html`.)

XP relies on the following 12 core practices:

1. The customer defines application features with user stories (essentially, a monologue of how the user performs a particular task).
2. The development teams put small code releases into production early, which allows for early user testing.
3. The development teams use a common system of names and descriptions (theoretically, this practice includes everything from how variables are named to the name of the servers used to test the application).
4. The development teams use the simplest object-oriented code that meets requirements.
5. To ensure reliability, the designers write automated unit tests beginning with the first module and run them throughout the project.
6. The development teams revise and edit the overall code design frequently. XP refers to this practice as refactoring.
7. All programmers work side by side in pairs in order to see and discuss each other's code on a constant basis.
8. All programmers have collective ownership of the code and the ability to change it.
9. The development teams integrate code and release it to a repository every few hours. A development team never holds onto its code longer than a day.
10. Programmers work only 40 hours per week; there's no overtime. (Other staff members and management can theoretically work longer hours, although it's better if everyone gets enough rest during the project.)
11. At least one customer representative remains on site throughout the development project. (Access to expert users is essential to ensure success.)
12. All programmers must follow a common coding standard. Consequently, it appears that a single individual wrote all the code in the system.

Besides the XP goals and practices, it's also important to know about the XP values. The original version of XP included only four values, but the current version includes the five values shown here (the last value is the one that was added):

- **Communication:** In order to write any application, you must have communication. Older strategies relied on written documentation to accomplish this task. XP favors the use of simple designs (mock-ups), storyboards, or other methods of finding common communication metaphors, collaboration between users and programmers, frequent verbal communication, and feedback from a variety of sources (especially the user).
- **Simplicity:** Instead of taking a long-term view of the application, XP takes a short-term view. The goal is to create the simplest possible solution that will answer the programming requirement today, rather than look toward a solution that also answers the requirement tomorrow and next week. XP detractors say that this viewpoint could end up costing more in the end because of the time required to implement long-term solutions. However, because software changes so quickly today, it's quite possible that the long-term need won't even exist in the future.

- **Feedback:** Development without feedback means that small errors today will become large errors tomorrow, and large errors cost a lot to fix. Likewise, stakeholders with unrealistic expectations often drive software projects into the ground and force them to fail. XP proposes that the entire group responsible for the project receive input from three sources: the system through unit tests, the user through interface testing, and the development team who can assess the time required to implement additional requirements.
- **Courage:** It's often difficult for an individual programmer to have the courage required to drive a solution forward. XP includes the notice that the programmer should have courage in three areas. First, the programmer should have the courage required to continue working on a problem until the problem is solved. Second, sometimes the programmer has to throw code away and start over because the code is hopelessly flawed. Third, the programmer should have the courage to review code as needed and refactor (change it) as necessary.
- **Respect:** This value comes at two levels. First, programmers should respect themselves by writing high-quality code and seeking the best solution possible by refactoring their code as necessary. Second, programmers should respect the team by not introducing changes that will break compilation, cause unit tests to fail, or otherwise the delay the work of their peers.

Adaptive Software Development

The Adaptive Software Development (ASD) programming technique comes out of the RAD model. In other words, this technique adds to what RAD already provides (read more about RAD in the "Using the Rapid Application Development (RAD) Model" section of this chapter). ASD replaces the elements of the waterfall model with a series of speculate, collaborate, and learn cycles. Each of these cycles helps move a particular component or other aspect of the application forward. Here is a description of each of the elements:

- **Speculate:** The standard specification process postulates that someone has correct assumptions about the application. When working with ASD, it's taken for granted that everyone has some aspects of the application design correct and some aspects wrong. The team members speculate about the correct method of implementing the application design.
- **Collaborate:** During the collaboration phase, team members work through differences and define the predictable parts of the design. The team members guide the predictable portions of the design to completion. As part of this collaboration, the team members also decide how to handle the unpredictable changes wrought by technology, requirements, stakeholders, software vendors, and other external elements.
- **Learn:** At some point, the development team has software to test and the stakeholders want to see it. During the learn phase, each of the team members tests the software, documents problems, and presents these issues to the team. The team as a whole learns from the mistakes made during the current cycle and fixes them in the next cycle. The hope is that eventually the team will master the entire problem domain.

Most developers rely on ASD when they require a mission-focused or feature-rich environment in which to create the application. In most cases, ASD relies on specific time periods for each phase of a cycle, so ASD is time-boxed. In addition, because of the way ASD works, it's extremely flexible and fault tolerant. You can discover more about ASD at `http://www.adaptivesd.com/` or `http://www.softwareplanner.com/se_sp_adaptive_software_mkt.asp`.

Feature Driven Development

Feature Driven Development (FDD) focuses on the features in an application. Jeff De Luca initially created FDD to meet the specific needs of a 15-month, 50-person software development project at a large Singapore bank in 1997.

A typical FDD project encompasses five activities as described in the following list.

1. **Develop the overall model:** This method relies heavily on models. The process begins with a walk-through of the application as a whole. This walk-through provides everyone with the same view of the application and helps the group see the application in context. The next step is to provide a detailed walk-through for each modeling area. The team then breaks into small groups to discuss the individual domains. Peer review happens next. Eventually, the entire group chooses a model for each domain or combines elements of various models, which becomes the model used for the application. This process continues until there's a domain model for every aspect of the application.
2. **Build the feature list:** The team analyzes the models and derives a list of application features from them. Each feature becomes part of the feature list eventually used to create the application. The list uses a special format of `<action> <result> <object>` to make it easier to understand each feature. For example, a particular feature may state, "Calculate the total of apples in the bin." One of the requirements for a feature is that it not require more than two weeks for the team to implement. When a feature requires more than two weeks, the team should split the feature into smaller pieces. For example, if "Print the output of the inventory." requires more than two weeks to implement, then you might split it into "Print the output of the in-store inventory" and "Print the output of the warehouse inventory" features.
3. **Plan by feature:** At this point, the team has a group of features that it wants to implement. The project manager categorizes the features, derives classes from them, and assigns groups of classes to lead programmers on the team.
4. **Design by feature:** The lead programmers take the list of classes the project manager assigned and develop a design for each of them. The lead programmers then break the classes into groups that they can program in two weeks. During this phase, the lead programmers also create sequence charts for each feature and perform tasks such as writing class and method prologs. Finally, the project manager holds a design inspection.
5. **Build by feature:** Individual programmers receive assignments from the lead programmers and write the code required to implement the feature. When the feature passes code inspection and unit testing, the project manager promotes it to the main build.

The developers perform the first three activities once for each application. They then perform the last two activities iteratively for each of the features. One of the best places to obtain additional information about FDD is on Jeff De Luca's Web site at `http://www.nebulon.com/fdd/index.html`. You'll also want to visit the Feature Driven Development community Web site at `http://www.featuredrivendevelopment.com/`.

Combined Methods or Create Your Own

The ideas for a development strategy presented in this part of the chapter are only the tip of the iceberg — pick a great developer and you're likely to find yet another in a long series of development techniques. The bottom line is that there's the technique that works and the one that doesn't. The proof of usefulness and adaptability is in the software. When you deliver a great application that's easy to maintain, the customer is unlikely to worry whether you used the waterfall method or RAD to create the application. In the long run, the method you use matters only to you and your team.

It's impossible to say that a particular method presented in this chapter is the right one for you and your application. In fact, none of these methods may work when used in their pure form. Consequently, one of the best facts you can take away from this chapter is that there are times when you have to come up with your own method. If it's a great method and you write it up, someone may present your method in a book as the best method of creating software the world has ever seen. The savvy developer knows that every project and development team is different, so the methods needed to accomplish the tasks are also different.

When you start your next software project, you should review the methods in this chapter again. It's easy to forget about the one method that you thought would work great in a particular situation — perhaps the situation you're facing today. When you look for a programming strategy, consider these factors:

- Application type
- Development team
- Management style
- Delivery schedule
- Stakeholder needs

If you don't find a precise match in this chapter, don't be afraid to look online, because there are many other methods available. Try not to reinvent the wheel. Of course, even online sources can run out. When this happens, take time to combine elements of the various strategies you find to create your own hybrid. Experience will eventually tell you what works and what won't.

Developing Your Design Strategy

This chapter begins by explaining the application lifecycle. Although you may initially think that the lifecycle is black and white steps in a process, think more of a shades-of-gray transition between phases. In fact, the application lifecycle can be quite hard to nail down unless you choose an organized method of viewing it, which is the purpose of the lifecycle models found in this chapter. You may find that you want to review other lifecycle models as part of your research before settling on a particular model for your application. In fact, you may even have to mix and match elements from several models to create a comprehensive view of your application. Once you understand the lifecycle for your application, you'll want to spend time considering a programming strategy for it. This chapter reviews agile programming strategies because they represent the method that seems to guarantee success most often. However, the programming strategy you choose must consider the management style of your organization, application type, developer skills, and environmental parameters.

Before you write one line of text describing your project, begin thinking about the application lifecycle — the entire lifecycle, not just the beginning. A woodworker doesn't build a dresser without considering every element of the lifecycle of that dresser — at least, not if the woodworker is successful. Likewise, you must understand your application's lifecycle completely before you can design anything. As part of your lifecycle management, you should decide on a lifecycle model and a programming strategy. Only after you complete these three elements can you move on to the next chapter.

Chapter 3 is probably where you expected to begin this book. It finally considers the elements of a thriving design strategy. Your application's life begins with the design strategy. When you get to Chapter 3, you're finally beginning to create an application — something that has a beginning, middle, and end. As with any starting point, you may find that Chapter 3 is a little hard, but it's less difficult when you complete the requirements found in this chapter.

3

Defining a Design Strategy

After you've decided on the application you want to create and the method you'll use to create it, and have all the stakeholders and development team in place, it's time to work out a design strategy. A design strategy normally involves creating some type of application structure. You want to begin thinking about how the application is going to go together.

The first task you'll want to tackle is creating an object model. Objects can help you define any sort of real-world situation. The most common way to view application objects is as a computer representation of a real-world object. For example, if you were to model an apple as an object, the apple object would contain properties such as `Color` and `Smell`, methods such as `Ripen`, and events such as `ChangeColor`.

Application objects normally interact with some type of data, so the second step is to create a data model. You'll need to consider issues such as the data sources and define data classes to create a connection to these sources. Once you have a connection, you need other classes to read, add, delete, edit, and update the data content. The data model must encompass concepts such as data integrity and connection reliability.

The user has to have some way of interacting with your application, so the third step in defining a design strategy is to create a list of user requirements and then convert them into user classes. The user classes include all sorts of concerns, such as the layout of the forms and the kinds of reports the user sees. Of course, you must also decide how best to serve user needs. For example, whenever possible, you should use something other than a textbox as input because the user will make incorrect entries relatively often in a textbox. Instead, you can help the user provide correct input by using drop-down list boxes or other controls.

The final portion of this chapter shows how you can use the Unified Modeling Language (UML) to make the modeling process go faster. UML isn't a design or implementation strategy. Rather, it's a method of graphically presenting the object model. You won't end up with an application as output; you'll end up with an object map of your application instead. Although this chapter relies on Visio as a UML tool, the principles apply equally well with other tools as well. The important information to get out of the UML section is that UML makes it easier to create and present your object model rather than trying to write everything down as text.

You can still follow the UML section of this book, even if you don't own a copy of Visio 2007. Microsoft provides a free 60-day trial version that you can download from `http://office.microsoft.com/en-us/visio/default.aspx`*. The trial version provides all the functionality of the full version — the only difference is that you can only use it for 60 days. The download Web page also includes a Try It Online link. Click this link to try the application online without having to download anything.*

Creating an Object Model

What will your application do? The answer to that question is the purpose of an object model. The object model displays a list of real-world objects that you plan to use in some way within your application. The methods, properties, and events the object exposes determine how you can interact with it. However, a set of objects sitting somewhere in cyberspace isn't very interesting or useful. Consequently, you create an object model to perform two tasks:

- Describe the objects that your application uses.
- Define how those objects interact with each other.

The interaction part of the object model is especially important. The interactions define the tasks your application can perform and the features it provides to the user. Remember that you're not defining data interaction or the user interface at this point. Remain focused on the functionality of the application itself.

You'll perform a number of steps in order to define your object model. For example, you must consider whether the class is an internal class (part of the application) or an external class (possibly part of a library). The following sections help you understand the concepts behind creating an object model for your own application.

Defining the Class Concepts

Developers don't simply begin choosing classes and then code them to create an application. The application process demands that the developer spend time considering the functionality that the application must have in order to meet user needs. Application features translate into tasks — tasks that the application performs and tasks that the user performs using the application. Some tasks are automatic, some manual, some occur when the application detects an event, and still others are inside the application and assist other tasks in the performance of their duties. The following sections describe functionality and the associated tasks as part of a feature set.

Understanding the Feature Set

The user is your main source of information for the feature set. Some books claim that you should work with expert users alone. There's some validity to the statement — expert users can provide the most information on the tasks that the application must perform. However, expert users have worked with a particular process for so long that it's easy for them to forget special needs and requirements. In fact, if you watch expert users work for a while, you'll see that they perform some tasks automatically — they aren't even aware that the task is completed because they've done it for so long. Consequently, it often helps to have a less-experienced user as one of the stakeholders to obtain a different point of view, one that considers the less-advanced-user needs.

When users define a feature, they describe it from their perspective. The user might say something like, "I need to type text and then print it." The tasks that must occur to answer this seemingly simple need are numerous. The user hasn't stated the need to save the text to disk because often the user takes this need for granted. You know that you have to save the text, so you add it to the list of features. The user also hasn't mentioned anything about formatting the text before the application outputs it, yet you know that the user will want the text formatted. It always pays to ask the user about these assumptions, because some developers have created monstrosities that no one can use, by assuming too much about what the user has left unstated.

The feature set will always include unstated needs that you need to ask about in your initial conversation with the user. For example, if users are writing letters, then they'll probably want a source of addresses for the letters. They may even want to see the letters preformatted and want a wizard to lead them through the writing process to ensure the letters meet company requirements. (I've written an application or two for companies that want letters and other correspondence in a precise form.) As you ask about these unstated requirements, you should make notes about the tasks that the application will have to perform to meet the requirements, such as accessing a database containing the company's customer list.

Defining the Class Candidates

Eventually, you have a list of features the user needs. However, you don't have a list of classes at this point. What you have are the user concerns. In order to begin creating the list of classes, you need to create a list of class candidates — essentially descriptive phrases that you eventually turn into class names. Let's look a little further into the simple text editor described in the previous section. You may start with a list of features, but you need to rewrite them into verb/noun pairs like the list that follows:

- Create new document
- Save document to disk
- Open document file
- Write text
- Edit text
- Format text
- Print text
- Format printed output
- Obtain application information
- Provide user help

These aren't strictly verb/noun pairs, but they're close enough and the list provides what you need to start building a class candidate list. In some cases, such as "create new document," the item in the list is probably complete by itself. However, "format text" is a large topic — too large for a single class because you need to perform a number of tasks to format the text. Consequently, you might split format text into the following list of class candidates:

- Change font
- Set tabs

- ❑ Add bullets and numbering
- ❑ Add border and shading

Of course, you need to verify that the user actually wants all this formatting. Perhaps the user wants additional formatting, such as specialized paragraph formatting. As you create your list of class candidates, you'll come up with other questions that you must ask the application user. In some cases, you may need to ask other stakeholders about the requirements. The point is that by the time you finish this process, you should have a rather lengthy list of class candidates that you need to work with.

Adding documentation to your candidate list is always a good idea. For example, make sure you explain what you mean by "change font" in the list. This may mean something as simple as choosing a typeface and size, but it could also mean adding effects such as bold and italics. It's important to think about every feature and to document precisely what that feature should do. Make sure the customer reviews the list and understands each of the entries or you may find that you have to make changes to your design later.

Choosing Classes from Candidates

You now have a candidate list. It's time to decide which items on the list will make good classes. You still have to provide the functionality required by all the entries, but some entries will work better as part of something else. For example, you may choose to handle bullets, numbering, borders, and shading as a single class.

As you choose classes from the candidate list, you need to think of class names. One of the reasons to format the candidate list in a certain way is to make it easy to sort any way you want. The other reason is to make it easy to create unique class names. For example, the "set tabs" candidate may become the `SetTabs` class. Using a name derived from the candidate name also makes it easier to show your implementation to the customer later.

When you create the list of classes, you should also consider how those classes interact. In some cases, thinking about these interactions will show the need for additional classes. These classes aren't on the candidate list because they don't provide an actual application feature, but you need them anyway to make the rest of the classes work. For example, in order to change the font of existing text, you need a text selection. Consequently, you might need to create a `SelectText` class. This particular class is going to come in handy for a number of purposes, such as editing the document content.

Group the classes next. For example, the list of classes definitely includes a document category. These functions interact with the document, rather than with the text. In this case, you might want to create a `Document` class that performs general work with the document, such as ensuring the user saves changes, and have all the document features inherit from this class. This is the time to begin looking for relationships between classes and ensure you create the optimal model for your application. Thinking about the document editor, you could group the classes into the following categories:

- ❑ Application
- ❑ Document
- ❑ Text

The application group will include an `Application` class that provides support for items such as the application version number. The application group also includes classes such as `UserHelp` and `About` that affect the application as a whole. You place these classes in the application group because they won't change over time unless you perform an update of the application. The document group contains classes that affect the entire document (the container), such as `PrintDocument`, `SaveDocument`, or `OpenDocument`. Finally, the text group contains classes that affect the content of the document, rather than the container, such as `SelectText` and `FormatText`.

Choosing between Classes and Structures

When creating an object model for your application, you also have to make a choice between using classes and structures. A class creates an object on the heap, whereas a structure creates a value on the stack. When you create a new object based on a class, C# only creates a reference to the object on the heap until you instantiate the object using the new keyword. However, when you create a new value based on a structure, C# immediately sets the memory aside for that value and assigns the structure members default values.

The main reason most developers use structures in C# is to interact with the Win32 API using platform invoke (P/Invoke), because you can modify the way C# allocates structure memory using the `[StructLayout()]` attribute (see the articles at `http://www.vsj.co.uk/articles/display.asp?id=501` and `http://blogs.msdn.com/ericgu/archive/2004/08/12/213676.aspx` for details). You use the structures to pass data to and from Windows API calls. Structures can also prove slightly more efficient from a memory usage perspective, and using them correctly can improve application speed.

Both classes and structures can include methods, events, and properties. However, only classes have destructors, so you must use a class when you want to create an object with a special destructor. Microsoft also places strict limits on the use of constructors in structures that you can read about at `http://msdn.microsoft.com/en-us/library/aa288208(VS.71).aspx`. You can read more about C# structures at `http://www.c-sharpcorner.com/UploadFile/rajeshvs/StructuresInCS11112005234341PM/StructuresInCS.aspx`. The article at `http://www.dotnetspider.com/resources/740-Difference-between-class-struct-C.aspx` also provides a nice comparison of classes and structures.

At some point, you'll want to create a visual representation of your object model called an *object model map* to make it easier for your development team to see how the various pieces interact. You can see a number of examples of object models online. For example, look at the Word Application Object Model Map at `http://msdn.microsoft.com/en-us/library/bb288731.aspx`. Of course, the example discussed in this chapter isn't nearly as complex. Figure 3-1 shows an example of the object model map for the simple document editor.

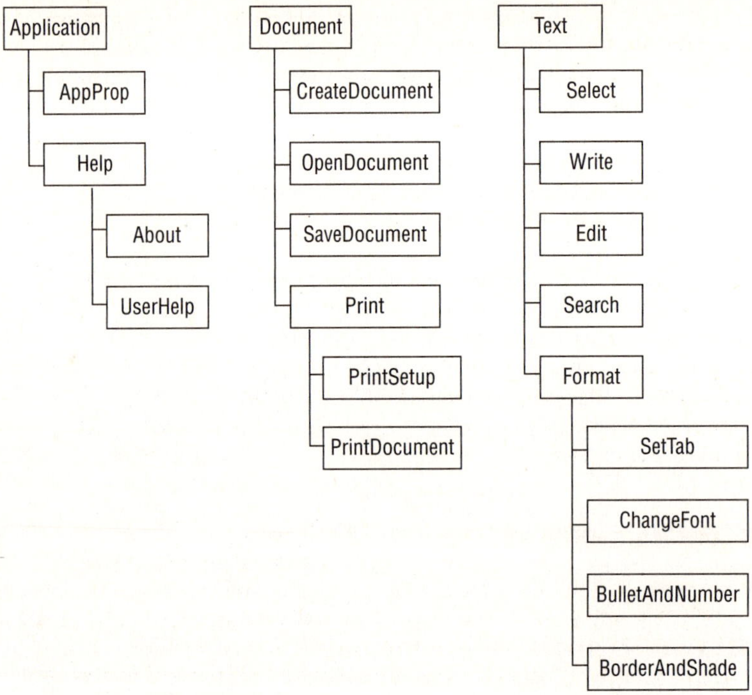

Figure 3-1: Create an object model map for your application to keep class interactions clear.

Developing Internal Classes

Part of the reason to develop the object model map shown in Figure 3-1 is to determine which classes you must write as part of the application. Any class that performs a specialty task should appear as part of the internal classes for the application. For example, it's unlikely that any members of the `Document` class are common classes. Consequently, you must create all these classes as part of the internal classes for the application. As you begin working with the classes, think about potential holes in your coverage. Sometimes it's easy to miss a class that your application requires to function properly because it performs a background task, rather than interacting directly with the user or the user interface. This need was more common in older, unmanaged applications. For example, every unmanaged application requires a background task to manage memory — you get this functionality free as part of the .NET Framework when working with C#.

As you work though the list of internal classes, you may also find cases where you can combine classes to provide a better class model. Some purists want to create a class for every little need. It's not enough to create a class for obtaining application settings — the purist also wants a class for individual settings. In short, rather than deliver an easily used structure containing all the settings, the purist might provide separate classes for the last update date and the version number of the application. In some cases, you want to combine classes simply because doing so makes the application easier to develop and upgrade later.

This is also the time to start thinking about potential connectivity requirements. Your application may have to access a database for particular needs such as obtaining client name and address information or the current price for a widget. Most business applications today require some kind of database connection, even if the business exposes the database using a Web service. At one point, you could say that applications such as a word processor wouldn't require a database connection, but that's no longer the case. Modern word processors include the capability to research data online, access an online thesaurus, and add objects such as maps (obtained online) to a document. In short, think through the connectivity requirements for your application thoroughly before you consider your object model complete.

Don't be afraid to begin adding some method, property, and event names to your object model. It's not essential that you provide every little detail yet, but whenever adding a method, property, or event helps you create a better object model, feel free to add it. This is the point of the development process where changes are cheap. You should feel free to move things around, break them apart, and combine them as needed to obtain the best possible object model. In fact, it's the need to organize the application that makes using a graphics application to draw the object model so attractive. Most developers benefit from the combination of abstract and visual when working through the object model.

Adding External Classes

It's important not to forget the importance of the code you've already written. Your organization probably has entire libraries of code that could help make creating this application easier. Look again at Figure 3-1. It's probable that you already have an `About` class available that has all the required information defined in it. It's possible that the About dialog box programming may require nothing more than creating an instance of the `About` class in a library and then calling the resulting object, which represents a second or two of development time.

The problem is that many developers do forget to look through the list of available software and waste time by reinventing the wheel every time they have to write the same tired class yet another time. Many of the applications on the market today probably include duplicate code because the developer didn't think to look for the class in an existing library. Part of the modeling process is to look for cases in which you can use library code or other external sources.

> *If you haven't started a database of reusable code for your organization yet, it's time to do so. When you provide developers with an easily searched database of existing code, it's more likely that the developer will actually reuse the code — saving both development and debugging time. Most organizations can write off the cost of creating a code database very quickly.*

Third-party products and libraries are also something to consider. You should plan for these add-on products as part of your initial design process so that they don't end up feeling like a bolt on that you added because you ran out of time. The downside of using third-party products is that they do cost you money. You'll have to weigh whether the third-party product saves enough time to warrant the investment in buying the product.

Libraries are the old standby that most developers know about today. However, you have access to other sources of external code. For example, you might choose to rely on a Web service to provide some of the functionality you need. A Web service is a kind of hybrid when you think about it. From a developer perspective, you're using someone else's code. On the other hand, a user is likely to view a Web service as an alternative source of data. No matter how you view the Web service, it's important to realize that it does provide an external method of accomplishing tasks that doesn't require you to write the code. In fact, you have the additional benefit of not having to maintain the code, either.

Don't forget to use internal Web services as needed. For example, many developers forget that they can reconfigure COM+ applications to appear as a Web service, making the COM+ application significantly easier to use in a managed application.

As companies merge and decide to use alternative technologies, the code base you have at your disposal grows to other platforms. Using various technologies available today (see the "Multiple Platform Scenarios" section of Chapter 1 for details), it's possible that the solution you need resides on a Linux system. Connecting to a Linux system using Web services, bridging solutions, and cross-compilation solutions is no longer a significant problem. Some of these tools make it appear that the external code is actually part of your Visual Studio solution — the bridge becomes invisible and your application development experience is significantly better.

There are actually a number of external class sources to consider. However, not all external classes are created equal. Here are the external classes you can consider in order of difficulty of use and of risk to your project:

- Internal managed library code
- Internal native library code
- Internal Web service
- Third-party product library code
- Private Web services
- Public Web services
- Cross-compiled code from another platform
- Bridged code from another platform

Considering Class Trade-offs

At some point, you have an object model in place. You know how the application is going to look, at least when it comes to the classes you plan to use. In many cases, you also know some of the methods, events, and properties the classes will contain. Some organizations actually begin color coding the blocks in the object model at this point (much as Microsoft does at `http://msdn.microsoft.com/en-us/library/bb288731.aspx`). Using color coding is a great idea because it adds to that visual aspect of the object model. Now is the time to consider the trade-offs in your object model. Here are some of the questions you should ask yourself:

- Should I implement a particular class as a class or as a structure?
- Is the functionality for a particular class completely encapsulated?
- Does the class rely on the services of other classes too heavily?
- Do the classes appear in a logical order?

- Are the class names logical and easy to understand?
- Will using external classes really work for a particular need?

You probably have other questions that you feel you need to ask yourself. Always write down the questions and your responses to them. This development diary comes in handy later when you start to doubt a particular aspect of the design. Going back to your development diary helps you understand the thought process involved in coming to a particular design decision. It's easy to get lost in the middle of a development effort and cost yourself time by reversing a design decision because you forgot why you made it in the first place.

While you consider the class trade-offs, you should also look at the way objects interact and determine whether you need a class factory to enhance some functionality. Class factories are higher-level classes that provide functionality to a number of lower-level classes. For example, you might need functionality to write documents to disk. The functionality to perform the writing process can appear as a class factory, while the actual process to write the data belongs in a lower-level class. The `WriteDocument` class might act as a factor for the `WriteText` and `WriteImage` classes. You'll want to display this functionality as part of your object model.

Don't confuse an object relationship with inheritance. For example, a `Document` *object may contain zero, one, or more* `Page` *objects. The* `Document` *and* `Page` *objects have a relationship because the* `Document` *object acts as a host to the* `Page` *object, but the* `Page` *object doesn't inherit anything from the* `Document` *object — the two classes are separate. Your object model will contain instances of inheritance. For example, you may define a single* `Page` *object from which all the* `Pages` *objects inherit. As another example, an object model may display an abstract* `Printer` *object from which the application derives the* `LaserPrinter` *and* `InkJet` *objects.*

Improving the Class Design

Some managers are quite certain that it's never acceptable to solicit advice from the people working for them and end up making a host of errors as a result. Starting with the object model, you should begin soliciting advice from your development team, if for no other reason than to have a fresh pair of eyes look at the development problem. Something as simple as a spelling error can cause problems later — imagine the chaos of having to work with the `PrintDocment` class for years on end until you finally get it fixed. In fact, the development team can help you locate and squash the following problems in the object model:

- Name consistency errors
- Object flow problems
- Object interactivity issues
- Logic errors
- Spelling errors
- Missing objects
- Objects displayed as internal that are available from an external library
- Classes that would work better as structures (and vice versa)
- Objects that you should split into smaller pieces

Even at this early stage, you should also consider how the objects will work. For example, you need to consider whether objects will have the potential to hinder application speed, present a security hole, or cause reliability issues. If you have a number of objects all calling the same central object, you have to wonder whether you've designed the central object properly or whether you need to divide it into smaller pieces to eliminate a potential central point of failure.

You should also take this time to mark some objects as critical. An application can work without some objects, albeit with reduced functionality. For example, objects that help the application print aren't critical unless the whole purpose of the application is to print other objects. However, when viewing the object model in Figure 3-1, you know that the ability to open a document is critical, because otherwise you can't perform any other task with an existing document.

Building a Data Model

Very few business applications can get by without some source of data. The report you viewed yesterday required a data source, as does the Web site you're using today. Data sources come in a vast array of forms — everything from the traditional database to Web services. In many cases, data need not even reside locally. Many applications rely on remote sources of data today. In some cases, a single application relies on multiple data sources, some local, and some remote. Consequently, it isn't too surprising that you'll spend a lot of time working through the data model for your application. The following sections describe the requirements for building a good data model for your application.

The vast array of data sources and the multiple techniques required to access them have caused developers no end of woe when it comes to C# development. Consequently, Microsoft recently provided a new method of accessing data, Language Integrated Query (LINQ). This new technique is a SQL-like language that works equally well with all data sources. This book contains a number of LINQ resources to help you get acquainted with this new technology. Chapter 9 describes how to use LINQ in scripting. Chapter 13 shows how to use LINQ to make your documentation easier to access. Chapter 23 provides a great overview of using LINQ in standard applications. Finally, Chapter 25 discusses how LINQ can make your multithreaded applications run faster.

Defining the Data Requirements

It would seem at first that defining data requirements should be relatively easy. After all, you have an application designed to work with a specific kind of information. When you create an application to add customer names and addresses to a database, you don't expect that the application will also need to access the Amazon Web Service (AWS) to look for books. Unfortunately, as computers become more connected to the Internet and other companies, and the data sources available through this channel become more diverse, any assumption you make about data requirements today can quickly change tomorrow. In fact, you should consider these scenarios when defining the data requirements for your application:

- The application can interact with a generic form of data, which means that users will attempt to use it to modify data from sources you may not know exist at the time you create the object model.
- Your organization is expanding and may need to handle data from remote or external sources (external here means from some other organization).

- Your organization merges with another organization and now needs to handle the other organization's data.
- The application can interact with multiple kinds of data, which means that users will almost certainly try to combine two or more data types to create a new, unique data type.
- The users don't communicate the data requirements well, which means that you must add data sources later.
- The data source vendor makes changes to the data source functionality that present compatibility problems with your application.

Any or all of these problems can occur and you have to consider them when defining the data requirements for your application. The goal is to create a flexible data requirements specification that can accommodate change. If you don't, you'll find yourself spending many hours reworking any diagram you create.

You model the data requirements using an entity-relationship (ER) diagram such as the one shown in Figure 3-2. The goal of this diagram is to create a picture of the data that you expect your application to use, no matter what the source may be — you expect the data to appear in this form whether the application receives them from a Web service or SQL Server.

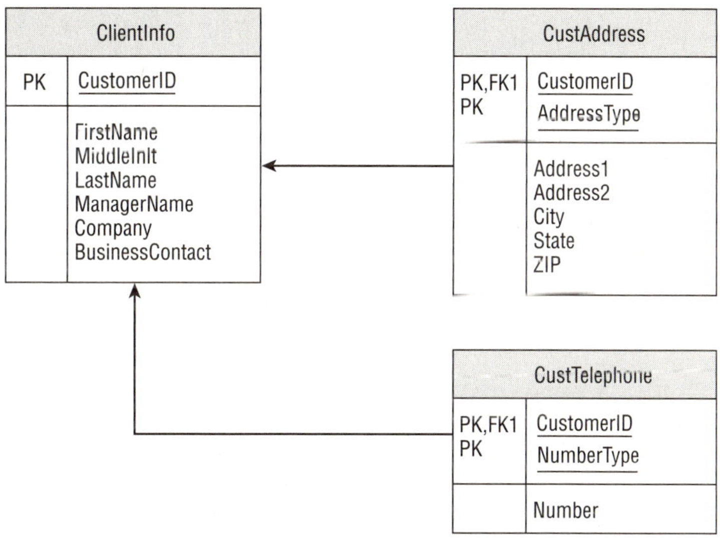

Figure 3-2: Use an ER diagram to create a model of your data.

In this case, the database accommodates a client who has one or more addresses and one or more telephone numbers. Obviously, the data model for your application can become extremely complex — this is a simple example. However, it demonstrates the principles you need to consider when creating a data model for your application. In this case, you'd probably create three classes for your application:

- `ClientInfo`
- `CustAddress`
- `CustTelephone`

These three classes would include logic to read, create, update, and delete records. The properties would provide the means to get and set the information for each field using properties. In addition, the classes would include code to maintain the database integrity. The classes would also include methods for moving between records and performing other database-related tasks.

Considering Access, Reliability, and Security Requirements

Databases are naturally tricky to work with because you have multiple applications and multiple users accessing a central resource that's the bread and butter for most companies. One major accident by any user at the wrong time can spell disaster for your company. Of course, the user has to have access to that data to perform useful work and access leads to accidents. No matter how carefully you construct your application, accidents will happen.

Creating any application that requires access to a data source is a matter of balance. You must balance the user's need for access against the potential for damage that the access can cause. Good backups and other maintenance do reduce the risk, but there's always some level of risk. Consequently, your data model must account for the potential risk in some manner. To ensure that the user has safe, reliable access to the data required to perform useful work, you must consider the following facets of database access:

- **Roles:** Users fall into a number of categories. Each category is a potential role. One common role is manager, where a manager might add new users to the system and have limited rights to assign security. The better you can define the potential roles a user might fulfill, the better you can limit access to the database. Limited access translates into better security.
- **Location:** Applications often fail to account for the user's location. They give the user the same level of access from an Internet connection as from a local connection. In general, you want to reduce the dataset you present to the user when working with a remote location, for several reasons. First, reducing the dataset improves security. Second, a smaller dataset takes less time to transmit, which improves application speed. Third, a smaller dataset is less likely to receive damage over a remote connection, making it more reliable.
- **Task:** Limiting or enhancing access according to the task that the user performs is essential. A manager doesn't require constant access to employee records — the only time a manager requires this access is when making changes to the employee records, so you should remove the access at other times.
- **Time frame:** It's tempting to provide complete access at all times. However, users have normal working hours in which they require access to the data in most cases. Monitoring user access and restricting it during off hours is a great way to improve overall application security. Of course, the application must provide for those situations where the user does legitimately require off-hours access. In addition, it may not be necessary to remove all access. A salesperson may require just read access to the database during off hours, rather than both read and write access.
- **Policy:** One of the most overlooked access, reliability, and security requirements is company policy. Many companies write a policy on paper and expect employees to follow it. However, written policies don't work in some cases, especially when the employee feels that monitoring and enforcement are weak. A better way to handle this need is to implement the policy in the application software as well as part of a written document. Using a policy-based approach usually makes data access both more secure and more reliable.

Creating the Data Classes

It turns out that creating the data classes is almost too easy if you think through the data model carefully. Every version of Visual Studio sees further improvements in database technology. In most cases, you can simply drag and drop the database components you need into the application from Server Explorer.

However, when you consider your data classes, you do need to consider what happens before and after the automation takes over. For example, one of the first considerations is whether you want to use a stored procedure or custom classes in the application. Using a stored procedure means that any work required to obtain the data occurs on the server, which tends to help insulate your application from minor data changes and makes it possible to use the application on less capable hardware. Using custom classes in the application places the burden on the client system and makes the server run more efficiently.

Part of the requirement for the data classes you create is deciding how much information you need. In the past, developers often brought all the data available for a specific query in one lump sum. It was nothing to see a SQL Server query such as `SELECT * FROM Customers` in an application. This kind of query wastes server resources, network bandwidth, and client resources. What you need to do is decide which fields you need from the database and determine which records to select. A query such as `SELECT CustomerID, ContactTitle, ContactName, CompanyName, Region FROM Customers WHERE Country = 'USA'` greatly enhances query speed and makes it easier to diagnose query problems later because you're asking for something specific.

It's also important to consider whether you need a dynamic (live) or static (snapshot) connection. A dynamic connection keeps your application better informed about the state of the database and tells you when you need to update the data displayed to the user. The cost is speed. Using a dynamic connection uses a lot of system resources because every action occurs in real time. Microsoft and other vendors have started to move toward static connections because these work in disconnected scenarios (the client loses contact with the server) and reduce client/server interaction. However, static connections have their own problems. Because the connection doesn't maintain a lock on the data, there's a chance of data collisions where the application must arbitrate changes. When a data collision occurs, the application can drop changes made by the current client, overwrite the previous change, or create a record that's a combination of the two changes.

Considering User Requirements

Some developers consider the user the worst part of the application design experience. After all, the application would run smoothly and without error if there were no users to cause problems for it. When you think about that sentiment for a moment, it sounds silly because applications serve user needs; it's not the user who serves application needs. Unfortunately, many developers take an application-centric view of the entire user equation and ultimately fail to make their application appear usable to the users whom the application is supposed to serve.

The following sections of the chapter help you get a good start with the user part of the application equation. In these sections, you discover that communicating with the user need not be hard, and you understand that you can follow some best practices to make the experience easier. Most importantly, the following sections help you create a better user interface by designing the user interface as a series of useful classes from the outset.

The world's best application is one in which users cannot make any mistakes no matter how computer illiterate they may be. However, no one has invented this application yet (and it's quite unlikely that anyone ever will). Give users enough rope and there's some way in which they can cause problems for your applications, which is why you want to keep the user involved as much as possible in testing the user interface. Even with a great design, it's a mistake not to ask users to pound your application and find all the flaws before it goes to production. After all, a small embarrassment from a few users in beta testing is far better than a major embarrassment before management in production.

Defining the User Requirements

Many developers do a great job of designing the underlying application objects. The database connection and object also don't pose much of a problem. However, when it comes to the user interface, most developers drop the ball. Here's the problem in a nutshell. Most developers can simply look at most user interfaces and know what to do — call it an art, a talent, or a built-in capability, but most developers have no problem at all figuring out the user interface for most applications. It's important to remember that you, as a developer, are positively motivated to know how to use your computer system. After all, it's not only your livelihood, but let's face it — most developers consider computers fun or they wouldn't have gotten started in this business in the first place.

Users, on the other hand, not only can't figure out the user interface, they're afraid to try working with it because they've had far too many bad experiences with applications damaging their data or falling apart altogether, seemingly at the merest touch. In addition, users aren't motivated to discover anything about a user interface because discovery takes time and they don't have time to work with your application. All the user knows is that your application is supposed to provide the means to output letters quickly. As soon as the users get those letters out, they can go home and relax in front of the television. In short, users are positively motivated to get their work done, not discover your user interface. The perfect user interface is invisible — users need not see it to output the data they want.

Unfortunately, the perfect user interface is a myth. At some point, the user is going to have to know that there's a computer involved in the letter writing. This fact will disturb some users considerably — you see it as users grope blindly for menu commands, toolbar buttons, and fields on forms. If you're telling users how to perform a task and ask them to locate File ➪ Save on the menu, you'll find them groping about blindly looking for that darn File menu yet again, even though they've used it 20 or 30 times today. Soon you're fidgeting and sometimes grabbing the mouse and doing the work for them simply because you can't tolerate the annoyance even one second more. The user is frustrated and so are you. At some point, you both explode and go to separate corners like combatants in the boxing ring.

It's because users have no interest in the user interface that Microsoft has developed a number of technologies to make life easier for the overburdened developer. Here are some ways you can use to reduce the pain level for both the user and you:

- License the Office User Fluent Interface.
- Rely on wizards as often as possible.
- Create workflows in the user interface that make it easy for users to follow a list of controls as they would a set of instructions.

- ❑ Hide or disable controls that don't serve a useful purpose for the current task.
- ❑ Provide only the controls the user needs.
- ❑ Choose controls based on user knowledge level and organizational role.

These tips help you design a better user interface — one that minimizes the impact of the user interface on the user's work environment. For example, Figure 3-3 shows a solution that I built for a client (simplified for the book) for writing letters. It combines the workflow experience with the use of the Office User Fluent Interface.

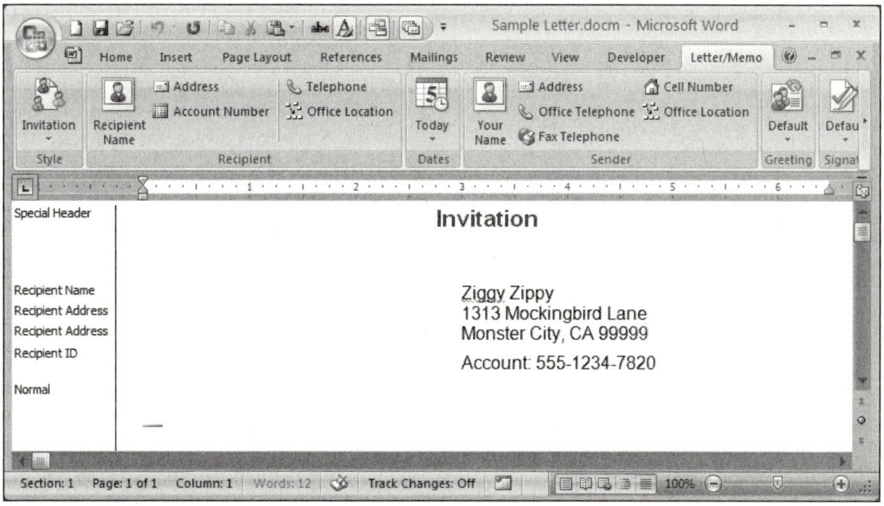

Figure 3-3: Rely on a combination of the Office User Fluent Interface and workflows to make the user interface mind-numbingly simple.

No matter how well you design your application, most users will require a help file to obtain additional information about any reasonably complex application. Make sure you couple the help file to your application so the user can obtain context-sensitive help (where the help directly relates to the task the user is performing).The help should include sections for performing specific tasks, as well as an overview that examines the application features. Try to present help in several different ways and use a combination of both text and graphics. Otherwise, you may simply confuse some users without helping them at all.

To use the Letter/Memo tab, the user simply moves from left to right and chooses the appropriate entries for each control. Yes, there's still an interface there, but using the technique shown minimizes the interface impact. More importantly, using this interface significantly reduces training time and user errors. This particular interface reduced training time by 75 percent and errors to an almost ridiculously small number (less than one per letter). Interestingly enough, using this application also improved user performance — a user requires less time to generate a letter when using an application of the sort shown in Figure 3-3. Chapter 4 discusses the whole issue of user interfaces in considerably more detail. For now, just consider methods of reducing the complexity of the user interface as you create the user classes.

Creating the User Classes

It's important to begin the user model process by defining the objects the user requires to perform useful work. The easiest possible method for designing user classes is to start with the forms that the user requires. Each of these forms represents a particular class. In fact, when you look at the way the Visual Studio IDE generates the forms for your application, you need to remember that each form is indeed an individual class.

The next step is to decide on which controls each form will contain. The controls determine the functionality of the form and establish what the user sees when working with the application. As part of adding controls to a form, you decide whether the control is private or public. In some cases, you must use public controls (or properties) to provide access to the data that the controls manipulate to a caller (the parent window).

As with any class, you can also add methods, properties, and events to provide custom behavior. For example, you might decide to provide multiple displays for a particular application. When something happens in a particular display, the associated form fires an event that gives the display focus so the user can see what's happening. You don't have to consider every aspect of the user forms at this stage of the design process, but it's important to start thinking about what the form will do.

Some developers have a tendency to place too many controls on a form, making it so cluttered that the user will never find anything. Forms should present an easily viewed, uncluttered appearance. A developer should find ways to present information in easily understood pieces. Forms are free — no one will ever charge you for them. If you need to use an overview form and several detail forms to ensure the user can understand them, then do so. It's almost never the case that the developer uses too many forms in an application or makes the data too easy to see.

Turning Your Design into UML

Before you go any further, put any ideas that UML is a design methodology out of your mind. A method implies a process — one that has an input, some type of internal data manipulation, and an output. UML isn't a method at all — rather, it's a modeling technique, or perhaps better still, a way you can present abstract ideas in graphical form. UML takes all the words you normally use to express a design idea and transforms them into a series of pictures that anyone can easily understand once they know the meaning of the graphics.

UML isn't really a new idea. People have used graphics for centuries to present complex ideas that didn't really work well with the written word. In fact, early programmers used flow charts for that very reason. Trying to describe program flow using words just didn't work out very well, but using a flow chart does. Unfortunately, most applications today are so complex that using a flow chart now doesn't work well. Flow charts are the yesterday solution for developers who work with procedural languages. UML is the today solution for developers who work with RAD programming environments and produce event-driven applications with complex inner workings.

It would take a book (or two) to describe UML adequately. The following sections present an overview of UML so that you have an understanding of what UML is all about, what it looks like, and why it's important to you as a developer. Instead of an abstract discussion that might not prove very useful, the following sections use Visio to show how UML works, at least, to the extent that it's possible to show UML within a section of a book.

Getting Started with Visio

I'm sure that someone's going to say that choosing Visio for a section about UML is the worst possible choice. It's amazing, but the choice of tool for working with UML is extremely political. If you already have a tool that you like using for UML, that's great! Please continue using it. I chose Visio for this book for a number of reasons, but the two important reasons are that Visio is extremely easy to use and it integrates well with Visual Studio. Make sure you review the note at the beginning of the chapter to obtain your free trial copy of the product.

After you install Visio, you can begin a UML diagram by choosing File ➪ New Software UML Model Diagram. You'll see a work area like the one shown in Figure 3-4 that contains a list of all the UML diagram types that Visio supports. To begin a diagram, simply choose the tab corresponding to the diagram type you want to create and begin dragging symbols to the design area. The "An Overview of the Visio UML Functionality" section of the chapter describes these tabs in more detail. Normally, you begin by creating a use case diagram for your application.

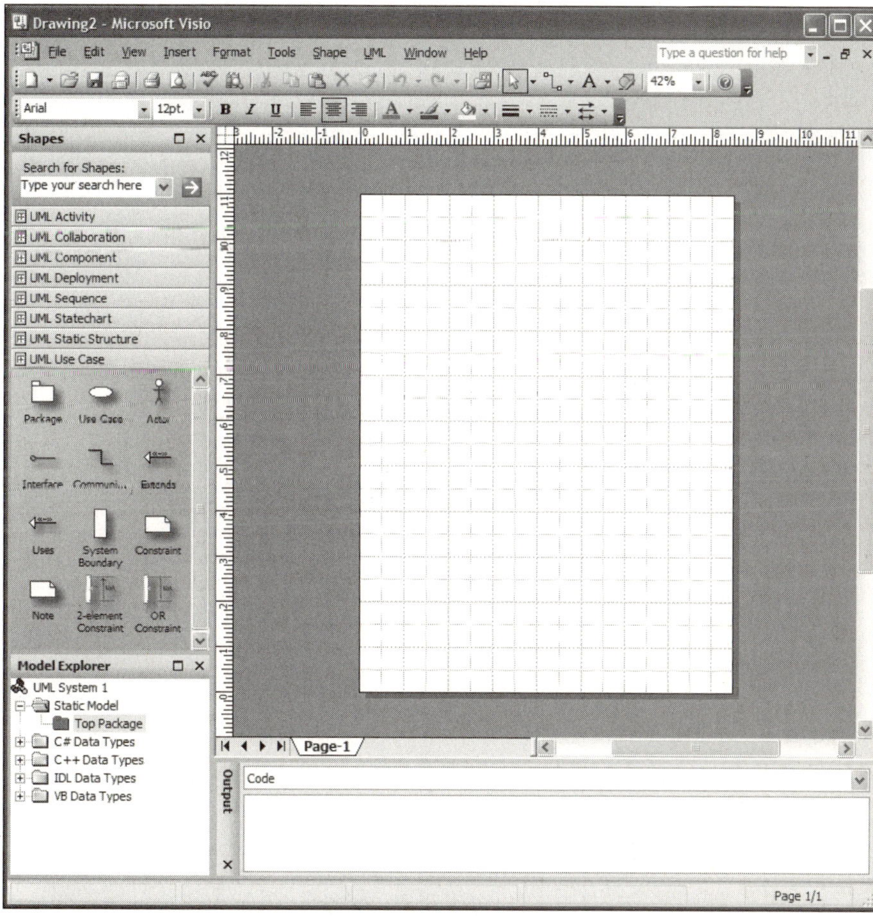

Figure 3-4: Visio provides a simple interface that works well with Visual Studio.

An Overview of the Visio UML Functionality

Visio provides great UML drawing functionality. You'll see all the standard drawing types and their associated symbols in the Shapes window. As with most UML products on the market, you create the drawings necessary to describe your application. The drawing you choose depends on which aspect of the application you want to describe. For example, a use case diagram helps you describe the actions that users take as they interact with your application. It's a script of what sequence of events must occur to accomplish a task successfully.

A single drawing can contain multiple pages, each of which is a different UML drawing type. To add a new page to your drawing, right-click the package you want to work with in Model Explorer (the default is Top Package) and choose the diagram you want to create from the context menu. Visio automatically adds the drawing you selected to the display. It also chooses the correct tab in the Shapes window for you. The following sections provide a brief overview of the UML drawing types that Visio supports.

Getting to Know UML

UML has become such a common development tool that you can easily find good tutorials online. One of the better basic tutorials appears on the Visual Builder site at `http://www.visualbuilder.com/uml/tutorial/`. This tutorial covers just the basics, but it's easy to follow. If you want a slightly more advanced tutorial, try the multi-part CRaG Systems tutorial at `http://www.cragsystems.co.uk/ITMUML/`. Some vendor sites can also prove helpful. For example, you can see a complete listing of the UML diagram types at `http://www.smartdraw.com/tutorials/software/uml/tutorial_01.htm`.

Activity Diagrams

The activity diagram models interactions with classes. It models the dynamic activity of a system by showing the flow of control from activity to activity. For example, a user may need to configure the application to perform a print job, choose a particular printer and configure it, and then print the document. Activity diagrams model the workflow that occurs when working with a particular object so that you can better see how the object will have to react to the various activities that the user performs.

It's also important to track the object state as part of creating an activity diagram. By including state information, you can determine what the object will need to do to ensure completion of the activity. The object states aren't limited to a single object. You also create relationships between objects to show how the state of one object affects the state of other objects in the application. In short, this diagram focuses on the object and shows how activities affect object state.

Collaboration Diagrams

A collaboration diagram shows the interaction between objects as a sequence of numbered messages. When you look at a collaboration diagram, you see the static nature of the object hierarchy. Each object that interacts with another object has a connection called an *association*.

The messages tell you about the dynamic nature of the objects. The numbers are in order of the sequence of object events. For example, when the user clicks a button, the event handler object may call on a print object to configure a print setup, which in turn calls on a print dialog object to display a Print dialog box. The message numbers can follow a hierarchical form. For example, you might use 1.1, 1.2, and 1.3 to describe the sequence that occurs when a user clicks one button, and 2.1, 2.2, and 2.3 to describe the sequence that occurs when the user clicks a different button.

Component Diagrams

Components are an essential part of any application. A *component* provides essentially a black box that has specific behaviors. When you provide a certain input, you know that you'll receive a particular output because the black box nature of the component provides consistency. You don't usually care how the component works on the inside. All you know is that a component is a black box that outputs certain data and generates specific behaviors.

A component diagram models the behavior of a component using the black box approach. You use interfaces to describe a group of operations that a component uses or generates. For example, Windows uses the `IUnknown` interface to interrogate a component and discover more about it. The interfaces describe what you can do with the component and often represent standardized behaviors that the component implements in order to interact with the system in a particular way.

In most cases, you see multiple components in a single component diagram. These components interact with each other in certain ways as modeled by the interfaces. The diagram can also show dependencies between components. A dependency says that if Component A doesn't behave in a certain way, then Component B can't perform its task.

Deployment Diagrams

A deployment diagram shows how the system interacts when deployed on a system — it consists of nodes, components, and connections. A *node* is a physical resource that executes the code within components. The *connection* shows a physical relationship between two nodes. Nodes can contain any number of components. Consequently, a client application may have a component that requests data from a server. The deployment diagram would show the client and server machines as nodes. The Ethernet communication between the two nodes appears as a connection. Within each node are the components used to solve a particular problem.

Sequence Diagrams

In some respects, a sequence diagram is a more complicated form of a collaboration diagram with a time perspective instead of a structural perspective. The sequence diagram displays a series of events in the form of objects and the messages they exchange. This diagram shows what happens given a particular set of circumstances over time.

Every object begins with a class role that describes how the object behaves in a certain context. A sequence diagram doesn't include the object attributes, but simply its behaviors.

When one object calls on another or reacts to events, the sequence diagram shows it as an object activation. The length of the activation indicates the time required for the object to complete a particular task and helps you define the anticipated performance characteristics of the object interaction.

Connections between activations show message traffic between objects. As you move from one activation to the next, you see the messages required to make the next activation occur. Messages come in a number of types such as synchronous and asynchronous.

Statechart Diagrams

The purpose of a statechart diagram is to model the dynamic behavior of a system in response to some type of external stimuli. For example, this kind of diagram can answer the question of what happens when a user clicks a button on a form. In practice, the statechart diagram focuses on the states and transitions of an object. In the beginning, an object achieves a particular stable state. An external event changes that state so the object transitions to a new stable state.

Transitions come in a number of forms. Think of the transition as the movement from one state to another. The transitions can fork to show multiple transition paths and join to show the result of the multiple state paths. It's also possible to include decisions within the diagram to show how an application chooses a particular transition path.

Static Structure Diagrams

Most of the UML diagrams show some type of activity. The static structure diagram is more along the lines of a blueprint — it shows detailed information about the static state of the application. This diagram shows all the classes associated with the application. In fact, Visio includes specialized symbols for specific kinds of classes. You can show the interfaces, data types, exceptions, and other elements of the classes in the application. In short, this is the diagram you use to model the entire application as a series of modules.

Use Case Diagrams

The use case diagram is the starting point for most UML projects. As mentioned earlier, the use case diagram provides a kind of script that describes a sequence of events that the user will perform. The use case diagram begins with one or more actors. An *actor* is simply a user in a specific role. Consequently, you might see a list of events such as this one:

1. Create new document.
2. Write some text.
3. Save document.
4. Close document.

An application can have multiple use case diagrams. In fact, it's typical that an application will have multiple use case diagrams — one for each method of using the application. The easiest way to think of a use case diagram is that it shows one method (case) for using the application. Depending on your application, you may create a number of use case diagrams to explore how the user interacts with the application fully.

A single use case diagram can also show multiple actors. For example, consider a supply request form. In this case, the user may fill out the supply request and send it for approval to a supervisor, who then sends it to the person who fulfills the supply request. In this case, the use case diagram contains three actors, one for each of the standard activities.

You don't always need to create a single diagram for every potential activity that the user may perform. An application may have multiple reports that it can output. Instead of creating a single use case diagram for each report, you create a "generate reports" use case that models all the report generating sequences (unless a particular report requires a special procedure to complete — in this case, you model that report separately).

Generating Code from UML

Unlike many UML products on the market, you can actually generate code by using higher-end versions of Visio (the Professional edition doesn't provide this feature). The UML doesn't generate the code — UML is simply a method of drawing a picture that corresponds to the software you want to create. Visio is actually interpreting your picture and creating output from it. You begin by choosing UML ➪ Code ➪ Check. Visio checks your drawing for potential problems and notifies you about any errors it finds.

After you check your drawing for errors, it's time to set the preferences for the output. Choose UML ➪ Code ➪ Preferences to display the Preferences dialog box shown in Figure 3-5. You can use the options in this dialog box to select the target language, location of the resulting project, and options such as the code template used to create the code.

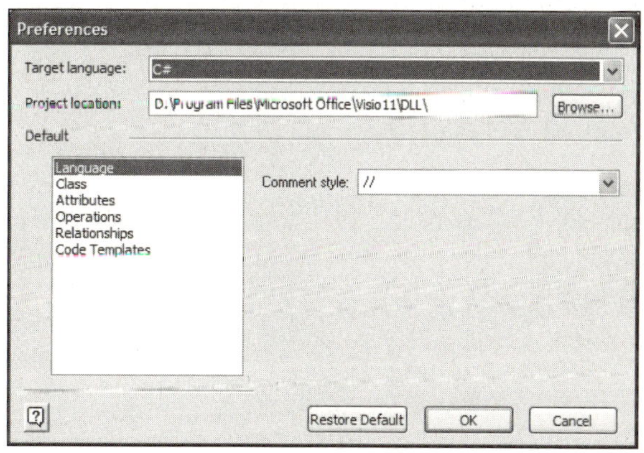

Figure 3-5: Set the output preferences to meet specific needs.

Your drawing must contain at least one class before Visio can generate any code for you. To add a new class to the drawing, right-click a package or class entry in Model Explorer and choose Class from the context menu. Visio displays the UML Class Properties dialog box shown in Figure 3-6 where you define the class characteristics. After you create a new class, you add UML drawings to it to define its characteristics.

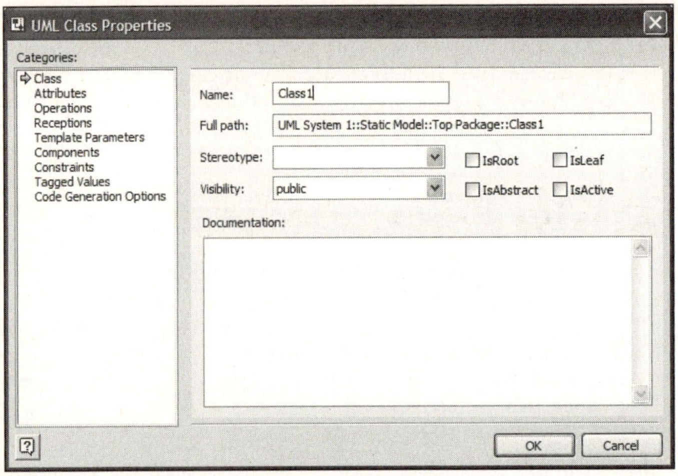

Figure 3-6: Define new classes as needed and add drawings to them to define their characteristics.

The next step is to generate the code. Choose UML ➪ Code ➪ Generate and you see the Generate dialog box shown in Figure 3-7. Clicking OK generates code you can modify to create an application. (The generation process requires several minutes at times, so be patient.) Of course, the code is only as good as your design. It's unlikely that the code is going to provide the perfect application at the outset, but you can refine your model and the application at the same time.

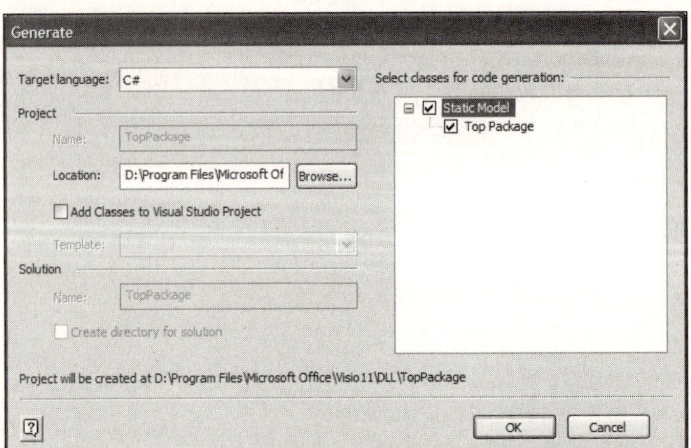

Figure 3-7: Select the generation options and then click OK to generate code from your diagram.

It's important to realize that there are limits to automatic code generation, which is the reason many UML aficionados don't want to have anything to do with the functionality that Visio provides. Even so, using this approach can give you a good start on your application. Given a well-defined model, you can usually get something prototyped to the point of usability with just a little coding.

Of course, the question that most people ask is whether you can use this approach to generate an application. Unfortunately, you don't get a complete application. Eventually, automatic code generation of this type may work. However, after 20-plus years of testing solution after solution and coming up empty, I'm convinced that the computer won't replace the developer anytime soon.

Developing Your Design Strategy

This chapter has demonstrated three essential steps or phases for creating a design strategy for your application. The first step is to create the underlying object model based on the tasks that the application must perform. Second, you define the data model used to interact with the data that the application requires to perform useful work. Third, you create a set of user classes that helps the user interact with the application and outputs the data the application provides.

In addition to the design strategy, this chapter discusses UML. Some people say that UML is a type of application design methodology — those people probably haven't used UML. What UML really provides is a way to present the object model for your application graphically. Instead of writing everything out and hoping everyone can grasp your abstract presentation, UML lets you present your design graphically, making it much easier for everyone to understand.

Now it's time for you to get into action. Don't wait until you've read the next chapter to design the object model for your own application. Remember to start with the underlying functionality for your application, move to the data model, and finally provide an interface for the user. It's not essential that you use Visio to create your model, but it's a good idea to use a modeling tool of some type when you create your model. The simple fact is that using a modeling tool of some type is easier than trying to write an easily understood specification.

Although this chapter provides a good start on the user interface design process, you really need more information to create a great user interface. Chapter 4 provides a wealth of techniques you can use to design the user interface for your application. Not only will you find the mundane standard interface elements, this chapter also discusses new approaches to the user interface such as licensing Microsoft's RibbonX interface (also called the Office Fluent User Interface). In short, Chapter 4 is the next step you need to take after you complete the modeling process described in this chapter.

4

Designing the User Interface

The user interface is your method of communicating with the user. The user may not see you, but when they see your interface, they're seeing part of you. Every developer puts something interesting into an interface. Sure, Microsoft and others have tried, somewhat successfully, to standardize the user interface, but there are always quirks to an interface that reflect the spirit of the developer who designed it. Because the user interface is your method of communicating with the user, you need to take special care in designing it so that your communication is both clear and efficient. Remember, in most cases, you won't be there to explain anything to the user who relies on your application.

Even though there is a movement toward interface standardization, there are many ways in which to differentiate your application. For example, the kind of interface (dialog box, standard window, tabbed, or free form) makes a significant difference in how the user views the application. Most users view dialog box applications as easier to use, even when they contain the same number and complexity of controls as a forms-based application or a windowed application. When it comes to the user interface, appearance is everything.

At some point, you must consider how to interact with the user in a complex way. Most applications today rely on a system of menus and toolbars to make the complete functionality of an application available to the user. However, task-based applications are becoming more popular because they tend to hide complex functionality from view until the user needs it. In some cases, an information-based interface works best. When working with an information-based application, the interface changes to match the kind of information the user is using or creating.

This chapter also considers the issue of how you interact with the user. A novice user requires a lot of handholding and complex functionality hiding. However, the same interface in the hands of an expert user is inefficient and tends to upset the user because of the view that everything is too difficult to find. You'll also find a special section on meeting the interface requirements of people with special needs. As the population ages, you'll find that more and more people have special needs — everything from poor eyesight to an inability to hear everything that goes on around them. The point is that you must provide some means of interacting with the audience for your application, which often means creating a user profile and modifying the design to match that user's needs. If you're creating a generic application, you may find that you have to add an expert mode that eliminates the feature hiding you provide for the novice.

Understanding the Application Form Types

A user interface begins with a form of some type in most cases. However, Windows supports a number of form types and you can configure them in a number of ways. One of the first decisions you must make when creating an application is the kind of forms that you'll use. Moderately complex applications often use several types of forms. For example, the main application component may require a window, while a configuration form requires a dialog box. The following sections describe the various application forms available through Visual Studio .NET.

It's important to remember that Windows truly does support a vast number of forms, not all of which are available in .NET. For example, you can't create property pages for the various Windows Properties dialog boxes without using special programming techniques. As another example, you can't create a Microsoft Management Console (MMC) snap-in without using special programming techniques — I've done it, and the P/Invoke techniques are quite esoteric. However, the forms supplied with the .NET Framework meet 99.99 percent of the requirements out there, so don't worry much about these truly esoteric alternatives.

Creating a Dialog Utility

You probably see several hundred dialog boxes every day. Most of them have certain similarities. For example, most dialog boxes include a Cancel button. You'll probably find a fair number of dialog boxes that also include an OK button or some equivalent. Of course, the content of the dialog boxes differs, which is where you come into play. The user expects to see dialog boxes with certain characteristics as a kind of unwritten standard. However, the content of the dialog box is unique because the dialog box has to complete a certain task in order to perform a useful function.

Users commonly rely on dialog boxes to provide access to something simple such as a configuration task. Dialog boxes also perform short tasks, such as printing a document. Theoretically, you could create a word processor in a dialog box, but it would be difficult to use and no one would really want to try. However, some developers do try to make dialog boxes do far more than they should by stuffing them full of controls. The result is that the reader finds the dialog box difficult to use and often makes errors with it. Here are some ways in which you can use the dialog box as an application form:

- Display application information, such as an About dialog box.
- Perform configuration tasks, such as setting up a printer for printing.
- Perform specific short-term actions, such as printing a document.
- Interactively adjust application function, such as adjusting the colors in a graphic display.
- Create a short response form, such as a bug report that requires few entries.

- Present status information, such as a warning that system memory is low.
- Provide user-to-user communication, such as a chat dialog box.
- Display application options, such as a text style picker.

Dialog boxes differ according to a number of properties. One of the more important properties, from a user perspective, is `FormBorderStyle`. This property controls the appearance of the dialog box border and its functionality, which is often the first clue the user has as to the dialog box function. Not setting this property can create unusual situations. For example, one user managed to resize a dialog box in such a way that the controls became invisible. The user couldn't figure out what to do next, so he called product support and product support spent several hours trying to figure out what purpose the dialog box served. Because the dialog box was modal and the application wouldn't respond without closing the dialog box, product support had to work through the problem with the user. The developer could have avoided this problem by changing `FormBorderStyle` to `FixedDialog`. Choosing the wrong setting cost everyone a lot of time. Table 4-1 describes the `FormBorderStyle` settings you can use and when you typically use them.

Table 4-1: `FormBorderStyle` **Options**

Value	Use	Description
None	This option can be used for tooltips or other informational messages.	Doesn't display a border at all. Don't use this option for modal applications.
FixedSingle	This is the standard option for tooltips or other informational messages. In some cases, the developer uses this option for interactive adjustments, such as graphic rollups found in higher end graphics applications.	Displays a thin fixed border. The user can't change the size of the border, so you need to modify the size of the dialog box when the user relies on a large font size.
Fixed3D	This option can be used for configuration dialog boxes and informational displays.	Displays a raised thick border. The user can't resize this border. Because of the decorative nature of this border, it probably isn't a good choice when you need to consider accessibility requirements.
FixedDialog	This is the standard option for small applications. You can also use it for informational displays and configuration dialog boxes. Some developers use it for interactive tasks such as chat dialog boxes.	Displays a thick fixed border. The user can't change the size of the border, so you need to modify the size of the dialog box when the user relies on a large font size.

Continued

Table 4-1: `FormBorderStyle` **Options** *(continued)*

Value	Use	Description
Sizable	This is the standard option for interactive dialog boxes where the user must type information.	Displays a thin sizeable border. The sizeable nature of this dialog box makes it possible for the user to enlarge the dialog box to provide more room for typing. Make sure you set a minimum dialog box size using the `MinimumSize` property so the controls don't disappear completely. This is an excellent option for accessibility purposes because the user can make the dialog box any size needed, but using it for every possible task also eliminates one visual cue that users rely on to determine the purpose of the dialog box.
FixedToolWindow	This is the standard option for configuration dialog boxes.	Displays a thick fixed border. The title bar is smaller for this option and the dialog box doesn't appear in either the taskbar or in the list of applications that appears when the user presses Alt+Tab.
SizableToolWindow	This option can be used for interactive configuration dialog boxes where the user must type a large amount of text.	Displays a thick sizable border. The title bar is smaller for this option and the dialog box doesn't appear in either the Taskbar or in the list of applications that appears when the user presses Alt+Tab.

There are other considerations when working with dialog boxes. For example, you normally make configuration dialog boxes modal so that the user completes settings before giving the main application the focus again. Using this technique prevents the application from doing odd things when the settings are incomplete or unchecked. In addition, using this technique prevents the user from complaining that the settings changes are incomplete. On the other hand, you won't normally make an interactive dialog box, such as a Search and Replace dialog box, modal because you might want the user to interact with the application while performing searches.

Some dialog boxes don't require user interaction at all. For example, when you display a tooltip, the tooltip should appear when the user places the mouse cursor on the target control and the tooltip should disappear when the user moves the mouse cursor away from the control. The display of the dialog box is automatic because the user expects this form of interaction.

Interacting with the Single Document Interface (SDI)

There are two kinds of basic windowed applications: Single Document Interface (SDI) and Multiple Document Interface (MDI). As you might imagine from the name of the window type, an SDI window contains just one document at a time. Microsoft experimented with this interface for Office once and found it didn't work particularly well (as evidenced by the loud outcry of protest from users). However, the SDI does have a significant number of uses. For example, Notepad is an example of an SDI. You create one window at a time and interact with it.

The SDI works well when an application manages only one document type and the user is unlikely to need to compare documents. Many developers associate the SDI with simpler applications because that's where you normally see it used. However, the SDI works fine with complex applications as well. The complexity of the application doesn't matter much — the way the user interacts with that application matters. If the user is expecting to work with multiple documents, it's a pain to have to open multiple copies of the application and carefully arrange them to accomplish the task. You're forcing the user to think about the software too much — the interaction should be natural.

An SDI need not prevent all forms of comparison. By using a splitter, you can divide the single window into two or more areas that the user can use to view different parts of the same document. For example, you might use this feature in a simple note taker to let the user see the previous day's entry while making new entries today.

When working with a windowed application, it's also necessary to divide the application into several discrete areas. These divisions can be quite formal, as when you work with C++, or less formal, as when working with C#, but they're something you must consider nonetheless. Each of these divisions has a specific purpose as described in the following list:

- **Application:** The application acts as a host. Don't get the idea that the host supports a particular kind of data or data representation. The host doesn't care about anything other than loading and unloading documents. For example, the consoles found in the Administrative Tools folder of the Control Panel are quite diverse. However, one application, MMC, hosts them all. The snap-ins you see are examples of documents. MMC loads and unloads them at your request and performs certain common interactions with them. After you spend a few minutes with MMC, you realize that an application that hosts documents doesn't care too much about what those documents contain.
- **Document:** The document is a container for a particular kind of content. If your application is like MMC and hosts a number of document types, you need one document object for each kind of content. The document provides functionality for the content you want to support. For example, the document saves and opens particular content.
- **Work area:** The work area is the view of the document. The work area and the document aren't necessarily connected. For example, you can view the same chart data as a line graph, bar chart, or area graph. The underlying document is the same; only the work area has changed. The same view can work for multiple documents as long as the view can understand the underlying data and present it to the user as anticipated.
- **Document content:** The document content is that actual data. In most cases, the document content is a complex type that can include multiple objects. For example, text documents include formatting. You can insert graphics into a text document, so the content becomes a mixture of text and graphics.

Interacting with the Multiple Document Interface (MDI)

The MDI is a windowed application just like the SDI. In fact, it shares many of the same features as the SDI. For example, it has the same four basic divisions as an SDI: application, document, work area, and document content. However, an MDI is more complex than an SDI because it can display multiple documents at once. It can also display multiple views of the same document. In most cases, you can minimize individual documents so that they appear as icons at the bottom of the MDI host display. A special menu, normally called Window, has options that let you arrange the individual views in a particular way.

In short, an MDI lets you do more with a number of documents than an SDI. More is always better, right? Actually, it turns out that more isn't always better and always results in reduced user efficiency, because users are distracted by the multiple windows. I worked in one place where an employee would open every document she intended to work on during the day. The documents would appear in windows and she fastidiously arranged the windows in the order in which she would work on them. After spending at least a half hour performing this task (during which time I had already typed quite a few paragraphs for my next book — I was writing government documentation at the time) she would start work. That's where the problems began. First, she'd complain she couldn't find the particular document she wanted and then she'd complain that the display area was too small. For this employee, MDI was a terrible time waster and made her computing experience far less enjoyable — an SDI would have been better.

Most of the time, I use Word in SDI mode. Yes, I could work on multiple documents at once, but it's distracting — it's far more efficient to work on one task at a time. I've actually timed myself and I always get more pages done per day when I focus on one task at a time — multitasking and humans spell poor efficiency (at least, it does for anyone I've worked with). The only time that the Word MDI functionality comes in handy is when I need to compare one document with another or update one document based on another. For example, when I update the table of contents (TOC) for my book, I open each chapter in turn in outline view and verify that the chapter outline matches my TOC. It doesn't take very long and having an updated TOC is mandatory if I want to track the progress of my book. Consequently, even though I seldom need the MDI capability of Word, it's nice to have when I do.

When creating an MDI application, you should default to an SDI view when opening the first document. Wait for the user to request to see multiple documents at once (maintain the SDI view during subsequent document openings). Otherwise, you may simply add to the confusion that can reign when a novice user sees a number of documents at once.

MDI isn't a free ride for the developer, either. Creating an MDI application requires significantly more time because you have to maintain the status of each document the user opens and sometimes need to coordinate information between views when the views all show the same document. Testing and debugging an MDI are also significantly harder than testing and debugging an SDI and it's far less likely that you'll find all of the bugs before you release the application to the users.

Overall, MDI seems like it's the interface to use for windowed applications, but it isn't always the right choice. You should consider these issues when you decide between SDI and MDI:

- ❑ Is the additional development time warranted?
- ❑ Will the loss of user efficiency result in a significant functionality benefit?

- Does the user actually need to view multiple documents at once?
- Will the application allow the user to see multiple views of the same document (some applications that support multiple views of a document only allow the user to select one view at a time)?
- Can the user accomplish the same goals using a split view in an SDI application?

Relying on a Tabbed Interface

The tabbed interface is a sort of dialog box with multiple pages. You use a tabbed interface for mini-applications that have too much configuration information to fit on a single dialog box. A developer normally groups related controls and places them on a single page. The page has a tab that you use to select it, and the name on that tab reflects the functionality of the group of controls. One of the better examples of a tabbed interface is the Display Properties dialog box used with Windows. The tabs include Themes, Desktop, Screen Saver, Appearance, and Settings. In this case, you configure the appearance of the Windows display by using the controls on the pages of this dialog box.

You normally use a tabbed interface for some type of configuration task. Many applications rely on the tabbed interface dialog box to provide a centralized location for configuring the application. Otherwise, the user would need to open individual dialog boxes for each configuration requirement. A tabbed interface can also work as a mini-application. For example, when you open the Remote Desktop Connection application provided with Windows, you initially see a standard dialog box. However, when you click Options, you see a tabbed interface. Each tab helps you create the connection to the remote server. When you click Connect, Remote Desktop Connection makes the connection to the remote system and displays its desktop for you.

Sometimes you'll see a wizard that uses a tabbed interface. Using this approach makes it possible for experienced users to skip directly to the configuration changes they need to make. Less experienced users can follow the wizard step-by-step as normal. However, you should only use this approach for a wizard that provides the necessary flexibility. Sometimes you really do need to follow the systematic course of the standard wizard application.

Theoretically, you can use the tabbed interface for specific kinds of user response forms. The trick here is that the user response form must provide default values for every optional field. A developer could employ this kind of form for common response requirements, such as trouble reports, which the user fills out often enough, so that there is no problem with being familiar with report content. Make sure you do leave required fields blank and check those fields before you let the user submit the form — otherwise, you might experience database corruption and other problems from incomplete forms.

It's a mistake to think that you can use the tabbed interface for anything more than a small application. For example, you probably wouldn't want to create a complete data entry application that uses a tabbed interface, because the tabbed interface could lead to data integrity problems. However, tabbed interfaces do find use within large applications as part of a solution. For example, Visual Studio uses a tabbed interface to display a list of open documents. Even though the tabs aren't part of the main application (which relies on the familiar toolbar and menu interface), they do make using the various child windows easier.

Developing Specialty Skinned and Free-Form Applications

The use of a skinned or free-form interface, such as the one you can create with Windows Media Player, is always optional. In fact, you probably won't want to use this kind of interface with business applications because a skinned interface can cause a significant amount of user confusion. A skinned interface is the equivalent of a dialog box or tabbed interface application in most cases, although it's possible you could create an SDI application using a skinned interface as well.

The motivation for using the skinned interface is to give the application pizzazz — to make it look appealing and snazzy. It might be interesting to try this approach for applications that users tend not to like in any form, such as bug report applications. However, you'll commonly find this approach used for fun applications such as the Windows Media Player because the developer wants to make the application a little more interesting.

A skinned interface presents a common list of controls, but in no particular order. The appearance of the application differs from the standard in that it's normally graphic in nature and lacks the usual square appearance of other applications. You can see a set of skins for the Windows Media Player at `http://www.microsoft.com/windows/windowsmedia/player/skins.aspx`. All these skins provide access to the Windows Media Player, but as you can see, the skins are quite different in appearance and the controls appear in different places for each skin. Consequently, a skinned interface usually works well for an intuitive application such as Windows Media Player, but would present a training nightmare for anything approaching the complexity of most business applications.

Of course, the seeming lacking of applicability of the skinned interface raises the question of why you're even seeing it listed in this book. I was surprised recently to see a skinned application used for information display and configuration purposes. Figure 4-1 shows an example of ASUS PC Probe II, an application designed to tell you about the status of the hardware for your system (fan speed, temperature, and the like).

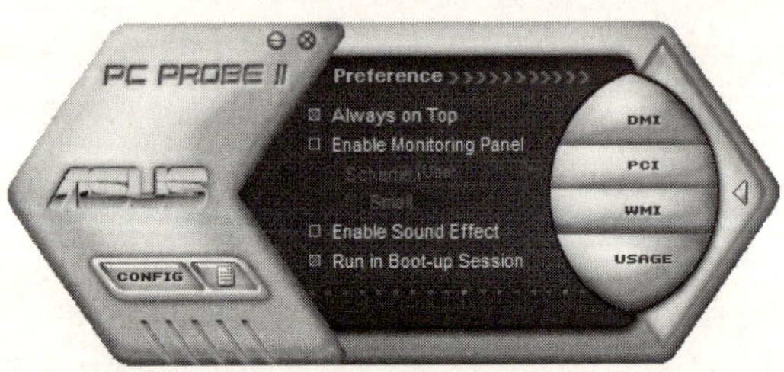

Figure 4-1: Skinned interface applications do have a place in the business world.

In this case, there is only one skin for the application, making it more of a free-form application than a true skinned interface. The lack of additional skins is the only difference between the skinned interface and the free-form interface. Using this interface is fun, yet it doesn't present any sort of training nightmare because the interface is the same for everyone using the application. Consequently, if you have a business application, such as a bug report form, and you want to dress it up to make users think about using it a little more often, the free-form interface approach taken in Figure 4-1 may be the answer you need.

Never assume you can't adapt an interface to a different use. Of course, adaptation always comes with risks. The designer at ASUS who came up with the PC Probe II interface was truly inspired, because it's not only fun, but it's quite functional and easy to use. For every one of the good adaptations on the market, there are probably a hundred more adaptations that fail by making life more difficult for the end user.

Working in the Visual Environment

Many users today are more visually oriented than users in the past. If you talk to older users, some of them may remember using punch cards and paper tape to communicate with the computer. Some of them will remember how nice it was to move to the green screen (a kind of monochrome screen used on early computers — some were orange and blue too). In these early days, a developer could get by creating a text display with a few graphical ASCII characters thrown in the mix.

Today, users consider it a crime if they have to use anything less than 24-bit color displays. Those displays often require fancy graphics and a lot of pizzazz. Most developers aren't visual — they're used to working in the abstract world of algorithms and interesting coding techniques. The old text displays no longer work very well.

Sometimes it's helpful to have someone visually oriented on your team. A graphic artist with lots of computer experience and a bit of programming experience can be a huge asset for complex applications. When you want to present information in an eye-appealing manner, it's important to have someone who understands how people view graphics so you can avoid some of the horrors of tacky icons and unusable graphic output. A development team need not always consist exclusively of developers — consider expanding your horizons a bit and adding people who have other skills, too.

Working with RibbonX Applications

RibbonX is a new API that Microsoft has developed. You see it in many of the Office 2007 applications where Microsoft refers to it as the Office Fluent User Interface. Microsoft even makes this API available to anyone who wants it, royalty free (check for details at `http://msdn.microsoft.com/en-us/office/aa905530.aspx`). You can get an overview of all of the RibbonX programming elements at `http://msdn.microsoft.com/en-us/magazine/cc163469.aspx`.

Microsoft marketing has a tendency to produce a wealth of names for the same technology. The longer the name, the more Microsoft marketing seems to like it. Even though Microsoft seems to like the Office Fluent User Interface moniker a lot, this book refers to the API simply as RibbonX.

The basic idea behind RibbonX is information hiding. Yes, you still have an entire interface for Office, but the user needs to see only part of it at any given time. Rather than present the user with a menu full of options, RibbonX hides all of the options except those that relate to a specific task such as laying out pages (using the Page Layout tab). In addition, the user sees only controls that relate to basic page layout functionality. In order to see advanced options, the user must click on special controls that display these features. Consequently, a typical user is probably going to use only the standard features — those that Microsoft feels are safe and easy to use.

Microsoft based RibbonX on the needs of the novice users commonly found in the enterprise environment. In fact, administrators can (and probably do) implement significant levels of information hiding to protect these users from themselves. Most power users find the RibbonX interface reduces productivity significantly. In fact, some are downright hostile to the entire idea of using the RibbonX interface in Office, so a third-party market has appeared that provides ways to circumvent RibbonX, such as the tools found on the pschmid.net site at `http://pschmid.net/office2007/index.php` and ToolbarToggle `http://www.toolbartoggle.com/`. These aids help the power user recover lost productivity, while letting novice users reap the benefits of the easier-to-use-and-understand RibbonX interface. The point is that RibbonX probably won't win you any points if your development environment has mainly power users and very few novices. Make sure you use this new interface in the correct environment.

Although the basic idea of RibbonX is to hide information, it does work exceptionally well for creating workflows. A *workflow* is a task-oriented environment in which the user follows a specific process to accomplish a task. For example, Figure 4-2 shows a typical workflow in which the user moves from left to right and simply clicks buttons or chooses options to create a letter. Even a power user is unlikely to complain about this use of RibbonX because it actually does speed work considerably. In this case, notice that all the default, simple options appear as controls. A user can select other options by clicking the down arrow near a button. For example, if the user wants to choose something other than the default date, clicking the down arrow under Today will display a date/time picker that the user can use to choose a new date.

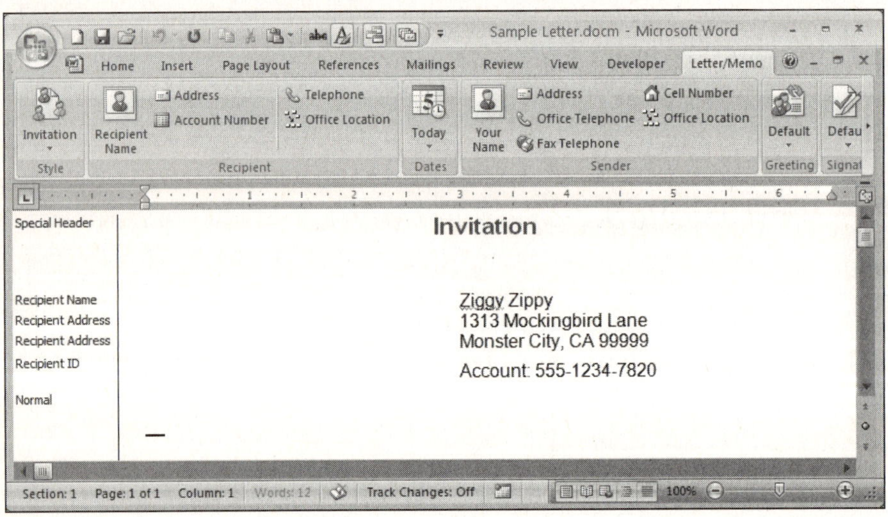

Figure 4-2: The best use of RibbonX is for workflows.

Overall, the RibbonX interface is what you make of it. The examples provided by Office aren't the best productivity aids out there — at least not for the power user who is always looking for a way to overcome them. However, workflows are a win for everyone because they help power user and novice alike to get more done in less time and with fewer errors.

Using the Notification Area

An application uses the Notification Area as a place to present its icon without having it sit on the Taskbar, taking up space. Of course, the most common icon in the Notification Area is the Windows volume control. Just about everyone is familiar with this little speaker icon that lets you change the volume settings for your current setting.

The Notification Area of the Taskbar is getting cluttered. Users seem to think they must have a host of icons in there, including a hardware monitor, sound device adjuster, DVD drive monitor, printer monitor, and who knows what else. In fact, it's the "who knows what else" part that prompted Microsoft to include a Windows feature that removes unwanted icons. Consequently, placing your application icon in the Notification Area isn't any guarantee that the user will actually see it and use it.

Creating an application that places its icon in the Notification Area, rather than in the Taskbar, isn't tricky, but you should have a good reason for placing the icon in the Notification Area. For example, I created a timer application for myself. I set it to alert me to the need to get up and move about once an hour or so. Getting up and moving about is good for someone who sits in front of the keyboard as many hours as I do. After I come back from my quick stretch and move-about break, I click another button and the timer starts again. The point is, this particular application has no need to sit on the Taskbar taking up space because I don't need to interact with it very often — the Notification Area works just fine in this case.

The application also provides status information through the icon. When you hover the mouse over the icon, it displays how much time is left before the next break. Right-clicking the icon shows all the functionality you need to control the application. Using just the icon, you can exit the application, pause the timer, or display the full dialog box where you can change the time interval. Most successful Notification Area applications present this kind of interface and provide similar levels of functionality.

One of the Notification Area icons that seems to bug users most is the one for Microsoft Office Outlook. The application already appears on the Taskbar, so why do you also need a Notification Area icon for it? This is an example of a situation where Microsoft has used the Notification Area incorrectly. You should always choose between a Taskbar and a Notification Area presentation for your application, but not both, because using both tends to irritate users. Consequently, you should consider whether your application is compatible with the Taskbar or Notification Area. Here are some of the guidelines you should consider for using the Notification Area:

- The application should normally work in the background and not require a lot of user interaction.
- In most cases, you use the Notification Area for relatively small or simple applications.
- Use a Windows service if the user won't need to interact with the application at all; the Notification Area is for applications that require some level of attention and provide the user with status information.
- Applications that appear in the Notification Area normally provide a service and start when the user logs into Windows.
- Use the Notification Area for supplemental applications that provide output to the user. For example, a printer provides monitoring software that interacts with a host application that provides access to the printer's full capability. The monitoring software also provides status information such as the current ink and paper levels.

Investigating the Command Line

After spending so much time talking about really cool GUIs, it may surprise you to learn that your next application may not sport a GUI interface at all. For many years, Microsoft seemed determined to wipe out any notion of the command line. It even came up with Windows PowerShell (see `http://www.microsoft.com/windowsserver2003/technologies/management/powershell/default.mspx` and Chapter 9 for details), which is a managed alternative to the command line. However, if you've been following the trade press news, you know that there is a new version of Windows out there called Windows Server 2008 Server Core (Server Core for short), which uses nothing but the command line as an interface. That's right; Server Core lacks a Taskbar, Notification Area, Desktop, icons, and a whole lot of other features that you normally associate with the GUI that is Windows. In fact, some GUI applications won't even run under Server Core because Server Core lacks basics like the common dialog boxes. (You can read more about Server Core at `http://msdn.microsoft.com/en-us/library/ms723891(VS.85).aspx.`)

You may wonder how, if Server Core doesn't support the .NET Framework due to limitations in its design, it's possible to run managed applications. Fortunately, you don't have to rely on Microsoft for .NET Framework support. An alternative to the .NET Framework exists in the form of Mono (`http://www.mono-project.com/Main_Page`*). You can easily install Mono on Server Core. As long as your .NET application doesn't rely on graphic elements that are outside the Mono domain of support, you can use it on Server Core.*

Server Core aside, many administrators in the know prefer using the command line because it's significantly faster to type a command than to navigate a GUI. Of course, commands require memorization, but administrators perform some tasks so often that memorization isn't a problem. In addition, using batch files makes working at the command line even faster and reduces the need for memorization significantly. Even so, there is that problem with potential typos and other errors when working at the command line.

Some management applications provide a dual interface. You can choose to use the GUI for error-free performance or speed your way along by using the command line. In fact, many applications are heading this direction. Exchange Server 2008 provides many features using both a GUI and a command line interface, so you have your choice of which interface to use.

The command line isn't just for management tasks. For example, if you have a program that you want to run just once at startup — say a program that changes the user's desktop wallpaper to show current events or something else that corporate thinks is important — you can create a program that relies on a command line interface. If you think you'll also need to interact with the application to change settings, you can add a GUI counterpart to it. The point is, you now can create a Windows shortcut to the application that includes all of the required command as part of the shortcut. Place the shortcut in the Startup folder and you're ready to go.

Lest you think that Microsoft really has given up on the command line, you'll find that there are hundreds of commands available at the command line today. Many of these commands are added when you install Microsoft applications. Microsoft isn't the only vendor interested in the command line; many third-party vendors rely on the command line, too. You can discover more about command line programming techniques in the "Adding Command Line Functionality" section of Chapter 12.

There are some caveats to using the command line interface as part of your application design strategy. The following list describes these potential concerns:

- The command line isn't for the novice. If novices mainly use your application and you don't intend to add Windows shortcuts to use the application, you may want to avoid the command line.
- Make sure the command line interface is fully documented using the `/?` command line switch. Nothing is worse than a mystery interface for administrators.
- Document the command line interface as part of the help file and tell the user when it's appropriate to use the command line interface to perform tasks. In addition, it's often helpful to provide batch file and other examples of working with the command line as part of your documentation.
- Use an application name that actually matches the functionality that the command line application provides. If you can't accurately define the command line application functionality, consider splitting the application into smaller pieces so it's easier to work with at the command line.

Understanding the Common User Interface Types

This section considers the problem of determining how the user interacts with your application. If you write an application for a power user, you might use a menu-driven application, because the power user will want full access to the complete power of the application. However, novice users often find menu-driven applications confusing. In this case, you might create a wizard-driven or a task-driven interface.

In some cases, you choose a particular interface because it's what the user expects, or because it has become standardized over time. For example, whenever you run a setup program, you rely on a wizard-driven application to perform the task because it has become traditional over time and because the wizard-driven interface reduces the risk that the user will make a major error. The following sections describe the various kinds of user interface types that you commonly find in C# applications.

Amaze me! If you have created a user interface that doesn't appear in this section, let me know about it. Write me at JMueller@mwt.net and describe (within reason — I don't want to know your company secrets) your exciting new interface. I'd love to hear how your organization chooses to interact with the user.

Menu Driven

Most applications today are menu driven. The question is whether they should remain menu driven. The menu and toolbar system used by most applications today has its roots in the beginnings of Windows and probably well before. Let's just say the menu and toolbar user interface is timeworn and well tested. The menu-driven interface is still the favorite with power users of all types, including administrators and developers, because it provides fast access to the full functionality of an application. You should consider continuing to use this interface for the advanced users of your application.

The menu-driven interface is most appropriate for users who don't perform precisely the same tasks in exactly the same way every day. Look at the random access nature of the menu-driven application and you see why it's so speedy for someone who needs to come up with new procedures because their tasks vary. Using the menu-driven interface makes it possible for the user to interact with the application in a free-form manner.

There are better interfaces than the menu-driven interface for novice or intermediate users who do perform largely repetitive tasks. The free-form nature of the menu-driven interface proves confusing to less experienced users. Some users actually have to write procedures for using this interface and never do learn what the menu options mean. For less experienced users, the menu-driven interface is a nightmare that they overcome by parroting the actions of those users with more experience.

Task Driven

The task-driven interface is relatively new and unique. The workflow application shown in Figure 4-2 is an example of a task-driven interface, but this isn't the only example. Some developers may be tempted to confuse the task-driven interface with a wizard. However, a task-driven interface differs from a wizard in that the steps aren't absolute. A user normally moves in one direction, but each step has multiple options that the user can employ. In addition, a user can choose to perform a step zero or more times, unless you specify that the user must perform the step at least once.

Another difference in the task-driven interface is that the user can see all the steps. In some cases, the user may perform the steps out of order, which makes the task-driven interface different from a wizard. Of course, you can always enforce a particular order of execution by enabling controls in the next step only after the user successfully completes the previous step.

The task-driven interface tends to use controls that restrict the user to specific choices. For example, in the letter-writing application shown in Figure 4-2, the greeting choices may include, "To whom it may concern" and "Dear Sir," but not "Hey You!" The addition of specific choices makes it less likely that the user will make mistakes and ensures that the resulting output conforms to any corporate policies you might have in place for creating the desired output.

The task-driven interface isn't specifically associated with the RibbonX API. You can create a task-driven application with any form you want. The idea is to present a flow of some sort. Although RibbonX does excel at this kind of development, many applications allow the same approach using toolbars or other means. In fact, using the old toolbar and menu interface, you could present the application options in a random form for advanced users using the menus and then rely on the toolbar to create a task-driven interface for novice users.

In short, the task-driven interface frees the user from thinking about procedure by providing a visual workflow of some type. The result is that the interface becomes nearly invisible and lets the user focus specifically on content. This interface is excellent for users of all skill levels. Even the expert user can find a task-driven interface both useful and efficient after using it for a short time.

Information Driven

An information-driven application provides a hierarchical method of accomplishing a task. The user begins by creating a starting point for the task. As the user makes selections, the application automatically follows a hierarchical route to an ending node. The previous entry always acts as input to limit the options for the current entry. In this way, the information that the user provides acts as a limiter to what the application has to offer, which makes the application significantly easier to use, especially for the novice.

This interface actually has many names. For example, when an administrator drills down into an information store, the administrator is using an information-driven interface. The previous selections limit the options that the administrator sees when drilling down to locate a specific piece of information.

Many search engines are a kind of information-driven interface as well. The user starts out with a basic query such as letters. The application then offers the kinds of letters that the data store holds. The user chooses a specific kind of letter and the application then presents the user with the next level of the search. The process continues until the user locates a specific letter in the company database.

Most information-driven applications rely on a rule base and a data store to function properly. The rule base controls how the user searches. Given a specific set of entries, the rule base can help the user choose the next logical level. The rule base can even employ rule-based artificial intelligence, or expert system, to make the choices based on a probability of correctness. The database includes not only the information the user seeks, but aids to performing the search such as keywords.

Information-driven interfaces work best when the user doesn't know what he or she is looking for, and we all fall into that category sometimes. The focus of this interface isn't the user's skill level, but rather the kind of information the user is attempting to find — the more complex the information, the better the information-driven interface tends to work. Building a good information-driven interface requires superior programming skills and you must tune the rule base as the user works with the application. In short, you should use this interface when you have complex information that the user tends to search more than to modify.

Wizard Driven

The wizard is a longtime friend of the developer. Anyone who has installed an application has probably used a wizard. A wizard-driven interface usually relies on a dialog box presentation and uses specific steps to perform a task. The user isn't allowed to deviate from the prescribed sequence, which makes this form of interface an excellent choice for the novice. It's also a necessary interface at times for someone of any skill level, including administrators who spend quite a bit of time installing applications. You commonly find wizard-driven applications used for the following tasks:

- Installation programs
- Setup and configuration programs
- Document or project creation routines (as part of another program)
- Report creation
- Procedural applications, such as a hardware interface where the user must follow a specific set of steps
- Workflow-based tasks that require stronger procedural support than other interfaces, such as RibbonX, support

The wizard-driven application focuses on controls that provide specific values. For example, you might give a user a choice of performing a standard or custom installation using radio buttons. A wizard does sometimes require written input from the user. For example, a wizard will often ask the user for a username, a company name, and a product identifier — all of which appear in written form. However, a wizard-driven interface application should keep written entries to a minimum to prevent user errors.

One mistake that many developers make when creating a wizard is to let the user enter paths directly. It's better to force the user to use a folder listing whenever possible (the TreeView control works well for this purpose). If the user must provide a new folder, use the folder listing as a starting point and ask the user to enter the location as a new folder on the existing tree. Always provide the user with a default entry so that most users can simply bypass making any changes to the entry.

Some power users find a wizard-driven interface annoying in certain situations. For example, a novice might require a precise set of steps to format a letter, but the power user can probably perform the task faster without the wizard's help. Consequently, even though you would make use of a wizard mandatory to install applications, you wouldn't make it mandatory for the power users when working with many application-specific tasks.

Administrators find wizards annoying for installation and setup, too. That's why many setup programs provide a command-driven interface in addition to the wizard-driven interface. The administrator provides a response file that provides answers to all of the questions that the installation program will ask. By using this approach, the administrator can completely automate application installation. However, most administrators will admit the need to use the wizard-driven interface at least the first time to see how the response file should work.

The short take on the wizard-driven interface is that it's probably the best way to ensure that a novice user completes a task successfully. Everyone relies on the wizard-driven interface to perform certain tasks such as installing applications, but you should provide alternatives, such as a command line interface, for use by advanced users whenever possible.

Role Driven

A role-driven interface is one that changes its appearance based on the role the user plays. For example, a novice user will see fewer commands than a power user does. The role-driven interface doesn't depend on a particular application appearance — it works as well with a menu and a toolbar application as it does with a RibbonX application. Here are some of the criteria that a role-driven application may consider for adding and removing controls:

- User organizational role
- Task user is performing
- Application location (remote or local, as an example)
- Hardware capability
- Network status (loaded network translates into fewer features)
- System status (high system load translates into fewer features)
- Server status (heavily loaded server translates into fewer features)
- User-specific company policy

The role-driven interface has a number of uses in your organization. Since you can combine this interface with other interfaces described in this chapter, you usually don't have to give up anything to get it, either. A role-driven interface does require more time to develop because it requires some kind of rule base to use when making decisions about which controls to display. When that rule base gets unsynchronized with your organization, the role-driven interface can also deny access to application features that users require. However, despite this potential limitation, the role-driven interface is exceptionally useful and you should consider using it as needed.

The main reason to rely on a role-driven interface is security. A user can't interact with controls that don't appear on the form. Consequently, any tricks that a user might try to gain unwarranted access are also unavailable. Instead of using all the truly horrid methods to control access that many developers have relied on over the years, the role-driven interface reduces the problem at the source. In some cases, the users may not even be aware that the missing controls exist.

Using a role-driven interface has other benefits, too. As previously mentioned, novice users don't face controls that are confusing or beyond their capability to use. However, the role-driven interface can have other, subtle benefits. For example, if you hide sensitive controls when the user is accessing the application from a remote location, you add a subtle reminder that remote computing has risks the user should consider. Always remember that an interface is your method of communicating with the user and this is a communication of the most subtle sort.

Modifying the available user controls based on the status of something is also helpful. More often than not, developers create applications that try to trudge along on the available resources, making everyone using the application unhappy. When the resources run out, the applications often fail gracelessly, flinging the user out of the system and rending data into unusable shards. Using a role-driven application that views the server, network, or system state lets you take a third course — one of making as much of the application available as reasonably possible, while restricting access to overburdened parts. Using events, it's possible to update controls as resources become available. The user with restricted access can still perform useful work, so everyone is at least a little happier.

Developing a User Interaction Strategy

You're probably getting tired of hearing about this whole concept of communication in this chapter, but it's an important concept to understand when defining a user interface. There isn't anything mystical about creating a user interface that communicates well with the user. It's not the same as having a face-to-face communication, though. For one thing, you aren't speaking — this is a nonverbal communication of the most esoteric type.

Communication follows certain rules. Consider e-mail for a moment. When you talk with someone in e-mail, you often use emoticons to express body language — why is that even necessary? If you're one of the people who hate emoticons and refuse to use them, have you ever had someone get confused and misunderstand what you had to say? The fact is that the words you say in a face-to-face communication are only part of the picture. You communicate most of your message through voice inflection and body language. Over time, you have made mistakes and learned communication rules that govern the use of nonverbal communication.

The nonverbal communication of a user interface has a completely different set of rules. No one is going to be able to hear your voice inflection when clicking a button in a user interface. In fact, no one will hear you scream when the user clicks the same wrong button for the hundredth time during the computing session. However, the user will notice that a button is disabled. By disabling the button, you communicate that using the button at this particular moment is wrong. Adding a tooltip that tells the user why the button is disabled provides confirmation that you have disabled the button for a reason and tells the user what to do to correct the problem. Using a combination of the button's enable state and a tooltip has provided communication with the user — a kind of communication you may not have considered in the past.

The following sections are all about communication. They discuss all the nonverbal communication rules that a developer needs in order to communicate effectively with the user. Once you master this nonverbal communication, you can begin to interact with the user in ways that you may not have thought possible. More importantly, both the user and you will be less frustrated, and you'll find that the user makes fewer mistakes using your application.

Keeping the User in Control

It's hard for the developer to give control of the application to the user. However, if you want the user to be pleased with the application and use it as intended, you often have to do just that. Of course, you need to consider precisely what giving control means. It doesn't mean making the application less secure or reliable. You probably don't want to give the user a bunch of toys to play with, either. Keeping the user in control means that the application automatically configures itself to match the user's Windows preferences. A major problem for many users is color. Some developers don't understand that the user may have specific color requirements (for example, the user may be color-blind). To avoid color problems, use settings from the System tab when making color choices for your application as shown in Figure 4-3. When you use these settings, the application automatically reconfigures itself to use the color settings the user chooses in the Windows Advanced Appearance dialog box.

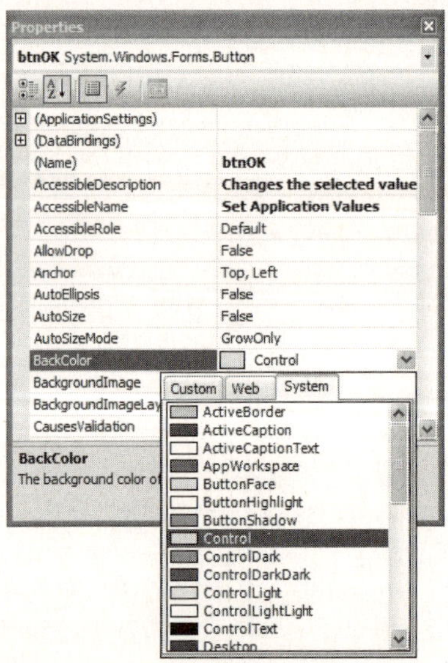

Figure 4-3: Choose colors from the System tab to keep the user in control.

Some user configuration options require modification of your application code. For example, if the user relies on a large font, your application should also use a large font. Of course, using a large font may mean resizing dialog boxes so that the content fits, so your code should have the flexibility to perform the task. In most cases, you check the user's selected font size when you start the application and size the display elements appropriately during the display process.

Make sure you read through the "Considering Accessibility Requirements" section of the chapter for additional hints on keeping the user in control. Anything you can do to make the user comfortable with your application is helpful.

Nudging the User in the Right Direction

Users often need a nudge in the right direction to accomplish tasks, especially novice users who may lack confidence. Nudging a user comes in a variety of forms. Some nudging is subtle. The use of a wizard to perform a task is a kind of subtle nudging because the user must accomplish the task in a specific order. In addition, the wizard dialog boxes tend to focus user attention on one specific part of the task at a time.

The use of descriptive labels is another form of user nudging. You can combine this kind of user nudging with tooltips that provide an example of what the user should type for textboxes. The point is to help the user understand what to do, which can be quite a feat at times. The smarter the users are in some other fields, the more often you'll find that they have a problem with your computer applications because their attention is focused on their particular need, not on your application. Consequently, helpful nudging is a requirement for most users in professional trades.

Some users benefit from the use of tips. You should always make sure that the user can turn this feature on or off. However, expert advice from you is usually helpful and the users appreciate that you're taking a personal interest in them. I used one application that actually had the guy's face plastered in the upper left corner of every dialog box. His mouth was open and it looked like he was talking with you about an application concern. The fact that he looked quite jolly made things even better — he really did look like he was happy to help. Of course, I can think of a less helpful experience: if I ever find Clippy in a dark alley — well, you get the idea. Just make sure a user can turn this feature off should you choose to include it. (Microsoft tried to get people to like Clippy for four years and was completely unsuccessful — read more at `http://www.microsoft.com/presspass/features/2001/apr01/04-11clippy.mspx`.)

Some nudging can become annoying — more annoying than Clippy. Some applications use colored fields to show missing data, which isn't nearly as annoying as applications that color the fields and have them flash on and off to attract attention. However, there is a helpful alternative to coloring the fields — simply place an asterisk next to the missing data.

Designing an Interface That Interacts

Interfaces can be a lot like people. Some people talk at you, others talk over your head, and a few talk with you. The application you design communicates with users, and one of the worst things you can do is design an interface that talks at them or over their heads. The application shouldn't treat users like idiots, but it should seek to work with them so they can gain maximum benefit from the application. For example, when the user makes an error, a message box saying that an error has just been made is unhelpful. What the user really needs to know is how to fix the error.

Consider the situation where the user needs to fill in a field before proceeding to the next step in a process. Many applications respond with a message like, "Error in form content." A more helpful message is one that tells the reader something like, "Type a username in the Username field." At least the user now understands what to type and knows where to type it.

Sometimes an interface needs to present more than messages. If the user needs to provide complex input or you think the user may not understand the content required, provide a custom dialog box that includes a Help button. The user clicks Help and obtains step-by-step information on precisely how to fill out the errant field. Advanced users won't take exception to this kind of help because they can simply choose to ignore the Help button.

Defining a Reliable Interface

The user has an expectation of an interface that performs in a predictable manner. If you suddenly start displaying a chorus line of dancing pigs in tutus every time the user makes an error, the user might be amused for a moment, but also distracted. You've wasted the humor because the user will probably make an error during the next step of using the application. Distraction is one of the biggest evils that an interface can exercise on the user. Even though it sounds mundane, a reliable interface is the best option because the user knows what to expect.

Reliability problems can come in a number of forms. For example, the user may see a left-to-right progression of controls on one page of a tabbed interface, but a right-to-left progression on the next page. The interface is unreliable because it doesn't behave according to user expectations. The display of controls should move fluently from one page of an interface to the next and from one form to the next.

Another reliability problem is the presentation of data and request of input. Using a drop-down list box on one form and a textbox on another form for the same kind of data is almost certainly going to confuse the user. Part of your design goals for the application should include consistent use of controls for particular kinds of data. If you use a drop-down list box to obtain state information on one form, you should use a drop-down list box for that information on all forms.

Even icons can pose a problem for the user's perception of reliability. A developer can choose to use different icons for the same purpose form by form. For example, consider the simple wait icon. If you use an hourglass icon on one form and a stopwatch icon on another form, the user will be confused. You should decide on specific visual and aural indicators for certain events from the outset of the application design process.

Considering Security Concerns

Interestingly enough, most users do have some expectation of security in applications. For example, they probably frown at an application that doesn't check their input and lets unusable input go through, mainly because they have to go back and edit the data later. Checking inputs has an important benefit for the developer as well. If you provide code that limits input in a textbox to alphabetical characters and the length to 10 characters, it's very tough for someone with ill intent to inject a virus into the application. Sometimes, the kinds of checking the user expects also serve your purposes. In some cases, the user may even suggest a useful check you hadn't considered.

Many security concerns occur under the covers today. The user can't tell that the application uses encryption to send data unless you provide some type of visual sign. Adding a visual sign to your application is a great idea. You might simply provide a message saying something like, "Sending encrypted data to server," so the user doesn't have to guess whether the data is safe from tampering.

More applications are providing visual cues today about secure conditions, such as encryption. However, most applications lack visual cues that tell the user that the system is unsafe. For example, if the application attempts to establish a Secure Sockets Layer (SSL) connection with the server, and can't do so, the application should display an error message and refuse to communicate with the server until it can establish a secure connection.

Security is an incredibly important part of application development today. If your application works with unusually sensitive data, then it should perform a check of the system during startup. For example, you should check to ensure that the user has the firewall enabled and that the virus checking software is updated. You can obtain some of this information using the Windows Management Interface (WMI). The "Working with WMI" section of Chapter 27 describes how to work with WMI.

Considering Accessibility Requirements

Many applications today are completely unusable by someone who has special needs. For example, if you're blind, you'll find it quite difficult to use some applications. In fact, sometimes it's impossible. Even if you have low vision, some applications make it so difficult to understand what's going on that you probably won't get very far using them. Many people who have low vision use larger fonts and high-contrast displays to make the forms they see viewable. Most developers never test their application in this mode, yet they should. Something as simple as color choices can make a great deal of difference to your user. They may not be able to see part of the display at all if you use the wrong color combinations.

Vision is possibly the most critical accessibility requirement to consider. Even if you have perfect vision today, it's quite possible (in fact, likely) that your vision will become worse as you get older. All it takes is a cataract or other vision difficulty to give you firsthand experience with the accessibility requirements described in this chapter. You're probably going to have special needs someday, so now is the time to start writing applications so that they can meet your future needs.

Of course, vision is just the start of the accessibility requirements. As people get older, they find it more difficult to perform certain physical tasks. Pressing Ctrl+T may not seem like much of a problem to most people, but anyone with a pressing case of arthritis in the hands will likely find it an impossible task to perform. Every application you write should consider mobility requirements because a vast number of people have problems in this area.

Business applications typically don't rely heavily on sound. However, if you're writing an application that relies on sound, then you probably need to provide some alternative means of communication. The recommended way of handling this issue is to provide some type of visual cue in addition to the sound, so that users with hearing problems don't have to guess about aural events in the application.

It would be nice if this small section of the chapter could express every accessibility requirement and help you understand it. However, the following sections do describe the basics you need to consider when designing a user interface. If you find that you want some additional information on this topic, consult my book, *Accessibility for Everybody: Understanding the Section 508 Accessibility Requirements*, Apress (2003).

Understanding Visual Element Considerations

Some applications are unfriendly because they assume something about the user that probably isn't true. Fortunately, you can make a few simple changes to your application to make it considerably easier for everyone to use. The first change involves adding a simple ampersand (&) to every control and field on a form. Adding the ampersand produces a speed key using the character after the &. For example, the `Text` property in Figure 4-4 shows that the V has the ampersand next to it. If the user wants to execute this command using the keyboard, he or she would press Alt+V. Try to use a standard speed key whenever possible. For example, you normally see an `E&xit` option when working with the `&File` menu.

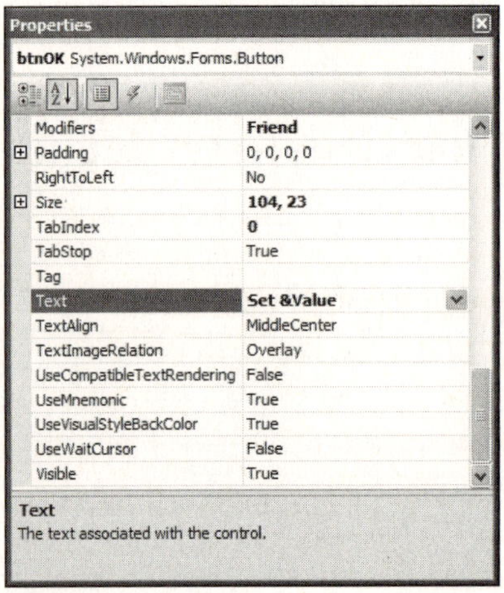

Figure 4-4: Provide speed keys for all controls, including fields.

The second step you can take to make your application significantly easier to use is to set the `TabIndex` property to ensure that pressing Tab chooses the controls in a logical order. The flow of control for most applications is from left to right and from top to bottom. When working with a dialog box, you generally provide access to controls before you provide access to fields, even when the fields are to the left of the controls.

If you're writing an application for someone who speaks one of the languages that buck the usual order, such as Hebrew, you might want to change the order. In this case, you would order the controls from right to left. When working with Chinese, you need to order the controls from top to bottom first, and then right to left.

Fields present some interesting challenges. To set the speed key for a field, you add the ampersand to the Label control associated with the field, rather than to the field itself. Consequently, you shouldn't have any fields that are simply sitting on the form without an associated label or you will make it difficult for users with special needs to access. The tab order that matters is the one set for the field, not the label. You associate a label with a field through proximity and tab order. If the field has a tab order of 4, then the label should have a tab order of 3.

The sizing and positioning of controls is also an issue. Make sure you align controls and make associated controls the same size as shown in Figure 4-5 for the Grab-a-Picture application. Formatting and aligning your controls isn't hard. All you need to do is rely on the controls found on the Layout Toolbar of Visual Studio. (Chapter 8 describes the IDE in detail.) Select the controls you want to size or align, and then click the appropriate button on the Layout toolbar. In a matter of moments, you have a form that looks better and is easier to use.

Never assume that your user is a rocket scientist. The forms you create should use descriptive terms for every control and field. Of course, it's easy to get carried away. You don't need to write entire sentences, as Microsoft is prone to do. Using complete sentences makes your application difficult to use with accessibility aids such as screen readers. Imagine having to listen to five or six minutes' worth of dialog for each form. After you listen to all this information, you have to use it to visualize what the form looks like and then choose the correct control from the list of controls that the screen reader presented. For some applications, the process is extremely long and frustrating.

Figure 4-5: Take time to properly format and position controls to make them easier to work with.

Adding Tooltips and Accessibility Descriptions

Imagine you're blind. In fact, take the time to see what it feels like for a few hours. I often wondered what it was like to use my application without vision, so I tried an experiment that truly opened my eyes to the needs of other people. Do what I did, and download and install a free trial copy of Job Access With Speech (JAWS) at `http://www.freedomscientific.com/fs_downloads/jaws.asp`. Now, put on a blindfold and try to use your application — no peeking. The screen reader will tell you when your mouse is over a particular control. Can you use the application? If not, think about how frustrating it would be to avoid using your application because it simply doesn't work properly with a screen reader. Many applications fall into this category — they're a nightmare to use if you don't have perfect vision.

Fortunately, you can make your application considerably easier to use for the novice user and the person with special needs at the same time. Microsoft provides three accessibility properties for every control as shown in Figure 4-6. Here's a description of each of these properties:

- **AccessibleDescription:** The accessible description provides a little more information about the control than the control name alone does. Sighted users will see a descriptive tooltip when they hover the mouse over the control. Don't use long sentences for a description because screen readers will read all of this text to the person who uses one. Instead, try to express the purpose of the control in five or six words. Actually, this field is helpful for the developer, too. If you find that you can't express the purpose of the control in five or six words, then perhaps you don't have a clear idea of what the control is supposed to do.

- **AccessibleName:** Some screen readers use this name in place of the control's `Text` property value. In most cases, you use slightly more descriptive terminology for the control name. Don't describe the control; make the purpose of the control clear by giving it a descriptive name.
- **AccessibleRole:** This field describes the role that the control plays. In most cases, you use the default setting of `Default`. However, a control may actually have a special purpose that matches one of the options in the drop-down list box, so you should verify that the `Default` value matches the control's role.

It takes less than a minute to fill in these three properties. Adding the appropriate values makes your application visible to those who require special aids. Without these values, you may be preventing someone from using your application — someone who might have really liked it.

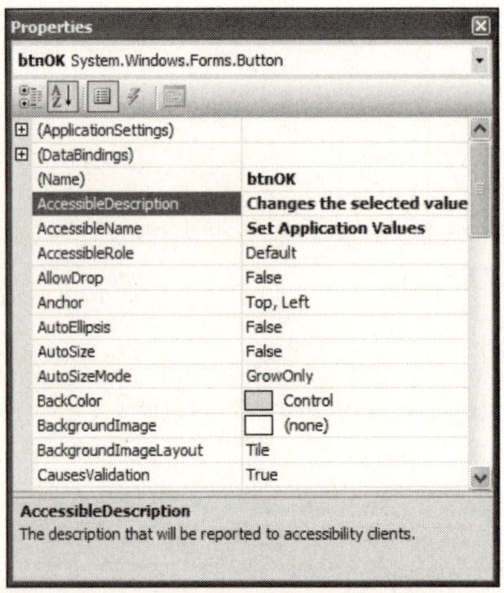

Figure 4-6: Microsoft provides three accessibility properties for every control, which makes it effortless to create an accessible application.

One of the best ways to ensure that your application meets all the required accessibility needs is to use the government's Section 508 requirements as a guideline. These requirements specify the parameters that an application should meet for government contractors. You can see a Section 508 checklist at `http://www.webaim.org/standards/508/checklist`.

Practicing Good Coloring Techniques

Most developers have gotten the word — no garish color combinations in applications, please. However, some developers still use color combinations that make their application nearly invisible to users with color blindness. If you're male, it's considerably more likely that you suffer from color blindness than if you're female. For example, 4.9 percent of the male population suffers from green color blindness, or deuteranomalia (there are six different kinds of color blindness). You can see an interesting write-up, with statistics, on color blindness at `http://msdn.microsoft.com/en-us/library/bb263953.aspx`. The Web site at `http://www.firelily.com/opinions/color.html` provides you with a better idea of how something would actually look to someone with color blindness.

Unfortunately, it isn't very easy to determine when someone will have a problem with your application when you yourself have full color perception. Unlike controls, it's hard to test for good color combinations. You won't find any hard and fast rules or best practices you can rely on either, because color use is subjective. However, you can use online color checkers such as Vischeck at `http://www.vischeck.com/vischeck/vischeckImage.php`. Grab a screenshot of your interface and upload it to the Web site to see how your form looks to someone with a particular color deficiency. If you have a lot of screenshots to process, consider downloading Vischeck from `http://vischeck.com/downloads/`.

Developing Your Design Strategy

This chapter has considered everything that you need to define a user interface from a design perspective. However, this chapter can't make you an expert in user interface design by any measure of the term. It takes time and experience to discover what the user is really telling you when it comes to an interface that doesn't feel right. What this chapter has provided are the concepts you need to design a good user interface for your application. Many developers need to team up with someone else to tease out the social, physical, and educational requirements of the user interface from users who don't necessarily like computers in the first place. It's important to remember that the user interface is your method of communicating with the reader, and you can't perform that task adequately with code, standards, and best practices alone.

It's time to put a user interface together. The best way to accomplish this task is to create mock-ups of every form, message box, or other visual or aural requirements for your application. In a few cases, you may even have to provide a mock-up of any touch elements of the interface. It's impossible to check a user interface design without mock-ups that precisely match the final application (the more closely they match the better). Take time to listen to what users have to say about your design. Record the conversation — it's important because you won't remember everything the user has said about the interface. If necessary, team up with someone who is skilled in reading body language and interacting with people. Developers often miss cues that are important to interpreting the usefulness of a design. An extra set of eyes is always important — you won't see everything the user has to offer no matter how skilled you might be in other aspects of application design.

After the hard grind of creating a user interface, you may find that Chapter 5 provides a nice diversion. In this case, you begin looking at the speed aspects of your application. This chapter answers the question of how fast you can make your application react to user input and define the speed at which it performs tasks. The reason this next chapter is so important is that creating a truly useful user interface often slows down an application. This is your opportunity to add the lost speed back into the application and even improve it some. Besides, everyone knows that speed is the wow factor of applications. When you go back to the user with those interface improvements, it's a good idea to say, "Look at how fast it works, too!"

5

Designing with Speed in Mind

Many developers equate performance with speed. Part of the reason for this confusion is that the media tend to confuse performance and speed. You hear about a high-performance engine for a car and automatically think about the speed that the engine delivers, because that's the area of performance on which the media focus. You can be sure the guys in the pits are thinking more about how reliably the engine can deliver that speed. In short, speed is only one component of performance. When you look at the speed of an application, you're asking how fast the application can perform a task. The application could have high speed and perform the task incorrectly, which would mean that it was getting nowhere fast.

This chapter explores the question of application speed. Speed is important because users quickly become dissatisfied when applications are slow. Speed is also extremely hard to quantify — fast for one person is slow for someone else, usually depending on the skills of the two people. Consequently, developers are always asking the question of how fast is fast enough. This chapter will help you define the parameters for answering that question, but you'll need to provide the specific answer for your application based on organizational requirements and user needs.

Once you get past the question of how fast is fast enough, it's important to consider how to add speed to an application without making it unreliable or insecure. Of course, there are many ways to modify the speed of an application. For example, you can view the application loops and attempt to reduce the amount of work they do. This chapter examines a number of techniques you can use to safely increase the speed of your application.

Finally, it's important to quantify the speed of your application and to do so within the environment in which it operates. Consequently, an application with great speed on your development system may be a creature of sloth on the production system. You must quantify the server speed to ensure that the application works as anticipated. The examples in this chapter help you build the ability to quantify application speed into your applications and then monitor performance over time to ensure that application speed doesn't suffer as the result of server changes.

Considering Speed vs. Performance

Speed is an essential element of performance because it determines how fast a user can accomplish a given task. However, speed isn't always a factor in application performance. When the application is waiting for the user to complete some part of the task, you can be certain that the user isn't paying any attention to speed. The user is concentrating on the task at hand and is happy that the application is waiting, ready to perform work. In fact, if the user had anything to say about an application, it would always wait for the user, and any task the user requested would complete automatically — in a split second. The real world has a habit of intruding on this ideal vision of speed, one in which the application always waits on the user.

At some point, you have to decide just how long the user is willing to wait for an application to accomplish a task. You'll need to perform some testing to obtain a precise number for your organization. The following factors contribute to the time estimate you create:

- **Environment:** An organization with a laid-back atmosphere is less likely to produce users who want to get everything done now. If you have managers checking with users every 10 seconds to determine the state of a project, the user is going to experience stress and is going to want to see those instant results more often. Temporary changes to the user's environment, such as a large number of interruptions, also can have an effect on the user's desire to wait on the application. Consequently, environment produces a range of wait values.
- **Task load:** Users tend not to react well to heavy task loads. A sudden increase in task load will make a user less likely to wait for an application to complete a task.
- **Skill level:** As the skill level increases, so does the desire for nearly instantaneous results. In fact, expert users may actually overwhelm an application that doesn't provide the required speed and cause it to fail. Of course, frustration also builds as an experienced user waits for an application that's perceived as too slow.
- **Personality:** The user's personality has a great deal to do with the required application speed. Type A personalities (read more about the Type A personality at `http://en.wikipedia.org/wiki/Type_A_personality`) tend to lose patience significantly faster than Type B personalities. Of course, not even a Type B personality will wait forever — the application must perform with some level of consistency to be useful.
- **Other:** There are many other factors that you may have to consider when creating your time estimate. For example, some organizations have a strict response policy. The response time may not have any basis at all — it's simply the amount of time that someone in the organization feels is the maximum they're willing to wait. Make sure you research any potential speed issues before you begin the development process. Otherwise, you might find that what you think is fast enough isn't fast at all from someone else's perspective.

Studies abound that define approximate values for the time a user is willing to wait. For example, the Web site at `http://www.useit.com/papers/responsetime.html` says that your application must react in as little as 0.1 second to give the user that instantaneous feel. If your application takes longer than 10 seconds to respond, it's quite possible that you should give users something else to do while waiting and definitely provide an indication of how long the task will take. These approximates are a good starting point, but you'll want to tune your estimate to meet your organizational requirements and user needs.

In most cases, a progress dialog box buys you only a few moments. The user will tire very quickly of watching the little progress indicator march across the screen. However, providing progress indicators and other indicators of activity does add to the performance value of your application. The perception that the application is doing something can help the user forgive any speed problems due to an unforeseen circumstance. Consequently, adding user interaction to your application helps it perform well, even though you haven't increased application speed at all.

Considering Perceived Speed vs. Real Speed

It's interesting to note that you often have to take a real-world speed hit in order to give the application an appearance of speed. A progress indicator requires additional time to develop, uses system resources, and requires processing cycles that you could use to increase true application speed. However, the presence of the progress indicator makes the user think the application is running faster and makes it more likely that the user will wait for the task to finish. Sometimes perception is more important than reality.

The need for perceived speed hasn't escaped the notice of companies such as Microsoft. All of Microsoft's product installation applications include a progress indicator. However, in addition to the progress indicator, you now see what amounts to an advertisement of the product's features. Users view these advertisements as they install the application. Because the user is spending more time viewing the application and interacting with it, the installation usually finishes faster. The installation still takes as long as it did before, but it doesn't wait as long for the user to respond to queries for information. Consequently, the application finishes faster even though it actually runs slightly slower.

Developing a High Speed Application

Code optimization has a place in every developer's toolbox. You need to run applications that check your code for optimization and take all the fat out of the application. However, code optimization can only do so much. You need to plan for speed as part of the application design process. For example, if you want to use multithreading as part of your application speed strategy, then you need to design the application to use multiple threads. Adding this functionality later just won't work. The following sections describe some of the techniques you can use to add speed to your application. These aren't the only techniques at your disposal, but you normally have to plan for these techniques as part of the design process.

Using Multithreading

Multithreading is a process by which you break your application into pieces and let each piece execute separately. For example, you might print a document in the background while interacting with the user in the foreground. Multithreading doesn't actually increase application speed — in fact, it reduces overall application speed because you now have the multithreading support to consider. Something has to track each of those threads and ensure that each thread executes when it's supposed to execute and only for its allotted time. However, multithreading does make your application more responsive to the user. Using multithreading makes it possible for an application to print in the background while the user continues to work with it in the foreground. The application may be slower as a whole, but because the application is more responsive, the user sees it as faster.

Some application features naturally lend themselves to multithreading. For example, printing in the background works exceptionally well. You can also update local resources from the Internet in the background. The user continues to work with the application while the application automatically performs these tasks in the background. It's also important to use multithreading when application responsiveness is a requirement. For example, when creating an installation program, you should perform the actual installation tasks as part of a thread, so that the foreground application can respond to user requests, such as canceling the installation. User aids, such as progress indicators, should also appear as part of a thread, rather than the main execution thread.

You often use threads as a means to smooth application performance. For example, an application that looks for new files in a certain folder and then processes them will benefit from multithreading. The application can use polling or some other technique to detect the new files, and then create new threads to process the file. The application will operate more smoothly because each file will have its own thread of execution.

Threads aren't a fix for application speed problems. An application with slow code that leaks resources won't get any faster by adding multithreading. A well-planned multithreaded application can provide the ultimate in responsiveness though, so it helps to hide intermittent problems, such as clogged network arteries.

It's important to avoid creating too many threads. Each thread requires some amount of resources to perform housekeeping chores. In addition, threads use memory and other system resources. As the number of threads increases, the time required to work with the individual threads becomes prohibitive and drags application performance down significantly. At this point, the user is certain to notice that the application is no longer working efficiently and will complain.

There's one case where using threads can help application speed. Using multithreading with multiprocessing can improve the measured speed of your application, but what you're really doing is spreading the load, not increasing application speed. Most systems today come with multiple processors, so multiprocessing is a useful way to gain some extra speed. However, you gain this extra speed at the expense of other applications running on the system, so it's not really a good trade-off in some cases. The section of this chapter on "Considering the Effects of Multiprocessing" discusses this approach in greater detail.

Understanding That Speed Doesn't Equal Code

Some developers are under the impression that they can overcome every speed problem by optimizing their code well enough. Unfortunately, optimized code doesn't always equate to improved speed. An application running on underpowered hardware will run slowly. Consequently, you must have the hardware required to do the job, and the only way you can make that determination is by monitoring the hardware during testing. Your high-speed application requires enough memory, a large enough hard drive, and high-speed hardware components to provide the speed you expect. Of course, there's always the obstacle for some organizations of not having enough money. Often, you have to balance the speed expectations of an application with the amount of money available to buy hardware to run the application. Management should know as soon as possible in the development process about any potential hardware issues that you might encounter.

Considering the Effects of Multiprocessing

One of the more important new technologies to consider is multiprocessing. Yes, multiprocessing has been around for years, but for most of that time only servers had multiple processors. It's common now to find workstations with two processors, and even four processors are becoming more common. It's important to note that these processors are often part of multi-core setups — the processors all reside within a single package. However, as far as Windows is concerned, the multiple cores are separate processors.

The .NET Framework doesn't currently include support for directly modifying the processors that your application uses. By default, your application uses all the available processors on a system and it tends to use them equally, whenever possible. You can't write code that tells a particular thread to execute on a particular processor in an attempt to move some background processing to a specific processor. However, Microsoft does provide guidance on setting your application to use certain processors. For example, the Knowledge Base article at `http://support.microsoft.com/kb/815156` provides information on modifying your ASP.NET application to use certain processors.

There are exceptions to just about every rule of speed. If you write a single-threaded application for a system with four processors, the application will use only one processor. In order to let an application use multiple processors, your application must have multiple threads.

Measuring Application Speed

You have to define some method for measuring application speed. Although the human measure of speed is subjective, the absolutes of a numeric measure are the best way to go. The Windows method of measuring performance is the counter. Essentially, the *counter* is a small piece of software that counts something. What it counts is up to you. For example, you could decide to count the number of records that your application processes per second. Counters can also provide a certain level of mathematical analysis. For example, you could calculate the percentage of processor time that your application uses or the percentage of the disk that it requires for data storage. Counters are quite flexible.

Of course, a counter need not always focus on your application to provide useful information. For example, you might want to monitor resource usage on the host system. Many applications monitor the local system for memory usage and report to the user when memory is too low to support the application properly. You can add standard counters directly to your application and monitor them there, or you can use the Performance console found in the Administrative Tools folder of the Control Panel to perform the task. The following sections show how to work with both standard and custom counters as part of your application and using the Performance console.

Viewing Standard Counters

System Monitor is a short-term, performance-monitoring tool. It provides all the displays used for analysis of performance data. The following sections describe some essential areas of System Monitor usage.

Using Counters

A monitoring session begins with the selection of performance counters. The easiest method to add counters is to click the Add button (the plus (+) sign) on the toolbar. You'll see an Add Counters dialog box like the one shown in Figure 5-1.

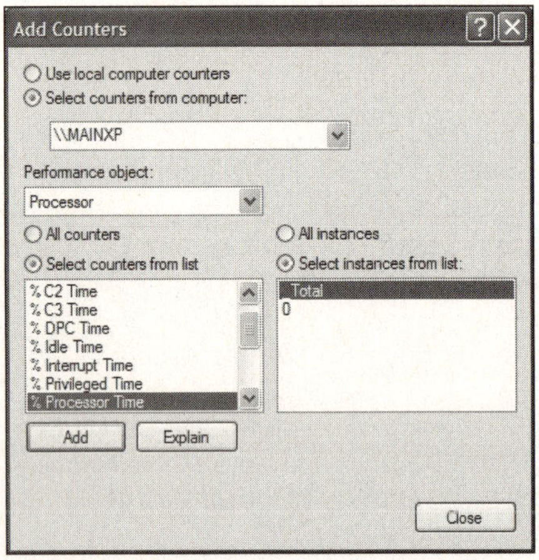

Figure 5-1: The Add Counters dialog box is the starting point for every System Monitor session.

The dialog box shows that you can choose four levels of performance monitoring. The following list describes each level:

- **Machine:** The machine you choose to monitor depends on the circumstances. For example, one performance monitoring scenario is to compare two machines with the same characteristics and application load. If one machine performs substantially slower than the other, the statistics might indicate the presence of a problem on the slower machine.
- **Performance Object:** This is the name of an application containing counters. There's a performance object for each major category of device or application on your machine. For example, Figure 5-1 shows the Processor object. You'll also find objects for the physical and logical disk drive, memory, and network. Applications appear in objects such as browser, job, and thread.
- **Counter:** This is a specific performance-measuring thread within the object. The counter is the portion of the performance monitor that acquires the data. The term *counter* is accurate in this case. The counters actually do count the number of occurrences of an event within a given time interval. For example, when determining the percentage of CPU cycles used to handle user requests, the counter counts both the total processor clock cycles and those used to handle user needs. It then performs a mathematical computation to calculate the percentage.
- **Instance:** In some cases, saying you want to count something doesn't define the problem. For example, if you have two processors and want to determine the percentage of user time, you have to indicate whether you want the user time for one or both processors. You also need to indicate which processor you want to work with if you choose only one.

As you can see, the potential number of performance-monitoring combinations for a single system is immense. A typical system provides a minimum of 40 performance objects. Each of these objects has a number of counters (two is a minimum and 30 is common). Many of these counters have at least two instances and a _Total instance (the combination of all instances of a counter). In addition, many applications such as SQL Server add their own counters to the mix. If you add multiple machine scenarios into the mix, you can see that System Monitor has a lot to offer.

Click Explain in the Add Counters dialog box if you want to know the meaning behind a particular counter. The explanation is relatively short, but usually helpful. It will always provide you with enough information to conduct additional research into the counters.

This brings up an important point. You don't want to overload a single display with too many counters. Tracking five or six of these counters is difficult on some displays. Adding more than that makes the information hard to track. Select carefully the counters you want to see. If you find that you've selected too many counters, remove a few by highlighting them in the listing and clicking Delete (the X next to the Add button).

After you add the counters, click Close. You'll return to the Performance console and see the counters you selected displaying data. Figure 5-2 shows a typical example of a Performance console display. The line extending from the top to the bottom of the chart area is the current drawing position.

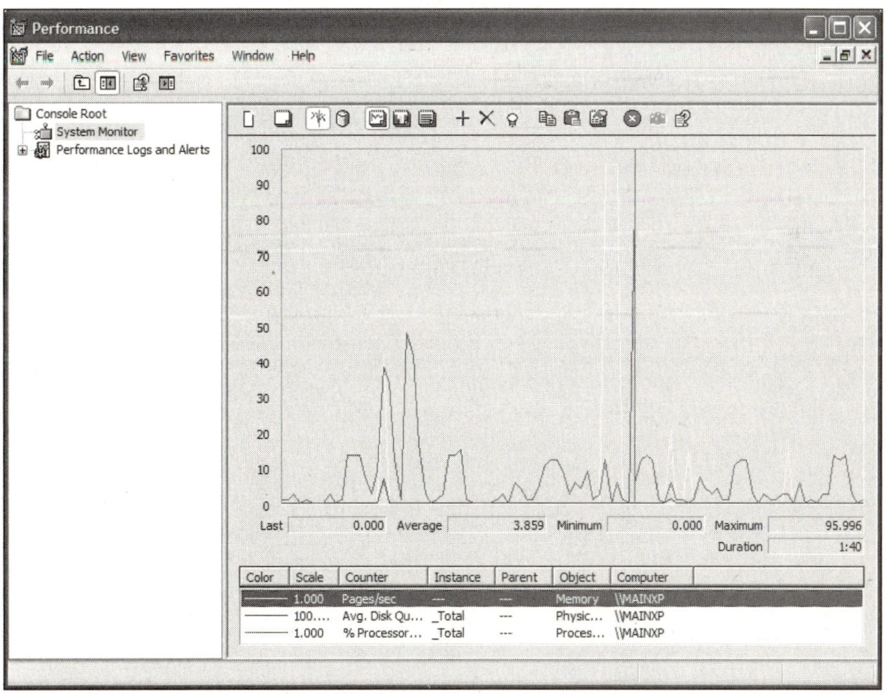

Figure 5-2: The Performance console displays the output from the counters you selected.

Once you find settings that you like, you can save the settings to disk and reopen them later. You can also study the settings if you want because the Microsoft Console (MSC) files are actually eXtensible Markup Language (XML) in disguise. If you open the file in Firefox, as shown in Figure 5-3, you can learn a lot about the way Microsoft structures these files. In some cases, you might be able to tweak a console setting after the fact to make the console more appealing.

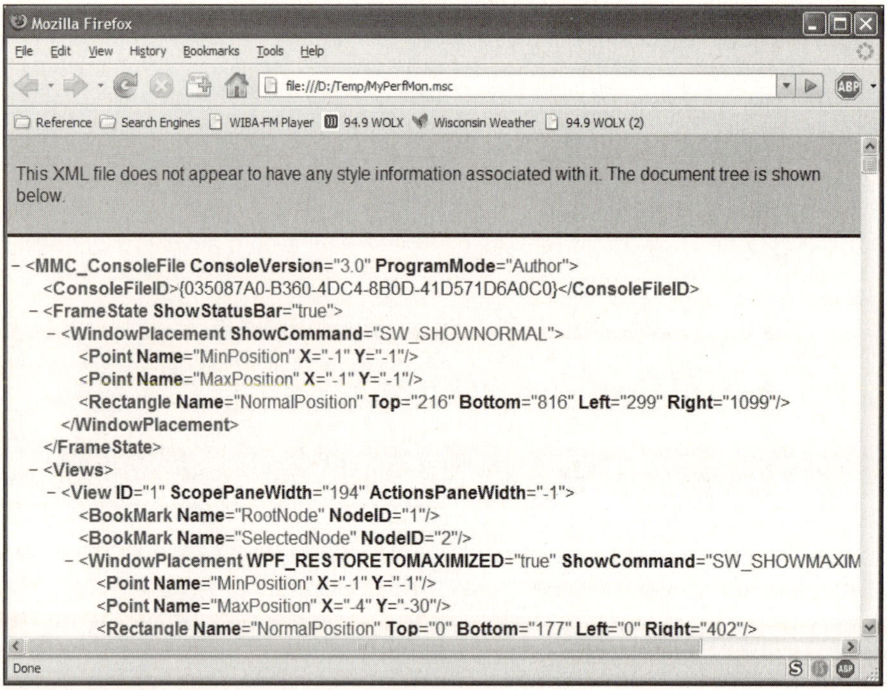

Figure 5-3: MSC files actually contain XML data.

Even with the few counters displayed in Figure 5-2, you still might have a hard time seeing a particular counter line. System Monitor fixes this problem with the Highlight button, which looks like a little light bulb. Click Highlight and the associated counter line will turn dark.

Sometimes you need to study the information you're seeing on screen for a while without interruption. If so, click Freeze Display (the red circle with an "X" in it). Click Freeze Display a second time to restart the display. Freeze Display just stops the display; System Monitor continues to collect data in the background. If you want to update the display quickly, click Update Data (the camera next to Freeze Display). Click Clear Display if you want to start the entire sequence over again. This allows you to see an entire screen without interruption.

Setting Graph Properties

Graph appearance is important. For example, you might want to add horizontal or vertical graph lines. Click Properties if you want to change any of the settings. Figure 5-4 shows the General tab of the System Monitor Properties dialog box.

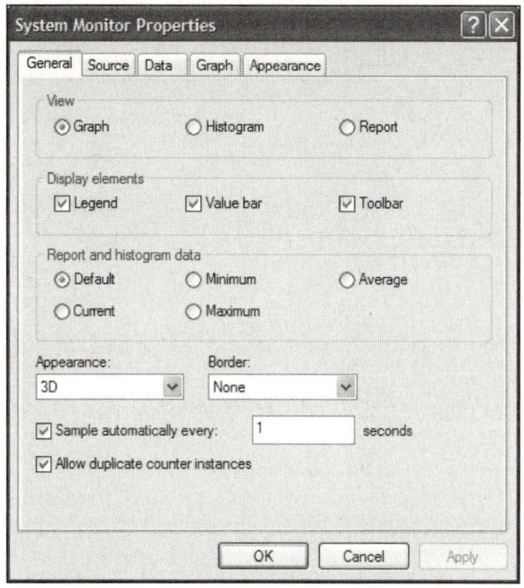

Figure 5-4: The General tab allows you to set graph elements such as the graph type.

As you can see, this tab allows you to select a view. System Monitor supports three views including graph, histogram, and report. You can also select a view using the appropriate button on the toolbar (as we'll see in the "Selecting Another View" section).

Below the views are three options for displaying the Toolbar, Value Bar, and Legend. The Toolbar contains all of the buttons we've discussed to this point. The Value Bar contains a list of all the vital statistics for the counter highlighted in the Legend. For example, you can learn the minimum, maximum, and average values for a particular counter. The Legend lists the selected counters. Each counter entry includes the instance, parent, object, and computer information.

The report and histogram views support only instantaneous data values. Sometimes it's beneficial to see something other than the default data. For example, you might want to see the average data value. The next section of the General tab allows you to change the histogram and report view values. The default setting displays the current (instantaneous) values.

The Sample Automatically Every setting permits you to update the display more or less often than the default setting of 1 second. Clearing this entry will freeze the display. The Allow Duplicate Counter Instances option tells System Monitor that it's OK to display more than one instance of the same data. This feature comes in handy in report view, but is actually detrimental in other views.

The Data tab shown in Figure 5-5 helps you configure the data display. You begin by selecting one of the entries in the Counters list. This view allows you to change the color of the data, along with the width and style of the line. The scale determines how the lines scale in comparison with the rest of the lines on screen. Using a larger scale can often bring out details about the data, especially if variations are small.

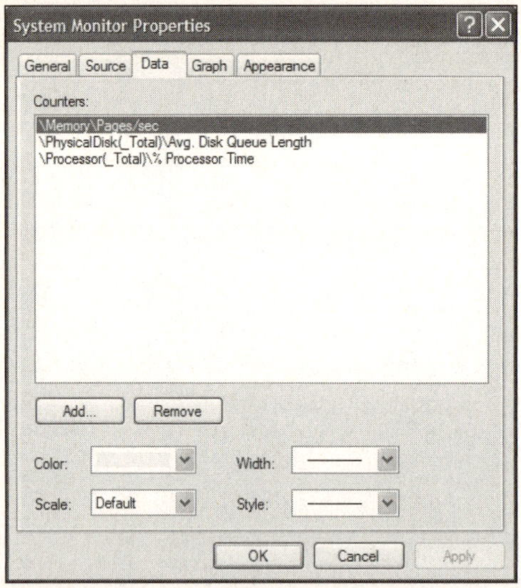

Figure 5-5: Use the Data tab to change the appearance of the data on screen.

The Graph tab contains settings that change graph display elements. This includes the use of a vertical and horizontal grid. You can also give your graph a title and assign a name to the vertical element (the horizontal element is always time). The Vertical Scale properties offer another chance to optimize the graph display. You can set the graph so it displays the data a little larger or smaller than the default settings allow.

Finally, the Appearance tab contains settings that change the colors used to display certain elements such as the graph background and time bar. This tab also enables you to choose a new font for the display. The use of a different font may make the information more legible or easier to print.

Selecting Another View

The default graph isn't the only view of the data you can get. System Monitor also provides histogram and report views of the data, both of which serve different purposes. To select a different view, click the appropriate button on the toolbar. There are three buttons: View Graph, View Histogram, and View Report.

The histogram view shown in Figure 5-6 is best for comparing instantaneous values between similar elements. For example, you might want to compare the statistics for two processors. The large bars make it easy to see how two values compare.

To gain the full benefit from the histogram view, you need to keep the number of bars small. A lot of pencil-thin bars are hard to compare and defeat the purpose of using this view. Remember that you do lose the time element in this display, so you may have to resort to a display of average values instead of instantaneous values.

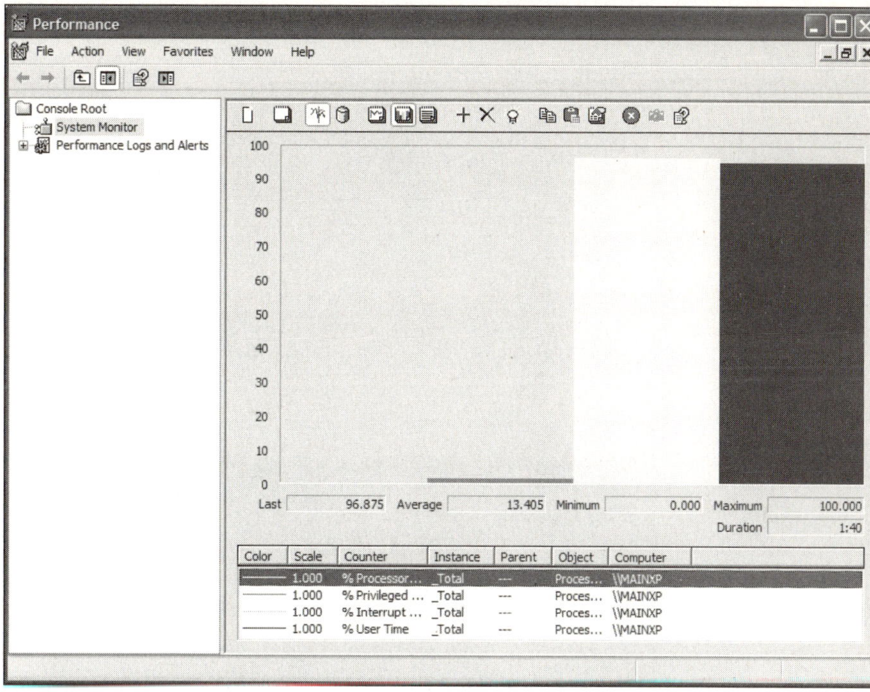

Figure 5-6: Use the histogram view to compare values between similar counters or counter instances.

The report view organizes the data by counter and instance. The System Monitor doesn't provide any means for changing the method of organization, so you'll need to consider the counters you use carefully. The strength of the report view is the organization it provides. You can view a large number of counters with this view without going crazy comparing the different lines or bar heights. The report view is also best when you select something other than an instantaneous value. The average value display works well, but you could also use minimum or maximum values in some cases.

Defining an Application Counter

A counter can appear as part of any project. Any application that requires a counter can use a counter. In fact, you should always add counters to a project of any significant complexity for the sole purpose of monitoring application performance over time. Adding a counter doesn't require much code and benefits are significant when you add the counter correctly. The following sections describe an example performance counter — the project isn't designed to model a specific performance counter; it simply shows a performance counter that could appear as part of any application.

Creating the Counter Project

The counter project is a simple dialog box application in this case. However, it's important to remember that you can add counters to any application using the approach described in this chapter. The application includes a button for starting and stopping the generation of random outputs (something to count) and a button to close the application. You use the Performance console as described in the "Viewing Standard Counters" section of the chapter to monitor the output of this application.

Before you can work with custom counters, you must create a custom category and counters for it. You can use a number of techniques, but the easiest technique is to work with Server Explorer. The following steps describe how to create the custom category and counter for this example.

1. Open Server Explorer within Visual Studio (press Ctrl+Alt+S if you don't see the Server Explorer window).
2. Right-click the Servers\<Your Machine Name>\Performance Counters folder and choose Create New Category from the context menu. You'll see the Performance Counter Builder dialog box shown in Figure 5-7. Figure 5-7 shows the values to use for this example. Normally, you'll add values as needed by your application.

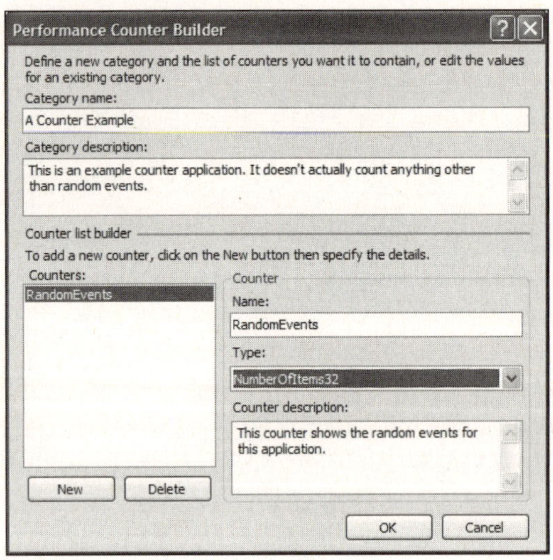

Figure 5-7: Add a new category and associated counters to your application.

3. Type a category name (usually the name of your application) in the Category Name field.
4. Type a description for this category in the Category Description field. Normally, you explain how the category monitors performance as a whole. If nothing else, describe your application so that anyone viewing the category knows what the category is all about.
5. Click New.
6. Type a name for a counter in the Name field. The counter name should reflect the specific use of this counter, rather than reflect the category or application use. If you're counting the number of port listening events that occur per second, call the counter PortListeningEvents/Sec, not something else.
7. Choose a counter type from the Type field. You can find a description of these types at `http://msdn.microsoft.com/en-us/library/system.diagnostics.performancecountertype.aspx`.

8. Type a description for the counter in the Counter Description field. Make sure the description describes the counter fully.
9. Repeat Steps 5 through 8 for all of the counters in the category you want to create.
10. Click OK. You'll see the new category added to the list in the Performance Counters folder.

Now that you have a shiny new category, drag and drop it onto your application form from Server Explorer. This is a custom counter, so it doesn't appear on other machines. To add the counter to other machines, you must create an installer using the following steps:

1. Select the performanceCounter1 entry in the design area and rename it to something such as OutputRandomEvents.
2. Click the right arrow on the OutputRandomEvents icon and you'll see an Add Installer link.
3. Click the Add Installer link and Visual Studio will add a performance counter installer to your application. The process is automated for the most part — all you're doing is telling Visual Studio to perform the task for you.

Visual Studio assumes that you spend most of your time reading counters. If you're working with an application that monitors system state, the assumption is true. However, this application is outputting counter data. Consequently, you must set the OutputRandomEvents `ReadOnly` property to `False`. You're ready to begin working with the custom performance counter.

Adding the Counter Code

The counter code is exceptionally simple in this case. The main purpose of the example is to show how you can add a counter to your application. Listing 5-1 shows the code you need to add.

Listing 5-1. Adding a counter to an application

```
public frmMain()
{
   InitializeComponent();

   // Initialize random number.
   NewNumber = new Random();
}

private void btnQuit_Click(object sender, EventArgs e)
{
   // End the application.
   Close();
}

private void btnStartStop_Click(object sender, EventArgs e)
{
   if (OutputTimer.Enabled == false)
   {
      // Start the timer.
      OutputTimer.Enabled = true;
```

Continued

Listing 5-1. Adding a counter to an application *(continued)*

```
            // Rename the button.
            btnStartStop.Text = "&Stop Timer";
        }
        else
        {
            // Stop the timer.
            OutputTimer.Enabled = false;

            // Rename the button.
            btnStartStop.Text = "&Start Timer";
        }
    }

    // Holds a random value.
    Random NewNumber;

    private void OutputTimer_Tick(object sender, EventArgs e)
    {
        // Generate a random value.
        // Output the value to the counter.
        OutputRandomEvents.RawValue = NewNumber.Next(100);
    }
```

In this case, the application relies on a timer, `OutputTimer`, to generate tick events. In almost every case, you need to provide some type of timer for your application as well. The timer generates the counter events at specific intervals, making it easier to display them on the Performance console.

The example relies on a random numeric output. The form's constructor instantiates the `NewNumber` object, and the random number update occurs during each `OutputTimer Tick` event. The application limits the output to a value of 100.

The `btnStartStop_Click()` method contains code to start and stop the timer. You should test this feature out as you view the output in the Performance console. The code has a practical value as well. A performance counter slows your application by a small but perceptible amount. Provide a feature for turning the counter on or off as needed — you don't want to monitor performance all of the time unless you really do need it for remote monitoring purposes.

The final bit of information to look at is the `OutputTimer_Tick()` method. The only line of code in this event handler sets the `OutputRandomEvents.RawValue` property to the new random value. Most of the counter applications you create set this property to a specific value. However, it's important to remember that you can also set the counter to intermediate values. For example, if you're counting user click events, it may be easier to rely on the `Increment` property to increment the counter value until you reach a specific number. Some counters require other techniques based on what they count. For example, you may want to time how long it takes to obtain a specific value, so that the counter output is a time, rather than a value.

Testing the New Counter

Using your new counter is the same as using any other counter. Simply open a copy of the Performance console and add the counter you created to the display as described in the "Viewing Standard Counters" section of the chapter.

A Word about Hardware

Writing a fast application doesn't mean that the application will run quickly. If you write a fast application, but run it on an antique system that lacks sufficient RAM, uses an old processor, and has an ancient hard drive, you can't expect the application to run fast. You have to have the hardware in order to run the application. Consequently, every application you create should provide some hardware requirements so the user knows what the application needs.

Hardware extends to all areas of the system. A faster server can't make the application run fast on old workstations. Likewise, your network connections must provide the speed required to run the application. Every part of the hardware must provide the support the application requires to run fast.

When you run into speed problems with the application and you know that you have tested the application in every way possible for speed, consider looking at the hardware. The hardware isn't always at fault, but reviewing every aspect of your setup is necessary if you want to find the source of potential speed problems. Don't forget to consider the effects of user loading — a hardware configuration that works fine for development won't provide the same results in a production environment.

Developing Your Design Strategy

This chapter has focused on the need for speed in applications. The essential piece of information to gain from this chapter is that speed does not equate to performance. In fact, you should stress this fact as you design your application. Trading reliability and security for speed is false economy and doing so will lead to disaster as you build your application. The measure of how fast an application runs is important, but how fast it performs the task correctly is essential. You've also discovered some safe techniques for making applications faster and for monitoring your application without dragging performance to a halt.

The reason this chapter appears so early in the book is that you must design speed into your application. You can't bolt speed onto the application design late in the process. Features such as multithreading and multiprocessing don't just happen; you have to plan for them from the outset. In addition, you must plan to monitor your application. Speed isn't a constant. The application will provide different levels of speed based on a huge number of environmental and internal factors. If you aren't monitoring your application, then you have no idea of just how much speed it's delivering on a given day. Of course, the big issues are to figure out what to monitor and define when to monitor it.

As mentioned earlier, speed is only one component of performance. Chapter 6 discusses the second element, reliability. In order to gain any benefit at all from the speed of your application, the application must perform its tasks reliably. However, just as with anything else, the faster you perform a task, the less reliably you do it in many cases. Applications aren't humans — they don't get tired. However, if you take out enough code to gain speed, the application will make errors nonetheless. These errors can cost in a number of ways and make any speed gain you achieve worthless. That's why you must consider reliability as part of your speed solution.

6

Designing with Reliability in Mind

Reliability: It's a term that you hear quite often today as the price of devices plummets and the quality of the components used to create them becomes an issue. Most businesses today run 24/7, so reliability is on the tip of many administrators' tongues. Reliability should be part of your vocabulary, too. Many developers wrongly associate reliability only with hardware — reliability is a software issue as well. As described in this book, reliability is a measure of how long something will work as intended without loss to an organization. The term *loss* requires a little explanation. You can probably define what loss means specifically to your organization, but any definition of loss should include:

- Lack of user access
- Hardware downtime
- Data corruption or outright loss
- Restrictions on software use or a complete crash
- Configuration or compatibility issues
- Financial considerations (such as lost customer sales)

Designing an application for reliability means keeping loss of all types at bay. In general, you ensure that all the components used to create the application are reliable and that the application structure itself supports reliable operation. You must also place constraints on user activity that would tend to reduce application reliability. In many cases, application reliability requires that you monitor the application for aberrant activities from any source, including the user.

Application reliability requires that you become invasive in your approach to defining application boundaries. It's important to keep the difference between security and reliability in mind. The most secure application in the world would disallow all access, keeping the application and its data safe from any outside activity. However, a reliable application means granting maximum access without any potential loss. The most reliable application in the world allows all access, even unforeseen access, without any potential for loss at all. Obviously, this goal is unrealistic. This chapter helps you get as close to this goal as possible by considering what's possible given the realities of application development today.

Verifying Resource Availability

One of the first issues you must address is whether the resources your application requires are available; if so, then you can determine the level of that availability. It's a trap to assume that nothing outside your application affects reliability. When your application lacks the resources that it needs to run properly, you can't assure any level of application reliability. For example, one of the most common application problems in times past was memory. Many otherwise reliable applications failed to work properly due to a lack of memory and often nothing else. Consequently, resources are the first issue you must consider as part of your application design. Here are some of the resource types you need to consider:

- Local hardware (memory, disk space, video, and so on)
- Remote hardware (routers, cabling, and other infrastructure)
- User (skill level, training, and so on)
- Network (bandwidth, availability, wireless access point, or WAP, and other networking elements)
- Server (local and remote hardware resources, network resources, application access, data access, and other server-based resources)
- Intranet (localized Web services, Web site access, and other Web-based technology access)
- Internet (remote Web services, third-party or partner server-based resource access, Web site access, and other Web-based technology access)
- Administration (administrator time, administrator skills and training, administration software, and so on)
- Infrastructure (electrical, air conditioning, and other infrastructure resources)
- Catastrophic failure (data recovery, failover servers, backups, and so on)

Whenever you check for resources, always assume a worst-case scenario. Test the resources to ensure that they actually exist and monitor them to determine the least normal level of access to that resource. Document your assumptions and use them as the minimum acceptable level of resource availability. Ensure that management and the administrators who will work with your application sign off on these requirements before you design your application around them. Creating a written document, a Service Level Agreement (SLA), is the best way to ensure that everyone knows what level of reliability to expect (see `http://www.service-level-agreement.net/` *for guidelines on creating an SLA).*

In most cases, you won't obtain additional resources. Whatever resources you have at the time you begin the design process are probably going to be the resources you have when you're done. It's important to look at the resource availability realistically. If you can't make the application perform all the tasks that the customer is asking with the resources that you have available, you must either ask the customer to increase the number of resources or reduce the number of application features. Tricks that use resources more efficiently can work, but there's always a trade-off to consider. For example, reducing the memory available for threads means that you can run fewer threads, and application speed will suffer as a result. Never assume you can reduce resource usage and still maintain a specific feature set, because it's unlikely that you'll succeed.

The biggest error that many developers make is assuming that the application won't grow or that it won't grow very much. Organizations have a tendency to grow far beyond anticipated levels and your application will have to scale with that growth. To keep costs under control, you need to avoid over-engineering your application. But you should also design your application with an eye toward future growth. Normally, you'll want to build the application so it can handle at least a 200 percent increase in load, unless you know that you need even more capacity for future needs.

Human resources are more precious than any other resource you must consider for your application. Of course, you must consider the user skill level and training as part of creating any particular application. However, it's not enough to consider those abilities based on the users you interact with today; you must also consider the abilities that future users will have. When a company has a high turnover rate or is considering expanding, you may find that the mix of users with a particular skill changes and that the well-planned application of today becomes tomorrow's support nightmare. So yes, you do have to consider the users you have today, but keep the overall skill level of users from a historical context in mind as well. You may find that creating an application for a user with fewer skills is actually to your benefit when it comes to support and training. In addition, supporting the lesser number of skills also tends to reduce reliability problems.

The administrators you interact with also have a considerable impact on reliability. In this case, you must depend on the administrator to perform certain tasks, which means assuming that the administrator also has certain skills. If you have only one administrator who's skilled at performing a particular task when you create the application, you must include cross-training or the hiring of another administrator with the same skills as part of your application strategy. Otherwise, you have a single failure point in your application, which means that one failure in a particular area will bring your application to its knees, despite having everything else in place to use it.

Redundancy is good to include as part of your application strategy. You don't know when the loss of an Internet connection is going to cause you woe. In fact, many organizations today have at least two Internet connections through different providers. However, to make this redundancy worthwhile, your application must provide automation to use it. The application should follow this sequence of events when an infrastructure error occurs:

1. Detect the loss of the primary infrastructure element, such as an Internet connection.
2. Test the secondary infrastructure element.
3. Automatically connect to the secondary element and begin using it.
4. Alert the administrator to the loss of the primary infrastructure element.
5. Check for the restoration of the primary infrastructure element.
6. Restore the primary connection as soon as the primary infrastructure element becomes available.
7. Notify the administrator about the restoration of normal service.

Depending on the complexity of the redundant resource, you may have to add verification code to the application. For example, if you have a primary and backup server, you may need to add additional code to the administration code to ensure that the data replicates between servers, depending on which server is active during the user's session. Otherwise, the user could end up with lost data.

This chapter doesn't consider a number of required resource management needs. For example, it doesn't matter how many redundant servers your organization has; you still need a great backup plan to ensure that your data remain safe. In addition, smart organizations usually have multiple sites in regionally separate areas so that catastrophic failure of one site doesn't also spell failure in the other site. These infrastructure decisions are outside the scope of this book, but you still need to consider them for a complete solution.

Saving Data, Settings, and State

Data are the most important part of your application. The software receives data from some source, usually centralized. It modifies the data, and then stores the changed data to some source (usually the same source from which it received the data, but you could also save the data to a different source). If an application fails to manipulate data correctly, then the software is useless and you may as well throw it away.

However, data storage isn't the only concern. Imagine how the user would react to software that requires configuration each time you start it. Users have the reasonable expectation that any software they use will store their configuration settings and restore those settings at the beginning of the next session. The saving and restoration of the settings should occur automatically — the user shouldn't have to do anything special to obtain this feature.

Settings affect the features that the user knows about — the things that the user can see. For example, a setting may contain the location of the user's preferred data storage folder or determine whether the software sends reports about application failures automatically. Software also relies on another set of settings called state. The state of the application determines how the software reacts. When a Mozilla Firefox session stops suddenly, rather than as part of an anticipated shutdown, the software offers to restore the browser state the next time you start Firefox. This is an example of state — the condition of the software that the user isn't normally worried about. The fact that Firefox offers to restore the previous state is an example of good programming practice.

Consequently, an application must work with three levels of information reliably: data, settings, and state information. The following sections discuss the design requirements for all three kinds of information.

Implementing Data Saves

Application data are the most important part of the information store because they have the potential to affect more than the local user — they can affect the organization as a whole. Storing data can also present the biggest problems for the application developer from a reliability perspective because data commonly appear on a remote system. Consequently, data have the highest value, yet also experience the highest potential for damage. Your application design should consider the following data needs:

- The application must read the data without damage (even from network sources).
- The application must write the data without damage, which means maintaining referential integrity and other data storage requirements.

- Reading and writing the data must occur without potentially exposing the data to someone else (which may mean using encryption).
- When a connection failure occurs, the application must have a backup plan for storing the data on permanent media, normally the local hard drive or on a flash drive when a hard drive is unavailable.
- The application must prevent remote data access when the conditions are unfavorable to reliable access.
- Data access must occur within the limits of corporate policy, even when reliable access could otherwise occur.
- The data store must be 100 percent reliable, which means rolling back unsuccessful data transactions (a feature an application should always provide).

Never use an application under development with an existing data store on a production system. Test the new application with a copy of the data store on a test server. Verify that the application does no harm to the data over an extended test period. Many organizations have suffered the consequences of moving their application from the test environment to the production environment too soon.

Considering Methods to Save Settings

Application settings are an essential part of the application because you don't want to reconfigure the application every time you use it. An application should provide a means to automatically store and load application settings when a session ends or starts. In addition, your application should provide some method for exporting and importing settings as required. Applications that fail to meet these requirements often make a significant amount of work for the administrator who often has to guess at the application's original configuration. Settings occur at four levels:

- Organization
- Local machine
- Individual user
- Session

Of these four levels, only the session level is optional. In fact, you usually won't save session settings. It's important to store the settings in the correct place. The individual user settings appear in the user's local storage such as the My Computer folder, the user's storage in the registry, or in a user-specific folder on the server. The local machine storage can appear within the application directory (a poor choice for Vista users who may not have access to the `\Program Files` folder), HKEY_LOCAL_MACHINE registry hive, within the `\WINDOWS` folder, or in a machine-specific folder on the server. Organization-level settings normally appear in a shared folder on the server.

Over the years, developers have also created a number of settings storage strategies. Each of these strategies has advantages and disadvantages as described in Table 6-1.

Table 6-1: Setting Storage Location Advantages and Disadvantages

Storage Location	Advantages	Disadvantages
Registry	The registry provides a centralized storage location that's familiar to all users and administrators alike. The .NET Framework provides a number of standardized method calls for working with the registry. Many applications use the registry today because it has become traditional.	The registry has become filled with so much detritus that it's impossible to separate the useful settings from the dross. In addition, it's not very easy to save settings found in the registry, making it necessary to create a custom export and import feature.
INI File	The standardized INI file appeared in the earliest versions of Windows and provides a consistent method of storing simple data. The INI file is easy to move to another machine, so you don't need a special input/export routine for your application.	Many developers view the INI file as limited because the file doesn't provide good hierarchical storage and only supports strings and integers for the most part. In addition, if you want true INI support, you must resort to using P/Invoke (see the article at `http://jachman.wordpress.com/2006/09/11/how-to-access-ini-files-in-c-net/` for details).
Serialized XML	Using serialized XML has many advantages because it supports every data type that the .NET Framework supports and you end up with an easily read XML file as output. Moving settings from one machine to another is trivial, so you don't need a special input/export routine for your application.	Using serialized XML means creating a special class that describes what you want to save to perform the work. The .NET Framework has all of the functionality required to use your custom class, so you don't have to resort to odd programming techniques. Serialized XML is more complex than using an INI file so the file is more easily damaged and harder to fix. (See the article at `http://www.devsource.com/c/a/Techniques/XML-Serialization-Better-than-the-Registry` and Chapter 22 for details on using XML serialization.)
CONFIG File	The CONFIG file that comes with your .NET application is a good place to store certain kinds of machine-level settings. The .NET Framework makes access to this file absurdly easy. In fact, this is the easiest method, from a development perspective, to save machine-level application settings.	The CONFIG file doesn't provide very good storage for individual user settings. You'd need to create special routines for reading and writing the settings and those routines would become error prone at some level of complexity. In addition, Microsoft normally reserves the CONFIG file for application-specific settings, so using it for user-level settings could make the file large and the application slow to load.

Storage Location	Advantages	Disadvantages
Binary File	A binary file offers significant settings storage space in a very small file. In addition, binary files provide access to any data type, even those not supported by the .NET Framework. For example, you could use this technique to store settings for a P/Invoke method.	The .NET Framework doesn't provide support for binary storage without special programming and neither does the Win32 API. Consequently, you must program this storage technique completely by hand. In addition, the binary format makes damaged file repairs extremely difficult.

Implementing State Saves

Applications usually have state information that you can choose to save based on the application requirements. Most of the state settings concern controls that the application uses to perform useful work. For example, as mentioned earlier, Firefox saves the browser state so that an unexpected crash doesn't leave the user without access to the Web sites that originally appeared in the browser. When you restart Firefox, the application asks whether you want to restore the Web pages that originally appeared in the browser. In some cases, Firefox takes the usage of state information further. Restarting the browser after an update automatically restores the Web pages.

It isn't always necessary, or even helpful, to save the application state. The key criterion for making the decision is whether the application can successfully restore its previous state based solely on the settings that you save. Many applications that save the application state today perform the task marginally and sometimes not at all. For example, most of the Office applications provide a restart feature, but it doesn't always work. Sometimes you have to restart the application cleanly and hope your data aren't damaged too severely.

An application normally stores state information in a temporary file in the application's executable folder or the user's data folder. As the user interacts with the application, the application stores information about those interactions in the file. When the user exits the application, the application deletes the temporary file as part of the required cleanup. During the start of the next session, the application looks for the temporary file. If it doesn't find the file, the application assumes that the application ended normally, or else it restores the application state from the settings it does find in the file.

When creating a state save file, you don't normally expect the file to exist long term. Consequently, most developers look for something very simple to implement. Table 6-1 shows alternatives commonly used for long-term settings storage. Given that you're storing control information for a control, the INI file solution is inappropriate. You probably won't want to store the data in the registry either. However, any of the other storage solutions should work well.

Expecting the Unexpected

Reliability has a statistical basis. Simply stated, reliability tells you the probability of any particular failure occurring in a specific situation. In many cases, the people responsible for making reliability predictions attempt to improve the calculation through empirical evidence or through tests, much as you test an application for bugs. An engineer expresses the result of a reliability calculation as the Mean Time Between Failures (MTBF). The MTBF states that within a certain time, half of the objects that are the target of the calculation will fail. However, the first error can occur immediately and the last error can occur at some time in the distant future.

The main use for hardware MTBF is to determine how many parts to stock to meet the predicted failures over some time interval, not to predict the likelihood of failure for a particular device, because a particular device can fail at any time. Likewise, software reliability helps define the support requirements for an application, not predict the likelihood that any particular user will cause the system to crash. The difference between hardware and software reliability prediction is that hardware reliability prediction considers manufacturing perfection, while software reliability prediction considers design and usage perfection.

In general, any user can cause any number of problems on any given day. Perhaps Murphy is working overtime with that particular user. Of course, you must also consider whether the user's training is inadequate for the task or whether external events are causing problems, such as resource shortages. The point is that increasing reliability does reduce the risk of potential failure, but it doesn't eliminate failure. You must always expect that at any given time a set of circumstances will conspire to produce a failure that can cost you time, money, data, user access, or any number of other problems. In short, reliability provides a certain expectation of consistent usage, but doesn't guarantee anything.

It's interesting to note that many administrators believe that reliability is somehow a guarantee of something. If you say that a piece of software will have a 100-hour MTBF, the administrator may assume that the first failure won't occur until the application reaches the 100-hour mark. At best, reliability is mathematical analysis of the predicted estimate of the software's longevity and nothing more. Consequently, when designing your software, you must emphasize the fact that something will eventually go wrong and have contingency plans in place to handle the software's failure modes.

Most software follows the bathtub model for reliability purposes. The bathtub model shows that the software will fail quite often at the outset due to the usual break-in period problems and bug fixes. The software will reach a low failure point and run for quite some time with few failures. However, as the software reaches the end of its useful life, environmental problems (such as updated hardware) and accumulated errors will begin taking a toll and the number of errors will increase to some unacceptable level, at which point most organizations retire the software.

The Web site at `http://www.ece.cmu.edu/~koopman/des_s99/sw_reliability/` provides some interesting insights into software reliability that you should consider as part of the design process. A number of vendors, including Isograph (`http://www.isograph.com/workbench.htm`) and Relex (`http://www.relex.com/products/relpredsoft.asp`), produce software you can use to perform software reliability prediction. Reliability prediction is a useful tool to help you define the support requirements for your application.

Considering the Reliability Benefits of RibbonX

The first rule of reliability is that less is better. The fewer components found in a piece of hardware, the fewer failure points, and the higher the reliability. The same holds true for software. As you add more features, you also add more potential failure points, making the software less reliable. Even though many developers don't think about it, the same holds true for the user interface. Add more buttons or other controls and you increase application complexity, which spells reduced reliability.

The recent move to feature hiding, such as that found in both Office 2003 and Windows — where a feature exists, but the software hides it from view when the user doesn't access it — does improve reliability somewhat. However, the feature still exists and when the user performs certain actions, such as hovering the mouse when looking for a needed feature, the feature becomes visible again. In short, the feature only helps reduce complexity when the user is already sure about which action to take. Feature hiding doesn't work when the user needs it most, when there's uncertainty about what to do next. You can see this phenomenon take place. Users often hunt for features with their mouse cursor because they simply can't remember which menu option to choose or which button to click.

> *The best way to make the user interface reliable is to reduce complexity whenever possible. Hide advanced features from view. Remove features unless you feel the user absolutely must have them. If possible, place advanced features in a separate application, rather than as part of the main application, in order to make your application more reliable. Get rid of old features when no one's using them — they only clutter the display and reduce user efficiency.*

The reason the RibbonX interface is so much better than its predecessors is that you avoid the whole question of hunting for a feature by reducing the user's view. A user can see only a particular set of features associated with a specific task. Consequently, the user engages in less mouse hunting and more productive work. The overall effect is to improve application reliability.

When you make the RibbonX interface perform as a workflow, the potential for error is reduced, because the user may now see as little as one correct control to perform a particular task. Theoretically, the presence of just one control to perform a task means that the RibbonX interface is 100 percent reliable for that task. Of course, other controls are visible and the user could inadvertently click one of them, making any potential decision less than 100 percent reliable. However, the use of workflows does make the reliability of the application significantly higher.

The RibbonX interface is easier to customize than other interfaces. It relies on a special container file that holds a number of XML files you can use to customize the look of the Ribbon. To see this arrangement for yourself, change the extension of an Office 2007 document, such as DOCX, to ZIP. You can now open the file using any ZIP archive utility and see the files it contains. The `CustomUI.XML` file found in the `CustomUI` folder contains the custom feature for the Ribbon interface you design. You can find the schema for this interface at `http://www.microsoft.com/downloads/details.aspx?FamilyID=15805380-f2c0-4b80-9ad1-2cb0c300aef9`.

Because you're working with standard file formats, you don't even need to perform odd conversions to change the interface in an Office 2007 file or template. The Custom UI Editor provides direct access to the underlying XML. You can learn about this tool at `http://openxmldeveloper.org/articles/customuieditor.aspx`. The article also includes a link to the Custom UI Editor tool.

Using the RibbonX interface isn't limited to Office applications you modify. It's relatively easy to include this functionality in your own applications and increase their reliability as well. Of course, the RibbonX interface works best with novice users and for workflows, not for applications focused on the needs of expert users. The article at `http://www.devsource.com/c/a/Techniques/Using-a-Custom-Ribbon-in-Your-NET-Applications/` tells you how to provide this functionality in your own applications.

Developing Your Design Strategy

This chapter has discussed the elements you should consider for a reliable application. Reliability is difficult to achieve and you have to spend a good deal of time designing it into your applications. The biggest thing to remember is that you can't usually add reliability to an application after the design process is complete. An application either starts out reliable or it never becomes reliable. This chapter has also helped you focus attention on some areas of reliability that provide the largest payoff from a time-spent perspective.

It's time to consider the reliability of your design. As you now know, it's impossible to create an absolutely reliable application — to achieve a state of application perfection so incredible as to be unbelievable. However, you can achieve a considerable amount of application reliability that also has a payoff so that management and user alike will support it. The payoff is an essential part of creating the reliable application because you require the participation of everyone involved in working with the application to obtain a high level of reliability. Most important of all, consider the unreliability of the user when designing your application. If the user can find a wrong set of keys to press, you can be sure that some user will try them. However, remember that only a user can test for these conditions, so make sure you have plenty of them as part of your test team.

Chapter 7 discusses the third part of the performance triad, security. As stated earlier in the book, an application that performs well is one that has a balanced view of speed, reliability, and security. An application that lacks any member of the triad is almost certainly going to disappoint anyone who uses it and cause you considerable woe as well. The balance you must achieve is based on the requirements of your organization and the needs of your user. The information you receive in Chapter 7 augments the information from Chapters 5 and 6 — you should use all three chapters together to help design an application that provides everything needed in today's world.

7

Designing with Security in Mind

Almost everyone talks about security. There are possibly more books and articles on security than any other single topic in computer science. Industry pundits have viewed the security issue from every potential angle and a few angles that some of us had never considered. Of course, the issue in nearly every developer's mind is whether all the fuss is worth it — whether any application can reach that magical state of complete protection. The answer is yes. If you design the application such that it has no outside access, no access by the user, no interchange with the network, and doesn't rely on any outside data whatsoever, you can make it completely safe. Unfortunately, no one can use the application, but it's quite safe.

It seems then that true security is a matter of making it difficult to gain unauthorized access and then providing some type of monitoring to make sure that the security measures work. Most applications today go through a vicious cycle where:

1. An expert attempts to break in (and always succeeds because it's easier to break down the wall than to build it).
2. The vendor attempts to constrain new attacks while creating a fix.
3. The fix is bungled.
4. The vendor creates an improved fix.
5. The vendor says the application is now bulletproof — as if it ever could be under the current circumstances.

The vendors usually ask that the experts not spend all their time breaking their applications, while the experts claim that the public has a need to know about these vulnerabilities. I don't personally want to end up in the middle of the debate. However, it does seem like a counterproductive way in which to spend time and effort. Many of the exploits that the experts describe are so odd and difficult to employ that the person relying on them would be better off doing just about anything else.

This chapter takes a different kind of look at security — one that emphasizes managed risk, not building an ever-higher wall that still fails to keep the intruder out. Someone's probably going to be able to find a way through the security you employ based on the strategies discussed in this chapter. However, they'll have to work hard to do it, which buys you time to detect their presence. Along with the managed risk, this chapter advocates monitoring the application in various ways to observe adverse behavior. The emphasis in this chapter is on:

- Keeping relatively honest people out of your software
- Detecting those who are determined to break in no matter what
- Protecting users from themselves

Assuming the Worst-Case Scenario

The glum view, the one that looks at every aspect of security as a potential for someone to break into your system, is probably the smart view. It's not that you should think the job of securing your application is impossible; with the right application code and some monitoring, you can achieve amazing things when it comes to security. However, all it takes is a good healthy look at the trade press and you know that many have gone before you and many have failed. You have to see security as something that's very hard for you to do and very easy for someone else to break. Those with ill intent seem to break into systems at will.

Part of the problem you face is that you can't focus exclusively on your application if you want to ensure success. Many external elements can thwart the best application design and you must consider them as well. Here are a few of the external elements you must consider as you work through your application design:

- Users
- Operating system
- Other applications
- Poor administration practices
- Business partners
- The Internet
- Fired employees
- Anyone who wants access to your organization

Unfortunately, you can't control any of these external elements. The best you can hope to achieve is to overcome some of the worst effects of these external elements as part of your design. For example, you can partially mitigate the user threat by checking user input and verifying that users provide only the input you expect. Using the right controls can help in this regard. It's very hard to embed a script in a drop-down list box (or to simply type the wrong thing as you could when using a textbox).

Although you can't completely eliminate operating system and other application threats, you can ensure that your company provides all the required updates. Yes, a security expert somewhere will find yet another hole in the operating system or application tomorrow, but at least for today your system won't have any known vulnerabilities. It's also important to check for compatibility problems, because these issues often act as a conduit for gaining unauthorized access to your system. Sometimes, two completely unrelated applications can work against each other and offer an avenue of attack for someone outside your company. A failure in one application provides access to another application without your knowledge.

Overcoming poor administrative practices is one of the harder parts of securing your application. In this case, training can help, but sometimes you need a combination of both negative and positive reinforcement to ensure proper performance. However, sometimes nothing will help and that's where monitoring comes into play. It's important to perform spot checks on the administrative practices of everyone in your organization.

Business partners and the Internet pose similar problems. By allowing access to your application by outsiders (and let's face it, any Internet-facing connection provides access, no matter how good your firewall may be), you open your application to potential fiddling by people you can't control in any way. Of course, good monitoring practices are a requirement in this situation. The outside sources shouldn't have access to sensitive data. In addition, the Internet portion of your application should provide significant restrictions on application access, even to employees on the road, because you simply can't trust the connection.

It sounds trite and timeworn, but it still works. The best way to keep a secret is not to tell anyone about it. The less access you provide to your application, the better. Provide only the access the user requires and not anything more. During testing, try various access levels and hide controls you think the user might not need. Put yourself in the user's place and see if you can accomplish a task. Use real users as part of the test. Offer some type of incentive for the user who finds the most controls to eliminate safely from the new application.

In the recent past, fired employees have become a significant nuisance when it comes to security. An employee who leaves the organization for any reason at all is a threat, but one the organization has fired is a significant threat. Obviously, you must lock the employee out of the system. Unfortunately, removing the employee's account isn't enough. You must also perform an audit of the system account to ensure the employee hasn't provided a back door into the system. It's also essential to monitor the system for unusual access — access that may point to someone who knows the system layout, rather than a complete stranger.

Eliminating Errant Input

Errant input, whether automated or manual, purposeful or accidental, is one of the biggest security risks for your application. Users constantly type the wrong thing into the fields of forms. Anything you can do to reduce the amount of typing a user performs increases application security simply because there are fewer ways for the user to enter the wrong data. Of course, some people insert the incorrect data on purpose. They're looking for some way to trick your application. Perhaps they're injecting a script to perform some dark deed.

Of course, many outsiders don't even do the work themselves any longer — so many Web sites to crack, so little time in which to do it. Determining whether your application is accessed by another application or a human is also a problem. In fact, the proliferation of Completely Automatic Public Turing Test to Tell Computers and Humans Apart (CAPTCHA) says a lot about the prevalence of this problem. You can read more about CAPTCHA at `http://www.captcha.net/`. Figure 7-1 shows an example of a

CAPTCHA screen (look at the word "morning"), complete with audio functionality for users who can't see the specially constructed graphic image.

Figure 7-1. Using CAPTCHA can help reduce the potential for automated access of your Web site.

If you do use CAPTCHA as part of your strategy, make sure you include the voice version of CAPTCHA as well for blind users who won't be able to see the graphics you provide. Otherwise, you may find that you lock out a number of legitimate human users. Computerworld *provides an article that discusses the topic of obstacles, including the use of CAPTCHA, at* `http://www.computerworld.com/action/article.do?command=viewArticleBasic&articleId=9077118`.

The combination of user mistakes and outright attacks points to a need to create smart user interfaces that reduce your risks. The following sections describe some of the methods you can use to make your applications less susceptible to errant input of all types.

Using the Correct Control or Component

Any time you can avoid using a control where the user can type in a value, you're ahead on security. Asking the user to type something isn't wrong, it simply opens the door for the user to type something incorrectly. Depending on how your application uses the information the user types, the results can prove interesting or devastating. The key to typed data is determining whether your application will interpret that data in the correct way. A user typing the wrong text into a word-processed document probably won't take your server offline, but a user typing the wrong text into the field of a data entry form can have unforeseen and terrible results. In fact, many nefarious individuals count on this very behavior to fool your application into doing their bidding.

It often helps to look at ways that other people create forms to pick up techniques for your own forms. In fact, you may want to maintain a notebook of techniques you can use to avoid text fields. The possibilities are amazing. Most people know that you can substitute a drop-down list box for a state entry. However, you can also obtain all the cities for an area based on the user's state entry. Once the user chooses a city from a drop-down list box, you can present a list of ZIP codes as well. Check out the Web service at `http://www.webservicex.net/uszip.asmx` for more details. In short, you can eliminate user error by entering the city, state, and ZIP code for any entry. Interestingly enough, you can also verify the area code for a particular ZIP code using this Web service. The Web service costs you absolutely nothing to use and it easily integrates into your application. Consequently, there isn't any reason to avoid using this Web service to make your application less reliant on a user's typing the right value.

You can probably find a Web service somewhere to meet just about any need. For example, you can find a database of Universal Product Code (UPC) values at `http://www.upcdatabase.com/xmlrpc.asp`. Relying on this Web service means that you can at least verify any value the user inputs. In fact, you can find a host of Web services just waiting for you to use them at `http://www.webservicelist.com/`. Use the Internet to your advantage — keep user-typed entries minimized by retrieving the correct data from the Internet and displaying it as a user selection. Sometimes one control works better than another for a particular situation. Use a drop-down list box when the user is likely to know the value needed for a particular form entry and when you need to save space. Option buttons work better when you have only a few choices to provide and you're not sure the user will see all the selections in a drop-down list box. A list box often provides the best functionality when the user must make multiple selections.

Part of your reason for conducting a user test as part of the design process is to determine which control works best in a particular situation. Create versions of the application that use different control combinations and then monitor the user error rate to determine which control combinations provide a better user experience. At some point, you'll obtain tested solutions that reflect the best user experience and most secure application setup.

Checking All User Input

It's nearly impossible to create a user application that lacks any form of text input. You can access every possible Web service out there and the user is going to have to provide input at some point. For example, given an address database, you can look up the city, state, and ZIP code. It's even easy to verify the address the user supplies as input. However, there's the matter of the name the user enters — it would be hard to create a method for verifying the name. Consequently, the best-designed address entry form in the world will still have a minimum of three text fields for first, middle, and last name.

It's still possible to manage the risk of a text field entry. You can verify that the data the user enters are within a certain range. Verifying the data length is also helpful and you can even use pattern matching to ensure the data appear in a certain form (such as a telephone number). Finally, you can restrict user input in free-form text fields by disallowing certain characters. For example, it's highly unlikely that a name will include the curly braces ({}), which are characters used for scripting. By not including these characters, you can keep someone from entering a script in place of the name you expected. The following sections describe three techniques you can design into your applications to make them safer.

Checking the Data Range

A data range defines the acceptable values for data input. For example, when you define a value in your code as `Int32`, it means that the user can enter any value from –2,147,483,648 through 2,147,483,647. However, your application might not find this range acceptable. When this happens, you must include special code in your application to check for potential error conditions. You might want to accept numbers from 0 to 40,000 in your code, which is outside the `Int16` value range, but well within the `Int32` value range. In short, a data range is specific to the need at hand.

Generally, you'll find that value data types are the easiest to range check because they have predefined ranges. The .NET Framework supports more value types than you might think. For example, the .NET Framework considers a color used for drawing (`System.Drawing.Color`) a value type. You can see the full list of .NET Framework value types at `http://msdn.microsoft.com/en-us/library/system.valuetype_derivedtypelist.aspx`.

Always use the .NET Framework–specific value types, rather than native types, whenever possible. Although the .NET Framework maps native types to their .NET equivalent, using a .NET type at the outset reduces potential confusion. These types are standard across all languages used for .NET development.

Data ranges can encompass a variety of types. For example, it's possible to create a discontinuous numerical set to address specific configuration needs. Strings naturally fall into a discontinuous set because words don't fall into any ordered pattern except as defined for language. In many situations, you can overcome this problem by defining an enumeration and then using that enumeration as input as shown in Listing 7-1.

Listing 7-1: Enumerating discontinuous data ranges

```
// Use the enumeration names directly for strings.
public enum SomeStrings
{
   One,
   Two,
   Three,
   Four
}

// Supply a specific value for numbers.
public enum SomeValues
{
   Value1 = 1,
   Value10 = 10,
   Value100 = 100,
   Value1000 = 1000
}

public class DoMsg
{
   public static void Show(SomeStrings Input1, SomeValues Input2)
   {
      // Convert Input2 to a number.
```

```
        Int32 IVal;
        IVal = (Int32)Input2;

        // Display a message box using the inputs.
        MessageBox.Show("The selected string is: " + Input1.ToString() +
                        "\r\nThe selected number is: " + IVal.ToString(),
                        "Selection Results",
                        MessageBoxButtons.OK,
                        MessageBoxIcon.Information);
    }
}
```

This simple example has two enumerations. The `Show()` method of the `DoMsg` class uses these enumerations to define acceptable input values. To any external program, the `Show()` method will appear to use specific data types. This technique does require more time, but the results are worth it. If an external program were to try to access the `Show()` method like this:

```
DoMsg.Show("Hello", 2);
```

the program wouldn't even compile. Visual Studio presents you with six errors as shown here:

```
Error 1: 'EnumeratingRanges.SomeStrings' is a 'type' but is used like a 'variable'
Error 2: The best overloaded method match for
   'System.Collections.Generic.List<EnumeratingRanges.SomeStrings>.List(int)'
   has some invalid arguments
Error 3: Argument '1': cannot convert from 'EnumeratingRanges.SomeStrings' to 'int'
Error 4: The best overloaded method match for
   'EnumeratingRanges.DoMsg.Show(EnumeratingRanges.SomeStrings,
   EnumeratingRanges.SomeValues)' has some invalid arguments
Error 5: Argument '1': cannot convert from 'string' to
   'EnumeratingRanges.SomeStrings'
Error 6: Argument '2': cannot convert from 'int' to 'EnumeratingRanges.SomeValues'
```

To make this feature work with the user interface, you need two list boxes. You fill them with the enumerated data using code like that shown here:

```
public frmMain()
{
   InitializeComponent();

   // Store all of the enumerated values in the list box.
   foreach (String ThisString in Enum.GetNames(typeof(SomeStrings)))
      cbSomeStrings.Items.Add(ThisString);

   // Choose a default item.
   cbSomeStrings.SelectedIndex = 0;

   // Perform the same task for SomeValues.
   foreach (String ThisString in Enum.GetNames(typeof(SomeValues)))
      cbSomeValues.Items.Add(ThisString);
   cbSomeValues.SelectedIndex = 0;
}
```

Use the `Enum.GetNames()` method to obtain all the names. Make sure you provide a type, rather than the actual enumeration, using the `typeof()` method. The act of adding all the names in the enumeration to the list box and then selecting a specific item in that list makes it impossible for the user to make an incorrect selection. Once the user makes the selection, you can access the `DoMsg.Show()` method like this:

```
private void btnTest2_Click(object sender, EventArgs e)
{
   // Convert the values in the list box into enums.
   Object SelString = Enum.Parse(typeof(SomeStrings), cbSomeStrings.Text);
   Object SelValue = Enum.Parse(typeof(SomeValues), cbSomeValues.Text);

   // Perform the request.
   DoMsg.Show((SomeStrings)SelString, (SomeValues)SelValue);
```

Checking the Data Length

Many of the exploits shady individuals use depend on your not checking the length of the incoming data. For example, the buffer overrun technique has become so popular precisely because few developers check the length of incoming data. Fortunately for the .NET developer, the Common Language Runtime (CLR) does much of the length checking automatically and raises an exception. Even so, CLR only checks for extreme cases — you still have to perform checks for your particular application.

Data that are too short can be just as much a problem as data that are too long. For example, if your program needs a string that it will then parse for appropriate data, it could fail if it suddenly runs out of data before the parsing is complete. Ensuring that the data are as long as you need before you begin any processing is the best way to avoid certain kinds of problems. Make sure you tell the user about these limits and present clear messages about the error when it does occur. Listing 7-2 shows a typical example of how you can handle a data length issue.

Listing 7-2: Detecting and handling data length errors

```
private void btnTest_Click(object sender, System.EventArgs e)
{
   try
   {
      // Process the input text.
      if (ProcessData(txtInput.Text, 8, 4))

         // Display a result message for correct input.
         MessageBox.Show("You typed: " + txtInput.Text,
                         "Input String",
                         MessageBoxButtons.OK,
                         MessageBoxIcon.Information);
   }
   catch (SecurityException SE)
   {
      // Display an error message for incorrect input.
      MessageBox.Show(SE.Message,
                      "Input Error",
                      MessageBoxButtons.OK,
```

```
                      MessageBoxIcon.Error);
   }
}

private void btnBadTest_Click(object sender, System.EventArgs e)
{
   try
   {
      // Process the input text.
      if (ProcessData(txtInput.Text, 4, 8))

         // Display a result message for correct input.
         MessageBox.Show("You typed: " + txtInput.Text,
                         "Input String",
                         MessageBoxButtons.OK,
                         MessageBoxIcon.Information);
   }
   catch (ArgumentException AE)
   {
      // Display an error message for incorrect input.
      MessageBox.Show(AE.Message,
                      "Argument Error",
                      MessageBoxButtons.OK,
                      MessageBoxIcon.Error);
   }
}

private Boolean ProcessData(String Input,
                            Int32 UpperLimit,
                            Int32 LowerLimit)
{
   // Check for an input error.
   if (UpperLimit < LowerLimit)
   {
      System.ArgumentException   AE;
      AE = new ArgumentException("The UpperLimit input must be " +
                                 "greater than the LowerLimit number.",
                                 "UpperLimit");
      throw(AE);
   }

   // Check for a data length error condition.
   if (Input.Length < LowerLimit || Input.Length > UpperLimit)
   {
      SecurityException SE;
      SE = new SecurityException("String is the wrong length. Use a " +
                                 "string between 4 and 8 characters " +
                                 "long.");
      throw(SE);
   }

   // If the data is correct, return true.
   return true;
}
```

This example actually shows two kinds of checking you need to provide — both of which are tested in the ProcessData() method. The first is the user input (demonstrated in the btnTest_Click() method). The input has to be a certain length for this application and the ProcessData() method checks to ensure it is. The second is the input argument (demonstrated in the btnBadTest_Click() method). The ProcessData() method uses a separate check for argument errors.

Notice that this example can create one of two exceptions. The ArgumentException object represents cases where the arguments are incorrect, while the SecurityException object represents incorrect user input. It's important to use the right type of exceptions when you track problems such as data that are the wrong length — even if you have to create new exceptions for the job. Tracking potential security problems such as incorrect data length begins when you provide good error documentation by using different exception objects for each error type.

In order to compile this application, you must add using System.Security; at the beginning of the code. It's important to remember that you can augment the security provided in this example. For example, if you set the control's MaxLength property to 8, then the user can't directly type a string longer than eight characters. However, someone could potentially change the string length in the background, so you still need to perform the length check.

Keeping Unnecessary Characters Controlled

Unnecessary characters are any characters that your application doesn't require as input. For example, if your application doesn't require any slashes, then you shouldn't accept them as input. Likewise, you should avoid any numeric or control character input unless you actually need them to make the application work properly.

You may think that checking individual characters in a string isn't worth the effort. Until you actually see some of the exploits unsavory individuals use, it may seem that character checking is a solution in search of a problem. The Security Focus site articled entitled, "Abusing poor programming techniques in webserver scripts V 1.0" at http://www.der-keiler.de/Mailing-Lists/securityfocus/secprog/2001-07/0001.html *shows that this is a significant problem. Pay careful attention to this example. Notice that it breaks several of the rules listed in this chapter, including allowing the use of nonstandard characters.*

Disreputable individuals have devised a number of interesting exploits over the years to make use of extra characters. The problem is especially severe for Web applications where an application could actually end up combining several fields if the correct input is used. However, even desktop applications need to be aware of unwanted characters because some control characters can damage data or cause other problems. Listing 7-3 shows an example of how you can control unwanted characters.

Listing 7-3: Avoiding unwanted characters in input

```
private void btnTest_Click(object sender, EventArgs e)
{
   try
   {
      // Process the input text.
      if (CheckChars(txtInput.Text))
```

```
            // Display a result message for correct input.
            MessageBox.Show("You typed: " + txtInput.Text,
                            "Input String",
                            MessageBoxButtons.OK,
                            MessageBoxIcon.Information);
      }
      catch (SecurityException SE)
      {
         // Display an error message for incorrect input.
         MessageBox.Show(SE.Message,
                         "Input Error",
                         MessageBoxButtons.OK,
                         MessageBoxIcon.Error);
      }
   }

   private Boolean CheckChars(String Input)
   {
      // Create a regular expression for match purposes.
      Regex R;
      R = new Regex("[A-Za-z]");

      // Check for a data length error condition.
      if (R.Matches(Input).Count < Input.Length)
      {
         SecurityException SE;
         SE = new SecurityException("String contains incorrect " +
                                    "characters. Use only A through Z " +
                                    "and a through z.");
         throw(SE);
      }

      // If the data is correct, return true.
      return true;
   }
```

The `CheckChars()` method relies on a `Regex` (regular expression) object to perform its task. In this case, the `Matches()` method counts the number of times the letters in the input string match the allowed letters in R. If the number of matches equals the length of Input, then the input string doesn't contain any unauthorized letters.

Of course, someone could provide characters that don't match R. This example uses a `SecurityException` object to raise an exception when the input contains incorrect characters. Your program could react in a number of ways, but displaying the default error message probably works best. The idea is to present the user with the list of acceptable input choices. This is one situation when you might want to track the number of times the user makes incorrect entries to detect evil individuals looking for weaknesses in your defenses. In order to compile this application, you must provide the following code:

```
using System.Security;
using System.Text.RegularExpressions;
```

Verifying Data Sources

As you put your application together, you need to consider the data sources you use. Some of the data sources are local and verification is easy. The most easily verified source is anything that comes from the local system. It would be hard for someone to spoof a connection to a SQL Server database on your LAN (never say anything is impossible). As you move out from the LAN, you have to start thinking about potential spoofing. For example, someone could spoof a remote connection to your own Wide Area Network (WAN) given the right tools. Although such spoofing is highly unlikely, it's always a good idea to ask the server for credentials and use encrypted communication. Likewise, the server should request client credentials to ensure that the communication comes from a known requester and that no one is engaged in a man-in-the-middle attack (read about the man-in-the-middle attack at `http://en.wikipedia.org/wiki/Man-in-the-middle_attack`).

Most organizations today don't rely strictly on home-brewed data. At a minimum, many organizations rely on data from partner organizations to augment their own. For example, you may need catalog data from a company you interact with regularly. Some companies share customer lists with each other for promotional or other reasons. In fact, it's amazing that the world hasn't become one huge database yet, because most organizations rely heavily on data from a host of sources. Everyone seems to have collaborated with everyone else in search of new data. Theoretically, data from a partner are reliable, at least to an extent, but now you're accessing a computer in another company and you can't be sure about the security surrounding that computer. Consequently, you have to build up your own security (and monitoring) to compensate.

The hardest data source to verify comes from public Web services. When you connect to Amazon.com to discover books, products, or services you need, you can't be sure that someone hasn't tampered with the information. In fact, you can't be certain that the information was correct in the first place. All you get are some data delivered to you in a particular format — it's up to you to decide whether that information is correct. You can get data delivered through a Web service today through most large companies including eBay, Google, and AOL. In fact, you can find literally thousands of sources out there that you know nothing about — all of them containing valuable data your company requires to beat the competition. When you must verify data from a public Web service, consider these design criteria:

- Verify the IP address of both sender and receiver for each call to ensure you haven't been spoofed.
- Use the .NET Framework functionality to verify the format of the data.
- Validate the incoming information to ensure it meets the Web service's published specifications.
- Don't send any more information than absolutely necessary to make requests.
- Keep track of changes in data format published by the Web service vendor.

Hiding Data from View

As part of keeping your data secret, you'll want to hide it from view as often as possible. Sometimes you'll hide the data in plain sight (such as using encryption); sometimes you'll completely hide it from view (using local data only). Some developers become good at placing data in locations that outsiders don't think to look at, and others protect the locations so that outsiders can't view them even if they do gain access to the network. These techniques have one thing in common: they make the data invisible to outsiders. The following sections discuss in detail techniques you can use to hide data from view.

Keeping Data Local

The application that has the most hidden data is one that one that stores data on the local hard drive and never makes a connection to any other machine. Of course, an application like this doesn't share data very effectively either. In addition, it's an error to think that the data are completely safe. Someone could stick a DVD in the drive and copy the data from the local hard drive to the DVD. If no other means exists, users will handwrite the data they want using pen and paper. Consequently, the only data that an application completely hides from view are the data that absolutely no one will ever see, making the data useless.

It's important to consider hardware as part of your security solution. If a PC or server doesn't require a DVD burner, then don't install one. If it doesn't require a DVD reader, don't install the DVD reader either. Keeping hardware to a minimum tends to protect it from security issues to an extent. If the hardware required for an exploit doesn't exist, then the evil person can't use it. If the hardware comes preinstalled and you don't need it, consider disabling the hardware for security reasons.

Local data resources do have their uses. Keeping a user's settings on a local drive is a good idea, because the user does have a need to some privacy in the organization (although legally it appears that the user has no expectation of any privacy while working for an organization of any type). You may want to cache data locally before writing them to the server to improve application speed. Temporary files are usually best left on the local hard drive as well. In fact, your application should delete temporary files when it exits, rather than leaving them lying around to gather dust.

Using local storage becomes a problem when the data are general in nature and others have the right to see them. Managers often complain about the user who keeps localized data as a means of not sharing them with others. These users do maintain an important security concept in their greed; no one else sees the data, making them more secure. Unfortunately, the data also don't help the organization as a whole. Their only purpose is to serve some political need and you should consider designing your application in such a way that it discourages users from storing generalized data locally.

Encrypting Data

Some developers view encryption as a hassle and an application speed killer. Suddenly, you have to translate everything that the application does before it sends or receives information. Fortunately, the .NET Framework makes encrypting data surprisingly easy. Chapter 21 shows you how to perform this task without using a lot of code at all. In fact, you may find that encryption becomes so easy that you'll use it everywhere, which is actually the idea behind this section. It turns out that if someone's monitoring the activity on your system, the best way to get rid of them is not to give them anything worthwhile. Here are the places where you should consider using encryption:

- Any communication you send to another machine to keep packet sniffers at bay
- All files containing any type of sensitive data on any hard drive or other storage device
- Data stored in memory as part of the application

- Data that are archived so that anyone losing the backup tape won't compromise your entire company's data store
- Any communication over a public network regardless of the data's sensitivity

Of course, encryption isn't any good if someone can break it. Many developers still remember the days of the Data Encryption Standard (DES). Now you can crack DES in a matter of minutes. Security experts no longer consider even Triple DES a good encryption method (read more about the cracking of DES at `http://en.wikipedia.org/wiki/EFF_DES_cracker`). Always use the Advanced Encryption Standard (AES) when possible for transferring data (read about AES at `http://en.wikipedia.org/wiki/Advanced_Encryption_Standard`).

Sometimes, you don't want to send the data at all. A *hash* converts data into a unique numeric value. If the sender and receiver can agree on a protocol, they can use a hash to send common information, rather than rely on sending the data. This is the method that Windows uses for your password. The server actually stores a hash of your password, rather than the password itself. When you type your password into the logon dialog box, Windows converts it to a hash and sends the hash to the server. Because this number is unique and Windows requires that you provide a password, and not the hash, the password is considerably safer.

Placing Data in Protected Locations

In general, you don't want to hide data so completely that no one can find them. However, you can make the data very difficult to find. For example, some developers will hide their data in unusual places, locations that an outsider won't know about, such as a flash drive. Theoretically, when the administrator suspects that someone may be looking for the data, removing the flash drive from the USB port hides the data completely until the administrator can resolve the issue. Realistically, this approach is limited, but it does give you the idea behind using protected locations.

The standard method to place data in a protected location is to create a shared folder on the server that has specific entry requirements — you must have the rights required to access the folder. This technique works well in situations where access is standardized to the Windows security methods. It works well for most situations where you need to protect the data.

However, you may encounter a situation where hiding the data in some obscure location won't work and the Windows security method won't work either. For example, you may want to restrict access by location. In this situation, you can begin with the standard Windows security method. You can also encrypt the data in the folder. Now, the user can't access the data without the proper rights and the simple act of accessing the data doesn't let the user read them. The data are locked in two ways that the application controls.

Now, you can add role-based security to the mix. The user must have Windows access to the file and also be in the proper role to decrypt the file. This two-tier system does take a toll on application speed and especially on application startup speed, but it's extremely effective.

Adding Application Monitoring

Monitoring occurs everywhere today. Walk through a shopping center and someone is probably monitoring you. Cross a busy street in the middle of a major city and someone probably knows about it at some point. We monitor our cars — OnStar (`http://www.onstar.com/`) probably knows that you have a problem with your car before you do. People who can afford it, and have the need to do so, monitor their homes. At some point, you'll probably find that someone is monitoring your refrigerator and telling you what you need to buy at the store. Monitoring has become a fact of life because it makes many people feel secure — personally, I get visions of *1984*, `http://en.wikipedia.org/wiki/Big_Brother_(1984)`, and avoid it as much as possible.

Whether or not you feel monitoring is a good idea, monitoring your applications is probably a requirement in today's world. The problem is that for every fix a vendor implements, someone finds two additional items that require repair, and every one of these errors appears to provide those with ill intent an avenue for invading your organization. Let's just say that the security dike you thought was secure has substantial holes in it and a finger won't be enough to stop the flow of data out of your organization. You have to monitor your applications to determine just how bad your data breaches have become and who is striking the dike wall with shovel and pick. The following sections describe in more detail monitoring that you should include in your application design.

Defining the Monitoring Strategy

How you monitor your application determines the kind of information you receive about it. For example, if you monitor the local system, you'll see how a particular machine interacts with the application. In order to obtain a valid statistical sample, you must monitor a number of machines. Monitoring the network will tell you about application connectivity and shows the files that users need most often. You can detect potential problems such as too many password requests (or not enough requests, as conditions dictate). Looking at the activities of a particular user can help you understand that user's needs better, help you locate potential security issues associated with that user, or define the reasons that the user is experiencing problems with the application. Sometimes you have to monitor the server in order to locate a problem. Outsiders often target the server because it's easier to hide on the server and the server offers access to information from a number of accounts instead of just one account.

Employee monitoring of any sort normally requires that you make the employee aware of the monitoring in advance. You should also provide the employee with a written policy that describes the monitoring, your reason for using it, and how you use the results of the monitoring. As this is not a legal tome, you'll also want to contact your lawyer and discuss any other requirements specified at the federal, state, or local level. Reading articles such as, "Is e-mail monitoring legal?" (`http://www.policypatrol.com/Email-monitoring-article.htm`) *is also helpful, but not a good substitute for knowledgeable help from a trained professional.*

The monitoring strategy you define must define the amount and kind of information you need to detect a particular issue. For example, if you collect too much information, it becomes hard to parse and you may actually bypass needed information because there's simply too much of it. Getting the right type of information is also important. Unless you want to store every packet that a network transmits, you need to provide a filter that detects specific packets. Any time you apply a filter, you could miss out on essential information. Information overload is a constant threat to good monitoring, as is information underload.

Developing a plan for determining how much to monitor is also useful. If you plan to monitor users' after-hours activities, then you don't want to include regular daytime activities in the database. Of course, limiting the information to after-hours activities means creating another kind of filter that may not provide everything you need. Filters tend to be precise mechanisms in a world of gray.

Always remember that the computer gathers data, but it doesn't make conclusions. Only a flawed human can come to a conclusion about the data and the conclusion is often flawed as well. It's always best to include a double-check or two as part of your monitoring strategy.

Implementing Logging

Logging is used for a number of purposes with applications. For example, when an application experiences difficulty in performing a task and normal debugging techniques are ineffective at showing the source of the problem, developers often resort to logging everything the application is doing. Yes, the logging slows down the application immensely, but the developer usually ends up with the information needed to troubleshoot the problem. Likewise, you can use logging for security purposes. You may suspect that the user is performing an application task in a manner that exposes the application, the user's system, or the entire network to potential harm. Asking some users about the issue won't result in a truthful response because the user normally has job safety or other concerns. The only method to detect and track the problem when this situation occurs is to log user activity and possibly application activity as well.

Never confuse application logging with employee monitoring. Application logging is an extremely selective tool designed to work only with one application. Employee monitoring usually requires a third-party tool such as 007 Spy Software (`http://www.e-spy-software.com/`) or KeyGhost (`http://www.keyghost.com/`). When you perform such invasive levels of monitoring, you have to consider the potential legal ramifications of doing so. For example, KeyGhost even provides a disclaimer about such activity (`http://www.keyghost.com/disclaimer.htm`). There are many legal opinions (such as `http://membersonly.amamember.org/hr/2001/3016.cfm` — you may need to sign on to use this Web site) on this topic and since I'm not a lawyer, I refer you to any of the numerous legal Web sites that discuss the issue.

The technique you use for logging user or application events depends on how you plan to use the information. For example, you may simply rely on a local log for the task if the user isn't suspected of illegal activity. In this case, you could simply rely on methods such as XML serialization (see Chapter 22) to get the job done. You could also rely on the event log (see the "Using the Event Log" section of the chapter) or messages sent directly to the administrator (see the "Sending Administrator Alerts" section of the chapter) when the situation requires.

If you plan to use the logging in a generalized way, you might want to send the reports to a central database instead. For example, you could set up a SQL Server database that not only monitors the application for security reasons but also as a means to discover usage patterns. You may find out that users never use a particular feature. Having this information in hand during the next application update can simplify the user interface and make the application easier to use. The point is that application monitoring helps you discover more about the application and look for potential misuses of application features so that you can improve the application later. Here are some events you may want to monitor:

- Feature selections (such as menu options)
- File usage

- Task completion scenarios (the keystrokes a user relies on to complete a task)
- Workflows (the order in which users normally access features)
- Connections made and broken
- Local versus remote resource usage
- Precise user entries for a given field

Using the Event Log

One of the features that developers come to appreciate about Server Explorer (press Ctrl+Alt+S if you don't see it) is that it helps you categorize information. You drill down to the information you need, but ignore everything else. For example, when you open the Application Event Log, you need to connect to the remote server, locate the log, and then search through the list of messages for the particular message you need. Server Explorer categorizes event messages by type, so all you see is the message you want.

If you want to build a quick application to monitor just certain types of messages, all you need to do is drag the requisite folder to a form and add some quick code to monitor it. Listing 7-4 shows a short example of how you could use this feature in an application.

Listing 7-4: Creating and reading event log entries

```
private void ApplicationEvents_EntryWritten(object sender, EntryWrittenEventArgs e)
{
   // Respond to the entry written event.
   MessageBox.Show("The Application Generated an Event!" +
                   "\r\nType:\t\t" + e.Entry.EntryType.ToString() +
                   "\r\nCategory:\t" + e.Entry.Category.ToString() +
                   "\r\nEvent ID:\t\t" + e.Entry.InstanceId.ToString() +
                   "\r\nSource:\t\t" + e.Entry.Source.ToString() +
                   "\r\nMessage:\t\t" + e.Entry.Message.ToString() +
                   "\r\nTime Created:\t" +
                   e.Entry.TimeGenerated.ToString(),
                   "Application Event",
                   MessageBoxButtons.OK,
                   MessageBoxIcon.Information);
}

private void btnCreateEvent_Click(object sender, EventArgs e)
{
   // Create an event entry.
   ApplicationEvents.WriteEntry("This is a test message",
                                EventLogEntryType.Information,
                                1001,
                                1);
}
```

You could place such code in a Taskbar Tray (Notification Area) application. The application will continuously monitor the event log in the background and let you know if something happens. This particular feature is even good for debugging, because many server-side controls only log errors in the event logs.

The Event Log entry created by dragging the Event Log from the Server Explorer will have a default configuration. The `EnableRaisingEvents` property will enable your application to detect changes to the log and notify you. However, this feature only works on the local machine. If you want to monitor events on a remote machine, your application will have to perform some form of polling or use a remote component (agent) that connects to your local application.

> *Older versions of the .NET Framework relied on the* `e.Entry.EventId` *property to obtain the event identifier. Microsoft has changed how the event log works in newer versions of Windows. In order to interact with these newer versions of Windows, you must use the* `e.Entry.InstanceId` *property instead.*

Before you can use this application, you must set the `ApplicationEvents` object `Source` property to reflect the name of the application (using the Event Log for the example). In addition, you must add the following code:

```
using System.Diagnostics;
```

Sending Administrator Alerts

Just as you might use the event log to record events that the administrator can see later, sometimes you need to send the administrator an e-mail or other alert to handle a problem immediately. For example, a user's entering the wrong data in a field a few times is something that can probably wait until later. Someone purposely trying to overcome application security in order to gain access to your data probably can't wait — you need to handle it now.

The .NET Framework does support sending e-mail through the features found in the `System.Net.Mail` namespace. You'll probably have to work with precise setup for a while to obtain the desired results. Listing 7-5 shows a sample of what you'll likely need to provide in order to send the administrator an alert using e-mail. The same technique works with other communication methods, but you need to adapt it to the transmission technique you want to use.

Listing 7-5: Sending e-mail to the administrator

```
private void btnSendEmail_Click(object sender, EventArgs e)
{
    // Define the mail message.
    MailMessage NewMail = new MailMessage();

    // Get the required arguments.
    NewMail.From = new MailAddress(txtFrom.Text);
    NewMail.To.Add(new MailAddress(txtTo.Text));
    NewMail.Subject = txtSubject.Text;
    NewMail.Body = txtMessage.Text;

    // Create the SMTP client.
    SmtpClient Client = new SmtpClient();
```

```
        // Define the SMTP host.
        Client.Host = "YourHostAddress";

        // Supply the user credentials.
        CredentialCache MailboxAccess = new CredentialCache();
        MailboxAccess.Add("YourHostAddress", 25,
                          "NTLM",
                          new NetworkCredential(
                             "YouEmailName", "YourPassword"));
        Client.Credentials = MailboxAccess;

        // Send the message.
        Client.Send(NewMail);
    }
```

You create a message in code much as you create a message using Outlook or some other e-mail program. The first step is to define all the message requirements such as sender, recipient, subject, and message body. After you create the message, define an `SmtpClient` object. The tricky part is defining the credential you need — different e-mail applications have different requirements. Once you have a client ready to use, send the e-mail using the `Send()` method. You must add the following code to make this example work:

```
using System.Net;
using System.Net.Mail;
```

Using a Team Overview

It may surprise you to learn that the security experts have the right idea. Part of your application should include break-in testing by members of your team. Obviously, you don't want the person who wrote the code testing it. Make sure team members test each other's code by attempting to do things that the coder never considered part of the standard application process.

Perform a code review as well. Ask team members to break into groups who look at each other's code and check it for potential security problems. The peer review process isn't an attack — it's a means of assisting the person who wrote the code. After you look at the same piece of code for several hours, it's very easy to overlook a potential security hole. Someone looking at your code with fresh eyes may see a problem quickly and help you fix it long before the code goes on the test server.

One potential problem with peer checks is when you match two teams of unequal skills. For example, if Team A writes code that accesses a DLL using P/Invoke and Team B doesn't have someone skilled in working with P/Invoke, Team B could easily miss potential security threats in the Team A code. Consequently, successful peer checks often rely on teams with equal skill levels, which means having two developers with each skill set required to develop the application. Having two developers also tends to reduce the risk associated with one developer's leaving the company and not having a replacement for that developer.

The hand checks you perform are important. You can't easily replace the hand checks, because only you know your code well enough to find something truly terrifying in it. However, you need to combine the hand checks with some level of automation or you might never finish your project. In addition, the automated tools on the market tend to check common threats against your software, making it more likely that you'll find a potential hole that someone is already exploiting. The Web site at `http://searchwindevelopment.techtarget.com/topics/0,295493,sid8_tax302936,00.html` provides a list of helpful aids for testing your application including:

- Security best practices
- Performance management
- Web application security
- Vista security and .NET 3.0
- NET security tools

Another good place to look for security testing information is the Microsoft Web site at `http://www.microsoft.com/learning/en/us/exams/70-340.mspx`. The exam described on this Web page shows what Microsoft is looking for as knowledge in developers. This information is helpful in deciding precisely what you need to look for in team members that you want to use as part of the testing effort.

It's important to look at all potential testing software when working with your application. For example, if you're working with a Web-based application, you have a much wider selection of tools from which to choose. In fact, using a tool such as IBM Rational AppScan (`http://www-01.ibm.com/common/ssi/cgi-bin/ssialias?infotype=AN&subtype=CA&htmlfid=897/ENUS207-254`) may give you an entirely different perspective on your application, which is always good when it comes to security. Desktop application testers can find a handy list of 15 security testing tools at `http://searchenterprisedesktop.techtarget.com/generic/0,295582,sid192_gci1162879,00.html`. The point is not to limit yourself to a specific set of tools. Security depends on adapting to what the bad guys are doing outside your network and inside your organization, and using a variety of tools helps reduce the risk of missing something important.

Developing Your Design Strategy

You've probably heard many views of security during your time as a developer. Security is a topic that receives the most press because it's the concern that seems to occupy most people's minds. The common line of thought seems to be that if you can build a high enough wall, then your application will remain secure. The fact that the security experts have never run out of exploits to publicize should tell you the silliness of trying to attain this goal. Rather, this chapter points out the need to use a balanced approach to security — one in which the application does deny access, but not to the point of creating an unbalanced application. Of course, every development team has a different view of this extremely volatile topic. Make sure the approach you take also complies with security policy and the environment in which the application runs — keep thinking about managed risk as you work through your own application design.

It's time to consider the security requirements for your own application. Let's hope this chapter has provided some thoughtful advice for creating a balanced application. Make sure you also review the concepts in Chapters 5 and 6 as part of the design for your application. Creating an application that performs well means considering speed, reliability, and security concerns as these apply to your application. You should include some security facets in any application. For example, it's always a good idea to monitor and limit user input. Any application can benefit from correct input, and any user can benefit from input that's easy to provide. The concepts go hand in hand when you use a well-considered security approach.

Chapter 8 moves in a new direction. This part of the book moves from designing your application to working with Visual Studio. In Chapter 8, you'll review the Integrated Development Environment (IDE) and may discover a few new techniques for making your coding experience both better and more efficient. Some developers rely on Microsoft to manage their IDE by not changing the default Visual Studio settings. Using the techniques in Chapter 8, you'll discover ways to make Visual Studio your programming environment, rather than simply something that Microsoft offered to you.

Part II: Coding Strategies

8

Customizing the IDE

If you're using the Visual Studio Integrated Development Environment (IDE) precisely as it came out of the shrink-wrap, you're missing an opportunity to work faster and smarter. Most developers find that they like some features that Microsoft configures for them, but there are also a lot of things they'd like to change. You may not like the colors that Microsoft uses, or the font size may be too small. These seem like minor issues, but you can literally configure every aspect of the Visual Studio IDE to make it easier and better to use. The Visual Studio IDE provides significant flexibility so that you can configure it any way that you see fit. It's possible to change the position of windows, remove windows as needed, and modify the toolbars. In short, you can make the Visual Studio IDE over into whatever you think it should look like.

Although good IDE modifications are extremely helpful in making you efficient and more productive, using snippets, macros, and add-ins can help even more. Snippets are bits of code that you store away for future use. Rather than having to hunt for that piece of code you used in another application, you now have it at your fingertips. Macros are mini-programs you use to perform repetitive tasks at the touch of a button. For example, many developers begin a programming session by performing the same setup each time. Rather than repeat yourself like a broken record, you can tell Visual Studio to make the changes for you. Finally, third parties are always looking for ways to cash in on Microsoft's success. Third-party add-ins can help you perform tasks faster and with greater ease.

You may think you have to start that big hulking IDE every time you want to perform the smallest task, but Visual Studio also provides significant functionality at the command line. Using the command line is often easier than working with the IDE, because you don't have to hunt for the commands you need. In addition, you can create batch files to perform custom compilations as needed. The command line even provides the means to execute tasks, as if you're using the IDE by remote control.

Configuring the IDE

Immediately after you install Visual Studio, you should begin configuring the IDE. Most people instantly see some items that don't look the way they expect — first impressions are important. Rather than allow the IDE to change the way you work, force the IDE to change. After all, the Visual Studio IDE offers a significant amount of configuration flexibility, so you should use it to make things work as you originally anticipated. If you don't want to see the Build toolbar because you prefer to use the menu commands, get rid of it. Keeping an extra toolbar around when you could use that screen real estate for some other purpose can be downright frustrating. The following sections provide you with a wealth of suggestions for modifying your IDE to meet your needs.

Using the Visual Studio Options

The first place to look for potential changes is the Options dialog box that you access using the Tools ➪ Options command. Figure 8-1 shows a typical view of the Options dialog box. In many cases, it pays to start at the top and work your way down the first time you use the IDE, if for no other reason than becoming familiar with the settings you can change.

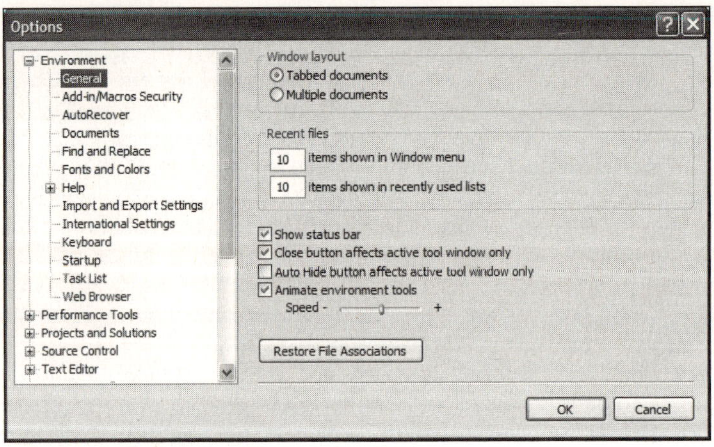

Figure 8-1: The Options dialog box provides a wealth of options you can change.

The appearance of the Options dialog box can change depending on how you install Visual Studio. If you choose the General Development Settings options during installation, your display will look similar to Figure 8-1. However, if you use another setting, such as Web Development Settings, then you may not see all the features shown in Figure 8-1. In this case, check the Show All Settings option to see the full list of settings. The number of options can also vary by the number of third-party products you install and whether you have a full-fledged version of SQL Server installed (among other things). Consequently, Figure 8-1 is more a view of how the Options dialog box generally appears, rather that how it specifically appears. You may also find that other features described in this chapter don't appear on your system due to your installation choices or the version of Visual Studio you own.

Visual Studio breaks the options into groups so that you can find the option you need faster. Here's a quick listing of each of the option groups:

- **Environment:** The Environment folder contains all the settings that affect how you interact with the Visual Studio IDE itself. This is where you go to change the frequency with which Visual Studio saves autorecovery information for your project. This is also the place you change one of my favorite settings — fonts and colors. Many developers prefer larger fonts than Microsoft seems to think they need. Users with color blindness or simply a desire for different colors can adjust the colors to suit their needs. Unfortunately, the Web Browser folder doesn't let you choose an alternative browser — you're stuck with Internet Explorer.
- **Performance Tools:** This folder contains settings that adjust how Visual Studio presents performance information. For example, you can choose between displaying the information using clock ticks or milliseconds.
- **Projects and Solutions:** Use the settings in the Projects and Solutions folder to modify the location of your projects, project templates, and item templates. You can also adjust how Visual Studio reacts to issues such as errors when you compile your application. The Build and Run subfolder defines what happens when you build a project and when you click Run without rebuilding your application first. The folder also contains some special settings for Visual Basic.NET and C++ developers.
- **Source Control:** This folder is a placeholder in a default setting — your source control solution will add settings to this folder.
- **Text Editor:** The Text Editor folder is one of the folders that you should always visit when you first install Visual Studio. The general settings let you change things such as whether to use drag and drop, and if the IDE tracks changes you make. The File Extension subfolder is especially handy because it lets you assign nonstandard file extensions to a particular editor and define an editing experience for that extension. Make sure you understand the difference between the All Languages folder and the language-specific folders. The All Languages folder contains settings that you can apply to all languages to provide a consistent editing experience. The language-specific subfolders override the All Languages settings and provide you with a language-specific editing experience. Consequently, if you want tabs to work the same way in all languages, you make a change to the All Languages/Tabs settings, rather than the language-specific settings.
- **Business Intelligence Designers:** This folder only shows up when you have SQL Server installed. The settings affect the Analysis Services Designers and Integration Services Designers configuration. You use these settings to change everything from the colors used in charts to the way automatic connections work.
- **Database Tools:** The entries in the Database Tools folder mainly affect SQL Server usage when working with a default installation. For example, you can choose the default SQL Server instance that you want to use for your application. Some options do affect any database with which you work. The Table and Database Designers subfolder contains settings that affect any database you use as a data source. It's possible to modify these settings to control properties such as the default size of column based on data type. Make sure you check out the Table Options settings because Microsoft doesn't check some items by default — Visual Studio won't warn you about null values in primary keys unless you check the Warn on Null Primary Keys option.
- **Debugging:** As you might imagine, the Debugging folder contains a wealth of entries, many of which are personal choice settings or options you choose based on a particular kind of application. Personal settings include features such as asking whether you want Visual Studio to ask

before it deletes all the break points in an application. The application type choices include loading DLL exports when working with a native-code module — an important feature for some types of P/Invoke applications.

- **Device Tools:** Many developers work with devices other than a PC today. The Device Tools folder contains settings that control how you interact with other devices — mainly device emulators because that's how most developers create applications for other devices. The default setup includes device emulators for the Pocket PC, Smartphone, Windows CE Device, and Windows Mobile devices, among others. You can obtain additional emulators at locations such as `http://www.microsoft.com/downloads/details.aspx?familyid=a6f6adaf-12e3-4b2f-a394-356e2c2fb114`, which provides you with a Tablet PC emulation. This folder also contains general settings, such as whether you want to display the skins associated with a particular emulation. A *skin* is a graphic representation of how the particular device will appear to the user.
- **HTML Designer:** The HTML Designer folder settings come into play only when you're working on Web applications. The general settings include personal decisions such as whether you want to start in Source view, Design view, or a split view of both Source view and Design view. This folder also lets you configure Cascading Style Sheet (CSS) support and visual elements such as the ruler and grid units. Most important is the View subfolder, which contains color settings for the various design elements, such as master pages and layout elements.
- **Office Tools:** The Office Tools folder settings come into play only when you create an Office application. The subfolders contain specific settings for Excel, Word, InfoPath, and Project. For the most part, these settings affect how Visual Studio handles the keyboard. For example, when configuring Excel, you have a choice of always using the Visual Studio keyboard, or you can switch between the Excel and Visual Studio keyboard layouts depending on which application has focus at the time.
- **Test Tools:** Visual Studio makes it easy to test your applications using a Test project. You create a Test project the same way you do any other project — using the New Project dialog box. For example, if you want to create a Test project for your C# application, you look in the `Visual C#\Test` folder. The Test Tools folder contains settings for configuring a Test project. The Test Project folder determines which elements Visual Studio automatically adds to a Test project, such as a Load Test or a Unit Test. You can also configure Visual Studio's response when specific test conditions occur and how you want to run the tests.
- **Text Templating:** You use *text templating* to generate code automatically based on the content of a text file. The full name for this Visual Studio 2008 feature is the Text Template Transformation Toolkit (T4). The default installation provides just one setting for this feature, the ability to turn the security message on or off as needed. Microsoft provides a wealth of information about T4 at `http://msdn.microsoft.com/en-us/library/bb126445.aspx`. However, Microsoft's support for T4 is weak at best. You'll probably want to obtain a third-party editor such as the Clarius editor font at `http://www.t4editor.net/`. Visual Studio 2005 developers can theoretically obtain this functionality with the Guidance Automation Toolkit (GAT) found at `http://msdn.microsoft.com/en-us/vsts2008/aa718948.aspx`. If you're really interested in T4, you'll want to check out the introductory article at `http://www.olegsych.com/2007/12/text-template-transformation-toolkit/` and the debugging tutorial at `http://blogs.msdn.com/garethj/archive/2006/01/09/t4debugging.aspx`.
- **Windows Forms Designer:** The Windows Forms Designer folder contains settings that control how this designer works. The settings control essentially two levels of the designer. First, you can control the physical appearance of the designer, such as the size of the grid used to

position controls on screen. Second, you can control how Visual Studio incorporates data user interface customization, which makes it easier for you to configure controls on screen. You can add your custom controls to the list (see the article at `http://msdn.microsoft.com/en-us/library/5554bf3a.aspx` for details).

- **Workflow Designer:** This folder contains a list of themes used to configure the workflows you create using Visual Studio. A theme can include background and foreground colors, styles, icons, and other elements normally associated with a theme. The default themes include one for Microsoft's custom workflow theme and a second for the operating system based on the user's current color selections.

This list covers just the standard option folders you see in the Options dialog box. Many third-party add-ins also create folders. Consequently, when you install a new add-in, you should check the Options dialog box to determine whether the add-in provides you with additional settings. Make sure you configure the add-in immediately so that the add-in also meets your needs.

This list provides you with only a glimpse of the features you can configure, but as you can see, that list is impressive. The important thing to remember for these settings is that there isn't a precise right or wrong to most of them. In most cases, you configure the settings to meet your particular tastes and needs. If you find that a particular setting isn't working for you as a developer, feel free to experiment a little. The worst thing you can do is assume that things are supposed to feel a bit uncomfortable at the outset and then "get used to" the setting that you feel Microsoft thinks is best. Even Microsoft wants you to change these settings — the company merely chose the setting that seemed to work best for the majority of their developers in most cases.

Customizing the Toolbars and Menus

As with the Visual Studio options, the toolbar and menu configuration isn't set in stone. You should feel free to change any of the toolbars or menus that Microsoft provides, or better yet, create your own toolbars or menus to meet specific needs. The point is, if you feel that the Visual Studio IDE is too difficult to work with as is, change it to meet your specific needs. You can literally remove or add any feature you want for either toolbars or menus. The following sections describe how to work with both menus and toolbars in Visual Studio.

I generally recommend adding changes to custom toolbars and menus. You can always hide a toolbar that you don't want to work with (removing a main menu item means rebuilding the menu from scratch or resetting all your changes later, so you don't want to remove a main menu without a lot of thought). However, when you receive instructions for performing a task from Microsoft or a third party, they'll assume that you have the standard toolbar and menu setup to work with. If you have changed the defaults, then you'll find it considerably harder to follow any directions that someone has given you to work with.

Working with Toolbars

Toolbars are easier to rebuild than menus. In many cases, toolbars are also faster from a usage perspective, so you'll want to modify a toolbar when you can, rather than work with the menus. Figure 8-2 shows all the standard toolbars that come with Visual Studio. Many of these toolbars appear automatically, depending on the task you're performing. For example, the Debug toolbar automatically appears when you debug an application. However, if you want to see the Debug Location toolbar, you must add it manually. To add a toolbar to the IDE, simply right-click in the toolbar area and check the toolbar you want to see. If you want to remove the toolbar, simply remove the checkbox next to its entry in the context menu.

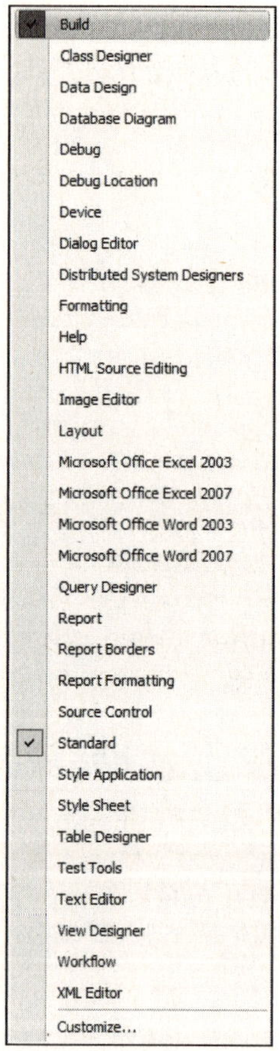

Figure 8-2: Visual Studio provides a number of standard toolbars.

Notice the Customize option at the bottom of the list shown in Figure 8-3. Selecting this option displays the Customize dialog box where you can choose the toolbars you want to use from a list. If you make a mistake on configuring a particular standard toolbar, you can highlight the toolbar in the list and click Reset, which changes the toolbar back to its default state. The Reset button isn't available for your custom toolbars because a custom toolbar doesn't have a default state — it contains whatever you choose to put there.

To add a new toolbar, simply click New, type a name for your toolbar in the New Toolbar dialog box, and click OK. At this point, you can begin customizing the toolbar to meet your needs. Microsoft doesn't allow you to change the names of standard toolbars. However, if you want to change the name of a custom toolbar, you select its entry in the list and click Rename. You'll see a Rename Toolbar dialog box where you can type the new name for the toolbar. Likewise, you can't delete any of the standard toolbars, but highlighting a custom toolbar and clicking Delete will remove it.

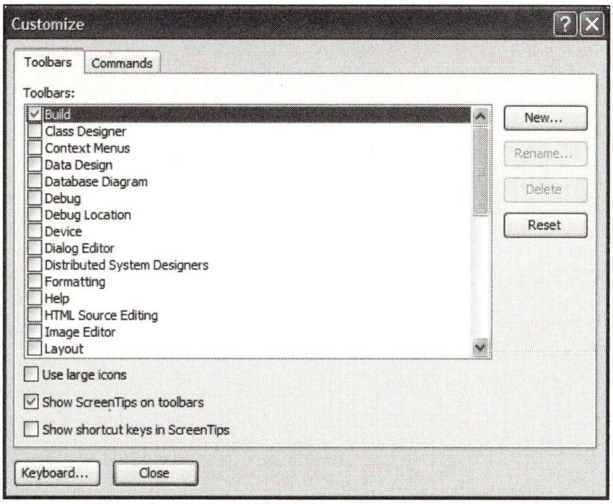

Figure 8-3: Use the Toolbars tab to modify how the standard toolbars work and to create new custom toolbars.

Notice that the Toolbars tab has three options you can select. Check Use Large Icons if you have a problem seeing the default icons that Microsoft provides. The Show ScreenTips on Toolbars (tooltips) option is checked by default — hovering the mouse over a control displays that control's function. If you're a big user of shortcut keys, as I am, then you'll want to check Show Shortcut Keys in ScreenTips as well, because you can discover the shortcut key while you're learning the use for the particular control.

The Commands tab shown in Figure 8-4 lets you add new buttons to your toolbars and menus. Simply locate the category of command you want to add and you'll see a list of commands associated with that category in the right window. Drag the command you want to add from the Commands list onto either the menu or toolbar. Visual Studio will display the new option for you. Of course, the new command will use whatever configuration Microsoft has chosen for it. To change the configuration (such as displaying text, an icon, or both text and an icon), select the new control, click the Modify Selection button (a list of configuration options will appear), and choose configuration options you want to use.

In most cases, you want to add an existing command from a menu to a toolbar. Locate the main menu command that you want to work with, such as File, and the particular option on that menu to add that command to the toolbar. Of course, there's nothing to stop you from adding commands from any other category in the list. Commands that have a default icon associated with them will display that icon to the left of the command text. You can also draw custom icons or choose an icon from the Change Button Image list as needed for commands that don't have a default icon.

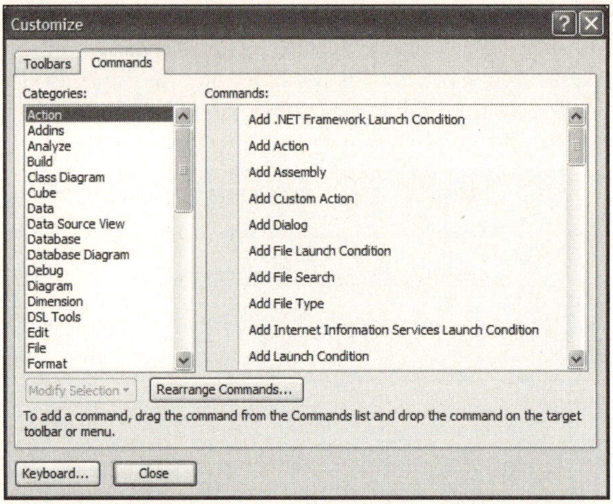

Figure 8-4: The Commands tab provides the means for placing commands on a standard or custom toolbar.

If you're a touch typist, taking your hands off the keyboard to mouse about can be a time-wasting experience. The best way around this problem is to associate a keyboard shortcut with the command you've created. When you click Keyboard on the Commands tab of the Customize dialog box, you see the `Environment\Keyboard` folder of the Options dialog box. To add a shortcut, select the command you want to modify in the Show Commands Containing field, select the scope of the keyboard shortcut in the Use New Shortcut In field, press the keyboard shortcut you want to use in the Press Shortcut Keys field, and click Assign. It's a straightforward process to make the association.

Working with Menus

As previously mentioned, working with menus in Visual Studio is considerably more difficult than working with toolbars. Adding and removing commands is just as easy, but some other tasks aren't nearly as easy. For example, to hide a menu entry, you actually have to delete it. Of course, deleting a menu presents a problem if you want to restore it later. For example, you could possibly delete the File menu accidentally. The following steps tell the easiest way to restore a missing standard menu:

1. Right-click in the toolbar area and choose Customize from the context menu shown in Figure 8-2. You'll see the Customize dialog box shown in Figure 8-3.
2. Select the Commands tab shown in Figure 8-4.
3. Click Rearrange Commands. You'll see the Rearrange Commands dialog box shown in Figure 8-5.
4. Choose the Toolbar option and select Menu Bar. Click Reset and Visual Studio will completely restore your menus. Unfortunately, you'll also lose any changes you may have made earlier. This is an example of the sledgehammer-used-to-swat-a-fly mentality of the menu system in Visual Studio, which is why I prefer to make changes to toolbars where they're easily changed.

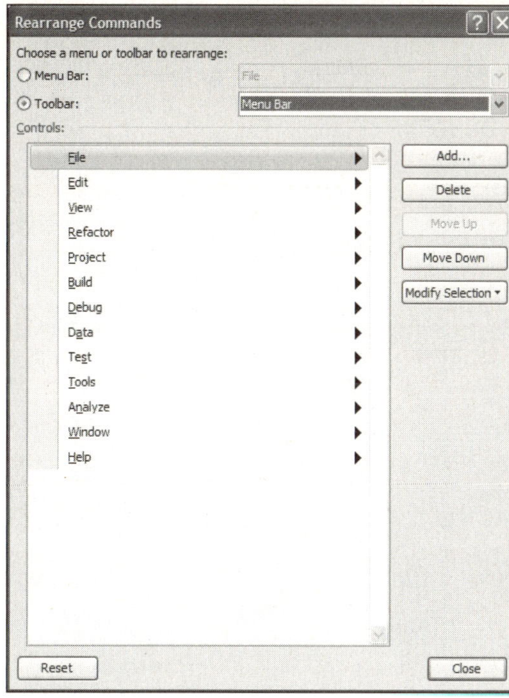

Figure 8-5: You may not think of certain tasks associated with this dialog box as rearranging anything.

Of course, you can always rebuild the missing menu by hand. To perform this task, you start in the Rearrange Commands dialog box as shown in Figure 8-5. However, instead of clicking Reset, you click Add. Locate the New Menu entry and click OK. Now you need to configure the new menu entry to match the missing menu entry. Use the drag-and-drop method to add the commands back onto the new menu entry. Although this technique does preserve any changes you made to the menu system, it's time consuming for larger menus and there's a high risk of not getting some of the configuration options correct, which means that you'll still face some compatibility issues. In short, deleting a standard menu is a very bad idea.

If you insist on using the menu system, you can use the technique described in the previous paragraph to add a completely new menu. You can then fill this custom menu with any commands you want. If you get tired of the menu later, you can simply delete it.

Microsoft makes it insanely easy to delete menus. All you have to do is go into customize mode (with the Customize dialog box showing) and drag the menu entry off the menu bar. Visual Studio gives you no notice at all that you're going to remove a menu — it's simply gone.

Adding External Tools

You can add any external tool you want to the Tools menu. For example, I always add the Registry Editor to my list of tools because I sometimes need to see how my application changes the registry during use. In fact, Microsoft provides connections to some external tools in the default Visual Studio configuration as shown in Figure 8-6. If you get the idea that the field entries work just like a Windows shortcut, you're right. You provide a title for the external tool, the executable location, any command line arguments the tool requires, and the initial directory for the tool (usually a data directory). The only entries you must provide are the Title and Command fields.

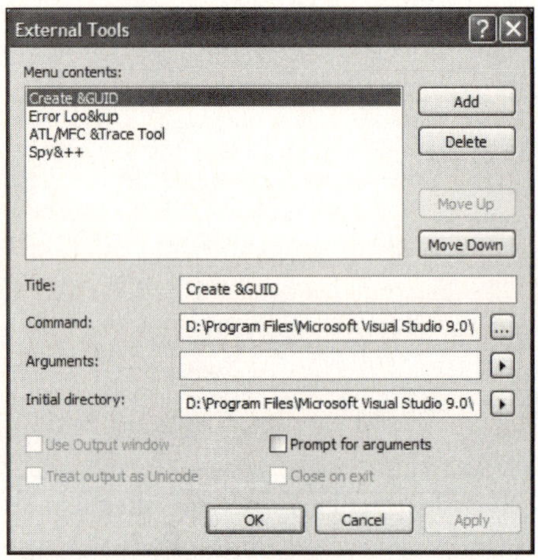

Figure 8-6: Add any custom commands you want to the Tools menu.

The commands you provide need not be graphical in nature. For example, let's say you want to add a command for seeing the directory tree of your application. Solution Explorer doesn't always provide the whole story, so you add a special directory command. Figure 8-7 shows an example of how you might configure such a tool. Begin by clicking Add, and then add all the entries shown. When you click OK, the command becomes part of your application arsenal.

This command requires a little explanation. The `Dir` command is part of `Cmd.EXE`; it's not a freestanding command. Consequently, you must start a copy of the command processor before you can use `Dir`. Now look at the Arguments field. The `/C` tells `Cmd.EXE` to execute a command and then exit. `Dir` is the command that you want to execute; you want to list all of the files starting in the project directory (selectable using the right-facing arrow), and you want to find all of the files in all subdirectories (the `/s` command line switch). The command starts in the project directory, so that's what you select in the Initial Directory field.

Now, you could open a command prompt to view the output, but why bother when you can use the Output window simply by selecting Use Output Window. Because you won't need the command any longer, you can also check Close On Exit. If you want to add some additional `Dir` or `Cmd.EXE` arguments, you can check Prompt for Arguments. It's possible to generalize this command simply by providing command line arguments every time you use it, but the specific command shown is significantly easier to use.

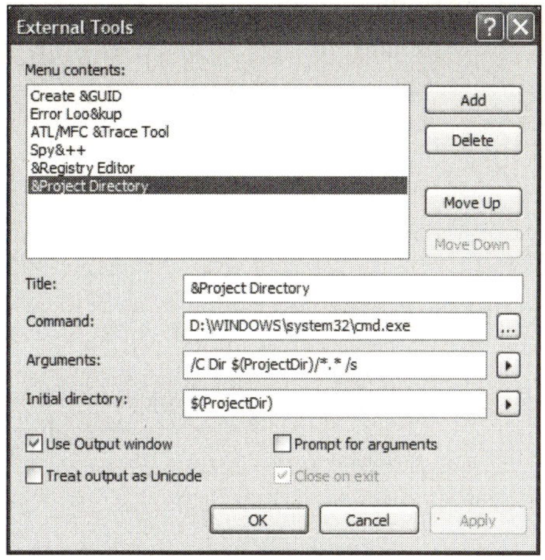

Figure 8-7: Use the command processor to access internal commands.

Using Snippets, Macros, and Add-ins

This section of the chapter describes three productivity enhancers: snippets, macros, and add-ins. It's amazing to discover that many developers don't use them and a few haven't even heard of them — and these three items can save you a huge amount of time. Here's how the three productivity enhancers differ:

- **Snippet:** A snippet is a piece of code that you use regularly. For example, when creating a console application, you may rely on a particular piece of code to determine whether the application is in a release or debug state. Because the console window normally closes immediately, you can use code within a define block to add a pause to the screen. Now, when you debug the application, the screen stays in place so you can see how the screen looks. This kind of code is too short to place in a library — really, it's something you'd add to an application as needed. Consequently, it's a perfect candidate for a snippet.

- **Macro:** Visual Studio has its own macro language. The macros perform tasks that you normally perform by hand, such as choosing the File ➪ Open command. By stringing commands together, you can create a kind of application to make creating applications faster, easier, and more consistent (since the macro will perform the steps in precisely the same order every time). Of course, you want to use macros only for tasks that you perform often enough to pay back the time used to create the macro.

- **Add-in:** An add-in is an external application designed to work with Visual Studio and enhance its capabilities. Microsoft encourages third parties to create add-ins. In fact, you'll find a number of articles on Microsoft Developer Network (MSDN) such as the one found at `http://msdn.microsoft.com/en-us/magazine/cc300778.aspx` that tell you all about add-ins. In most cases, an add-in is a feature that didn't attract enough attention for Microsoft to add it to Visual Studio, but does provide enough functionality that a group of developers wants it. In addition to the material in this chapter, you'll also want to view the chapters in Part V of the book to gain an understanding of how helpful add-ins can be in specific situations.

Avoid pack rat syndrome. A snippet, macro, or add-in is only useful as long as you use it. Once you stop using it, you should remove it from your system. Otherwise, Visual Studio is encumbered with additions that don't help you and slow it down. Eventually, the load becomes so great that Visual Studio stops working as it should and you get frustrated with Visual Studio as a result.

Now that you have a more formal definition of snippets, macros, and add-ins, it's time to discuss them in detail. The following sections show how to work with each category of enhancement.

Creating and Using Code Snippets

Visual Studio comes with a number of code snippets that you can use to enhance your productivity. The problem is that many developers aren't aware of them. Code snippets are a great productivity feature that Microsoft doesn't appear to promote heavily, but it should, because using snippets can also reduce programmer error by automating some coding tasks.

Using a code snippet is easy; simply right-click where you want to insert the snippet in the code editor. You'll see a context menu like the one shown in Figure 8-8. The context menu contains two code snippet options. The first option, highlighted in the screenshot, inserts a snippet at the position you selected. This first option lets you add something completely new to the application, such as a new region, an Excel control, or a workflow. The second option, immediately below the highlighted option, surrounds the code you highlight with a code snippet. You use this second option when you want to place existing code within a structure, such as an `if` statement. Both options work in a similar manner, but the second option is limited to structures that can hold other code.

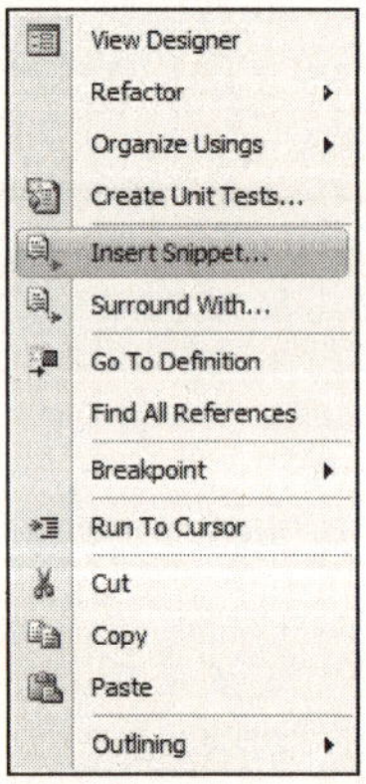

Figure 8-8: Two code snippet options appear on the context menu.

After you choose Insert Snippet, you see a list of snippet categories that includes NetFX30, Office Development, Other, and Visual C# for a default installation. You can add your own snippet categories, and third-party products may also add categories that you can use. Choose a category, such as Visual C#, and you'll see a list of snippets as shown in Figure 8-9. Select the snippet you want to use from the list and the IDE will automatically insert the code snippet for you.

Code snippets are actually a kind of XML file. The articles at `http://msdn.microsoft.com/en-us/library/ms165393(VS.80).aspx` show you how easy it can be to create your own code snippets. Normally, you place your custom code snippets into the `\Documents and Settings\<Your Name>\My Documents\Visual Studio 2008\Code Snippets\Visual C#\My Code Snippets` folder of your machine.

Developers should be aware of an important limitation in using code snippets with C#. The Visual Basic.NET version of a code snippet provides a references section that automatically adds the references required to use the code generated by the code snippet. The C# version doesn't allow the references section, so you must add the references manually. I suggest adding a comment to your C# code snippet to remind the developer to add the required references. This is especially important when the code relies on a reference that doesn't normally appear as part of the project.

You can also manage the code snippets supplied to your application. Simply open the Code Snippets Manager by choosing Tools ➪ Code Snippets Manager or by pressing Ctrl+K, Ctrl+B. Figure 8-10 shows the Code Snippets Manager where you can add or remove code snippets, import existing code snippets, or search online for new code snippets. When you select a code snippet, you see its descriptive information in the right pane as shown in the figure.

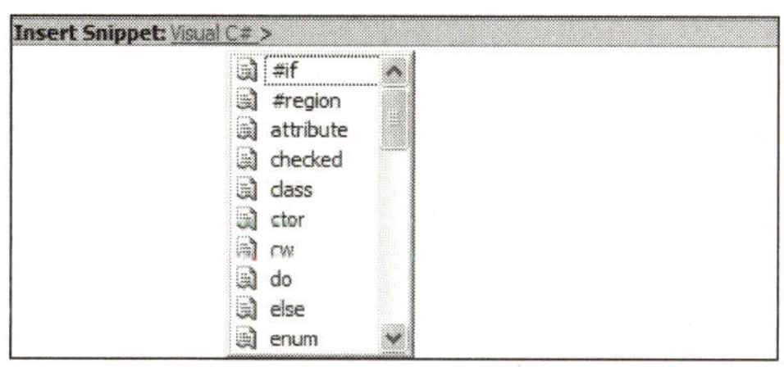

Figure 8-9: Select a snippet to use from the list.

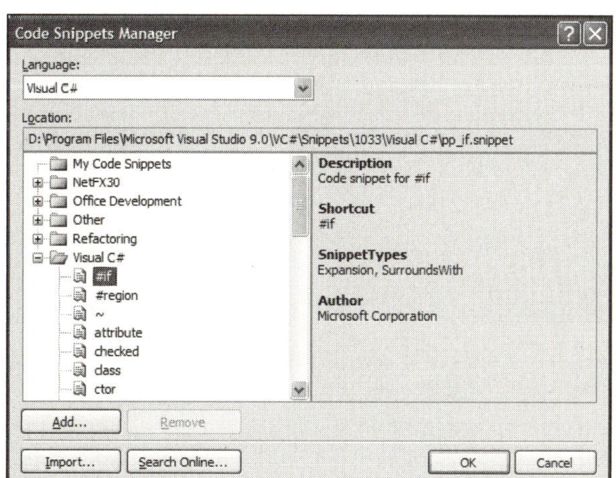

Figure 8-10: Use the Code Snippet Manager to manage your code snippets.

Using Macros to Automate Tasks

Instead of inserting code into your project, macros perform tasks — they repeat keystrokes that you ordinarily perform. Because you use these keystrokes so often, it pays to create a macro to perform them for you. A macro is a kind of mini-application designed specifically for Visual Studio. As with code snippets, Visual Studio comes with a host of predefined macros. You can view these macros by choosing View ➪ Other Windows ➪ Macro Explorer or by pressing Alt+F8. Visual Studio displays the Macro Explorer window shown in Figure 8-11. The Microsoft-supplied macros, such as InsertDate, appear in the Sample folder.

It's relatively easy to record your own macros. Simply press Ctrl+Shift+R to start the macro recorder, perform the task you want to perform, and then press Ctrl+Shift+R again to stop the macro recorder. You'll see a new macro named TemporaryMacro in the Macro Explorer window — the default name given to all new macros. Rename this macro to match its purpose and you're ready to use it as needed.

You can also edit macros as needed to add special programming to them by right-clicking the macro entry in the Macro Explorer window and choosing Edit from the context menu. The same context menu lets you delete, rename, and run the macros as needed. The articles at `http://msdn.microsoft.com/en-us/library/8h31zbch(VS.80).aspx` describe how to perform these additional tasks.

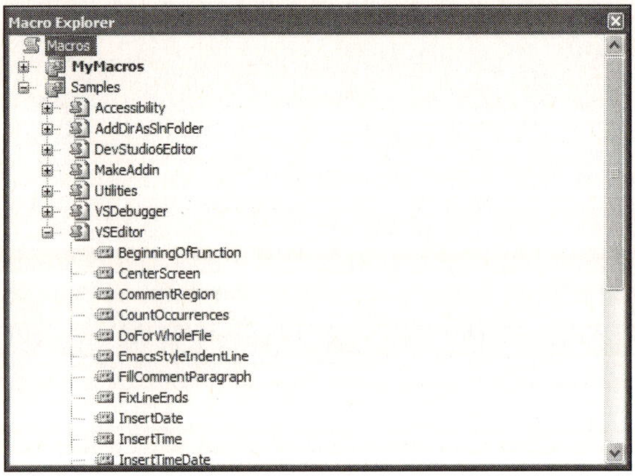

Figure 8-11: The Macro Explorer window displays a list of macros found on your system.

Relying on Add-ins for Extended Functionality

An add-in is the next step in complexity after a macro. While a macro can repeat keystrokes you make and modify the environment in other ways, an add-in actually adds new functionality to the Visual Studio environment. Unlike code snippets and macros, Microsoft doesn't supply any add-ins to you; they're always something you obtain from a third party. You can see if your copy of Visual Studio has any add-ins by opening the Add-in Manager by choosing Tools ➪ Add-in Manager. The article at `http://msdn.microsoft.com/en-us/library/xwdatdwh.aspx` tells you more about managing your add-ins, but you also need to consult the vendor documentation.

At some point, you're going to find a Visual Studio add-in need that no one has addressed yet. Fortunately, creating your own add-in isn't hard. The tutorial at `http://www.c-sharpcorner.com/UploadFile/mgold/AddIns11292005015631AM/AddIns.aspx` provides you with a complete set of instructions. You may also want to look for less-expected add-in resources, such as the visualizer article at `http://www.devsource.com/c/a/Using-VS/Write-Your-Own-Visualizer-for-VS-Debugging/` and `http://www.codeproject.com/KB/macros/dstags.aspx`.

Microsoft also supplies a number of articles on the topic of creating add-ins. Begin your journey with the "How to: Create an Add-In" article at `http://msdn.microsoft.com/en-us/library/80493a3w.aspx`. You'll also want to check out the "Walkthrough: Creating a Wizard" article at `http://msdn.microsoft.com/en-us/library/7k3w6w59.aspx`. Finally, the Creating Add-ins and Wizards Web site at `http://msdn.microsoft.com/en-us/library/5abkeks7.aspx` provides access to a number of helpful add-in resources.

Using the Visual Studio Command Line

Some developers might not even realize that the Visual Studio IDE supports command line switches, but it does. The command line switches can do everything from changing your work environment to compiling your application. One of the benefits of using the command line switches, rather than locating the corresponding feature using the menu system, is that you can automate some tasks. For example, you can compile your application without even displaying the IDE. In many cases, using a command line switch is simply convenient. For example, you can use the command line to load a local Web site directly, rather than waste time drilling down into your hard drive looking for the Web site you want to load.

Accessing the Command Line

You might think that accessing the command line is a simple matter of clicking the Start ➪ Programs ➪ Accessories ➪ Command Prompt shortcut. That shortcut will open a command prompt, but not the right one. This command prompt lacks the required environment variables, especially the path information to Visual Studio. Open a development command line by clicking the Start ➪ Programs ➪ Microsoft Visual Studio 2008 ➪ Visual Studio Tools ➪ Visual Studio 2008 Command Prompt shortcut instead. The command line you see is ready for use in development applications. Of course, you can easily create your own batch files with the required environment variables. Look at the `VCVarsAll.BAT` in the `\Program Files\Microsoft Visual Studio 9.0\VC` folder of your hard drive for an example of how to create such a batch file.

You access the development environment (the IDE) using the `DevEnv` command. If you ever forget the command line switches found in this chapter, you can display a list to refresh your memory by typing **`DevEnv /?`** and pressing Enter at the command line. Generally, you'll find that you can use the command line to open a solution, project, or specific file directly, with or without special environment- or task-related command line switches. Here's the command line syntax for `DevEnv`:

```
DevEnv  [solutionfile | projectfile | anyfile.ext]  [switches]
```

Loading Projects Using a Shortcut

You can load any project by typing `DevEnv`, followed by the solution filename, project filename, or single filename, and pressing Enter. The IDE automatically loads everything required to start the project. Of course, you perform this task quite easily with the IDE. What makes the command line special is that you don't have to search for the project on the hard drive. You create a shortcut that contains everything needed to load the project. Placing these shortcuts on the Desktop makes them fast loading and quite accessible. I usually place my shortcuts in a project folder. That way, no matter where a project is physically located, I can access it easily by double-clicking the entry in the project folder.

To create your own shortcut, begin by right-clicking an open area in the folder where the shortcut will appear and choosing New ➪ Shortcut from the context menu. The Create Shortcut wizard will appear. You must provide three pieces of information in the Type the Location of the Item field, such as, `%comspec% /c "C: \Program Files\Microsoft Visual Studio 9.0\Common7\IDE\DevEnv .EXE" DateTimeVisualizer.sln`.

The first entry, `%comspec%`, creates a command processor. The `/c` command line switch tells the command processor to execute a command and exit. The second entry is the command you want to execute, which is the development environment. Notice that you must place this entry in quotes because it contains spaces. The example shows my configuration; make sure you change it to match your setup. The third entry is the name of the solution, project, or file that you want to open. You could also add any of the command line switches provided in this chapter to the command line.

Once you enter the command line, click Next, and follow the remaining wizard instructions. After you create the shortcut, you must make one additional change. Right-click the new shortcut and choose Properties from the context menu. Type the full path to the solution in the Start In field on the Shortcut tab for the shortcut's properties dialog box. Now, whenever you double-click the shortcut, the project will start.

Understanding the Command Line Switches

The Visual Studio command line switches perform a number of tasks. You can combine the command line switches in any order needed to accomplish your goals. Here's a list of the tasks you can perform and the goals they help you achieve:

- **IDE environment:** Many developers set their environment one time and never change it. However, you may find that one environment works better than another when performing certain tasks. For example, you might want to use a Multiple Document Interface (MDI) environment in some cases (working with complex applications) and not in others (building a utility).
- **Automated compiles:** Depending on the size of your project, you might want to wait to compile it until everyone has gone home for the day. Of course, you might have multiple modules and a complex work environment. Unless you want to work all night getting compilation tasks completed, you should consider another course of action. By combining command line switches with the Task Scheduler, you can create nightly jobs for the development environment while you're at work, during daylight hours. Using this approach, the Task Scheduler ensures that the development environment completes the work while you're at home. Microsoft obviously expects developers to perform many different kinds of application build options because it

provides a number of command line switches for the task. You can even perform deployments after hours using the command line switches that the `DevEnv` command provides.

- **IDE errors:** Have you ever had the IDE suddenly decide not to work? If you experiment with third-party products at all, or build add-ins of your own, you've probably had the experience of not being able to work with the IDE. Some people approach the problem by reinstalling Visual Studio. However, there's a safer, easier, and more effective way to work through IDE problems.

Now that you have some idea of what tasks these command line switches perform, it's time to look at the switches. Table 8-1 contains a complete listing of the command line switches, their task group, and the goal they help you achieve.

Table 8-1: Visual Studio Command Line Switches

Switch	Task Group	Description
`/Build` *`ConfigurationName`*	Automated compiles	Builds the application according to the configuration name you provide. For example, you can use this command line switch to create either a debug or a release build. The development environment doesn't rebuild any existing source code that hasn't changed when you use this option. You must provide a solution name as input with this command line switch.
`/Clean` *`ConfigurationName`*	Automated compiles	Cleans up the object and executable files for an application without compiling it using the specified configuration file settings. This feature is handy when you want to send a project to someone without burdening the person with all the object and executable files as well. The source code is significantly smaller than the resulting executables. You must provide a solution name as input with this command line switch.
`/Deploy` *`ConfigurationName`*	Automated compiles	Deploys an application after the development environment builds or rebuilds it according to the configuration you provide. This feature works very well for team development where you want a group of testers to work with the current build (looking for bugs and usability problems) while your development team continues work on the application code. The source code is significantly smaller than the resulting executables. You must provide a solution name as input with this command line switch.
`/FN` *`FontName`*	IDE environment	Sets the name of the font used to display information on screen. If you perform many database and engineering-type tasks in Visual Studio, you'll find that the ability to change fonts can save your eyes. Sometimes, the font used to write code doesn't work nearly as well for creating a database design.

Continued

Table 8-1: Visual Studio Command Line Switches *(continued)*

Switch	Task Group	Description
`/FS` *`FontSize`*	IDE environment	Sets the size of the font used to display information on screen. If you're like me, those late-night coding sessions can become troublesome when the small font that works fine during the day becomes blurry at night. Using this option lets you upsize your viewing font without fiddling with the menus all of the time.
`/LCID` *`LocalID`* or `/L` *`LocalID`*	IDE environment	Specifies a locale identifier (LCID) for the development environment. This is an excellent option for someone who needs to work with multiple language environments. Using this command line switch, it's easy to change locales as needed during the development process. You can find a list of the common LCIDs at `http://krafft.com/scripts/deluxe-calendar/lcid_chart.htm`.
`/Log` *`Filename`*	Automated compiles	Specifies the name of a log file that receives all development environment activity information. You can use this feature to track IDE usage, check for the execution of macros, or verify that the IDE is working in a specific manner while performing tasks automatically. Unlike the `/Out` command line switch, this command line switch doesn't focus on build errors; it provides you with detailed usage information that can become quite large over time.
`/MDI`	IDE environment	Places the IDE into the Multiple Document Interface (MDI) mode. The MDI mode uses screen space more efficiently by eliminating features such as the tabs that you normally see at the top of the display. You can still switch between editing windows by pressing Ctrl+Tab or you can select a particular window from the Window menu. Use this option when you're focusing attention on a few documents, rather than making small changes to many documents. Using this command line switch also sets the Multiple Documents option found in the `General\Environment` folder of the Options dialog box.
`/MDITabs`	IDE environment	Places the IDE into the tabbed mode. The tabbed mode displays tabs for open documents across the top of the screen, providing faster access to documents, albeit with some loss of screen real estate. Use this option when you need to make edits on a number of documents and move quickly from document to document during testing. Using this command line switch also sets the Tabbed Documents option found in the `General\Environment` folder of the Options dialog box.

Switch	Task Group	Description
`/MigrateSettings`	IDE environment	Moves the settings from a previous version of Visual Studio to a new version of Visual Studio. Using this command line switch, you can configure a new Visual Studio setup quickly. Otherwise, you end up resorting to manual registry manipulation, which is error prone at best.
`/NoLogo`	Automated compiles	Performs the build without displaying the normal logo and copyright information. This command line switch is especially useful when you want to use automation to handle build errors.
`/Out` *`Filename`*	Automated compiles	Specifies the name of an error file to receive all errors. This command line switch is a requirement when you perform after-hours or unassisted builds. Otherwise, you can't be sure of seeing a complete error list.
`/Project` *`ProjectName`*	Automated compiles	Defines the name of a project to use during the compilation process. Instead of compiling an entire solution, the development environment compiles only a single project within that solution. You can't use this command line switch alone; it must appear with the `/build`, `/rebuild`, `/deploy`, or `/clean` command line switches. You must provide a solution name as input with this command line switch.
`/ProjectConfig` *`ConfigurationFilename`*	Automated compiles	Specifies the name of a file that contains configuration information. You can use this command line switch to add a new build configuration or overwrite an existing configuration of the same name.
`/Rebuild` *`ConfigurationName`*	Automated compiles	Cleans up any existing executables and object files first, and then builds the application according to the configuration name you provide. As with the `/Build` command line switch, you can create any named configuration and you must provide a solution name as part of the input for this command line switch.
`/ResetAddin` *`AddinName`*	IDE errors	Resets the specified add-in. Essentially, this means that you won't see the add-in the next time you start the IDE. The article at `http://msdn2.microsoft.com/ms228765.aspx` provides full details on how to perform this task.

Continued

Table 8-1: Visual Studio Command Line Switches *(continued)*

Switch	Task Group	Description
`/ResetSettings [SettingsFile]`	IDE errors	Resets the entire development environment to default settings. You can use this option when your development environment becomes so useless that you can regain control only by resetting everything. As an option, you can supply the name of a settings file. The development environment will use these settings in place of the standard defaults. See the article at `http://msdn2.microsoft.com/ms241273.aspx` for additional information before you use this option.
`/ResetSkipPkgs`	IDE errors	Resets the packages you've installed in Visual Studio. If you suddenly start receiving error messages such as the ones described in the Knowledge Base article at `http://support.microsoft.com/?id=823245`, you can use this command line switch to fix the problem.
`/SafeMode`	IDE errors	Starts the development environment using the minimal number of features. This is the command line switch to use when you're not sure whether a configuration setting is causing problems or your installation really is trashed to the point where you need to reinstall it. If the IDE won't start in safe mode, you can be sure that you need a fresh installation. See the article at `http://msdn2.microsoft.com/ms241278.aspx` for additional information.
`/Upgrade`	Automated compiles	Upgrades a project or solution to the latest version of Visual Studio. The development environment creates a backup of the old project or solution for you in a backup directory. You can use this backup to revert to the previous version of Visual Studio when desired.

Executing Visual Studio Commands

Perhaps the most powerful command line switch is `/Command`. You can follow this command line switch with any command that you can execute within the IDE. For example, if you always want to open the IDE with the project dialog box open, you could use:

```
DevEnv /Command File.OpenProject
```

Whenever you start the IDE using a command, the IDE doesn't display the Start page. Unless you actually use the Start page (and many people do), this shouldn't be a hindrance. To use a command, you must provide the correct alias for the command. In this case, `File.OpenProject` is an alias for the File ➪ Open ➪ Project menu sequence. You can find a list of aliases that the IDE recognizes at `http://msdn.microsoft.com/en-us/library/c3a0kd3x.aspx`.

You can also use this feature to execute macros. Consequently, you can create a macro to perform any level of processing you want and execute it from the command line. When combined with Task Scheduler, you can perform a wealth of tasks while you're sleeping. Here's an example of a macro execution from the command line:

```
DevEnv /Command "Macros.MyMacros.DoTasksModule.PerformProcessing"
```

Running your Application

Sometimes you'll work on an add-on (an external piece of code, usually in a DLL, that does something special), such as a library or service, to a main application. Every time you make a change to the add-on, you have to test the main application. Unless you want to run many copies of Visual Studio at the same time, you need a solution for running the main application quickly. That's where the `/Run` (or `/R`) command line switch comes into play. You can create a shortcut that includes the `/Run` command line switch to compile and run the application. Because the application compiles before you run it, any changes to the add-on will appear in the new run of the application.

If you don't need to keep the IDE open after the application runs, you can use the `/Runexit` command line switch. This command line switch works like the `/Run` command line switch. However, the IDE automatically closes when you finish running the application. You could use this feature with automated testing tools to run the tests and exit immediately. Any errors will appear in the test suite log files. You could take the process a step further and ask the computer to analyze the log files automatically as well. The point is that you can add a significant amount of automation to the application test process by using this one command line switch.

Coding Your Application

This chapter has shown you the unique features of the Visual Studio IDE. Although it's easy to think that the IDE doesn't provide much flexibility or that it's too complex to fiddle with because you have a deadline to meet, modifying the IDE to meet your needs is an essential task. Knowing how to use snippets, macros, and add-ins truly speeds your tasks by leaving out the mundane elements and letting you perform more creative tasks. Finally, using the IDE from the command line lets you further automate tasks using batch files or other techniques.

Now is the time that you should spend an hour or so configuring your IDE for optimum use. Remember that optimum is in the eye of the beholder. The environment you see as optimum may not meet anyone else's needs, but it meets your needs and that's important. It's not unusual for developers with the right environments to double their productivity, simply because they don't have to spend so much time hunting for the right option. It's also time to start building your library of snippets, macros, and add-ins. Don't overwhelm your environment, because doing so would reverse any productivity gains you might hope to achieve. However, having a library of snippets, macros, and add-ins at your disposal can make your next project significantly easier.

Before you go any further, you should probably bookmark this chapter in some way. The "Using the Visual Studio Command Line" section of the chapter is a handy reference that you should keep at your fingertips. If you've ever thought it would be nice to build your application at night without having to start it before you leave work, you can use the techniques in this section to create a Task Scheduler entry for doing those late-night compiles. Having the command line at your disposal is an immense advantage when working with the Visual Studio IDE — your colleagues will be amazed at the amount of work you do while they're sleeping.

This chapter has touched on scripting for the Visual Studio IDE. It won't surprise you to discover that scripting comes in handy for a lot of other uses as well. Chapter 9 explores another realm of scripting. You'll see how scripting can save you development hours, and make the code you create more accessible and easier to change.

9

Scripting

Many developers turn up their noses at scripts because they consider them a poor alternative to full applications. In the common developer view, a script is simply a tool provided to users and administrators who lack the skills required to create full-fledged applications. Unfortunately, this view is incorrect and counterproductive. Scripting, like any other tool, has its uses and you should be sure to add scripting to your developer toolbox. This chapter reviews a number of scripting options and considers how they can help you create better applications. You may find that using these suggestions really does improve productivity, make development easier, and enhance your relationship with the application user.

One of the essentials you should consider is adding scripting support to your application when appropriate. Obviously, you won't add scripting support to a simple text processor — at least, not unless the user truly needs the functionality. However, many higher-end applications can benefit from script-processing functionality. In many cases, you'll find that the scripting functionality you add also helps you, because scripting functionality usually makes it easy to add automation features to an application, rather than having to rewrite portions of the application to meet user needs.

Windows PowerShell also provides a solution for some development needs today. It's important to remember that this environment provides complete access to the .NET Framework, so you can build some extremely powerful scripts using Windows PowerShell. In fact, it probably won't surprise you to know that Microsoft relies on Windows PowerShell to provide scripting support for products such as Exchange Server. This chapter considers how you might use Windows PowerShell as part of your scripting solution.

Considering the Scripting Options

You have a tremendous number of scripting options as a developer. Of course, you can resort to batch files and VBScript or JavaScript, but this chapter doesn't consider those options because you have better options available through Visual Studio. This chapter does review some scripting options you should consider for your application. For example, instead of writing code to manage SQL Server, you can write a script and let SQL Server perform most of the heavy lifting for you. A C# application can easily access SQL Server scripts, but using scripts doesn't require nearly as much code. You can also use various existing scripting options and even use new technology options such as Language INtegrated Query (LINQ) to make your application easier to use. The following sections discuss a number of scripting options of this type.

Interestingly enough, the batch file and VBScript/JavaScript option does come in handy for working with certain Windows objects such as Windows Management Instrumentation (WMI). You can perform tasks such as using the WMIC utility to check the results of changes your application makes to the WMI database. The point is there are many options this chapter doesn't consider and you may very well want to explore them all.

Working with SQL Server

Anyone who's created an application that makes queries using a `SqlCommand` object knows the frustration of having the administrator ask for changes to the application. In addition, users often have reporting requirements and other needs that a `SqlCommand` object, with its programmed functionality, can't answer without additional development time on your part. Although using a `SqlCommand` object can often provide a little additional speed and it places control of the query directly in your hands, it often isn't the best solution to a given problem.

What you really need is to ask the administrator to create stored procedure (sproc), and then have your application query that stored procedure. Now the query code is outside your application, so you don't have quite as much control, but the fact that the code is outside your application means that someone else can easily change it. As administrator and user query requirements change, so does the output from your application, so everyone is happy.

Unfortunately, using sprocs isn't a silver bullet solution either. You must now write your application to expect just about anything as output from the sproc (with luck, the database administrator, DBA, will show a little restraint). Your application must now discover the output coming from the sproc and use the discovery phase to determine how to handle the output. Once you master the discovery technique, however, you'll be amazed at how easy it is to modify the output of reports without changing a single line of code in your application. The bottom line is that you need to use a `SqlCommand` object when control of the query is the most important criterion (such as creating a form for editing data) and a sproc when flexibility is the most important criterion (such as displaying data as a report).

Creating C# Scripts

It's possible to add scripting support directly to your application. Of course, the most common example of such support is the Visual Basic for Applications (VBA) support found in Office applications. In most cases, you won't want to provide such extensive scripting support in your application because it can prove cumbersome to maintain (as Microsoft has discovered over the years). However, many applications include some level of scripting support. In many cases, the scripting support merely provides a means of playing keystrokes back quickly. Internally supported scripting functionality can have the following purposes in an application:

- Provide a means of playing keystrokes back quickly, which provides a superior level of user productivity because users tend to make fewer mistakes and perform tasks consistently.
- Create a method for writing new reports or other output, which means that the user can play with the output to determine the best presentation.
- Define a method for formatting and structuring data that the application manipulates, making it possible to predictably recreate previous results.
- Support mini-applications within the main application so that the user can generate forms and other structures to make using the application easier, especially for novice users.
- Perform low-level interaction with application structural elements in a controlled manner so the user can adjust application features such as menus and toolbars.

As you add scripting functionality to your application, you increase application functionality. In many cases, the increased functionality makes it possible for expert users to improve their productivity greatly. However, the performance gain for the expert user comes at the cost of complexity for the novice user, who may eventually find that the application is so difficult to use that it no longer supports that user's needs.

Scripting functionality also comes at the cost of development and support time. As you add more scripting support, you must also consider the cost in maintenance time for the scripting functionality. At some point, the scripting functionality maintenance time outweighs the productivity benefits of adding the scripting support. The best course of action is to provide only enough scripting support to obtain the user performance benefit without encumbering the developer.

Evaluating C# Expressions

An *expression* is simply a kind of description of a particular abstract concept or idea. For example, when you create a math equation, your expression is an abstraction of some real-world concept in most cases. A building construct becomes an equation that expresses the particulars of the construct, such as the amount of weight it will hold or its physical dimensions. You use C# expressions as a means to add flexibility to your application. The user defines an abstraction that your application turns into code and then executes, providing a result as output.

Using Windows PowerShell

Windows PowerShell is the new command line. Unfortunately, it hasn't taken off as fast as Microsoft may have initially envisioned. Essentially, you gain access to a managed-code environment that replaces the native-code environment for the original command prompt that administrators have used since DOS.

You can write two forms of code for Windows PowerShell. The first form is a script that works most like the VBScript/JavaScript scripts used at the native-code command prompt. This is the form discussed in this chapter. The second form is a Windows PowerShell cmdlet that works very much like an executable application. (If you aren't familiar with cmdlets, the articles at `http://www.microsoft.com/technet/scriptcenter/topics/msh/cmdlets/index.mspx` provide a basic overview that you can use with the material in this chapter.) In both cases, you gain complete access to the .NET Framework, so anything you can do in a C# application, you can do with Windows PowerShell.

One of the more interesting uses of the scripting functionality provided with Windows PowerShell is to provide administrators with access to application configuration. You see this use of Windows PowerShell with Exchange Server. Administrators can work at the Windows PowerShell prompt instead of relying on the GUI. It's possible for an administrator to write batch files to automate tasks, and the overall feel of the Windows PowerShell prompt is the same as the old command line — everything is simply monitored more, especially application security.

If you decide to include Windows PowerShell functionality with your application, you must provide some type of configuration file or other data element that Windows PowerShell can access. In general, you want to use this form of scripting for configuration tasks. The main environment for this kind of configuration is complex applications that administrators must work with on an enterprise level. However, just about any application could benefit from Windows PowerShell management given the right circumstances.

Using LINQ

LINQ is one of the newest technologies available to make your development experience better. It's akin to using SQL, but not quite the same — there are differences. Even so, if you already know SQL, then discovering how to use LINQ isn't time consuming or difficult. The essential goal of LINQ is to reduce the complexity of making queries, while improving the flexibility of the resulting output, and LINQ serves both purposes admirably.

The reduced complexity part of the equation is the real reason to use LINQ. You can use the same syntax to query just about any data source you can imagine, and, possibly, a few that you hadn't considered queryable in the past. For example, if you want to model data using the Resource Description Framework (RDF) and then query that data using LINQ, you can do so quite easily using third-party providers. The articles at `http://www.devsource.com/c/a/Architecture/Modeling-with-RDF-Part-1/` and `http://www.devsource.com/c/a/Architecture/Using-Resource-Description-Framework-Files/` tell you precisely how to perform this task.

Using LINQ also lets you query multiple sources using a single query. For example, you can query a list box in your application and a SQL Server database at the same time. Consequently, using LINQ can make your code significantly shorter than if you had to perform those queries separately. In addition, you'll normally find that the LINQ query is considerably shorter for the same given output than using SQL or some other query language.

The interesting part about LINQ is that you can also easily include LINQ functionality in your application. If you constantly have to upgrade your application to meet specific user reporting or query needs, adding LINQ functionality to your application may be a better alternative. Because LINQ is consistent for most data sources, the user doesn't have to write a query. Rather, the user will fill in a form that expresses the substance of the query and your application will convert the form data into an actual query. Because the user doesn't input a query, you don't have to worry quite as much about potential spoofing or script injection. In addition, because your application controls the query, it's more likely that the user query will succeed.

Interacting with SQL Server

SQL Server is one of the mainstays of the .NET application developer. Consequently, anything you can do to make this environment more efficient will continue to pay off as long as you develop applications. Someone could write an entire book on the topic of making interaction between SQL Server and Visual Studio more efficient, because the relationship between the two products is so complex. The following sections don't presume to explore every potential benefit you can obtain from efficient SQL Server and Visual Studio interaction, but you'll find some interesting suggestions.

Working from Visual Studio

Visual Studio provides a significant amount of automation you should consider using as you develop your application. In fact, your development plan should include applying the automation as a strategy. Microsoft has worked out a number of the kinks in the Visual Studio automation, making it a worthwhile choice for larger projects.

Some developers don't like to use the Visual Studio automation because they say it doesn't work well and it produces code that the developer can't easily read later. Some of this feeling is due to the exceptionally poor automation found in early development products. Developers really did need to know how the automation worked because they had to fix the code later. However, newer products do a better job of automating development tasks, and you should try them. If nothing else, create some test projects so that you can determine the level of automation you want to use for a particular project in advance.

The main productivity enhancement from a Visual Studio perspective is Server Explorer. Developers often misunderstand this feature, partly because some of the more interesting features haven't received much press from Microsoft. Essentially, Server Explorer is a drag-and-drop interface. You locate the item you want and then drag it to the form of your application. Figure 9-1 shows a typical example of Server Explorer with one database connection in place and a typical list of server features that you can access directly from your application.

It's helpful to spend a little time looking on the Internet for potential Visual Studio add-ins that enhance SQL Server interactivity. For example, Craig Riter has created a Visual Studio add-in that helps you write SQL statements. You can see how this add-in works and download it at `http://www.builderau.com.au/program/windows/soa/Create-a-VS-NET-add-in-to-write-SQL-statements/0,339024644,320266978,00.htm`.

When working with SQL Server, you must first create a connection to the server instance and database you want to use. You perform this task using the Data Sources window (open it using the `Data\Show Data Sources` command). Clicking `Add New Data Source` starts a wizard where you create a connection to a data source you've opened in Server Explorer or create a new connection to any other kind of object. Figure 9-2 shows a typical example of the data sources you can select from SQL Server. Later, you can use drag-and-drop techniques to modify the data you work with using the Dataset Designer. As an alternative, you can always use the wizard to make any data source changes. The result is that you're still relying on automation, rather than hand coding, to create the connection.

Visual Studio 2008 now provides support for SQL Server 2008. In order to gain this support, you must download Service Pack 1 (SP1) from `http://www.microsoft.com/downloads/details.aspx?FamilyId=FBEE1648-7106-44A7-9649-6D9F6D58056E` *and install it on your system.*

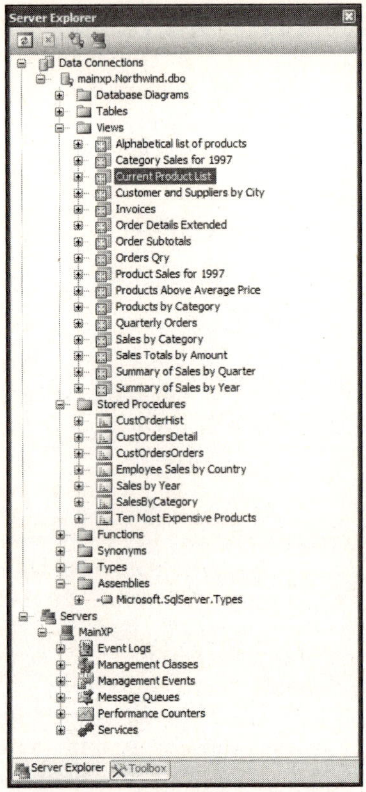

Figure 9-1: Server Explorer is a significant productivity aid when working with Visual Studio.

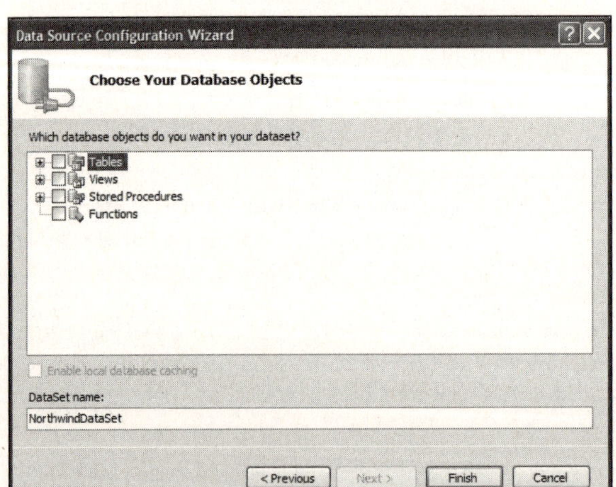

Figure 9-2: You can use automation to access tables, views, stored procedures, and functions in SQL Server.

Using Built-in SQL Server Features

The main scripted interaction for SQL Server is built-in SQL Server features. You can access two main kinds of SQL Server functionality — stored procedures (the old standby from times past) and .NET add-ins (a new technology that has a lot of promise). The following sections discuss these two forms of interaction.

Using Sprocs

Sprocs are a phenomenal way to work with SQL Server in your applications. Using sprocs helps you interact more easily with the DBA. They also make your application more flexible. The DBA can make changes that help your application adhere to company policy or give the application a slightly different view of the data.

When working with sprocs, you typically need more than one sproc to accomplish a given task. For example, if you do design a data entry form around sprocs, you need a minimum of four sprocs to make the form fully functional:

- Data retrieval
- Data update
- Deletion
- New data entry

Most developers understand how sprocs can make reports work better. The sproc retrieves the necessary data from the server and sends just that data to the application. In fact, with a carefully crafted application, a DBA can change the data that the sproc provides to the application and change the output of the report — all without modifying the application code.

However, sprocs can become more tenuous for form-based applications because the data source is no longer under the developer's control. An errant change by the DBA can cause significant problems for the application, and debugging such an error is incredibly hard. Consequently, if you use sprocs for a form-based application as a means of improving both performance and flexibility, you need to lock down the sprocs to ensure that only authorized personnel can change them. Otherwise, you may find that you're in for a nasty surprise when users suddenly find that their form-based application is no longer reliable.

Using Views

Views are exceptionally useful for reports. A view provides a specific look at data. A DBA can use a view to restrict what the user can see. For example, you don't want everyone to see everyone else's salaries, but you may need access to a list of employee names for a particular task. Using a view ensures that the user sees only the data that the user is authorized to see — enhancing security.

Because a view restricts access to the data on the server, many of the techniques that despicable individuals employ to obtain unwarranted access to the data won't work. For example, sniffing the network won't provide any data access because the data never leaves the server in the first place. In addition, using a view enhances performance at several levels:

- The server performs better because it manipulates fewer data.
- The network performs better because it transports fewer data.
- The application performs better because it sees fewer data and has to filter fewer data.

If you're experiencing performance problems with your application, consider using views instead of direct database access. You should be able to improve performance by carefully crafting the view to provide access to just the data the user requires to accomplish a task.

Using .NET Assemblies

SQL Server 2005 and above provide support for managed code. You can write a .NET add-in that installs directly into SQL Server. These entities appear in the Assemblies folder as shown in Figure 9-1. Using assemblies can greatly increase the flexibility of your SQL Server interaction. It's possible to find a wealth of articles on this topic online. For example, check out the tutorials at `http://www.devsource.com/c/a/Using-VS/Introducing-SQL-Server-2005s-CLR-Integration/` and `http://www.codeproject.com/KB/database/CLR_in_Sql_Server_2005.aspx`. The Microsoft article at `http://msdn.microsoft.com/en-us/library/ms189524.aspx` tells you about the T-SQL needed to create a new assembly in SQL Server.

Scripting Your Application

Many applications have some level of scripting support added to them. The more complex the application, the greater the chance you'll find scripting support. Adding scripting support to your application has three potential purposes:

- Making it possible for developers to add expanded functionality without writing new code
- Helping the administrator to perform administration tasks from the command line
- Increasing user efficiency by letting the user create new application functionality based on existing features

One section of a book can't provide a complete tutorial on adding scripting support to your application, but this section does discuss some design issues you must consider as part of the scripting process. The big thing to remember is that scripting support is almost certainly an optional part of your application, so you should always design with the idea that this feature is optional.

The first task you must perform before you can add scripting to your application is to define the goals of the scripting language. It's important to consider the uses to which you expect the user to put the scripting languages — whether it's merely to play back keystrokes or to perform other tasks as complicated as a full-fledged programming language (which is quite an undertaking).

The second step is to define how to achieve the goals you have for your scripting language and to consider issues such as security. Every time you add a feature like scripting to your application, you also open the door for someone to discover a way to add viruses to your application environment. Worse, you might make it possible for users to damage data or the application environment. Remember to weigh the benefits of a scripting language against potential penalties such as reduced application reliability and security.

The third step is to define the method used to run the script once the user creates it. At this point, you have to consider the same elements that anyone designing an interpreter has to consider. For example, you have to define how the application will parse the code that the user supplies.

An ongoing step for this kind of undertaking is maintenance. No matter how well you perform your task, a scripting feature will require constant maintenance. Users and administrators will ask you to add new keywords and other functionality. In addition, languages require updates to make them useful and clear. Finally, you must consider that bugs in your application are hard to find — locating them in an interpreter is a magnitude of difficulty harder.

Using C# Expressions

Using C# expressions relies on the .NET Framework's ability to use the Code Document Object Model (CodeDOM) and reflection to build new code out of strings. In many cases, you see this functionality used to parse math expressions and then use the resulting code to evaluate the expression. You can see examples of this kind of application at `http://www.c-sharpcorner.com/UploadFile/mgold/CodeDomCalculator08082005003253AM/CodeDomCalculator.aspx`, `http://www.codeproject.com/KB/cs/runtime_eval.aspx`, and `http://www.codeproject.com/KB/recipes/matheval.aspx`. However, the same principle applies any time the user has a need to provide an expression of some type and have it evaluated. Theoretically, you could parse English-like sentences and use the result as output.

C# expressions are seeing use in a number of forms. In every case, you provide some type of textual input, parse it, create code, and provide an output based on that code. However, the techniques used to perform these four steps differ. The discussion at `http://weblogs.asp.net/esanchez/archive/2006/06/06/C_2300_-Expression-Evaluators.aspx` recognizes four different techniques for working with C# expressions to achieve a particular result (summarized here):

- Procedural
- Object oriented
- Visitor pattern
- Layered solution using partial classes

Expressions work extremely well for scientific, engineering, or business applications where the user must evaluate something. It need not be an equation, although that does seem to be the major use for this technology. Of course, you can use the expression in any way. For example, you could use it to perform "what if" analysis or simply come up with a better query to use for a report based on SQL Server data.

Developing Windows PowerShell Solutions

The .NET developer has something to gain from working with Windows PowerShell. In some cases, you can work out details of a new technique using scripting, versus trying to write it as a full-fledged application. In addition, you can turn your hard-earned application development skills into a scripting skill as well.

Windows PowerShell provides a number of benefits over using the command line, including the reliability and security that the managed-code environment provides. In addition, you can create scripts of significant complexity because you have the full power of the .NET Framework at your disposal. The following sections describe how to work with Windows PowerShell to create scripts.

Microsoft is using Windows PowerShell more often as part of its application solution. For example, when you install Exchange Server 2007, the installer automatically installs Windows PowerShell as well. Windows PowerShell requires a separate installation when working with Windows Server 2008, but you don't have to download anything to obtain Windows PowerShell support. However, you may not have an application that automatically installs Windows PowerShell on your system. In this case, your can download Windows PowerShell from `http://www.microsoft.com/windowsserver2003/technologies/management/powershell/download.mspx`.

Understanding the PS Utility

Windows PowerShell, like `CMD.EXE`, is essentially a command interpreter — a special kind of utility. In this case, you're using the `POWERSHELL.EXE` file.

You may see a number of User Account Control (UAC) error messages when using Windows PowerShell under Vista or Windows Server 2008. In addition, you may find that security is generally tighter when using these operating systems. Whenever you encounter an error under Vista or Windows Server 2008, consider the error source before you attempt to resolve the problem. If the problem is from the operating system, you may have to look at the rights you've given yourself or whether you have an administrator-level Windows PowerShell prompt open. To open a Windows PowerShell prompt in administrator mode, right-click the entry in the Start menu and choose Run as Administrator from the context menu.

As with `CMD.EXE` (the executable for the old command prompt), `POWERSHELL.EXE` has a number of useful command line switches. You use these command line switches to change the way that Windows PowerShell works and the environment it provides to the user. This utility uses the following syntax:

```
PowerShell.exe [-PSConsoleFile cf | Version version] [-Help] [-NoLogo]
   [-NoExit] [-NoProfile] [-NonInteractive]
   [-OutputFormat {Text | XML}] [-InputFormat {Text | XML}]
   [-Command { - | <script-block> [-args <arg-array>]
   | <string> [<CommandParameters>] }]
```

The following list describes each of the command line arguments:

- **-Command:** Executes the remainder of the command line arguments as though you typed them at the command line. The command line interpreter exits when it completes the commands unless you provide the `-NoExit` command line switch. You can use the following formats for a command:
    - -: Specifies that the command input come from the standard input device. In other words, you'll type the commands at the command line.
    - `script-block [-args arg-array]`: Specifies one or more commands as a script block. You can only use the option if you're currently running the PS shell. Enclose the script box within curly brackets ({}). The parent shell automatically serializes any data to the child shell using a pipeline. Always send arguments to the child shell using the `-args` command line switch as an array.
    - `string [CommandParameters]`: Specifies a single command as a string. If you specify a dash (-) as the command, PS reads the command text from the standard input. PS passes all text after the command string to the command as part of its input arguments.

- `-InputFormat {Text | XML}`: Specifies the format of the input data. The current shell values can include TEXT for text string output and XML for serialized XML format.
- `-NoExit`: Forces the command line interpreter to continue running after it completes running all startup commands.
- `-NoLogo`: Forces the command line interpreter to start without displaying the copyright banner.
- `-Noninteractive`: Performs one or more tasks without presenting an interactive prompt to the user. This feature lets you execute commands or cmdlets in the background without disturbing the user.
- `-NoProfile`: Initializes the command line environment without executing a user initialization script. Normally, you want to run the initialization script to obtain specific command line functionality.
- `-OutputFormat {Text | XML}`: Specifies how the shell formats output data. The current shell values can include `TEXT` for text string output and `XML` for serialized XML format. The text format is most useful for entering commands manually. The XML format works well with scripts, especially when you intend to send the data to a database.
- `-PSConsoleFile cf`: Loads the specified PS console file during startup.
- `-Version version`: Starts a particular version of PS. This feature goes along with general side-by-side execution for the .NET Framework.

Creating a Script

As with most scripts, a Windows PowerShell script is simply a series of executable statements that the system interprets to perform tasks. However, a Windows PowerShell script is built on a combination of the C# language, special objects that the Windows PowerShell developers create for you, the .NET Framework, and any special cmdlets that you create. You can find a great overview of the language on the Ars Technica Web site at `http://arstechnica.com/guides/other/msh.ars`. If you want the short version, check out the basic list of elements on Arul Kumaravel's WebLog at `http://blogs.msdn.com/arulk/archive/2005/02/24/379732.aspx`.

This chapter isn't going to provide a description of the Windows PowerShell scripting language or its programming elements, but will show you how to use them to create a script. The authoritative resource for the Windows PowerShell scripting language is the current documentation available from Microsoft at `http://www.microsoft.com/downloads/details.aspx?FamilyId=B4720B00-9A66-430F-BD56-EC48BFCA154F`. *In fact, you may want to review the entire list of Microsoft resources for Windows PowerShell at* `http://www.microsoft.com/technet/scriptcenter/hubs/msh.mspx`.

Script files are text files with a PS1 file extension. However, if you try to edit a file with a PS1 extension under newer versions of Windows, such as Vista (assuming you haven't changed the security settings), the system will display an error message. You must rename the file to have a TXT or other editable file extension and perform any required changes. Just in case you're thinking about creating scripts with a TXT extension, that won't work either. The file must have a PS1 extension to execute it as a script. If you give the file some other extension and load it, Windows PowerShell won't execute it. These security features prevent you from accidentally executing a partially created script. In addition, the security feature reduces the risk of someone modifying your script later.

A Windows PowerShell script can include a wealth of features. As with any command line script, you can include any command that the command interpreter supports, as well as calls to utilities. In addition, Windows PowerShell scripts support all the same statements that full-fledged programming languages do, including both conditional and looping statements. Unlike JavaScript, Windows PowerShell scripts also include the concept of data type.

Windows PowerShell scripting has taken off. You can find sample scripts on many Web sites. However, some samples are better than others. The first place you should look for sample scripts is on the Microsoft site at `http://www.microsoft.com/technet/scriptcenter/scripts/msh/default.mspx`. *You'll also want to check out the community scripts at* `http://www.reskit.net/monad/samplescripts.htm`.

The example script shown in Listing 9-1 shows how to map a network drive using Windows PowerShell. You could easily perform this task using JavaScript, VBScript, or some other scripting language. The point of this example is to show something simple (and reliable) you can do with Windows PowerShell. If you're working with a newer version of Windows, create a text file, add this content to it, and then rename the file `MapNetwork.PS1` in order to execute it.

Listing 9-1. Mapping a network drive with Windows PowerShell

```
#Input arguments Local Drive and Network UNC location.
Param ($DriveLtr = "", $UNCName = "")

# Detect the correct number of input arguments.
if (($DriveLtr -eq "") -or ($UNCName -eq ""))
{
   # Detect a request for command line help.
   if ($DriveLtr -eq "/?")
   {
      # Display the help information
      [system.console]::Out.WriteLine(
         "Usage: MapNetwork <letter> <UNC target>")

      # Exit the script and provide an error level of 1 to
      # indicate a help request.
      return(1)
   }
   else
   {
      # Ask whether the user wants to continue.
      [system.console]::Out.WriteLine(
         "No input provided! Provide it interactively? [Y | N]")
      $Answer = [system.console]::In.ReadLine()

      # If the user doesn't want to continue, display help and exit.
      # Use an exit code of 2 to indicate a data entry error.
      if ($Answer -eq "N")
      {
         [system.console]::Out.WriteLine(
            "Usage: MapNetwork <letter> <UNC target>")
         return(2)
```

```
            }

            # Input the drive letter.
               [system.console]::Out.WriteLine(
                  "Type the local drive letter (X:).");
               $DriveLtr = [system.console]::In.ReadLine();

            # Input the UNC drive on the remote machine.
               [system.console]::Out.WriteLine(
                  "Type the UNC location (\\MyServer\MyDrive).");
               $UNCName = [system.console]::In.ReadLine();
         }
      }

      # Define the network object used to map the drive.
      $oNetwork = new-object -COM WScript.Network

      # Attempt to create the connection.
      Trap [Exception]
      {
         # Display an error when the task fails.
         [system.console]::Out.WriteLine("Couldn't map the drive!")
         [system.console]::Out.WriteLine($_.Exception.Message)
         return 3
      }

      # Perform the drive mapping function.
      $oNetwork.MapNetworkDrive($DriveLtr, $UNCName);
```

If you're familiar with other scripting languages, such as JavaScript, you'll see that Windows PowerShell performs some tasks differently. These differences actually make creating a Windows PowerShell script significantly easier than its JavaScript counterpart and can also result in a shorter script in most cases.

Notice the way that this example creates the input arguments. Instead of accessing an argument list, this example simply places the values directly in the variables, which ends up saving time because you don't have to check the argument list several times before you can even create the variables.

The example uses the pound sign (#) for comments. In addition, you might notice the odd method of performing logical operations with `-eq` (for equals) and `-or` (for or). You'll find a complete list of these logical operators in the Getting Started document provided as part of the Windows PowerShell documentation. All variables in a Windows PowerShell script must begin with the dollar sign ($), as shown in the example.

For anyone who has worked with .NET console applications, the `[system.console]::Out.WriteLine()` method call will look familiar and that's precisely what it is. The example makes a call to the console class of the system namespace. The console class contains an `Out` property that's actually a container for the standard output stream. The stream object includes the `WriteLine()` method that the example uses to output text. You can use any .NET Framework feature in precisely the same way, which means that Windows PowerShell has a very large list of language features from which to choose.

One feature that differs from standard .NET application coding is the lack of a `try...catch` structure. When working with Windows PowerShell, you use a `Trap` instead. The `Trap` relies on the .NET Framework exception classes. Once you set a trap, it remains in effect until it either goes out of scope or you set another trap. To access the data that the exception provides, you use the `$_.Exception` property, followed by the exception property that you want to access. The example simply displays the `Message` property so that the user knows what happened during an attempted drive mapping.

Windows PowerShell can use COM objects, just as your JavaScript scripts do. In this example, the script creates the `WScript.Network` object. To perform this task in Windows PowerShell, you must use the `new-object` cmdlet and call it with the `-COM` command line switch. The result is the `$oNetwork` object that calls the `MapNetworkDrive()` method using the same syntax as the JavaScript counterpart. The `Trap` statement that appears before the `MapNetworkDrive()` method call provides error trapping in this case.

> *Now that you have a taste for Windows PowerShell scripting, you might want to obtain some additional tutorial type resources. You can find a series of articles about Windows PowerShell script on Computerworld. These articles use the Monad code name that Windows PowerShell originally used, but the information is still useful. The four-part scripting series begins at* `http://www.computerworld.com/softwaretopics/os/windows/story/0,10801,107669,00.html`. *The second part is at* `http://www.computerworld.com/softwaretopics/software/story/0,10801,107673,00.html`. *You'll find the third part at* `http://www.computerworld.com/softwaretopics/os/windows/story/0,10801,107681,00.html`. *The fourth part is at* `http://www.computerworld.com/softwaretopics/os/windows/story/0,10801,107683,00.html`.

Executing the Script

You're ready to try a script. However, running a script with Windows PowerShell is nothing like running a script under the old command line. You can't simply type the script name (in most cases) and let the process take over. The first step is to load the script into memory. To perform this task, type **`get-content MapNetwork.PS1`** and press Enter. When working with another script, you type the name of that script. You'll see Windows PowerShell load your script into memory. In fact, the entire script flashes by on screen as Windows PowerShell loads it.

Now that you have the script loaded into memory, you can execute it. Type **`./MapNetwork`** and press Enter. At this point, you're probably seeing an error message if you're using one of the newer versions of Windows. The default Windows PowerShell setting doesn't allow you to execute any scripts at all, which means that you have to do something special to get this application to run.

You have to make a decision now. The issue is what level of scripting to allow on your system. Before you disable the protection that Windows PowerShell provides, consider using the security to your advantage and set the system to execute only signed scripts. To set the system to use only signed scripts, type **`Set-ExecutionPolicy AllSigned`** and press Enter. However, if you really don't want to have to sign that script before you run it, type **`Set-ExecutionPolicy Unrestricted`** and press Enter instead. Windows PowerShell won't display anything when the call is successful; otherwise, you'll see an error message telling you what has gone wrong.

Now that you have the permission problem solved with Windows PowerShell, try running the script again by typing **`./MapNetwork`** and pressing Enter. This time the script will tell you that it requires input. You can add the required input and map a drive. The script also accepts the input arguments from the command line. Type **`./MapNetwork /?`** and press Enter to see the help screen. Try entering incorrect arguments and you'll find that the exception handling works fine, too.

Successful script completion doesn't show any output at the Windows PowerShell prompt; otherwise, you'll see an error message as usual. To see the results of this script, open a copy of Windows Explorer. You should see the mapped drive under the My Computer folder.

Obtaining Debugger Support

One of the problems that you'll experience when working with scripts is that they often lack formalized debugging support. You can create a Windows PowerShell script using any text editor — even Notepad — so there's nothing special to purchase. However, the lack of an IDE does present a problem for debugging when using the Windows PowerShell 1.0 support found in this chapter. Fortunately, you can get around this problem by installing Windows PowerShell 2.0 (`http://www.microsoft.com/technet/scriptcenter/topics/winpsh/pshell2.mspx`), which was unreleased at the time of writing. It turns out that the development team chose to include debugging support as part of Windows PowerShell, so that you can add commands to your script to perform application debugging. Learn more about this technique at `http://www.microsoft.com/technet/scriptcenter/topics/winpsh/debug.mspx`.

Coding Your Application

This chapter has considered a number of scripting aspects. Developers often leave scripting out of their development plans because they see it as a crutch used by less skilled users and administrators, but that's a mistake. Scripting is a wonderful solution for certain requirements and you should include scripting in your developer toolbox. Any developer without scripting knowledge is at a disadvantage, especially when you consider that some products, such as Exchange, rely heavily on powerful scripting products such as Windows PowerShell. Scripting is all about empowerment at a low learning cost and reduced cost later.

This chapter isn't a plea to add scripting support to your next application — scripting is appropriate in some cases and not appropriate in others. When thinking about scripting, consider the complexity of your application, skill set of your users, need for flexibility, and desirability of expansion potential. If you do add scripting to your application, consider precisely how you should add the scripting support. You may decide to use an existing solution such as Windows PowerShell (as Microsoft has) to create the solution or a more traditional approach of including a command processor as part of the application itself. Adding the appropriate scripting is just as important as adding the scripting in the first place.

The one opportunity that you shouldn't miss is to add scripting to your personal toolbox. If you haven't worked with Windows PowerShell before, you should consider doing so now. Take time to look at the scripting support in Visual Studio and work through scripting in other environments, such as SQL Server, as well. Most important of all, don't miss new technology opportunities, such as LINQ, because by doing so you let your skill set lapse and may find that someone else has the scripting skill you desperately need to make use of an opportunity.

Chapter 10 looks at data as viewed from the Visual Studio IDE. Your applications interact with data constantly, so knowing the best ways to access data is important. Some of the techniques in Chapter 10 even build on the scripting approaches used in this chapter. The Visual Studio IDE provides a surprising number of ways in which to interact with data. Some of these techniques will likely look familiar, but others may be new. No matter whether the techniques are new or old to you, you should consider all the available techniques and choose the most appropriate technique for your application when you design a new application.

10

Viewing Data in the IDE

Seeing your application data (the data that the application manipulates as you use it) is possibly the most important aspect of working with the code in your application, yet it's one of the skills that many developers only partially develop. The "good enough" approach to viewing data often holds sway. Unfortunately, the "good enough" data view often leads to errors in code because the developer can't see the data adequately. Subtle problems make the developer think that the data are fine, when they really aren't. Careful viewing would show that the data really aren't as healthy as they should be and that the code needs some additional tweaking to obtain the desired result.

Visual Studio provides two main methods for viewing data: special windows and visualizers. You can use any of the windows that Visual Studio provides to see collections of data. These views provide a drill-down interface that you can use to locate specific data. However, the views only provide textual views of the data, which may not be enough to determine that the data are correct. After all, it's very easy to miss a closing angle bracket in XML data.

Careful viewing is where the second method of data viewing comes into play. Using visualizers helps you to interpret the data — to see it in a completely human-readable form that makes errors a lot easier to see. Instead of simply seeing text, you see the text as a human would see it — XML really looks like XML. Visual Studio comes with four visualizers:

- Text
- XML
- HTML
- DataSet

As nice as these four visualizers are, they don't cover all the viewing needs you have. Consequently, once you get used to working with visualizers, you might want to look for visualizers that other people have created. There's a growing list of third-party visualizers on the Internet and most of them provide valuable services. If you still don't find what you need, you can create your own visualizer — it really isn't very hard to do. The last part of this chapter shows how to create a custom visualizer to meet any need.

I'm always on the lookout for new products and code examples to add to my books. If you create a custom visualizer, write me about it at JMueller@mwt.net. I'm amazed at how many different ways this particular technology is used, but I think the inventive minds out there can come up with significantly more ways and I'd like to know more about them. I'll be sure to give you full credit if I mention your visualizer in one of my books.

Working with the IDE Elements

Microsoft provides a number of windows for viewing data in the IDE. Precisely how you use these windows is a matter of personal choice. However, using the correct window for a particular situation can save you time and frustration. The four main windows for viewing data are:

- **Autos:** Shows all of the objects associated with the current task, no matter where those objects are declared.
- **Locals:** Shows all of the objects associated with the current method, including the `this` object.
- **Watch:** Doesn't contain anything initially — you add the objects that you want to track as you debug your application.
- **Command Window:** Lets you ask questions of the debugger and perform what if–type analysis on your application.

Using these four windows, you can get an overview of your application from a number of perspectives. For example, the Autos window is usually the best choice when you're working on a specific problem in your application, but the Locals windows is probably a better choice for performance tuning or when you're looking for a bug in a method. The following sections describe each of these IDE elements in detail and provide some usage instructions that may help you debug your application more efficiently.

Using the Autos Window

The Autos window shows you what your application is currently using. This window focuses on the current task, which makes it exceptionally useful when you want to see something that's specifically wrong with your application. The view tends to focus your attention on the task and keeps you from getting distracted with other objects that appear in the current method. For example, consider a coding session that stops at the last line of the following code:

```
// Define the mail message.
MailMessage NewMail = new MailMessage();

// Get the required arguments.
NewMail.From = new MailAddress(txtFrom.Text);
```

What you see in the Autos window is something like the view shown in Figure 10-1. The `NewMail` object is at the top of the display because that's the focal point of this code. You also see the `NewMail.From` property because the code specifically changes that property. When you stop at the next line of code, you see the property changed by that line — the `NewMail.From` property disappears from view. The constant change of view keeps the information you're seeing relevant. Sometimes, if you don't see something that you expected to see, it's a pointer to potentially bad code — missing objects tell you as much as those that are present.

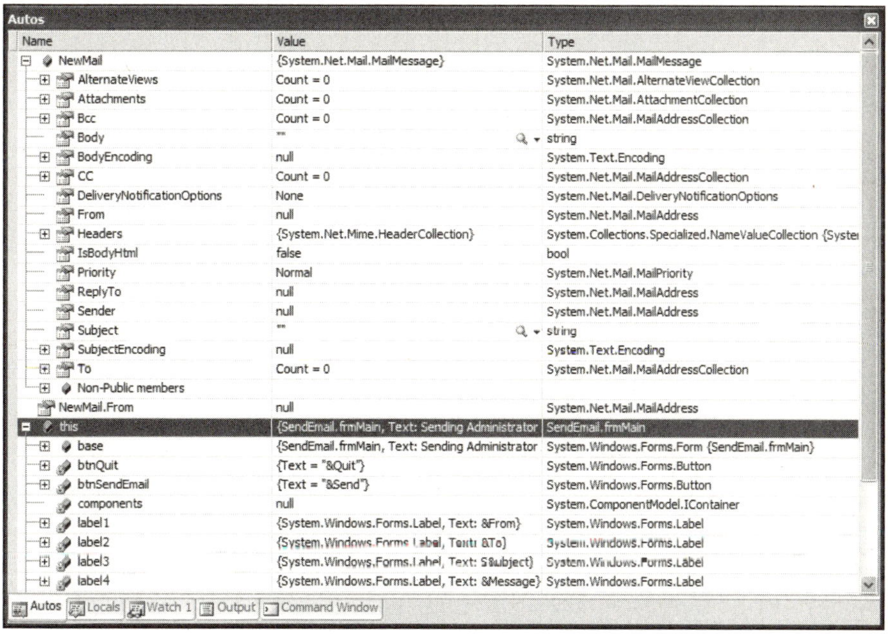

Figure 10-1: The Autos window always contains objects that relate to the task at hand.

It's important to realize that the `this` object is available to you in both the Autos and Locals windows, as shown in Figure 10-1. You can also add specific `this` object elements to the Watch window or query them in the Command Window. The `this` object is important because it provides access to the application as a whole. Notice that Figure 10-1 shows that you can access all the controls quite easily using the `this` object. As you work through your application, you'll find use for the `this` object in checking things that are happening outside the current focal point.

Using the Locals Window

The Locals window presents all the objects found in a particular method. What you see is an overview of the method, as shown in Figure 10-2. In this case, the list of objects begins with `this`, moves on to method input arguments, such as `sender` and `e`, and then begins listing all the internal objects, such as `NewMail` in this case. The Locals window normally lists objects in order of appearance, rather than based on the current task, to make them easier to find. Unlike the Autos window, you won't see any properties listed in this window — just objects. Consequently, if you want to find the `NewMail.From` property, you must open the `NewMail` object to do it.

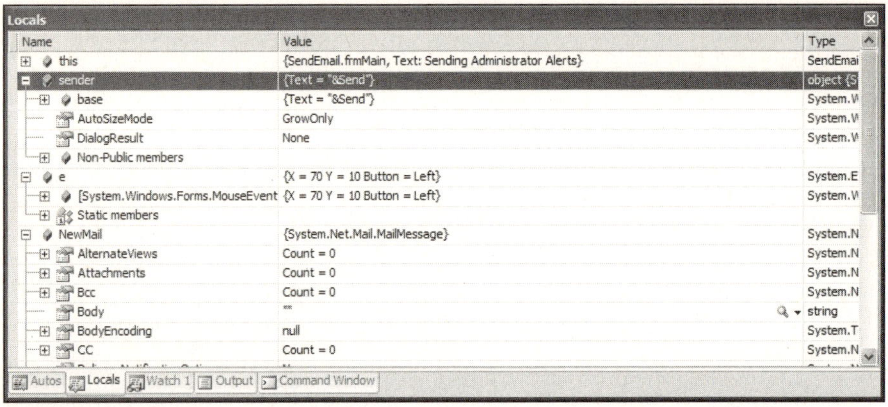

Figure 10-2: The Locals window contains variables that are local to the current method, along with the this object.

It's easy to miss the importance of the input arguments, especially if you aren't coding against them in your application. For example, the `sender` argument in the Locals window shown in Figure 10-2 tells you that the Send button called the method. If you were expecting some other button, then this indicator would tell you the source of your problems. The event arguments, `e`, can also provide helpful information. All of these additional bits of information work well in an environment suited to getting an overview of a particular method, rather than looking for something specific.

Using the Watch Window

Some developers eschew use of the Autos and Locals windows because they feel the windows are too cluttered. The Watch window provides you with a blank slate on which to put any objects or properties that you want. The result is a view of your data that's customized specifically for your needs, as shown in Figure 10-3.

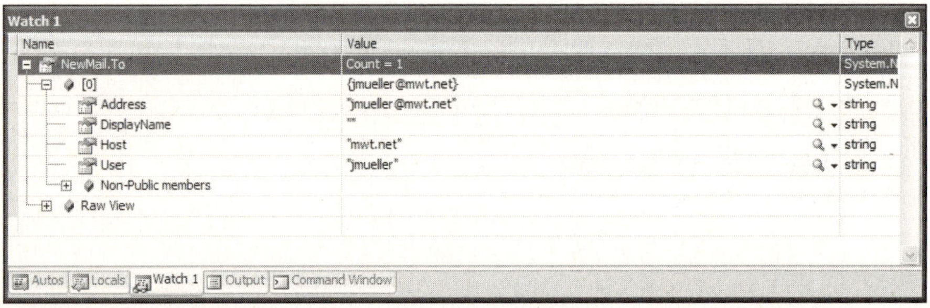

Figure 10-3: The Watch window comes into play when you want to specifically monitor a particular object.

Microsoft must think the Watch window is important. Although Figure 10-3 shows only one Watch window, you can access up to four Watch windows using the Debug ➪ Windows ➪ Watch options. Visual Studio labels the Watch windows from Watch 1 to Watch 4 and all of them are independent. You can place anything needed in each Watch window to address complex debugging needs.

The easiest way to use a Watch window is to highlight whatever you want to view in the Debugging window, right-click the entry, and choose Add Watch from the context menu. As an alternative, you can drag and drop an object from the Debugging window onto the Watch window of your choice. If you don't see a precise representation of what you want to watch, you can place the cursor on a blank line in the Watch window and type what you want to see.

Using the Command Window

The Command Window lets you issue commands to Visual Studio. You can use it to query Visual Studio about aspects of your application or to gain access to any menu or command that Visual Studio supports. Consequently, this is an extremely powerful window, but only if you know what to type.

The most common use of the Command Window is to interrogate the application. For example, if you want to know what the `NewMail.Subject` property contains, you type **`? NewMail.Subject`** and press Enter. The output shows the current value of the `NewMail.Subject` property. Likewise, if you want to set the `NewMail.Subject` property, then you type **`? NewMail.Subject = "Hello"`** and press Enter. You can access any object or property using this technique.

> *As an alternative, you can use the Immediate window to change values. To access the Immediate window, type* **`immed`** *or* **`Debug.Immediate`** *and press Enter in the Command Window. To get back to the Command Window, type* **`>cmd`** *and press Enter in the Immediate window. You can learn more about the Immediate window at* `http://msdn.microsoft.com/en-us/library/f177hahy.aspx` *(this information also appears in the MSDN library that comes with Visual Studio).*

The secondary use for the Command Window is to access any menu or command that Visual Studio supports, even those that don't appear on a menu or toolbar. For example, if you want to access a feature on the File menu, you begin by typing **`F`**. The Command Window instantly displays a list of F items that you can access, including the entire File menu.

It's also possible to use the Command Window to perform debugging tasks you can't perform in the other windows, including "what if" analysis. For example, you can use the `Debug.EvaluateStatement()` method to evaluate a statement as part of the debugging process. In fact, you'll find a host of `Debug` commands that you can use.

Perhaps the most interesting use of the Command Window is to execute actual commands, as you would from within Windows. You accomplish this task using the `Tools.Shell` command. For example, if you want to see a directory listing of your root folder, you might type **`Tools.Shell ""CMD.EXE /K Dir C:\*.*""`** and press Enter. You'll see a command prompt open with the information you requested. Type **`Exit`** and press Enter to close the command prompt window.

Understanding the Use of Visualizers

Visualizers were a new addition to Visual Studio 2005. Since that initial release, developers have worked out a number of visualizers to meet specific needs. A visualizer is a special debugging tool that helps you to see the data you work with in a human-readable form — as a user would see it. The following sections describe visualizers in more detail and help you get started with the visualizers that Visual Studio provides.

Defining a Need for Visualizers

A problem for developers viewing data in Visual Studio is that the data may not look anything like the data that developers normally interact with. For example, a Web page might appear as a run-on text string of tags that lacks any white space. Viewing a Web page this way is difficult to say the least. More importantly, you can't see how the Web page will look — you see only the code used to create the Web page. Consequently, it's extremely easy to miss errors that are extremely easy to see when you view the Web page itself. As humans, we don't speak computer very well, so visualizers make it possible for us to see data in the form most useful to us.

Visualizers also address practical concerns. Most developers can see strings in the debugger just fine, but the string may contain a lot of text. In this case, the text rambles on to the end of the Debugging window and you lose sight of it. The debugging windows don't provide a practical method of seeing the entire string. Consequently, the developer has to copy the entry from the Debugging window and paste it into Notepad or simply assume that the rest of the text is accurate. Neither solution is efficient or particularly helpful. Using the Text visualizer helps you see the string as you'd expect to see it, in addition to seeing the entire string.

Not every property in the debugging windows provides access to a visualizer. You can always determine when a property provides access to a visualizer by looking for the magnifying glass in the Debugging window. For example, in Figure 10-3, the `Address` property is of type `string` and it provides access to a visualizer. The same holds true for the `DisplayName`, `Host`, and `User` properties. As you add visualizers to your system, more of the properties will have a magnifying glass next to them. You select a particular visualizer by selecting the down arrow next to the magnifying glass and choosing a visualizer from the list.

Most visualizers provide a minimum of two fields. The first, Expression, contains the expression used to create the output you see in the visualizer. In many cases, this expression is complex and you need to verify that you're seeing the data that you expect to see. In addition, it's fascinating to see how the visualizer is interacting with the data. The second field is some type of value. This field contains the interpreted results you use to visualize the data.

With few exceptions, you can't edit data you see in a visualizer. The visualizer simply displays the data in an easily recognized form. None of the visualizers provided with Visual Studio offer editing functionality. If you want to make a change, you must close the visualizer and use one of the debugging windows.

Using the Text Visualizer

The text visualizer is the easiest and most straightforward of the visualizers. When you open a property in the text visualizer, you see the text as you'd see it within a text editor such as Notepad. All the control characters are gone because the visualizer uses them to format the text for easier viewing. The three essential control characters used for formatting text are tab, carriage return, and line feed. Figure 10-4 shows typical output from the text visualizer.

Notice that the Text Visualizer window includes a Wrap option. Even with the wide display that you can create with the text visualizer, some strings may not contain the carriage return/line feed control characters required to format the output of the text in easily read lines (the text will simply continue right off the end of the display area, making it very hard to see). The Wrap option tells the text visualizer to display long lines as several lines of text in the Text Visualizer window.

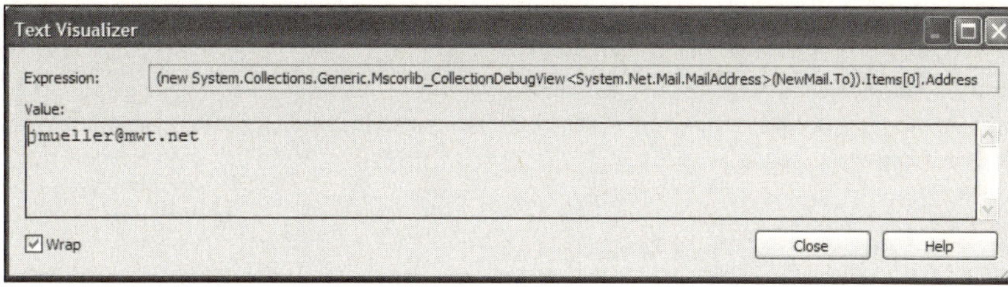

Figure 10-4: Use the text visualizer to see long pieces of text.

Using the XML Visualizer

XML is especially difficult to read as a string. You can probably make out some of it, but trying to figure out whether the application has properly formatted the elements proves impossible. Any reasonably complex XML becomes a nightmare to view. If you really want to look at it, you have to copy the data out of the debugger and create a new XML document, which you then view using a browser or XML utility. What a mess.

The XML visualizer shown in Figure 10-5 takes care of the process of copying the data, creating an XML document, and displaying it in a browser for you. What you're really seeing in Figure 10-5 is an Internet Explorer window that contains the formatted XML. As with Internet Explorer, you can collapse or expand elements as needed to view your data. The XML Visualizer window also provides the XML with color coding, making it easy to track the different processing instructions, namespaces, elements, and values. Using Internet Explorer also ensures that you see the proper white space, rather than a continuous line of text.

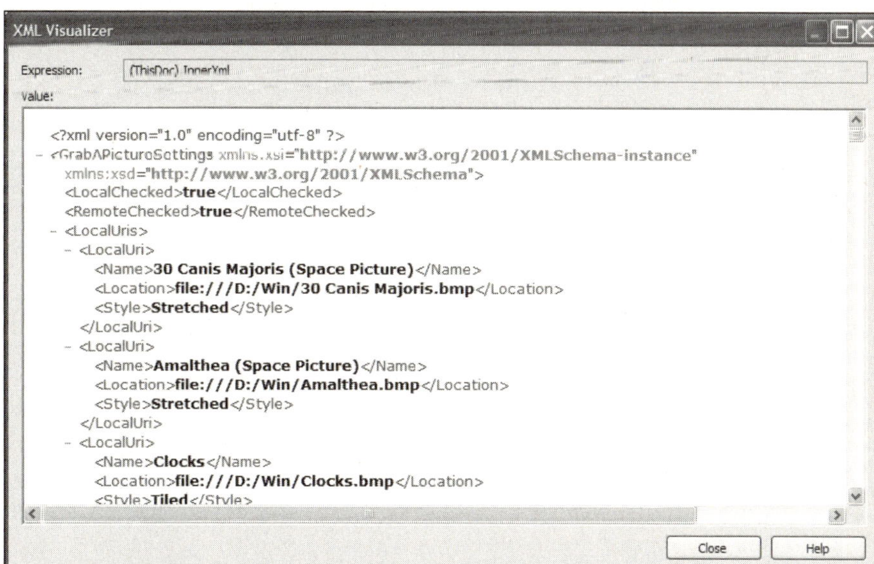

Figure 10-5: The XML visualizer helps you see XML data as color-coded XML.

The XML Visualizer window displays only well-formed XML. If your XML isn't well formed, you'll see an error message instead of the XML you expected. This feature makes it quite easy to locate a problem in the XML output of your application. The error is obvious and therefore easier to fix. If you want to see the unformatted XML so that you can locate an errant tag with greater ease, use the text visualizer instead. The text visualizer can display any kind of text, even if it isn't well-formed XML.

Using the HTML Visualizer

Like XML, trying to view HTML in the debugger windows is nigh on to impossible. However, even if you could read the HTML tags used to create the Web page, you still might not gain any useful information from it. The problem is that the human-readable form of a Web page isn't the tags — it's the visual output. Consequently, you need a different kind of view from what the XML visualizer provides in Figure 10-5. What you really need to see is the Web page as it appears to the user.

If you want to see the tags used for an HTML document, you normally need to use the text visualizer to see them. The XML visualizer will normally complain that the HTML document isn't well formed, and you'll see an error message rather than the tags.

The HTML visualizer shown in Figure 10-6 converts the HTML tags into a document that you can understand. This view helps you see misplaced controls, features that don't work properly, and other issues that the user might experience with the Web page without ever leaving the confines of the Visual Studio IDE. One limitation of this visualizer is that it may not display every Web page element, depending on your browser settings.

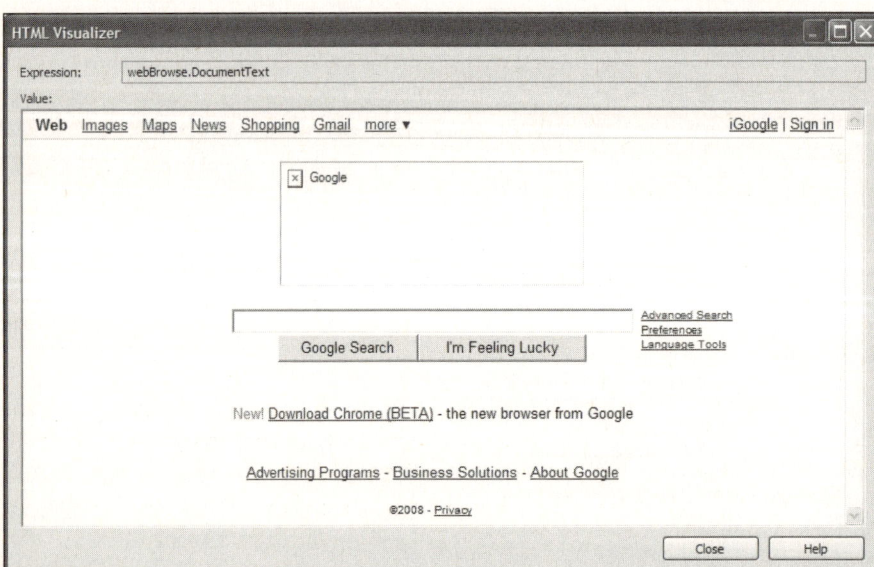

Figure 10-6: The HTML visualizer shows most elements of a Web page you've loaded into an application.

You can use this view to move from page to page. Buttons and links do work. However, you don't have access to the Internet Explorer controls. For example, pressing Alt+Left Arrow won't take you to the previous page. If the Web page doesn't provide a method for getting to the previous page, you can't go there unless you reload the page by closing the visualizer and reopening it.

Using the DataSet Visualizer

The DataSet visualizer helps you interact with the `DataSet` and `DataTable` objects. These objects are pretty much unreadable in the debugger. The best you can hope to achieve is to drill down into the objects and interpret the data they provide, but you can't obtain an overview of the information in anything approaching human-readable form. As shown in Figure 10-7, the DataSet visualizer makes it easy to interact with DataSets in your application. You can see the data contained within specific `DataTable` objects in a format that looks very much like a grid view in an application.

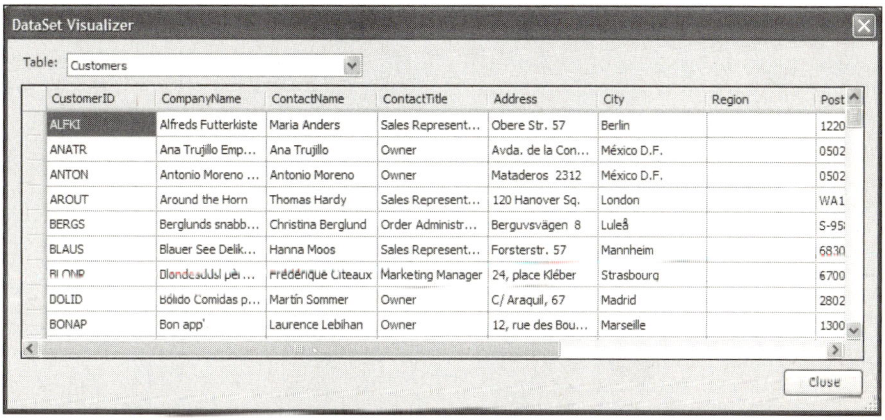

Figure 10-7: The DataSet visualizer helps you to see information found in DataSets with greater ease.

Unlike the other visualizers, you won't see an Expression field in the DataSet Visualizer window. What you see instead is a Table field where you can choose from any of the tables contained within the `DataSet` object. The Table field is still available when working with a `DataTable` object, but obviously, there's only one choice to make.

In addition to the Table field, the DataSet Visualizer window also supports editing. You can modify any of the table entries. The modifications remain in place for the current session only, unless you provide code for saving the `DataSet` or `DataTable` to the database. However, the ability to change values and test them in your code is a significant advantage over trying to do the same thing with the debugging windows.

Odd as it may seem, the DataSet Visualizer window doesn't include a Help button. You can obtain additional help with this visualizer at `http://msdn.microsoft.com/en-us/library/d480bk47(VS.80).aspx`.

Obtaining Third-Party Visualizers

You won't find a lot in the way of shrink-wrapped third-party visualizers. In fact, the best visualizers are part of a grassroots movement. They often appear as part of someone's blog or on the Web site of someone who has an interest in making Visual Studio better. For example, you can find two visualizers on Brett Johnson's blog at `http://blog.bretts.net/?p=11` and `http://blog.bretts.net/?p=9`. The first is a cache visualizer for ASP.NET, while the second is a custom control visualizer.

Articles often include interesting visualizers. For example, Saqib Ullah, the author of Custom Visual Studio Visualizer, shows how to create a visualizer for in-memory graphics (`http://geekswithblogs.net/technetbytes/archive/2008/06/11/122792.aspx`). Download the associated project and you now have a visualizer to perform this task. You may even find ways to improve this particular visualizer to support a wider range of graphics. The main consideration is that you have a good starting point and a functional visualizer to use now.

Sometimes you need a visualizer for a nonstandard data type. For example, you may have created a custom class and want a visualizer to work with it. Mike Gunderloy tells you how to create such a visualizer at `http://www.codeguru.com/columns/experts/article.php/c11713`. In addition, you get to see an interesting-looking task class that could come in handy for your own code.

The market does have a few commercial products you can buy. For example, Mole v4.2 provides visualizer support with properties that you can edit (`http://karlshifflett.wordpress.com/mole-for-visual-studio/`). Normally, a visualizer supports viewing data alone, so this is a new and interesting twist on the whole concept of working with visualizers.

If you think the DataSet visualizer supplied with Visual Studio is interesting, you might want to look at the RightHand.DataSet.Visualizer at `http://www.rthand.com/DesktopModules/Articles/ArticlesView.aspx?ItemID=15&mid=10244`. This visualizer adds significant functionality to the whole concept of working with a DataSet visualizer. Not only do you see a hierarchical display of the data structure, but you also see properties associated with the DataSet. This product is amazing because it gives you a complete, structured view of your data.

Creating a Custom Visualizer

The interesting thing about visualizer technology is that it adds so much to your debugging experience, yet doesn't require a lot of effort to create. The "Obtaining Third-Party Visualizers" section of this chapter discusses the many third-party offerings you can find for this technology. However, you may eventually exhaust these sources and need to create a visualizer of your own. The process isn't hard, but you do need to test the resulting visualizer carefully, because a debugging tool with bugs in it isn't very useful. The following sections take you through the process of creating and testing your own visualizer.

Configuring the Visualizer Project

A visualizer is essentially a special kind of class that you install within a designated location on your machine. Visual Studio looks at this location for DLLs that contain the correct class information when it initializes. It loads all the DLLs that match the required criteria and calls on the functionality the DLL provides when you debug the application. Select a string variable in the Watch window of the debugger and you'll see options for displaying the string as text, HTML, or XML using the standard visualizers.

Of course, the trick is to create a class DLL that Visual Studio will recognize as a visualizer. This section of the chapter shows how to create a project and set it up so that Visual Studio will recognize the resulting DLL as a visualizer. In this case, the example shows how to create a visualizer that will display `DateTime` object values in an easily recognized form. However, the techniques presented here will work for any visualizer you want to create because the essentials are the same for any visualizer project. The following steps get you started:

1. Create a new Class Library project. Give the product an appropriate name — the example uses DateTimeVisualizer, but you can use any name that makes sense to you.
2. Rename the `Class1.CS` file to something appropriate — the example `DateTimeVisualizer.CS`. The IDE should automatically rename the class to `DateTimeVisualizer` as well.
3. Right-click the References folder entry in Solution Explorer and choose Add Reference from the context menu. You'll see the Add Reference dialog box shown in Figure 10-8.

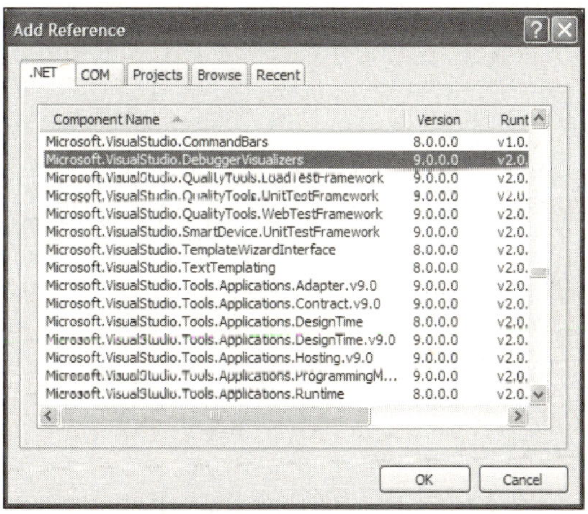

Figure 10-8: Add the `Microsoft.VisualStudio.DebuggerVisualizers` namespace reference.

4. Choose the `Microsoft.VisualStudio.DebuggerVisualizers` entry and click OK.
5. Type the following line of code to the beginning of your class file:

```
using Microsoft.VisualStudio.DebuggerVisualizers;
```

6. Change the class declaration so it derives from the `DialogDebuggerVisualizer` class. Type a colon after the class entry and type **`DialogDebuggerVisualizer`**. Visual Studio will display a smart tag asking whether you want to implement the abstract class 'DialogDebuggerVisualizer' as shown in Figure 10-9.

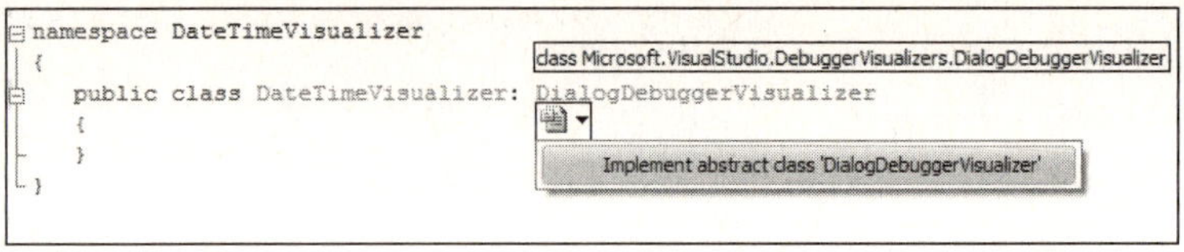

Figure 10-9: Implement the `DialogDebuggerVisualizer` class to create your visualizer.

7. Select the Implement abstract class 'DialogDebuggerVisualizer' option. The IDE will automatically create all the required method stubs for your class. It's time to make the class recognizable as a visualizer.

8. Open the `AssemblyInfo.cs` file found in the Properties folder of Solution Explorer. Add this code to the end of the file:

```
[assembly: System.Diagnostics.DebuggerVisualizer(
  typeof(DateTimeVisualizer.DateTimeVisualizer),
  Target = typeof(System.DateTime),
  Description = "View DateTime Forms")]
```

9. Save the changes you've made, and the visualizer is ready for coding.

Before you go any further, you should know a little more about the `System.Diagnostics.DebuggerVisualizer` attribute you added to the `AssemblyInfo.cs` file. The three arguments for this attribute include the type of the class that contains the visualizer, the type of the target object, and a description of the visualizer. In this case, we're targeting the `DateTime` object. However, you can target any kind of object you want. If you want to target a custom type, you have to provide a reference to its declaration. The description you provide appears in the window when the developer using the visualizer debugs an application. Consequently, it's important that you provide a description that's both clear and related to the object at hand.

Adding the Visualizer Code

At this point, you have a shell. The shell defines this visualizer as a visualizer that works with the DateTime data type. Other than that, the visualizer shell you now have could work for any visualizer you want to create. It's time to add some visualizer-specific code to the project. A visualizer consists of two objects: the viewing window and the underlying visualizer code. To make things easier to understand, the following sections cover each visualizer area separately.

Defining the Viewing Window

A visualizer, by definition, provides some kind of window for seeing the data in a new way — one that the debugger doesn't currently provide. Add a new window by right-clicking the project entry in Solution Explorer and choosing Add ⇨ New Item from the context menu. Choose the Windows Form template and call it `DateTimeWindow.cs`. Click Add. You can add controls to the form, as shown in Figure 10-10.

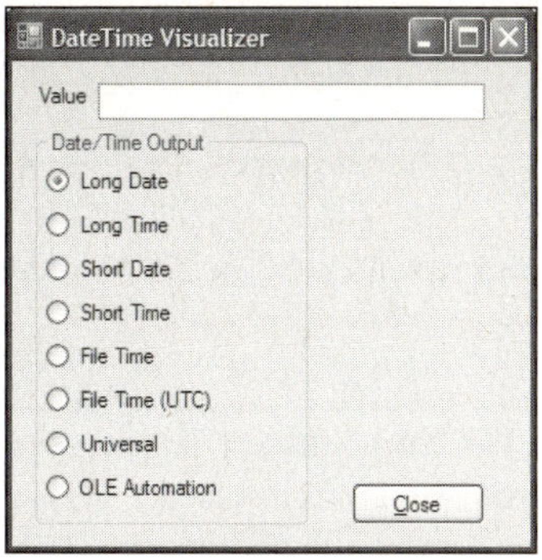

Figure 10-10: This `DateTime` object viewer will help you see dates and times in a number of new ways.

The code for the window is relatively straightforward. You need to change the constructor to accommodate an input value from the visualizer class. Because the caller can never call this window without providing a value, you don't need to include a default constructor. In fact, it's a bad idea to include a default constructor for the simple reason that no one should call the constructor without the proper `DateTime` value. Listing 10-1 shows the constructor for this example.

Listing 10-1: Create the constructor for the visualizer window

```
private DateTime _Value;

public DateTimeWindow(DateTime Value)
{
   InitializeComponent();

   // Display the value.
   txtValue.Text = Value.ToLongDateString();

   // Save the value.
   _Value = Value;
}
```

The example displays the current value as a long date string. It then saves the value in a local variable for later use. Each of the radio buttons on the form will also have code attached to its `CheckedChanged()` event, as shown here.

```
private void rbLongDate_CheckedChanged(
   object sender, EventArgs e)
{
   if (rbLongDate.Checked)
      txtValue.Text = _Value.ToLongDateString();
}
```

In this case, the code ensures that the control is actually checked. If so, it displays the correct time format as output.

A few of the time formats require additional processing. For example, when you display universal time, you need to create a string based on the input because `ToUniversalTime()` produces a new `DateTime` object. The example uses the technique shown in Listing 10-2, but you can certainly use any output you want.

Listing 10-2: Converting a date time object to universal time

```
private void rbUniversal_CheckedChanged(
   object sender, EventArgs e)
{
   if (rbUniversal.Checked)
      txtValue.Text =
         _Value.ToUniversalTime().ToLongDateString() +
         " " + _Value.ToUniversalTime().ToLongTimeString();
}
```

Theoretically, you could display another dialog asking the user to select an output format for the universal time. The complexity of the window code is up to you. Simply decide how much information you want to display and in what form you want to display it.

Adding the Visualizer Code

Now that you have a shiny new visualizer window, it's time to complete the visualizer class. The first thing you have to remember is that this code always executes halfway between the Visual Studio IDE and the test application, so you can't assume some of the things that you'd normally assume about a class. For example, you don't really know how a change will affect the application environment, so you always have to use the built-in classes to communicate with the application. Listing 10-3 shows the class code for this example.

Listing 10-3: Creating a visualizer class

```
protected override void Show(
   IDialogVisualizerService windowService,
   IVisualizerObjectProvider objectProvider)
{
   DateTime ThisValue;

   // Verify the object isn't null.
   if (objectProvider.GetObject() == null)
      return;

   // Make sure the object converts to a DateTime.
   try
   {
      ThisValue = Convert.ToDateTime(objectProvider.GetObject());
   }
```

```
        catch
        {
           return;
        }

        // Create the visualizer window and pass it the data.
        DateTimeWindow DTW = new DateTimeWindow(ThisValue);
        windowService.ShowDialog(DTW);
    }
```

The focus of a visualizer is the `Show()` method that the IDE automatically adds when it implements the `DialogDebuggerVisualizer` class. The example begins by making some necessary checks. For example, you need to know whether the object is `null`, because the visualizer shouldn't process `null` objects. Always perform conversions within a `try...catch` block to ensure the application environment doesn't crash due to a problem with the input from the Visual Studio IDE.

Now that you have a data value to process and it's in the correct format, you can display the visualizer window created earlier. Creating the window is the same as any other window you've created in the past. However, notice that you don't use the form's `ShowDialog()` method to display the window. If you use the form's `ShowDialog()` method, the Visual Studio IDE is unaware of your visualizer status and could continue execution before your visualizer window is closed. Always use the technique shown in the example to display the visualizer window.

Testing the New Visualizer

The visualizer you created in this section is basic, but it does do something useful. Before you can use it with a real project, however, you must test it. The best way to test the visualizer is to create a test project as part of the visualizer solution. The following sections describe how to create a test project for this visualizer, and then test the visualizer functionality. You can use the same approach for any visualizer you create.

Creating the Visualizer Test Project

The example visualizer uses a console application for testing. Because this visualizer works with a specific data type, it's possible to use a console application. However, when working with complex visualizers, you want to use a project that best matches the environment in which you want to use the visualizer. For example, if you plan to work with `DataSet` objects, then you need to create a project that incorporates the `DataSet` objects in the same way you plan to use them in the real world. The following steps configure the test project:

1. Choose File ➪ New ➪ Project. You'll see the New Project dialog box.
2. Highlight the Console Application template, type **`VisualizerTest`** in the Name field, select Add to Solution in the Solution field, and click OK. Visual Studio creates the new project for you.
3. Right-click the new project and select Set as StartUp Project from the context menu to ensure the test application runs when you click Start Debugging.
4. Right-click the References folder entry in Solution Explorer and choose Add Reference from the context menu. You'll see the Add Reference dialog box shown in Figure 10-8.

5. Select the Projects tab, highlight the `DateTimeVisualizer` project entry, and click OK.
6. Right-click the References folder entry in Solution Explorer and choose Add Reference from the context menu. You'll see the Add Reference dialog box shown in Figure 10-8.
7. Choose the `Microsoft.VisualStudio.DebuggerVisualizers` entry and click OK.
8. Type the following line of code to the beginning of your class file:

```
using Microsoft.VisualStudio.DebuggerVisualizers;
```

At this point, the project is ready for coding.

Adding the Visualizer Test Code

It's important to make the test code as simple as possible. Remember, you're testing the visualizer, not your ability to write complex code. Listing 10-4 shows the testing code used for this example.

Listing 10-4: Creating a test application for the visualizer

```
static void Main(string[] args)
{
    DateTime ThisTime = DateTime.Now;
    VisualizerDevelopmentHost host =
        new VisualizerDevelopmentHost(
            ThisTime,
            typeof(DateTimeVisualizer.DateTimeVisualizer));
    host.ShowVisualizer();
    Console.WriteLine("The current date and time are:");
    Console.WriteLine(ThisTime.ToLongDateString());
    Console.WriteLine(ThisTime.ToLongTimeString());
    Console.WriteLine("Press Any Key When Ready...");
    Console.ReadLine();
}
```

It's important to remember that the Visual Studio IDE doesn't know about the visualizer at this point, but you can simulate this recognition using the `VisualizerDevelopmentHost` object. The constructor for this object accepts the name of the object you want to test, as well as the type of the class that performs the visualization. Calling the `ShowVisualizer()` method simulates the act of selecting the visualizer in one of the debugging windows. The example test code includes a sanity check that verifies the output shown in the visualizer window. In addition, this extra code ensures that you can verify the visualizer stops application execution as intended.

Before you perform the test, make your visualizer available as a standard visualizer. This means placing the visualizer (`DateTimeVisualizer.DLL` in this case) in a location where Visual Studio expects it. Compile the solution, and then copy the visualizer to either the global or personal visualizer location. Global visualizers appear in the `<VS Install Dir>\Common7\Packages\Debugger\Visualizers` folder. Personal visualizers appear in the `My Documents\Visual Studio 2008\Visualizers` folder.

To perform the test, set a break point at one of the lines after you instantiate `ThisTime`. The example uses the `Console.WriteLine(ThisTime.ToLongDateString());` line of code. Start the application, and the first thing you see is the Visualizer window due to the call to `host.ShowVisualizer()`. Close the visualizer window. When the debugger breaks the second time, you can select `ThisTime` in the Autos window and see the View DateTime Forms visualizer, as shown in Figure 10-11.

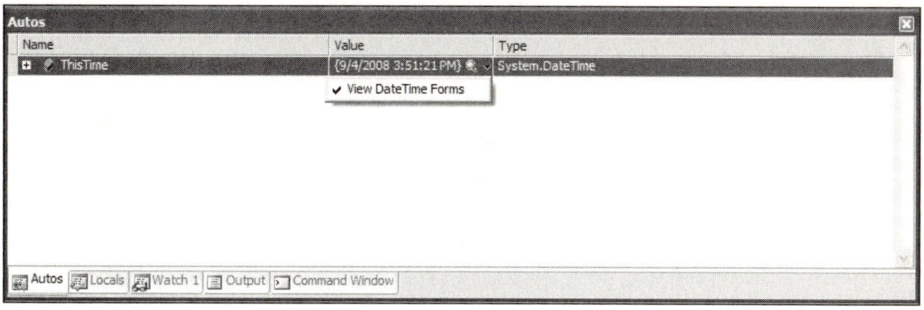

Figure 10-11: The new visualizer is ready for use when you can select and use it in the debugger.

Coding Your Application

This chapter considers the question of viewing data while you debug your application. The technique you use is a personal one — what works for me may not work for you at all. However, you need to know about the various techniques at your disposal in order to make a reasonable choice. The better you can see your data, the easier it is to locate potential security, reliability, and speed problems, as well as those ever-present bugs. In this chapter, you discover two main methods of viewing data, specialty windows and visualizers.

The only way you become proficient with the technology that Visual Studio provides is to use it. While this chapter exposes you to potential methods of seeing data as you debug your application, it only provides the overview that most articles and books can provide. It's up to you to try out the various technologies using your applications to determine what works best for you. In some cases, that means setting aside several hours to play with the IDE (yes, I said play — play is important for developers, too). The time you spend with the IDE features now will save you considerable time debugging your application later.

Chapter 11 moves into a new area — components and controls. Now that you have a better idea of how to view data, it's time to look at the objects that generate that data. Components and controls form the basis of most applications. Sure, you have to write glue code to make those components and controls perform useful work, but the component or control is the initial feature of the application, the one that you use to begin planning your application. While you work through Chapter 11, try the various viewing techniques described in this chapter — you might be amazed at what you see.

11

Working with Controls and Components

The vast majority (if not all) GUI applications rely on controls and components to create part of the application infrastructure. Controls and components are specialized objects that encapsulate code and make it remarkably easy to reuse. Most developers associate controls and components with the user interface for an application. However, components can fulfill a number of non-user interface requirements as explained in the "Understanding the Differences between Controls and Components" section of this chapter.

Whether you need the material in this chapter depends on the kind of application you want to create. All GUI applications use controls and components. However, if you create a command line application designed for an environment such as Windows Server 2008 Server Core, you may not use any controls or components. Check out the articles at `http://www.devsource.com/c/a/Add-Ons/Win-Command-of-the-Command-Line-Interface/` *and* `http://www.devsource.com/c/a/Architecture/Mixing-Server-Core-with-NET-Applications/` *for examples of this type of .NET application development. Writing command line applications isn't the only time you tend to avoid controls and components. Some specialized development, such as writing a service, may also not require use of controls and components. The article at* `http://www.devsource.com/c/a/Using-VS/Writing-a-Managed-Windows-Service-with-Visual-C/` *discusses some of the issues to consider when writing a managed service.*

An important issue to consider about controls and components is that many developers use them without ever building a control or component of their own. The control and component are essentially black boxes that you incorporate into your application. As with any object, you interact with controls and components using the methods, properties, and events that the developer supplies. This chapter describes a number of control types and shows you how to build a simple one of your own. After you look at controls, the chapter also describes how to build a component and explains some of the differences you'll encounter when creating a component.

Microsoft provides the Object Test Bench as a means for testing your controls and components. You discover how to use this tool at the end of the chapter. Although you can't use this tool to test controls and components designed by other people, you can use it to test your own controls and components. In addition, this tool comes in handy for testing any class within your application. All you need to do is access it from the Class View window.

This chapter doesn't provide a comprehensive view of how to build components and controls; rather, it focuses on how to design and develop better components and controls. As you read this chapter, ask yourself the question, "How do I use this material to build better components and controls?" While many books focus on implementation of a specific component or control, this chapter focuses on building better components and controls in general.

Considering the Usefulness of Nontechnical Input

Developers often rely exclusively on technical input for elements, such as controls and components, to their detriment. Users often have a unique perspective of application elements that escapes developers completely.

It's best to illustrate this principle using a story. An eye doctor notices that Americans are visiting the eye doctor more often and that they have symptoms associated with close work more often than before. The eye doctor blames computer screen usage, because the symptoms do occur when using a computer screen. Consequently, the eye doctor decides to recommend that his patients rely on timers to alert them to the need to get up and walk around for a while to ease eyestrain (among other things).

Someone who is neither computer literate nor has any knowledge of eye diseases notes that the eye doctor has potentially come to the wrong conclusion. She works on crafts and knows that fellow crafters suffer from the same issues. In fact, these issues have been around for as long as she remembers (and being 85, she has been around for a while). This person surmises that the eye doctor is seeing more patients because people have better access to eye doctors today — after all, you can find them in most major stores. In addition, because these large stores encourage customers to use a credit card to pay for glasses and other eye needs, customers are willing to get the kind of help they need. Finally, many stores have stopped carrying the large selection of reading glasses that many people once used in place of going to the eye doctor for this problem.

Is the eye problem one of increased stress or one that reflects our society's changing way of dealing with eye problems? No one will ever know because the problem is lacking the one datum required to answer the question — no one is asking the eye doctor's customers the right question.

The story shows that two people, one a professional and one not, came up with two completely different views of the same problem. When you write applications without the nonprofessional input, you're potentially coming to the wrong conclusion. You need the nonprofessional to help you better understand the problem or at least look at the problem from another angle.

Understanding the Differences between Controls and Components

Some developers have a problem differentiating between a component and a control. It's important to know the difference because you have different design decisions to make for each item. Although there are many differences between components and controls, you have a simple way to tell the two apart. A *control* is a visual object, such as a button or checkbox. A *component* is a nonvisual element, such as a tooltip or timer that the user may not interact with directly (for example, a tooltip adds functionality to an existing control — the user doesn't interact with it directly). In both cases, you find these objects listed in the Visual Studio Toolbox.

Dragging and dropping a control onto the Design window places a representation of that control on the form you're designing. However, dragging and dropping a component onto the Design window places the component in a special area below the form called the Component Designer, as shown in Figure 11-1. As shown in this figure, button1 is a control, while timer1 is a component.

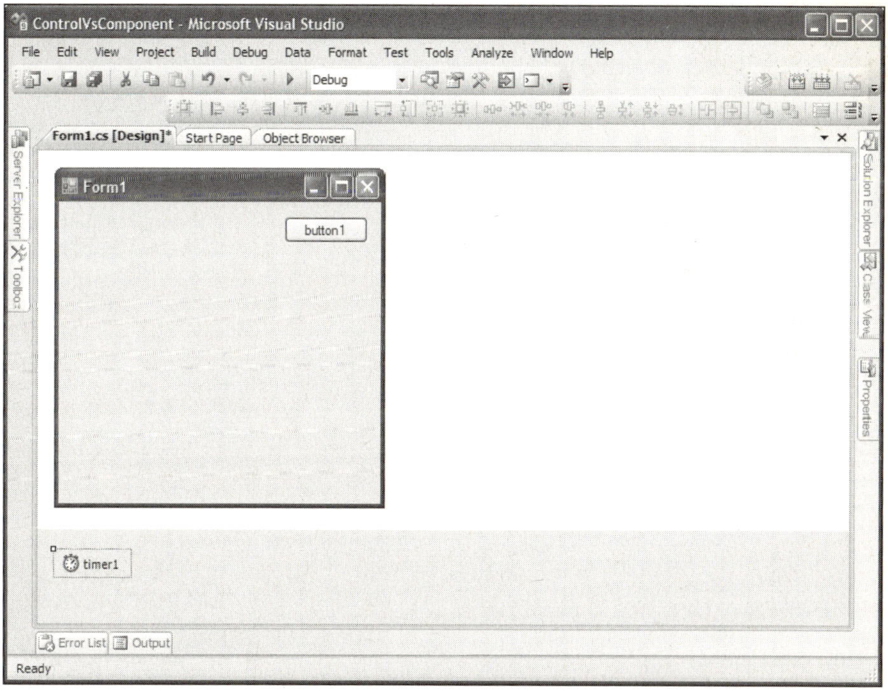

Figure 11-1: Controls and components display differently in the IDE.

As you can see from the figure, timer1 has no visual element — nothing that appears on the application form. It has properties, methods, and events, just as button1 does, but it lacks a visual element (the icon displayed at the bottom won't appear in your application). Components normally fulfill a background function that affects the user interface in some way, but not always. In this case, timer1 can fire an event that updates the display at an interval. For example, you may want to create a scrolling display of system status information. However, you could just as easily use it to time internal events that the user doesn't even realize occur. For example, an application could use a timer to know when to look for new files in a particular folder.

Controls tend to have certain restrictions placed on them because they do provide a visual element. For example, most controls provide some specific properties because you need them in order to work with the control on the form. Here are some typical properties found in most (if not all) controls (see `http://msdn.microsoft.com/en-us/library/system.windows.forms.control_members.aspx` for a fuller description of base control members).

AccessibleDescription
AccessibleName
AccessibleRole
AllowDrop
Anchor
CausesValidation
ContextMenuStrip
Cursor
Dock
Enabled
Font
GenerateMember
Location
Locked
Margin
MaximumSize
MinimumSize
Modifiers
RightToLeft
Size
Tag
UseWaitCursor
Visible

You implement these properties in your controls and assign them typical behaviors. For example, the `Anchor` property determines how the control reacts when the user resizes the form. The `Cursor` property lets you assign a particular cursor to the control so the user associates that control with a specific task. Likewise, controls have common properties, as shown below:

BindingContextChanged
CausesValidationChanged
ChangeUICues
ClientSizeChanged
ContextMenuStripChanged
ControlAdded
ControlRemoved
CursorChanged
DockChanged
DragDrop
DragEnter
DragLeave
DragOver
EnableChanged
Enter
FontChanged
GiveFeedback
HelpRequested
Layout
Leave
LocationChanged
MarginChanged
MouseCaptureChanged
MouseDown
MouseEnter
MouseHover
MouseLeave
MouseMove
MouseUp
Move
ParentChanged
PreviewKeyDown
QueryAccessibilityHelp
QueryContinueDrag
RegionChanged
Resize
RightToLeftChanged
SizeChanged
StyleChanged
SystemColorsChanged
TabIndexChanged
Validated
Validating
VisibleChanged

Of course, controls also have custom properties, events, and methods that they implement. Each control also has customized behavior and appearance. However, all these elements are in addition to the common elements.

Unlike controls, components have no common or typical properties, methods, or events. For example, timer1 has just a few properties, such as `Interval`, that modify its performance. The only event that timer1 supplies is `Tick`, which fires every time the interval you set expires. While controls always have events, it's entirely possible that you might create a component without events and it will work fine. In short, there are fewer rules when working with components than with controls — components are more free form in nature.

One property that tends to appear in controls and components alike is `Tag`*. This particular property provides the developer with a means of storing custom data. Generally, you should provide this property and not assign it any specific functionality — Microsoft designed it for use by the application developer. Many components also include the* `Enabled` *property, but providing this property isn't a requirement.*

Defining the Control Types

Before you can create your own control, you must decide how to create it. Controls require more work than components to create, especially if you want to create a completely customized solution. However, you don't have to create a completely customized solution. In fact, you have three options from which to choose, as described here:

- **Derived:** A derived control lets you begin with an existing control and add to or subtract from it. You use a derived control in situations where an existing control almost meets your requirements, but not quite. For example, you may want to augment a standard `Button` control to include an on/off state. You could even change the appearance of the control so that it has two standard captions, On and Off. The advantage of using a derived control is that you don't have to start from scratch — you only need to modify the functionality of the existing control so that your new control performs tasks with greater ease. This is the most common method for creating a new control because it offers significant flexibility at a relatively low development cost.
- **UserControl:** A `UserControl` is actually a container. You stuff one or more existing controls in the `UserControl` and then customize the existing controls to meet certain needs. When someone uses the resulting `UserControl`, it already has common code and functionality in place, so all the developer needs to do is perform a few small configuration tasks to use the `UserControl`. For example, you might create a `UserControl` from a list box and configure it with a list of regions (states) or countries. Special settings may determine whether the resulting `UserControl` displays all the regions it holds, or just those in a certain country. A `UserControl` is extremely helpful in team projects where you want to ensure that everyone's using the same control configuration. Most developers begin experimenting with the `UserControl` because it provides a simple environment and moderate flexibility.
- **New:** In some cases, Microsoft hasn't supplied an existing control that even comes close to what you want to do and you can't create a `UserControl` that meets your needs either. A new control starts from ground zero — you have to do just about everything to create one. This option provides you with the ultimate in flexibility. In addition, select this option when you can't afford any of the performance hits that you would take when creating a derived or `UserControl` solution. Creating reliable, fast, and secure controls requires the expertise of an experienced developer, so you won't want to choose this option for your first control project.

Someone has probably invented hybrids of these three methods and you might even find other alternatives, but these are the three standard techniques for creating a new control. (If you've invented a truly interesting control creation method that works well, write me at `JMueller@mwt.net` — I'd love to hear about it.) The following sections demonstrate how to create controls using all three methods. The final section describes testing techniques that you can use to check your controls as you develop them.

Building Derived Controls

The derived control is the most commonly used control basis, so the chapter discusses this option first. Remember that a derived control starts with another control, such as `Button`, as a starting point, and adds or subtracts features as needed. The following sections describe how to create a specialized button that provides several specific states.

Essential Considerations for Developing a Derived Control

Before you begin writing any code, you want to plan your derived control carefully. Of course, one of the biggest questions to answer is how this control should look and act. The decisions you make determine which control to use as a starting point. You may find you originally thought that a `ListBox` would work just fine, but after working through the details, the `ListBox` control falls short and you really need a `ComboBox` control as a starting point. A little extra time at the outset usually provides better results.

One mistake developers make is assuming that they can rely only on the standard controls that come with Visual Studio. While it's true that using the standard controls does have benefits, such as not forcing you to buy additional copies of a third-party library, the standard controls can also limit your choices. Relying on a third-party library may save you considerable time and effort — more than repaying the cost of buying additional copies of the library.

Whenever you use a third-party library as a starting point, always check into licensing and usage details. Otherwise, you may find you have a lovely new control that you can't use anywhere due to the sometimes terrifying licensing terms that third-party vendors place on your use of their controls. If there's any doubt, contact the vendor and obtain vendor input in writing (telephone conversations won't do in this case).

Derived controls always use a single control as a starting point. Consequently, you can't easily combine a `Button` and `TextBox` control to create an aggregate (combined) control. If you need an aggregate control, then you want to rely on a `UserControl` as described in the "Building UserControls" section of the chapter. As an alternative to building an aggregate control, you can always create several discrete controls and place them within the same library. In fact, you'll probably end up with libraries that have several related controls in them just to make things easy.

Defining the Derived Control Project

This section shows how to create a basic derived control project. You can use these steps to create any control you want. The section does focus on the example application — simply substitute the specifics for your control as needed.

1. Choose File ⇨ New ⇨ Project. You'll see the New Project dialog box shown in Figure 11-2.
2. Select the .NET Framework version you want to target from the list box in the upper right corner. Select the `Visual C#\Windows\Windows Forms Control Library` template, as shown in Figure 11-2. Provide a component library name in the Name field (don't use the name of an individual control — especially if your library will contain multiple controls). Click OK. Visual Studio creates the new project for you.

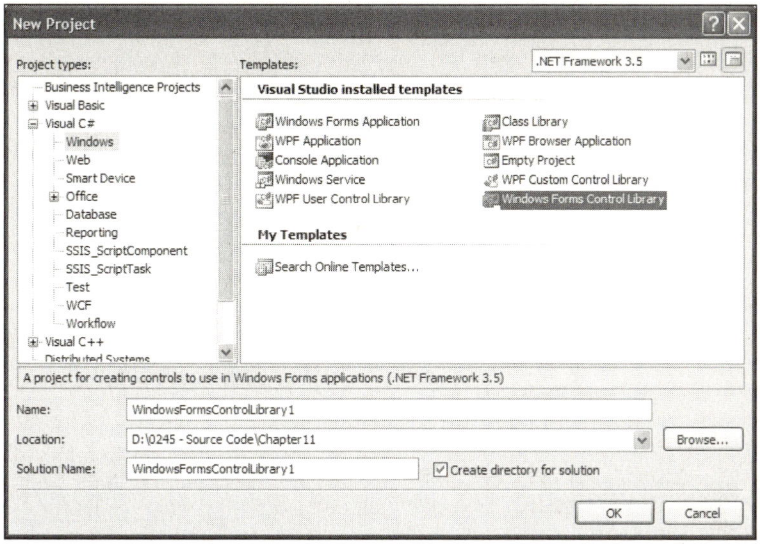

Figure 11-2: Choose the Windows Forms Control Library template as the starting point for a derived control.

Choosing a .NET Framework Version

One of the first things you should do when creating any kind of control project is determine the .NET Framework version you want to use. Visual Studio 2008 defaults to the newest version of the .NET Framework available on the host system, which is .NET Framework 3.5 SP1 as of this writing. Using the newest .NET Framework version isn't always the right choice; sometimes you need the flexibility provided by an older version of the .NET Framework.

The .NET Framework version appears in the upper right corner of the New Project dialog box. Before you do anything else, select the version you want to use for your control project. You'll notice that the entries in the Templates list change to match the .NET Framework version you select.

All three versions of the .NET Framework support the Windows Forms Control Library template used for the controls in this chapter. However, when you select an older version of the .NET Framework, you also lose the ability to use features found in a newer version of the .NET Framework. Therefore, you must balance the need to provide version flexibility in your controls with the requirement to access newer product features.

3. Right-click the `UserControl1.CS` entry in Solution Explorer and choose Rename from the context menu. Type a name that matches the name you want to use for the control. The example uses `StartStopButton.CS`.
4. Close the Designer (sometimes called Design) window.

5. Right-click the control's entry in Solution Explorer and choose View Code from the context menu. You'll see the Editor window where you can change the class from which the control is derived.

6. Delete the `UserControl` entry and add a standard control entry in its place. Your code should look like this if you plan to derive from the Button control:

```
namespace DerivedControl
{
   public partial class StartStopButton : Button
   {
      public StartStopButton()
      {
         InitializeComponent();
      }
   }
}
```

7. Choose Build ➪ Build `<Project Name>` to build the control. At this point, you see a terrible-looking error message in the Error List window regarding `AutoScaleMode`. The error message isn't your fault — it's a bug in Visual Studio and you can overcome it easily.

8. Double-click the error entry and you see the `StartStopButton.Designer.CS` file open with the

```
this.AutoScaleMode = System.Windows.Forms.AutoScaleMode.Font;
```

`AutoScaleMode` keyword highlighted. Comment out this line of code and try to compile the component again. The code should compile this time. At this point, you're ready to start adding code to your project.

Adding the Derived Control Code

After you've configured the derived control, you can begin adding code to it. The example doesn't do anything very complicated. All it does is toggle the button between two states using the code shown in Listing 11-1.

Listing 11-1: Creating custom properties and methods for a derived control

```
public StartStopButton()
{
   InitializeComponent();

   // Configure the component.
   _UseStartStop = false;
   _IsStart = false;
}

// True when the button is in start/stop mode.
private Boolean _UseStartStop;

[Category("StartStop")]
[Description("Determines the button start/stop mode.")]
public Boolean UseStartStop
{
```

```
      get
      {
         return _UseStartStop;
      }

      set
      {
         // When the UseStartStop property is true,
         // set the button text and properties
         // appropriately. Don't change the button text
         // the the UseStartStop property is false because
         // that would change the design setting.
         if (value == true)
         {
            _UseStartStop = true;
            this.Text = "Start";
            _IsStart = true;
         }
         else
         {
            _UseStartStop = false;
            _IsStart = false;
         }
      }
   }

   // True when the button shows Start.
   private Boolean _IsStart;

   [Category("StartStop")]
   [Description("Returns the current start state.")]
   public Boolean IsStart
   {
      get
      {
         return _IsStart;
      }
   }

   protected override void OnClick(EventArgs e)
   {
      // Always perform the base processing.
      base.OnClick(e);

      // Perform special processing when the
      // UseStartStop property is true. This
      // code simply toggles the button.
      if (_UseStartStop == true)
      {
         if (_IsStart == true)
         {
            this.Text = "Stop";
            _IsStart = false;
         }
```

Continued

Listing 11-1: Creating custom properties and methods for a derived control *(continued)*

```
            else
            {
                this.Text = "Start";
                _IsStart = true;
            }
        }
    }
```

The code begins by initializing the private variables in the constructor. You must exercise care when initializing control elements because you could inadvertently overwrite a developer setting. For example, if you set the `Text` property in the constructor, the custom control will never display the text that the developer provided while interacting with the control in the Designer.

Properties work in a control just as they do in any class. However, you want to make things easier for the people using your control, so you add two attributes to each property. The first, `Category`, places the property in a custom location within the Properties window. Using a custom category always makes the properties easier to find. The second, `Description`, provides a description of the property's purpose at the bottom of the Properties window. The more information you provide here, the better. The developer is normally going to look at the bottom of the Properties window first to determine how to work with the control property.

> *Controls can use a number of additional helpful attributes for description purposes, depending on the user's needs. Most of these attributes appear as part of the* `System.ComponentModel` *namespace, which you can find described at* `http://msdn.microsoft.com/en-us/library/system.componentmodel.aspx`. *For example, you can use the* `AmbientValue` *attribute to assign an environmental value to the property, so that the property obtains a value from another source. Given the example of a color, you can set the color to match something else, such as a standard Windows color, when the developer selects a particular value from the list, such as* `Color.Empty`. *Compare this attribute to the* `DefaultValue` *attribute, which assigns a default value to a property until the user changes it.*

The `UseStartStop` property is of type `Boolean`. Use nontext types whenever you can to reduce security risks. It's very hard to set a `Boolean` to the wrong value. When you do use a `String` or other text type, make sure that you check the input carefully. A `Regex` object can be your best friend, in this case, because it helps you quickly eliminate unlawful characters, such as the curly braces ({}) used for scripts. (See the "Keeping Unnecessary Characters Controlled" section of Chapter 7 for details on using the `Regex` object.)

Many properties require behavior modification when the developer changes the property value. In the case of `UseStartStop`, the code determines whether the developer has set the property to `true` or `false`. Setting the property `true` initiates the behavior change and sets the button to toggle between states.

You'll also find that you need to override the behaviors associated with the control. In this case, you must override `OnClick()` to provide the toggle action the developer expects. IntelliSense makes it quite easy to determine which control features you can override. The example control performs the toggling action when `_UseStartStop` is `true`. The button displays Start or Stop based on its previous setting. It isn't necessary to provide the `Category` and `Description` attributes, in this case, because the control automatically inherits these attributes from the parent control.

Checking the Derived Control Functionality

You have a number of options for checking the control you create. However, the easiest way to perform a quick check is to add a Windows Forms project to your application. The following steps describe how to perform the required configuration:

1. Choose File ➪ New ➪ Project to display the New Project dialog box shown in Figure 11-2.
2. Choose the Windows Forms Application template. Type a name for the application such as `StartStopButton_Test` in the Name field. Select Add to Solution in the Solution field. Click OK. Visual Studio creates a Windows Forms application for you.
3. Right-click `StartStopButton_Test` in Solution Explorer and choose Set as StartUp Project in the context menu. This step ensures you can compile and start your application for debugging purposes.
4. Open the Toolbox and look at the top of the list. You'll see a special folder that holds the new control you created, as shown in Figure 11-3.

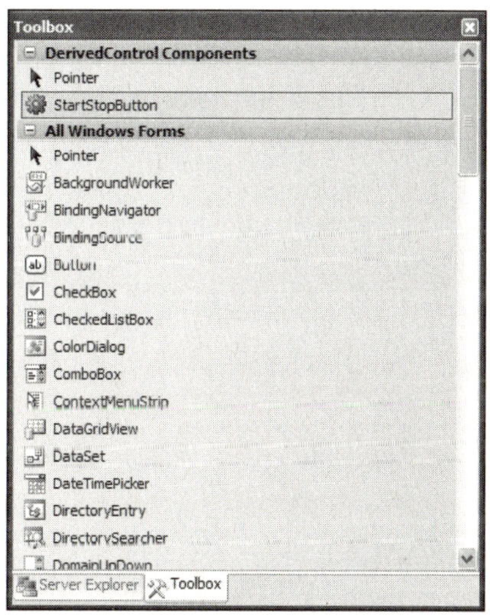

Figure 11-3: The Toolbox automatically holds a copy of the control you create.

5. Drag and drop the `StartStopButton` control onto the form. You'll see what looks like a standard `Button` control added to the form. However, when you start reviewing the properties, you notice that the button has all of the custom properties defined in the "Adding the Derived Control Code" section of the chapter.
6. Select the new `StartStopButton` control and set its `UseStartStop` property to `True`. If you list the properties by category, the StartStop category is easy to find, as shown in Figure 11-4. Notice that changing the `UseStartStop` property also changes the `IsStart` property and modifies the `Text` property to `Start`.

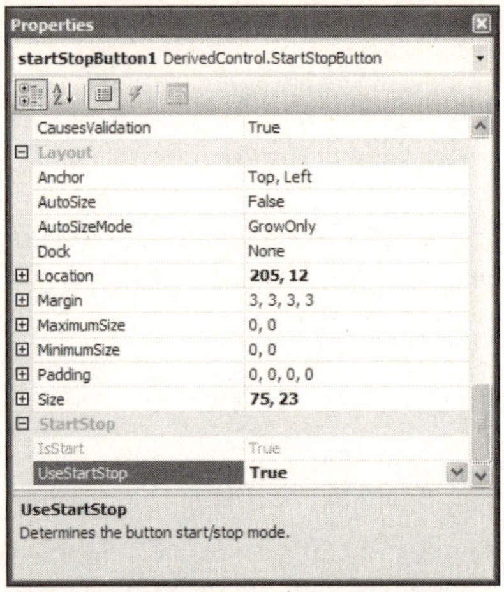

Figure 11-4: Using a special category for custom properties makes them easy to find.

7. Drag and drop a second `StartStopButton` control onto the form. Whenever you test a derived control, you should also test the original functionality to ensure you haven't modified it in an undesirable way. This second button will use the default settings. Change the `Text` property to `Hello` so that you can ensure the change sticks.

8. Double-click each of the controls in turn. Add the following code to check their functionality.

```
private void startStopButton1_Click(object sender, EventArgs e)
{
   MessageBox.Show(startStopButton1.Text);
}

private void startStopButton2_Click(object sender, EventArgs e)
{
   MessageBox.Show(startStopButton2.Text);
}
```

At this point, you can build the application. Click Start Debugging (F5) and you can test the new control's functionality. The first control should toggle between Start and Stop, while the second control displays Hello each time you click it.

Adding the Control to Another Application

Your custom control won't automatically appear in the Toolbox. If you want to use it with another application, you must add it to the Toolbox using the following steps.

1. Right-click in the Toolbox and choose Add Tab from the context menu. Type a name for the tab such as `My Custom Controls` and press Enter. You'll see a new tab added to the Toolbox. Storing your custom controls in a separate tab makes it easier to find them.

2. Right-click `My Custom Controls` (or whatever you named your tab) and select Choose Items from the context menu. After a few seconds, you'll see the Choose Toolbox Items dialog box shown in Figure 11-5. Don't worry about not seeing the control yet.

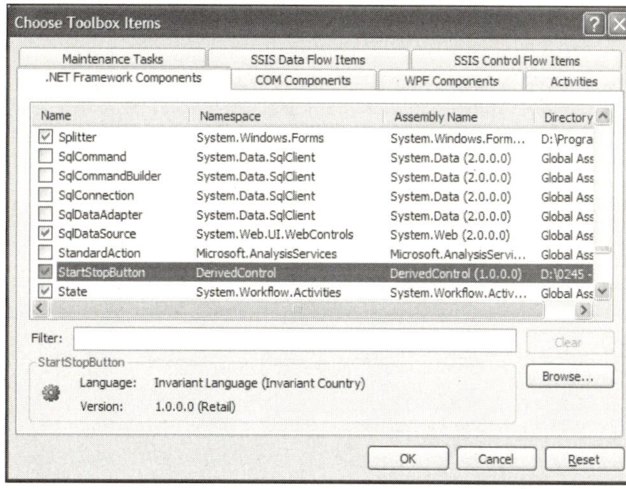

Figure 11-5: Add the control to the Choose Toolbox Items dialog box.

3. Click Browse. You see an Open dialog box where you can locate and select the control you created. Highlight the control and click OK. You'll see it added to the Choose Toolbox Items dialog box, as shown in Figure 11-5.

4. Ensure the entry for your control is checked (Visual Studio automatically checks it for you in most cases). Click OK. You'll see the control added to your custom tab in the Toolbox.

Building UserControls

As previously mentioned, the `UserControl` is the simplest control project you can create. It's the best project to use for learning the techniques you need to build the other two control types. In fact, you should probably try out several `UserControl` projects before you move on to the more popular derived control. Ease of use aside, you also need to realize that a `UserControl` can slow application performance because a `UserControl` has more linkage and more goes on behind the scenes. A `UserControl` has some impressive uses, but you also need to use it carefully. The following sections describe how to work with the `UserControl` in detail.

Essential Considerations for Developing a UserControl

When working with a `UserControl` project, you drag and drop existing controls onto a work area and then begin configuring the result. A `UserControl` project saves time and effort because you start with one or more existing controls to create a new control. However, there's a tendency to include too many features in a `UserControl` project. A developer may choose to make every property, method, and event of the original controls available, which ends up only making the control difficult to use. A

`UserControl` project should limit the number of available features in order to reduce complexity and make the resulting control easier to use.

Some `UserControl` projects are too limiting. A developer may combine a slider control with a textbox to create a volume control. However, the same project may see use as a color control. If the developer doesn't see this other use, the set of exposed properties may prove insufficient for use as a color control. Yes, it's important to limit the exposed properties, methods, and events to ensure the control is easy to use, but when the control becomes limited to one specific task, it probably won't provide a sufficient level of code reuse to make the project worthwhile. Developers need to balance generic functionality against ease of use to achieve a balanced approach to solving a range of problems.

There's a tendency to think of a `UserControl` as too simplistic to provide value as a control. However, by creating control packages in the form of a `UserControl`, you can help maintain consistency within team development projects. During your design discussions with team members, you must consider situations where two or more controls commonly appear together. These situations warrant a `UserControl` to ensure that all developers implement the control group the same way — reducing training costs and potential support headaches.

An example of an interesting `UserControl` *is the OK/Cancel button combination that often appears on dialog boxes. You can create a* `UserControl` *to make adding this button combination simple. In addition, relying on a* `UserControl` *ensures that the buttons always provide the same order and suggest positioning of the control on the dialog box form. If desired, you could also add an Apply button to the mix and provide a property for making it appear only when needed. Because the behavior of these three buttons is well defined, they make a perfect example of a* `UserControl` *project.*

Working with the UserControl Project

A `UserControl` project begins precisely the same way as a derived control project does (steps 1 through 5 of the procedure in the "Defining the Derived Control Project" section of the chapter. However, you don't change the inherited control from `UserControl` to something else. Instead, you begin adding controls to the `UserControl` in the designer. Figure 11-6 shows a typical example. Notice that you can add both controls and components as needed.

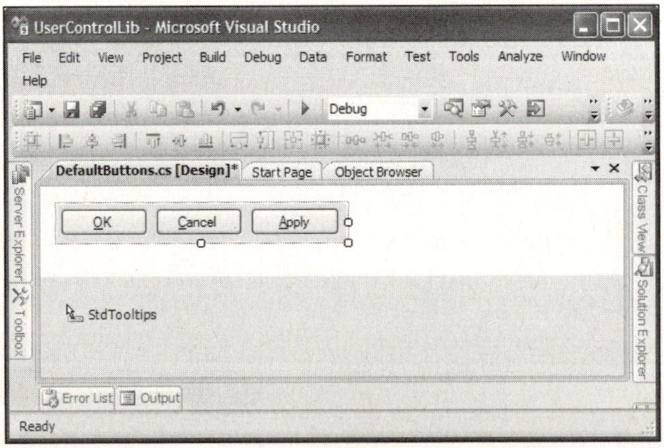

Figure 11-6: The `UserControl` setup lets you add as many controls and components as needed to define basic functionality.

At this point, you need to add code to make the `UserControl` do something. In this case, the developer using the control needs to know which button the user clicked, so the control includes a `DialogResult` property where the Apply button has a `DialogResult` of `Yes`. You may wonder where the `UserControl` gets a `DialogResult` property. In this case, you use the counterintuitive code shown here:

```
[Category("Default Buttons")]
[DefaultValue(DialogResult.None)]
[Description("Shows the result of clicking the buttons.")]
public DialogResult DialogResult {get; set;}
```

Because the `UserControl` doesn't have a `DialogResult` property, you can add it directly without overriding anything. Notice that this control provides the standard `Category` and `Description` properties. The `DefaultValue` property assigns a value to the `DialogResult` property to ensure it has a value when the developer begins working with it.

It isn't always necessary to keep the controls and components in a `UserControl` *private. If you want all the functionality of a control or component exposed, simply change the* `Modifiers` *property to match the level of visibility you want to provide (which is* `Public` *in most cases). Of course, exposing the control partially defeats the purpose of creating the* `UserControl`*, which is to exercise control over the control appearance and behavior.*

It's important to provide connectivity between the controls on the `UserControl` and the `UserControl` container. For example, if you want to let the developer using your control see the result of an OK button click, you have to provide the required connectivity. Here's an example of one of the event handlers for this example:

```
private void btnOK_Click(object sender, EventArgs e)
{
   DialogResult = DialogResult.OK;
   this.OnClick(new EventArgs());
}
```

Remember that this is the event handler for the OK button. When the user clicks OK, this event handler responds, but the user doesn't see any effect from it. The code is relatively simple. It begins by assigning the appropriate dialog result value to the `DialogResult` property associated with the `UserControl`. It then raises (fires) the `OnClick()` event associated with the `UserControl`. The developer handles this event as part of the application code.

Testing a `UserControl` is the same as testing a derived control. You add a Windows Forms project to your component project and add the `UserControl` to it. Using the `UserControl` in other applications is the same as well.

Building New Controls

Creating completely new controls is a job for an experienced developer and even experienced developers will want to forgo this daunting task whenever possible. The problem is that new controls require you to think of every aspect of control behavior — an extremely complex undertaking. You must consider everything from how the control draws itself on screen to the way common features behave. The Common Language Runtime (CLR) has no template on which to base control behavior, so you must define it all. Creating a new control does give you maximum flexibility, however, and you can tune the performance of a new control well beyond the limits imposed by either derived controls or the `UserControl`. The following sections provide insights into how you can create new controls — this section doesn't include the complex code required to create a new control.

Essential Considerations for Developing a New Control

When working with a new control, it's essential to keep in mind that it's entirely new. You must consider every aspect of the design carefully, including the control's physical appearance. All the design principles discussed in the earlier chapters of this book apply. To create a new control successfully, you must design every element before you write the first line of code. When you create a new control, your class inherits from the `Control` class, which implements the following basic functionality for you:

- User input through keyboard and pointing devices
- Message routing
- Security
- Control bounds (size and position)
- Window handle (`hWnd`) for drawing the control
- Ambient properties that include `Cursor`, `Font`, `BackColor`, `ForeColor`, and `RightToLeft`

Windows Forms automatically provides accessibility support for your control. However, you may want to provide additional accessibility support by changing the `AccessibleName`, `AccessibleDescription`, `AccessibleDefaultActionDescription`, and `AccessibleRole` property values. You can expose these properties to the developer as Microsoft exposes them for standard controls. If your application has special accessibility requirements, you can also derive your own class from `AccessibleObject` or `Control.ControlAccessibleObject`.

The `Control` class does provide access to a significant number of properties, methods, and events that you can implement in your own control. However, you must expose these properties, methods, and events before a developer can use them. The Web site at `http://msdn.microsoft.com/en-us/library/system.windows.forms.control_members.aspx` provides a full listing of the properties, methods, and events you can access using the `Control` class.

Working with the New Control Project

Creating a new control project is somewhat different from creating a derived control or `UserControl` project. The following steps help you create a new control project:

1. Choose File ⇨ New ⇨ Project to display the New Project dialog box shown in Figure 11-2.
2. Choose the Class Library template. Type a name for the new control such as `NewControl` in the Name field. Click OK.
3. Close the Class1.CS Editor window. You won't use this window because you're creating a component, not a class.
4. Right-click the `Class1.CS` entry in Solution Explorer and choose Delete from the context menu.
5. Right-click the `NewControl` entry in Solution Explorer and choose Add ⇨ New Item from the context menu. You'll see the Add New Item dialog box shown in Figure 11-7.
6. Highlight the Custom Control item template. Type a name for the control you want to create in the Name field. Click Add. Visual Studio adds the custom control to your library.

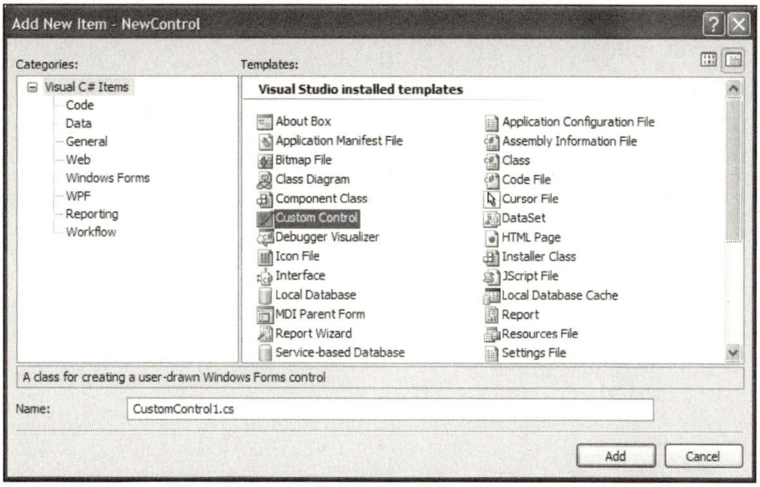

Figure 11-7: Locate the Custom Control entry to add a new control.

At this point, you have a new control ready for whatever you want to provide. You can drag and drop controls from the Toolbox onto the Designer to add existing controls to your new control. However, these controls won't appear in the resulting control — a new control doesn't share this feature with the `UserControl`. When you view the default code, you see something like this:

```
namespace NewControl
{
   public partial class SampleControl : Control
   {
      public SampleControl()
      {
         InitializeComponent();
      }

      protected override void OnPaint(PaintEventArgs pe)
      {
         base.OnPaint(pe);
      }
   }
}
```

As a minimum, you must provide a visual presentation for your control using the `OnPaint()` event handler. In addition, you provide the methods, properties, and events for the new control.

Building Components

As previously mentioned, components are nonvisual elements that you add to your application to perform specific tasks. For example, you can add a timer to your application to fire an event each time an interval you set expires. However, components have significantly wider usage in .NET applications. For example, if you add an `Event Log` object to your application from Server Explorer, you're adding a specialized component. The `Event Log` object, such as `Application`, appears in the Component Designer area of the Designer view shown in Figure 11-1.

Components are so useful that some developers have embraced a programming methodology called Component-Oriented Programming (COP). In this approach, almost none of the application code resides within the application itself — every major aspect of the application appears as part of a component. Whether you find this methodology useful depends on the kind of application you create. You can find an interesting paper on this topic at `http://www.cs.jhu.edu/~phf/pub/thesis-uci-2003.pdf`. *The book,* Component-Oriented Programming *(Wiley-Interscience, 2005) by Andy Ju An Wang and Kai Qian provides interesting insights into this programming strategy and includes some helpful tips for .NET developers.*

This book doesn't delve deeply into component creation. Someone could easily write two or three books on the topic. Creating a component is both easier and harder than creating a control. The easier part is that no one has expectations of specific methods, properties, and events. You also won't need to consider any visual elements. The harder part is that it truly can be difficult to create a useful component — one that's both easy to use and still meets everyone's needs. Components can also present security and reliability problems because developers tend to use them in unanticipated ways. The following sections help you understand the process of creating a component better.

Essential Considerations for Developing a New Component

Clear your mind and throw out any preconceived notions of what a component should do or how you should create it. Components are truly an art form — a creative endeavor of the highest sort. There aren't any rules when creating a component — only results. If your component provides a successful list of methods, properties, and events that helps a developer use them in the way in which you intended, then you've achieved success. The problem is that success is often elusive because developers overdesign the components they create. Consequently, the first rule of components is to keep it simple.

Just because the outside of your component is simple is no reason to assume that the inside is simple as well. You have no idea of how people will use your component. Consequently, you must include code to check everything. For example, you need to consider whether someone has sent your component a script, rather than the text you expected. Your code must ensure that numbers are in range and you must provide a means of dealing with errant input. The second rule of components is to make the code robust so it handles the unexpected without failure.

The previous paragraphs don't address the question of balance — making the outside simple and the inside robust. The problem of not knowing how your component will appear within an application means you can make errant decisions. The component user can also make errors in using your component. The third rule of components is to document how the component is supposed to work and to provide as much useful help information as possible. This third rule is especially important because nothing is worse than the frustration suffered by a developer who doesn't understand your component. All kinds of terrifying things happen when developers get frustrated.

Some developers confuse classes and components because both object types are nonvisual and seem to perform essentially the same tasks. The biggest difference between the two is that a class implements `System.IDisposable` *or derives from a class that implements* `IDisposable`. *A component implements* `System.ComponentModel.IComponent` *or derives from a component that implements*

`IComponent` so that you can use it on a design surface. The most common way to create a component is to derive it from `Component`. This seemingly small difference lets you add a component to a design surface. You can't add a class to a design surface. The overhead of implementing `IComponent` does give components a performance hit when compared to classes, so you should choose the implementation based on how you plan to reuse the code.

Defining the New Component Project

Components require a special setup. This section shows how to create a basic component project. You can use this technique to create any component you need. In this case, the example shows how to create a component named `DingDong` that raises an event on the quarter hour. You could use it for something like a clock application or possibly for specific monitoring events. The following steps show how to create the component project:

1. Choose File ⇨ New ⇨ Project to display the New Project dialog box shown in Figure 11-2.
2. Choose the Class Library template. Type a name for the component such as `ComponentLib` in the Name field. Click OK.
3. Close the `Class1.CS` Editor window. You won't use this window because you're creating a component, not a class.
4. Right-click the `Class1.CS` entry in Solution Explorer and choose Delete from the context menu.
5. Right-click the `ComponentLib` entry in Solution Explorer and choose Add ⇨ Component from the context menu. You see the Add New Item dialog box shown in Figure 11-8. Notice that Visual Studio automatically selects the `Component Class` entry for you and supplies a default name.

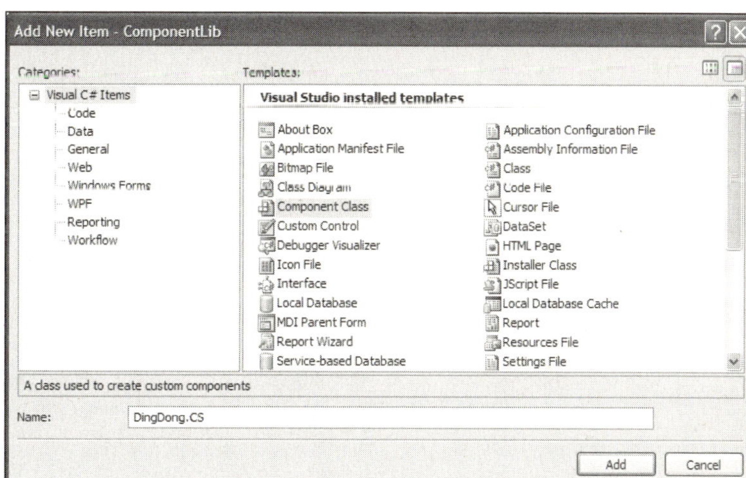

Figure 11-8: Add a new component class to your application.

6. Type a name for the component in the Name field. The example uses `DingDong.CS`, but you can use any name that suits your needs. Click Add. Visual Studio adds the new component to your library. Visual Studio automatically opens the new component in design mode where you can add components used by this component to perform a task. At this point, you can start creating your custom component — the remaining steps affect the example used in this section of the book.

You can mix controls, components, and classes in a single library if desired. There isn't any law that says you must keep the three object types separate. However, you should strive to create libraries that contain a single theme. For example, you might place all the financial database controls, components, and classes in a single library to make them easier for developers who work with that database to access.

7. Drag and drop a `Timer` control onto the Designer. Visual Studio adds the new component to the design surface.
8. Change the name of this `Timer` control to `ShortTimer`. Modify the Interval property to 1000 so that the timer ticks once per second.
9. Drag and drop another `Timer` control onto the Designer. Visual Studio adds the new component to the design surface.
10. Change the name of this `Timer` control to `QuarterTimer`. Modify the Interval property to 900000 so that the timer ticks once every 15 minutes.
11. Double-click `ShortTimer` to add a `Tick` event handler for it. Double-click `QuarterTimer` to add a `Tick` event handler for it.

Often, you can start with existing components to create new functionality, as with this example component. It's important to remember that any component you add to your custom component does present a performance hit because you have an additional layer to consider.

Adding the New Component Code

It's time to add some code to your component. Writing component code is very much like writing control code. You consider the same attributes and techniques. The only difference is that you don't consider the visual element. Listing 11-2 shows the component code for this example.

Listing 11-2: Creating a component

```
[DefaultEvent("OnQuarterHour")]
[DefaultProperty("Enabled")]
public partial class DingDong : Component
{
   public DingDong()
   {
      InitializeComponent();

      // Initialize the local variables.
      _Enabled = false;
      _WaitingForQuarterHour = false;
   }

   public DingDong(IContainer container)
   {
      container.Add(this);

      InitializeComponent();

      // Initialize the local variables.
```

```
      _Enabled = false;
      _WaitingForQuarterHour = false;
   }

   // Tells the user when the clock has started.
   [Category("DingDong Timer")]
   public delegate void TickStarting();
   [Category("DingDong Timer")]
   [Description("Shows that the timer is starting.")]
   public event TickStarting OnTickStarting;

   private Boolean _Enabled;

   [Category("DingDong Timer")]
   [DefaultValue(false)]
   [Description(
      "Enables generation of quarter hour timer events.")]
   public Boolean Enabled
   {
      get
      {
         return _Enabled;
      }

      set
      {
         // Set the current state.
         _Enabled = value;

         if (value == true)
         {
            // Generate a starting event when true.
            OnTickStarting();

            // Start the short timer.
            ShortTimer.Enabled = true;

            // Show that we're waiting for the quarter hour.
            _WaitingForQuarterHour = true;
         }
         else
         {
            // Turn off both timers.
            ShortTimer.Enabled = false;
            QuarterTimer.Enabled = false;

            // Show that we're not waiting for the quarter hour.
            _WaitingForQuarterHour = false;
         }
      }
   }

   // The clock has to wait for the quarter hour before
   // it begins generating events.
```

Continued

Listing 11-2: Creating a component *(continued)*

```
      private Boolean _WaitingForQuarterHour;

      [Category("DingDong Timer")]
      [Description(
         "Set to true while the timer waits for the quarter hour.")]
      public Boolean WaitingForQuarterHour
      {
         get
         {
            return _WaitingForQuarterHour;
         }
      }

      private void ShortTimer_Tick(object sender, EventArgs e)
      {
         if ((DateTime.Now.Minute == 0) ||
             (DateTime.Now.Minute == 15) ||
             (DateTime.Now.Minute == 30) ||
             (DateTime.Now.Minute == 45))
         {
            // Disable the short timer.
            ShortTimer.Enabled = false;

            // Enable the quarter hour timer.
            QuarterTimer.Enabled = true;

            // Show that we're no longer waiting for the
            // quarter hour.
            _WaitingForQuarterHour = false;

            // Fire the quarter hour event for the first time.
            OnQuarterHour();
         }
      }

      // Occurs each quarter hour while the timer is enabled.
      [Category("DingDong Timer")]
      public delegate void QuarterHour();
      [Category("DingDong Timer")]
      [Description("Shows that it's the quarter hour.")]
      public event QuarterHour OnQuarterHour;

      private void QuarterTimer_Tick(object sender, EventArgs e)
      {
         // Fire the quarter hour event.
         OnQuarterHour();
      }
   }
```

This example starts with two new attributes: `DefaultEvent` and `DefaultProperty`. You use these attributes to define the name of the event and property that the developer using your component is most likely to require. It's also a helpful way to show a mandatory event or property. For example, when working with this component, you must create an event handler for OnQuarterHour or you won't see any results from using the component. Likewise, you must set Enabled to true before the component will do anything.

The component has two constructors by default. You normally won't need to provide additional constructors. The only thing the constructors do, in this case, is initialize two variables.

Everything begins for this component when the Enabled property becomes true. Because this component doesn't do anything right away, I've included a special event, OnTickStarting, to tell the developer using the component that something has happened. It's important to provide status indicators with components that you create so that developers don't have to guess about the component status. Otherwise, developers using your component may worry that they have done something wrong — sometimes developers are even less willing to wait than users are.

The Enabled property comes next. Notice that this property includes the standard Category and Description attributes. However, it also adds a DefaultValue attribute. This attribute adds a default value to the property, ensuring that the component doesn't start in an undefined state. This property is a simple toggle. When the user sets Enabled to true, the property raises (fires) OnTickStarting(), starts the ShortTerm timer, and sets _WaitingForQuarterHour to true. Setting Enabled to false stops both timers (you don't know which one is running) and sets _WaitingForQuarterHour to false.

This component includes a second status indicator in the form of the WaitingForQuarterHour property. The developer can query this property to ensure that it's still waiting for the initial quarter hour to expire.

The ShortTimer_Tick() event handler performs a simple check. Whenever DateTime.Now.Minute shows a quarter-hour value, it disables itself, enables the QuarterTimer, sets _WaitingForQuarterHour to false, and fires the first OnQuarterHour() event. You may wonder at this point why the code simply doesn't reset ShortTimer to the new value and continue using the single timer. Relying on a second timer makes the code simpler, more easily read, and provides a specific object for each task.

The final bits of code deal with the OnQuarterHour() event. Once the initial waiting period expires, all the component really has to do is raise the OnQuarterHour() event every quarter hour. The QuarterTimer_Tick() event handler performs precisely this task.

Testing the Component

You use essentially the same process to start testing a component as you do for testing a derived control (see the "Checking the Derived Control Functionality" section of the chapter for details. The example there uses a test application name of DingDong_Test).

After you create the new application, you'll want to add some components and controls to it. Of course, you'll want to add the DingDong component, which appears in the ComponentLib Components tab of the Toolbox. Name this component ChimeTime. In addition, you'll want to add a Timer component. The controls include two buttons and a label. The first button, btnStartStop, provides a toggle between the start and stop states for ChimeTime. The second button, btnGetStatus, shows the current WaitingForQuarterHour property status. The label, lblCurrentTime, simply shows the current system time so you can determine whether the quarter is up. Figure 11-9 shows how the example dialog box appears.

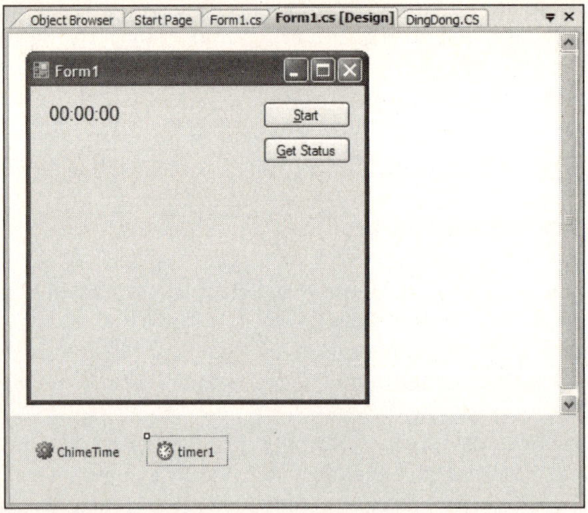

Figure 11-9: Create a form to test the `DingDong` component.

Now that you have some components and controls to work with, you can begin adding some code. Listing 11-3 shows the code used for this example.

Listing 11-3: Monitoring the `DingDong` component

```
private void ChimeTime_OnQuarterHour()
{
   MessageBox.Show("It's the quarter hour!");
}

private void ChimeTime_OnTickStarting()
{
   MessageBox.Show("The timer is waiting for the quarter hour");
}

private void btnStartStop_Click(object sender, EventArgs e)
{
   // Toggle between start and stop states.
   if (btnStartStop.Text == "&Start")
   {
      btnStartStop.Text = "&Stop";
      ChimeTime.Enabled = true;
   }
   else
   {
      btnStartStop.Text = "&Start";
      ChimeTime.Enabled = false;
   }
}
```

```
private void btnGetStatus_Click(object sender, EventArgs e)
{
   // Show the current status.
   MessageBox.Show(
      "Waiting for Quarter Hour: " +
      ChimeTime.WaitingForQuarterHour.ToString());
}

private void timer1_Tick(object sender, EventArgs e)
{
   lblCurrentTime.Text = DateTime.Now.ToLongTimeString();
}
```

The first two event handlers simply show the output of `ChimeTime`. When you start the timer, you see a message that the timer is waiting for the quarter hour. When the quarter hour occurs, you see another message telling you so. These are simple checks to ensure that the events provided by `ChimeTime` work.

The `btnStartStop_Click()` event handler enables or disables `ChimeTime`. It also changes the button text to show the change in status. Whenever the button enables `ChimeTime`, you should see the Waiting for Quarter Hour message.

The `btnGetStatus_Click()` event handler shows the current `ChimeTime` status during the initial waiting phase, when it needs to wait for the first quarter hour to occur. The associated message box should display a true result until the first quarter hour elapses. Afterward, the message box should return false. The message box should also return false when `ChimeTime` is disabled (stopped).

The `timer1_Tick()` event hander simply displays the current time on screen. This added test feature makes it easier for you to track the component's behavior. Consider adding touches like this to your own test environment.

Testing Classes Using the Object Test Bench

The Object Test Bench takes a different view of your classes. You use it to explore the class from a developer perspective, but that exploration is more on a visual level than working with the debugger to check your code. The benefit of the Object Test Bench is that you can see how the class interacts without actually starting the debugger. The best way to discover Object Test Bench is to use it, which is what this section is going to do.

You might think that you can test your controls directly using Object Test Bench. However, the controls have to have a container, the test applications used in each section of the chapter. Object Test Bench works with the class view of your application, so you need to press Ctrl+Shift+C to display the Class View window. Figure 11-10 shows a typical view of the Class View window for a control test setup (this is a separate solution that contains the code for the derived control).

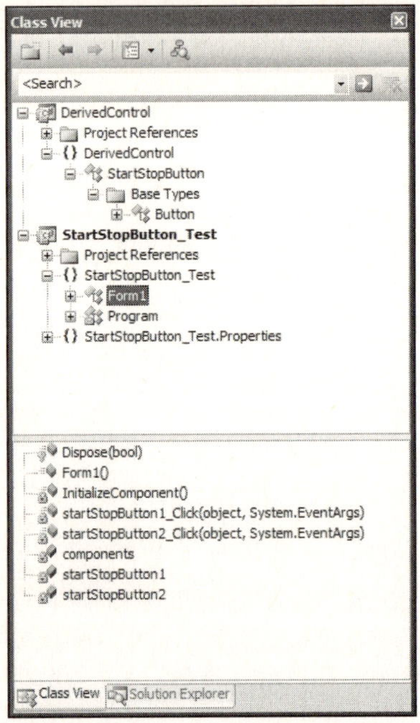

Figure 11-10: Class View shows the classes in your application.

To bring up a copy of Object Test Bench, right-click the form holding the controls in Class View (Form1 in this case), and choose Create Instance ⇨ Form1() from the context menu. You'll see a Create Instance dialog box where you type a name for the class. What you type doesn't really matter because it isn't permanent — choosing the default name is just fine in most cases. Visual Studio displays Object Test Bench with your class loaded, as shown in Figure 11-11.

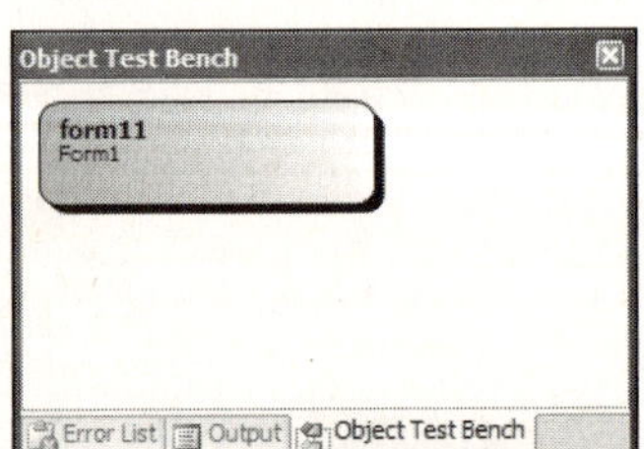

Figure 11-11: Object Test Bench contains an instantiated copy of your class.

Now that you have an instance of an object to use, you can work with it in a number of ways. For example, you may simply decide to test the `Click()` methods for the Start button. To perform this task, right-click the `form11` object shown in Figure 11-11 and choose Invoke Method ⇨ startStopButton1_Click (object, EventArgs) from the context menu. You'll see the Invoke Method dialog box shown in Figure 11-12.

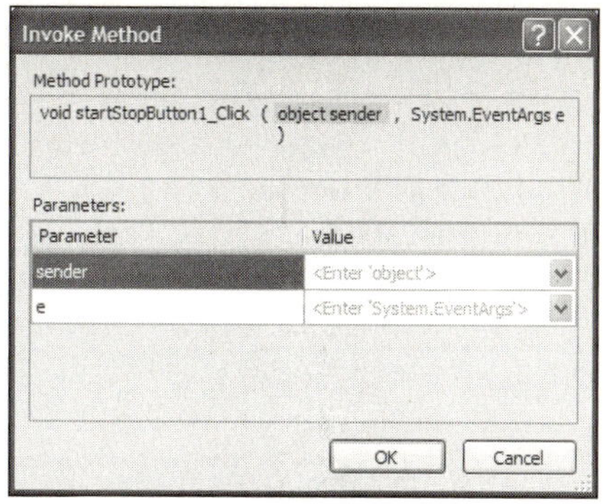

Figure 11-12: Invoke specific methods without creating the form.

Before you can do anything else, you must provide arguments for "sender" and "e" or the call will fail. In both cases, you can choose null from the drop-down list box in the Value column. Click OK and you'll see a message box appear with the word Start in it. Click OK in the message box and you see a Method Call Result dialog box like the one shown in Figure 11-13. This dialog box tells you whether the method call was successful and provides you with the result value. Click Retry if you want to try the method call again or OK to do something else.

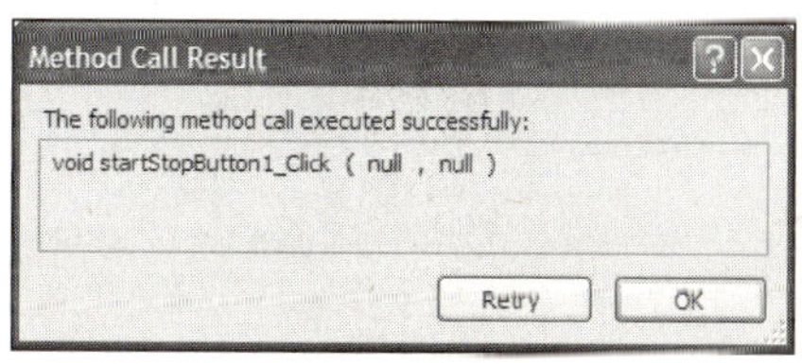

Figure 11-13: View the results of a method call and execute it again if desired.

Many of the methods you need come from the base classes. To access these methods, right-click the `form11` object and choose Invoke Method ➪ Inherited Methods from the context menu. Leave the mouse in place for a few seconds. Eventually, you'll see a list of inherited methods. Let's say you want to display the form. In this case, you choose `Form.ShowDialog()` from the list. You'll see the same Invoke Method dialog box (see Figure 11-12) as before. When you click OK, you'll see the form appear as before and you can use the form to interact with the controls.

When you close the form, you'll see the Method Call Result dialog box as before (see Figure 11-13). However, this time the dialog box contains a Return Value field because the method call returns a result. You won't normally see this return value in the debugger, which is why the Object Test Bench is so useful. The default settings save the result for you so that you can make several tests and compare the results. Clear the Save Return Value option if you don't want to save the results, and click OK. Otherwise, you'll see the result added as an object to the Object Test Bench. Interestingly enough, you can interact with this object in the same way that you interact with any other object. If you want to change the result value to a string, you can invoke a method to do it.

The Object Test Bench also lets you see how the control classes interact. Hover the mouse over the `form11` object and you'll see a popup appear. Click on the various elements to see the structure of the test application and the controls it contains. Let's say you want to change the text for the Start button to see what will happen. In this case, you follow the hierarchy to the `System.Windows.Forms.ButtonBase` class, as shown in Figure 11-14. It may surprise you to know that this is where the `Text` property actually resides, but there it is. If you click on this entry, you can edit its value. When you finish, you can try working with the control again to see how the change affects it.

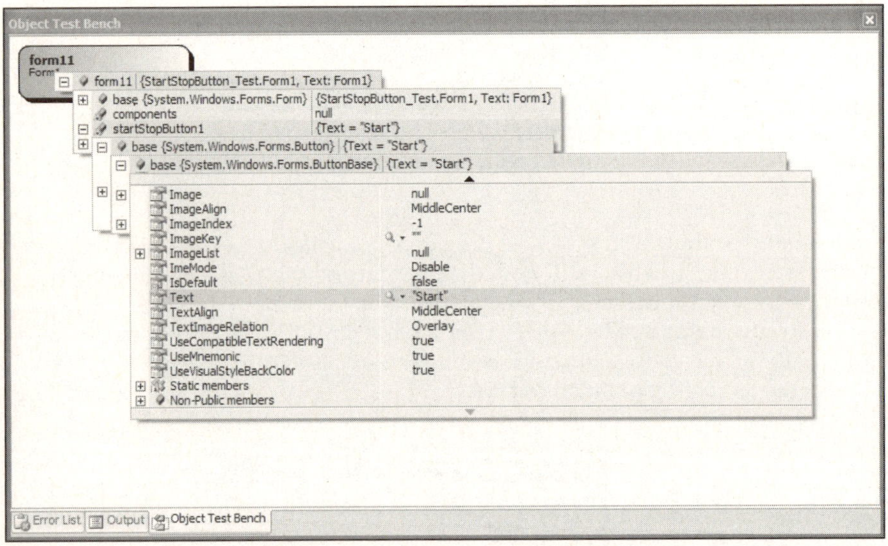

Figure 11-14: View and change property values as needed by drilling down to correct class.

One of the more interesting things to view is the `CreateParams` entry. Look at the `System.Windows.Forms.Button` entry and you'll see a `CreateParams` child property, which contains all the arguments that Windows uses to create the button on screen. Viewing information like this helps you see the connection between the managed environment and the native environment that Windows supports. You can use information like this to create better low-level applications, especially when working with P/Invoke.

This is an extremely short tour of the Object Test Bench. The best way to learn more about this tool is to create an object and play with it for a while. Even though this tool seems simple, you can use it to perform an amazing number of tasks that you can't perform with the debugger. More importantly, you can use this tool to understand your application better. For example, you can perform "what if" analysis to see how changing things will affect the application. The Object Test Bench tends to model the real world better than the debugger does, so you get a better view of how changes will affect your application. In addition, unlike the debugger, you can save the results of method calls for comparison purposes, which makes it considerably easier to view the results of your "what if" analysis.

Coding Your Application

The first piece of information you should walk away with after reading this chapter is that you may not always use controls and components in your application. Some application categories don't use them. The next piece of information is that controls and components aren't the same. The simple way to remember the difference is that controls are visual in nature. This chapter has also provided you with examples of building your own controls and components, and then testing them using the Object Test Bench. Always remember that the Object Test Bench can test any class in your application — not just controls and components.

Most developers will build a number of controls and components during their careers. However, most developers won't use custom components and controls nearly as often as they could to solve specific application issues. Instead, they'll reinvent the wheel every time they need to perform a task. Of course, you don't have to follow the crowd. You can change things now by creating a list of components and controls you've always wanted and begin building them. Many libraries begin when someone decides to brainstorm solutions to problems that we all know exist, but haven't done anything about. When making your list, be sure you prioritize it. Create the components and controls you need for your current project first, and then work on those nice-to-have components and controls. In many cases, components and controls make a good diversionary project — you can work at them when you need a break.

You have all the building blocks for your application — a good design, a data source, components and controls, and other elements including an enhanced IDE. Chapter 12 takes the next step — coding your application. Just as this chapter doesn't provide a comprehensive view of everything you need to know for components and controls, Chapter 12 isn't a comprehensive view of coding applications. Rather, just as this chapter focuses on design and development issues, Chapter 12 helps you build better applications by pointing out ways to implement your design more consistently.

12

Coding the Application

After the initial design phase, many developers head directly to their editors and start typing. If you're working alone on a simple project, you can probably take this approach without experiencing any problems. However, when working on a complex team project, the immediate typing approach seldom works because you must consider some code writing issues such as the naming convention the team will use and determining how certain features will appear in the application.

This chapter begins by addressing the mundane sounding, yet politically charged, issue of using a consistent naming convention. In the end, it doesn't matter which naming convention you use — they all work. What matters is that all coders on your team use the same naming convention so they can read each other's code. This chapter doesn't espouse a particular naming convention — it simply tells you what's available so you can make your own decision.

How an application begins and exits has always been important. However, in an age when Microsoft has introduced Windows Server 2008 Server Core — a special version of Windows that lacks a GUI — the manner in which an application begins and ends has taken on special significance. This chapter provides you with techniques you can use to begin and end a .NET application at the command line or simply use the command line as an intermediary to standard GUI use. Having command line functionality gives you a big advantage when it comes to making the application flexible.

Finally, this chapter provides a view on custom feature usage. A custom feature is a new way to perform a common task, such as error trapping. The two most common custom features are attributes and error classes. You'll discover when it's most appropriate to use custom features and when to avoid them. In some cases, using a custom feature is the only way to accomplish a particular task.

Using an Appropriate Naming Convention

I'd love to say that there's a standardized approach to naming conventions in coding, but there isn't. Naming conventions have sparked more than a few protracted discussions online, with the protagonists declaring that only imbeciles would use any alternative to the naming conventions they promote. This section of the chapter isn't meant to spark another in a long series of political debates — it exists only to tell you what naming conventions are available so that you can make an informed decision on which approach you want to use. Any of these methods produces good code that compiles and works just fine within the application. This is a stylistic consideration akin to asking whether you want cheese on the burger that you ordered. Everyone has a preference and I'm certain that you'll find your own style, too.

Computer scientists have created more than a few naming conventions — this chapter doesn't even begin to scratch the surface. For example, the chapter doesn't discuss positional notation, which is a method of naming variables mainly found in mainframe applications today. The three naming conventions found in this chapter are the most popular conventions in use today. However, you may want to research other naming conventions if you don't find a solution that works for you in this chapter. Of course, you must find a solution that works within the constraints set by C#.

Using Hungarian Notation

You've likely seen Hungarian notation, even if you don't know what it is. Hungarian notation has been around for a very long time. Charles Simonyi originally created Hungarian notation during the days of the Disk Operating System (DOS) to make the functional type of identifiers apparent. The naming convention grew from there to see use in Windows programming where, at one time, the purpose of an identifier was even harder to determine. You can see a write-up of the history of Hungarian notation at `http://msdn.microsoft.com/en-us/library/aa260976(VS.60).aspx`.

In some respects, Hungarian notation is no longer standardized (not that it was ever standardized by a committee). The original use for Hungarian notation was for languages such as C/C++. You can find one presentation of this older notation at `http://www.gregleg.com/oldHome/hungarian.html`. Many developers have adapted Hungarian notation for use with newer languages such as Visual Basic. You can find a discussion of this use at `http://support.microsoft.com/kb/173738` and `http://support.microsoft.com/kb/110264`. The Visual Basic convention also works great for C#.

How you use a Hungarian notation–like naming convention depends on your organization. The basic idea is to provide some means of identifying coding elements. You could create your own code to perform this task. Nothing says you have to precede every label with lbl.

Many people have said that Hungarian notation is no longer appropriate because it replicates the type checking performed by compilers today. In addition, you can discover type information using IDE features such as IntelliSense. Microsoft is among the companies that discourage use of Hungarian notation. Others still rely on Hungarian notation either because they've used it for so many years or because they find it still works as an organizational aid. For example, if you use the Visual Basic form of Hungarian notation, you'll find all labels, forms, and so on organized by notation type when you look for them. In addition, Hungarian notation still has value when the code appears outside the IDE, such as when you copy and paste it into an e-mail message.

Using Camel Case

You've already seen camel case in use in popular culture because it's a technique for combining multiple words while retaining the original words. For example, the surnames MacLean and VanDyke are both examples of camel case. In this case, the surnames reflect the original language's use of two words for the surname, but the English language's preference for a single word. You also see it for company names. RadioShack is an example of a company name that uses camel case. In some cases, technology uses camel case, such as VistaVision, which is a widescreen format for movies. It's little wonder that camel case appears in application code — everyone already knows how to use it. Camel case for development purposes has a number of other names, so you may have already seen this naming convention using a different name. Among them are:

- CamelCase
- Camel caps
- Medial caps

Microsoft and other industry leaders have modified the standard use of camel case. When you talk about camel casing for .NET, what you really mean is that the first letter of each word, except the first word, is capitalized. For example, if you want to create a variable that contains the background color for an object, you might call it `backColor`. Microsoft generally recommends using camel casing for parameters and protected instance fields.

Using Pascal Case

What most people call camel case, Microsoft calls Pascal case. The original source of Pascal case is the same as camel case — it was adopted from what people were used to using in real-world situations. See the "Using Camel Case" section of the chapter for a discussion of the source. Using again the example of a variable that holds a background color, the Pascal case version is `BackColor`. Notice that the first word is in initial caps, instead of in lowercase. Microsoft recommends using Pascal case for the following purposes:

- Class
- Enum type
- Enum values
- Event
- Exception class (always end the name with the word Exception)
- Read-only static field
- Interface (always begin with the letter *I*)
- Method
- Namespace
- Parameter
- Property
- Public instance field

Many industry experts have focused on a combination of camel case and Pascal case for variable names. Unfortunately, they tend to disagree with each other. One of the more interesting and comprehensive efforts in this area is the naming conventions found at `http://www.irritatedvowel.net/Programming/Standards.aspx`. *You may also want to check the MSDN sites at* `http://msdn.microsoft.com/en-us/library/ms229045.aspx` *and* `http://msdn.microsoft.com/en-us/library/ms229002.aspx`.

Adding Specialized Syntax

A naming convention can consist of more than capitalization, prefixes, and suffixes. In some cases, you apply specialized syntax to standardize the coding elements in some way. For example, even if you don't normally use Hungarian notation, you might add an *I* to all interface classes. As a practical matter, you may want to follow Microsoft's lead in this regard. If you see a particular syntax used for the .NET Framework, you may also want to use it for your code. The following sections list some of the most common syntax elements.

It's always bad form to use a specialized prefix for some other purpose in your code. For example, you wouldn't want to create an integer variable that has an I *prefix, such as IMyInt. Anyone looking at the variable would assume that you mean some type of interface, not an integer.*

Applying I for Interface

Interfaces receive special attention in .NET coding because they provide a standard from which developers create classes. Microsoft has used interface definitions for a very long time. An interface describes the methods, properties, and events that a class must implement in order to provide a certain type of functionality. This functionality provides a means for applications to communicate with each other, including native-code applications.

In some cases, you must define an interface to ensure that other developers can interact with your code. Because an interface could potentially look like a class, Microsoft recommends that you prefix all interfaces with an *I*. In fact, you'll notice that Microsoft follows this practice not only for the .NET Framework but also for languages such as C/C++. When you see an *I* prefix, you can always be sure that you're looking at an interface.

Applying m_ for Local Memory

You won't always see the m_ prefix used for local memory, but it still appears commonly. Some developers wondered how to approach the issue of private variables used to hold property values. The method that's seen the longest use is to prefix the variable with m_ and give it the same name as the property. For example, if you have a property named `MyProperty`, the local variable for that property is `m_MyProperty`.

Unfortunately, Microsoft views the m_ prefix as a leftover from Hungarian notation. Consequently, many Microsoft developers initially decided to use just the underscore (_) for private variables. In this case, the private variable for `MyProperty` is `_MyProperty`. Some developers found this naming convention confusing.

The new Microsoft method seems to rely on a camel-cased variable, with a Pascal-cased property counterpart that ends with the word Property. Consequently, if you declare a variable named `myVar`, then the associated property is `MyVarProperty`. Because Microsoft has been so inconsistent in this area, you must consider that you'll see all three of these variations.

Working with Uppercase, Abbreviations, and Acronyms

Sometimes you need to use a naming convention that relies on special characteristics such as uppercase, abbreviations, or acronyms. For example, a user interface element may rely on the UI abbreviation, such as `ObtainUIParameters`. An object specifically designed to work with the Windows Internet Naming Service may contain the WINS acronym, such as `QueryWINS`. In a very few cases, you may rely on uppercase for emphasis or some other special need, such as `TODOAttribute`.

The emphasis that these naming conventions provide can make the name considerably easier to understand. When working with uppercase, abbreviations, and acronyms, you must ensure that the team member will understand the term. Otherwise, it serves no purpose. For example, most developers won't know the alternative WINS acronym, Web Invoicing System. Microsoft generally asks developers to avoid uppercase, abbreviations, and acronyms because of the understanding issues that they can present.

Always document the abbreviations and acronyms you employ in an application. Use consistent meanings for abbreviations and acronyms — don't assign different meanings to the same abbreviation or acronym. When a conflict does exist, use the most common definition for the abbreviation or acronym, and spell out the other meaning.

In some cases, you also create abbreviations of common words. For example, you could possibly use `CmdLineArgs` for command line arguments. Most developers will understand the abbreviations used for this name.

One of the biggest issues in using uppercase, abbreviations, or acronyms is consistency. If you decide to use a particular capitalization, abbreviation, or acronym somewhere, you should use it everywhere. The reason is simple — developers will come to depend on the presentation you provide and could actually miss the term if it appears in some other way.

Using Numbers

Numbers can appear as a naming convention in several ways. In many cases, you see them used in place of words, such as `Hex2Dec`, for a method that changes hexadecimal to decimal. Another use is as a direct reference. For example, you might see `ErrorHandler412` for an error handler for the 412-error code. Microsoft doesn't say much about numbers used as part of a naming convention. However, when you use numbers, you need to consider whether the viewer will understand what you mean. Most developers will understand the use of 2 in the previous example, but they may not understand the use of 412.

As with other naming conventions, consistent use is important. Unfortunately, numbers present a number of consistency issues. Developers may forget to use the number 2 in place of "to" and create an alternative method, `HexToDec`. As with any naming convention, documentation and training are essential.

Numbers and special characters present a special problem for C#. You can't use them everywhere. For example, a variable name can't begin with a number, so `2Test` *wouldn't work. The C# compiler places extreme limitations on special characters. For example, you can't use ! anywhere, so* `HelpMe!` *won't work.*

Considering Other Special Cases

It's important to realize that the techniques you use to identify various kinds of variables are entirely up to you. The compiler certainly doesn't care. The human-readable naming convention is there for your use. Consequently, if you decide that you want to add a certain suffix to objects of a specific type, that's up to you. As long as your naming convention doesn't break the compiler's rules for naming things, you don't have any worries. Here are some things to consider when adding your own naming conventions:

- Make naming convention additions consistent so they make sense.
- Keep naming conventions to a minimum to ensure that members of your development team can memorize them for easy use.

- Document naming conventions so that new members of the team can discover what they mean.
- Avoid naming conventions that have use for only one project, because single-use naming conventions tend to increase maintenance costs.

Adding Command Line Functionality

Developers often don't realize just how important the command line has become. After working with administrators long enough, however, you realize that the command line is often where they live — at least that's where the best administrators live.

The command line can help you perform tasks unimaginably fast, and you can also use it to automate tasks. Not only can the administrator automatically schedule tasks using the Task Scheduler, but reliance on batch files and scripts means that the administrator need not even remember arcane command sequences. Consequently, unless the application you build works only with a graphical interface (such as an application that monitors system performance using graphs), you probably want to add a command line interface to it.

Always adding command line functionality (except where it absolutely won't work) sounds like a rather broad statement, but you might be surprised to discover just how often administrators use the command line. For example, you might find it interesting to know that you can perform many Exchange Server 2007 tasks at the command line considerably faster than by using the GUI. Some Exchange Server 2007 tasks actually require that you use the command line exclusively because the GUI just gets in the way. The following sections get you started adding a command line interface to your application.

When to Use Command Line Switches

Some of the simplest applications in the world provide command line switches. For example, type **`Notepad /p MyDoc.TXT`** and Notepad will send the document to the printer for you. If you print the document regularly, adding this command to a batch file or as an entry in the registry can save you considerable time. Consequently, if your application prints something from a file, you can add the same functionality and save administrators time — it really is that easy to come up with a good reason to add command line functionality.

Of course, adding the right command line switches is as important as adding the functionality in the first place. Microsoft made a mistake with Notepad. The `/?` command line switch is the most common you'll find offered. Any application that offers a command line interface should implement the `/?` command line switch. However, type **`Notepad /?`** and press Enter at the command prompt. You'll find that Notepad starts and displays an error message, rather than providing help. Now, try the directory (`Dir`) command. Type **`Dir /?`** and press Enter. You'll see a helpful screen of information that shows how to use the `Dir` command. Here's a list of common command line switch types:

- **Help (`/?`):** Always include the help command line switch. The application should also display help when the user doesn't provide any command line switches at all.
- **Context-sensitive help (`/A /?`):** Some command line switch arrangements are so complex that you must provide several layers of help. In this case, you see help for the `/A` command line switch, which is part of a larger application.

- **Variable data (MyDoc.TXT):** Variable information can be anything — the name of a file, a username, a location in the registry, anything at all. The variable information appears on the command line without any associated command line switch. An application can have one variable data entry at most because otherwise you can't determine how the user means to use the data.
- **Optional variable data ([MyDoc.TXT]):** You can make the variable data optional. The traditional way to make variable data optional is to show them within square brackets. Use this form only when the application runs fine without the data or you want to ask the user about the data after the application begins.
- **Exclusive command line switch (/A):** Most applications with a command line interface include one or more command line switches. A command line switch always begins with a slash (/), followed by any number of letters, numbers, or special symbols (except spaces and reserved characters) desired. You typically use a command line switch to tell the application to perform an action.
- **Optional exclusive command line switch ([/A]):** In many cases, the user won't want to perform all the actions that an application can perform using a single command line. Optional command line switches, always found within square brackets, provide the means to perform some tasks and not others.
- **Specific data input (/F "MyDoc.TXT MyDoc2.TXT"):** When your application requires several pieces of information and you want the user to specify the kind of data, then combine a command line switch with a variable data string. If the data contain spaces, then enclose the data in single (') or double quotes (").
- **Default data input (/F [<Filenames>]):** You can assign a default value to data input. The user provides just the command line switch when using the default data value. The command line switch says to use the default data. The command line includes both the command line switch and the data value when the user wants to override the default value. As always, optional values appear within square brackets. The name within the angle brackets defines the kind of data input the application expects (one or more filenames in this case).
- **Nested command line switch and data input ([/A [/F [<Filenames>]]]):** Nesting lets you define a sequence of command line switches and data input. You can arrange the sequence in any order. In this case, if you want to use the default file or specify a file, then you must also provide the /A command line switch. The square brackets appear within each other to define the syntax order so the user doesn't provide them in the wrong order.
- **Optional command line switches and data input ([/A | /B | /F <Filenames>]):** In some cases, command line switches and data input are mutually exclusive. For example, in this situation, you can use the /A, /B, or /F command line switches, but you can choose only one of the three. In addition, when using the /F command line switch, you must provide a filename. Separate the members of an optional command line switch group using the pipe (|) symbol.

This list touches on the most common command line switch configurations, but there are many more. In fact, try typing **WMIC /?** and you'll begin to appreciate just how complex command line switch setups can become. In this case, you're viewing a complex array of command line switches, data input, and positional keywords. For example, try typing **WMIC ComputerSystem /?** and you see another help screen. Drill down further by typing **WMIC ComputerSystem GET /?** and the listing becomes even more complicated.

Adding Command Line Switches

It's important to understand how the command line works before you begin this section, and the best way to obtain that information is to spend some time working with it. Of course, this means having a list of commands you can execute. You can find such as list on Web sites such as `http://www.ss64.com/nt/` or within my book, *Administering Windows Server 2008 Server Core* (Sybex, 2008).

After you've worked at the command line for a while, you discover most of the commands don't have a GUI — you type a command and they display the output as text. This kind of application is a console application — one that lacks a GUI. Creating a console application is one of the easiest ways to discover the command line. The example in this section uses a console application to display the current date or time in the format you specify.

Before you begin creating a command line application, you want to define the list of commands it will perform. This process is akin to designing the user interface for a GUI application, except you work with text commands. This example uses the following command line switches:

- `/?`: Displays the help screen.
- `/FD DateTimeString`: Displays the date and/or time using the specified formatting characters.
- `/LD`: Displays the date in long format.
- `/LT`: Displays the time in long format.
- `/SD`: Displays the date in short format.
- `/ST`: Displays the time in short format.
- `/UTC`: Displays the date and time in Coordinated Universal Time format.

The name of this example is `ShowDT`. To begin, choose the Console Application template in the New Project dialog box in Visual Studio. A console application begins with a very small `Main()` method and that's about it. The `Main()` method receives an array of strings that tells you which command line arguments the user supplied at the command line.

One potential addition to this application would be to display the time and date using a specific locale. In fact, this application is easy to extend, and you should expand it as necessary to meet your particular needs.

Defining the Help Screen

Every console application has at least two cases. The user can ask for help or the user can execute a command. For this example, when the user supplies either the `/?` or doesn't supply any command line arguments at all, the application displays a help screen. Otherwise, the application searches for valid command line arguments. As a safety feature, this application displays the help screen when the user doesn't supply any valid command line switches. Because you'll display the help screen a number of times, it's better to place the information in its own method. Listing 12-1 shows the help screen code for this example.

Listing 12-1: Providing a help screen

```
static void ShowHelp()
{
   Console.Write("Displays the date and/or time in the format");
   Console.WriteLine("you request.");
   Console.WriteLine();
   Console.Write("ShowDT [/?][/FD <DateTimeString>][/LD][/LT]");
   Console.WriteLine("[/SD][/ST][/UTC]");
   Console.WriteLine();
   Console.WriteLine("/? - Displays the help screen.");
   Console.Write("/FD DateTimeString - Displays the date and/or");
   Console.WriteLine("time using the specified");
   Console.WriteLine("      formatting characters.");
   Console.WriteLine("/LD - Displays the date in long format.");
   Console.WriteLine("/LT - Displays the time in long format.");
   Console.WriteLine("/SD - Displays the date in short format.");
   Console.WriteLine("/ST - Displays the time in short format.");
   Console.Write("/UTC - Displays the date and time in Coordinated");
   Console.WriteLine("Universal Time format.");
   return;
}
```

As you can see, there isn't anything too complicated here. I did format the help text for a nice appearance in the output, as shown in Figure 12-1. It's standard practice to provide a minimum of three pieces of information as part of your help screen: a summary of the purpose of the command line application, the command line syntax, and an explanation of the usage of the command line switches.

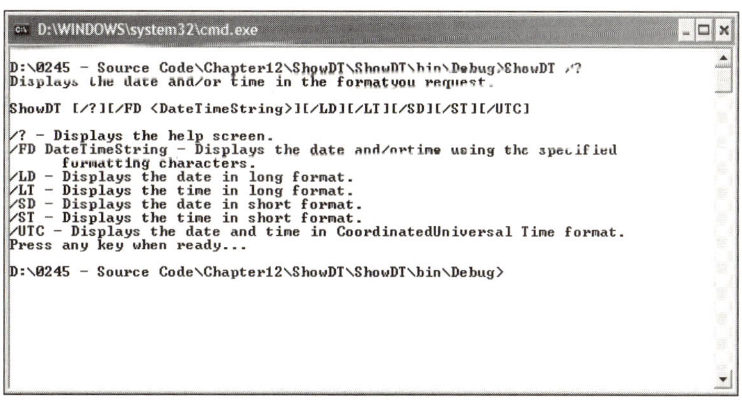

Figure 12-1: Every command line application requires a help screen accessed with the /? command line switch.

As your command line application becomes more complex, you should add a fourth section that shows usage examples. Some command line applications become even more complex and rely on multiple help screens to accomplish work. The "When to Use Command Line Switches" section of the chapter provides more information about how to implement command line switches, what types of command line switches are available, and the use of multiple help screens to make your application significantly easier to use.

Handling Debugging

One of the problems with console applications is that they execute and immediately exit. Therefore, when you try to debug your application, you see a quick flash of the output and that's it. Of course, you could place a break point into the IDE, but that only helps when debugging from within the IDE. You might want a debug version of your utility to use with a batch file or script. The example application includes a special method called `CheckDebug()` that appears here:

```
        static void CheckDebug()
        {
#if (DEBUG)
            Console.Write("Press any key when ready...");
            Console.ReadLine();
#endif
        }
```

Visual Studio automatically creates a constant called `DEBUG`. You can set this constant on the Build tab of your project's Properties dialog box, as shown in Figure 12-2. (To access this dialog box in the example project, choose Project ➪ ShowDT Properties.) The code shown in Listing 12-2 relies on the `DEBUG` constant. When you create a Debug build, the `DEBUG` constant is defined and the compiler adds the pause code into your application. When you create a Release build, the compiler doesn't add the code, so the command line application works as normal.

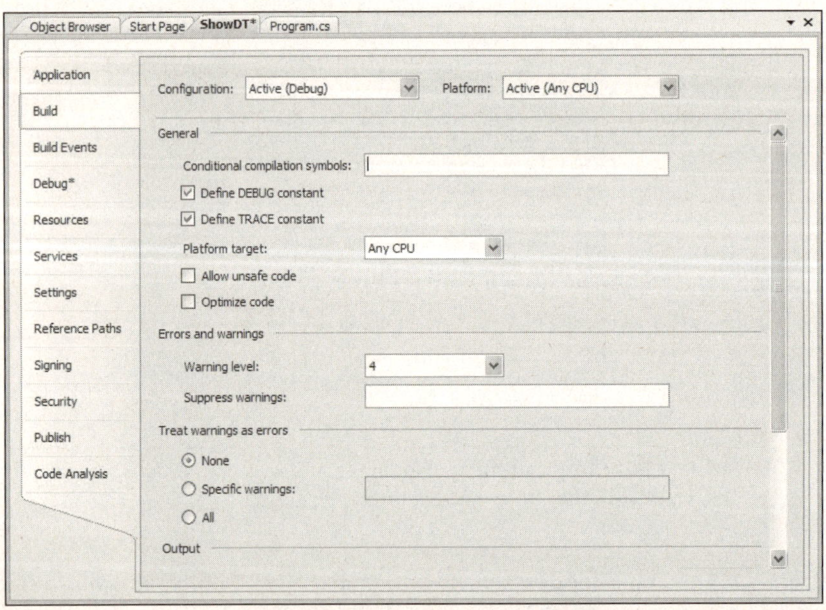

Figure 12-2: The IDE adds both a `DEBUG` and `TRACE` define to your application by default.

When you create an application that uses the `CheckDebug()` *method described in this chapter, you must provide the user with a release version of the application. Otherwise, the user may report errors due to any pauses you include in the application. Error reports of this sort can prove irritating and difficult to locate because the application is actually performing as expected.*

Creating the Main Code

It's time to look at the `Main()` code for this application. What a command line application does is look for command line switches that control its operation. It then acts on those command line switches in a specific way. The example application normally builds a string that contains the requested date and time information, as shown in Listing 12-2.

Listing 12-2: Processing the command line switches

```
static void Main(string[] args)
{
   // Display help when requested.
   if ((args.Length == 0) || (args.Contains("/?")))
   {
      // Display the help screen, pause when in debug mode
      // and return.
      ShowHelp();
      CheckDebug();
      return;
   }

   // Contains the output.
   String Output = "";

   // Contains the current Date/Time.
   DateTime Current = DateTime.Now;

   // Begin checking for the other command line switches.
   for (int Count = 0; Count < args.Length; Count ++)
   {
      // Add a long date to the output string.
      if (args[Count].ToUpper() == "/LD")
         Output = Output + Current.ToLongDateString() + " ";
      // Add a long time to the output string.
      if (args[Count].ToUpper() == "/LT")
         Output = Output + Current.ToLongTimeString() + " ";
      // Add a short date to the output string.
      if (args[Count].ToUpper() == "/SD")
         Output = Output + Current.ToShortDateString() + " ";
      // Add a short time to the output string.
      if (args[Count].ToUpper() == "/ST")
         Output = Output + Current.ToShortTimeString() + " ";

      if (args[Count].ToUpper() == "/FD")
      {
         // Holds the formatting string.
         String TheFormat = args[Count + 1];
```

Continued

Listing 12-2: Processing the command line switches *(continued)*

```
            // Define the output string.
            try
            {
               Output = Output + Current.ToString(TheFormat) + " ";
            }
            catch (FormatException FE)
            {
               Output = FE.Message;
            }
         }
      }

      // Check for an empty output string. If the string is empty
      // show the help screen.
      if (Output.Length == 0)
         ShowHelp();
      else
         Console.WriteLine(Output);

      // Pause for debugging.
      CheckDebug();

      return;
   }
```

The example begins with the `Main()` method. This method receives an array of strings in `args`. Whenever the user types a space at the command line, it creates a new `args` string. Consequently, if the user types **`ShowDT /LD /LT`** at the command line and presses Enter, the application sees two arguments, `/LD` and `/LT`. The exception to the rule is delimited arguments. For example, if the user types **`ShowDT /FD "dd MMM yyyy"`** and presses Enter, the application sees only two arguments, `/FD` and `dd MMM yyyy` (making the `/FD` switch special). The double quotes act as delimiters for the date/time string. You can also use single quotes as delimiters.

The first task is to determine whether the user has supplied any command line switches at all, or has supplied the `/?` command line switch. In either case, the application calls `ShowHelp()` to display the help screen described earlier in the article. It then calls `CheckDebug()` to place the pause shown earlier in Figure 12-1 during debugging. Finally, it returns, because you don't want to process any other command line arguments after displaying help.

When the application detects that there are one or more command line arguments, it enters into a loop to process them. This way, if the user supplies the formatted output requests in a certain order, they appear in that order in the output. Notice that the code uses `args[Count].ToUpper()` to extract the current command line switch. This approach ensures that the user can enter the command line switches in upper-, lower-, or mixed case as desired. Some command line utilities are case sensitive, but the normal approach is to use case-insensitive command line switches.

Many of the command line switches for this example are simple. If you want to display the long date, then all you need to do is call the `ToLongDateString()` method and store the result in a string. The example processes all the simple formats first and builds a string that contains the requested date and time information.

Processing the `/FD` command line switch isn't as easy as processing the other command line switches. First, you must obtain the format string by peeking at the next argument in the `args` array. There shouldn't be a problem in using this approach because the next argument won't match any of the command line switches. However, interactions are always a problem with command line applications and you need to exercise care to peek at the right time. The next step is to create an output string that contains a date or time in the specified format. However, you don't know whether the user has supplied a valid format string or has supplied a format string at all. Consequently, you must perform this task within a `try...catch` block.

The final section of code checks to determine whether Output has any information in it. If not, the user hasn't supplied any valid command line switches, so the application displays the help screen. Otherwise, the user has supplied valid information and the application displays the results on screen.

Testing Command Line Functionality

At some point, you can start testing your console application. Of course, that means providing command line switches. The Command Line Arguments field of the Debug page of the project Properties dialog box shown in Figure 12-3 is where you supply command line arguments (choose Project ➪ ShowDT Properties to access this dialog box). You supply only the arguments as shown in the figure and not the name of the application.

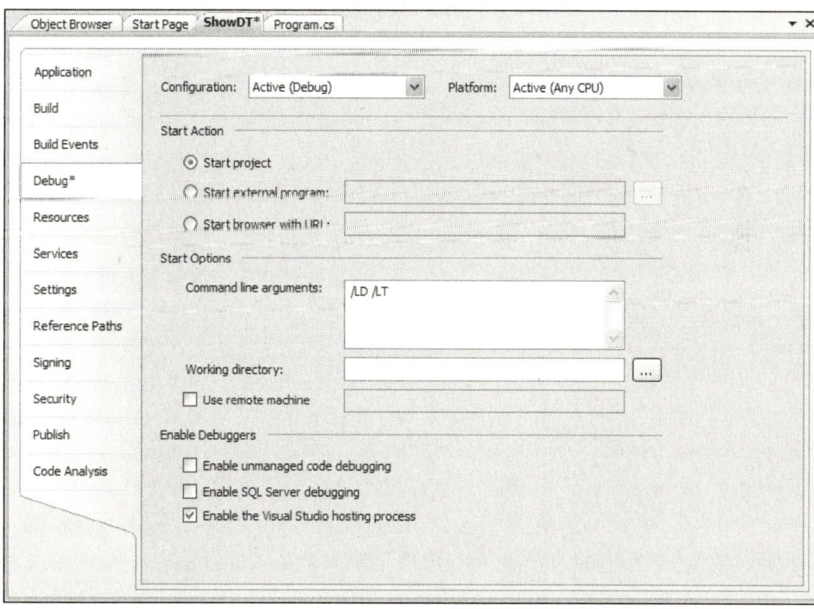

Figure 12-3: Set the command line switches for your application before you debug it.

Make sure you supply the arguments in the order you expect to see them in the output. In addition, the `/FD` command line argument requires two switches, such as `/FD "dd/MM/yyyy"`. When you run this application in debug mode and supply the /LD /LT command line arguments shown in Figure 12-3, you see the output shown in Figure 12-4.

You can find the standard formatting strings at http://msdn.microsoft.com/en-us/library/az4se3k1.aspx. *The custom formatting strings appear at* http://msdn.microsoft.com/en-us/library/8kb3ddd4.aspx.

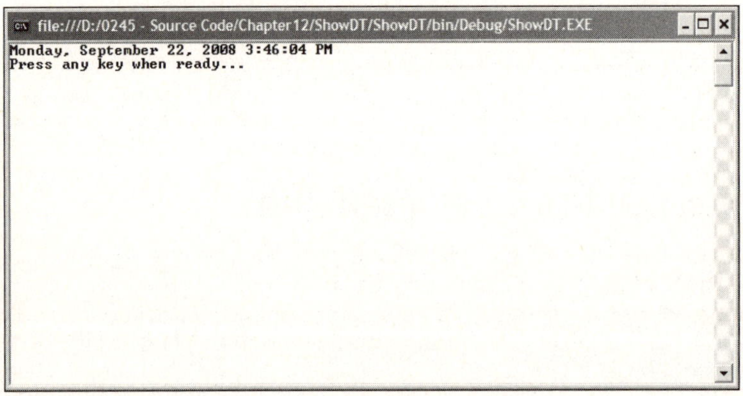

Figure 12-4: Typical output of the ShowDT application.

I actually use this utility when I work at the command line. I use it to add a date and time stamp to files I create for other purposes. I'll show you one way in which I use it after we look at the example. Interestingly enough, there isn't a way to perform this task easily using the existing commands, so you'll end with a new tool for your command line toolbox. (You can use the Time /T *command to output the time, but you have no choice in formatting that output; likewise with the* Date /T *command.)*

Exiting the Application Properly

You have a number of ways in which to exit an application. If you're used to working with relatively simple GUI application, you may use only the Form.Close() method. This approach works relatively well for the basic application, but there are many times when you aren't working with a basic application and you must think about how the application exit affects the system. The following sections discuss application exit techniques and show how you can use them to your advantage.

When Simply Closing the Form Isn't Enough

Most texts about application development focus on what happens inside the application. You discover how using the Form.Close() method affects the application internally. Normally, when you call Form.Close(), all the objects within the form are closed and the form itself disposed of. If this is the main form of an application, the application ends. However, there are two situations where closing the form doesn't dispose of it:

- The form is part of a Multiple-Document Interface (MDI) application and the form isn't visible when you close it.
- You displayed the form using the ShowDialog() method.

If either of these conditions is true, you need to call the `Dispose()` method manually to mark the form and the controls it contains for disposal. Otherwise, the form and its controls continue to use memory and other system resources.

The problem with simply closing the form is that no one outside the form knows why the form closed or whether it has closed at all in some cases. Older applications always provide a return code that signifies failure or success. When a failure occurs, an error code tells the external application how the form failed.

An exception to the rule is the `DialogResult` property. You set this property for the buttons on the form that causes a `Form.Close()` call. When you create and call the form using the `ShowDialog()` method, you can catch the `DialogResult` value and determine which button caused the form to close. However, this kind of information is still different from knowing specifics about the internal workings of the form, such as when an error occurs. Here's an example of how you can detect the `DialogResult` value.

```
private void btnDialogResult_Click(object sender, EventArgs e)
{
   // Create the form.
   frmDialogResult DialogDemo = new frmDialogResult();

   // Display the dialog result.
   MessageBox.Show(DialogDemo.ShowDialog(this).ToString());
}
```

Notice that the `DialogResult` value is the output of the `ShowDialog()` method call and that you can convert it to a string for display on screen. In most cases, you want to use the current window as the parent for the dialog box to preserve the application hierarchy, so you pass this along with the `ShowDialog()` method call. Here are some interesting facts to know about using the `ShowDialog()` method:

- The form returns the `DialogResult` value for the `AcceptButton` property of the form when the user presses Enter. If the `AcceptButton` property is set to `(None)`, then pressing Enter doesn't have an effect on the `DialogResult` value unless the user has selected a button with a `DialogResult` on the form.
- The form returns the `DialogResult` value for the `CancelButton` property of the form when the user presses Esc. If the `CancelButton` property is set to `(None)`, then pressing Esc has no effect unless the application has special Esc functionality programmed within it.
- The form returns `DialogResult.Cancel` when the user clicks on the Close button (the red square with an X in it in the corner of the dialog box), no matter what the form property settings are.

Setting an Exit Code with System.Environment

Many developers are used to working with the `System.Environment` class to obtain information about the system. For example, you use this class to obtain a list of the system environment variables or to determine the user's name. You also use this class to obtain special folder paths, such as the system folder. However, the `System.Environment` class also offers three different techniques to exit your application and you use different techniques for specific exit requirements. Listing 12-3 defines these three methods and shows how you use them.

Listing 12-3: Using System.Environment members to exit an application

```
private void btnSystemEnvironment_Click(object sender, EventArgs e)
{
   if (rbExitCode.Checked == true)
   {
      // Set the exit code.
      System.Environment.ExitCode = 0;

      // End the application.
      Close();
   }
   else
      if (rbExit.Checked == true)

         // Exit immediately.
         System.Environment.Exit(0);

      else

         // Exit without finalizing anything.
         Environment.FailFast("This application failed big time!");
}
```

The first technique doesn't actually exit the application, but it provides a means to tell the outside world how the application exited. You set the `ExitCode` property and then perform any required tasks before ending the application, using any of the methods described in this chapter. The resulting exit code is available anywhere, including batch files. Consequently, you can use the `IF ERRORLEVEL` construct in a batch file to catch the error code and act appropriately. (You can find information on using `ERRORLEVEL` at `http://www.robvanderwoude.com/errorlevel.html`.)

The second technique, `Environment.Exit()`, exits the application immediately. The application calls all finalization code, assigns the exit level, and then ends. You must supply an exit code using this technique. As far as the user is concerned, the application exited normally. However, you can check the exit code using any technique desired (such as from the calling application).

It's important to note that `Environment.Exit()` *doesn't check to determine if any application forms are still processing data. This call does provide for an orderly exit, but the exit is forced, which means the application must exit. Use the* `Application.Exit()` *method if you want to provide additional control over whether the application should close.*

The third technique, `Environment.FailFast()`, is actually a method of exiting the application after a massive application failure. In this case, you provide a string describing the error in as much detail as possible, which may not be much detail at all. You use this approach when exiting any other way will cause more harm than good. For example, finalizing anything could cause more data damage than will already happen due to the fast exit. The user does see an error message like the one shown in Figure 12-5.

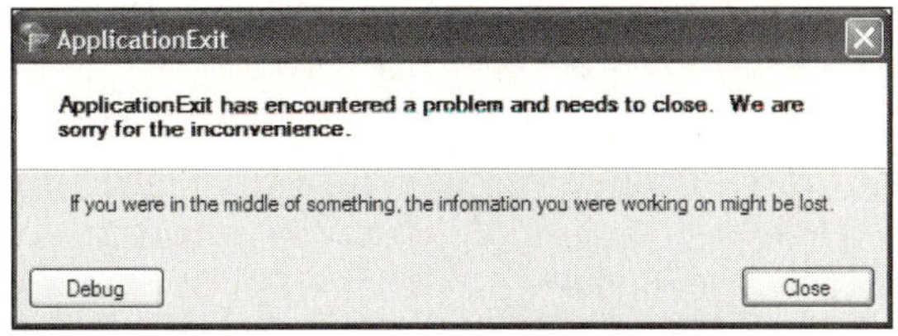

Figure 12-5: The user sees an error message when you use `Environment.FastFail()`**.**

The error message doesn't tell the user much about the application error, just that the error has closed and the application must close. Developers can click Debug when this error occurs — users generally click Close and tell someone that they saw an error. The paucity of the error information tells you something about this approach — you should use it only in extreme emergencies. Even raising an exception provides more information than this approach. The `Environment.FailFast()` method does generate a `System.ExecutionEngineException` exception, but you can't catch it, so placing the call in a `try...catch` block won't serve any purpose.

Fortunately, you can determine some information about the error. The string you provide to the `Environment.FailFast()` method is used as part of the input for an Event Viewer entry like the one shown in Figure 12-6. Notice that the error information is nebulous. All you know is that the source is the .NET Runtime. You don't even know the name of the application that generated the error.

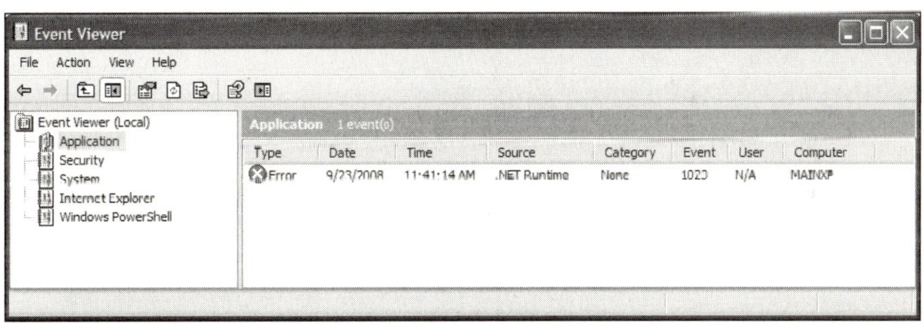

Figure 12-6: Look in the Application log to determine what caused your application to fail.

Double-click the event log entry, and you'll see the Event Properties dialog box shown in Figure 12-7. This dialog box finally contains the string that you provided as part of the call to `Environment.FailFast()`. You want to provide an error string that's more substantial than the one shown for demonstration purposes in the example.

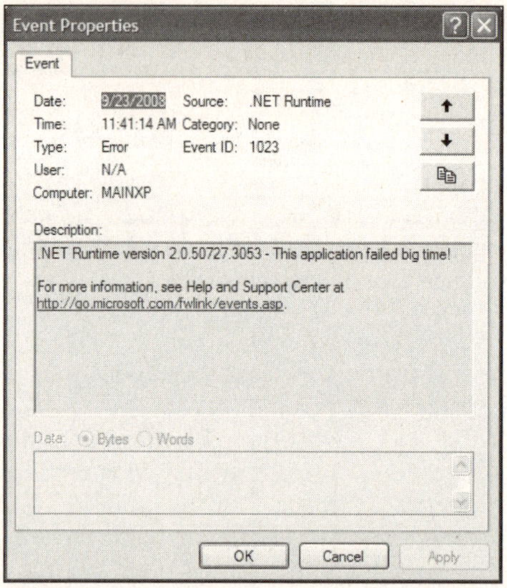

Figure 12-7: The Event Properties dialog box contains the error message provided as part of the call to `Environment.FailFast()`.

Relying on Application.Exit()

The `Application.Exit()` method provides a means for you to control how an application exits or whether it exits at all. This is the safest method of exiting your application, in most cases, because you can detect why the application is closing.

> *Prior to the release of the .NET Framework 2.0, a call to* `Application.Exit()` *meant that the application would end without firing either the* `Form.Closing()` *or* `Form.Closed()` *events. This omission often meant that end of form processing didn't occur, which could lead to data damage and other nasty problems. Newer versions of the .NET Framework do fire the* `Form.Closing()` *or* `Form.Closed()` *events, so there isn't any need to worry about using the* `Application.Exit()` *method.*

This method relies on two calls. First, you must call `Application.Exit()` to start the closing process. Second, you must create a handler for `FormClosing()`. When the application calls `Application.Exit()` or any other exit method except for `Environment.FailFast()`, the `FormClosing()` event handler can review the reasons, as shown in Listing 12-4.

Listing 12-4: Controlling application exits

```
private void btnApplicationExit_Click(object sender, EventArgs e)
{
   // Create a variable to hold the cancel state.
   CancelEventArgs Cancelled = new CancelEventArgs();
```

```
        // Try to exit the application.
        Application.Exit(Cancelled);

        // Display a message when the exit is cancelled.
        if (Cancelled.Cancel == true)
            MessageBox.Show("Application Exit Cancelled");
    }

    private void frmMain_FormClosing(object sender, FormClosingEventArgs e)
    {
        // Don't allow the user to close the form using the Close button.
        if (e.CloseReason == CloseReason.UserClosing)
        {
            MessageBox.Show("Don't close the application using the Close button!");
            e.Cancel = true;
        }

        // Ask before performing an Application.Exit() close.
        if (e.CloseReason == CloseReason.ApplicationExitCall)
        {
            if (MessageBox.Show("Are you sure you want to exit?",
                                "Exit Application",
                                MessageBoxButtons.YesNo) ==
                DialogResult.No)
            {
                e.Cancel = true;
            }
        }
    }
```

The `btnApplicationExit_Click()` event handler comes first. In this method, the code creates a new `CancelEventArgs` object, `Cancelled`. This object returns the result of the `Application.Exit` call attempt. The next step is to call `Application.Exit()`. When the application exit is cancelled, the application displays a message with the status information.

Of course, you have to have a means for cancelling the application exit. The `frmMain_FormClosing()` event handler receives a `FormClosingEventArgs` object, `e`. This object contains two properties of interest. The `CloseReason` property is an enumeration that contains various reasons for closing the form. If the user clicks the Close button or you issue a `Close()` call, the reason for closing the main form is `CloseReason.UserClosing` and the application cancels this approach to closing the form by setting `e.Cancel` to `true`.

When the `CloseReason` is `ApplicationExitCall`, the application displays a `MessageBox` where the user can choose Yes or No. If the user clicks No, the application sets `e.Cancel` to `true` and the application doesn't close. Clicking Yes closes the form. The point is that the closure process is controlled and you don't have to allow the application to close at all.

Using P/Invoke to Exit Applications

The .NET Framework doesn't always act as a good citizen with native-code applications that rely on messaging to perform tasks. Messages are a method of sending data between applications and they're still very much in use, even in .NET applications. However, your .NET application doesn't provide notification, in the form of a `WM_QUIT` message that it's closing to other applications. None of the methods described so far in the chapter outputs the `WM_QUIT` message. Consequently, a native-code application that relies on your application can fail when your application exits unexpectedly. The most common method of exiting an application with the `WM_QUIT` message is using `PostMessage()`. Using `PostMessage()` is an example of relying on Platform Invoke (P/Invoke) to overcome deficiencies in the .NET Framework. Because the `PostMessage()` function is part of the Win32 API, you must add the following code to the beginning of your application:

```
using System.Runtime.InteropServices;
```

You use the `PostMessage()` function to send a message to a particular window, to the current thread, or to all the top-level windows (generally, applications and background processes such as services) in the current session. Here's the definition for the `PostMessage()` method:

```
// Define the external function for posting a message.
[DllImport("User32.DLL", SetLastError = true)]
public static extern Boolean PostMessage(
   IntPtr hWnd, UInt32 Msg, Int32 wParam, Int32 lParam);
```

After you define where to find the `PostMessage()` function, you can begin using it as you would any other method in your application. You create the `WM_QUIT` message by using the `PostMessage()` approach like this:

```
PostMessage(this.Handle, WM_QUIT, 1, 0);
```

You'll always want to provide the application handle so that other applications know which application is ending. The `WM_QUIT` message has a value of 0x0012, so you also need to add a constant for it to your application, like this:

```
const int WM_QUIT = 0x0012;
```

One handy way to find this value is to open a command prompt at the `\Program Files\Microsoft Visual Studio 8` folder. Use the `FindStr /s "WM_QUIT" *.h` command to locate the value of `WM_QUIT` in the C++ header files. The `WParam` argument contains the exit code for this application, making this technique similar to the `Environment.Exit()` method. In this case, the application exits with a code of 1. Interestingly enough, all you have to do is post the `WM_QUIT` message and your .NET application will exit, just as if you had used one of the standard .NET Framework methods.

A full description of working with messages is outside the scope of this chapter. However, you can find a good tutorial about using messages in the four-part DevSource series:

- Working with Windows Messages in .NET (`http://www.devsource.com/c/a/Using-VS/Working-with-Windows-Messages-in-NET/`)
- Hooking Windows Messages in .NET (`http://www.devsource.com/c/a/Using-VS/Hooking-Windows-Messages-in-NET/`)
- Globally Hooking Windows Messages in .NET (`http://www.devsource.com/c/a/Using-VS/Globally-Hooking-Windows-Messages-in-NET/`)
- Special Windows Message Hooking Techniques for .NET (`http://www.devsource.com/c/a/Using-VS/Special-Windows-Message-Hooking-Techniques-for-NET/`)

Relying on Custom Features

Custom features can help you create better applications. Of course, you want to design custom features as part of the overall application design. Custom features can include anything that you create as a specialized tool. The most common custom features in applications today are attributes and exception (error) classes. Both these features add to the default attributes and error classes that Microsoft already provides. The following sections consider the use of custom features in your application.

Considering When to Use Custom Features

It's always tricky using custom features in your application. The best way to view the problem is that you're turning a standard feature into a feature that you must maintain. In other words, you're adding seemingly unnecessary work to the application maintenance cycle. Consequently, you must think through the advantages for your custom feature carefully before you add it to your application design. Here are some potential benefits of using a custom feature:

- Added flexibility in dealing with application issues
- Increased information flow
- Reduced debugging time
- Improved application performance (however, custom features are one area in which the most common performance factors are reliability or security, not speed)
- Enhanced application code readability

Custom features can add significantly to your application. However, there's always that maintenance factor to consider, which can become quite cumbersome. Selling management on your idea to use a custom feature in place of a standard feature that Microsoft maintains for you is always a hard sell. You want to arrive at any design discussions with a range of reasons to use the custom feature. Of course, you must counter these potential negative side effects of using a custom feature:

- Cost is one of the issues that will hit you hardest. Management doesn't care whether your custom feature does some neat technical feat — management is interested only in return on investment. You must be willing to provide some type of cost advantage for using your custom feature.
- Development time is another issue to consider, because many projects today are on a short time schedule. Adding custom features will always add to the development time for your project. If possible, show how spending a little time creating the custom feature at the outset will save development time later. Make sure you use accurate measures when making this claim.
- Maintenance time is something already covered in this chapter. Any custom feature will cost maintenance time. You must prove that the maintenance time spent on the custom feature will provide a payback of reduced maintenance time in some other area.
- Standards-based application design requirements may also come into play. Custom features always cause problems with the standards. No one's tested your custom feature, so it isn't known whether you've broken any rules of the standards your application may need to support.

Using Custom Attribute and Exception Classes

You can easily find a wealth of custom attribute and exception samples on the Internet. Of course, the first places you should visit are `http://msdn.microsoft.com/en-us/library/84c42s56.aspx` for attributes and `http://msdn.microsoft.com/en-us/library/ms229064.aspx` for exceptions. These sample applications and associated articles all help you create attributes and exceptions, but you might find that they lack a few bits of information for designing attributes and exceptions.

One of the first design decisions you must make is which class to use for inheritance. If you want a very basic attribute, you inherit from `System.Attribute`. Likewise, you can create a very basic exception by inheriting from `System.Exception`. Of course, this is the smart decision only when you can't find an attribute or exception that already provides part of the functionality you need. In general, it's easier to locate an attribute or exception that performs most of what you need to do, and then add functionality to it. Using this approach means that Microsoft will do more of the maintenance work for you and that you'll make better use of tested code for your custom feature.

The second design decision is deciding how to make that attribute generic enough that developers can use it for a range of tasks, while making exceptions specific enough to convey precise error information. The goal is to focus these custom features so they maximize the benefits they can provide. In fact, the dichotomy between attribute and exception in this regard is an indicator of how hard it can be to create a good custom feature. Part of your design task is to discover what the class delivers as a whole — it isn't always obvious.

Finally, the third design decision is considering the alternatives to a custom attribute or exception class. It's important not to become blind to the issues surrounding anything custom. If you have another alternative you can use, even if that alternative is a third-party library you must purchase, take it. Often, the cost of updating a third-party library is far less than creating your own solution.

Coding Your Application

This chapter has shown you some techniques you can use to write better applications. When everything is said and done, the techniques that last are those that produce consistent, reliable results. You can have as many academic arguments as you want, but the real-world benchmark is the results you achieve using a particular technique — even a nonstandard technique. After all, every technique starts out as a nonstandard technique. The focus of this chapter has been on using a consistent coding style, avoiding odd programming techniques, providing a standard startup and exit strategy, and relying on custom features when necessary. Obviously, you can find other techniques for writing great applications, but these four areas sum up what you really want — coding techniques that provide consistency both within and outside the application — coding techniques that make it easier for developers to understand the code in an application.

A local radio station has run an advertisement for painting your house. They'll provide the paint and the labor, but you must choose the color. The ad goes on to say that color is a personal choice — one that only you can make. This chapter has provided you with the paint and part of the labor, but you must still choose the color of your coding. What the content of this chapter really comes down to is making a choice of your coding style — the style your team will use to create an application. There aren't any right answers here, only answers that work for your organization. It's time to make some coding color choices.

Chapter 13 covers the developer-despised topic of documentation. In this chapter, you'll consider the issue of how to document your application, including the coding style choices you'll make. It's one thing to choose a consistent style for your project, but you must also document those choices so that others who follow can also use the correct coding style. Nothing's worse than trying to maintain an application where you don't understand any of the rules. Administrators and users also rely on you to create application documentation. Otherwise, they don't know how to use the application. The fancy command line options you provide for your application are meaningless when the administrator lacks information to use them. Documentation is an essential topic, even if you aren't very happy about doing it.

13

Considering the Documentation

Not every developer out there hates writing documentation, but you'll likely find that a vast majority of developers do hate the job. Writing documentation is a difficult task — writing great documentation that other people will understand is even harder. Unfortunately, without documentation, you can't expect anyone to understand and use your application. Most people can't simply look at the user interface and know what to do immediately. Even developers need help when it comes to working with someone else's documentation. This chapter helps to ease the pain. Fortunately, there are guidelines you can use to write good documentation. You'll find guidelines for the three main user types of your application: developers, administrators, and users.

In addition to user-level documentation, you must document the application code. Poorly documented code is hard to follow, difficult to maintain, and impossible to fix. Some projects become so difficult to fix that the developers who have to work on it throw up their collective hands and ask to start from scratch. This chapter looks at a number of ways to create comments and use them to generate XML documentation that others can use with your application to maintain it with greater ease. Once you have an XML file containing code comments, you can use it in a number of ways, employing the technologies that Microsoft provides. This chapter also reviews these alternative uses for your documentation.

> *Some developers claim that their code is self-documenting. The term* self-documenting *is the lazy developer's way out of writing good comments — comments that everyone working with the code will find useful. The concept of self-documenting code is a myth. Yes, you can often see the purpose of a piece of code when you have sufficient programming skill and experience with the application, but you must also consider the needs of the developer who lacks experience.*

Adding Documentation Support to Your Application

Many people view documentation incorrectly by saying it's a document (essentially text) that describes an application. Documentation is far more than mere text. The following sections view documentation from several angles. Most importantly, they provide advice on how to approach documentation as a living part of the application, rather than as a dusty book in the library.

A View to a Document

James Bond may like sleuthing out the details of a particularly important case (as in *A View to a Kill*), but most developers don't like sleuthing out anything. Unlike 007, most developers want all the details spelled out because they don't have time to discover the details on their own. Documentation does more than simply describe. In fact, documentation performs the following tasks:

- Demonstrates the use of the application.
- Shows how to operate the application.
- Defines the flow of information through the application.
- Considers the flow of work used to manipulate data.
- Provides details on administering the application.
- Informs the administrator about the structure and manipulation of configuration files.
- Supplies an overview of the application design.
- Details the inner workings of the application code.
- Illustrates particulars of the data store structure.

In short, documentation examines the application from every possible angle for every potential audience. You can probably add application-specific tasks to this list.

Of course, it's easy to fall into the trap of looking at documentation as some kind of text. In fact, documentation can take a number of forms, most of which won't appear in this chapter. Here are some ideas that you can pursue:

- Text, of course
- Code samples
- Videos of all types (everything from usage to programming techniques)
- Audio presentations (such as developer notes)
- Diagrams and other graphics
- Scripts or other code that automates and demonstrates procedures
- Presentations (including podcasts and Webinars)
- Slide shows

- Hands-on seminars
- Video games
- e-books
- Version control software (the complete documentation of your application at a developer level)

Yes, even video games can help document your application. A number of prominent organizations, including the military, now use video games to help people understand applications. A developer may erroneously assume that everyone learns in the same way, but the fact is that there's no one way to teach people about your application. Consider using all the senses for your documentation.

Considering the Needs of the Developer

Most developers have had the experience of trying to modify another developer's code and not being able to understand the application code at all. Of course, good comments and using a standardized naming convention (see the "Using an Appropriate Naming Convention" section of Chapter 12 for details) can help, but these aids to development aren't the entire documentation story. Developers need considerably more documentation than the bits of text that appear within an application's source code to perform maintenance and updates correctly.

If you think that comments are for someone else, think again. Good comments can make it easier for you to understand your own code because we all forget. However, good comments also force you to think about your code. When you're forced to think about your code in a new way, you often find logic errors and other bugs that weren't apparent before.

The original design document is a helpful source of information for the developer, but this document is only useful when the team developing the application updates the documentation when the application is complete. The design document should also include notes on any updates and show precisely how the updates affect the application code. A well-maintained design document can help the developer move around the application code considerably easier. However, even this document isn't quite enough to do the job.

A third piece of standard developer documentation is a listing of all the application elements, classes, methods, properties, attributes, enumerations, event handlers, and so on, along with their use. Fortunately, you can create this kind of documentation automatically as you define your comments using the techniques found in the "Creating Documentation Comments" section of this chapter. The resulting XML file can help a developer in a number of ways. The "Alternative Uses for Documentation Output" section of this chapter helps you understand some of these techniques.

At this point, if you implement these three levels of documentation (comments and naming convention, design document, and exported usage documentation), you have an average level of documentation. Yes, developers who follow can probably figure your application out now, but they could still get lost on some of the finer points of application maintenance.

With today's technology, a developer has no reason to avoid using alternative documentation techniques. For example, a developer could maintain a blog-like daily diary of events or create an audio record of pertinent activities. It's possible to make a recording of techniques a developer uses to perform certain tasks, such as configuring a data source. Because the recording isn't intrusive, a developer could create it without much thought. The same recording techniques come in handy for development meetings.

Whenever possible, record the history of the application using multiple methods so that developers in the future don't have to guess as to why you did something in a certain way.

Ambiguity leads to confusion and confusion leads to bugs. Anything you can do to make your actions and motivations less ambiguous will produce less confusion in future developers and reduce application bugs. Documentation makes your life easier by reducing the bugs you have to fix.

Considering the Needs of the User

Some developers regard the user as a *blissninny* (a wonderful word coined by writer Finn Wilcox). In this view, users are mindlessly happy in their cubicles and oblivious to the developer's toil in creating exquisite applications. The users are happy-happy, at least until they're unable to make the applications function, at which point they turn snarling on the developer. Doubtless some users are like this, but most are not blissninnies — they're smart enough and realistic enough — just less interested in the superb features of the application than the developer is. They'd like the application to work so they can finish and go home.

The user needs to know how to use your application to perform useful work. Simply knowing how to use the application isn't enough — the user isn't interested unless the documentation includes that useful work element. In fact, forget about usage completely: focus on that useful work element and you have a winner for user documentation.

The documentation shouldn't even begin by looking at the user interface — the documentation should begin by describing how to use the application to perform useful work. For example, you could give the users a procedure for opening a file, modifying it in some way, and then saving it. The users will nod their collective head (after waking up) and promptly forget anything you told them. However, if you tell the users that they can write a letter in five minutes, rather than the usual 15, using your application, you'll garner their attention. At this point, you provide the users with a procedure specifically aimed at writing that letter. It's become common to view this kind of application approach as a workflow. Essentially, you forget there's a user interface, because the user isn't interested in it anyway, and focus exclusively on getting work done.

Now that you've refocused your user documentation, perhaps you should stop killing trees (or, at least, writing text) to present it. Create an audio tape titled "How to Leave Work 15 Minutes Early Using My Application," and I guarantee that you'll have users beating down your door trying to get a copy. Every one of them will listen to that tape on the way home from work and possibly again on the way into work the next day. It's audio — they don't have to look at any words — it's easy. If you can add some infomercial pizzazz to your presentation, so much the better because you have to keep those users interested.

If you can invest a little additional time, make a video showing how to perform specific tasks with the application. Ensure that the user can access individual tasks on the video. You've probably seen an instructional tape or two — it comes with that SliceMaster 2000 that you bought last year that not only slices and dices, but accurately cubes fruits and vegetables to within 0.0001 inches. Grit your teeth, put the tape or DVD in your player, and view it. Notice that the video contains discrete sections for each task — now, create your video the same way. Using a video saves time because you can hand it out whenever someone new joins the organization. In fact, you can put these newcomers in a room with a pot full of coffee on their first day to ensure they don't destroy their PC in the first five seconds of use.

Although I haven't found any scientific study to back this up, it appears that most users will watch, at most, 10 minutes worth of video unless you're a dynamic presenter. In looking at some of the videos I've collected over the years, it appears that other people feel this time interval works, too. Some videos will use up to 15 minutes per task, but you'll likely find that 10 minutes or less is the normal interval. The point is to make the training interval short and break the tasks up into the smallest elements possible.

When you find that a number of users are making the same mistake, create a podcast or Webcast (whatever proves most popular in your organization). Put it on the company Web site and encourage everyone with that problem to download and view it. Now, whenever you find you're having that support issue, you can direct people to the podcast. The point is, use multiple methods to get your training plan across to people — use modern techniques whenever possible.

Don't forget to include hands-on activities as part of your documentation. A hands-on activity could consist of performing a simple procedure and checking the results against a document of some type. Of course, you can create an actual script-based tutorial for using the application. The tutorial interacts with the user as the user performs tasks using the application. The basic idea behind hands-on training is to get the user comfortable performing tasks with your application using a certain procedure.

Enter the Power User

You can't answer every user need using task-oriented articles, audio tapes, or videos. A few users, power users, actually want to know about everything your application can do and want to know how to do it the fastest way possible. The power user is the audience for your tome that includes a complete description of the user interface and all the things you can do by right-clicking. If your application has a command line interface, the power user will want to know about that, too.

Power users often need the same user-level information as administrators because they help teach other users and get those users out of their messes when they occur. A well-informed power user saves you time by answering those silly questions other users have. In addition, a power user usually understands the application well enough to provide you with useful application feedback. Consequently, it's a bad idea to forget the power user in your documentation plans.

Considering the Needs of the Administrator

The administrator's needs begin with the same requirements as a user. The administrator needs to perform tasks using the application, just like anyone else. If you can show the administrator the most efficient way to perform a task, then the administrator can get more done and you'll find that you get disturbed by user requests less often.

An administrator is a kind of power user. In addition to the needs of normal users, an administrator also requires complete documentation of application usage. See the "Enter the Power User" sidebar for more information on these requirements.

Administrators spend most of their time configuring applications and working with data. Consequently, your administrator documentation should include detailed information about configuration. The administrator not only needs to know how to configure the application but needs to know where the configuration information is stored as well. In addition, the administrator should have detailed information about the structure of that data. Often, an administrator has to recover application configuration information after an error causes the application to crash and damage the configuration file or registry entries. Every detail you can provide is important, right down to the acceptable values for each configuration file entry. Present the configuration information using a combination of text, graphics, and tables. Use tables to discuss the entries, default values, allowable values, and purpose.

The data requirements for an administrator depend on how the application data is stored. If you use a database, then you must completely document the database tables, views, scripts, and other elements. Don't assume anything about the data. The administrator may not realize how data obtained from a Web service work, so you need to document the interaction, too (unless, of course, you really enjoy waking up at 2 A.M. to locate a faulty router that's preventing access to the Web service). As with configuration information, you should present the data design using a combination of text, graphics, and tables. Make sure you supply graphics that use standard database symbols to ensure the administrator understands them.

Don't forget to make use of built-in database features to help document data sources. For example, when working with SQL Server, you can rely on database diagrams to help you document the database structure.

Administrators come in a number of forms, so you may need to target the documentation for specific groups. For example, if your organization is large enough, you probably have one or more administrators, called database administrators (DBAs), whose sole task is to manage the local SQL Server, Oracle, MySQL, or other setup. These administrators probably won't have much interest in the documentation you provide to the network administrator for configuring the application on the network.

Creating Documentation Comments

Comments in your code are mandatory because no one, including you, will ever figure out what the code means without them. At one time, the best developers could slug their way through an uncommented piece of spaghetti code and figure it out; but as developers create applications using advanced coding techniques, even those with expert capability have found it more difficult to repair the omissions of other developers.

Of course, you can't just write any comments and expect someone to follow them. A comment must contain enough information to help the developer figure out what the code is doing. Consequently, many companies now concentrate on helping developers create truly useful comments. You can find a number of formats for comments today. Most focus on forcing the developer to provide everything that someone following behind the developer will need. The following sections consider the kinds of comments you can make, along with some idea on where to place comments for maximum efficiency.

Considering the Kinds of Comments

When you talk to some developers about comments, they tell you about the standard // comment. It's true; you use the standard comment most often. For example, whenever you create a new variable, you document it using a technique like the one shown here:

```
// Define the output string.
string Output = "";
```

This kind of comment helps other developers, but you have other options. In fact, it may surprise you to learn that C# provides six kinds of comments as shown below:

- Standard // and /* ... */ comments
- XML /// comments
- Custom XML comments
- Attributes
- Custom attributes
- Task list

You get four kinds of comments with C#: standard comments, XML comments, attributes, and task list, plus you can create both custom XML comments and custom attributes. If you aren't using all four of the comment types in your applications, then you're missing opportunities to maximize the benefits of using comments. In general, the standard comments appear within code blocks such as methods, while XML comments and attributes appear outside major code blocks.

In many cases, you combine comment types to receive maximum benefit. For example, you might want to document a property within a component. In this case, you can combine the XML comment with attributes, as shown here:

```
/// <summary>
/// Contains the current changed value of the string.
/// </summary>
[Category("Change Strings")]
[Description("Contains the current changed value of the string.")]
[DefaultValue("")]
public string CurrentString {get; set;}
```

Whenever you type three slashes (///), the Visual Studio IDE automatically creates an XML comment for you. This comment has special tags that define how the information should appear in an XML file (see the "Using the Resulting XML File" section of this chapter for details). In this case, the comment contains a single field of information, `<summary>`, for the `CurrentString` property. The XML comment affects IDE features such as IntelliSense. You can also use the resulting XML file to create reports or perform class queries.

The attributes document the `CurrentString` property in another way. These entries change how the Properties window views the property. When you add attributes to your class, the Properties window displays additional information about it, making the component considerably easier to use. Chapter 11 contains additional details about working with components and controls.

Some XML comments provide a lot more than a simple summary. For example, when you create a method that has input and output values, the XML comment reflects this fact, as shown here:

```
/// <summary>
/// Performs a specific string change.
/// </summary>
/// <param name="Value">
/// The string you want to change.
/// </param>
```

```
/// <param name="Type">
/// The type of change you want to perform on the string.
/// </param>
/// <returns>
/// Provides the changed string as a return value.
/// </returns>
[Category("Change Strings")]
[Description("Performs a specific string change.")]
public string PerformChange(string Value, ChangeType Type)
```

Notice that this XML comment includes a lot more information. Each parameter has a `<param>` tag associated with it. The `<param>` tag includes the `name` attribute, which contains the parameter name. You type information about the parameter between the opening and closing tags. Any return value relies on the `<returns>` tag. All this information appears within the XML file, and IntelliSense (see Figure 13-5 on page 276) makes use of it as the developer works with the method.

XML comments always appear before attributes when the two appear together. Otherwise, the compiler will display a warning message stating that the XML comment is missing. In addition, you'll see a warning stating that the XML comment doesn't appear on a valid language element. The code will still compile, but you'll have to deal with the warning messages.

The task list feature is important because it helps you document tasks you must perform while writing or updating the code. A task list comment looks very much like a standard comment, except you provide a keyword at the beginning of the comment. For example, you can add a TODO item by typing the following comment in your code:

```
// TODO: Add a property for the change type.
```

This comment appears in the Task List window (choose View ➪ Task List to display this window) when you select Comments in the Categories list. Figure 13-1 shows a typical example of a task list entry based on a comment. (You can also add user comments to the list by choosing the User Comment entry of the Categories list — user comments aren't associated with a particular location in the code.) Simply double-click a task list entry to go to its location in the code.

Figure 13-1: Use the task list entries to define tasks you must perform.

The word, TODO, is a *token*. Visual Studio comes with a number of tokens already defined, but you can also define your own tokens for tasks you want to perform. To create your own tokens and to see the tokens that Visual Studio provides for you, choose Tools ➪ Options. You'll see the Options dialog box. Select the Environment ➪ Task List folder shown in Figure 13-2.

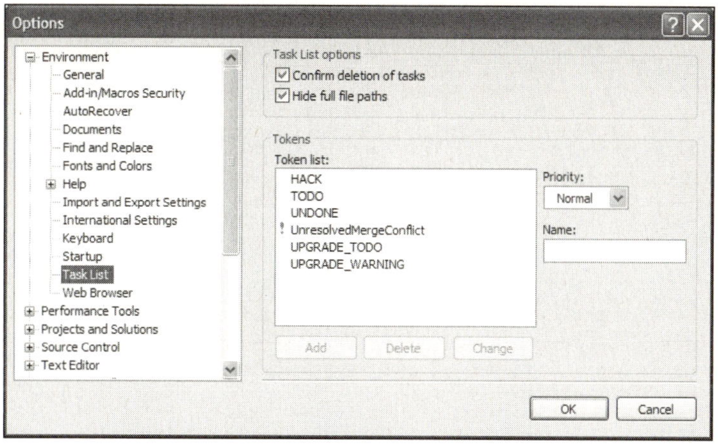

Figure 13-2: Create custom task list tokens as needed.

Notice that Visual Studio normally comes with six predefined tokens (your installation may vary). These special words always appear at the beginning of the comment. A token has a priority of low, normal, or high associated with it. To change the priority of a particular token, highlight its entry and choose a new value in the Priority field. To add a new token, type a token name in the Name field and click Add. A token never has spaces in it, but you can use the underscore to simulate spaces as needed.

Using custom comments or attributes makes sense when your organization has a special need. In general, it's easier to use the standard features that Visual Studio provides. The "Using Custom Attribute and Exception Classes" section of Chapter 12 provides some guidelines on using custom attributes with your application. These guidelines are also useful when making the decision to use custom comments.

Placing Comments in the Correct Place

Comments are only useful when they appear in the right place. A single comment for 30 lines of code isn't sufficient. You need more comments than that to describe the code correctly. Of course, you don't necessarily need to comment on individual lines of code either. It's important to maintain a balance between too many and too few comments. Comments should address specific needs. When you write comments, consider answering the following questions:

- What task is the code performing?
- Why is it performing the task in this way?
- When does the application activate the code?
- How does the code use the variables?
- Why does the application require variables of a specific type?
- Where does the application obtain the data used to fill the variables?
- Who created the code and how can you contact them?
- What revisions has the code received?
- What revisions has the organization planned for the code in the future?

Interestingly enough, Visual Studio tells you when you miss an important XML comment location. The omission appears in the Warnings tab of the Error List window, as shown in Figure 13-3, after you compile your application.

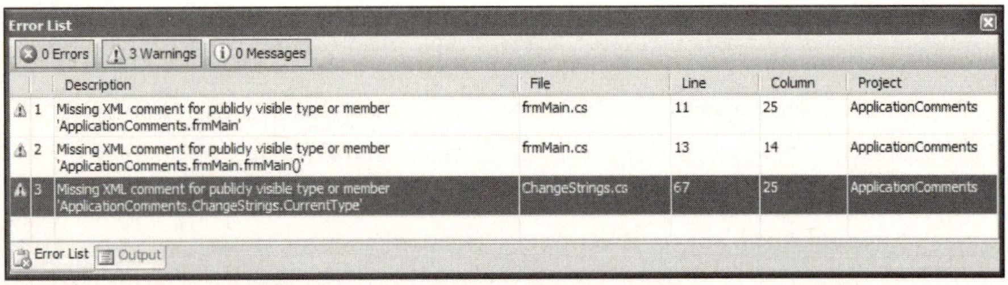

Figure 13-3: Visual Studio helps you document your application thoroughly.

All you need to do to fix the problems with the XML comments is to double-click the entries. The IDE takes you to the location of the missing comments in the code. Type the required XML comment and you're ready to go. Your best clue that you don't need an XML comment is that nothing happens when you type the starting ///. Normally, when you type the triple slash, the IDE expands the comment to provide the required XML comment format.

In many cases, you need to place XML comments within code blocks. For example, when working with an `enum`, you include an XML comment for each enumeration member, as shown here:

```
/// <summary>
/// Contains a list of the acceptable change types.
/// </summary>
[Category("Change Strings")]
[Description("Contains a list of the acceptable change types.")]
[DefaultValue(ChangeType.Lowercase)]
public enum ChangeType
{
   /// <summary>
   /// Reverses the order of the string elements.
   /// </summary>
   Reverse,

   ... Other Members ...

   /// <summary>
   /// Moves the characters around so they appear in a
   /// random order.
   /// </summary>
   Randomize
}
```

In this case, each of the members has a separate XML comment that appears when you work with that member in the editor. You see the comments when you work with the enumeration in the editor, so it's important to provide a comment that applies directly to that member.

If you have a choice between using XML comments or attributes, the XML comments normally provide greater flexibility and offer you more ways to use the comments later. However, the attributes generally provide greater support for IDE features. Consequently, you need to choose between post-design or design-time support when making this choice.

Once you have all the XML comments in place, you have to generate a file based on their content. By default, this file appears in the same folder as the executable for your application. However, Visual Studio doesn't generate the XML file unless you tell it to. To add XML file output to your application, choose Project ⇨ `<Project Name>` Properties. Select the Build tab of the resulting project Properties windows to modify the XML output options.

Figure 13-4 shows a typical example of how the project Properties window appears. Notice the Output section near the bottom of the window. Normally, all you need to do is check the XML Documentation File option and close the window. The next time you build your application, Visual Studio also generates the XML file for you. However, you can also choose to change the Output Path property when you want to place the XML file in a centralized location. (Don't worry about the Generate Serialization Assembly option — it doesn't affect the XML file output, but you can learn about it at `http://msdn.microsoft.com/en-us/library/bk3w6240(VS.80).aspx`.)

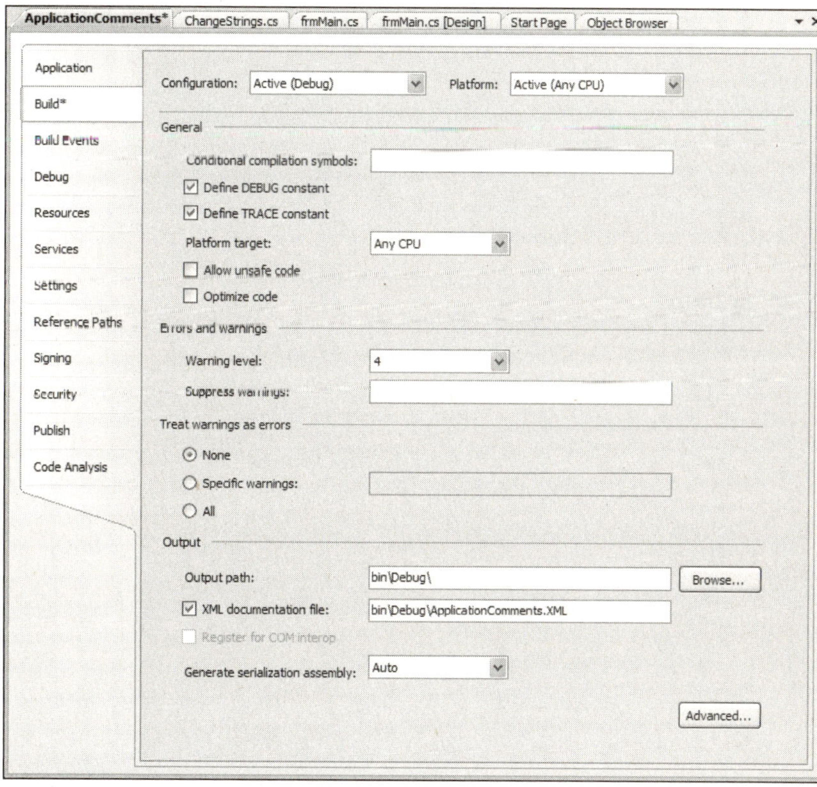

Figure 13-4: Set the application to create the XML file.

Using the Resulting XML File

Generating the XML file has an immediate effect on the Visual Studio IDE. For example, when you use one of the class features, IntelliSense tells you about the feature, as shown in Figure 13-5. This use of the XML file is automatic. The addition of IntelliSense support makes adding the XML comments well worth the effort.

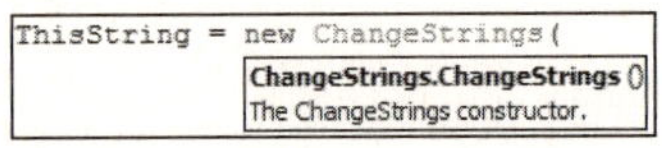

Figure 13-5: Set the application to create the XML file.

Of course, you can also view the XML file directly. Figure 13-6 shows a typical view of the file from Firefox. It may surprise you to discover that the Visual Studio IDE automatically adds some XML comments for you, so the resulting XML file contains more entries than you expect. Obviously, the XML file in Figure 13-6 is a little difficult to read and most developers on your team won't want to use it directly. Therefore, it may initially seem that your only benefit is to obtain additional support from the IDE. However, this is an XML file, so you can manipulate it directly using eXtensible Stylesheet Language Transformation (XSLT) to display it in a specific format.

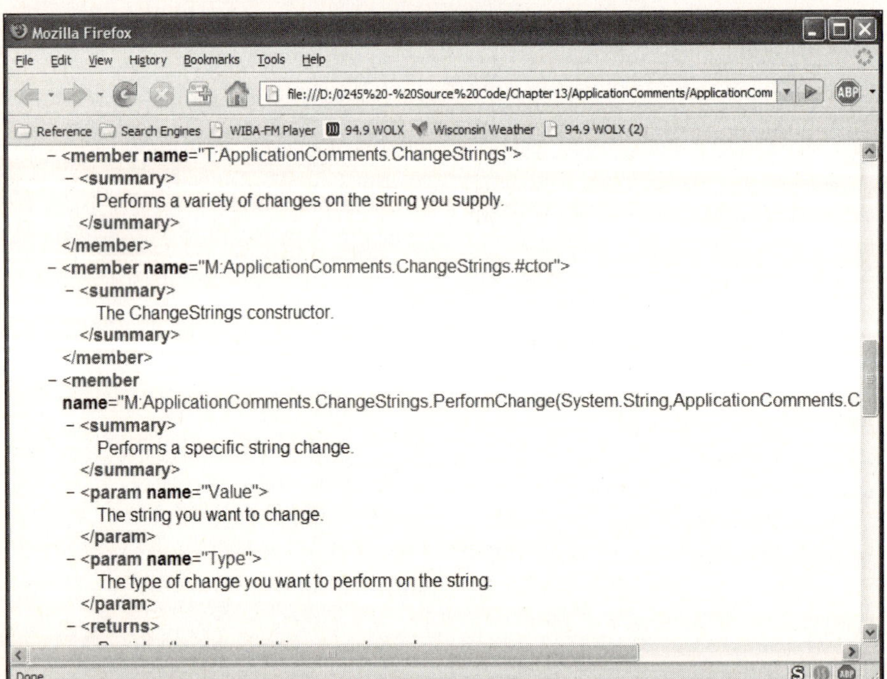

Figure 13-6: The XML file contains a significant amount of application information, but in a nearly unreadable form.

Fortunately, both Microsoft and third-party vendors have been busy creating utilities that turn that XML file into something else, such as a help file. One of the commonly used XML file compilers is Sandcastle. In order to use this tool, you must first download the Sandcastle product from Microsoft at `http://www.microsoft.com/DOWNLOADS/details.aspx?FamilyID=e82ea71d-da89-42ee-a715-696e3a4873b2`. However, most developers find that using Sandcastle alone is difficult, so they also download the Sandcastle Help File Builder from `http://www.codeplex.com/Wiki/View.aspx?ProjectName=SHFB`.

Some third-party products don't support modern versions of the .NET Framework. For example, NDoc (`http://ndoc.sourceforge.net/`) provides support for Mono, the .NET Framework 1.0, and the .NET Framework 1.1, which is fine if you want to use an older version. However, despite the antiquated nature of NDoc, it's still one of the easiest-to-use documentation generators available and lets you output the help file in a number of formats, including native MSDN format.

After you download and install these two products, you can start the GUI by choosing Start ➪ Programs ➪ Sandcastle Help File Builder ➪ Sandcastle Help File Builder GUI. You'll see the initial display shown in Figure 13-7.

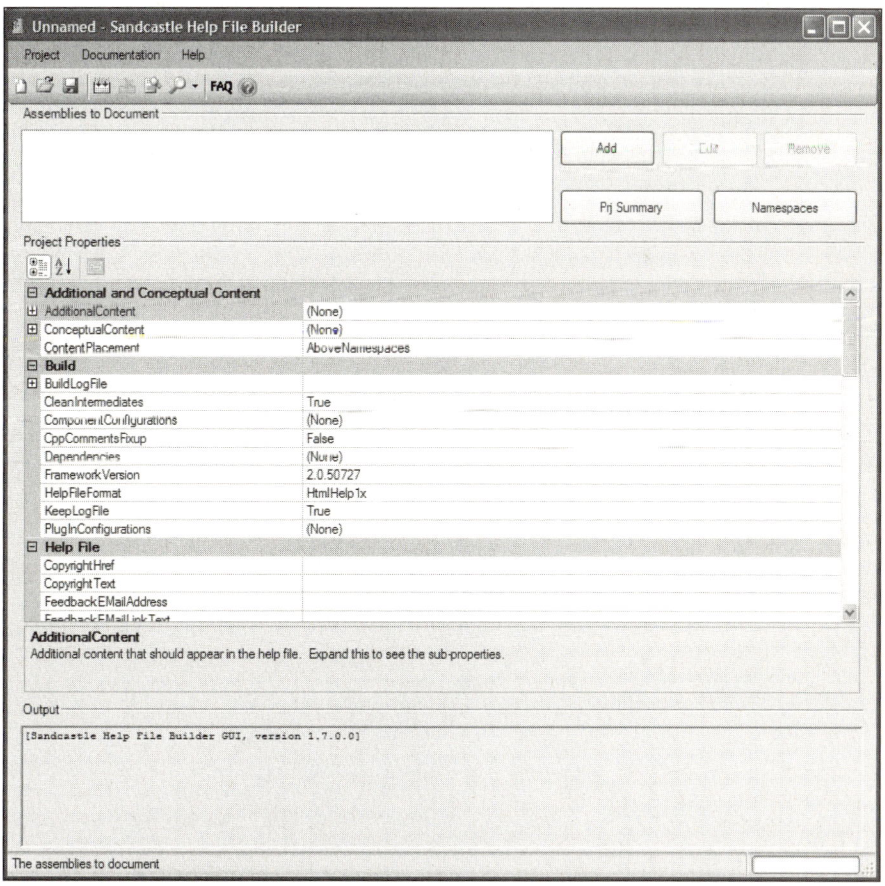

Figure 13-7: Sandcastle makes it relatively easy to build comprehensive help based on your XML comments.

You modify this window using the same approach that you normally use for working with the Properties window in the Visual Studio IDE. However, you'll find that the default settings provide a reasonably nice help file. Before you can generate a help file, though, you must provide the location of the project's XML file by clicking Add. Use the Select the File(s) to Document dialog box to locate the XML file you created earlier. Double-click this file and you see it added to the Assemblies to Document. If you have multiple assemblies that you want to document in a single help file, simply add them to the list using the same technique.

The only default setting that may pose problems is Framework Version found in the Build category. Make sure you set this property to match the version of the .NET Framework that you're using. In addition, you may want to define the properties in the Help File category.

After you add all the assemblies that you want to work with to the list, click Save the Current Project on the toolbar (the disk icon). Save the project file. At this point, you can click Build the Help File on the toolbar (the icon looks the same as the build icon in Visual Studio). The help building process takes a while, even for a small project, so you can get a cup of coffee. When the process is done, the GUI automatically launches the new help file for you. Figure 13-8 shows typical output.

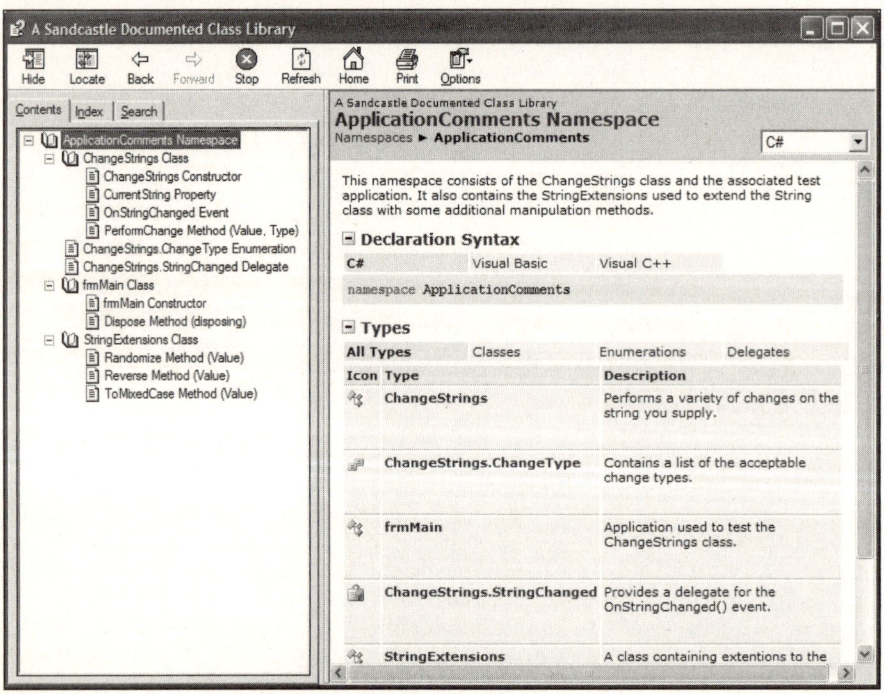

Figure 13-8: Sandcastle produces an exceptionally nice help file with many useful features.

If you've defined all the elements of your application with XML comments, the help file will contain everything you provided in a form that's both easy to understand and to use. Anything you miss will appear as an error message in the help file, so going through the help file makes it easier to locate anything you should define. Of course, now that you have a help file, you can start testing it on the developers in your organization. You'll find the help file in the `\Help` folder that appears below the application folder.

You'll see one error in the help file that Sandcastle creates for you, complaining that the XML file automatically generated by Visual Studio is missing a namespace XML comment. Interestingly, Visual Studio doesn't provide a means to create this comment. It's possible to create a custom XML comment to solve this omission, but there's an easier way to fix it. Right-click the solution entry in Solution Explorer and choose Add ➪ New Item. Select the XML File item template in the Add New Item dialog box and give the XML file a name that represents the content the file will contain, such as `ProjectAndNamespace.XML`. Add the project and namespace comments, as shown in Listing 13-1.

Listing 13-1: Defining project and namespace comments

```
<?xml version="1.0" encoding="utf-8" ?>
<doc>
   <assembly>
      <name>ApplicationComments</name>
   </assembly>
   <members>
      <member name="R:Project">
         <summary>
            This project demonstrates the use of application comments
            and shows how to test them.
         </summary>
      </member>
      <member name="N:ApplicationComments">
         <summary>
            This namespace consists of the ChangeStrings class and the
            associated test application. It also contains the StringExtensions
            used to extend the String class with some additional manipulation
            methods.
         </summary>
      </member>
   </members>
</doc>
```

The code begins with the `<assembly>` element that holds the actual name of the file that holds the assembly without the file extension. If your application contains more than one assembly, you can create an `<assembly>` element for each assembly. Within the `<assembly>` element is a list of `<member>` elements. Each `<member>` element must include a name that consists of a special code letter (R for project and N for namespace), followed by the project or namespace name. Each `<member>` element has a `<summary>` child element where you place the comment that Sandcastle requests. When you create your help file, add this `ProjectAndNamespace.XML` file as a second entry.

Alternative Uses for Documentation Output

The XML file you create using the XML comments in Visual Studio can see more use than simply creating a help file (as nice as that help file might be). The flexibility of XML files means that you can interpret the contents using any of the technologies that work with other XML files. For example, you could use XSLT to create formatting output of any sort you might want. The following sections provide some ideas for alternative uses. I'd love to hear your ideas about how to use the XML file as well — write me at JMueller@mwt.net with your ideas.

Using LINQ to Query the Documentation File

The .NET Framework 3.5 provides a new search technology called Language INtegrated Query (LINQ). The interesting feature of this technology is that you can query just about any data source, even an XML file, using a standardized query language. (To see one of the more flexible uses of LINQ, read the articles at `http://www.devsource.com/c/a/Architecture/Using-Resource-Description-Framework-Files/`, `http://www.devsource.com/c/a/Languages/Understanding-LINQ-Expression-Trees/`, and `http://www.devsource.com/c/a/Languages/Extension-Methods-LINQ/`.)

Using LINQ, you could create an application for the developers on your team that could help you locate particular namespaces, classes, methods, properties, events, or anything else for that matter, based solely on a partial recollection of something the developer had seen in the past. The key to this technique is to build LINQ queries to access the XML files that Visual Studio creates based on your XML comments.

Creating Automated Application Reports from Documentation

The XML file created because of your XML comments provides source information for any reports you need to create. For example, you could create an application that queries this XML file and builds a report from it. Perhaps you want to show that you've completed certain parts of the design specification or that you're at least working on them. The Build Events page of the project Properties dialog box contains a Post-build Event Command Line field where you can add events such as calling on this application. Every time you build the application, the build process automatically generates the report needed to show project progress.

Coding Your Application

You may have started this chapter thinking that documentation means providing others with information about your application. Yes, it does do that, but documenting your application properly can also provide a big payoff for you as a developer. Using the new technologies that Microsoft provides lets you use the documentation you create for all kinds of purposes. This chapter doesn't even scratch the surface of what you can do with good documentation.

The best way to learn how to write documentation is to perform the task. Write documentation, lots of it, to build your writing skills. Documentation writing isn't an engineering skill — it's an art. Of course, when you review your documentation, you'll think it's a combination of *War and Peace* mixed with *I, Robot*. Most people don't write well enough to make a claim of parity with either book. Make sure you rely on peer review to help you learn how to write better — people usually can't review their own work objectively. Be prepared to take a few lumps when you start. Some people will say your writing skills stink and you'll never be a writer — don't listen to them, keep practicing.

Chapter 14 tackles another topic that developers love to hate — error trapping. People assume that the task should be easy, but the entire industry knows otherwise. If error trapping were so easy, we wouldn't have to deal with all the viruses out there today. Believe it or not, good documentation is your first step toward good error handling. As you write your documentation, you discover things about your code and often locate problems that directly affect your error-trapping efforts. Chapter 14 is an exciting way to build on what you've learned in this chapter.

14

Implementing Error Handling

Your application, no matter how well crafted, examined, optimized, quality controlled, tested, or user stressed, is going to have errors. It's possibly the saddest fact of life for developers, because most developers would like to think that error-free applications are at least possible. However, errors are part of human nature and even if human nature didn't intrude, the law of life is that errors exist in nature as well. The perfect application, should it exist, would have to run on flawed hardware and be used by imperfect users. Consequently, no matter what you do, your application will experience errors. Your best defense against errors is to assume nothing about the application, the hardware, the user, the environment, or anything else for that matter. When you assume nothing, it's less likely that your error handling will contain flaws (although it will likely contain at least a few problems that you'll need to fix).

Error handling becomes more reliable when you use specific error-handling techniques. Using such techniques means relying on an almost engineering view of application design. You apply the error-handling techniques consistently and attempt to solve problems as precisely as possible. Instead of trapping a generic error, you trap specific errors and act on each error according to type. Of course, this type of error handling requires more development time, but it also produces significantly better results. Generally, better error handling costs time and money, but more than pays back the investment you make in it.

At one time, instructors told aspiring computers scientists that applications shouldn't crash — they should fail gracefully. Most organizations today can't afford to have applications that fail gracefully. Organizations require applications that keep running no matter what happens. Of course, that's a very tall order and you can't always fulfill it. In fact, anyone who has a realistic view of applications at all knows that the "always running" application is a myth. However, you can create self-healing applications that have a reasonable chance of continuing to run even in circumstances that would bring older applications to their knees.

This chapter considers error handling from the practical perspective — what's possible, rather than what would be nice. What would be nice is a perfect application running on flawless hardware with automaton users who never make mistakes in an environment devoid of natural occurrences such as lightning. However, this environment doesn't exist, so it's not even a good idea to strive to achieve it. Instead, this chapter will help you discover the application that runs most of the time and catches the majority of errors that happen while users type on flawed hardware during a lightning storm.

Discovering the Advantages of Assuming Nothing

When it comes to error handling, any assumption you make will almost certainly end in disaster, so the safest course of action is to assume nothing at all. This sounds like an impossible task, but it really isn't. When designing the error-handling part of your application, you need to consider how you make decisions about the error-handling code you create. For example, many developers provide data-type checking code for portions of the code that face outward — that interact with the user, the environment, other systems, or networks. However, you can't assume that the inner parts of your application have any significant advantage, so you must also check the type of any incoming data for the inner parts of the code as well. In addition, you must perform range and content checks. In short, all the checks described in Chapter 7 also apply for error handling. By creating a secure application, you also create one that performs a certain level of error handling as well.

Of course, the next question is how often you should check the input. After all, once you know that someone's reliable, shouldn't you assume that they're trustworthy enough to provide the correct input all the time? Even if you have the most reliable person in the world, that person will make mistakes. In addition, you can't discount environmental effects such as lightning, bad lighting, static electricity, and myriad other data contaminants you can't control. Consequently, the answer is that good error handling demands that you assume nothing and that you check everything, every time.

The lesson of assuming nothing was driven home to me early in my career. A customer kept complaining that a PC was rebooting for seemingly no reason at all. A test of the equipment showed nothing wrong. Bringing the computer to my shop demonstrated that the computer was working just fine. However, taking it back to the customer resulted in more calls. It turned out that the person operating the computer generated a static potential by walking across the carpet. Every time the person touched the keyboard, the system would reboot. Because the soles of my shoes were of a different material, I didn't generate the static potential, so I didn't see the problem. The point is that when you assume nothing about your application, you can't be disappointed when something happens.

Error handling comes in a number of forms. Yes, it begins with checking the inputs and outputs. However, errors can occur within the application code, too. Of course, you have the usual bugs to deal with. The best coder in the world produces code with bugs, so get used to seeing bugs in your code, too. Adding error handling, in this case, means placing sensitive code in `try...catch` blocks. The "Reviewing the Importance of Specific Error Handling" section of this chapter describes this kind of added error handling.

You also need `try...catch` blocks for those unexpected events. For example, when you attempt to use a Web service as a source of data, you know that you need to place any interactions within a `try...catch` block. However, you also need to follow the same practice with the server on your local network. It's easy to assume that the server is going to be available or that you'll be able to tell the user when the server's down, but the reality is that you can't assume anything about that server. Who knows, someone could walk into the office, disconnect it, and walk off with it somewhere — you don't know.

The paranoid view of error handling has significant advantages. If you always check absolutely everything, you won't get hit with as many unexpected problems. The problem with this approach is consistency. Checking for a particular error once isn't enough; you must do it every time that the error can occur. The "Providing Consistent Error Handling" section discusses this topic in detail. In order to create an environment with maximized error handling, you must be willing to create a consistent error-handling regimen that quality assurance or some other responsible, outside part of your organization verifies. By adding consistency to good error checking (and therefore handling), your application will experience significantly less down time and fewer security problems as well.

Everything comes with a price, and error handling is no exception. The entire concept of error handling is a combination of security and reliability. When you improve error handling, you also improve these two important performance features of your application. However, remember that performance has a third element, speed. Error handling does reduce the speed of your application. In fact, many developers assume that the speed hit is going to be so high that they refuse to entertain the idea of intense, proactive error handling at all. Obviously, you must maintain a balance between speed, security, and reliability in your application, but to keep all error handling out of your application is simply a silly way to develop applications. It's akin to driving down the expressway at 65 mph with a blindfold on and hoping you don't hit anyone — the sure bet is that you will and that it will hurt when you do.

Understanding Exceptional Events

Many developers today use exceptions as a means of writing sloppy applications. They don't want to take the time to code properly, so they raise an exception and let someone else handle it. Unfortunately, this approach is entirely incorrect and it leads to many of those speed problems that developers hate about error handling.

Exception handling gets its name from the concept that it only happens when an exceptional (extraordinary) event occurs. An exceptional event is one that you didn't anticipate happening. In fact, it's possible to say that it's impossible to anticipate the event occurring, so an exception is the only way to handle it.

When the user types the wrong input — that's expected and you should handle it with code other than an exception handler. If the client loses its connection with the server, that's expected — you should handle it as part of your regular code. However, when lightning hits your network cabling and turns your data into crud, that's an exceptional event and you probably need an exception to handle it. Using exceptions only when necessary will make error handling a lot speedier and make it possible to create applications with higher reliability and security.

Reviewing the Importance of Specific Error Handling

It's easy to write nonspecific error handling. All you need to remember is one thing — the `Exception` keyword. However, when a developer writes nonspecific error handling, it's possible to miss a considerable amount of information about the error. Using generic code that essentially says, "Oops, we've experienced an error, folks" is potentially worse than not catching the error at all. At least if the developer doesn't catch the error at all, the user can think that the developer simply missed it. When a generic equivalent of a shrug appears on screen, it says the developer didn't care enough to handle the error correctly. The following sections show how you can add specific error handling to your applications.

Using the Standard Exception Classes Correctly

All the standard exception classes, those that represent errors of various kinds, have the word *Exception* in them. In fact, Microsoft recommends that any custom exceptions you create also have the word *Exception* (including the capital E) in them. Whenever possible, you should use one or more of the standard exception classes to handle exceptional conditions in your code. It's important to catch all the specific exceptions you can and then move on to the more generic exceptions. Table 14-1 shows the 68 standard exception classes and provides a basic description of them. Note that this table contains only the exceptions that you're likely to use with C# — the Microsoft documentation shows a total of 88 upper-level exception classes, including `System.Exception`.

Even though many of the terms in the Host Namespace or Class and Exception Name columns appear on multiple lines, you use them on a single line in your code. For example, the `Microsoft.Build.BuildEngine` *class would appear on a single line, as would the* `InternalLoggerException` *exception.*

Table 14-1: Standard Exception Classes

EXCEPTION NAME	HOST NAMESPACE OR CLASS	CAN INHERIT?	DESCRIPTION
ActiveDirectoryObjectExistsException	System.DirectoryServices.ActiveDirectory	Yes	Specifies that an Active Directory Domain Services object you want to create already exists in the underlying directory store.
ActiveDirectoryObjectNotFoundException	System.DirectoryServices.ActiveDirectory	Yes	Shows that the Active Directory object you requested doesn't exist.
ActiveDirectoryOperationException	System.DirectoryServices.ActiveDirectory	Yes	Provides a general indication that an underlying Active Directory operation has failed. The `ForestTrustCollisionException` and `SyncFromAllServersOperationException` exceptions are more specific than this one.
ActiveDirectoryServerDownException	System.DirectoryServices.ActiveDirectory	Yes	Occurs when the Active Directory server is unavailable. However, any subsidiary errors can trigger this one, such as a loss of network connection.
AddInSegmentDirectoryNotFoundException	System.AddIn.Hosting	Yes	Shows that the segment directory is missing from a pipeline directory structure. Whenever an application activates an add-in, the system constructs a pipeline to its host using the pipeline directory structure. The add-in system requires that the pipeline segments appear within a particular directory structure. See `http://msdn.microsoft.com/en-us/library/bb384240.aspx` for additional details.

EXCEPTION NAME	HOST NAMESPACE OR CLASS	CAN INHERIT?	DESCRIPTION
ApplicationException	System	Yes	Indicates that a nonfatal application exception has occurred. The `System.Reflection.InvalidFilterCriteriaException`, `System.Reflection.TargetException`, `System.Reflection.TargetInvocationException`, `System.Reflection.TargetParameterCountException`, and `System.Threading.WaitHandleCannotBeOpenedException` exceptions are more specific than this one.
CardSpaceException	System.IdentityModel.Selectors	Yes	Specifies that one or more CardSpace service-level exceptions have occurred. The exceptions appear in the event log, rather than as part of the exception.
ChangeConflictException	System.Data.Linq	Yes	Indicates that a database update has failed because the database record content changed since the application read it. See the usage examples and suggestions at `http://msdn.microsoft.com/en-us/library/system.data.linq.changeconflictexception.aspx`.
DirectoryException	System.DirectoryServices.Protocols	Yes	Used as a base class for all other `System.DirectoryServices.Protocols` exception classes—you don't use this exception directly. The `BerConversionException`, `DirectoryOperationException`, `DsmlInvalidDocumentException`, `ErrorResponseException`, and `LdapException` exceptions are more specific than this one.
DirectoryNotFoundException	System.IO	Yes	Indicates that the system couldn't locate the specified directory. See the usage example at `http://msdn.microsoft.com/en-us/library/system.io.directorynotfoundexception.aspx`.
EventLogException	System.Diagnostics.Eventing.Reader	Yes	Used as a base class for event log exceptions—however, you can use this exception directly in some cases. The `EventLogInvalidDataException`, `EventLogNotFoundException`, `EventLogProviderDisabledException`, and `EventLogReadingException` exceptions are more specific than this one.
ExceptionCollection	System.ComponentModel.Design	No	Contains a collection of exceptions that you can query. Applications use this class to hold multiple exceptions in a single object.
IdentityValidationException	System.IdentityModel.Selectors	Yes	Shows that the recipient certificate is invalid.

Continued

Table 14-1: Standard Exception Classes *(continued)*

EXCEPTION NAME	HOST NAMESPACE OR CLASS	CAN INHERIT?	DESCRIPTION
InstrumentationBaseException	System.Management.Instrumentation	Yes	Used as a base class for all other `System.Management.Instrumentation` exception classes—however, you can use this exception directly in some cases. The `InstrumentationException` exception is more specific than this one.
InternalLoggerException	Microsoft.Build.BuildEngine	No	Defines a logging exception generated by the build engine.
InvalidActiveXStateException	System.Windows.Forms.AxHost	Yes	Shows that the application has referenced an ActiveX control in an invalid state. See the usage example at `http://msdn.microsoft.com/en-us/library/system.windows.forms.axhost.invalidactivexstateexception.aspx`.
InvalidChannelBindingException	System.ServiceModel.Channels	Yes	Occurs when the binding specified by an application isn't consistent with the contract requirements for a particular service.
InvalidDataContractException	System.Runtime.Serialization	Yes	Shows that the `DataContractSerializer` or `NetDataContractSerializer` experienced an invalid instance type during serialization or deserialization. See the usage example at `http://msdn.microsoft.com/en-us/library/system.runtime.serialization.invaliddatacontractexception.aspx`.
InvalidPipelineStoreException	System.AddIn.Hosting	Yes	Indicates that the system couldn't locate the specified directory and that the user doesn't have permission to access the pipeline root path or an add-in path. Unlike the `DirectoryNotFoundException`, this exception doesn't provide any path information, which means that an evil user can't use this exception to obtain true path information after purposely making an invalid method call.
InvalidProjectFileException	Microsoft.Build.BuildEngine	No	Signifies a problem with the XML file used to build a project. Any XML file validator can determine whether the project file is well formed. Use an XSD file to catch problems with the file syntax. Only manual editing will help you locate file semantic issues.
InvalidTimeZoneException	System	Yes	Indicates that the time zone information supplied by a `TimeZoneInfo` object is invalid. The system uses the `TimeZoneNotFoundException` when the time zone information is missing completely.

EXCEPTION NAME	HOST NAMESPACE OR CLASS	CAN INHERIT?	DESCRIPTION
InvalidToolsetDefinitionException	Microsoft.Build.BuildEngine	Yes	Signifies a problem with the user's custom toolset definition file. Any XML file validator can determine whether the project file is well formed. Use an XSD file to catch problems with the file syntax. Only manual editing will help you locate file semantic issues.
IOException	System.IO	Yes	Specifies that an input/output (I/O) error has occurred. Although you can use this exception directly, the `DirectoryNotFoundException`, `DriveNotFoundException`, `EndOfStreamException`, `FileLoadException`, `FileNotFoundException`, `PathTooLongException`, and `PipeException` exceptions are more specific than this one. See the usage example at `http://msdn.microsoft.com/en-us/library/system.io.ioexception.aspx`.
IsolatedStorageException	System.IO.IsolatedStorage	Yes	Indicates an error during an isolated storage operation. The most common sources of this exception are security failures (you didn't provide sufficient evidence to validate the identity of the caller) and invalid operations (isolated storage doesn't support all FileStream operations).
LinqDataSourceValidationException	System.Web.UI.WebControls	Yes	Signifies that one of many errors occurred during a LINQ data update, delete, or insert. See the usage example at `http://msdn.microsoft.com/en-us/library/system.web.ui.webcontrols.linqdatasourcevalidationexception.aspx`.
LockRecursionException	System.Threading	Yes	Indicates that a recursion into a lock isn't consistent with the lock recursion policy. See the usage example at `http://msdn.microsoft.com/en-us/library/system.threading.lockrecursionexception.aspx`.
LoggerException	Microsoft.Build.Framework	Yes	Defines a method for a logger to stop a build for a particular reason. See the usage example at `http://msdn.microsoft.com/en-us/library/microsoft.build.framework.loggerexception.aspx`.
MembershipCreateUserException	System.Web.Security	Yes	Indicates that a membership provider has not successfully created a user. See the usage example at `http://msdn.microsoft.com/en-us/library/system.web.security.membershipcreateuserexception.aspx`.

Continued

Table 14-1: Standard Exception Classes *(continued)*

EXCEPTION NAME	HOST NAMESPACE OR CLASS	CAN INHERIT?	DESCRIPTION
MembershipPasswordException	System.Web.Security	Yes	Shows that the application couldn't retrieve a password from the password store.
NoClickablePointException	System.Windows.Automation	Yes	Provides information about the exception raised when an application calls `GetClickablePoint` on a UI Automation element that doesn't have a clickable point.
ParseException	System.Management.Automation	Yes	Shows that errors have occurred while parsing a script. The `IncompleteParseException` exception is more specific than this one.
ParseException	System.Web.Query.Dynamic	Yes	Shows that errors have occurred when LINQ attempts to parse values to create a query.
PeerToPeerException	System.Net.PeerToPeer	Yes	Represents an error that has occurred within the peer-to-peer infrastructure.
PolicyValidationException	System.IdentityModel.Selectors	Yes	Indicates that the system can't validate a policy passed by the recipient.
PrimarySnapInDataException	Microsoft.ManagementConsole.Advanced	No	Indicates an error in the data passed by a primary snap-in to an extension snap-in through the Microsoft Management Console (MMC) host. The snap-in extension receiving the exception can catch it and continue functioning without the data provided by the primary snap-in.
PrimarySnapInDataException	Microsoft.ManagementConsole.Internal	No	Indicates an error in the data passed by a primary snap-in to an extension snap-in using internal connectivity. The snap-in extension receiving the exception can catch it and continue functioning without the data provided by the primary snap-in
PrintDialogException	System.Windows.Controls	Yes	Shows that an error has occurred while opening, using, or accessing a print dialog box.
ProviderException	System.Configuration.Provider	Yes	Represents a configuration provider error. Configuration providers also throw this error when an internal error occurs that doesn't map to other preexisting exceptions.
ProxyAssemblyNotLoadedException	System.Windows.Automation	Yes	Defines an error that occurs when loading an assembly that contains client-side providers.
RemoteErrorException	Microsoft.Build.BuildEngine	No	Shows that an error has occurred on a remote node.

EXCEPTION NAME	HOST NAMESPACE OR CLASS	CAN INHERIT?	DESCRIPTION
RightsManagementException	System.Security.RightsManagement	Yes	Indicates that a rights management operation can't continue. See the usage example at `http://msdn.microsoft.com/en-us/library/system.security.rightsmanagement.rightsmanagementexception.aspx`.
RuleException	System.Workflow.Activities.Rules	Yes	Used as a base class for all other `System.Workflow.Activities.Rules` exception classes—however, you can also use this exception directly. The `RuleEvaluationException`, `RuleEvaluationIncompatibleTypesException`, and `RuleSetValidationException` exceptions are more specific than this one.
RuntimeWrappedException	System.Runtime.CompilerServices	No	Wraps an exception that doesn't derive from `System.Exception`. In general, only C++ uses this exception class because exceptions created with C# and Visual Basic.NET must derive from System.Exception. See the usage example and additional details at `http://msdn.microsoft.com/en-us/library/system.runtime.compilerservices.runtimewrappedexception.aspx`.
SequenceFullException	System.IO.Log	Yes	Indicates that a sequence of log records is full.
ServerManagerException	Microsoft.Web.Administration	Yes	Indicates an error has occurred within the Windows Server 2008 Server Manager console.
ServiceBusyException	System.IdentityModel.Selectors	Yes	Indicates that CardSpace is busy processing other requests.
ServiceNotStartedException	System.IdentityModel.Selectors	Yes	Shows that the requested service (generally CardSpace) isn't started and can't respond to commands.
SettingsPropertyIsReadOnlyException	System.Configuration	Yes	Signifies that the application has attempted to write to a read-only `SettingsProperty` object.
SettingsPropertyNotFoundException	System.Configuration	Yes	Signifies that the application has attempted to write to a non-existent `SettingsProperty` object.
SettingsPropertyWrongTypeException	System.Configuration	Yes	Signifies that the application has attempted to write data of the wrong type to a `SettingsProperty` object.

Continued

Table 14-1: Standard Exception Classes *(continued)*

EXCEPTION NAME	HOST NAMESPACE OR CLASS	CAN INHERIT?	DESCRIPTION
SmtpException	System.Net.Mail	Yes	Shows that the Simple Mail Transfer Protocol (SMTP) client was unable to send the requested message. See the usage example at `http://msdn.microsoft.com/en-us/library/system.net.mail.smtpexception.aspx`.
StsCommunicationException	System.IdentityModel.Selectors	Yes	Represents an inability to communicate with the Security Token Service (STS).
SUDSGeneratorException	System.Runtime.Remoting.MetadataServices	Yes	Indicates an error has occurred during the generation of a Web Services Description Language (WSDL) file using SOAPSuds.EXE (see `http://msdn.microsoft.com/en-us/library/xd176a6c.aspx` for additional details).
SUDSParserException	System.Runtime.Remoting.MetadataServices	Yes	Indicates an error has occurred during the parsing of a WSDL file.
SystemException	System	Yes	Used as a base class for all other System exception classes—in most cases, you won't use this exception directly. See `http://msdn.microsoft.com/en-us/library/system.systemexception.aspx` for a list of exceptions that derive from this class—all of which are more specific.
TimeZoneNotFoundException	System	Yes	Indicates that the system can't locate a time zone. In most cases, this means that the time zone doesn't exist or that the time zone doesn't provide the required configuration data.
UnsupportedPolicyOptionsException	System.IdentityModel.Selectors	Yes	Indicates that the policy provided to the system contained unsupported options.
UntrustedRecipientException	System.IdentityModel.Selectors	Yes	Shows that the recipient provided as part of a call doesn't have the required security credentials.
UserCancellationException	System.IdentityModel.Selectors	Yes	Occurs when a user cancels an operation during the `GetToken(arrayViewStateException`
WebManagementServiceException	Microsoft.Web.Management.Server	No	Indicates that an error has occurred with the Web Management Service (WMSvc), which provides remote management for Internet Information Server (IIS) 7.0.
WmiProviderInstallationException	System.Management.Instrumentation	Yes	Represents an error that occurs when Windows Management Instrumentation (WMI) provider installation fails.

EXCEPTION NAME	HOST NAMESPACE OR CLASS	CAN INHERIT?	DESCRIPTION
WorkflowMarkupSerializationException	System.Workflow.ComponentModel.Serialization	Yes	Signifies that an error has occurred during data serialization or deserialization.
WorkflowOwnershipException	System.Workflow.Runtime	Yes	Defines an environmental problem where the workflow runtime engine attempts to load a workflow that's already loaded by another workflow runtime engine instance. This exception also occurs when a workflow runtime engine attempts to save a workflow after the time interval specified during loading expires.
WorkflowTerminatedException	System.Workflow.ComponentModel	No	Indicates that a workflow runtime engine has terminated a workflow.
WorkflowValidationFailedException	System.Workflow.ComponentModel.Compiler	No	Shows that the workflow didn't validate properly after a workflow runtime engine loaded it.
XpsException	System.Windows.Xps	Yes	Used as a base class for other `System.Windows.Xps` exception classes—however, you can also use this exception directly. The `XpsPackagingException` and `XpsSerializationException` exceptions are more specific than this one.
XpsWriterException	System.Windows.Xps	Yes	Indicates that the application has called a method of either an `XpsDocumentWriter` or a `VisualsToXpsDocument` object that's incompatible with the current object state.

Table 14-1 shows many exceptions that provide more details than `System.Exception`. For example, check out `UserCancellationException`, which occurs only during a specific method call. In fact, `System.Exception` should seldom see the light of day except as a general error handler when you can't catch an exception any other way.

Make sure you reference to the correct exception when writing your code. For example, the `ParseException` *appears in multiple classes (not all of which appear in Table 14-1). Using the wrong version of* `ParseException` *could cause more problems for your application than the original error.*

Remember that you can also throw these exceptions, as well as catch them. Consequently, when you encounter an error in your code that you can't handle at the current level, remember to throw a specific error and provide as much detail as possible about it.

When you don't see the specific exception you need in Table 14-1, you can always use one of these exceptions as the basis for your own custom exception class. The "Implementing Custom Error Handling" section of the chapter provides more detail on this topic. Of course, rather than starting from scratch, it's always important to review the list of exceptions to determine whether you can repurpose an existing exception. For example, you could probably use the `SettingsPropertyIsReadOnlyException`, `SettingsPropertyNotFoundException`, and `SettingsPropertyWrongTypeException` for properties of any type. If nothing else, derive a new exception from these existing exceptions and simply change the name to something more acceptable for your use.

Implementing Custom Error Handling

Custom error handling should always have a place in your toolbox. Table 14-1 shows that Microsoft provides a combination of relatively specific (`ActiveDirectoryObjectNotFoundException`) and generic (`Exception`) exceptions, many of which you can easily override. It's important to think about how you can override these exceptions. For example, even a relatively specific exception such as `ActiveDirectoryObjectNotFoundException` doesn't always provide every piece of information you want. For example, you might want to include additional information about the particular Active Directory object or the other objects around it. The important issue to remember is that you can always inherit a particular exception and make it even more specific to ensure that your application handles it correctly. Listing 14-1 shows the essentials of creating a new exception.

Listing 14-1: Defining a custom exception class

```
public class CustomException : Exception
{
   // As a minimum, you normally override the Message
   // property.
   public override string Message
   {
      get
      {
         // Return a custom message.
         return "My Custom Message";
      }
   }

   // You'll often override the Source too.
   public override string Source
   {
      get
      {
         return Application.ProductName +
            "\r\n" + Application.ProductVersion;
      }
   }
}
```

An exception works the same as any other class. In this case, the class inherits `System.Exception` — however, you can inherit from any of the classes in Table 14-1 that allow inheriting. Deriving a custom exception class from the class that best matches your specific needs saves time and effort. You can add any methods, properties, or events desired to an exception class. Most exception classes rely on the same basic set of properties, which may lead some developers to think that they can't customize in any way they see fit. As with any class, you can make any customization you see fit.

In most cases, you override the `Message` and `Source` properties. These two properties provide unique identification information, and most developers rely on these two properties, plus the `StackTrace` property (see Listing 14-3 for an example), to display error information on screen.

After you create your custom exception class, you need to know how to call it. Listing 14-2 shows how to perform this task and how to catch the exception after you throw it.

Listing 14-2: Using a custom exception class

```
private void btnTest2_Click(object sender, EventArgs e)
{
   // Throw and handle a custom message.
   try
   {
      throw new CustomException();
   }
   catch (CustomException CustomE)
   {
      MessageBox.Show(
         CustomE.Message + "\r\n" +
         CustomE.Source);
   }

}
```

Remember that an exception travels up the call stack. If you call a method from another method, the two methods form a hierarchy of calls. If the second method throws an exception, but doesn't handle it, the exception bubbles up to the next level of the call stack. When the application doesn't handle an exception, the exception bubbles up into the Common Language Runtime (CLR) and finally displays as an unhandled error — not a very dignified way to address an application error. Consequently, you should normally try to address errors at the lowest possible level in your application hierarchy.

Considering the Importance of the Error Hierarchy

Most code doesn't generate a single exception. In fact, you'll find that code generates a number of exceptions in most cases and you may not even know the exception type unless you test the application thoroughly. Consequently, you'll generally add several catch statements to your code, as shown in Listing 14-3.

Listing 14-3: Using multiple exception levels

```
private void btnTest_Click(object sender, EventArgs e)
{
   try
   {
      // Generate a divide-by-zero exception.
      int First = 3;
      int Second = 0;
      int Third = First / Second;
   }
```

Continued

Listing 14-3: Using multiple exception levels *(continued)*

```
      catch (DivideByZeroException DBZ)
      {
         MessageBox.Show(
            DBZ.Message + "\r\n" +
            DBZ.Source + "\r\n" +
            DBZ.StackTrace);
      }
      catch (Exception Except)
      {
         // This error handler normally won't call this
         // error handling code.
         MessageBox.Show(
            "This exception isn't specific: " + Except.Message +
            "\r\nIt is of type: " + Except.GetType().ToString());
      }
   }
```

In this case, the code begins with the most specific exception first, `DivideByZeroException`. If the exception is of some other type, then the code moves on to the next exception in order. Consequently, you always want to place the most specific exceptions first, followed by those that come next in code listing order. In this case, the next exception is the general `System.Exception`, but you can include any number of exceptions in the list.

Sometimes, you won't know what exceptions your code will display because Microsoft doesn't always document the possible exceptions thoroughly. Of course, it would be nice to know the exception type so that you can add specific code for handling it. Notice that the general exception `catch` includes `Except.GetType().ToString()`. This bit of code displays the exception type when the application displays the generic exception. When you see the general message, you also see the specific exception type so you can add code to handle it in your application.

Providing Consistent Error Handling

Handling errors is important. However, handling them consistently is essential. The users, administrators, and even developers who interact with your application will become used to a particular way of working through errors. If you choose not to handle the errors consistently, the application will behave illogically according to those who use it. The following sections describe some consistency issues you need to consider.

Consistent error handling doesn't require that you handle errors in the same order all the time, but doing so can help. The list of exceptions you track can almost become a checklist when you handle them in the same order every time. Your eye will naturally begin to detect that a particular exception is missing from the list and then you'll wonder why you left it out. These questions help you consider how error handling should proceed in a particular section of code and help your application behave more logically as a result.

Working with Single-Source Errors

Some application code is critical and you can't easily recover from errors in it unless you plan carefully. In many cases, the code in question encompasses a single line that you must execute correctly every time in order to ensure proper application results. One of the best ways to handle such code is to place the single line within a `try...catch` block, and then place the `try...catch` block within a loop that includes a retry count. For example, when attempting to attach to a database, you may place the code for creating the connection within such a loop. Every time the code raises the error, the application attempts to fix the connection or asks user help in fixing it. When working with a retry counter, use a consistent count for the entire application and provide the administrator with settings to change this count to reflect the realities of a particular usage environment.

Trapping Multiple-Source Errors

In some cases, the result of a process is only useful when the entire process succeeds. In some respects, you can view this process as a sort of transaction. For example, when obtaining data from a Web service, the process is only useful when the entire sequence of events needed to create the connection and obtain the data succeeds. In these situations, placing the entire code sequence within a single `try...catch` block usually works best. Of course, every one of the statements can produce a number of exceptions, so the list of `catch` statements can become long in such a situation.

Working with multiple lines of code means that the error-handling situation becomes more complicated and takes longer to resolve. In this case, you should include a user query in the loop that lets the user stop the process without exhausting the retry counter. The message you present to the user shouldn't contain technical information, but should strive to explain the facts in human-readable form. A message that says, "DivideByZero Error" isn't helpful. However, a message that says, "The application has experienced a math error — you can't divide a number by zero" is helpful because it helps the user understand what is wrong using nontechnical terms.

Finalizing Error Handling

Many developers view the `finally` statement as something that protects application code or data. In many cases, you use the `finally` statement for just this purpose. However, the `finally` statement can also help you correct, or at least reset, the application to reduce the risk of a second error. Listing 14-4 shows an example of using the `finally` statement for this task.

Listing 14-4: Finalizing error handling

```
private void btnTest3_Click(object sender, EventArgs e)
{
   try
   {
      // Parse the input.
      Int32 Value1 = Int32.Parse(txtInput1.Text);
      Int32 Value2 = Int32.Parse(txtInput2.Text);
```

Continued

Listing 14-4: Finalizing error handling *(continued)*

```
         // Perform the division.
         Int32 Output = Value1 / Value2;

         // Display the result.
         MessageBox.Show(Output.ToString());
      }
      catch (FormatException FormatE)
      {
         MessageBox.Show(FormatE.Message);
      }
      catch (DivideByZeroException DBZ)
      {
         MessageBox.Show(DBZ.Message);
      }
      catch (Exception Except)
      {
         MessageBox.Show(Except.Message);
      }
      finally
      {
         // Reset the inputs.
         txtInput1.Text = "1";
         txtInput2.Text = "1";
      }
   }
```

In this case, the application receives input from two textboxes. The user can make a number of errors when entering the data. The application catches two specific exceptions: `FormatException` (where the user inputs something other than numbers) and `DivideByZeroException` (where the second input is a zero). Of course, the code includes generic exception handling as well. However, the point of interest is the `finally` statement. Notice that the code resets the two textboxes to provide correct inputs. Using this kind of finalization is a form of self-help. Even the most stubborn user will eventually become curious and try the values that work, which will likely help the user provide the correct input values in the future.

I've taken a little license with this example to demonstrate a technique. In the real world, a developer would validate the input first, so this error wouldn't occur. However, even if it wouldn't occur, you should still include the error-handling code. Often, applications fail because the developer didn't think to check for something — it's always best to provide the code so the application can overcome errors that even diligent developers miss.

Devising Self-Healing Applications

A self-healing application is one in which an error doesn't cause the application to crash. Instead, the application follows this procedure:

1. Locate the source of the problem.
2. Log it.

3. Notify the administrator.
4. Fix the error.
5. Resume operation from the point of failure.

Of course, self-healing applications require extremely specific exception information and significant proactive error handling. A self-healing application will always attempt to overcome errors by not letting them occur in the first place. When a user provides errant input, no matter what that input might be, the application rejects it. The user may become frustrated that the application won't accept the input and try devious methods of getting the application to accept the input, but the application continues to reject the input nonetheless. Eventually, the user calls support or deigns to read the manual to discover what input is acceptable.

When an error does occur, the exception that generates the error must provide specific information — nothing nebulous will work. For example, a database record may contain errant information. In this case, the application receives an exception that the data are in error. The application can use a standardized error record in the place of the errant record to overcome the problem. The user becomes aware of the error by seeing the error record in place of the requested data. The outcome is that the application continues to run, allowing the user to continue working after noting the errant data. This example serves to show that self-healing doesn't translate into perfection. In a perfect scenario, the application would somehow determine the error in the data and repair it. Unfortunately, until applications become artificially intelligent at a level that gives them the same capability as humans, displaying the error record will likely need to suffice.

Using precise exceptions will make the application self-healing most of the time. It's impossible to provide a correct statistic. Only your testing can provide such as statistic for a particular application, but you should see self-healing occur at least 80 percent of the time (some self-healing systems can handle up to 99 percent of the errors experienced by a well-designed application), when an error does indeed occur. The other 20 percent of the time, you must rely on user assistance to repair the problem, which would seem counterintuitive.

Fortunately, you can use well-established expert system techniques to repair most of that remaining 20 percent. An expert system database consists of three components:

- First, you must provide a means to determine the problem solution, such as a list of exceptions, the call stack, or other criteria. The application tracks the specific sequence that causes the exception and locates the entries in the database that the experts say will fix the problem. For example, an errant record could have multiple causes, such as a lost connection.
- Second, you must define the answer to the solution based on the problem determination. In most cases, you could rely on code that you compile and execute locally. Using the errant record as a starting point, the application could use code to reestablish the connection. The Microsoft Knowledge Base article at `http://support.microsoft.com/kb/304655` provides you the technique for performing this task. This Knowledge Base article demonstrates how you can compile and execute C# code from within a running application. In short, it demonstrates that you can create code dynamically to meet specific needs, such as healing application errors.

- Third, you must provide a means of tracking results and use the technique that obtains the desired results most often. For example, you could ask the user whether the requested data appears on screen. If the user says yes, then the application updates the database to show that the technique has worked. If not, then the application tries the next technique listed in the database, such as checking security. The application always tries the solution that works most often first, next often second, and so on. By maintaining statistics on solutions that work, the system learns and the application becomes more resilient through use.

Expert systems work exceptionally well once you create the database and test the results it provides. In the meantime, you still need to rely heavily on support to answer the 20 percent of user needs not handled by the self-healing system.

Relying on an expert system means that you can continue to add solutions to the database and have them automatically deployed to every application. However, an expert system can't build itself. You build the expert system during beta testing. As users encounter exceptions that a single routine can't handle, you add it to the expert system database. The growing database handles more and more of the exceptional conditions that the exception handler can't handle on its own. By the time the application reaches the production phase, most of the common sources of problems already appear in the expert system database, making the application essentially self-healing.

The problem you must avoid when creating self-healing applications is assuming that the application will fix every problem every time. Even with user interaction and a fantastic expert system database, a self-healing application won't fix absolutely every problem. You can reduce the support staff required to support the application, but some problems will still require support staff intervention. Of course, as soon as the support staff finds and verifies a particular problem, the developers need to locate the precise code source of the problem and add it to the expert system database. The point is that the self-healing application reduces support requirements significantly, but can't eliminate them completely.

Coding Your Application

This chapter has demonstrated one important fact — no matter how hard you try, your application will crash and people will point fingers at you — sort of like the pod people in *Invasion of the Body Snatchers* (check it out at `http://www.imdb.com/title/tt0077745/`). Your goal is to create the best application you can, and then provide procedures to deal with those little failings that you expect the application to have. Of course, you'll maintain lists of things to fix, and immediately after you fix them, someone will find more things to fix. It's the nature of applications to have errors. If you walk away from this chapter with nothing else, it's the knowledge that every other developer is suffering the same as you are, but no one tries to talk about it much.

Of course, you can use the techniques in this chapter to make your applications more reliable — to handle errors with aplomb. What you really need to do is build error handling directly into your application design. Assign part of the team to play devil's advocate in order to build a list of everything that you think might go wrong. Design your error handling to trap all these specific errors, and then trap anything that you didn't think about, with the knowledge that you'll have to add specific error handling in the future to address these needs. Document every possible failure that the .NET Framework documentation tells you can happen when making a call and assume that the error will happen. After all is said and done, however, placing the application in the hands of clueless users (the more clueless the better) is the only way to wring out every error you can during testing.

Chapter 15 takes you on to other less-than-inspiring topics: testing, debugging, and quality assurance. This chapter tells you just how wrong you are about your error-handling assumptions. In fact, this chapter often points out flaws in your documentation (Chapter 13), coding problems (Chapter 12), errors in your custom controls and components (Chapter 11) and those of third-party vendors (sorry, I can't help you there), and even the need for new tools (Chapter 10). Yes, Chapter 15 ties everything together and helps you get the full impact of the need for a great design before you start writing any code at all.

15

Testing, Debugging, and Quality Assurance

Many developers think of testing, debugging, and Quality Assurance (QA) as acts that you perform after you write the application — that these have nothing to do with designing the application. However, if you don't design these three tasks into your application, they won't accomplish the job that they should perform — that is, ensuring your application is ready for use by the customer. Testing, debugging, and QA should be part of the design scenario and you must consider them as you write the application as well. It's especially important to include testing during the writing process, because otherwise your code will lack essentials needed to make the testing process easy. Anytime you make these three tasks hard, they won't get accomplished — at least, they won't get accomplished correctly.

This chapter breaks the tasks of testing, debugging, and QA into three major areas, each with its own requirements. You should break down these three activities when designing your application as well. The design document should include separate areas for each activity and describe how you plan to incorporate them into your application from the first day of writing. For example, you often need to include debug code as part of the application as you write it — while you understand how a particular piece of code is supposed to work. If you add the debug code later, you'll often miss tests that you would perform.

This chapter uses Microsoft-supplied products to perform testing, debugging, and QA. In many cases, these tools provide everything you need to create applications successfully. However, many third-party products exist that provide additional capabilities and features. If you find that the Microsoft tools don't do everything you want, it's a good idea to look at third-party alternatives. You may also find that you don't have all the tests listed in this chapter. The tests that you see depend on the version of Visual Studio you have installed on your machine.

Testing Your Application

It used to be that testing an application was an error-prone task of monumental proportions because you accomplished it using human input. The results were seldom even close to perfect because humans test inconsistently and incompletely. Today, tests go considerably faster due to automation. In addition, automation makes it possible to test the application consistently. However, testing is still generally incomplete, in part because humans must determine what to test, and there usually isn't time to test every application feature. Even so, testing today produces better results than in the past, even if the results aren't perfect. The following sections describe how to use Visual Studio automation to test your application. In addition, you'll discover that human testing provides some useful input and that you need to include human (manual) testing to ensure your application works as intended.

One of the rules of testing is that the test results are only good as long as the code remains precisely the same. The minute you add new code, change existing code, or delete code you no longer need (even if that code isn't in use at the time), the old test results are invalid — you must retest the application.

Creating a New Test

Before you can create a test, you need an application to test. For presentation purposes, this chapter uses a simple Windows Forms application. Of course, when creating your own test, you'll use your own application. The principles are the same as shown in the chapter. After you create the test application, you choose Test ➪ New Test to display the Add New Test dialog box shown in Figure 15-1. In order to create a new C# test, you must select Create a New Visual C# Test Project in the Add to Test Project field, as shown in the figure.

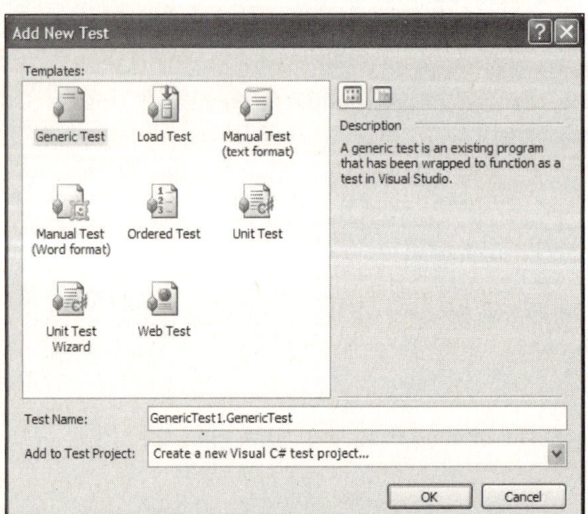

Figure 15-1: Choose the kind of test you want to perform from the list of available tests.

After you create your first test project, the Add to Test Project field will include an entry for that product. Normally, you want to keep like tests together in one project, but place tests that use a different approach or work with other modules in a separate project. Using this technique makes it easier to reuse tests later so that you only have to create them once.

As you can see from Figure 15-1, Visual Studio provides a number of test templates, so choosing the correct test is important. The following list describes each of these tests.

- **Generic Test:** Many organizations have a test suite that they developed before Microsoft created the testing functionality for Visual Studio. A generic test lets you load the existing test suite into Visual Studio by wrapping that test code in interface code that helps Visual Studio understand how to use it. Generic tests have special criteria:
    - The test must execute at the command line.
    - The test must provide a pass/fail output response.
    - The test optionally provides details of inner tests that it performs.

  You can read more about this test at `http://msdn.microsoft.com/en-us/library/ms182622.aspx`.

- **Load Test:** At some point, you want to see how your application will react when loaded. This is a reliability test, rather than a speed test, because you load the application to see whether it will break under stress. The load test combines multiple other tests to hit the test application in multiple ways simultaneously. Even the performance test, which tests application responsiveness, is a kind of reliability test showing how the application works under pressure. Not all tests check the application using heavy stress, however. The smoke test checks how your application performs under a light load (a problem for some applications designed for work in a real-time or critical environment). You can read more about this test at `http://msdn.microsoft.com/en-us/library/ms182561.aspx`.

- **Manual Test:** Manual tests provide a means of performing testing tasks that you can't automate, such as verifying that the tab order of the controls on a form are correct. Theoretically, you could write an automated test to perform the task, but the code would be difficult to write and a human can perform this task considerably faster. Manual tests use two forms of input:
    - **Text Format:** You use a text document to hold the test information when working on a Web application or at the command line. Text documents are the universal means of holding test procedures, so you can use them anywhere. However, they lack formatting, which can make it hard to convey nontext meaning to the test procedure.
    - **Word Format:** You use a Word document to hold the test information when working with an application within a GUI environment. Using Word documents helps you convey nontext information, such as warnings shown in red or italics used to define terms. A Word document can also contain graphics, which make it easy for you to convey procedures or show how the output of a test should appear. When using a Word document, you need to avoid the ransom note look where the document contains so many odd font types and styles that reading becomes difficult.

  You can read more about both forms of the manual test at `http://msdn.microsoft.com/en-us/library/ms182615.aspx`.

- **Ordered Test:** An ordered test contains other tests that you want to run in a specific order. This kind of test provides the means to perform a test suite as a procedure. In most cases, you begin building a test suite by creating the individual tests. Once you know that the individual tests work as anticipated, you can begin tying them together in a test suite using the ordered test. The ordered test output shows both overall test statistics as well as the results of individual tests, so you don't lose any depth of information by using this technique. You can read more about this test at `http://msdn.microsoft.com/en-us/library/ms182629.aspx`.

- **Unit Test:** The unit test normally performs a check of an individual method within a class. You use the unit test to validate that the method accepts specific input and provides a particular output using that input as the source of information. The unit test provides the basis for test automation by letting you test multiple inputs and anticipated results for a method quite quickly. This option lets you create the unit test criteria manually. You can read more about this test at `http://msdn.microsoft.com/en-us/library/ms182515.aspx`.
- **Unit Test Wizard:** The Unit Test Wizard option is similar to the Unit Test option, except that you rely on a wizard to help you create the unit test criteria.
- **Web Test:** A Web test specifically checks Web applications for desired output based on the input you provide. The Web application receives Web requests, just as it would from a Web page. In short, what you're testing is the ability of the Web application to handle Web requests in a specific way. You can read more about this test at `http://msdn.microsoft.com/en-us/library/ms182536.aspx`.

After you choose one of the tests, click OK. Visual Studio will ask you to provide a test project name. Type a name and click Create. At this point, the wizard for the specific test starts and you begin providing any required information for that test. For example, when working with the Unit Test Wizard template, you see a point-and-click interface like the one shown in Figure 15-2 for selecting applications features to test.

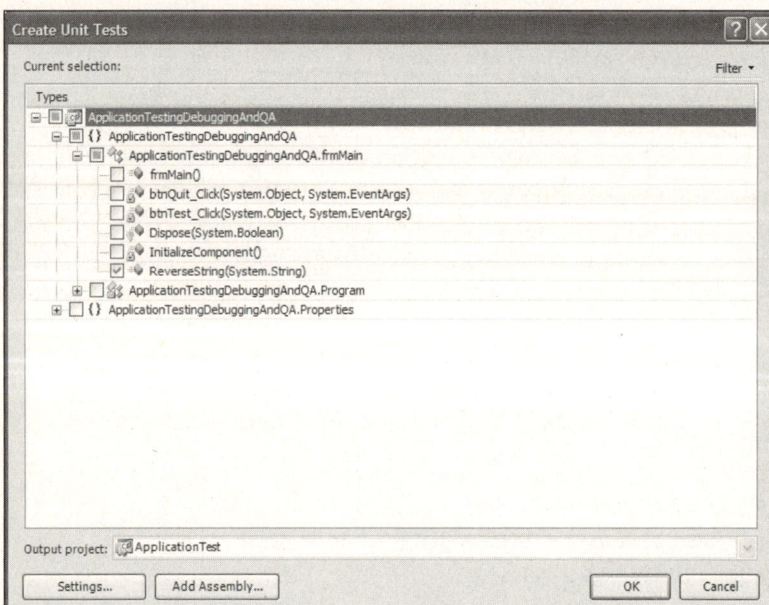

Figure 15-2: Choose the items you want to test from the list provided by the wizard.

In this case, the example tests a method called `ReverseString()`. It's important to note that you can test any method in the application. Using this wizard makes it relatively easy to create a unit test that checks any part of the application. The wizard also reduces the amount of hand coding you must perform to accomplish the task. The other templates include other helpful aids to make creating a test application relatively easy.

You'll eventually see a change in Solution Explorer and potentially some new code. Some of the changes, such as the addition of the `ApplicationTestingDebuggingAndQA.VSMDI` file shown in Figure 15-3, are especially important. The file with the VSMDI extension contains testing information that you can reuse later.

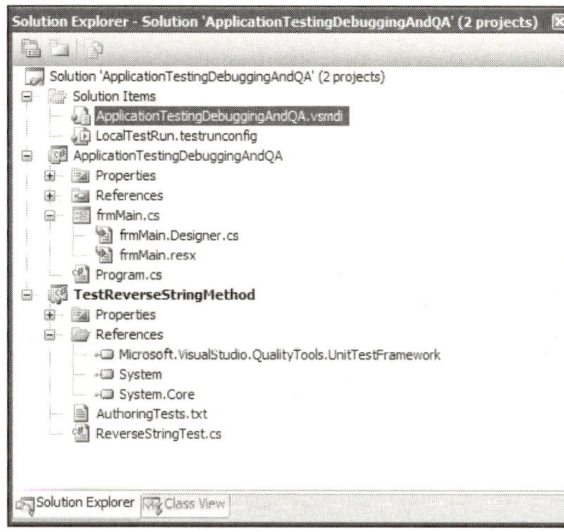

Figure 15-3: Creating a test adds a new project to the solution and generates a VSMDI file.

At this point, you can begin adding specific test code or configuration information for the various tests you create. For example, when you use the Unit Test Wizard template, you see one or more methods such as the one shown in Listing 15-1. You still have to modify these methods to check the application completely, but the wizard provides you with a good starting point.

Listing 15-1: Default unit test code generated by the wizard

```
/// <summary>
///A test for ReverseString
///</summary>
[TestMethod()]
public void ReverseStringTest()
{
   frmMain target = new frmMain(); // TODO: Initialize to an appropriate value
   string Input = string.Empty; // TODO: Initialize to an appropriate value
   string expected = string.Empty; // TODO: Initialize to an appropriate value
   string actual;
   actual = target.ReverseString(Input);
   Assert.AreEqual(expected, actual);
   Assert.Inconclusive("Verify the correctness of this test method.");
}
```

In this case, you modify the three TODO comments to provide the desired testing environment. You can also add more tests to the `ReverseStringTest()` method to verify a number of input and output scenarios. The point is that using the wizard does save you time over working with the Unit Test template, which tends to require considerably more coding on your part. After you complete the modification of the default unit test, make sure you remove the `Assert.Inconclusive("Verify the correctness of this test method.");` line of code or the test will never pass, even when the output value is correct. Any copies of the unit test that you make must include the `TestMethod()` attribute or the IDE won't use them to test the application.

Running Tests

After you create and configure the tests you want to run, you can run them by making the test project the default project. Right-click the test project in Solution Explorer and choose Set as StartUp Project in the context menu. The test suite will run faster if you press Ctrl+F5 or choose Debug ⇨ Start Without Debugging than if you perform the test with debugging in place. Figure 15-4 shows the preliminary tests used for the example application. In this case, the tests check a single method, `ReverseString()`.

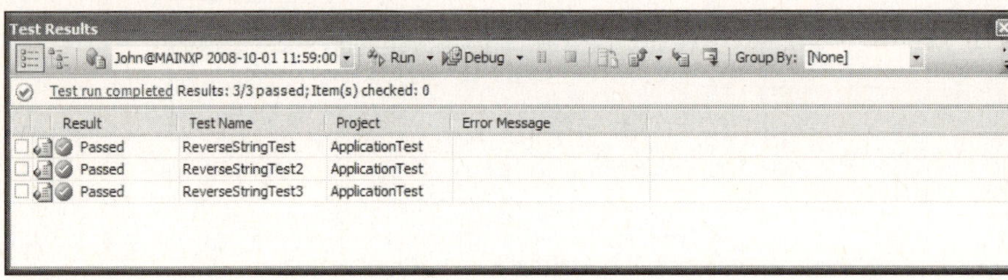

Figure 15-4: Running the test suite shows the success or failure of every test you create.

The display in Figure 15-4 is more than just the simple Test Results window implied by the window title. For example, let's say one of the tests fails and you want to find out why. Check the failed test's entry, set your break points in the code, and then click Debug in the Test Results window. You actually have three debugging options available from the Debug drop-down list box:

- Debug Checked Tests (default when you have a test checked).
- Debug All Tests in Test Results (only available option when none of the tests are checked).
- Debug Deployed Checked Tests.

It's also possible to recheck failed tests or to run all the tests a second time. The Run button also includes a drop-down list box from which you can choose the following options:

- Run Checked Tests (default when you have a test checked).
- Run All Tests in the Test Results (only available option when none of the tests are checked).
- Run Deployed Checked Tests.

Some test suites can require a long time to run. You may find that you need to pause a test suite, by clicking Pause, to perform some other task. In addition, you can click Stop to stop the tests completely (perhaps due to a severe error).

Visual Studio collects all your test results in the TestResults folder associated with the solution. All these XML-based files have a TRX extension. The Select Run list contains the last three runs you've made. If you want to review an earlier test, click Import Test Files, highlight the TRX file you want to view, and click Open. The Test Results window will now contain the results of the test you select. The test filenames include the login name of the person running the test, the machine name, date, and time of the test. It's also possible to export all or part of a test to another file by choosing one of the Export Test Run Results options.

The view shown in Figure 15-4 is relatively simple because it includes only a few tests. However, when working with a large application, you can have hundreds of tests in the list. The filtering options provided by the Test Results window let you sort the test results by any of a number of criteria. For example, you can group the results by class name. You can also filter the content by column name or by entering a specific keyword.

Understanding Smart Testing Design

It's tempting to create a single unit test that does everything. Because a unit test is just a bit of code in a class, Visual Studio certainly won't stop you. However, the smart way to test is to check a single kind of input in each test and to use as many tests as needed to check each input type.

The example application uses three tests to check the `ReverseString()` method. The first test checks a standard input string to ensure that the method works as anticipated. The second test checks how the method reacts when you send it a blank string, which could occur if the user doesn't enter anything into the textbox. The final test checks to see what happens when `ReverseString()` sees an empty string. This error could occur when someone wants to probe your defenses for a possible hole or simply when a careless developer fails to initialize a string before sending it to `ReverseString()`.

The goal of smart testing is to have a particular test for each kind of input so that you can quickly judge how a method is failing. Creating tests of this type reduces the amount of debugging required to find a problem and also ensures that you test each method consistently by enforcing a particular set of tests as part of your strategy. In short, defining multiple short tests normally provides better results than a single big test that checks everything.

Setting the Test Properties Using Test View

All the tests that you create have properties. When you run a standard unit test, it's likely that you won't have to change these properties because the defaults normally work fine. However, once you begin working with data tables or you need to set a timeout value to ensure the test doesn't stall, you need to set the test properties.

The easiest way to perform this task is to use Test View, which is a sort of Solution Explorer for tests. You won't see the Test View window by default. In order to display the Test View window shown in Figure 15-5, choose Test ➪ Windows ➪ Test View. After you display Test View, you can highlight a test and modify its properties in the Properties window, as shown in the figure. As with the Test Results window, you can apply filters to make finding a particular test considerably easier.

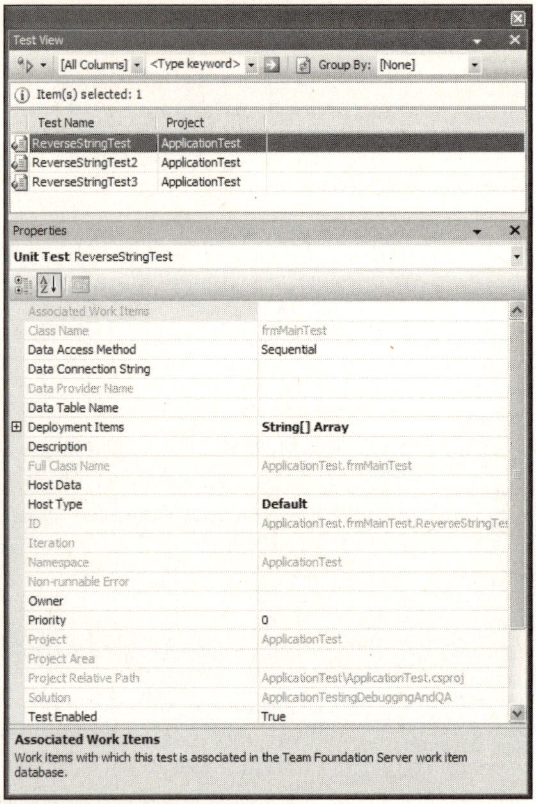

Figure 15-5: The Test View is a kind of Solution Explorer for tests.

In addition to helping you set test properties with greater ease, you can also use the Test View window to interact with individual tests. The Run Selection button actually has two purposes: you can use it to run a test or to debug a test by choosing Debug Selection from the drop-down list. Use the Ctrl+Click method to select multiple tests within the lists and run or debug the group of tests at one time.

As you change some properties shown in Figure 15-5, you'll notice changes in the test code as well. For example, when you change the `Description` property, Visual Studio adds or modifies the `Description()` attribute for that test. Likewise, modifying the `Owner` property adds or modifies an `Owner()` attribute in the code. Consequently, you can modify many of these properties simply by adding the appropriate test method attributes.

The information changes you make take effect the next time you compile the application. However, you may not see them immediately. In order to see property changes such as `Description` and `Owner`, you must modify the Test Results window view. Right-click anywhere within the window and choose Add/Remove Columns from the context menu. You'll see an Add/Remove Columns dialog box like the one shown in Figure 15-6. Check the columns you want to add and click OK. You'll see the new columns added to the Test Results window. If you want, you can reorder the columns by dragging a column heading to a new location and dropping it. The IDE lets you know where a column will end up by showing a bar at the entry point.

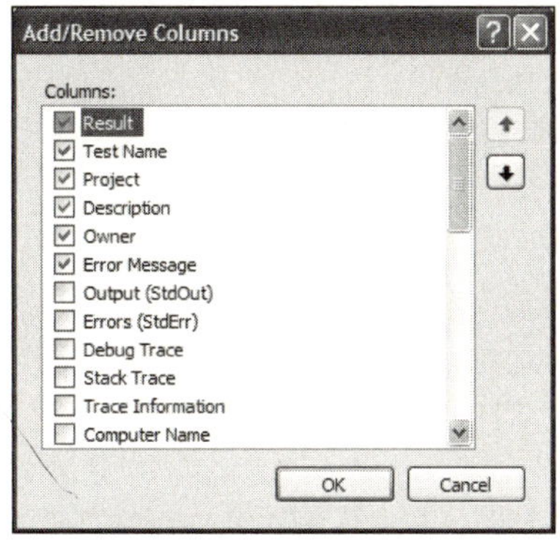

Figure 15-6: Add and remove columns as needed to obtain full information about the tests.

Organizing Tests Using the Test List Editor

You can begin amassing a considerable number of tests to check even a simple application, especially if you decide to use the smart testing methods described in the "Understanding Smart Testing Design" sidebar in the chapter. Organizing these tests is important because you may not want to run the entire test suite every time you want to check the application. Locating a single test can become a nightmare unless you provide some method of finding it quickly. Fortunately, you can create test lists — a method of creating a hierarchy of tests that you can execute. To display the Test List Editor, choose Test ➪ Windows ➪ Test List Editor. You'll see a display similar to the one shown in Figure 15-7 (this display is already organized to show what you can do).

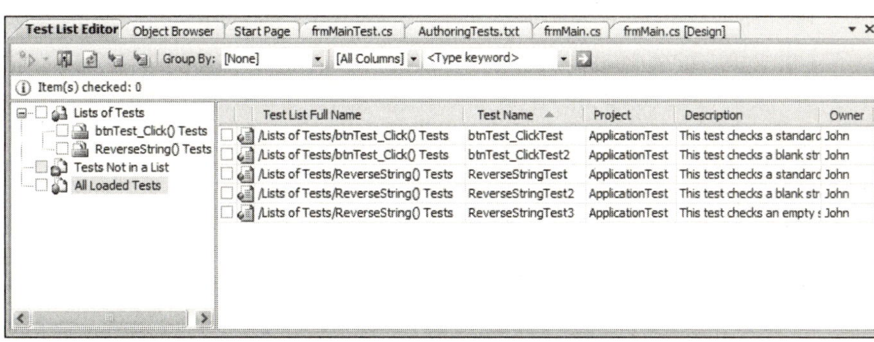

Figure 15-7: Organize your tests to make them easier to locate and use.

The window will actually begin with just two lists: the Tests Not in a List and All Loaded Tests, which make the window next to useless. In order to make the window useful, you need to add Test Lists. To perform this task, right-click anywhere in the Lists of Tests folder of the left pane and choose New Test

List from the context menu. You'll see the Create New Test List dialog box shown in Figure 15-8. This dialog box provides a place to add a test name (it can include spaces) and a test list description.

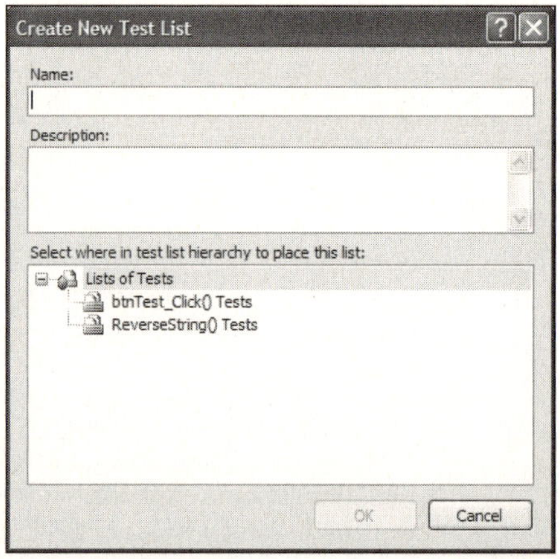

Figure 15-8: Add new test lists as needed to organize your tests.

The important part of the Create New Test List dialog box is the tree view at the bottom of the display. Notice that this tree shows three items. You can add the new test list to any of these three items, which means that you can create lists within lists if desired.

After you create a new test list, drag and drop tests from the All Loaded Tests or Tests Not in a List folder to the new test list. The test won't disappear from the All Loaded Tests folder, but it will disappear from the Tests Not in a List folder and will appear in the test list you're using to store it. In addition, the Test List Full Name column in the All Loaded Tests folder will now contain the location of the test.

Notice the checkboxes in Figure 15-7. By using test lists, you can choose to run an individual test, all the tests in a particular test list, or all the tests in a test suite, simply by checking the appropriate checkboxes. You must check at least one test to enable the Run Checked Tests button. Clicking Run Checked Tests executes the tests you selected. You can also choose Debug Checked Tests from the drop-down list associated with the Run Checked Tests button to debug the tests you select.

Understanding the Code Coverage Results Window

The problem with testing is knowing whether you've covered all the important pieces of code. When creating an application, you may not want to test the Quit button because the only task it performs is to cause an application to end. Then again, you may want to check it to ensure that any required end of application tasks occurs. Other methods definitely require testing. For example, the `ReverseString()` method is a required test subject in the example application. The Code Coverage Results window shown in Figure 15-9 helps you understand just how much coverage you provide with the tests you create for your application. To display this window, choose Test ➪ Windows ➪ Code Coverage Results or click Show Code Coverage Results in the Test Results window.

Not all versions of Visual Studio support the Code Coverage Results window. Consequently, you may not have access to the information that this window provides when testing your application. Because of this omission, you may also see differences between your copy of Visual Studio and the screenshots displayed in this section of the chapter. Your display will show the features available to you in your copy of Visual Studio.

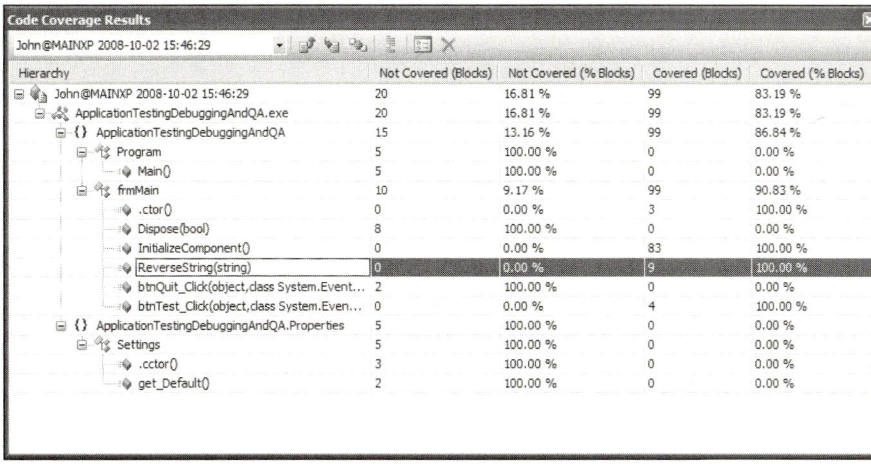

Hierarchy	Not Covered (Blocks)	Not Covered (% Blocks)	Covered (Blocks)	Covered (% Blocks)
John@MAINXP 2008-10-02 15:46:29	20	16.81 %	99	83.19 %
ApplicationTestingDebuggingAndQA.exe	20	16.81 %	99	83.19 %
{} ApplicationTestingDebuggingAndQA	15	13.16 %	99	86.84 %
Program	5	100.00 %	0	0.00 %
Main()	5	100.00 %	0	0.00 %
frmMain	10	9.17 %	99	90.83 %
.ctor()	0	0.00 %	3	100.00 %
Dispose(bool)	8	100.00 %	0	0.00 %
InitializeComponent()	0	0.00 %	83	100.00 %
ReverseString(string)	0	0.00 %	9	100.00 %
btnQuit_Click(object,class System.Event...	2	100.00 %	0	0.00 %
btnTest_Click(object,class System.Even...	0	0.00 %	4	100.00 %
{} ApplicationTestingDebuggingAndQA.Properties	5	100.00 %	0	0.00 %
Settings	5	100.00 %	0	0.00 %
.cctor()	3	100.00 %	0	0.00 %
get_Default()	2	100.00 %	0	0.00 %

Figure 15-9: Verify that your tests cover all the important methods using the Code Coverage Results window.

To ensure you see the code coverage for your test, you need to enable the code coverage testing in your test run. A test run is a file that defines how the Visual Studio runs the test. The IDE creates a test run for you automatically when you create your first unit or other test. The default filename for this configuration information is `LocalTestRun.TESTRUNCONFIG`. You find it in the Solution Items folder of Solution Explorer. Double-click this file to open it and you see the `localtestrun.testrunconfig` dialog box shown in Figure 15-10.

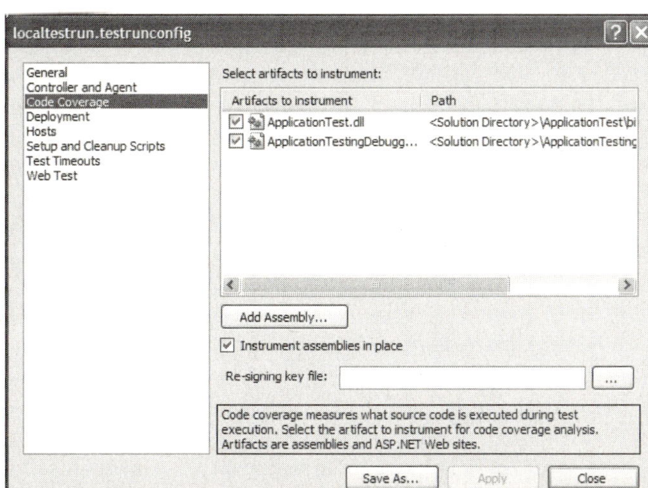

Figure 15-10: Configure the test run to provide code coverage results.

The Code Coverage page contains a listing of the executable files in your project. Check the DLL for all of the application tests, as well as the application executable. You can skip any files that the application tests don't check (or you don't want covered in the results). Click Apply, and then Close, to make the changes permanent.

There's a bug in the code coverage feature of Visual Studio. If you see a message stating, "Code coverage is not enabled for this test run," yet you've made the proper selection for the test run, the problem isn't in your configuration. Select one or more tests in the Test View window and choose Run Selection from the Run Selection button drop-down list. Visual Studio remembers if you select Debug Selection while in this window and the code coverage feature doesn't work when you use debug mode.

The Code Coverage Results window has one additional interesting feature. If you select the Show Code Coverage Coloring feature and then view your application code, the IDE colors code that you've tested in light blue and code you haven't tested in a pinkish red. This feature lets you go through your code to see which features you haven't tested completely.

Viewing the Test Runs

Every time you perform one or more tests, Visual Studio records the results in a separate file. This file remains loaded until you either unload it or close Visual Studio. The Test Runs window shows you which tests are loaded into memory and the status of the tests you have loaded, as shown in Figure 15-11. To see this window, choose Test ➪ Windows ➪ Test Runs.

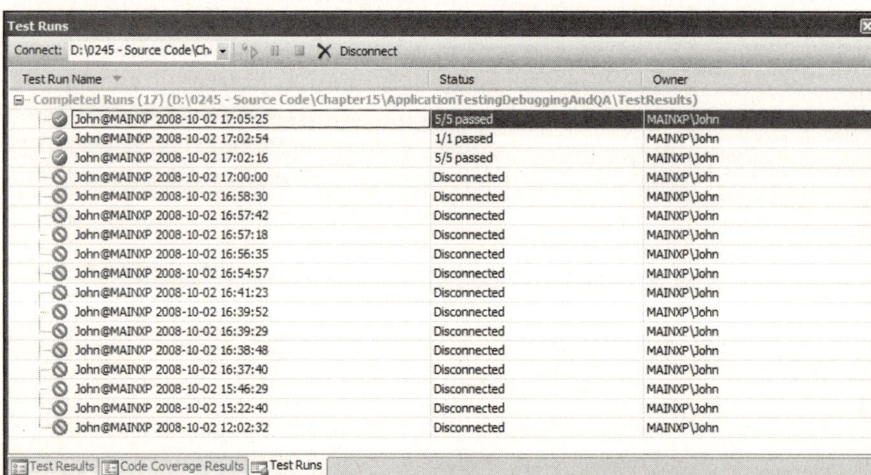

Figure 15-11: The Test Runs window shows which test results are loaded and the test status.

The Test Runs window shows loaded test runs with a green checkmark icon and unloaded test runs using a red circle with a slash through it. In order to load a particular test run, highlight its entry in the table and click Connect. Likewise, to unload a test run from memory, highlight its entry and click Disconnect. When you no longer need a test run, highlight its entry and click Delete. Deleting the test run from the list also deletes it from disk, so use this option with care. If you want to see the results of a particular test run, right-click its entry and choose View Results from the context menu.

Visual Studio provides a default of 25 test runs that you can store. Once the number of entries in the `TestResults` folder for an application reaches this number, the IDE automatically begins deleting the oldest test run. Visual Studio does display an error message so you know that the deletions are taking place, so you have the option of not deleting the test runs before you export them to another location. As an alternative, you can change the number of test runs the `TestResults` folder will hold. Choose Tools ➪ Options to display the Options dialog box shown in Figure 15-12. Select the Test Tools ➪ Test Execution folder. Change the Limit Number of Old Test Results To field to reflect the number of test runs you want to store.

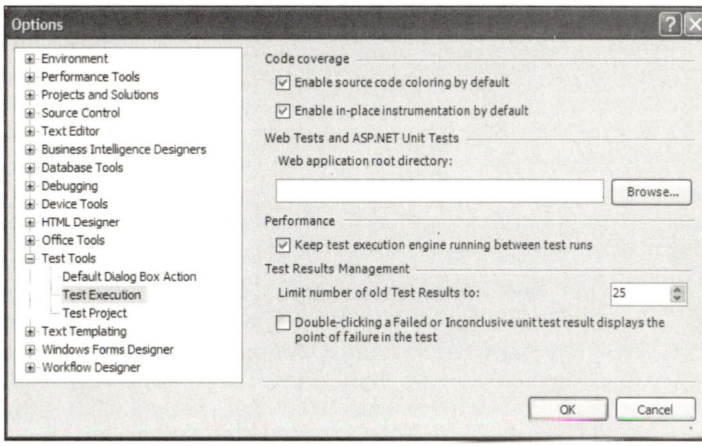

Figure 15-12: Modify the number of test runs that Visual Studio stores for an application as needed.

Considering the Human View of Testing

Most texts on testing today emphasize the need for automation with good reason: applications are more complicated than ever before and hand testing every potential bug simply isn't possible. In fact, the task is likely impossible with automation as well, but at least using automation makes it possible to test the application consistently and you can test more of the application in less time. Unfortunately, if you remove the human from the testing, you can add a significant level of new bug types to the application, because automated testing can't do everything.

An application requires a certain amount of human testing to ensure that things humans tend to notice — but automated tests don't — receive testing too. For example, many applications on the market today contain typos, nearly unreadable help text, and other language problems that you simply can't detect accurately using an automated test. In fact, most applications today could use the services of a good copy editor because the language elements are poorly worded and easy to misunderstand. Whenever prompts and help text becomes unreadable, errors become more significant and support costs increase dramatically.

Human testing fulfills another need. Sometimes an automated test sees a success, when the result is actually a failure. Consider the situation where the application must perform an action that only a human can judge. For example, you might create an application that mixes paint colors to match a particular environment. Although the computer can probably provide an adequate guess, a human will likely need to "bump" the color to make it aesthetically pleasing. You can't write an automated test to check this kind of application feature — only a human tester will do.

It's also impossible for an automated test to check for ergonomic requirements. An application may complete the task properly, but while it performs the task, the screen flashes at a rate that gives the user a headache. You can't test for a flashing display using an automated test.

Debugging Your Application

Most developers view debugging as more art than engineering. It's true: there's little science behind the art of debugging — some people do it well, most people stumble along and hope for the best. The problem is not one of technique. In fact, the technique portion of debugging is the only part that is scientific. You know that you need to step through the application one line at a time, check the variables to determine whether they contain the correct information, verify the results of tasks the code performs, and so forth.

The problem occurs in finding the problem — the bug. It's more of a scavenger hunt — you have some idea of what you want to find, but knowing where to find it is where the art of debugging comes into play. Even experience has only so much value for the developer debugging the application — knowing where the error occurred in the past doesn't mean that it will happen in the same place again. When all is said and done, technique, experience, and engineering skill play subordinate roles to the real skill of debugging, which is intuition. Some people understand code well enough that they can debug an application simply by looking at it. You'd think they had a sixth sense — perhaps they do. However, you can reduce the pain of debugging by using all the features Visual Studio provides. The following sections provide an overview of some of these features.

Working with the Debugging Windows

Some developers will use a single debugging window to the exclusion of everything else. Of course, using a single debugging window to debug your application is akin to running a marathon using a single leg and no arms. Hopping to your goal of a perfectly functioning application is going to require more time than most developers have today.

No matter how many windows you use, a tired developer will usually require significantly more time to locate a problem than a well-rested developer will. When debugging an application, set a timer. Work for an hour, then take a 10-minute break. Do some stretches. Get a cup of coffee. Walk about for a few minutes and visit with a friend about the video game you played last night. In fact, doing anything other than looking at the problem usually helps you become more productive. If nothing else, go outside and scream at the top of your lungs — people may look at you funny, but you'll feel better.

Using multiple debugging windows buys you something extremely valuable — different perspectives of the problem at hand. Figure 15-13 shows the debugging windows that I normally provide for myself — your display will likely vary from mine because each developer uses a different approach to debugging. The important issue, here, is that the display shows multiple tabs — each of which has a different view of the test application.

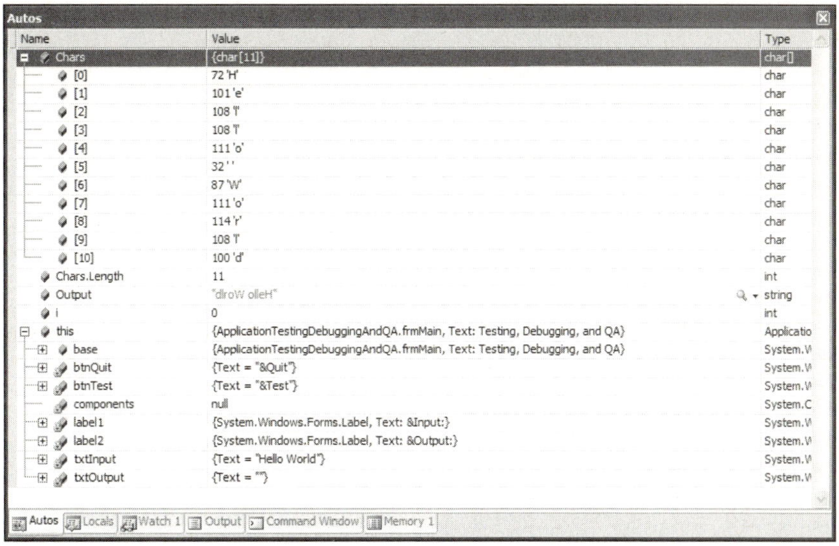

Figure 15-13: Use all the debugging windows, not just one or two of them.

Each of these windows has a specific purpose. For example, the Autos window contains a list of all the variables currently in use. The Locals window shows you all the variables within the current code block. The Watch 1 window contains only what you put in there. Finally, the Output window contains informational messages from your code as it runs (the other two windows appear later in this chapter).

Visual Studio always displays the data of interest — the data with the latest changes in red. If you're colorblind, then you'll want to change the colors so that you can see the difference. The important issue is that the red text is your focal point — everything else revolves around it and contributes to it. Focus is important when debugging an application. By setting up the various windows correctly, you can see different views of this focal point and possibly find the problem in your application significantly faster.

Asking the IDE a Question

Many developers fail to talk to Visual Studio often enough. They probably think that Visual Studio will fail to respond or that other developers will think them odd for talking to software. However, go ahead and give talking a try. You can use the Command Window to ask the IDE questions about your code, using the question mark (?), as shown in Figure 15-14.

Figure 15-14: Visual Studio is ready to answer any question you want.

In addition, you can execute any command that Visual Studio provides by typing its name in the Command Window. Visual Studio will help you type the command correctly, as shown in the figure. Using the Command Window lets you communicate with Visual Studio and the outside world in all kinds of interesting ways. For example, you can use the `Nav` command to navigate to a Web site, another location on your system, or even a network drive. Simply type the location as you would in Windows Explorer.

Remember to use the `Shell` command as necessary, too. You can execute any external command you want using the `Shell` command. For example, type **`Shell Cmd`** and press Enter to display a command prompt where you can type any console command you want.

Viewing Memory Content

Many developers fail to consider memory. It's easy to assume that the Autos, Locals, or Watch windows provide everything you need. However, the Memory window can show you how data actually appear. Figure 15-15 shows an example of this window. In this case, you're looking at the Output variable. The Memory window won't normally appear as one of the standard debugging windows. You access the Memory window by choosing Debug ➪ Windows ➪ Memory ➪ Memory 1. (Most of the debugging windows require that you be in debugging mode to display them.)

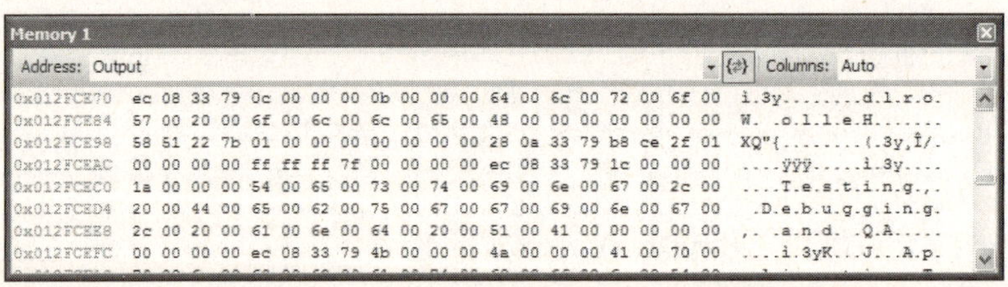

Figure 15-15: Viewing memory can help you understand how your application performs tasks in the background.

To make the Memory window easier to use, click Reevaluate Automatically. It's the only button on the toolbar. This feature lets you see the variable names in human-readable form.

Notice that the Output variable relies on Unicode characters. You can make this determination by observing that each character requires two words. Each of these characters has one word that contains the ASCII character code and a second word that contains a 0, which is typical of Unicode characters for English. However, you couldn't make this determination without looking at the Memory window. In some cases, using ANSI characters rather than Unicode characters can cause significant problems for your application.

It's also possible to use the Memory window to see how your application structures data. In some cases, a structural flaw will cause an error that you simply can't find any other way. The point is that you may not use the Memory window very often, but you should at least consider it as one of the tools you use to correct problems in your application.

Obtaining Bugs from Users

We've all seen those terrible bug forms used to register application deficiencies. The user sees a bug and tries to report it in as much detail as possible. Unfortunately, the forms often result in less than useful feedback because they ask the wrong questions. For example, every form created asks the user to provide the exact sequence of steps used to display the error. Users don't know how they got to the current place in the application, however, so asking them is pointless. If you really want to know how the user got to a particular place in the application, you need to log the user's actions and review the log as needed.

It's also important to log exception data. Chapter 14 discusses error handling and describes how to work with exceptions. One of the reasons to create custom exception classes, even if these classes don't do anything special from an exception perspective, is to make it possible to create detailed logs that describe precisely what error has happened. Using this approach, you don't rely on the user to provide information that the user probably can't provide due to a lack of technical expertise.

If you automatically record both the sequence of steps and the precise error information that describes a bug, you might wonder what the user provides, except for a body that tests the application for you. A user can provide you with a wealth of information that automated methods can't address. For example, a user can tell you whether a particular workflow works smoothly. Users can help locate logic bugs in applications and point out places where the interface doesn't react as expected. In short, users help you find soft bugs — the kinds of bugs that you often discover long after the application is in production, when changes are expensive.

Performing Quality Assurance Checks

QA checks are one of the few places where you absolutely don't want any member of the development team or original test group involved. By the time an application reaches the QA phase, it should be fully functional — ready to deploy. The application shouldn't have any major bugs to fix and it should be feature complete. When an application reaches QA, everything freezes for a while and the development team holds its breath. You can always tell which development team has an application in QA; they're the people who sweat uncontrollably and have that faraway look in their eyes. Of course, the development team that does its job right has nothing to worry about. The following sections tell how a QA team should work to reinforce the belief of the development team that its application is ready to go — at least, when the development team does a good job.

Interacting with Team B

The QA team, or Team B as many organizations call it, consists of peers of the development team. The best QA team includes professionals in every area as the original development team does, because otherwise you can't be certain that the QA team won't miss something. Under no circumstances should the QA team contain any members of the original development team — to do so contaminates the test environment and makes any results you obtain suspect to say the least.

When you prepare the QA team, you should begin by having its members go through the original design document to become familiar with what the application is supposed to do. In fact, this is the first test of the application. If the original development team members didn't keep the design document updated, it's likely they missed other documentation requirements as well and perhaps missed requirements that the application is supposed to fulfill.

After the QA team becomes familiar with the application design, it should also become familiar with known issues for the application under tests. Even though the application should never enter QA with major issues, it's quite likely that the application will have minor faults. The QA team needs to know that the development team already knows about these problems so QA doesn't spend a lot of time documenting them.

A QA team normally begins by validating the application using the test suite and also working through its functionality using manual testing. However, this is only the starting point for QA. The QA team also needs to perform these checks:

- Match the application against the design document to ensure that the development team met all its design goals.
- Validate that the comments within the code adhere to company policies.
- Check any documentation the development team provides and ensure that the development team has provided all requested documentation.
- Ensure the application data sources meet design specifications.
- Verify the hardware requirements for the application.
- Performance test the application to ensure it meets responsiveness requirements.
- Load test the application to determine whether it will scale well.
- Confirm that the application can communicate efficiently with both users and external data sources.

Your organization may require other QA checks. These checks should appear as part of an organization policy document so that the development team knows what the organization expects during the QA phase. It's also important to realize that an application may fail QA multiple times before the organization accepts it. Failure isn't a bad outcome — in fact, it's likely that when the QA team does its job correctly the application will normally fail at least once.

In many cases, the issues discussed in this section aren't addressed by QA as they should be. Even though it's a bad idea, many of the tasks end up being part of the development or environment team responsibilities. Avoid making this mistake because shifting responsibility can cause significant problems later. The tasks discussed in this section really do belong with QA to ensure they're performed correctly and consistently.

Constructing Useful Feedback

Anyone can be critical. Making comments such as "This doesn't work" is extremely easy. A QA team that provides critical, nonconstructive feedback is worse than useless — such a team kills the morale of the development team and causes significant infighting. Making comments in such a way as to make the other team feel bad is simply a poor way to do things, because eventually the QA team will have its work checked, too, and people will likely not provide benevolent input. The QA team should receive instruction on providing useful feedback, and managers should constantly check the work of the QA team to ensure that the comments they provide are both respectful and constructive. Good feedback usually contains the following elements:

- The person making the comment provides the precise location of the error whenever possible.
- Error information should include the reason why the feature is at fault.
- The QA team should provide helpful suggested fix information whenever possible.
- All input that the QA team provides should reflect the design document and company policies, rather than personal agendas.
- Whenever the QA team sees something outstanding, it should note this as part of its comments — everyone likes to hear something positive during an event that is normally associated with negative input.

You may find additional elements to add to the useful feedback list. This list reflects some common elements that every organization should adopt. While it's possible to create an application without using these techniques, you'll find the process significantly more enjoyable and the results far easier to achieve if you do.

Getting the User Involved

Just as you rely on users to test the application, you should involve users in the QA process. As with the development team, you should rely on a different set of users to perform QA testing of the application. The users should reflect the same general cross section of your organization as those who performed the original testing. Make sure you have users comment on all the screens, look at reports, and report any displays that they find confusing or hard to read.

The one problem that can occur at this stage is the user who wants more. Users at this stage of testing need to realize that the design is frozen. Yes, they can report any flaws in existing features, but, no, they can't request any new features, no matter how nice those features might be to have. Of course, some users will likely play the politics card and try to get their pet feature added by pursuing someone in management. Normally, you need to talk about this scenario with management at the outset and verify that management will also maintain the frozen status of the application. Otherwise, costs for changes can quickly mount and you may never get the application out of QA.

It's important that you also let the user know that new feature suggestions are acceptable. These features won't appear in the current version of the application, but they could appear in a future version. New feature suggestions are the basis on which you make updates. Make sure you provide some standardized method for recording these new feature suggestions and don't simply let them fly out the window.

As with user debugging and testing, you need to provide some automated method for recording errors and other problems the user sees. Just because you're relying on a different set of users doesn't mean they're any more adept at telling you precisely how they arrived at a certain place in the application or that they will be able to tell you any technical details of a flaw they discover. Users are best at locating and telling you about flaws that the automation can't find, such as spelling and grammar errors, reports that won't work, and problems with displays that work illogically.

Coding Your Application

Testing, debugging, and performing QA checks can seem like mundane tasks designed to make your life boring. However, they represent an incredibly important part of the development process and you need to plan for them the second you begin designing your application. Ensuring that you set these processes up correctly is also important. Some companies use the same developers who put the application together to perform QA. Such a policy is reckless to the extreme. If you take nothing else away from this chapter, it's that testing, debugging, and QA are planned activities and you must design them into your application.

Before you run back to your current project to determine whether it has the proper testing, debugging, and QA designed into it, you have to ask whether your organization has the policies in place to enforce the correct method of performing these tasks. In most organizations, performing these tasks is an afterthought, so you have to start any changes at the organization level. Once you have management convinced of the need to perform these three tasks correctly, you can begin to add them to your application design and reap the benefits of better application results.

Of course, once you have this truly inspiring application completed, you'll want to let others use it. Chapter 16 discusses the deployment. Surprisingly, some applications fail during the deployment — after they have already passed every other check. Having an application fail during deployment is akin to snatching defeat from the jaws of victory, but it happens. Interestingly enough, your best assets for ensuring a smooth deployment are the testers you drafted in this chapter. All those experienced users who've already tried your application now act as advertisements and help prepare the rest of the organization to use the new application. Make sure the testers understand the honor you're giving them!

16

Deploying the Application

Eventually, you'll have a shiny new application that you'd like everyone to use. Deploying your application is an important step in the application process. A good deployment gives everyone a good feeling and, more importantly, makes it easier for them to accept your application. Not everyone will think your application is the best move for the organization. In fact, people tend not to like change of any kind, so your deployment will make people uneasy. You must convince them that the new application is in their best interest and will make their lives easier. People love easy — hence the easy-button commercial on television.

Third-party vendors provide a wealth of deployment alternatives. For example, you can discover the AppDeploy Repackager in the "Creating MSI Files Using The AppDeploy Repackager" section of Chapter 30. Of course, AppDeploy Repackager is only an example of a much larger group of potential product selections. Make sure you take time to research the alternatives if the Microsoft offering doesn't completely meet your needs.

Every deployment is unique. Here are some of the issues you must consider as part of deploying your application:

- Unique characteristics of your application
- Environment in which you plan to deploy the application
- Size of the deployment
- Application complexity
- People who will use the resulting application setup
- Organizational policies regarding new applications
- Deployment range (local or enterprise-wide) and environment
- Rollback or backout plans should the deployment fail

In addition to basic deployment characteristics, you must also consider the kind of deployment you want to perform. Many people instantly think about the standard setup application, but developers have significantly more choices. For example, a well-designed application can rely on an XCopy installation, which refers to the XCopy utility used in times past to copy the application to the user's local drive. Of course, you can use the standard Setup application or you can rely on a Microsoft Installer option. The range of choices is huge, so picking the right type is essential.

You also have access to a number of media types when deploying an application. Of course, you have the traditional choices, such as installing the application from a network location or relying on a CD/DVD. Some organizations rely on Web installations now, which is simply an extension of the network method. A few (very few) organizations still rely on floppy disks for small applications. However, you can also choose newer methods, such as placing the application on a flash drive or using other media such as a replaceable hard drive. The application may not even appear on the local system, but reside on a network drive or Web site. The installation process may consist of setting up local user data files and configuration information.

After you make all the required deployment decisions, you still need to test the deployment to determine whether it will work as you anticipate. It's also important to track deployments on production systems and evaluate the results. Nothing's worse than trying to service a partially or improperly installed application, so keeping deployment logs is essential. In short, this chapter is your guide to deployment Microsoft style.

This chapter focuses on Microsoft offerings. It's important to remember that Microsoft isn't the only company in the world offering installation software. You may find that a third-party product serves your needs better. Some of these tools, such as Caphyon Advanced Installer (`http://www.advancedinstaller.com/`*), are even free, so looking around online is a great idea if you have any questions about the suitability of using the Microsoft solutions.*

Determining the Deployment Type

The kind of application deployment you want to make determines a number of other decisions that you make, such as the media type and the technique you use to distribute the code. An application can have more than one distribution type. For example, most organizations will produce a testing release of any reasonably complex application to ensure that the application runs as anticipated on a select group of production systems. A larger organization may perform a localized deployment next so that any support problems are in easy access of support personnel. Once an application has proven itself, the organization will likely perform an enterprise-wide deployment so that satellite offices also receive the application. More than a few applications also end up in shrink-wrap (commercial) form, which requires an entirely different kind of deployment. Finally, you must consider both major and minor releases for bug fixes and maintenance purposes. The following sections deliberate on each of these deployment types.

Considering the Testing Release

The testing release is the most common kind of initial release. In fact, it would be a good idea if even small projects had an initial testing release. A testing release is one where the application has gone through testing, debugging, and QA and is deemed as ready as possible for production use. You create a setup program that matches the setup you intend to use for your initial deployment and deploy the application to a select group of machines that statistically reflect the systems that will eventually receive the application. Most testing releases deploy on no more than 10 percent of the systems in an organization. However, you can use a higher or lower percentage based on your organization size and testing requirements. For example, a testing release in an organization that has 10,000 systems will likely be for fewer than 1,000 systems unless you really want to test the application fully.

When you configure the testing release, it should have all the features of a full release. In addition, the testing release shouldn't have any debugging code in it. You might include additional performance counters, however, along with additional logging functionality. Make it possible to turn these additional features on or off using a configuration file or menu setting (set the default setting to off), and let the users know that the application will run slower when they have the features enabled. Ideally, the users should see precisely the same application everyone else will see after the initial testing period is over; otherwise, you won't obtain accurate testing results.

A testing release should also go to a statistically representative group of users — people of every background in your organization and at every level of training. You should choose users who haven't seen the application before, if possible. Users who've seen the application during testing and other phases may compensate for application shortcomings and give you a false sense of security about the readiness of the application. In addition, relying on users who haven't seen the application before will also increase the user base that has some experience with the application, which will reduce training and support costs in the long run. It's important to think of the testing release phase as one more step in an incremental deployment that ends when everyone in the organization is using the application.

Use a testing release to also test all the application infrastructure — everything from the people who perform the installation and configure the application, to those who support the application later. Even your training staff should begin trying out their lesson plans on the people using the testing release. This dry run will help you locate any potential problems associated with application deployment and work them out before the other 90 percent of the organization obtains the application.

Deployments never work when rushed. Take your time and ensure that all the pieces are in place. Once you begin deploying the application, people will expect it to work more or less perfectly. Many applications fail because of a poorly planned deployment, rather than any actual faults in the application.

Considering the Local Deployment

A local deployment usually refers to an application installation that occurs within the confines of a single building — normally the central building for an organization. A local deployment lets you perform a scaled deployment where only the part of the organization that's easy to service and support obtains a copy of the application. Using a local deployment reduces immediate support and training costs and makes it possible for you to react quickly.

Some organizations will have only a local deployment because the entire organization resides in a single building. In this case, you should also read the information in the "Considering the Enterprise Deployment" section of the chapter before you begin your local deployment.

You have an extremely good reason to perform a local deployment before you perform an enterprise deployment. It's possible that your testing release deployment didn't find a potentially harmful bug. For example, some bugs won't appear until the servers are under nearly full load, making them particularly annoying to fix because they're usually buried in a location where you least expect to find them. In addition, these bugs make your team look particularly bad in front of the entire organization. Using a local deployment makes it possible to fix the bugs quickly and reduces the effects of the bad application impression.

Performing a local deployment can also reduce the risks of certain application installation problems, such as network connections. Reduce the complexity of an application deployment any time you can, so that it's easier to locate potential problems and fix them. Ironing out local problems first makes it more likely that an extended deployment will work. In addition, when you do perform the enterprise deployment, you'll find that you can reduce the number of potential errors you must consider as part of the problem. For example, you already know that the setup program itself works fine, but you may not know whether the database connectivity works over a remote connection, so you still need to check the database connection.

Considering the Enterprise Deployment

The enterprise deployment can occur in one or many phases. Depending on the size of your enterprise, you may want to deploy the application in pieces to reduce costs. Using a phased deployment means that your training and support staff can move from area to area and you can rely on a smaller, highly trained staff to perform the work. Enterprises regularly divide deployments using the following criteria:

- Location (one physical location at a time)
- Department or workgroup
- User or organizational need
- User training level (normally power users first)
- Project (high-priority projects receive the application first)
- Risk (groups who will experience fewer problems from a failed installation receive the application first)

An enterprise deployment normally occurs after you've performed both a testing release and a local deployment. By the time the application reaches this phase, you've probably received a significant amount of input on potential issues including:

- Data access
- Security
- User interface issues
- Bugs
- Remote application access
- Hardware compatibility

It's always a good idea to fix these issues before you begin the enterprise deployment, so that the enterprise as a whole receives the best possible application as a starting point. You shouldn't expect that the application will provide perfect functionality at this point. Users will still find a number of issues as the application receives additional use on every platform you designed to use it. Because users are the way they are, you also shouldn't be surprised to learn that the mob mentality takes over and users begin abusing your application in some very interesting ways, such as putting your Windows-only application on Linux, just to see if it will run using Mono. Some users will try to use your application on their cellular telephones, even if the application doesn't provide such support. Look for Web application users to rely on just about every browser ever invented, including all those old or beta browsers you didn't test.

By the time you get done performing the enterprise deployment, the support staff for the application should have a considerable amount of experience under its collective belt. In addition, the people who have trained the users will likely have more than a few fascinating anecdotes. This is the time to begin writing up all this information and putting it in some permanent form. The highly trained support and training staff of today will need those notes tomorrow because people tend to forget as time progresses. Unless you want to lose all that information, you should get it in written form as quickly as possible. In addition, you should perform some lessons-learned sessions based on the information you collect. These sessions could lead to future updates to keep the attention-grabbing acts from happening again.

Considering the Shrink-Wrap Deployment

The shrink-wrap deployment occurs after the enterprise deployment. A company should never send out a shrink-wrapped product that it hasn't tested completely. In fact, the application should receive daily use at the organization that created it. Nothing's worse than to call a vendor for support and know beyond a ghost of a doubt that you're receiving help from someone reading from a sheet, who has never used the application.

The most important difference to consider between an enterprise deployment and a shrink-wrap deployment is that the enterprise deployment is under your control. The systems that receive the deployed application will have hardware and software specifications that you already know about (or should know about at least). When you put software in shrink-wrap and sell it to buyers outside your organization, you have no idea how they plan to use that application or how they'll load it onto their systems. It's for this reason that every shrink-wrapped application should also go through extensive beta testing. You want your potential customers to begin working with the application as soon as possible.

A shrink-wrap deployment may not have anything to do with a physical product today either. For example, most game vendors now provide methods for purchasing and downloading a game directly from their Web sites. Business software vendors are following suit. It may eventually happen that you won't be able to buy software on physical media in a brick-and-mortar store. The concept of shrink-wrapped essentially says that you sell the software to the public. In short, the deployment method you use may not have anything to do with installing the software from physical media such as a DVD.

One of the more interesting approaches to distributing software online is taken by Stardock games (`http://www.stardock.com/`). You download an application called Stardock Central where you can see current news about new releases, purchase and download new games, update existing games, interact with other users, obtain free products, and perform a wealth of other tasks. This centralized application makes it easy for Stardock to set up the equivalent of a virtual store directly on your system. It's an interesting approach and one that vendors offering shrink-wrapped software are likely to pursue in greater numbers in the future.

Some vendors are also pursuing Software as a Service (SaaS). In this case, you keep just your data and settings on the local drive and rely on application access through an Internet connection. Whether this approach gains a critical mass of adherents depends on a number of issues, such as continued performance increases in Internet connections and safe application access. However, SaaS does present another distribution method that definitely works for some types of applications.

A full discussion of shrink-wrap deployment is outside the scope of this book. Distributing software to people you've never met and can't control is a complex undertaking. The best thing to remember is that you can't test shrink-wrapped software too much or too often.

Comparing Major and Minor Releases

As users beat on your software mercilessly and you create fixes for the problems they find, you'll need to get the updates to your users so their applications will work better. Precisely how you perform this task depends on the deployment type you use. For example, when working with a testing release, you don't worry about the concept of a major or minor release — you simply release an entirely new version of the software to your testers. Of course, you'll want to make certain that everyone is using the same build when you start receiving bug reports and other notifications of problems.

Every other level of software deployment requires that you provide updates as some type of patch or new media. Most organizations use *patches*, simple updates of some files, configuration settings, and data files, for minor releases. Users receive new media for major releases where the update replaces all or part of the existing application. The idea is that the application is essentially a new release — something that the user didn't have earlier. Major releases normally represent a departure significant enough that a patch will prove troublesome to install.

The designation of major release versus minor release depends a great deal on the organization and the policies it sets. In fact, as part of your design process, you should define the terms major release and minor release in the design document. Otherwise, you open the door for major infighting and political intrigue later as your successors grasp for the power you left unclaimed (it really does happen).

Of course, the words *major* and *minor* have no defined meaning within computer science. People with strong opinions may try to convince you that such meanings exist, but they don't, and you shouldn't buy into meanings that don't fit in with your organization's management style. However, if you're completely lost and need a starting point for your deliberations, many organizations define a minor release as an update that provides only bug, usability, and security fixes. In addition, minor releases normally affect fewer than half the application assemblies, data files, and configuration files. Of course, there's a lot of wiggle room here for interpretation. Major releases normally contain significant changes to more than half of the application assemblies, data files, and configuration files. In addition, major releases often provide application tweaks and small feature additions.

A problem occurs when you pass a certain, ill-defined line in the sand. When an application update begins acquiring major new features, it's no longer an update — it's a new product version. Users get confused when you try to pass off a new version as a major update or a major update as a new version. In fact, the latter scenario often makes users hopping mad, because most vendors charge for new versions but give major and minor updates away free.

Some developers also have a problem with the whole application-numbering scheme, so they number their updates incorrectly. Here's a typical application number:

```
1.2.3.4567
```

You see these application numbers all the time. Most people use the Help ➪ About (or equivalent) command of their application to see it. The resulting About dialog box tells you the application name, the vendor name, and a number of other items, including that application number. (Of course, you may see any amount of ancillary information that the vendor chooses to provide as part of the About dialog box.) Figure 16-1 shows a typical example for Firefox, but most applications provide you with equivalent information. For the sample application number, 1 is the version number, 2 is the major release number, 3 is the minor release number, and 4567 is the build number. The build number changes every time you build your application, but typically doesn't change to reflect a new version, major release, or minor release. The other three numbers change when you release a new version, major release, or minor release of your application. The lower numbers change in response to a change in the upper numbers. For example, if you provide a major release, then the minor release goes to 0. Likewise, when you provide a new version, both the major release and minor release numbers go to 0. For example, if you released version 2 of this application, the About dialog box might show 2.0.0.4567.

Figure 16-1: The About dialog box tells you the application number, which is 2.0.0.17 in this case.

You change the version, major release, minor release, and build numbers using the `AssemblyVersion` attribute. This attribute resides in the `AssemblyInfo.CS` file found in the Properties folder in Solution Explorer. This attribute begins with version 1, major release 0, minor release 0, build 0 as shown here.

```
[assembly: AssemblyVersion("1.0.0.0")]
```

If you want the IDE to automatically update any of these numbers (updating the build automatically is recommended), then replace the appropriate 0 with an asterisk (*). For example, here's how you'd change the default `AssemblyVersion` attribute to update the build automatically:

```
[assembly: AssemblyVersion("1.0.0.*")]
```

Selecting a Deployment Method

The deployment method you choose determines how you, the support staff, or the user will install the application. At one time, all applications relied on an XCopy installation. Using this approach, you simply copy the application files from the distribution media to the folder of your choice and begin using the application. However, as applications became more complex and developers began to store data in the registry, Microsoft developed other deployment methods. Now, Microsoft is expending considerable effort trying to persuade developers to use the XCopy deployment method again, because developers have encountered too many problems using other approaches.

In reality, unless your application has some very special needs, you can probably use the XCopy deployment method for most applications today. However, the following sections describe a number of deployment techniques you can use for applications that vary by complexity, user needs, data requirements, and other criteria. The best advice you can take from this section is to use the simplest method available that will meet your needs. Complex deployments are doomed to failure.

> **Considering the Presence or Absence of the .NET Framework**
>
> Your .NET application will rely on a copy of the .NET Framework to run. If your application runs in an enterprise environment, you can make sure the .NET Framework support is available when you install the application on the user's machine. You could also specify that all new systems have the .NET Framework installed by default. Ensuring that you have the proper .NET support in the enterprise usually isn't hard and you probably won't run into many problems with it.
>
> However, once your application moves outside your immediate control, you can run into problems because now you have to check for the .NET Framework using a technique other than personal verification. A common technique to address this need is simply to state that the application requires a specific version of the .NET Framework, provide an URL for that version, and rely on the user to download and install it. Another technique relies on the setup application to scan the hard drive, detect the presence or absence of the .NET Framework, and then download and install the .NET Framework as needed. Still another method places a copy of the .NET Framework on the distribution media and installs it from there. This third approach is troublesome because your distribution media could contain an older version of the .NET Framework that lacks the proper updates.

Using the XCopy Deployment

The XCopy deployment method gets its name from the `XCopy` command — a relic from the days of the Disk Operating System (DOS) that still provides extremely useful functionality. In fact, every developer should know how to use XCopy because it can save you considerable time in moving your projects around. You can obtain help with using XCopy from `http://technet.microsoft.com/en-us/library/bb491035.aspx` or obtain a more extensive view at `http://www.scriptlogic.com/support/CustomScripts/XCOPYCommandLineParameters.html`.

Newer versions of Windows come with an updated version of XCopy called RoboCopy (or Robust File Copy Utility, not the movie from the 1980s — see `http://www.imdb.com/title/tt0093870/` *for details on the movie). This new version comes with significantly more command line switches and lets you perform tasks that XCopy can only dream about. You can find a description of the command line switches at* `http://technet.microsoft.com/en-us/library/cc733145.aspx`*. If you think RoboCopy is too complex, you can obtain a GUI for it at* `http://technet.microsoft.com/en-us/magazine/cc160891.aspx`*. Developers who want a copy of RoboCopy for their Windows XP or Windows 2003 system can get it at* `http://www.microsoft.com/downloads/details.aspx?familyid=9d467a69-57ff-4ae7-96ee-b18c4790cffd`.

The XCopy deployment is the simplest method of installing your application because all you do is copy the files from the installation media (whatever that media might be — including a network location). The XCopy deployment is also simple to understand and use. Creating a batch file to perform the installation is straightforward. You could also call XCopy from a script or from within a .NET application. However, an XCopy installation has a number of rules, none of which you can violate because this results in a failed installation (and XCopy won't provide any indication of the failure):

- All the application files must appear in a single directory or within a single hierarchical directory structure.
- The configuration settings must not appear in the registry unless you set them up as part of the application initialization and you have no desire to move the settings later. Using a CONFIG or INI file is the recommended course of action from Microsoft to make it easier to move the application later.
- None of the application files can reside in common system folders such as `\Windows\System32`.
- The application must rely on data files found in the local application folder or in a centralized location on the server. You can't use a local copy of SQL Server or another database to store data.
- The application must not rely on specialized security schemes except those that the application enforces through internal code for access to a remote data source.
- Deleting the application directory should leave the target system without any trace of the application.

Creating a Basic Setup Project

The basic setup project is probably the most familiar alternative for most developers. The output from this project is an extremely simple wizard. The only choices that the user has to make are the application location and a determination whether the Start menu addition applies to the user or to everyone who uses the machine. Consequently, you can use this project for even semi-skilled users. The application could download from the network drive during system startup and start automatically. The setup project provides the setup executable and a Microsoft Installer (MSI) file.

The only negative about this project is that it's incredibly inflexible. If you add a shortcut to the user's Desktop, the user will receive the shortcut no matter what, because the setup application doesn't ask for permission to add it. Some users will complain about unwanted features. However, even this negative is a positive of sorts because your support team will know precisely what each user has installed. The following sections describe this project in detail.

Creating the Project

You'll begin with an application you've developed. This section doesn't make any assumptions about your application, except that you want to add a setup project to it. The application and the setup project are separate, so realistically you could simply create a new solution for the setup application. Many developers put the setup project with the target application so the two don't become separated.

To begin this process, choose File ➪ New ➪ Project. You'll see the New Project dialog box shown in Figure 16-2. The figure already has all the appropriate information filled out for the example. You select the Setup Project (rather than the Setup Wizard) template. Type a name for the setup program (the executable will receive this name, so make it something friendly for the user). Make sure you choose Add to Solution in the Solution field unless you're developing a stand-alone Setup Project solution. You'll also want to choose the proper .NET Framework version — the version that matches your application. It doesn't make sense to have a setup application that requires one version of the .NET Framework and an application that uses something else.

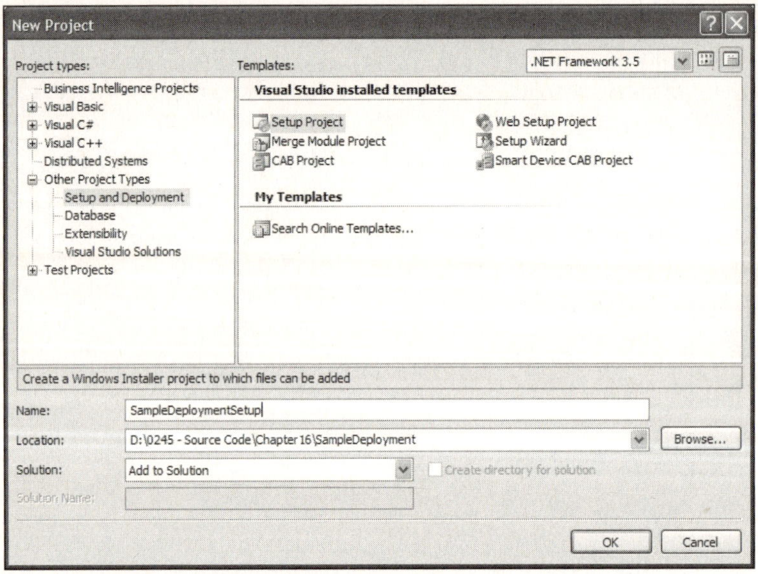

Figure 16-2: Choose the kind of setup product you want to create.

When you click OK, Visual Studio adds a new project to your solution. As part of this project, Visual Studio adds a number of files and then displays the File System window shown in Figure 16-3 where you provide the locations of the files used by your application. As you can see, Visual Studio assumes that you have a fairly basic setup that works with the application folder, user's desktop, and the Start menu. However, don't worry; you can make a considerable number of modifications to this basic setup as described later in this chapter.

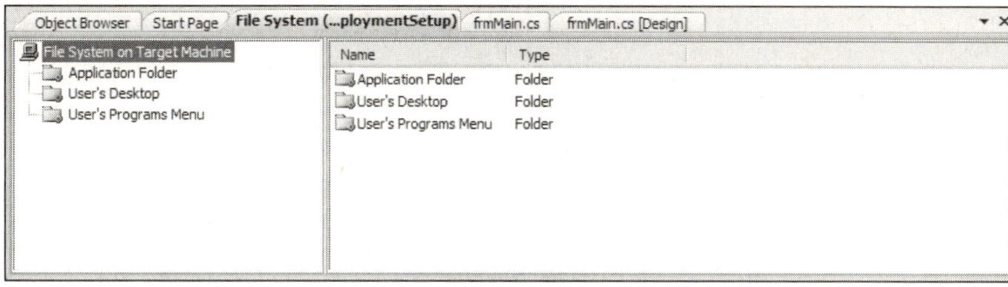

Figure 16-3: Define the locations of the various application elements.

Adding Special Folders

The Setup Project template provides you with three basic folders for your setup application. These folders represent the selections that most developers need. However, you may need additional folders, such as the `\System32` folder. In this case, you can right-click the File System on Target Machine entry in the File System window and choose Add Special Folder on the context menu. The Add Special Folder menu entry has a list of special folders that you can add to your project as shown in Figure 16-4. Simply click on one of these special folders and Visual Studio adds them to your project for you.

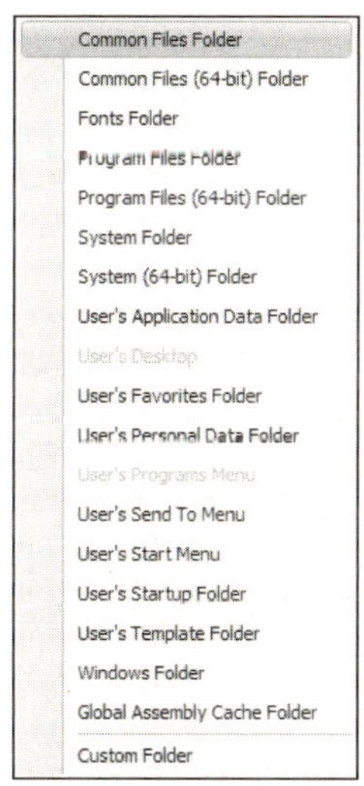

Figure 16-4: Define the locations of the various application elements.

You can also add special elements to any of the folders in the File System window. In this case, right-click the target folder, such as Application Folder in Figure 16-3, choose Add, and then select the special element you want to add. These elements are:

- **Folder:** A subfolder of the current folder. You use subfolders to organize application content.
- **Project Output:** A specialized kind of output including: primary output, localized resources, debug symbols, content files, source files, documentation files, and XML serialization files. You select these options using the Add Project Output Group dialog box.

- **File:** A file of any type.
- **Assembly:** Any assembly — even those outside your application.

To make your setup project as flawless as possible, try to create a complete folder structure. It's important to figure out where you want to put things before you start filling the folders. Otherwise, you could end up with an unusable directory structure or an application that fails because it can't locate resources it needs.

Adding Setup Content

After you create a directory structure for your application, you begin to add content to each of the associated folders. One of the first bits of content that you add is the application you want to install, and you add it to the Application Folder shown in Figure 16-3. You can add the application using a number of approaches. For example, you can add it directly as a file or as an assembly — either approach works just fine. However, the best approach is to add it as a project output. To use this approach, right-click the Application Folder and choose Add ➪ Project Output from the context menu. You'll see the Add Project Output Group dialog box shown in Figure 16-5.

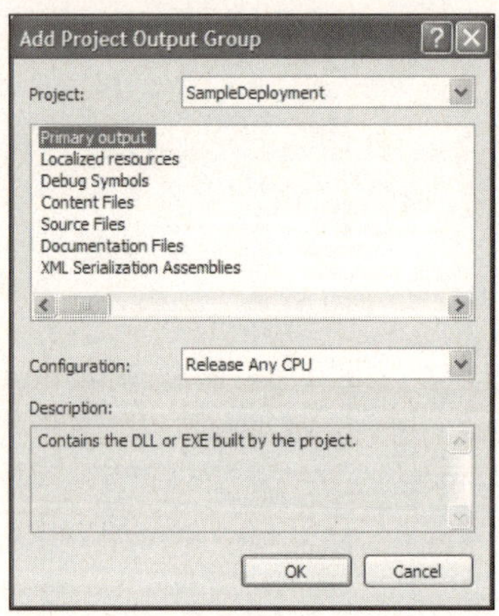

Figure 16-5: Add the project output to your installation program.

In this case, you choose Primary Output from the list. Notice that you can choose a particular configuration in the Configuration field. Using this option ensures that you don't send out a debug version of your application when you really meant to send a release version. Consequently, instead of receiving a file from a dubious location, the user receives the needed application executable. If your application works with multiple languages, you can also add any required localized resources. As you can see from Figure 16-5, using the project output option usually results in more precise installation application choices.

One of the more interesting choices in the list shown in Figure 16-5 is XML Serialization Assemblies. This option is extremely helpful when you produce an application that relies on XML serialization to store configuration settings.

Don't forget to add shortcuts to your application. Most developers add an application shortcut to the User's Desktop folder. Even if you don't provide a Desktop shortcut, you should always include a User's Programs Menu shortcut. The common strategy is to create a subfolder for your organization and then a subfolder below that for the application. To add a shortcut to either location, right-click the Primary Output from `<Application Name>` entry in the Application Folder and choose Create Shortcut to Primary Output from `<Application Name>` from the context menu. The shortcut will appear in the Application folder — not where we want it. Don't worry about this problem for now.

Setting Installation Properties

The folders and content you provide for your installation program have properties that help you adjust how the installation program works. Given that a basic setup project doesn't give the user many choices, you need to set these options carefully. For example, except for the Application Folder entry, the Visual Studio defaults don't assume that you want to install the User's Desktop and User's Programs Menu features — you must configure the folder properties to provide this functionality as shown in Figure 16-6.

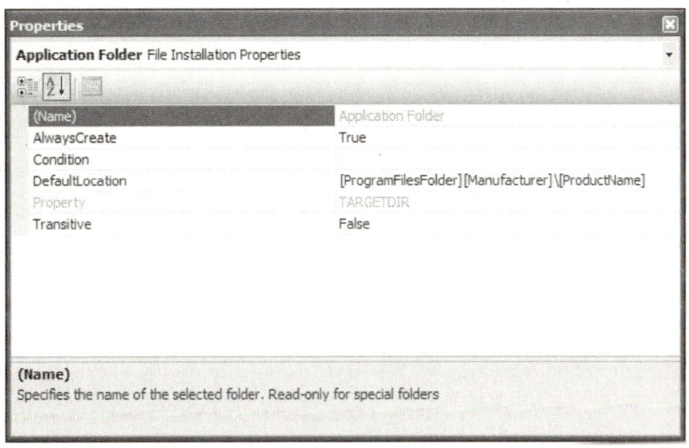

Figure 16-6: Make sure you set the folder and content properties correctly.

Notice that `AlwaysCreate` property. If you don't set this property to `True`, a basic project won't create the folder because it never asks the user whether it should do so. In fact, the compiler even presents you with an error message, such as the one shown here, for the example application:

```
The target of shortcut 'Sample Deployment Application' is invalid. The
  'AlwaysCreate' property of folder 'User's Desktop' must be set to 'True'
```

Some folders also come with the `DefaultLocation` property. You can use this property to assign a default location to the folder. The names in square brackets, such as `[ProgramFilesFolder]`, are Windows Installer properties. You can see a complete list of these properties at `http://msdn.microsoft.com/en-us/library/aa370905.aspx`.

In some cases, you may wish to control installation of a feature based on some special requirement, such as the operating system version or the user's language. In this case, you set the `Transitive` property to `True` so that Windows Installer will reevaluate the `Condition` property every time you install the application. The `Condition` property contains a statement that Windows Installer evaluates. When this statement evaluates to `True`, Windows Installer installs the feature. For example, if you want to keep the user from installing the application a second time, you provide a `Condition` property value of `NOT Installed`. You can learn more about creating conditional statements at `http://msdn.microsoft.com/en-us/library/aa368012.aspx`. The Web site at `http://msdn.microsoft.com/en-us/library/aa368561.aspx` provides a number of examples of `Condition` property syntax.

Once you set the folder properties, move to working on the individual file properties. Some files won't require any changes. However, most shortcuts will require at least a few changes. For example, Microsoft provides them with the inopportune name of Shortcut to Primary Output from `<Application Name>`. As with the folders, you want to select the shortcut to see its properties in the Properties window shown in Figure 16-7. Figure 16-7 shows the changes to the properties for this example; your Properties window will look different. Notice that the `Target` property shows a value of `Primary Output` — you must not change this value.

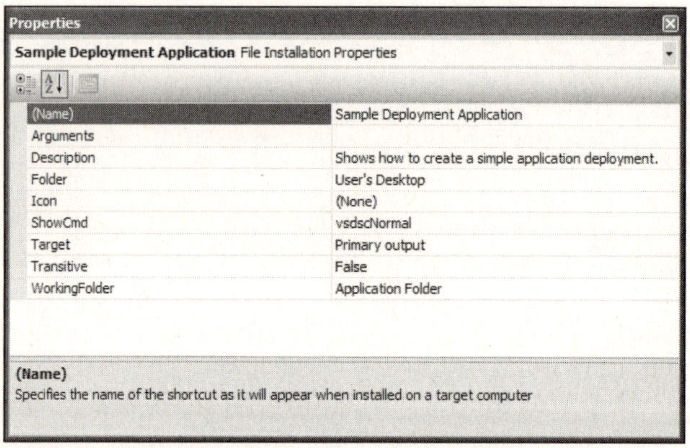

Figure 16-7: Configure the shortcut properties to match your application requirements.

In addition to changing the shortcut name, you need to move the shortcut to the appropriate folder by changing the `Folder` property to match the folder you want to use (the user's Desktop in this case). If you want to provide shortcuts from more than one place (user's Desktop and Start menu), you need to create a second shortcut and move it to the appropriate folder on the Start menu.

The shortcut properties include everything that you normally provide as part of a Windows shortcut. For example, you can use the `Icon` property to provide a special application property as part of the shortcut. The `ShowCmd` property controls the initial appearance of the application window. You can also provide a list of arguments to send to the application when the user executes the shortcut. As a minimum, you probably want to change the `(Name)` and `Description` properties to make the shortcut friendlier.

The application file settings may also require adjustment depending on how you configure your application. When you select your application, you see settings like the ones shown in Figure 16-8 (assuming that you added it as a primary output as described in the "Adding Setup Content" section of the chapter).

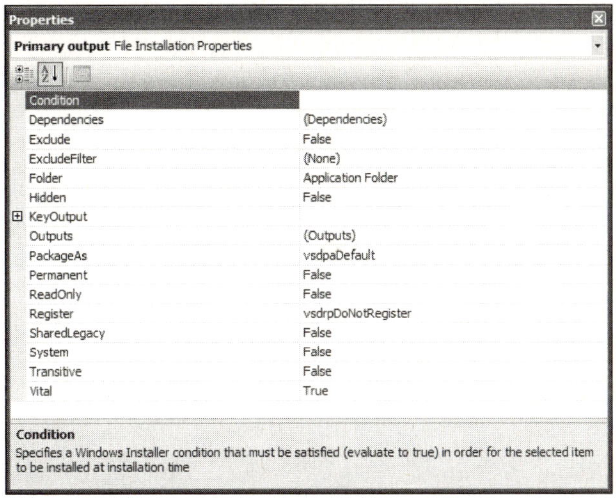

Figure 16-8: Verify that application file settings match the application requirements.

The property list shown in Figure 16-8 contains a few interesting entries. The `Dependencies` property contains a list of dependencies for the executable. Click the ellipsis for this property to see the Dependencies dialog box. If this list is incorrect, right-click the Detected Dependencies folder for the setup project in Solution Explorer and choose Refresh Dependencies from the context menu. The list of dependencies should change to match those of the application.

The `Permanent` property makes a particular file permanent. When you uninstall the application, the file remains in place. Because you don't want to clutter the user's hard drive with useless files, it's best to leave this property alone unless you really do want to make the file permanent. The only good time to use this option is when you want to preserve the user's configuration file after uninstalling the application.

The `Hidden`, `ReadOnly`, and `System` properties reflect the file system attribute settings. Setting these properties to `True` can reduce the risk of a novice user's doing something truly awful to the application files. However, it's relatively easy to override these settings and the determined person can change them when desired. Even so, the protection these settings provide can prove helpful.

If your application contains Component Object Model (COM) functionality, then you need to change the `Register` setting to match the registry requirement. In most cases, you'll choose the `vsdrpCOM` option. You can learn more about the options for this property at `http://msdn.microsoft.com/en-us/library/z5s1e2wh.aspx`.

Building the Installation Application

At this point, you can finally build your installation application. Choose Build ➪ Build `<Setup Application Name>` or click Build `<Setup Application Name>`. Building the solution doesn't appear to build the installation program for some reason. If you add your application to the setup project as a project output, the act of building the installation program will also rebuild the application. The output of the build process consists of two files: `Setup.EXE` and `<Setup Application Name>.MSI`. You place these two files on the distribution media of your choice and you're ready to go.

Modifying the Details

A setup project has a number of details that you can change for the installation. For example, you can modify the registry during a setup. In fact, you can modify a number of elements to change a simple setup into something more complex. The trick is to right-click the setup project entry in Solution Explorer and choose the View menu. You'll see the list of other views shown in Figure 16-9.

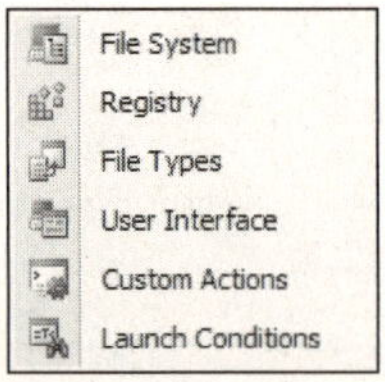

Figure 16-9: Your setup program need not remain simple; you can add any level of complexity needed using views.

To select a view, simply select its entry in the list. Visual Studio displays the editor required to use the view. Here's a short summary of each of the views shown in the menu:

- **File System:** This is the default view that Visual Studio displays when you create a setup project. It's the only view in which you must make changes in order to create the setup project. See the "Creating a Basic Setup Project" section of this chapter for details.
- **Registry:** This view provides access to the HKEY_CLASSES_ROOT, HKEY_CURRENT_USER, HKEY_LOCAL_MACHINE, HKEY_USERS, and User /Machine Hive sections of the registry. You can use this view to add new keys and values, just as you would using the Registry Editor. The value types are string, environment string, binary, and DWORD. In most cases, you use these entries to create registry settings that your application doesn't create by default, but requires to run.
- **File Types:** This view helps you create file type entries in the registry for your application. You use it to associate a particular file extension with your application. As with the registry entries, you provide command line syntax for common verbs such as `&Open`. These verbs appear on the file's context menu when the user right-clicks the file. Make sure your application provides the appropriate command line handling if you provide a file-type entry.
- **User Interface:** This view shows both the standard installation and the administrator installation sequence. You can use this view to add or remove dialog boxes from the installation sequence. Microsoft provides a number of predefined dialog boxes such as one for entering customer information. It's possible to create custom dialog boxes as needed. You set the dialog box properties to display special information on screen. The dialog boxes are broken down into three major installation sections: Start, Progress, and End. You place the dialog boxes in each section as needed.

- **Custom Actions:** This view lets you add custom actions to perform during the install, commit, rollback, and uninstall phases of application installation.
- **Launch Conditions:** This view lets you add launch conditions to the installation application. The default condition is that the machine must have the proper version of the .NET Framework installed on it. If the target system doesn't include the proper version of the .NET Framework, the installation program displays a predefined message and tells the user where to download the program needed. At that point, the installation program terminates — the user can't install the application until the target system meets the required launch conditions.

Using the Setup Project Wizard

A setup project that relies on the wizard begins by choosing the Setup Wizard template option shown in the New Project dialog box (see Figure 16-2). You can use this project on a stand-alone basis or as part of a project, just as you use the Setup Project template described in the "Creating a Basic Setup Project" section of this chapter. After you fill out the required information, click OK and you'll see a Setup Wizard dialog box. The following steps describe how to use this wizard.

1. Click Next to get past the Welcome dialog box. You'll see a Choose Project type dialog box like the one shown in Figure 16-10 (depending on the version of Visual Studio you use, you may see small differences in the dialog boxes). This is where you choose the kind of setup project that you'll create. Remember that these options affect the setup project itself, not your application. You can easily distribute a desktop application using a Web-based setup program. Notice that you can create one of four project types: typical Windows setup application, Web-based setup application, MSI file, or cabinet (CAB) file.

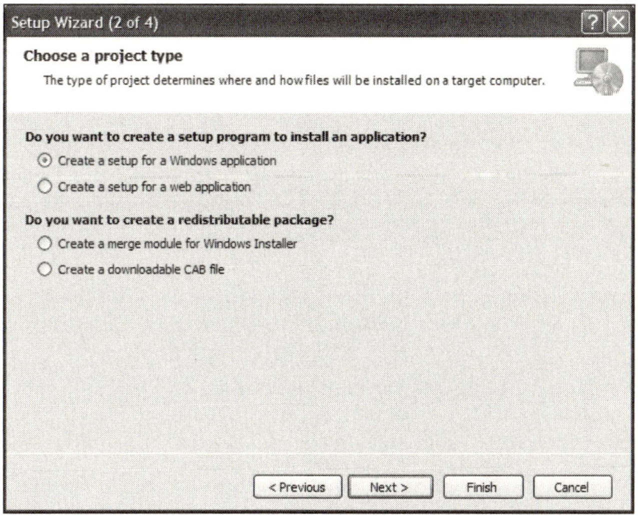

Figure 16-10: Select the configuration options for your setup application.

2. Select a project type and click Next. You'll see a Choose Files to Include dialog box like the one shown in Figure 16-11. In this case, the dialog box already contains the file the setup application will use. Click Add and use the resulting Add Files dialog box to add files to the list. If you make a mistake, highlight the errant file and click Remove.

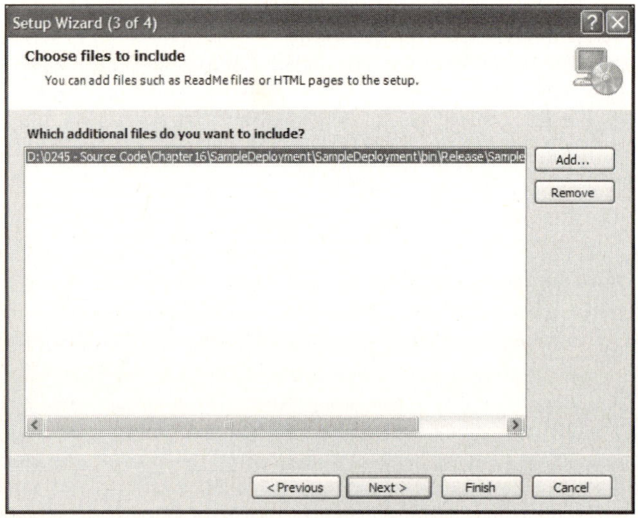

Figure 16-11: Add the files you want to install.

3. Add the files you want to add to the installation program and click Next. You'll see a Create Project dialog box that contains a summary of the project you want to create.

4. Verify the project settings and click Finish. Visual Studio creates a project that looks very similar to the one you'd normally create manually. The project includes any files that you selected. All you need to do is perform any configuration tasks and add installation-specific features such as application shortcuts.

Using the CAB Approach

CAB files have been around for a very long time in Windows. A CAB is essentially the same as using a ZIP file except that you have access to a number of other utilities when using one. The basic purpose of using a CAB is to package all the pieces of an application together into one convenient package. A CAB project begins by choosing the CAB Project template option shown in the New Project dialog box (see Figure 16-2). It may seem a bit odd, but nothing appears to happen when you create the project — you don't see any designers or editors. What you'll see is a new entry in Solution Explorer.

You build a CAB project directly in Solution Explorer. When you right-click the project entry and select the Add menu, you see options for adding project output or files to the CAB. There isn't even an option for placing the files in a separate folder, so this is about as simple as things can get for distributing files. After you add all the project output or files you want to appear in the CAB, build it as usual and you'll see a CAB file in the output directory.

The utility that you normally use with CAB files is Expand. The Expand utility is quite simple and you can script it or place it in a batch file (the batch was the option of choice for developers of old). You can see the command line switches and an explanation of the Expand utility at `http://technet.microsoft.com/en-us/library/cc722332.aspx`. Fortunately, you don't have to rely on Expand if you don't want to. Modern utilities such as WinZIP (`http://www.winzip.com/index.htm`) work just fine with CAB files.

You may wonder at first why you should even use such an old technology when newer technologies exist. The CAB has lost some of its luster over the years, but it's still the most common packaging format available for Windows machines. Yes, starting with Windows XP, Microsoft also includes ZIP file support, but some users turn this support off — the Internet contains more than a few sites that tell how to remove the support from a system. No matter what the user does, CAB support is always available and always accessible using Expand.

> *A number of people on the Internet are CAB file commandos. For example, you can find an interesting utility for working with CAB files at* `http://christian-helle.blogspot.com/2007/07/generic-multiple-cab-file-installer-for.html`. *If you find the Visual Studio approach for working with CAB files a little too cumbersome, you can also rely on a number of third-party CAB file makers such as the one found at* `http://www.softpedia.com/get/Compression-tools/Cab-File-Maker.shtml`. *In short, CAB files may be old, but definitely not forgotten.*

The CAB file that Visual Studio creates for you contains an `OSDFE.OSD` file. This XML file describes the CAB as a package. The package description is part of a standard that you can read about at `http://www.w3.org/TR/NOTE-OSD`. This description can also appear in Java ARchive (JAR) files (see `http://en.wikipedia.org/wiki/JAR_file` for details). You can modify the OSD file as needed to provide specific information for your CAB file. Make sure you read the section entitled, "3. Specific uses and benefits of OSD" of the standard to understand how CAB files use the OSD file.

It turns out that the OSD file is also part of a solution that relies on CAB files to provide automatic downloads of your application from a Web site. All you need to do is enclose the CAB file within a particular set of tags such as the ones shown here:

```
<OBJECT CLASSID="clsid:9DBAFCCF-592F-101B-85CE-00608CEC297B"
        VERSION="1,0,0,0"
        CODEBASE="http://www.mysite.com/CABExample.CAB"
        HEIGHT=100 WIDTH=200 >
</OBJECT>
```

Using this simple approach, you can download your application to a client machine and install it to support functionality on a Web site. Read the section entitled, "5. 'Pull' or 'push' models of software distribution on the Web" of the standard to learn more about using CAB files to enhance your Web site.

Choosing a Media Type

The media type you choose determines how distribution of your application flows throughout an organization or through a commercial market. Current technology partially affects the available media types, but the technology installed by a particular target group also affects number of types. For example, the enterprise environment in which you work may rely on workstations without any external media, such as CD/DVD. In this case, the media type you choose must work with a feature the workstation does possess, such as a network connection or a USB port where you can connect an external drive or new technology such as a flash drive. When you design your installation strategy, you must consider the target audience for your application and the kind of media that this audience can support.

In some cases, you must resort to older technology because you can't be sure that a particular group will have a newer technology. For example, home users will very likely have CD media at their disposal and you might possibly think that they'll have DVD at their disposal as well. However, it's unlikely that this group will have enough dual-layer DVD or Blu-ray drives on hand to make distribution using these media worthwhile. Of course, the distribution could always improve in the next few years, so you must also reevaluate your strategy as you provide new product releases. The important issue is that the media must match the target.

Some companies have embraced the network download as their major method of software distribution, because using network downloads reduces costs. In addition, it's easier to create a network download to update software at regular intervals, which tends to ensure that users will have the latest version of the software on their machines. Having the latest version of the software available tends to reduce risk and support costs. It's also easy to script network download installations so they occur on all affected systems without the user's interaction. Getting deployment statistics is also easier with a network installation because you already have a connection to the system. Finally, when a user has a problem with the installation, support staff find it easier to locate and fix the problem when working with a network installation because they already have a connection to the user's system.

Using a network download can prove successful, especially in the enterprise environment. However, using this approach makes an assumption that may not be true — the workstation performing the download must have a network connection. In many cases, a workstation error occurs that makes it impossible to connect to the network. If the workstation needs the software found on the network to fix the problem, you encounter a chicken or egg sort of a problem where the user can't resolve the problem. In this case, you must have physical media available that the user can use to perform the installation and fix the workstation problem in order to reconnect to the network.

Network installations can also encounter problems that don't plague physical media. When you place a DVD in a drive and use it to begin an installation, the DVD has direct, local access to the system. A network installation may flow through antivirus software and firewalls that make the installation fail at a critical juncture. At some point, the user will become frustrated and commit errors that further complicate the installation scenario. In short, even though network downloads have significant benefits, you should consider having a physical media option as an alternative.

Whatever media you choose, always verify the media before you send them out. Ensure that the media are complete in every detail so that there's a smaller risk of potential installation failures. In addition, check the media for potential viruses, adware, and other forms of infection. Verifying that your media are completely clean and usable is an essential part of the process and you should perform this check as the last item before you send the media off for duplication or make them available through a network connection.

Performing the Deployment

Once you've produced media that contain the installation program, it's time to install them on other systems. You have a number of deployment choices to make at this point. First, you must determine who will install the software. Here are some typical choices:

- Developer (testing scenarios only)
- Administrator
- Support personnel
- Manager
- Power user
- Average user
- Novice user
- Home user
- Professional (such as someone in the sciences)
- Military/Police

Of course, many other user types exist and you'll need to choose based on the target user for your application. Second, once you choose who will install the software, you must determine how they'll install it. Here are some options you have for installing the application:

- Scripted (where the user uses a written script to provide answers to the installation program)
- Controlled (where the user performs a particular kind of installation, but without using a script)
- Uncontrolled (where the user performs the installation based on personal need)
- Automated (where the user doesn't interact with the installation process at all)

You'll often begin by using a scripted installation for the testing release so that you can see how the software reacts under specific conditions. If the scripted installation works well, you might move onto a controlled installation and finally an uncontrolled installation so that you see how the software works in all these environments.

When working with a local deployment, you often rely on support personnel or the people actually responsible for installing the software. In many cases, these people will use a script to ensure that every machine has a particular setup. Using an automated installation is also a possibility in this environment. Unless you're working in a scientific environment, where each machine has a different purpose and differing capabilities, you probably won't perform an uncontrolled installation.

Due to the scale of the installation, an enterprise deployment normally relies on an automated installation based on information that you've collected at other installation phases. However, it's not unusual to have smaller rollouts performed by support personnel using a scripted installation. In fact, when someone in support encounters a problem machine, using a controlled installation may help get around problems.

At one time, all shrink-wrapped installations fell into the uncontrolled category. In addition, just about anyone could become involved in a shrink-wrapped installation. Consequently, the shrink-wrapped installation often feels like a controlled crash where the software works accidentally, when it works at all. Of course, the results depend a great deal on the person performing the installation as well as the software used to create the installation program. Today, more and more shrink-wrapped software provided over a network connection relies on automated installation, with the software asking the user as few questions as possible (and sometimes none at all). The software automatically detects machine characteristics, operating system version, other software installed on the machine, and as many environmental factors as possible, and then performs the best installation for the user automatically.

Completely automating shrink-wrapped software installations without giving power users a chance to make their own choices can cause a backlash from power users who like to fiddle with their machines. Developers often walk a fine line between providing too much help and not enough. You don't want to expose the grandmother in Sheboygan to the terrifying realities of the computer, but you also don't want to deny the expert in San Francisco the pleasure of working with your application. The best choice is the one where you offer to automate the process at the outset and let the user choose the best course for that person's particular needs, but even this option can lead to unanticipated and unwanted results. Experimentation is often the best teacher when it comes to designing the perfect installation program for your target audience.

Evaluating the Results

The method you use to evaluate the results of a deployment depends on the kind of deployment you're performing. For example, when performing a testing release, you want to maintain significant logs of every activity the user performs and the results that the user sees during the installation. You should also record all the events that occur behind the scenes. The testing release is the time during which you find the most bugs in your deployment strategy. Consequently, you need to obtain as much information as possible during this time frame.

The local deployment can also help you garner a lot of installation information. This deployment is considerably larger, so it provides better statistical reliability. However, the very size of the deployment also makes data analysis more difficult. If you gather absolutely every piece of information during this deployment, you might spend months evaluating it, which is far too long in most cases. Automating your analysis can help. Using XML files to store the data and then relying on a technology such a LINQ can make querying the data and evaluating the results easier. However, in general, you'll limit the amount of data you retrieve during a local deployment.

By the time you reach the enterprise deployment, it may prove difficult to store much data about the deployment at all. Not only is time more critical at this point, but the amount of potential data is staggering. Even with automated diagnosis and advanced-query techniques, making use of the data can prove hard. Some companies store only negative results at this point — installation faults or user choices that don't make sense. However, given a large enough database and the right questions, you can still use automated log data at this point to see general installation trends for the application. The installation trends often point to usage trends that the user will exercise later. Therefore, the data, while cumbersome, are still useful.

At one time, people would have stated emphatically that gathering installation log data for a shrink-wrap deployment would be insane. After all, you're talking about potentially analyzing thousands of installations from systems with which you have no contact. However, you might have noticed that Microsoft has begun gathering even this data in hopes of determining how people use their products. Of course, not everyone has the resources of Microsoft to analyze such data properly, but the fact that anyone does it proves that you could potentially track even shrink-wrapped installations.

The amount of data you collect determines how much analysis you can perform. You can target your analysis by choosing which data to collect or you can collect as much data as possible and filter it to meet specific analysis needs. No matter what you collect and how you analyze it, developers generally look for the following kinds of information when viewing the results of an installation:

- What installation choices did the user make?
- Do these installation choices make sense (for example, did the user choose what you would normally consider mutually exclusive options)?
- What are the installation choice trends of users by group (do specific groups tend to make particular installation choices)?
- How are the user groups related?
- Are users ignoring any product features?
- When do users normally install the product (is there a correlation, for example, between time of day and installation errors)?
- Did the installation succeed?
- Which faults occur most often?
- Is there any correlation between faults and user type?
- How long is the typical wait for a user to answer an installation question (this metric can point to everything from the user's leaving the desk to being confused by an installation choice)?
- How often does the user click the Back button and make a different installation option choice?
- How often does the user cancel the installation and at what point does the cancellation occur most often?

The list of questions can go on for quite a while. The point of asking these questions is to determine whether your installation package actually works as intended. The better you can target the installation package to meet user needs, the more successful the installation becomes. Successful installations tend to produce fewer support problems because the application is starting with a firm foundation.

Coding Your Application

This chapter has explored a number of deployment alternatives offered by Microsoft. Software deployment is important because it provides the first view of your application to the user. Many users feel that if you can't even get the deployment right, then perhaps the software won't be all that usable either. Of course, the application has to work great, too, or the best installation in the world won't make the user happy. The point is that you must carefully choose the correct deployment technique and the right media, and provide significant testing to ensure that the problems support sees relate to the application and not to a faulty installation.

Now it's time for you to look at the deployment of your application. As with many other parts of your application, you need to begin reviewing this issue as you design your application. Before you write a single line of code, you should have some idea of how you plan to get the application onto the user's machine. The reason is simple — the deployment method you use directly affects some of the decisions you make as you design the application. For example, if you want to use an XCopy installation, then you must keep all the application files in a single location. Running the application from the network means designing application security to allow for safe remote execution. In sum, if you wait until you have an application built to start making deployment decisions, the application itself will limit your choices, so it's better to make those decisions now.

Chapter 17 is a kind of "what happens next" chapter. After you complete your application installation, you face the possibility that your application will require some level of maintenance. In addition, you must provide application support. It's important to remember that both maintenance and support are user driven to an extent. Users will begin asking for application changes almost from the moment that you complete the installation — count on it. In addition, no matter how carefully you design the application, some users will require help using it. The best application in the world will cause some angst for users who aren't sure how to turn their computers on, much less how to use the mouse and the keyboard. Maintenance and support are standard phases of your application and they always occur after you install the application the first time — no matter where that installation occurs.

17

Supporting and Maintaining the Application

Your work doesn't end when you deliver a new application to the users. Even the difficulty of a successful deployment doesn't end the application process. In fact, from a certain perspective, your work has just begun, because now the test of your application design and implementation begins by vicious users who will show no pity whatsoever. You may quickly find yourself longing for the days when you spent hours, coffee cup in hand, writing and debugging the initial application — the days when your hopes were high. I'm not trying to terrify you too much, but once the application leaves the test environment and goes onto user machines, everything will change. People will do the inconceivable to your application and that's just the good days — the bad days will be worse.

Supporting and maintaining your application is hard because you often have to fix errors on a short schedule without much in the way of helpful information. The best developers do listen to the user and try to understand precisely what's gone wrong with the application they're using. However, even the most coherent users won't deliver everything you need to fix the application, and all the jumping up and down in the world won't change the situation. That's why the best developers also add capabilities to their applications that make the support and maintenance process easier. This chapter describes many of the techniques that developers use.

Creating Error Logs

The focal point of most support and maintenance tasks is the error log. Error logs take a number of forms. For example, some developers actually rely on the Windows event logs to store error information, but sometimes that approach doesn't work particularly well. Most developers today rely on a custom error log setup and at least a few are relying on a serialized XML file to provide the required error information, because XML files are easier to incorporate into databases.

(Chapter 22 provides additional information on working with XML serialization.) However, the kind of error log that you use matters less than the fact that you do use one to store error information. The following sections describe one technique for creating an error log within an application.

Defining an Error

The example in this section shows one way to create an error log. It certainly isn't the only way to create such an error log, but it's one of the easier ways to provide relatively comprehensive support of exception logging. Of course, you may eventually want to add support for tracking TRACE and DEBUG statements in your code, too. The level to which you extend this code depends on your personal needs. Before you can do anything else, you need a method that generates an error, catches it, and then reports it, as shown in Listing 17-1.

Listing 17-1: Defining an error condition, catching it, and reporting it

```
private void btnTest_Click(object sender, EventArgs e)
{
    try
    {
        int Value1 = 1;
        int Value2 = 0;

        // Create an error.
        int Value3 = Value1 / Value2;
    }
    catch (DivideByZeroException DBZ)
    {
        // Output the error information to the error log.
        ErrorHandler.RegisterError(
            DBZ.Message,
            DBZ.Source,
            DBZ.TargetSite.Name,
            DBZ.TargetSite.GetParameters(),
            DBZ.StackTrace,
            DBZ.Data,
            DBZ.InnerException);

        // Display a user friendly message.
        MessageBox.Show("A Math Error Has Happened!");
    }
}
```

The error isn't hard to understand — the code is dividing a value by zero on purpose to generate the error. The catch code is also typical for a DivideByZeroException exception. The important piece of code is the call to ErrorHandler.RegisterError(). This special class records all the exception information you see in the parameter list for later use by you in diagnosing the problem. Not every potential piece of information appears in the list, but you obtain enough to make it easier to understand the application error. You'll see how the ErrorHandler.RegisterError() method works later in this section.

Handling Error Log Settings

One of the problems you'll encounter when working with error logs is where to put the log. You could place it on the local system, but the user might erase it, mangle it, or simply not understand what you mean when you ask for it. It's important to understand that the user's machine may not be accessible from the network after the error occurs, so you may not be able to obtain the log yourself without walking over to the user's machine and getting it. Of course, you can always rely on a network storage location, which works fine unless the user's machine has lost network access as well.

The best solution for the location problem is to provide log settings as part of the application. Using this approach lets you tune an error log location for particular systems so that you have the best possible chance of catching the information you need. As part of the log settings, you'll also want to control the log size, so you'll probably want to add a size setting as well. To add the settings to your application, choose Project ➪ `<Project Name>` Properties and choose the Settings folder. You'll see a display similar to the one shown in Figure 17-1 (the window will initially contain a message telling you to click a link to create your first setting). The figure already has the settings used for the example in it. A good addition to this list is settings that control the amount of information the logging class records, but I chose to keep the example relatively simple.

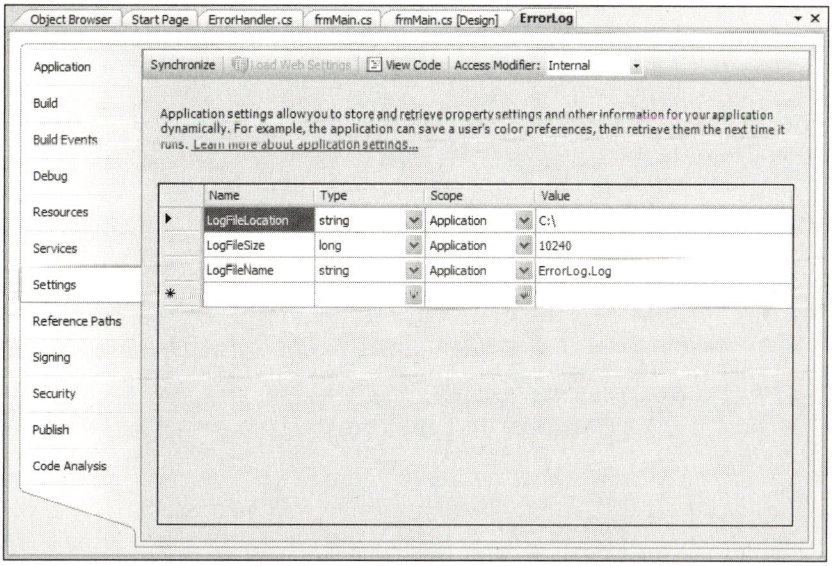

Figure 17-1: Define settings for the error log so that an administrator can easily change the location later.

Creating the Error Logging Class

Now that you have an error to record and settings to describe where to place the information, it's time to look at the error class itself. Normally, you'd create an assembly with your error handler and include that assembly with your application. To make things simple, the example provides the error logging class as part of the application. Listing 17-2 shows the error logging class code. The class contains a single static method, `RegisterError()`. You could possibly create special methods for certain kinds of errors or to include the content of `DEBUG` and `TRACE` calls as part of your error log (you need to use a custom trace listener to perform this task — see the example at `http://msdn.microsoft.com/en-us/library/ms180974.aspx`).

Listing 17-2: Logging the error to disk

```
class ErrorHandler
{
   public static void RegisterError(
      String Message,
      String Source,
      String MethodName,
      ParameterInfo[] Parameters,
      String StackTrace,
      IDictionary Data,
      Exception InnerException
      )
   {
      // Obtain the log file settings.
      String LogFileLocation =
         Properties.Settings.Default.LogFileLocation;
      String LogFileName =
         Properties.Settings.Default.LogFileName;
      Int64 LogFileSize =
         Properties.Settings.Default.LogFileSize;

      // Check for the log file.
      if (File.Exists(LogFileLocation + LogFileName))
      {
         // Verify the log isn't too large.
         if (
            File.OpenRead(
               LogFileLocation + LogFileName).Length >= LogFileSize)

            // Delete the old file if the file is too large.
            File.Delete(LogFileLocation + LogFileName);
      }

      // Open the log file for writing.
      TextWriter LogFile =
         new StreamWriter(LogFileLocation + LogFileName, true);

      // Write an error header.
      LogFile.WriteLine(DateTime.Now.ToLongDateString());
      LogFile.WriteLine(DateTime.Now.ToLongTimeString());
      LogFile.WriteLine(Environment.MachineName);
      LogFile.WriteLine();
```

```
        // Write the error information.
        if (Message != null)
           LogFile.WriteLine(
              "Message: " + Message);
        if (Source != null)
           LogFile.WriteLine(
              "Source: " + Source);
        if (MethodName != null)
           LogFile.WriteLine(
              "Method Name: " + MethodName);
        if (Parameters != null)
        {
           foreach (ParameterInfo ThisInfo in Parameters)
              LogFile.WriteLine(
                 "\tParameter: " + ThisInfo.ToString());
        }
        if (Data != null)
        {
           IDictionaryEnumerator DataEnum = Data.GetEnumerator();
           while (DataEnum.MoveNext())
           {
              LogFile.Write(
                 "Key: " + DataEnum.Key.ToString());
              LogFile.WriteLine(
                 " Value: " + DataEnum.Value.ToString());
           }
        }
        if (StackTrace != null)
           LogFile.WriteLine(
              "Stack Trace:\r\n" + StackTrace);
        LogFile.WriteLine();

        // Process the inner exception.
        if (InnerException != null)
        {
           LogFile.WriteLine("Inner Exception Message: "
              + InnerException.Message);
           LogFile.WriteLine("Inner Exception Source: "
              + InnerException.Source);
           LogFile.WriteLine();
        }

        // Close the log file.
        LogFile.Flush();
        LogFile.Close();
     }
  }
```

The example code illustrates a number of principles that are essential for you to provide in any disk-based error log solution. The code begins by obtaining the error log parameters from the application settings you created earlier. The code then checks the status of the error log before it does anything else. If the error log is too large, the example deletes it. Of course, you could simply rename the log, but then you also need to provide logic for removing old logs or the hard drive will end up with a host of potentially useless log information.

When you open the log file for writing, the easiest approach is to use a `TextWriter` object as shown in the example code. A `TextWriter` can handle most data types easily, and the code for using it is relatively simple, too. Make sure you open the log file for appending by adding `true` as the second method call parameter or you'll overwrite old log entries.

Error logs aren't particularly useful if you don't provide some time and location specifics in them. The example adds this information as a header at the beginning of every log entry to make it easy to identify individual entries. You can add other information, such as the username, if desired. However, don't fill up the log with information you really don't need. If there's only one user per machine, you already know who's using the machine, so it's not necessary to record that information in most cases (unless users routinely share machines).

The next step is to write the error information for this particular exception. You must check every parameter passed to the method because some exceptions generate more information than others do and you don't want to create another error by trying to process information that isn't there. Most of the information you receive is straight text. However, notice that some of the parameters, such as `Data`, require special processing because they contain multiple pieces of information. It's easy to overdo the information from these complex sources — make sure you actually need the information they provide before you record it in the log file. The example code shows a typical level of information, but there isn't any reason to avoid other specifics if you need them.

The final step is to record the information found in the inner exception, when it exists. An exception can have multiple levels of inner exceptions. Depending on the complexity of your code, you may want to process every level iteratively. However, most error logs need, at most, one additional level of error information, because it's quite possible that the inner exception has already appeared in the error log. You may choose not to process the inner exception at all in some cases. One way to handle this variable level of processing is simply to pass a null value as the `InnerException` parameter.

Viewing the Error Log Output

It's time to run the application. When you click Test, you'll see a simple message telling that the error has happened, but the message box doesn't provide much information. The developer-level information actually appears in the error log, which you can open using Notepad. Figure 17-2 shows a typical example of the error log output for this example. The information you see when you run the example will probably vary a little from the information shown in the figure, but it should be essentially the same.

In this case, the `DivideByZeroException` exception provides some basics that tell you where to find the error and which control caused the error. The source is the ErrorLog application, of course, and it occurred during a call to `btnTest_Click()`, which provides two parameters, "`sender`" and "`e`". The stack trace tells you that the error actually occurred on or near line 33 of the code.

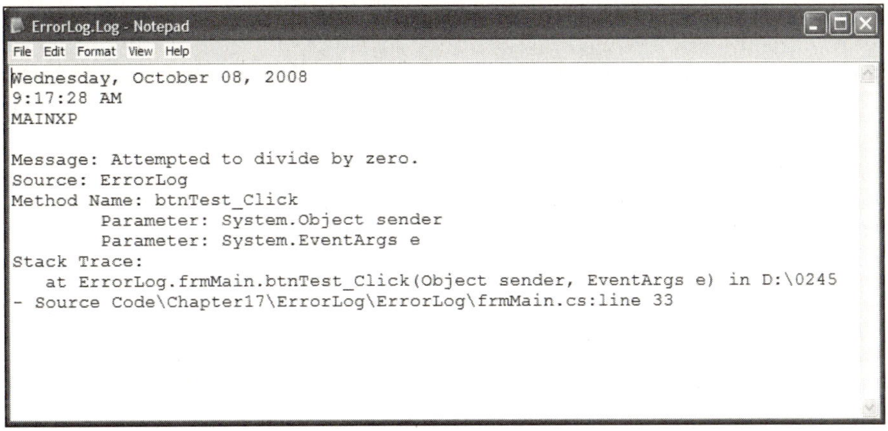

Figure 17-2: The error log provides enough information for you to start debugging.

Sometimes the stack trace is quite accurate about the location of an error. In this case, line 33 has the `int Value3 = Value1 / Value2;` *code associated with it. However, you can't always count on the stack trace providing completely accurate information. The stack trace may simply show the point at which the application first detected the error, rather than the point at which the error occurred. For example, in this case, someone could make the point that the error actually occurs on line 30 when the code first assigns a value of 0 to* `Value2`.

Using Error Logs to Provide Support

Error logs can do a lot more than simply provide the developer with a good idea of where to look for information — error logs can also help determine the approach an organization uses to deal with a particular problem. For example, if you notice that a particular error occurs when someone clicks the Test button after typing a specific value in an application field, you can use that information to provide better user training. The support staff can also rely on that information as part of its troubleshooting strategy. In other words, the patterns you see in the error log are important to everyone, even though you might be the only one who understands the error log content completely. The following sections discuss using error logs for support tasks in more detail.

Defining Errors, Sources, and Solutions

An error log alone doesn't provide much information. However, when you place a number of error logs into a database and perform analysis on that database, you can begin seeing the patterns that support staff need to provide better application support. You can divide the output of the analysis into three categories:

- **Errors:** The easiest information to obtain from the error logs is the errors. However, errors alone don't say much. It's when you say that errors are occurring for a specific group or when users perform specific activities that the error information becomes most useful. You may even find that the error information occurs in a certain area of the organization or on a particular machine type. All these patterns help support provide better information to users.

- **Sources:** Errors occur due to a specific cause or source. For example, typing `Hello` into a field and clicking Test may not cause an error, but typing `Hello World` into the same field and clicking Test does cause the error. Meanwhile, clicking an associated button, Test2, never causes the problem. This source information is essential when creating scripts that support can use to localize a problem before arriving at a specific solution.
- **Solutions:** Sometimes the error log data suggests a solution to a problem. Even before you create a fix for the problem (and all problems do require a fix at some point), you can use the error log information to provide a solution that overcomes the issue. Often, you can analyze the error logs and create such a short-term solution in hours, rather than the days needed to implement the permanent fix.

The error logs you obtain represent a source of information. In order to get the most from this information source, you normally must analyze the logs and then deduce a course of action based on that information. As with many aspects of computer science, analyzing error logs is more art than science, so you need to exercise your skills before you begin to see the patterns that error logs can provide.

Determining the Need for Direct Developer Interaction

As previously mentioned, no one understands the error log content like the developers who create the application do. This fact may frustrate developers who can look directly at the log and see that something terrible's happening that the user could easily prevent, but that's why, as they say, you earn the big money. In many cases, the support staff can look at the logs until they're quite blind and never figure out the solution that you can come up with in a few seconds. It's times like these when it's best not to hide in your office and hope no one sees you, but to roll up your sleeves and fix the problem.

Of course, once you prove your skill at resolving problems, users and support staff alike will have a tendency to come to you with every little problem. Most developers don't have time to address every problem that occurs with their application, so you need to provide a priority system to ensure the problem is handled at the lowest possible level. Yes, this approach is quite annoying and frustrating for the user who really doesn't care about your application in the first place. But the situation still requires that less skilled staff at least take a crack at the problem before you attempt to address it.

A proactive approach on your part can provide a sort of middle ground where you can reduce stress for everyone. Analyzing error logs over time and showing trends in problems can help you direct your efforts to the fires that you need to put out today so you don't encounter the wrath of the user tomorrow. For example, an error that occurs inconsistently, but at an increasing level, is a potential target for your attention. If you address the problem before too many people encounter it, you'll have the time to think about it properly — without the stress of the boss breathing down your neck.

Creating Support Logs

Error logs are only part of the solution. As you encounter problems, analyze them, and create solutions that support uses, you must also determine whether these fixes actually work and define how well they work. Most problems have multiple fixes. If you settle for the first fix that seems to address the problem, you may actually buy yourself more trouble later. Consequently, you need to create support logs that help the support staff track the efficiency of your solutions.

Relying on Error Log and Support Logs for Maintenance

The error logs you create can have a significant impact on how you perform application maintenance. For example, the error logs may show that only one or two people are encountering an error that's not only difficult to fix but expensive as well. Because the error logs help you understand the nature of the error better, you can use this information to place the maintenance task of fixing this error at a lower priority. However, error logs can also show that everyone is encountering a particular error, so you need to give the fix a high priority, no matter how much it costs to fix. The following sections describe using error logs for maintenance in more detail.

Prioritizing Maintenance Activities

Everyone wants their problem fixed today. The problem is that you only have so many hours in a given day and they aren't all available for fixing problems. It's quite likely, in fact, that even if you give up eating and sleeping, you won't address every problem in a single day, or a week for that matter. Problem resolution requires time, a lot of it in many cases. Besides, if you resolved every problem in your application today, what would you do tomorrow? Each day has a specific amount of work you can perform in it. In short, you need to prioritize maintenance activities to ensure that you address the tasks that you need to perform most, first.

Most prioritizing schemes have problems. In almost every case, a problem will appear on the list year after year and never receive the attention it needs. The unresolved problem will likely cause issues for someone who really does want to see a fix. To prevent the unresolved problem from appearing on your list, you should review the work list from time to time and increase the priority of longtime problems to ensure they receive a review. It's also important to clean your list — verify that the problem still exists before you do anything else with it.

Error logs can help you prioritize maintenance activities by pointing out how critical a particular application error has become. In fact, you should consider the following criteria when prioritizing maintenance activities for your applications:

- Severity of the error (application crash versus inconvenience)
- Number of people seeing the problem
- Error source
- Error effect (lost data is always bad)
- Area affected (if you run a catalog business and data entry is experiencing the problem, you should probably fix it sooner rather than later)
- Potential noncoding short-term problem solution effectiveness

Verifying Maintenance Requirements

Before you begin any maintenance task, make sure you understand all the maintenance requirements. You need to understand the problem completely and should already have a fix in mind. The error logs you collect can help you significantly in this regard, because they can provide you with precise information about the source and potential cause of the error. Of course, the error logs have to have the required information in them before you can use them in this way and you must perform specific exception handling to determine the particular cause of an error. If you handle every error using the `System.Exception` class, your error logs are going to be relatively useless and you'll waste hours looking for the problem before you can fix it.

Testing Maintenance Actions

After you complete a maintenance action, the error logs you create can help you define testing scripts. It's important to test any new code you create completely, but users are definitely going to complain if the fix you create doesn't actually fix anything. The very error logs that alerted you to the problem in the first place can provide the input you require to test the fix. A comparison of error log output can help you verify the effectiveness of a fix and make it possible to verify that you haven't introduced new problems as a result.

At no time should you consider abandoning the testing techniques described in Chapter 15. The maintenance action testing described in this section of the chapter is in addition to the normal testing you perform. It's still important to validate the application as a whole to ensure the user sees an increase in application reliability due to the fix you provide. Some developers will put a quick fix in place and end up creating more problems than the application had in the first place. This problem even occurs with shrink-wrapped software, as witnessed by the patch recalls a number of vendors have had to perform.

Deploying Patches

The final step in maintaining your application is to issue a patch. The patch must go through the complete testing and QA process that your application normally relies on to maintain application quality. Of course, you'll have to perform these checks while users are protesting outside your door, but you need to perform them nonetheless. One of the major problems with software today is that developers often bend to the will of the users to get a patch out quickly without the proper testing.

You'll very likely want to deploy the patch in stages. Distributing a testing release is always a good idea because you can't be sure how the patch will react on the production system. If the testing release works as anticipated, perform a local deployment next to see how the patch works with a larger group. Finally, distribute the patch on the enterprise level.

The final task to perform is to ensure everyone actually has the patch installed. Often, a small group of machines somehow misses the patching process. When these users begin calling into support with an error that looks very much like the one you just fixed, it could create chaos. Consequently, making sure that everyone has the patch installed will save you both time and effort.

Coding Your Application

This chapter has helped you understand some of the tools you can use to make support and maintenance of your application easier. What you should take away from this chapter is that the user won't provide the information you need, so you must have some type of error log support for your application, even if that support is based on the event log. If you have a large application, you may want to use a third-party product to provide the error log support you require. However, most developers can get by with one of the hand-rolled solutions found in this chapter.

If you haven't included plans yet for an error-logging module in your application, now is the time to do it. Error logging is incredibly important for your sanity, not to mention the sanity of your coworkers. You don't have to create anything fancy. In fact, when it comes to error logs, simpler is better because the application is in an unstable state in most situations when you need an error log. Make sure you define the specifics of error-log handling for your application at the outset. For example, many developers make the mistake of not making the error log available at the right times. Select a format that will work well for your organization as well. Finally, decide on a method for handling log file recycling.

Chapter 18 begins a new section of the book. In Chapter 18, you examine the performance triangle in detail. By using the techniques in this chapter and those that follow (Chapters 19 through 21), you can reduce your need for the error log techniques found in this chapter. No, you won't get rid of the error log completely, but consider each time you don't need it to answer a support or maintenance need as a gift. The best way to avoid problems is to prevent them from happening at all, which is the purpose of this next section of the book.

Part III: Speed, Reliability, and Security

18

Developing around the Performance Triangle

It's important to realize that development and design are two completely different tasks. In a perfect world, the development would always match the design perfectly. After all, you've put a lot of effort into the task of designing the application, so it would be nice if the application looked precisely like your design after you complete the development. In the real world, however, things change during development. The perfect design is no longer so perfect after all. The application runs too slowly, doesn't meet specific security needs, or seems to fail a little too often. These three issues are related to the performance triangle:

- Speed
- Security
- Reliability

During the design process, you worked through the theory of the performance triangle. The development process also requires that you rely on the performance triangle. However, now you're putting the theory into practice and you may find that you must make some changes. Every change you make should reflect good coding practice and you should quantify each change to ensure the change is necessary.

Notice that the chapter doesn't mention anything about new requirements, additional features, extra reports, or anything of that nature. Starting the development process doesn't give anyone carte blanche to make changes of this sort. In this case, you should stick by the design and make changes as updates later to keep the project on track. You don't want to be completely rigid, but a certain level of inflexibility will keep your project on schedule and within budget. Unnecessary or extraneous change in an application is necessarily bad in most cases.

This chapter discusses the performance triangle you originally encountered in Chapters 5, 6, and 7 from a development perspective. Now that you have a great application design, you need to incorporate that design into real-world code. By the time you complete this chapter, you'll have a better understanding how theory sometimes doesn't end up working as anticipated in the real world of the developer. In addition, you'll have a better idea of how to make changes to your design that will ease the transition from paper into code. Will the best practices in this chapter always speak to your specific organization's needs? Probably not. However, the best practices in this chapter will help you form your own opinion of how your design needs to change to meet specific development goals.

Acting after the Initial Development Phase

You've finished the application design. All participants wipe the sweat from their brows and feel incredibly good about the application you plan to put together. You may have already done some prototyping as part of the design process; the team members feel exceptionally good because the design is *proven* in their minds. However, your design is only paper — it isn't working code. Consequently, your design isn't proven yet — you only think it will work. The difference between the paper design and the living development is that one is what you think will work and the other is what you know will work.

Most development teams begin the initial development phase hoping that everything will work as designed. Even the senior, seasoned members of the team fall into this trap. Hope is an essential part of the human experience. If you're the senior member of the development team, you can't afford to be hopeful about anything. No, like a gloomy Gus, you must consider every potential pothole, enlarge it to twice the size, and think about all of the potholes you don't see yet. The senior member of the development team must act to put the brakes on unbridled optimism because the higher your team sails after the design process is complete, the greater the fall when the team experiences the first real-world development difficulties.

A good part of the team leader's job after the application moves into the development process is to keep the development team on an even keel. Sometimes this means telling people not to jump to conclusions — after all, you've already done that during the design phase. During the development phase, every team member must prove that changes will work as intended, or the team must not implement the changes as part of the application. In some cases, you also need to assure team members that things will improve. A good team leader doesn't spend every moment telling people to get things right or to do things better. The members of your team are good people; sometimes they just need a little encouragement.

Of course, as head of the development team, you also need to reassure other stakeholders that things will get better and that the application really is on track. Rumors are the worst possible thing for your application right now. Get any rumors you hear out into the open and replace gossip with facts whenever possible. The important consideration at this point is to view the design from the perspective that it presents a theory you're trying to prove. Don't worry too much about making changes to safeguard application speed, reliability, and security as needed. Here are some best practices to consider following:

- Make sure people know that you're the only reliable source of information and that anything else is a rumor.
- Squash rumors whenever possible by providing the facts to everyone involved in the project.
- Provide encouragement to everyone involved on the team as needed, but also be assertive with rules on acceptable coding and testing practice.
- Be willing to listen — actively — for real (instead of simply looking like you're listening). If you're thinking about what you want to say next, you're not listening.

- Admit your mistakes and don't pounce on development team members when they make mistakes.
- Keep in mind that every problem has a solution, even if you haven't found it yet.
- Use other team members as a resource — not everyone knows everything about every topic. When you get stuck on a problem, another team member may know the answer, but you'll never find out if you don't ask.

Defining the Performance Triangle

When you begin developing your application, you realize that the design performance triangle is relatively simple because all you need to consider is the concerns of the triangle itself. Making an application more secure necessarily makes it less reliable and less speedy. Likewise, speed improvements usually come at the expense of reliability and security. An application that performs well is one that has balanced these three elements as required by your organization. However, during the design process, you don't need to consider the other forces that act on the triangle — all you need to consider is your design.

Things change when you move to the development process. The design you create is a kind of promise that people expect you to keep. However, each stakeholder in a project likely has a different interpretation of precisely what that promise means. In addition, you must consider the realities of application development. Team members don't wake each morning with a smile on their face and the words, "Today I will be brilliant!" on their lips. Consequently, the performance triangle looks more like the triangle shown in Figure 18-1 in a development environment.

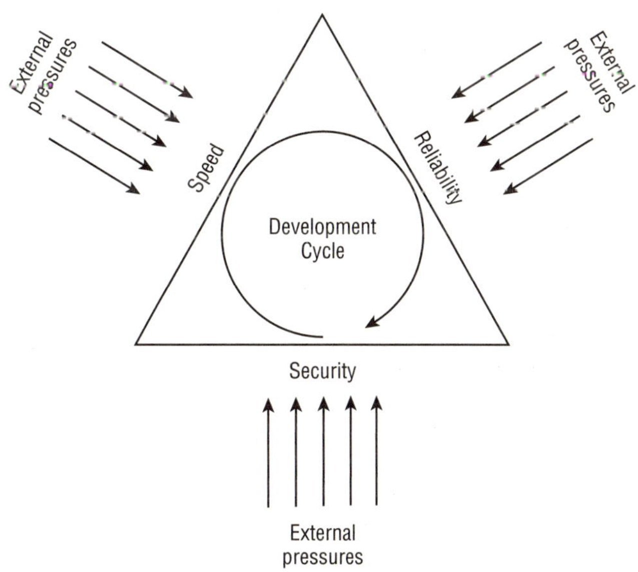

Figure 18-1: Tension exists between elements of the triangle, internal development pressures, and external pressures.

As you can see, the performance triangle is more complex now with both external pressures and development cycle concerns to consider. These forces don't act on your performance triangle consistently, nor do these forces interact with the performance triangle the same way all the time. The frustration that team members often feel is due to the forces they can't control that cause changes in the application design and that make the development process harder than it should be. In most cases, you can't control these forces; but by understanding how they act on your design, you can mitigate or eliminate some of the undesirable effects.

A major concern in this case is the development cycle itself. You won't ever find a development team that can work on speed, reliability, and security simultaneously. The development team will focus its attention on only one aspect of the performance triangle. Consequently, application development progresses unevenly, creating even more stresses. In some cases, you can compare it to someone putting a finger in the dike — there are three holes, but the person can only stop up one of those holes at a time. In the meantime, the town is flooding from the dam leakage. It's your responsibility to keep the town from ending up under water. The following sections consider the way in which these forces react with the performance triangle.

Characterizing the Speed Component

The major players in the speed component are the users. The users want an application that's fast because they want to get home earlier. In addition, users don't want to have to see the application any more than necessary. The user is interested in data, reports, and other application input and output, but not the application itself. Users will rely on pen and paper if necessary to get their jobs done faster. It happens regularly even today in many enterprise environments. The user will also leave that piece of paper that's brimming with company secrets in plain sight because security matters not at all, in most cases, to the user — the user views your application simply as a tool to get the job done. Consequently, this stakeholder's main concern is whether the application is fast, followed by whether the application is easy to use.

Before you get the idea that I'm engaging in user bashing, consider the fact that your application has no purpose whatsoever without users. Users play an important role in application design and development. However, the prudent developer considers the user's motivation, which is to complete the work and the user will do whatever it takes to accomplish that. Contrary to being a user basher, I try to be quite aware of a user's needs and desire to get work done — some of my best friends are users!

None of these components are specific to a particular group, however. Administrators also want fast applications because they don't want to hear users complain about the application speed. The administrators also want to get home as early as possible after a long day, and applications that perform slowly tend to cause maintenance problems. However, most administrators are more concerned about the application performing the task reliably and securely, than quickly.

Managers also have a stake in the speed component. However, the manager's view is different in that speed isn't necessarily efficiency. The manager needs to get the job done correctly as quickly as possible, which sometimes means slowing the process down so that users make fewer mistakes. Consequently, the manager view of speed is different from that of the other two stakeholders in the application.

A fourth group exists. Most organizations have to consider the needs of an outside customer. Whether the organization sells products directly to a customer or provides them through a third party, someone is waiting for a product. Customers aren't prone to waiting patiently for anything. They don't care that the user wants to go home early, that the administrator is concerned about security, or that the manager wants efficiency. The customer wants a product and wants it now. If the application can't provide immediate and correct gratification, the customer will go somewhere else. This group places pressure on everyone. You can characterize the speed component of external pressures, as shown in Table 18-1.

Interestingly enough, after surveying more than 500 developers, most of them aren't very interested in speed, except as it affects the users. In other words, when the user is happy, the developer is happy. Consequently, Table 18-1 groups the user and the developer together. If you'd like to participate in one of my surveys, please write me at JMueller@mwt.net.

Table 18-1: Speed Component Characteristics

Group	Performs Task Fast	Performs Task Securely	Performs Task Accurately	Performs Task Efficiently	Provides Immediate Results
Users (Developers)	X				
Administrators	/	X	/		
Managers	/	/	X	X	/
Customers			X		X

Characterizing the Reliability Component

The major players in the reliability component are the managers. The devastation caused by even one application failure can cost managers their jobs, so no manager is willing to give up anything that would tend to impair application reliability. Managers have a very practical and simple view of reliability — the application should never fail, ever. In addition, the application should always protect the data, even when a failure affects the application's output. In short, the manager is most concerned that the data remain undamaged and that users have no reason for not working. Because managers place such an emphasis on 24/7 application availability, they don't want to hear about applications that fail gracefully — they want applications that heal themselves and keep running.

Of course, administrators also have a major stake in reliability. Because administrators have to listen to user complaints, they're very interested in correct application output. The organization also makes the administrator responsible for the application data. Consequently, the administrator is very concerned that the application not damage the data. Administrators do expect application failures and are willing to put up with them as long as the application fails predictably — even so, the administrator would rather work with a self-healing application that requires less work on the part of the administrator to maintain.

Developers want an application that doesn't cause them any grief. Consequently, developers are most concerned with applications that please everyone — that don't fail unexpectedly or cause any form of data corruption (either input or output). Like the administrator, the developer knows that the application is probably going to fail at some point. Unlike the administrator, the developer doesn't care how the application fails as long as someone else can get it back up and running without developer intervention. It may sound surprising, but more than a few developers view an application with a few small problems as a kind of job security (even though they'd never admit to it in public). Developers usually understand that the 24/7 application is a myth and don't even attempt to achieve it.

Reliability from the user level means that the application won't hold up users. Consequently, users like applications that are self-healing, even when they have no idea of what the term means. Users also want an application that presents the correct output every time. Incorrect results mean having to go back to the application and perform tasks a second time, which means working slower than necessary. Users may accept an application that fails, but you can be sure they'll grumble about it. However, if the application fails in an inconsistent manner, which means that the user can't rely on the same trick as usual to fix the problem, the user becomes confused, and confused users cause significant problems for both the administrator and ultimately the developer. As a result, even though it may appear that the user is concerned only with getting the right output as quickly as possible, the user is also concerned about a number of other background issues.

Customers don't really care about application reliability except as it affects their orders. Just try charging customers too much for a particular item or sending them the wrong items, and you'll find out how much reliability means to them. Of course, delays of any kind are unacceptable. If a customer makes an order at midnight on Saturday, at least a percentage of them will expect a response from your organization in no more than an hour or so. Consequently, even though the customer has no idea of what 24/7 processing means in many cases, they want it. You can characterize the reliability component of external pressures, as shown in Table 18-2.

Table 18-2: Reliability Component Characteristics

Group	Provides Correct Output Every Time	Stores Data Correctly Every Time	Fails Gracefully and Consistently	Self-healing	Available 24/7
Users	X	/	/	X	
Administrators	X	X	/	X	
Developers	X	X	X	X	
Managers	/	X		X	X
Customers	X				X

Characterizing the Security Component

The major players in the security component are administrators. It doesn't take long to find trade press articles that tell who pays the highest price when security is lax. Many administrators have lost their jobs in a blink of an eye over security concerns. Administrators want to know that the application provides security in every possible way, from data input to data output and the data storage in between. Because the government is so involved in every aspect of security today, you'll find that administrators have a very strong desire to meet government regulations and be able to prove compliance through reports (the more, the better). Consequently, the government will place stresses on your application development through regulations. Administrators also want to make sure that the application doesn't provide any access to other applications. Even though they would rather applications not provide remote access, administrators understand that users want this feature. The administrator's main concern is that the user obtains remote access securely so that the home system doesn't become an unauthorized point of access for revolting people with designs on the data the administrator protects.

It's interesting to note that the reporter has become the administrator's nemesis. The trade press seems to delight in running any and every story that concerns any security breach whatsoever and presenting all the gory minutiae in exquisite detail. Reporters just love it when administrators haven't followed all the government regulations or have let data out that should have remained secret. Consequently, reporters, in an odd sort of way, exert their own pressure on your application development through the administrator.

Managers also have an incredibly strong interest in security. In some cases, administrators have been able to move blame from their shoulders onto a manager's shoulders for a security breach. It's true that this movement doesn't occur very often, but it has happened often enough to make managers nervous. Of all of the groups described in this chapter, managers are most likely to work from home, so they also have a strong interest in secure remote access to their applications. In most cases, managers monitor application security through reports. However, because managers lack technical expertise, they're less likely to worry about lower-level security, such as protection between applications. Finally, because managers are most concerned about data breaches that will appear in the trade press and embarrass them, it's quite likely that a manager will unduly restrict data access on the assumption that less data out translates into fewer security risks.

Customers have a fairly strong interest in your application security simply because the trade press has beaten them over the head with the need to track security measures your organization provides. Customers are interested in one security aspect only — the protection of their personal data. Identity theft (whether personal or corporate) has become such a big issue that customers want to ensure that you handle their data correctly and safely. In many cases, customers also have enough understanding of government regulations to know to ask you about security. You shouldn't expect the customer to ask for proof of compliance, but the customer will want to know whether you're following the rules. If customers feel uncomfortable with the answers you provide, you can expect them to seek help from the government, which may mean an auditor banging on your door. Developers often underestimate the security pressures presented by customers, but they're quite real and you should be prepared to handle them as you go through the development process.

The final group is users, who usually have an antipathy toward security of any kind because it hinders them from getting their work done. Users do care about security in three ways. First, many users now work from home and don't want the hassle of a data breach affecting that privilege, so they are often quite willing to put up with a lot of security when it comes to remote access. Users also want moderate security for data input because inaccurate input is hard to fix later (costing the user a lot of time). Finally, because users do have concerns about their organization, you'll find that users have at least a little interest in knowing that the company is following all the government regulations. In addition, because users usually need to work with your customers, you'll want to be sure they have the right conformance information for your application. You can characterize the security component of external pressures, as shown in Table 18-3.

Table 18-3: Security Component Characteristics

Group	Provides Secure Remote Access	Protects against Inaccurate Input	Protects against Unwanted Output	Protects Data from Unauthorized Change	Provides Security Reports	Conforms to Government Regulations	Secures Application against Other Applications
Users	X	/				/	
Administrators	/	X	X	X	X	X	X
Developers		X	X	X	/	/	X
Managers	X	X	/	X	X	X	
Auditors and the Government				/	X	X	/
Reporters		/	/	X		X	
Customers		X	/	X		/	

Creating the Perfect Triangle for Your Application

Some people get the idea that the performance triangle is something concrete and immovable. More than a few people ask me for specific guidelines on implementing the performance triangle in their applications. The triangle is fluid — it depends on a number of factors, none of which I can quantify for you in this book. The performance triangle is what you make it and the perfect performance triangle is the one that works for your application. However, here are some considerations for creating the perfect performance triangle for your application from a development (rather than a design) perspective:

- Does the application perform tasks as quickly as you expect it should? In some cases, measurements are misleading — a tapping finger is far more telling. You may have to observe people to determine whether fast is fast enough to meet user expectations.
- Can users actually find the product features they need to use? Your support staff can often provide you with this information. If the support staff spends too much time helping people find common features, the user interface isn't working or the users don't have enough training.
- Do users enter the wrong data with any regularity? If users can enter the wrong data at all, it probably indicates the need for additional safeguards in your application. However, you can often overcome this problem through additional training.

- Have users accidentally damaged data? In most cases, this means that your application doesn't provide enough data protection and that you should look for potential security and reliability problems.
- Does the application crash in ways that prevents your error logging from revealing the source of the problem properly? Application crashes are bad enough. However, if the error logging isn't revealing the source of the problem, it means that you don't have the right kind of error logging in place or that there's a major flaw in your design. You should fix this high-priority problem immediately.
- Does the application respond reliably when the unexpected happens? In many cases, applications behave in unexpected ways. When a failure occurs, unexpected or not, the application should react in a specific, dependable way that keeps the application running and prevents data loss.

By now, you can probably ask questions that reflect the design of your application. Creating the perfect performance triangle means asking questions — a lot of them. When you get done asking questions, you should welcome questions from your development team and the stakeholders working on the project as well. Get questions from the customers who will use the application. In short, make sure that all participants have asked their questions about the potential problems in your application.

Perfection is unattainable with any application. However, you can get close to perfection given enough time and resources. It's important to remember that perfection costs money. As you near perfection, the cost for making even incremental application improvements becomes higher. Part of the search for the perfect performance triangle, therefore, is how much you can afford to spend. You must ask that final question of how good is good enough.

Employing Technical Writers as Part of Your Team

Many development teams forget the usefulness of a good technical writer in locating application problems. A technical writer usually has expertise on par with the rest of the development team, but also has writing skills. Consequently, a technical writer can see problems with grammar and spelling in your application that the rest of the team will miss. Technical writers also have training that helps them focus attention on fit and finish issues, such as the regularity of information flow within an application.

Using technical writers to review an application after you complete it, but before you give it to other people for testing, can help you locate problems that are more typos than coding errors. It's amazing to see how many user issues end up being a poorly phrased prompt, rather then the wrong code. The words in your application are one of the major forms of communication, so you must ensure that you use the right words, which is where a technical writer can help most.

Making Your Application Reliable and Secure

This chapter is all about the real world bursting in on your perfect design and ruining it in some way. A good design won't have many changes, but it may have some changes. In fact, you can probably count on making at least one or two changes simply because a designer's visualization of a problem can't possibly consider every aspect of a real-world problem coded by a developer. Consequently, this chapter is about transitions — moving your code from the design to the development stage.

The act of moving from design to development phases of a project is jarring. Your development team will find that some things simply won't work as designed. There's a temptation during the transitional phase to play the blame game — to point fingers and try to make yourself feel better at the expense of someone else. Unfortunately, this whole transitional phenomenon occurs in every project. Here's what you do to handle the situation:

1. Remember that everyone on your team is human and that the finger pointing is a normal reaction to the dashing of one's expectations. As the project leader, you need to put a stop to the grousing and finger pointing immediately, and help everyone get back to work.
2. Take time to look at the design and determine where things simply aren't going to work. Write up a hit list of items you want to change.
3. After that first look, get everyone out of the office — play volleyball, go to dinner, do something different to remove the tension your entire team is feeling. You won't be able to think immediately after discovering the flaws in your design anyway — it's important to come back to the problem with a clear mind.
4. When you come back, work on the solutions you need to fix the design flaws. Use the hit list you created as a starting point and then work through the design again.
5. Get the design team together as needed for additional updates. However, don't make your work area "meeting central." Use e-mail or other communication methods when possible to consider small changes — keep everyone working on the project rather than wasting time in meetings.

Now that you're over the initial shock of the design to development transition (you are over it, aren't you?), it's time to look at each element of the performance triangle in detail. Chapter 19 discusses the speed element and shows you ways to make your development process work better when it comes to speed. This chapter addresses the important issues of how to measure speed and determine when your application is fast enough. Chapter 20 follows with a detailed discussion of reliability from the development perspective. Finally, you'll encounter the security part of the performance triangle for developers in Chapter 21.

19

Considering Application Speed Implications

Most applications go through a series of pretests as developers put the pieces together. The development team wants to see how the pieces are going together and determine if they work well with each other. In addition, the development team wants to see whether the design is working at all. In some respects, the pretesting stage is curiosity. Most people who create something want to see how things are looking as they create it. A sculptor steps back to view a creation, a cook tastes to see how the ingredients taste together — a developer is no different.

Sometimes the pretests are more than simple curiosity, however. They serve an important purpose in making your application work as it should. The sculptor steps back and notices that part of the ear isn't formed correctly, the cook notices that the pinch of salt is missing — the developer sees that the application is lacking something that causes speed to suffer. The sculptor conforms, in some respects, to engineering standards and artistic norms, and the cook uses a recipe, but these design statements can't address the artistic part of each trade — the artist's eye and the cook's sense of taste prevail. Likewise, the seasoned developer follows the design and relies on best practices, but the pretest provides the artistic touch that defines the difference between an application that works and one that works well.

Fortunately, Microsoft provides some tools to make pretesting more practical. Yes, you could theoretically add counters to your application and run it through its paces while you watch it, using the Performance console found in the Administrative Tools folder of the Control Panel. However, using the counter approach is inconvenient and overly formal for the kind of testing you need to perform during development — that's why using the testing tools in Visual Studio is important. The Performance Wizard and Performance Explorer make the task of performing a pretest easier and more convenient. These tools let you take a little sample of your application to see how it works without going through a strict process. This chapter helps you understand speed as it applies to the development phase of your application.

Defining the Trade-offs of Speed

Applications that run slowly aren't very useful. As described in Chapter 18, users expect speedy applications, as do your customers. Even managers expect applications that work efficiently, which includes running quickly. From the very first computer until now, speed has been an essential concern for every application. Even the fastest application can run faster still — no one's completely satisfied with the speed of any application. That said, most applications reach a point of acceptable or reasonable execution speed. After all, if the application spends 90 percent of its time waiting for the user to do something, making it faster probably won't result in any substantial time savings.

Too much speed can become detrimental. Like a recipe without salt or a statue with an ill-formed ear, the application that places speed over any other consideration lacks balance and will almost certainly fail. To put this issue in a different light, the application will taste bad to the user because it lacks the elements needed to provide everything the user requires. Most ill-advised speed trade-offs take two forms:

- Missing code that the application doesn't require to perform a task, but does require to service user needs.
- Code that the application requires to ensure the output is correct, even when this code isn't directly involved in performing the task.

The following sections consider these two forms of speed trade-off. When you read these sections, consider your current application design again. Sometimes a necessary element doesn't appear in a design and won't ever make it into the application as a result. Remember the cook adding salt to the dish and the sculptor refining the statue's ear. You may find that you must add a little salt to your application and refine it in other ways to give the user a good experience — sometimes sampling your application is the only way to see these needs.

Cutting Code in the Wrong Places

As the development process evolves, developers often find that their code isn't as fast as expected, and because they're short on time they look for a quick fix that they hope no one will notice. For example, explanatory dialog boxes and progress information often disappear as unnecessary. In many cases, no one notices until the application is released and the user complains. If the person receiving the complaint is astute, they will probably notice the missing feature and wonder why it doesn't appear in the application as originally anticipated in the design. Whether the developers maintaining the application rely on the original design or duplicate someone else's tired solution, the feature ends up as part of the application anyway and someone else will have to come up with a way to produce more application speed with the feature in place. In short, cutting needed features will always cost the organization time and frustration because someone will eventually notice that they're missing and add them back into the application.

You might wonder whether there's ever a good reason to cut code, even seemingly unneeded code, to produce a speed gain. Most applications do have low-priority features that you can cut. The design document usually lists these features. However, you should never cut a feature from the design without first discussing the matter with the development team. Other team members may be relying on that feature for a particular need or have code they're required to create to support it. Unfortunately, cutting low-priority features almost never improves application performance in the right area. You normally end up improving your code in some other way — possibly by tightening loop code or relying on any of the myriad techniques that developers have used to improve performance for years.

Still, the temptation to find a quick fix is very high when the pressure to produce reams of code is high, so some developers will look at other areas. The second most common false cut is code that verifies data inputs to a method, checks user identity for each call, or performs some other background task associated with either application reliability or security. In many cases, these cuts go unnoticed until some foul person breaks into your system, steals your customer database, and promptly sends an extortion letter to your organization's owner. Although this may seem like a far-fetched result of removing a line or two of code, it happens nearly every day. You can't gain speed at the expense of necessary reliability or security features, even if you feel that no one will miss these features.

Novice developers often remove safety code from an application. For example, an application may include code to verify every data write by reading the data back and matching it to the original data. Such a check can reduce application speed, but it does ensure that the data you write actually makes it to the destination. Because such code is time consuming, the novice developer will eye it gleefully and remove it in a heartbeat. Months down the road, someone finds out that the data in the database is corrupted or missing completely. Removing safety code is never an option.

A final area where developers often err in removing code is in flexibility areas. A design calls for code to appear in a specific form so that the organization can reuse or repurpose the code later. However, developing code like this can reduce overall application speed. A developer may come along and place the code within the application or change it in other ways to make it faster. However, now the code is embedded in the application, so the organization can no longer reuse it. An ill-advised fix becomes a maintenance nightmare for the organization and eventually costs the company money when the code becomes unavailable for the next application.

Creating Wrong Answers Really Fast

One of the worst possible speed scenarios is when an application performs tasks extremely fast, but performs them incorrectly. Errors can range from subtle to gross, but they always affect the organization in some way and eventually someone sees them. Regrettably, the mistakes are often found only after the organization suffers from them in some major way — sometimes the error is so great that the organization doesn't recover. The consequences of any wrong output from your application can be severe enough to cause harm to someone, even if you can't see how that harm will occur.

The effects of error often snowball in ways that no one can determine in advance. For example, you may work for an organization that makes alarm clock software for digital clocks — nothing too dangerous in that, is there? However, because your software is off by a little and a hospital uses the digital clock to time doses of medicine, a patient receives their medication too late. The patient dies because your clock was off. Is this example a little extreme? Sure, but it illustrates a point. Every piece of software you create is important and must provide error-free results within your ability as a developer to produce them. You can't ever assume that a slightly wrong answer of any sort is okay.

When you must choose between speed and accuracy, accuracy should always win. Of course, in very exceptional times this rule doesn't hold. For example, if you're creating an application that calculates the distance between earth and another object in the universe, an error of an inch or so probably won't cause any problems for anyone. Some applications don't need to calculate a result to the nth degree simply because the result of the calculation is so huge that the tiny fractional error won't result in any harm to anyone and won't change the human perception of the results. Obviously, these situations are far and few between. Normally, you want as much accuracy as your application can provide to ensure precise output.

You can create code that performs a task quickly and still provides the right answer. In most cases, you can avoid disaster by using the following process:

1. Try various techniques until you find the fastest method you feel will work properly.
2. Verify the results locally. Make sure you test the results completely — even relying on inputs that you know you won't normally use. Test outside the box.
3. Have the results independently verified by another group in your organization.
4. If necessary, request that an auditor also certify the results. When you take this step, don't change the code again for any reason unless you get the auditor to verify the new code.
5. Test and monitor the code in a production setup to ensure users don't come up with some quirk that will cause incorrect output.

Measuring Speed

You have many options for measuring the speed of your application. However, most of these options only work well after you have the application in final form. What you really need is a method that works while you develop the application. Visual Studio provides some tools that make obtaining speed predictions easier while developing your application. The following sections describe these tools in detail.

Understanding the Psychological Effects of Sampling

A cook discovers a new taste treat, samples it, and makes sure that it's fit to eat. When the taste treat is just right, the cook takes it to a friend and says, "What do you think of this?" Because the cook is an excellent chef, one would wonder why there's any need to have someone else sample the treat. The point of the exercise isn't to get a second opinion — it's to share the new taste treat and the excitement that goes with sharing something.

Everyone has the same psychological need to share. A developer discovers a new method for writing a routine that shaves minutes off the output time. The developer already knows that the routine works, yet has a strong desire to share it with others. In most cases, the developer is excited and wants to share that excitement with other people.

Of course, there are other forces at work here. The developer may want to obtain a certain level of prestige for the discovery. Some developers will also want to save others time and effort discovering the same technique. Developers also have a need for peer approval — just like anyone else. Finally, getting the boss's approval is a significant need for anyone, no matter what profession you work in.

It's the last need, the need for the boss's approval, where the team leader comes into play. You can't give your approval easily, because then it has no value. However, when the developer both earns and deserves your approval, you must give it or your team will starve psychologically. You must feed the minds of the people who work on the project.

A Quick View of the Sample Code

Before you can measure the performance of anything, you need some sample code. The example includes two sections of code for comparison. Listing 19-1 shows the first sample.

Listing 19-1: Displaying a list of files and file sizes

```
private void btnTest_Click(object sender, EventArgs e)
{
   // Obtain the starting time.
   DateTime Start = DateTime.Now;

   // Clear the listbox.
   lstOutput.Items.Clear();

   // Obtain a list of files to process.
   String[] FileList =
      Directory.GetFiles(
         Environment.GetFolderPath(Environment.SpecialFolder.System));

   // Get the filesize for each file.
   foreach (String ThisFile in FileList)
   {
      try
      {
         // Add the data to the list box.
         lstOutput.Items.Add(
            "Name: " + ThisFile + " Size: " +
               File.OpenRead(ThisFile).Length.ToString());
      }
      catch (IOException IOE)
      {
         // Add the data to the list box.
         lstOutput.Items.Add(
            "Name: " + ThisFile + " Error: " +
               IOE.Message);
      }
   }

   // Obtain the ending time.
   DateTime End = DateTime.Now;

   // Display the time difference.
   TimeSpan Difference = End - Start;
   MessageBox.Show("Processed " +
      FileList.Length.ToString() +
      " Files In " + Difference.TotalSeconds.ToString());
}
```

The example isn't very complicated, but it'll do the job. In this case, the example begins by obtaining the starting time. It then clears the list box used for output data and collects a list of the files to process.

The example uses the `Environment.SpecialFolder.System` folder because it usually contains a lot of files so you can see performance differences between two processing techniques without using extra code.

The next step is to process the files. In this case, the example uses the `File.OpenRead(ThisFile).Length.ToString()` method to obtain the size of each file. The second sample will use a different technique. Because this method can generate an `IOException` exception when a file is busy, you must place it within a `try...catch` block.

The code ends by obtaining the ending time, finding the difference, and displaying it in a message box. You see the time used to execute the example on screen, along with the list of files in `lstOutput`. The first time you run this code, the execution speed will lag. You have to expect this problem from some code because Windows needs to fill a cache or some other action must occur the first time (such as compiling the assembly). The first run of this code on my machine is 35.519 seconds. However, the second run is a mere 0.515625 seconds.

It's possible to improve on the initial processing time using a different approach to obtaining the file size. The example contains a second sample that uses the processing technique shown here:

```
// Get the filesize for each file.
foreach (String ThisFile in FileList)
{
   // Create an object to store the data.
   FileInfo FileData = new FileInfo(ThisFile);

   // Add the data to the list box.
   lstOutput.Items.Add(
      "Name: " + ThisFile + " Size: " + FileData.Length.ToString());
}
```

Everything else about the sample is the same. Notice that this example creates a special `FileInfo` object, `FileData`. This new technique doesn't require a `try...catch` block because it doesn't generate an error if a file is busy. When you run this example, you'll see a performance improvement. The run time now is a svelte 0.3125 seconds, or a 39.39 percent improvement.

A release build will generally run faster than a debug build. Make sure you run the two samples consistently — either both as release builds or both as debug builds. Otherwise, you'll receive inconsistent results.

Launching the Performance Wizard

The Performance Wizard is the first stop for seeing how your code will work. You can choose to explore application performance using one of two approaches:

- **Sampling:** Use this approach when you want to check the performance of the entire application. The sampling approach takes a snapshot of your application at intervals. It doesn't collect as much information as the instrumentation approach, so you can use the sampling approach for a longer duration. However, because the sampling approach stores less data, it doesn't provide a good view of individual modules.

- **Instrumentation:** Use this approach when you want to check specific methods within your application. When using the instrumentation approach, you insert diagnostic probes into the code, so the performance monitoring is extremely targeted. The instrumentation approach collects detailed data about the instrumented binaries and the external binaries they call. Because of the large amount of data this approach collects, you may want to limit data collection using the Data Collection Control explained later in the chapter.

Not all versions of Visual Studio have the performance tools described in this and other sections of the chapter. These sections assume that you're using the Visual Studio Team System Development Edition (or a similar high-end edition that includes the performance tools).

It's time to see how these two approaches work with the example program. The following steps show how to configure the sampling and instrumentation approaches using the Performance Wizard:

1. Choose Analyze ➪ Launch Performance Wizard. (You can also launch the Performance Wizard by clicking Launch Performance Wizard in Performance Explorer.) You'll see the Performance Wizard dialog box shown in Figure 19-1. This dialog box will normally have your application already selected. However, you can also choose Profile an Executable (.EXE), Profile a Dynamic Link Library (.DLL), or Profile an ASP.NET Application from the drop-down list box.
2. Select a target for your performance check. If you choose your application, go directly to Step 4. The Profile an Executable (.EXE), Profile a Dynamic Link Library (.DLL), or Profile an ASP.NET Application options require an additional setup step.
3. Click Next. You'll see target specific information you must provide. Figure 19-2 shows how the information appears for an executable. The information for a DLL is similar. When you choose the Profile an ASP.NET Application option, all you must provide is an URL for the application. Fill out the information required to locate and execute the target you want to profile.
4. Click Next. You'll see the Select the Profiling Method dialog box shown in Figure 19-3. This is where you choose between the sampling and instrumentation approaches. Note that if you're working with an executable, DLL, or ASP.NET application, the title bar will say Step 3 of 4.

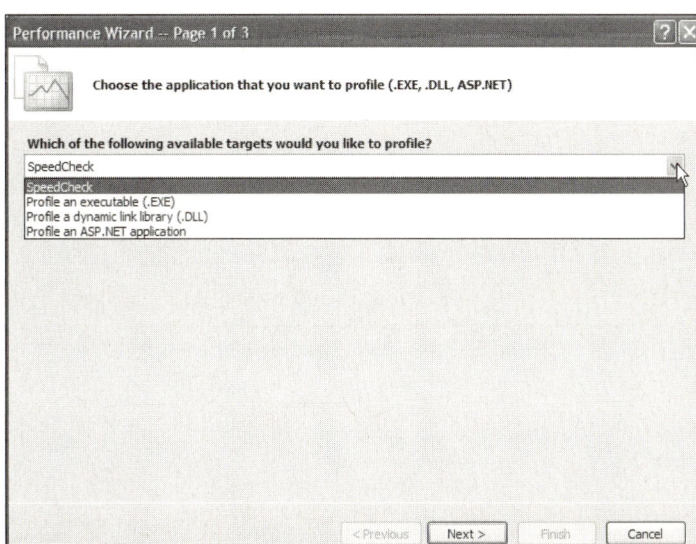

Figure 19-1: Select a target for analysis.

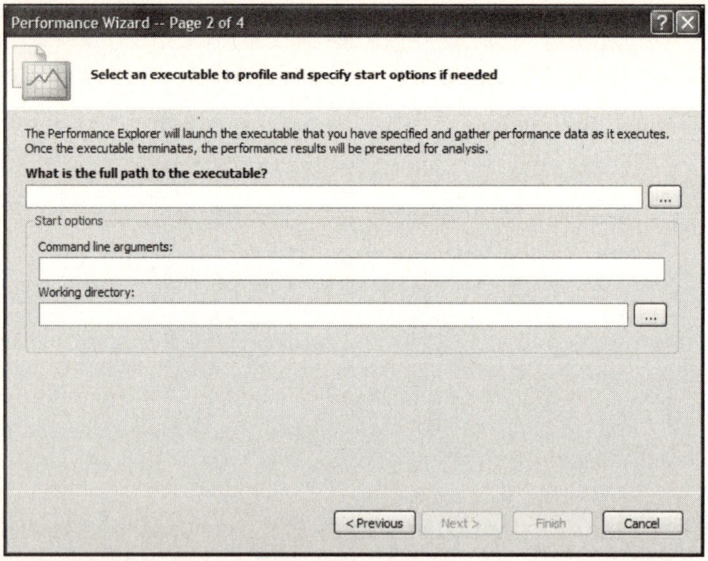

Figure 19-2: Provide the information required to locate the target you want to profile.

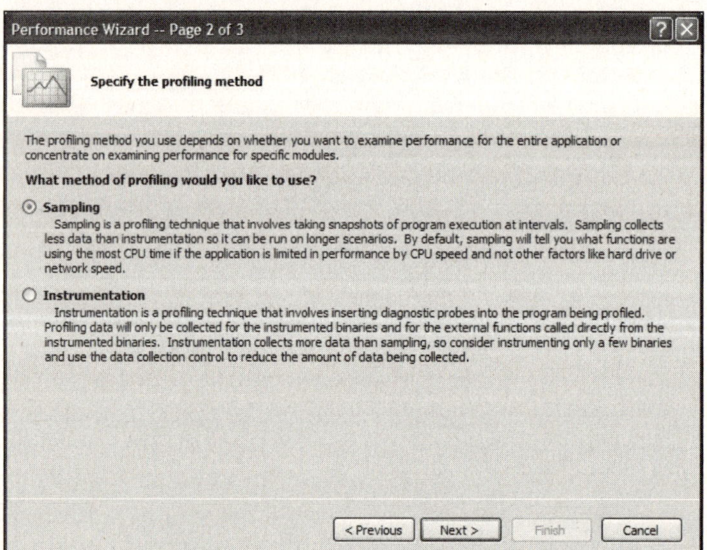

Figure 19-3: Select the profiling method you want to use.

5. Select Sampling (for full application profiling) or Instrumentation (to profile individual modules) and click Next. You'll see a summary dialog box that tells you about the selections you've made. Verify that the selections are correct. Click Previous if you find some of the information is incorrect.

If you choose the wrong approach, you can modify it by changing the option in the Method drop-down list box of Performance Explorer. Simply complete the wizard and modify the method as needed. You can also use this approach to switch between the sampling or instrumentation approaches as needed.

6. Click Finish. You'll see the Performance Explorer window shown in Figure 19-4. You're ready to begin profiling your application. The "Profiling Performance" section of the chapter tells you how to begin the profiling process. The "Viewing Performance Results" section of the chapter tells you how to interpret the results using Performance Explorer.

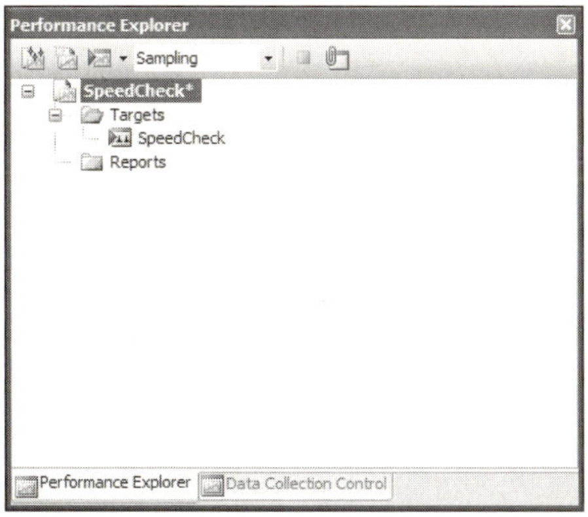

Figure 19-4: Use the options in Performance Explorer to begin profiling your application.

Profiling Performance

In most cases, you'll want to provide some special setups to profile your application. This means setting up features in Performance Explorer to ensure the profile works as anticipated. If you haven't already created a performance session using the Performance Wizard as described in the "Launching the Performance Wizard" section of this chapter, you'll need to create a new session using the technique described in the "Starting a New Performance Session" section that follows.

Once you have a performance session in place, you can configure the individual targets to provide specific input to the applications. It's also possible to limit the amount of data the instrumentation approach collects. Finally, if you really want to check out one of the more interesting features of the performance session, try connecting to a running application. The following sections describe how to perform these setups.

Starting a New Performance Session

If you don't use the Performance Wizard to create a new performance session, you must create one manually. The following steps describe how to create a performance session manually.

1. Choose Analyzer ➪ Profiler ➪ New Performance Session. You'll see a Performance Explorer window like the one shown in Figure 19-5. Compare this window to Figure 19-4, and you'll see that this new window doesn't have any targets defined.

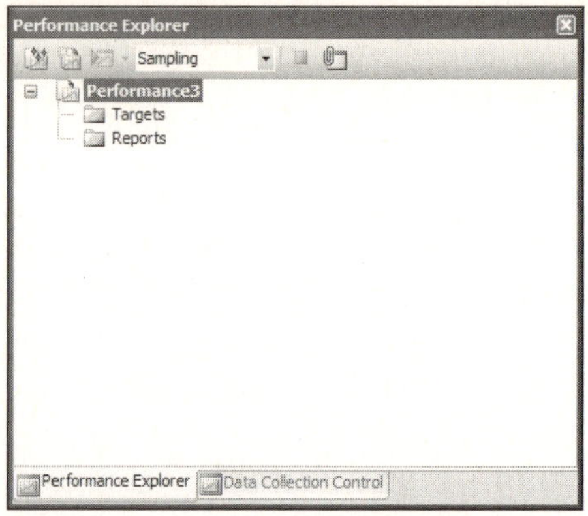

Figure 19-5: Creating a performance session manually means defining a target.

2. Right-click the Targets folder and choose one of the options on the context menu. You have the following choices:
   - **Add Target Binary:** Adds the current project, as shown in Figure 19-4. You don't have to supply any additional information when adding this option.
   - **Add Target Project:** Displays an Add Target Binary dialog box where you can choose the executable that you want to target. Simply select the EXE, DLL, or OCX file that you want to work with.
   - **Add Existing Web Site:** Displays an Add Existing Web Site dialog box where you type the URL for the Web site you want to test.
3. Perform Step 2 as often as necessary to add all the targets you want to monitor. That's right; you can add as many targets as desired and profile them all. Of course, the targets should be part of one application.
4. Choose either Sampling or Instrumentation in the Method drop-down list box. The performance session is now ready to configure.

Configuring the Targets

If you highlight a target in the Performance Explorer window, the Properties window will show you some information about it, but won't let you modify any of the characteristics of that target. In order to change the characteristics of a target, right-click its entry and choose Properties from the context menu. You'll see a `<Target>` Property Pages dialog box like the one shown in Figure 19-6. This dialog box contains three pages you can use to configure the target, including the way that Visual Studio launches the target. This particular feature is especially important for console applications, because you have to provide command line arguments to obtain useful information from a console application. The default setting simply executes the application. To add command line arguments, check Override Project settings, as shown in Figure 19-6, and type the arguments in the Arguments field. You can also change the working directory, as needed, to ensure that the executable can access its data as intended (some applications require a specific working directory).

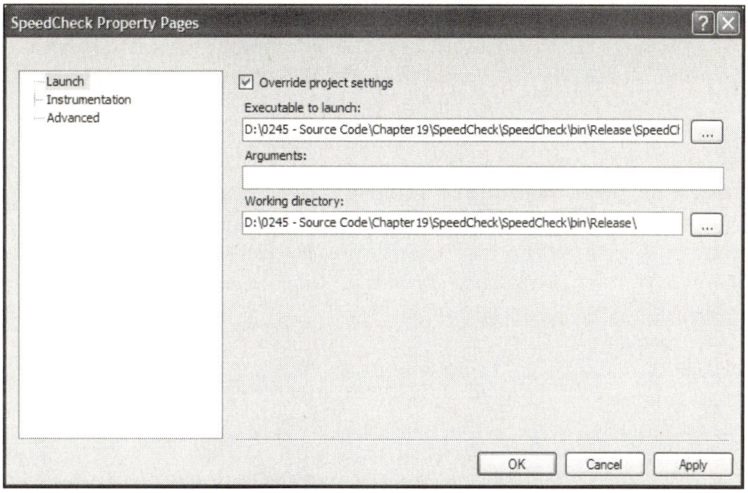

Figure 19-6: Modify the target launch characteristics as necessary to ensure the application works.

If you're using the sampling approach, the Launch page is the only one you should change, because the other settings don't matter. However, if you're using Instrumentation, you'll want to view the settings on the Instrumentation and Advanced pages. Figure 19-7 shows the basic instrumentation settings.

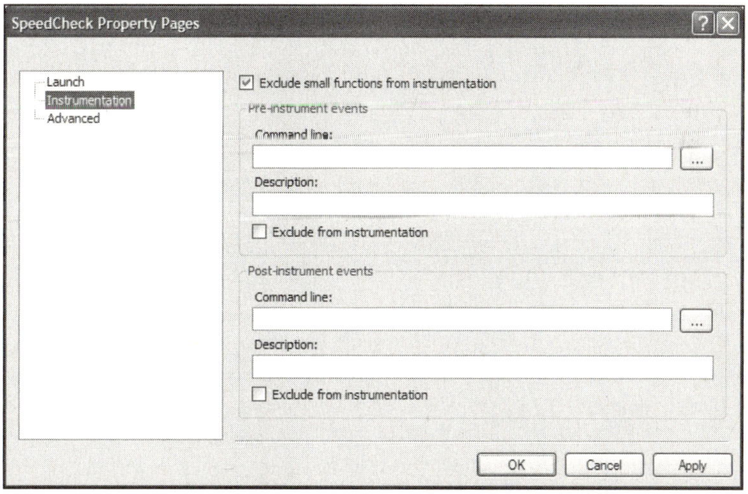

Figure 19-7: Change the instrumentation settings as needed to provide specific levels of monitoring.

When you use the instrumentation approach, the IDE checks the Exclude Small Functions from Instrumentation option by default. Unfortunately, nowhere does Microsoft define small. You won't find anything that specifies small in the documentation or online. However, this blog entry gives the best description of the setting: `http://blogs.msdn.com/profiler/archive/2008/07/08/excluding-small-functions-from-instrumentation.aspx`. Essentially, the setting excludes any small function (method) that doesn't make calls — it's a leaf function. Consequently, when you check this option, the instrumentation approach normally won't record data for property getters and setters, among other small functions.

The other entries on the Instrumentation page are for pre-instrumentation and post-instrumentation events. The pre-instrumentation events occur before you begin the instrumentation monitoring and the post-instrumentation events occur after you stop monitoring. In both cases, the system lets you specify special commands to run. By checking Exclude from Instrumentation, you can prevent these commands from appearing as part of the report.

The Advanced page contains a single field where you type special options that Visual Studio uses to fine-tune the instrumentation approach. These settings won't affect the sampling approach results. The basic use of these options is to control the amount of data that appears in the instrumentation report as described in the article entitled, "How to: Specify Additional Instrumentation Options" (`http://msdn.microsoft.com/en-us/library/ms182382.aspx`). The options you can provide are the same as those supported by the VSInstr command line tool. You can find a listing of these options at `http://msdn.microsoft.com/en-us/library/ms182402.aspx`.

Contrasting Speed and Efficiency

This chapter spends considerable time discussing the issue of speed. However, you should also consider efficiency when constructing your application. While speed measures how fast your application can perform a task, efficiency measures how fast your application and the human using it can perform a task. If your application is fast, but ends up impeding the human part of the equation, the overall effect is to make the application less efficient.

The problem of efficiency is that it's incredibly hard to measure, and managers like easily quantified data. Consequently, most developers spend all their time measuring speed because you can easily quantify speed. This chapter shows that the Performance Explorer provides you with a speed rating for your application. The data is quantifiable and should make for a nice report, but the report only tells you about the application speed, not its efficiency.

In order to determine application efficiency, you must perform tests that time the interaction between application and user. However, the timing must occur without the user's knowledge. If the user knows about the timed test, you can be sure of inaccurate results. The best way to complete the test is to use the error-logging approach described in Chapter 17. However, instead of recording error information, you record timed test information instead. Listing 19-1 shows how you can add timing information to a method — simply output this information to a log instead of displaying it in a dialog box.

Users aren't machines. Consequently, you can't test just one user — you must test a number of users with the full range of capabilities you expect from users interacting with the application to obtain accurate results. The report you generate will show soft information — given a range of user experience, machine performance, and application speed, this is what you can expect from the application in the form of efficiency.

Running the Profile

Now that you have a profiling session configured, you can run it. Performance Explorer provides two options for running your profile:

- **Launch with Profiling:** The logger engine starts immediately recording performance data from your application, which means that you see all the startup code associated with your application as part of the profile report.
- **Launch with Profiling Paused:** The application starts, but the logger engine doesn't. Data logging doesn't begin until you specifically start it by clicking Resume Collection in the Data Collection Control window. Using this option lets you obtain a subset of the normal performance data, making it easier to locate precisely what you need, but making the report less useful for long-term analysis.

Choose either of these options from the drop-down list box associated with the Launch with Profiling button on the Performance Explorer toolbar. To start the process, choose either of these options. You can exercise your application at this point to see how things work. When you get done, you can close the application as usual. At this point, you'll see a report appear on screen. Figure 19-8 shows the Summary page of this report, which is the first page you see. The "Viewing Performance Results" section of the chapter describes how to work with the report.

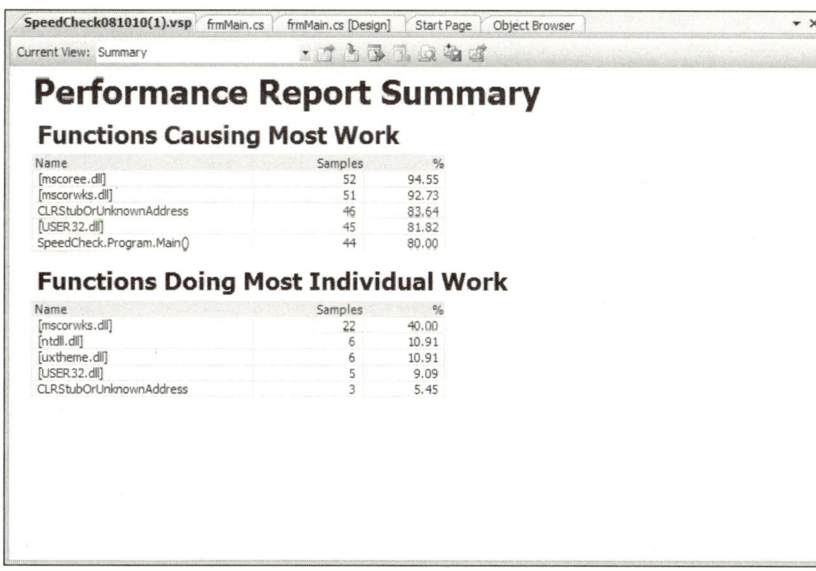

Figure 19-8: After you run your application, you see a report summary about it.

Using the Data Collection Control

The Data Collection Control window is an integral part of performance monitoring within Visual Studio. However, when you first view it, you might be distrustful about the value of this feature because its value isn't evident. In addition, Microsoft stuffs the window with useless entries that don't tell you anything about using the window. The Data Collection Control window always appears with Performance

Explorer as a second tab. The IDE automatically selects this window for you when you launch the performance session.

However, before you run anything, you should configure this window with something more useful than what Microsoft has provided, as shown in Figure 19-9, for the sample application. In this case, you see the three method names that you'll see filtered in the "Viewing Performance Results" section of the chapter. These entries represent marks that you'll place inside the performance report as described later in this section. For now, remove all the marks that Microsoft provides by highlighting the mark and clicking Remove Row (the red X). Add the three rows shown (or any rows required for your application) by clicking Add Row (the yellow plus sign) and typing the name of the mark. It's a good idea to use something you recognize, such as a method name.

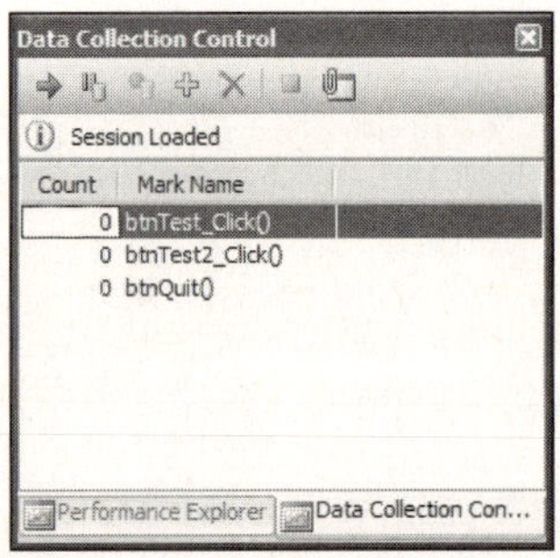

Figure 19-9: Configure the Data Collection Control window to provide useful information.

You need to know what the sample application looks like to understand how the marks are used. Figure 19-10 shows the sample used for this example. It contains three buttons, as shown, which call the methods shown in Figure 19-9. The list box displays the application output.

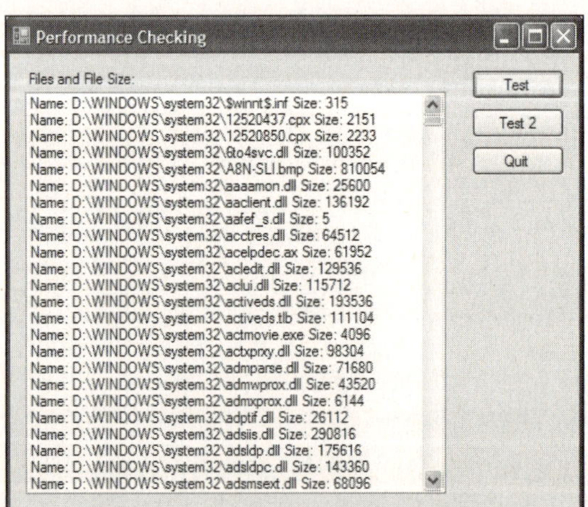

Figure 19-10: The three buttons in this application are the focus of the monitoring.

Now that you know about the marks and the application features, you need to know how to connect them. Here's how you'd use these marks for the sample application shown in Figure 19-10.

1. Start the application by clicking Start with Profiling in the Performance Explorer window.
2. Highlight `btnTest_Click()` in the Data Collection Control window and click Insert Mark (the blue right-pointing arrow). Notice that the count for the `btnTest_Click()` mark increases by one.
3. Click Test in the Performance Checking application. When you see the results dialog box, click OK.
4. Highlight `btnTest2_Click()` in the Data Collection Control window and click Insert mark. The count for the `btnTest2_Click()` mark increases by one.
5. Click Test 2 in the Performance Checking application. When you see the results dialog box, click OK.
6. Highlight `btnQuit()` in the Data Collection Control window and click Insert mark. The count for the `btnQuit()` mark increases by one.
7. Click Quit. The application ends and you see the report. At this point, you can filter the report using the marks you creating as described in the "Viewing Performance Results" section of the chapter.

Attaching to an Existing Process

You don't have to rely on starting your application in Visual Studio to use performance monitoring. It's possible to attach to any running application and monitor its performance. Simply click Attach/Detach in either the Performance Explorer or Data Collection Control windows. You'll see the Attach Profiler to Process dialog box shown in Figure 19-11.

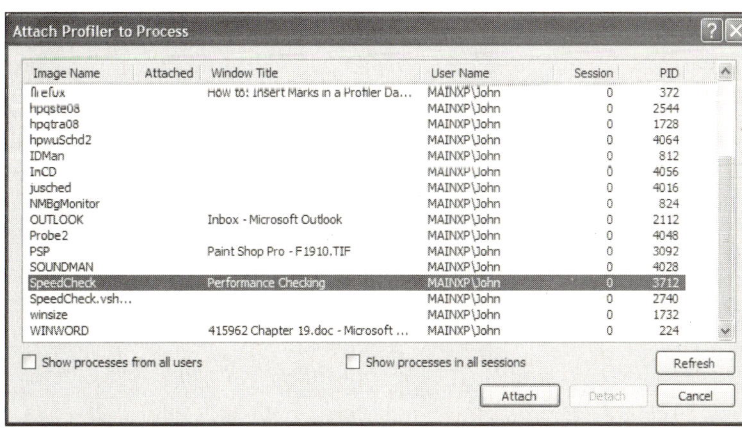

Figure 19-11: Attach the profiler to an application that's already running on your system.

When you get done profiling the application, you can close the application and see the report as usual. As an alternative, you can reopen the Attach Profiler to Process dialog box, highlight the application entry, and click Detach. Even though the application is still running, you'll see a report of the application's performance. When using this approach, you still have full access to the filtering and other features of Performance Explorer.

Viewing Performance Results

At this point, you have a report sitting in front of you. Visual Studio selects the Summary page, as shown in Figure 19-8, by default. However, the report contains a wealth of other pages as described in the following list:

- **Summary:** Presents an overview of the application, showing which methods cause the most work and which functions perform the most work.
- **Call Tree:** Displays a list of the calls made during the performance evaluation. Interestingly enough, the report includes both managed- and native-code modules. For example, you'll see calls to `User32.DLL`. Consequently, this report is helpful in seeing how your application interacts with Windows.
- **Modules:** Shows all the modules called by the application, including native-code modules. For example, you won't be surprised to learn that your application calls on `ComCtl32.DLL` for any common controls that it uses. However, it's interesting to know how much time your application spends working with `ComCtl32.DLL`.
- **Caller/Callee:** Helps you see the relationship between callers and callees in the application. You start at the top of the stack. Double-clicking an entry in the Functions That Were Called By list takes you down one level in the stack, while double-clicking an entry in the Functions That Called list takes you up one level. In the center, you see the Current Function list, which always contains a single entry for the module you've selected.
- **Functions:** Displays a list of all of the functions called by a particular application. When the profiler can't determine a specific function name (as with a native code module), it shows the module name instead. When you double-click one of these entries, the IDE presents the Caller / Callee page so that you can see the relationship between the selected function and other functions that application accesses.
- **Marks:** Presents a list of the marks you made within the profiler file and when you made them. You can use this part of the report when creating filters for making the report more readable.
- **Process:** Shows a list of the processes used to execute the application. Of course, your application is one process. However, you'll normally see `_CorExeMain` (see `http://msdn.microsoft.com/en-us/library/xh0859k0.aspx` for a description of this entry) and `MSCorWks.DLL` (part of the Common Language Runtime, CLR) as well. The entries tell the process identifier (PID), start time, and end time.

If you're interested in how the low-level hosting works for CLR, the article at `http://msdn.microsoft.com/en-us/magazine/cc301479.aspx` *describes how to create a custom host. Even if you don't implement a custom host, the article is helpful in explaining how hosting works.*

- **Lines:** Displays a list of source lines executed during sample profiling. This particular page isn't useful when using the sampling approach because the sampling approach looks at the whole application. You may not even see some methods listed in the report.
- **IPs:** Displays a list of specific instructions executed during sample profiling. This particular page isn't useful when using the sampling approach because the sampling approach looks at the whole application. You may not even see some methods listed in the report.

When you start looking through a report, the first thing that will hit you is that it contains a lot of information, probably more information than you ever wanted to see.

Adjusting the Filters

Filters are an essential part of working with the reports generated by the profiler. Without filters, you can spend hours trying to find what you need and still not find it. Visual Studio supports a wealth of filters, but you use them in the same way:

1. Click Show Filter on the report's toolbar. You'll see a new pane in the report window, as shown in Figure 19-12. The figure shows the filtering criteria used for the sample application.

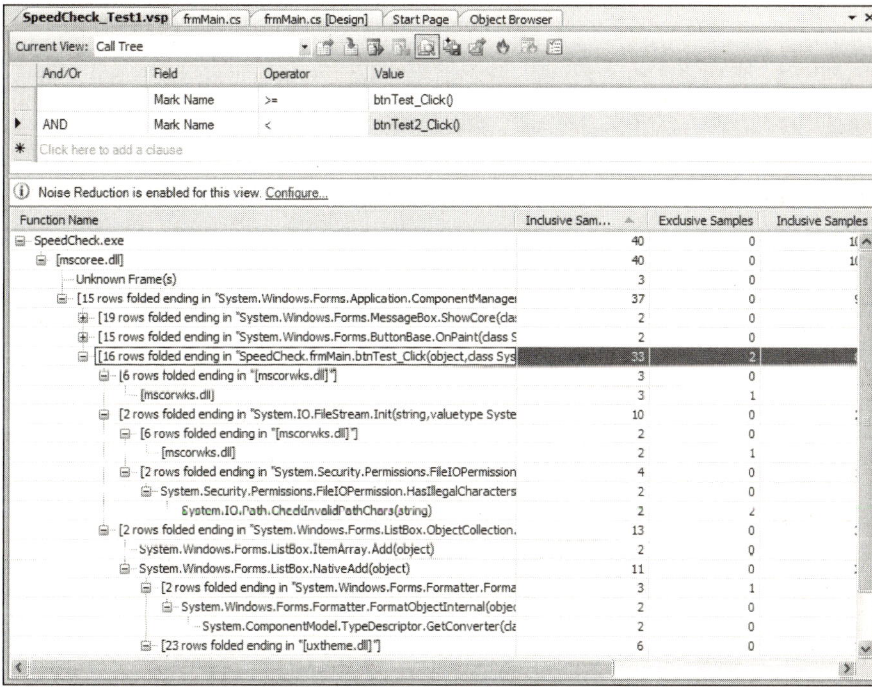

Figure 19-12: Display and configure the filtering criteria for a report.

2. Enter the filtering criteria. You have a lot of choices. The example uses the Mark Name field (see the "Using the Data Collection Control" section of this chapter for details). However, you can also filter by specifics such as the process or thread identifier, as well as by statistics, such as the time as a percentage.

3. Click Execute Filter. This act applies the filter to the report so that you see only the data you want. In this case, the report has far fewer items to consider in the Call Tree report shown in Figure 19-12. Filtering eliminates unneeded data, even though the data still exists in the background.

4. Choose the report page you want to review from the Current View drop-down list.

Working with Paths

The Call Tree page is probably the most difficult to use because it contains an exceptional amount of information. Visual Studio provides a special feature to help with this particular page. Click Expand Hot Path and you'll see the focal point of the report, as shown in Figure 19-13. The flames next to `btnTest2_Click()` and `btnTest_Click()` show that these are the hot-path items. You can remove the highlighting shown in Figure 19-13 by clicking Show Hot Path Highlighting.

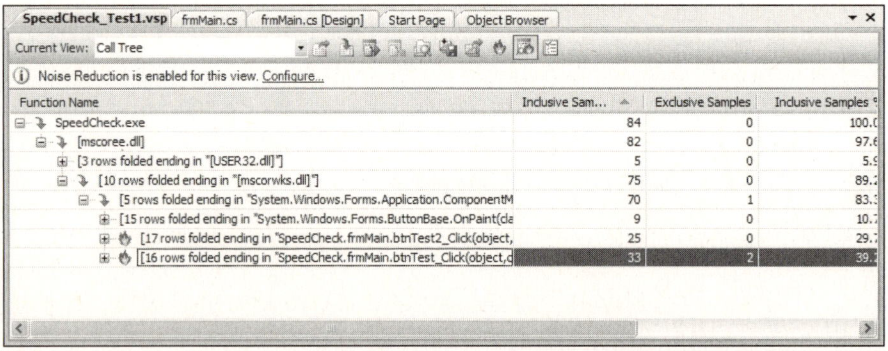

Figure 19-13: Get right to the focus of your report using the hot-path feature.

Reducing Noise

By default, Visual Studio enables a feature called noise reduction for your reports. Noise reduction removes entries that fall below a certain threshold, so you don't have to wade through reams of useless information. In fact, the top of the report includes a notice: Noise Reduction is Enabled for this View. It also has a Configure link. When you click the link or choose Analyze ➪ Profiler ➪ Noise Reduction Options, you see the Noise Reduction dialog box shown in Figure 19-14.

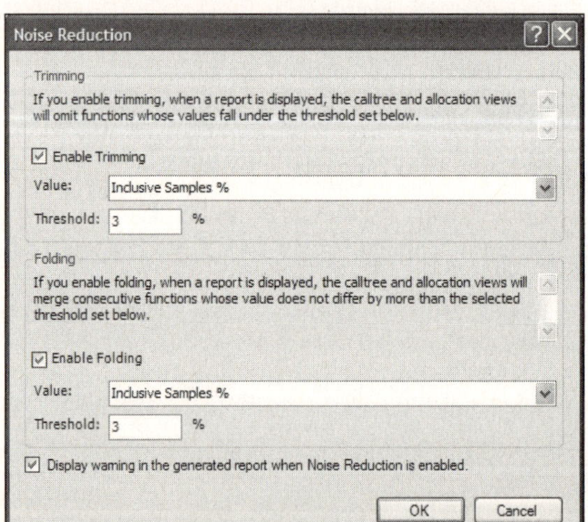

Figure 19-14: Get right to the focus of your report using the hot-path feature.

As shown in Figure 19-14, noise reduction involves two kinds of special filtering. First, you can enable trimming, which removes any entries that fall below a certain threshold value. The default setting removes entries whose Inclusive Samples % value falls below 3 percent. Unfortunately, the only Value entry is Inclusive Samples %, so you have to wonder why Microsoft even included the drop-down list box. Perhaps they plan to allow other options later. In most cases, you won't disable this option unless you really want to delve into the innermost workings of your application.

Second, you can enable folding. Folding merges entries that fall below the Inclusive Samples % level. Merging means that you're really seeing the output of multiple entries as a single entry. In some cases, you want to see these entries (such as when you're relying on native-code modules to perform certain tasks), so you'll clear the Enable Folding option. As with Enable Trimming, you don't have any options other than Inclusive Samples %.

Comparing Performance Reports

As you work with your code, you'll want to see how the changes you make are affecting speed. Of course, you could go through the mind-numbing process of comparing numbers manually, but Visual Studio offers a better option. You can use Visual Studio to perform the task for you. To start this process, choose Analyze ➪ Compare Performance Reports. You'll see the Select Analysis Files for Comparison dialog box shown in Figure 9-15.

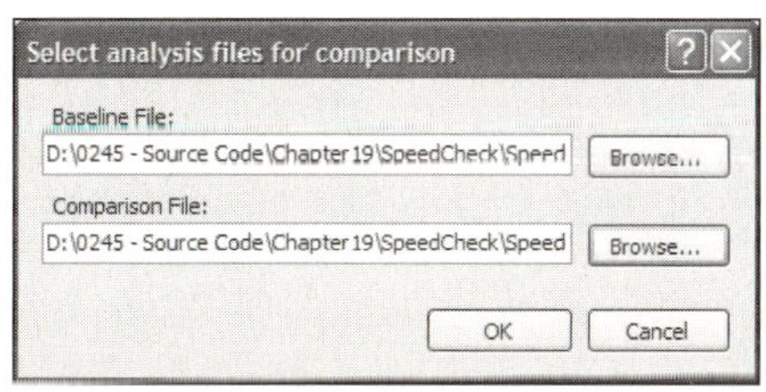

Figure 19-15: Choose the analysis reports you want to use for comparison purposes.

The Baseline File entry is the file you saved from your first run of the profiler. The Comparison File entry is the current run, the one that has the improvements you made. After you add the two files, click OK and Visual Studio creates a report similar to the one shown in Figure 19-16.

The comparison shows only the items that have changed. An up arrow shows an improvement, while a down arrow shows a place where application performance needs to improve. You can choose one of four tables to view:

- Function
- Module
- Line
- IP

These tables correspond to the pages of the report with the same name. You can also choose the column to use for comparison purposes and the threshold to use for the delta between two tests. The Threshold field is exceptionally important. If you set this value too low, you'll see items that vary only because of a natural variance during tests — in short, you're seeing noise. If you set the value too high, the comparison won't show you places where you really have experienced a positive change. In some cases, you'll need to set the threshold at 10 or so in order to filter out enough noise to obtain a useful comparison.

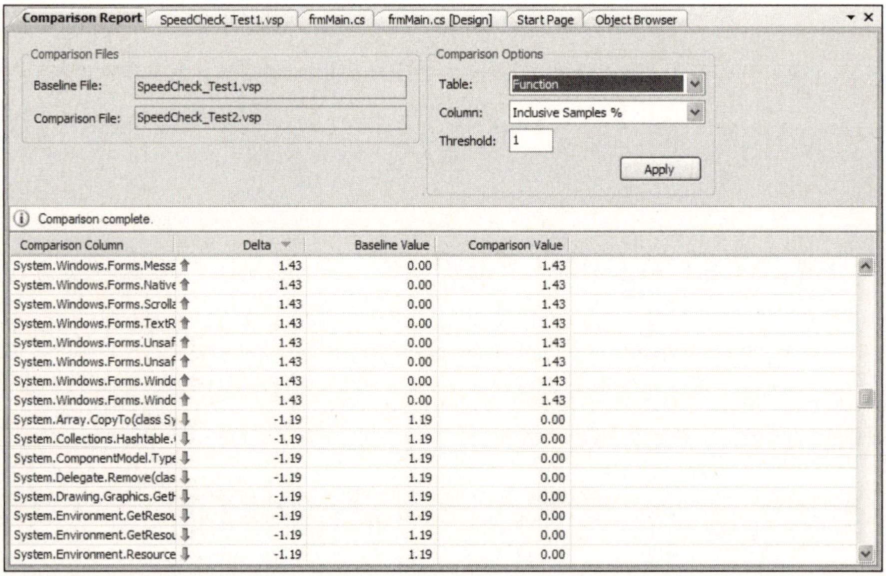

Figure 19-16: The comparison shows which elements have improved or gotten worse.

Making Your Application Reliable and Secure

This chapter considers the role of speed during the development phase of your application. It demonstrates techniques you can use to sample the application to determine whether you have the correct mixture of elements in place to produce an overall pleasing application. However, it's important to remember that sampling takes time and too much sampling is as bad as not enough. In most cases, you want to sample the application enough to ensure that when you begin the testing phase you won't encounter any nasty surprises.

Sampling the speed of the modules that will eventually make up the application you're building is important. Of course, you want to satisfy your curiosity, but it's also important to verify that your application is on track. Sampling serves a social function as well as a technical need. People want to demonstrate that they are creative and that they're finding new techniques that serve the project and the organization as a whole. When you create the schedule for your application, make sure you set aside sampling time. Otherwise, you may find that your development team is significantly less creative than it could be.

It's important to remember that this chapter is the first of three components of your performance triangle. Speed is important, but not to the detriment of the other two performance components. Chapter 20 presents the second leg of the triangle, reliability. In most cases, you must measure speed against reliability to ensure that changes you make don't cause your application to fail. Speed is useful only when it doesn't affect application output and won't create unsafe situations for your data. Chapter 20 helps you understand this relationship and shows how to move your application in the right direction.

20

Considering Application Reliability Implications

Reliability is never noticed. If no one's paying any attention to your application (they just use it without thinking about it), it's probably because you've achieved that most desired of all application traits reliability. Think about it for a moment. When you go home tonight and flip the switch for the lights, you probably won't think about it. In fact, you may not even remember flipping the switch. The only time you notice the electricity in your house is when the power is out — when the power has become unreliable. Otherwise, you pay no attention to it at all, and that's how things should be. Likewise, no one should notice your application — users should simply sit down and start using it. If you can achieve that state of nothingness, where the user doesn't even remember using the application, you've really done something, because it's quite likely that few developers will ever attain this status.

Reliability is also never complete. Consequently, you'll always have something to work on from a reliability perspective. The reason that people talk about five nines, or 99.999 percent, reliability is that you simply can't achieve the other 0.001 percent. What this means to you as a developer is that you can't afford to oversell the reliability of your application. No matter what you do, your application will fail at some point. Telling someone anything different will always land you in trouble.

This chapter emphasizes real-world reliability that you'll probably begin testing during the development cycle. The theory of reliability offers the hope of 100 percent success, but the reality is somewhat different. Part of the goal of this chapter is to help you consider reasonable reliability — the sort of reliability that makes your application work well, without hindering the user or impacting speed so much that the application becomes unusable.

> *All applications are unreliable to some extent. The most unreliable application in the world, however, is the application that no one uses. An unused application has no up time, which means that it has zero reliability. Only by creating applications that others like to use can you hope to achieve any level of reliability at all. Consequently, the first rule of reliability is not to attempt to achieve perfection through an unusable application — that path leads to the very antithesis of what you hope to achieve.*

Defining the Trade-offs of Reliability

For most developers, reliability is one of those features they must somehow include in the application, even knowing that no one will notice. However, reliability is easy to add incorrectly. In some cases, reliability concerns overshadow other needs such as usability. Stifling the application with checks and counterchecks can be as bad as not checking often enough. The following sections describe some ways in which developers can add reliability to an application incorrectly, despite the best of intentions. Of course, the last word in reliability is that there isn't any last word — reliability is always a process.

Avoiding the Overly Pessimistic Application

You've probably seen an application in the past that's pessimistic — the kind of application that asks whether you're sure you want to perform a particular act. Immediately afterward, it asks whether you're really sure. In a final act of desperation, the application asks whether you know that it can't undo this particular act. Finally, the application performs the task that you requested three dialog boxes ago.

Application pessimism can appear in a number of other forms, too. For example, you've probably encountered the application that won't use network resources — even local network resources — without requiring that you set a huge number of privileges and perform other configuration tasks. These applications make network access quite visible and reduce the user's ability to complete tasks in a reasonable time frame. In most cases, you can better handle these kinds of security situations by asking the network administrator to provide a list of clean drives and keeping the user out of the equation completely.

Considering the Microsoft Vista UAC Debacle

Not to pick on a particular application, but the User Account Control (UAC) (sometimes called User Access Control) in the Vista operating system is a great example of an overly pessimistic application. If the operating system were any more pessimistic, it wouldn't accomplish anything at all.

This feature is so maligned that Microsoft has been publishing guides such as the User Account Control Step-by-Step Guide found at `http://technet.microsoft.com/en-us/library/cc709691.aspx` to divert some UAC criticism. Some experts are even trying to explain why UAC is important (see `http://weblog.infoworld.com/securityadviser/archives/2008/08/user_access_con.html` as an example), but I'm sure their words are falling on deaf ears.

UAC is simply an example of reliability run amok. A key indicator that an application or an operating system is overly pessimistic is when you begin seeing explanations of why it must be inflexible (normally for the user's own good). Fortunately, you can turn off UAC and put both you and the operating system out of misery.

Creating Applications that Do Absolutely Nothing

It's possible for an organization to miss something big when creating an application. For example, the developers may use a test system that has a slightly different setup or hardware configuration than the production system. The application can work fine on the development system, but when the developers move it to the production system, the application fails. In many cases, the issues that the developers are facing are bugs — something not covered in this chapter to any degree (see Chapters 14 and 15 for error handling and debugging). However, in other cases, the failure point is something that should work, but doesn't.

The failure point is sometimes obvious. The developers made an assumption about the hardware that simply isn't true on the production system, so the application doesn't have the resources needed to perform the required task. This particular problem happens far more often than you might think, because the developers will often soup up the test system (sort of a hot rod for developers). Software that doesn't run on the production system points to a potential reliability problem. In this case, something in the software is preventing it from working on all platforms for which it's designed. In looking for the problem, you must find the reliability issues before you can fix the application so it runs correctly. Often, the code itself is fine.

Some failure points aren't obvious at all. For example, the administrator may not know how to configure the application properly. When you move the application from the testing system to the production system, a configuration error keeps the application from working properly. In many cases, the configuration error is small — something as simple as an error in a database connection string can cause considerable woe when it comes to making the application work. The first impulse for many developers is to look for a coding error. However, the application code is fine. Perhaps the only issue is that the connection string points to the test database server, rather than the production database server.

In some cases, hidden failure points aren't even part of the main application. For example, you install an application on a client system where the user has installed a favorite game program (unauthorized). The game conflicts with your application. If you think the user will admit to installing the game, think again. You'll need to go to the client system, dig out the failure source, and remove it. Even if you confront the user with the impossibility of the application's getting on the user's system through any legitimate means, some will continue to lie to you and try to convince you that they haven't a clue as to where the application came from. (Personally, I prefer a strong company policy against user applications suddenly appearing on systems from nowhere — a policy such as "install the application and find a new job somewhere else.")

Reliability has to consider any potential failure point, even if the possibility of that failure point occurring is miniscule. That a failure can happen at all means that it can, and possibly will, happen to you. The probability that you'll end up with an application that does nothing when you move it from the test system to the production system, or from your system to the client system, is actually quite high. It's always embarrassing, too. The client has likely seen the application work on your test system and seeing the working test system makes the client wonder why it doesn't work on the organization's system. In the meantime, you're trying to fix the application while the eyes of everyone in the room bore into your skull, making you feel quite uncomfortable.

The basic way out of the application that does absolutely nothing is to duplicate the production system in every detail. If the production system has a particular piece of hardware, then the test system should have the same piece of hardware. If the production system uses a particular driver, then the test system should, too. The test system should include every piece of software that the production system has and you should apply the same patches to the test system. Even the configuration should be the same, right down to how the administrator of the production system sets up the Desktop. If you're working with multiple desktop systems, configure multiple test systems — one for each desktop configuration. Mobile device testing requires precisely the same device for both testing and production setups. Likewise, Web application testing should mimic the client system as closely as possible.

> **Considerations for the Consultant**
>
> Consultants need to work a little harder to ensure their applications will work on a given client system. The consultant should create a complete list of all applications on the client system and then create a duplicate of that client system for testing purposes. As part of your research for building the duplicate client system, sit with one of the users for a few hours to see how the user interacts with the computer and which third-party applications receive the most use.
>
> Of course, the duplicate client system you build today is outdated tomorrow. A consultant needs to constantly check for changes in the target client system or the application may not work as anticipated. Don't just ask the network administrator for a list of new applications — verify the list by physically viewing several of the client systems yourself. As a consultant, you owe it to your client to take extra care in checking for potential interoperability problems.

Defining External Threats

The first step in avoiding a trap is to know that it exists. External threats are a kind of trap. You make an assumption about your application that simply isn't true. Some terrible person comes along and discovers the false assumption — and then calls you on the false assumption by adding a virus to your system or exposing your data for the entire world to see. Most people view external threats as someone trying to break into the system — that's the trap. In many cases, the problem is that you left the door open — the intruder was simply using your mistake against you.

I wrote a book once on home security. I was surprised to discover that most homes are robbed because the owners left a door or window open. The burglar didn't even have to work hard to get inside. In more than a few cases, I read about the burglar simply walking down the block while people were away at work and trying each door. Normally, the evildoer dressed up as someone delivering those cheesy advertisements that everyone seems to get tied to their screen door, so no one even suspected the burglar's real intent. If real-world burglars can make use of such an obvious means of gaining entry, you should think twice about the security of your applications — make sure the door is closed. Of course, part of closing the door is to disallow any form of back door or testing feature in a production environment.

External threats can include internal sources. The term *external* here means outside the application. For example, many companies are now finding that they shouldn't give the keys to the system to one individual. A basic security rule is the two-man rule — essentially, no one works alone and no one individual can do anything major to the system. In most cases, you want to create your application in such a way that most activities that could do major harm to your organization require the participation of two people — making it less likely that the event will occur.

One of the activities you should perform as the development cycle proceeds is to identify external threats. As developers write application code, they should be thinking about ways in which someone could use that code to damage the application or its data in any way, or gain unauthorized access to the system. Make the list a prominent part of the development process and consider ways in which you can keep these outsiders at bay. Think in terms of failure points, not necessarily the security threats described in Chapter 7. One of the best ways to keep people out of your system is to know how they can break into it.

Developing a Reliability Plan

Every organization should have a reliability plan for each of its applications. The reliability plan specifies how you plan to address reliability issues. For example, the plan should provide categories of reliability issues so that you can organize maintenance actions you want to perform. Assign each reliability need a priority so that you fix the problems with the biggest impact first.

Part of your plan should include the construction of a database to hold reliability-related issues. A reliability-related issue might be anything from changing the user interface to updating code so it relies on a new technique. A reliability issue need not always point to a bug. Later in the chapter, you'll learn about two Visual Studio features that can help you find reliability problems in your code: code analysis and code metrics. Using these tools won't point out bugs in your application, but it will point out potential reliability issues. Consequently, your reliability-related database may not contain what most developers would term as actual errors.

The reliability plan should include preventive maintenance. Your system, the hardware and software, constantly changes. Any change in any environmental factor can cause new failure points to appear in your application. However, you won't see the new failure points unless you test the application for them and perform regular reviews of the application and its environment. Reliability is fluid and changes constantly in response to other changes. Even a change in user training can create new reliability problems, because users who interact with the application differently will cause new failure points to appear. As you update the reliability plan and the content of the database that supports it, you should also update priorities to make sure you focus on the most important issues first.

Your reliability plan should emphasize the fact that reliability issues are unique — they're failure points. The reliability issues aren't necessarily security related — even though the reliability database will likely contain security issues. They aren't necessarily related to new external threats, but some of the issues in the database will reflect this reality. In short, reliability issues are failure oriented. Anything that tends to cause a failure is a reliability issue.

Placing Users in Monkey Mode

Although many developers view their users as monkeys (ill-behaved monkeys at that), it's probably best not to let the monkeys, uh, users know. All kidding aside, users are probably the best reliability testers you have because users do unexpected things. It's not inconceivable that a user will find a way to break a perfectly usable application when the best testers on your development team feel that the application is bulletproof. In fact, users all too often find that the application isn't bulletproof for a very good reason. Developers usually don't have a good grasp of the user's job — only the user has that understanding. Without a good understanding of the job, it's impossible to test the application properly. The following sections describe a few elements of application testing that your development team should emphasize as part of the testing process.

Care and Feeding of the Reliable Developer

You probably have a reliable developer on your team. No, it's not the guy who wears the funky orange pants that blind everyone in the room. It's the gal who's sitting in the corner minding her own business. Every day she puts out several hundred lines of very good code that don't require much, if any, work from you. She's quiet and doesn't stand out very much. Unless you look carefully, you won't even notice her. She'll just come in every day and output the same good work without anyone saying very much — she does it because she honestly likes writing application code.

One day you may notice her and think that you'll present her as a model to the rest of the group. Avoid the temptation! The reliable developer doesn't crave public notice or fame of any sort. However, you should do something. Make sure you tell the reliable developer that you appreciate her fine work and that she should continue doing it. Give her a day off to express your appreciation (or do something else nice).

The other bad thing that happens to reliable developers is promotion. Sure, some of them want to receive a promotion, but they'd rather have a pay raise in most cases. You should make a point of talking about career paths with the reliable developer. Make sure you understand where this person wants to be in the near and far future. It may surprise you to discover that the reliable developers really aren't all that interested in becoming a CEO — they're happy writing code because it's what they know and it makes them feel comfortable.

With proper care and feeding, the reliable developer will do more to advance your project that any other two or three developers on your team combined. The reliable developer is someone you should treat with due respect for her particular needs.

Breaking Applications during Testing Is Good

Users need permission to break your application. That may not sound realistic considering how often they break your application without trying, but it's true. All too often, users won't try an application feature for fear of the repercussions of breaking it. Even when users break the application, they often try to hide the breakage — often making things even worse. The biggest problem with user fears over breaking the application during testing is that you won't find the reliability problems in your application until the application is in production. At that point, fixes becomes expensive in terms of coding, testing, QA, user training, and deployment. It's best to find as many reliability problems as you can during the testing phase.

Users aren't easily encouraged to break your application during testing. However, if you make a game out of it, you'll usually find that the users are more than up to the task of locating reliability problems for you. In many cases, an organization will host some type of contest where the winner receives something in recognition of their ability to break the application. It sounds counter to the normal way application usage is supposed to work, but this is testing time and you want the users as active as possible.

A failed technique for encouraging user participation is to give everyone the same reward. The problem with this approach is that it doesn't build any competition. You want lots of competitive spirit when it comes to testing. People should be hitting your application from all sides trying to find the next reliability issue. Consequently, you must make the prizes worthwhile and offer them only to the few who truly excel at breaking the application. Now, it's fine to offer everyone a T-shirt — something on the order of "I tested the company's widget application and all I got was this lousy T-shirt," but don't make the T-shirt the major prize.

As part of the breaking process, you should publicize the places where people have found breaks so that your team doesn't have to process endless repeats of the same reliability issue report. You should also publicize areas of the application that no one has broken or that have received only a few breaks. It's important that users know where to look for potential reliability problems.

Remember the game aspect of this whole event. Users are far more likely to provide you with good reports if they know they're expected to excel at something that you normally dissuade them from doing. Anything you can do to make breaking your application fun is good. You might even add bells and whistles to the exception handling routine so that users will do things to ensure they get to see the "Easter egg" you've planted. Easter eggs are extremely popular. All you have to do is look at the huge listings at places such as `http://www.eeggs.com/tree/154.html`.

Creating a Lessons-Learned Journal

Any reliability scenario is all about things breaking. Of course, it's a good idea to go back to the breakage event and discuss why the break occurred and how you can fix it. However, if all you get out of the event is a fix for your application, you're really missing a big reason for this whole event to take place. Reliability testing of your application doesn't just serve the need of making your application better — it's training for you as a developer as well. If you're not learning something from the whole process, then you're missing out in a big way.

The first thing you should do when you start performing reliability testing on your application is to create a journal. This journal should contain entries for every bug that every user finds for the application. You should include obvious information, such as how you fixed the problem. However, the more interesting information to include in such a journal is how the user caused the problem in the first place. Knowing how a user breaks your application is important because this information often proves useful later. Many security researchers use this technique because it produces good results. For example, you won't learn about typing in a certain key phrase without asking the user for this information.

After a testing cycle is complete, you should go through the journal you created and attempt to discover some commonality in the errors you recorded. Generalizing your findings will make the journal useful for new projects that you design. For example, if users find it difficult to press Ctrl+Alt+Shift+C to capitalize words in a document in one application, they'll find it equally difficult in every other application you create. Generalizing your findings can help you understand these problems. In fact, difficult keystroke combinations are one significant cause of user error. When the user makes an error in using the keystrokes you provide, unfortunate things can happen to the application or its data. In short, using unviable keystroke combinations makes your application unreliable.

Sometimes a generalized error also forms the basis for policy in your organization. If you encounter a problem often enough, it makes sense to get rid of the cause of that problem. In many cases, this means making a policy designed to help others avoid the problem. Of course, you won't be able to follow trends in errors without some type of formalized documentation such as your journal.

Your journal should also contain personal revelations. A personal revelation is something you've done that had consequences and that you found a way to fix even though it doesn't appear to affect anyone else. For example, you may have a brainstorm for reducing glare on your screen — closing the drapes. It turns out, however, that closing the drapes also promoted sleep and you ended up wasting an entire afternoon that way — at least until the boss knocked on the door. Personal revelations can be anything that helps you understand your personal skills as a developer.

Don't make the mistake of thinking that your personal journal somehow replaces public documentation. Your organization should also have a database set aside to document application errors and behaviors. The public database probably won't have the charm of your personal notes, but it will serve the needs of anyone who works on your project in the future. Always ensure that any error that appears in your journal also appears in the public database. Obviously, your personal revelations, whatever they might be, won't receive the same treatment.

Checking Your Code

Visual Studio does provide some tools that you can use to check the reliability of your code. It's true that these tools also serve other purposes, but they really do affect reliability most. The following sections describe how you can perform code analysis and obtain code metrics for your applications, and how these measures will help you discover more about the reliability of your application.

The Visual Studio tools provide a good starting point, but many third-party products on the market provide in-depth information. If you have a large project and want to be sure that your code offers the best reliability possible, consider using products such as FxCop (see Chapter 30 for details) in addition to the tools offered with Visual Studio. Of course, Microsoft provides a wealth of tools too. Make sure to check out SyncToy — a tool that makes it easy to move files about your system — even between computers (see Chapter 29 for details).

Running Code Analysis

Performing a code analysis with Visual Studio is relatively easy. After you write your code, choose Analyze ➪ Run Code Analysis on `<Project Name>`. Visual Studio will compile your application and then perform analysis on it. After a few seconds, you'll see a list of warnings appear in the Error List window as shown in Figure 20-1. It doesn't matter whether you have a debug, release, or other type of build selected.

Figure 20-1 shows the typical appearance of code analysis warnings. The warning always includes a CA number to tell the reason for the warning. If the warning affects a particular section of the code, you'll see a filename, line number, and in some cases, a column number. The Project column always contains `CodeAnalysis` as the keyword so that you can sort by code analysis issues. The CA numbers reflect specific rules that Microsoft has created for writing safe code. You can find these numbers described at `http://msdn.microsoft.com/en-us/library/ee1hzekz.aspx`. The CA numbers use the following categories:

- **Design:** Issues that affect library design as specified by the .NET Framework Design Guidelines.
- **Globalization:** Application features that affect use by locales other than the one supported by the application developer. Normally, you only need to worry about these issues when you expect people in other countries to use the application.
- **Interoperability:** Potential support problems that can affect your application's ability to interact with Component Object Model (COM) clients.
- **Maintainability:** Design issues that could make it more difficult for you to support the application.
- **Mobility:** Issues that affect the power usage of your application. At one time, these warnings were only significant for mobile device applications. However, given the current emphasis on green computing, even desktop applications should adhere to these guidelines.

- **Naming:** Warnings that state you've decided to use a naming convention other than the one Microsoft suggests. As long as you use a consistent naming convention, you can ignore these warnings.
- **Performance:** Design issues that affect the speed of your application. In some cases, you can make your application run faster without affecting either security or reliability by following the advice provided.
- **Portability:** Implementation issues that affect application portability across different platforms. Given that the .NET Framework only supports one platform, you shouldn't worry too much about these warnings. They normally occur when you must use P/Invoke to perform a particular task (see Chapter 27 for details). However, these issues are important if you plan to run your .NET application using Mono (see the article at `http://www.devsource.com/c/a/Architecture/Mixing-Server-Core-with-NET-Applications/` for details).
- **Reliability:** Implementation issues that directly affect application reliability such as incorrect memory or thread usage.
- **Security:** Implementation issues that directly affect application security.
- **Usage:** Indicates that you've used the .NET Framework incorrectly. In most cases, these warnings are severe and will affect application reliability. For example, calling an exception within an exception class will definitely cause problems for the application — generally, it crashes.

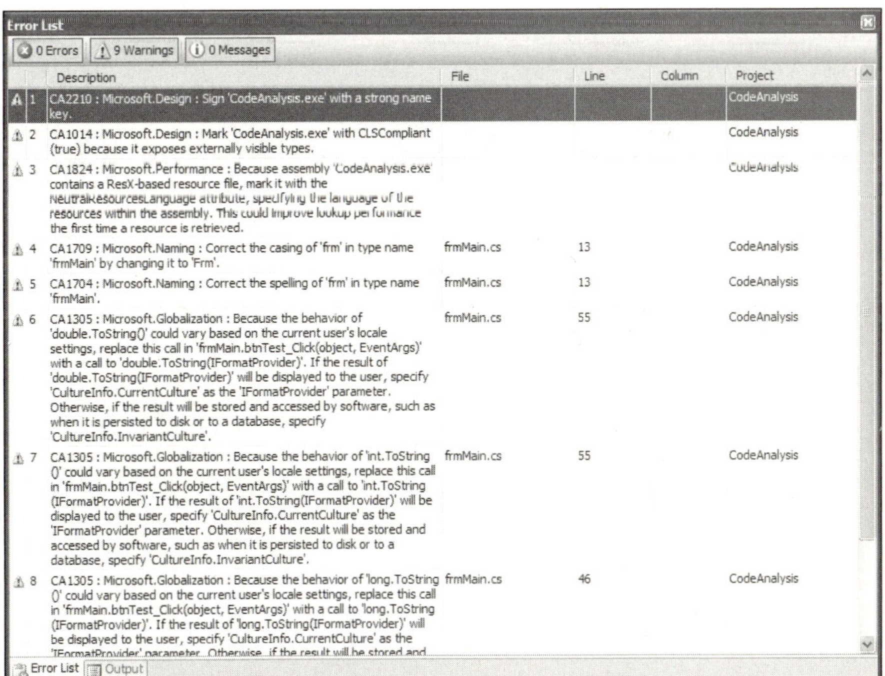

Figure 20-1: The Error List window shows the results of any code analysis you perform.

Microsoft provides information on every one of the CA numbers you see in the Error List window, but it doesn't tell you how to find that information. In general, you'll find the information fastest if you search for the CA number within MSDN. However, if you perform a Google search using the CA number, you'll probably find more ideas on how to fix the problem.

The Microsoft materials provide one essential piece of information in the Breaking Change field of the documentation. If you see the word *Breaking* there, you really need to fix the error or else your application isn't as reliable as it could be. Microsoft doesn't use the Breaking indicator lightly. For example, a globalization issue doesn't warrant such an indication. If you decide to use a different variable naming scheme from the one that Microsoft prefers, it isn't a problem. You can even use P/Invoke in your code and it's not an issue. However, when you decide to declare static members on generic types — it's a breaking problem.

Calculating Code Metrics

Code metrics provide statistics about your code. By performing this kind of analysis, you can determine where to spend your time to obtain the most benefit from a maintainability perspective. Improving maintainability makes your code easier to understand and fix, which improves your ability to perform bug fixes, which improves application reliability. In short, maintainable applications tend to have fewer problems.

You can run code metrics at any time. To run code metrics on your application, choose Analyze ➪ Calculate Code Metrics for `<Project Name>`. Figure 20-2 shows the code metric output for the sample application.

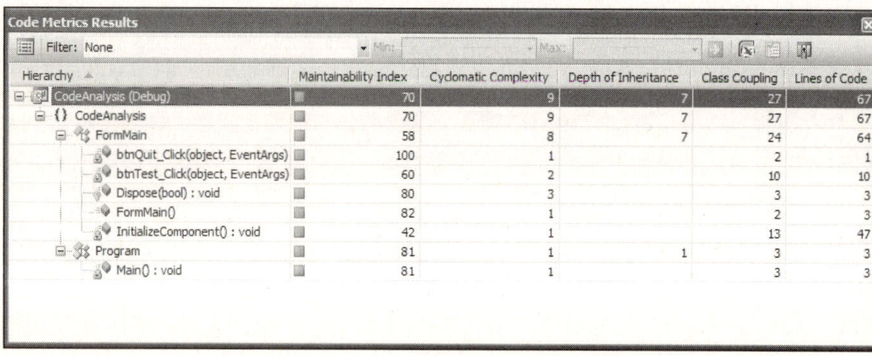
Code Metrics Results

Filter: None Min: Max:

Hierarchy	Maintainability Index	Cyclomatic Complexity	Depth of Inheritance	Class Coupling	Lines of Code
CodeAnalysis (Debug)	70	9	7	27	67
{} CodeAnalysis	70	9	7	27	67
FormMain	58	8	7	24	64
btnQuit_Click(object, EventArgs)	100	1		2	1
btnTest_Click(object, EventArgs)	60	2		10	10
Dispose(bool) : void	80	3		3	3
FormMain()	82	1		2	3
InitializeComponent() : void	42	1		13	47
Program	81	1	1	3	3
Main() : void	81	1		3	3

Figure 20-2: Verify that your code is easy to maintain by checking the code metrics.

The important thing to remember about this window is that green is good. If you see green squares for every entry, the application is maintainable. The higher the number in the Maintainability Index column, the better. Here's a description of the column contents:

- **Maintainability Index:** Contains an index value between 0 and 100 that tells you the maintainability of the code. A higher number is always better. Values between 0 and 9 display a red square and show that the code isn't maintainable. Values between 10 and 19 indicate that the code is marginal and display a yellow square. Visual Studio calculates this value based on the content of the Cyclomatic Complexity and Lines of Code columns. It also relies on a Halstead Volume (metric) calculation. You can read more about this calculation at `http://www.verifysoft.com/en_halstead_metrics.html`. The essence of this calculation is that it measures the number of operands and operators in your code — or in plainer terms, the complexity of the task that your code performs. You can see the calculation at `http://blogs.msdn.com/fxcop/archive/2007/11/20/maintainability-index-range-and-meaning.aspx`.

- **Cyclomatic Complexity:** Defines the general complexity of the code as measured by code blocks and structures (such as loops). Each element counts as a value of 1 and the analysis adds 1 to the result. Consequently, the `btnTest_Click()` method shown in Figure 20-2 receives a value of 1 because it includes a `for` loop. A higher value, here, indicates code with lots of loops and structures that require more unit tests to verify and more time to maintain.
- **Depth of Inheritance:** Shows the number of class extensions that reach to the root of the class hierarchy. In short, the number indicates the number of times that you've inherited from another class. A higher number shows a greater level of inheritance, which makes the code harder to understand and maintain because someone coming after you will have to move up through each level of the hierarchy in order to understand the code. At the class level, the number in this column shows the number of levels of inheritance starting from the root class. At the namespace and project level, this number is the same as the class with the highest number.
- **Class Coupling:** Indicates the amount of coupling between the element and other classes. A high level of class coupling shows that the element has a high dependency on other classes and types, which can make it hard to maintain. The interdependencies also make the code less reliable because a fault in any dependent class will also affect the current element. This measurement doesn't reflect use of base types such as `int`. It does include any of the following dependencies:
    - Attribute decoration
    - Base classes
    - Fields that are defined on external types
    - Generic or template instantiations
    - Interface implementations
    - Local variables
    - Method calls
    - Return types
    - Unique classes accessed through parameters
- **Lines of Code:** Shows the number of lines of code that appear in the Intermediate Language (IL) file for the element. Consequently, this number may not match the number of lines in your source code file. As the number of lines of code increase, maintainability and reliability decrease.

A general rule for reliability calculations is that the more items that can fail, the lower the reliability. That's the reason why many vendors strive to decrease the number of components in the devices they create. Software acts in the same way. Increasing the number of lines of code increases the number of failure points in your application and makes the code less reliable as a result.

Making Your Application Reliable and Secure

This chapter has discussed reliability from a number of perspectives. The one rule you can take away from this chapter is that reliability is attainable, but it will always be less than perfect. What you need to achieve is the highest possible reliability without impacting either speed or security to the point that the application becomes unusable. In addition, reliability is a long-term process — something that you continue to perfect as people use the application. Consequently, you shouldn't view short-term setbacks as failures, but as indicators of how to improve your application.

Are people complaining about your application crashing, providing a less than perfect user interface, or causing data errors? If they are, you're in good company. Most applications have some type of problem that the developer has to fix. It's important to understand how to measure reliability in your application and then work to improve those numbers. You should also realize that reliability is a process. Consequently, you need a reliability improvement plan for your application and should continue to update that plan as you see new areas in which it can improve. Most important of all, don't get discouraged. When discouragement does set in (and it will), take a break, review what you're actually trying to achieve (it isn't perfection), and then come back to the problems in your application.

Chapter 21 completes the performance triangle from a development perspective. This chapter considers the question of security. Because security is such a hot topic, you'll find that you have to battle hard to achieve the level of security that people expect. Unlike reliability, which no one notices unless you haven't achieved it, everyone notices security. When you have too much security, people complain about access. Not having enough security opens your application to attack. Consequently, security is like walking on a tightrope and hoping you don't fall off.

21

Considering Application Security Implications

Security is an illusion at times. It's good to remember quotes from some of the best warriors the world has ever seen when considering real-world security. For example, General George Patton once noted, "Fixed fortifications are monuments to the stupidity of man" (see `http://www.military-quotes.com/Patton.htm` for other quotes). The implications are obvious for application security, because every piece of code you add to an application is a fixed fortification. Yes, they'll keep the novice at bay or someone who is not truly interested in overcoming your security, but the truly determined adversary will overcome your fixed fortifications — count on it. During the development cycle, you begin to realize just how tenuous the security arrangements in Chapter 7 are when the application testers find ways to overcome them. You don't even have to wait for the reprehensible individual to arrive to test your fortifications.

Of course, the counter to the argument that no amount of fortification in the world makes your application safe is to think about not adding any security at all. Unfortunately, this view is akin to your bank leaving the money piled in the middle of the room because someone who is determined will make it into the safe. Adding security, the best security possible, to your application is always worthwhile; you just can't convince yourself that the fortifications are the end of the road. Security is a process where you erect a new fortification and someone else considers a new way to tear it down — security is war and only the vigilant survive.

It's important to remember that security is only one part of performance. When you make an application too secure, you deny access to the user who really needs it, without necessarily denying access to the person of evil intent. Security is a matter of balance. While there are techniques you can use to improve security, the most successful strategy involves monitoring, evolving strategies, and good damage control when someone breaches your security. This chapter discusses all three requirements, along with the need to maintain application reliability and speed.

Defining the Trade-offs of Security

Security, like any other element of your application, has trade-offs. As mentioned earlier in the book, the most secure application in the world is the one that no one can use. Of course, such an application is useless. However, keeping an application completely open to attack, simply to make things a little more convenient for the user, is also a terrible idea. You have to pursue the middle ground as described in the following sections.

Keeping Data out of the Hands of Users

Users are responsible for more security breaches than any other single source. In fact, users are often responsible for more security breaches than all other sources put together. You may find it tempting to find ways to keep data out of the user's hands. The fewer users that touch the data, the more secure those data become. However, you again run into the paradox that the data become less useful when users can't interact with them. The larger the obstacles for using the data, the more likely it is that the data will become worthless at some point — if for no other reason than that they'll become outdated.

Of course, you also don't want the user to have unnecessary information. For example, a user may need to know the name, e-mail address, and office telephone number of the other users in the organization — but few users require access to the home addresses and telephone numbers, and even fewer users need access to pay or Social Security information. Selective data hiding is a prudent way to keep data exposure to a minimum, without inhibiting a user's ability to perform useful work.

An interesting approach taken by one company to protect customer information was to use selective data hiding. I called a company to order some parts for my computer. They had my credit card on file, but the sales representative could only see the last four digits of the credit card number and the expiration date. This is all the salesperson needed to make the sale. Without the full credit card number, the rest of the information is less useful. Letting the sales representative have less information made me feel a little more comfortable about the transaction and didn't inhibit the sales representative's ability to complete the transaction.

You can and should design selective data hiding into an application. The selective data hiding may even work during initial testing. However, be prepared to work on selective data hiding code as the needs of users or the organization change. Be prepared to hide data just as quickly as you make them visible. In fact, part of your application maintenance should focus on hiding information that users really don't need in order to do their job.

Consider partial data hiding. Users may only need to verify data by knowing the last four digits of a phone number or a credit card. When the data require change, a supervisor or other responsible party can address the issue. Creating a two-level change mechanism does have benefits. Even though the user can't make the required change, the user does know about the supervisor's need to make the change and what change the supervisor should have made. If you start seeing unnecessary changes — those that the user can't verify — you can reconsider the reliability of the supervisor. The point is that you have a two-person monitor on the process.

Creating Performance Roadblocks

An application that has too much security applied may seem secure, but you must consider an important issue with the application that is too secure. Security affects the overall performance of the application in the following ways:

- **Speed:** Every security check you add to an application reduces application speed. In addition, these checks can also increase the need to retry some tasks, such as accessing data, further reducing application speed. You must also consider the human interaction time of additional security because the user will need to interact with supervisors more often. In short, security affects application speed on a number of levels, and adding too much security reduces application speed noticeably. Of course, the application requires a certain amount of security and the speed reduction that this required security inflicts is simply part of the cost of doing business.
- **Reliability:** Security issues can create failure points in your application. For example, denying access to needed data can cause the application to fail. Entering the wrong password, losing access to a needed resource, and other security issues all make your application less reliable. It seems counterintuitive, but security and reliability work together at some times, but against each other at other times.
- **Security:** Too much security can actually impact security negatively. If you secure data to the point that the user can't accomplish a particular task, the user will find another source for that data. Because users tend to view applications as evil and other users as best friends, the user will find someone with the required access to provide the data. In fact, you may find users sharing IDs and passwords with other users and circumventing security completely. Once your organization goes down the shared ID and password road, you can count on having a hard time getting reasonable security reestablished.

The best way to look at security is that you want to set up roadblocks for the obnoxious intruders bent on getting your data — you don't want to create roadblocks for users who are simply looking to accomplish a task and go home. Consequently, the question to ask is whether a particular security measure will cause more problems for intruders than for users, rather than whether the security measure will potentially block intruders. Many security measures block intruders, but only well-balanced security measures block intruders while helping users get their work done.

Considering Big Brother Syndrome

Most people have a negative reaction to what they consider Big Brother syndrome, a reference to the novel *1984* and the Orwellian sense of impending doom that too much monitoring evokes. Many organizations now take the view that any data a user generates using a company machine belong to the organization. The ownership of the data has been the focus of more than a few court cases as users try to take ownership of something at the company, but the fact of the matter is that the organization does own the data. The user has no right to the data, the machine on which it resides, or the application used to manipulate the data.

Still, despite the news articles, the court cases, and even common sense, people have a strong desire to own the data that they create and manipulate each day. Unfortunately, both the developer and the administrator are right in the middle of the controversy. The developer is in the middle because the developer adds the code required to monitor everything the user does with the application. The administrator is in the middle because most organizations make the administrator responsible for monitoring the usage logs that the application creates. You have little wiggle room when it comes to being the enforcement arm of Big Brother — monitoring the application is required from many perspectives, not the least of which are the government laws that require such monitoring.

Even with the requirement to perform monitoring, overly obvious monitoring or monitoring that somehow affects the user's ability to accomplish useful work is counterproductive. The monitoring process should occur in the background and not impede the user in any way. In most cases, logs should provide the administrator with indicators that activity is suspicious, but the administrators should also realize that an application can't provide complete monitoring. Administrators need to review the log for activities that appear legitimate, but result in actions that aren't.

No matter how hard you work, some user-related problems will always exist. The best way to keep a secret is not to tell anyone. Users will give out your secrets when they are properly motivated. In addition, social engineering attacks have no defense. Consequently, some user security risks defy easy fixes and you must perform a certain amount of monitoring to detect when they occur.

How Big Is Big Brother?

In general, it's hard for developers or administrators to spend too much time tracking the activities of every user on the network. Given a substantial base of users, some users are likely doing something they shouldn't do and they may not get caught, because the developers and administrators are too busy performing other tasks. However, both administrators and developers can make things easier for themselves by looking for specific patterns.

One of the things to consider is that the machine a user has for work shouldn't contain any private or personal data. Consequently, you can perform automatic monitoring for applications or data that don't appear to have any organizational use. Removing these extraneous bits of data will make the job of scanning the hard drive for potential problems significantly easier. Of course, it won't make you a favorite with users who think they own the machines they use, so you need management support for this activity.

You can also look for differences in usage patterns. A user who suddenly starts coming into work early may simply have a need to pick up a child at day care. However, this user may also be trying to hide illegal activities from view. You need to verify which category the user's activities fall into as part of your monitoring.

Sometimes changes in system condition are also indicators of something gone wrong from a security perspective. Look for data files that the user can't account for as part of the application, even when the user's machine is otherwise clean. In this case, the user may sincerely not know anything about that file, but an intruder using this machine as an access point to your network will know all about it. Monitor the system for processes that don't belong. Often, outsiders will leave these little tidbits simply because they can't hide them.

Yes, you need to be intrusive. It's part of your job to add code to the application to look for unusual patterns as well. For example, you could add a bit of code to look for extraneous data files in the application folders. Sometimes you have to think as someone with evil intent thinks in order to ferret out the security problems on your system. Big Brother has to be very big indeed in today's computing environment.

Breaking into Your Application

You've probably seen reports from security experts describing ways they have broken into popular software. In fact, there are whole conferences where the topic of discussion is techniques for breaking into software. People who attend these events swap exploits with the same abandon as someone else might trade baseball cards. The exploits created by these people often make the front page of the trade press, and nasty individuals who break into systems follow the discussions with glee. It's quite possible that no one would discover these methods of breaking into systems if it weren't for these experts. The point is that if you aren't diligent in looking for points of entry into your application, someone else will find them.

Your application may see only internal use within your organization, and you may therefore feel that your application is secure. Unfortunately, insiders break into applications quite often and steal everything that isn't tied down. They'll move on to another organization after the break-in and potentially sell the information they stole to your competitor. At the very least, they'll use it to advance their own careers at the expense of your organization. Don't think that your application is safe — it isn't. That's why the suggestions in the sections that follow are so important. As you develop your application, you need to look for ways that someone can gain unauthorized access and to look for ways to seal the holes. (As always, assume that someone will find something you missed and be sure to perform the appropriate monitoring.)

Don't assume that any level of security will provide complete protection. Your application relies on an operating system that may have security holes that someone can use to attack your application. Likewise, some security-related software, such as firewalls, has holes that outsiders will exploit as well. The .NET Framework, on which your application relies, has security holes. The application may rely on a third-party library, which could also have security holes. In fact, the list of potential security holes you can't control is long and somewhat depressing. You must account for these uncontrolled security holes through monitoring and by applying patches the moment they become available.

Testing application security boundaries, literally breaking into your application, is an important part of the development process. You should try to break into the application as a whole, but breaking into individual modules is also important. Often, the act of breaking into a module illustrates security flaws you may not have considered from an application perspective. In fact, security experts often review individual methods to locate weaknesses — seldom do they look at an application as a whole. The following sections provide techniques you can use to break into your applications for security testing purposes.

Relying on Internal Testers

Before you do anything else, tell your testers to break into the application. Don't tell them how to break into the application, simply that they should perform the task. Your testers may amaze you with their creativity. You may be tired of hearing it, but users view applications differently than you do. They see things you can't see because of your training and experience. Asking a tester to break into your application makes sense, because the testers can see things from the much-needed outside-the-code perspective.

If you have any security professionals on your testing team, you should also ask them to check for any new exploits and use them against your application. Of course, you want to check these exploits at the following levels:

- Individual method
- Module
- Assembly
- Application

Security holes can occur at one level and not another, but all it takes is one unguarded hole for someone to get through. Thorough, multi-level testing requires time and effort, but the results are worth it because you can at least detect potential security problems. Even if you can't fix the security issues (or don't want to fix them for some reason), knowing about the security risk means you can monitor the application for the problem.

Make Your Security Tasks Easier

Take time to look for third-party products you can use to test for common exploits. Web-based applications have the most number of available tools, but they also have the greatest potential to present security problems. Don't discount the value of free tools such as SpeedGuide Security Scan Information (`http://www.speedguide.net/scan.php`). Some open source tools, such as those found at `http://www.opensourcetesting.org/security.php`, are also a good value for the .NET developer. (Of course, you'll want to check Chapters 29 and 30 for third-party tools as well.)

Make sure you check out security organizations, such as the Open Web Application Security Project (OWASP) (`http://www.owasp.org/index.php/Main_Page`). Many Web pages also provide good information. You can find some of the more interesting security testing techniques at `http://searchsoftwarequality.techtarget.com/generic/0,295582,sid92_gci1215847,00.html`.

Don't forget to use automation whenever possible. The testing software you use to check for errors in your code can also provide help in locating potential security issues. In some respects, code errors are directly related to security issues because many (not all) security holes occur due to a flaw in the construction of application code.

The more testing you can perform internally, the better. You can control the use of data generated by internal testing and keep the data from prying eyes. Don't give outsiders any more ammunition than they already have. Keep the security holes in your application within the organization. However, always assume that someone has blabbed. Fix security issues as quickly as you can and issue patches. Make sure every installation receives the required update to reduce your risk. Otherwise, you may find that someone is already inside your firewall, with hands on your data.

You'll encounter exceptions to every rule. If you create a shrink-wrap application and it has security holes, you must let your customers know about the security problem as soon as possible. Vendors have many different ways of viewing this issue. Most vendors will provide patches for critical security problems as fast as possible and announce both the security issue and the patch on the same day. In some cases, vendors will announce noncritical security problems sooner, along with potential workarounds for the problem. If you sell shrink-wrapped software, sooner is always better when it comes to telling the public about potential security issues and the fixes you provide. Whenever possible, make the update process automatic, much as antivirus software does today, to make things as easy as possible for the user and improve the chances that users will actually apply the patches needed by your application.

Using a Third Party

Third-party testing of your application can become necessary when that application has any kind of outside access. In fact, third-party testing is an exceptionally good idea when your application interacts extensively with the Internet. Third parties, normally consultants with specialized skills, can help you locate problems that internal testers lack the skills to find. In addition, these security professionals often know all the latest exploits, so they can help you make your code secure against the latest threats. In some respects, the services that third parties can provide will inoculate your application against the latest viruses. Of course, even third parties lack the crystal ball required to check against future viruses.

You have many choices when it comes to third-party verification. Given what you're asking the third party to do, using someone reputable is a necessity. For example, VeriSign is a well-known company that happens to provide application security services (`http://www.verisign.com/products/applicationsecurity/consulting.html`). If you choose someone less well known — at least by you — look for indicators that the company is legitimate and that you can trust it to do a good job. For example, FishNet Security (`http://www.fishnetsecurity.com/Services/Assessment+/Application+Security/default.aspx`) works with both Microsoft and OWASP to provide security services. This company also has connections with the government.

Not everyone has need of a high-powered consultant to check security, so you might look for someone who is less expensive, but still provides good quality. Although certifications don't guarantee good quality or success in finding errors, two certifications can help:

- Certified Information Systems Security Professional (CISSP) (read more about this certification at `https://www.isc2.org/cgi-bin/index.cgi` and `http://certification.about.com/od/certifications/p/cissp.htm`)
- Certified Information Systems Auditor (CISA) (read more about this certification at `http://www.isaca.org/Template.cfm?Section=CISA_Certification`)

Before you allow security professionals to check your application, make sure they actually have any certifications they say they do and that they're in good standing with the certifying organization. It's also important to check their references and do your homework on what they should check in your application. Take time to interview potential security professionals before you let them look at your application. If you don't feel comfortable with the individual, look for someone else.

Checking for the Impossible, Too

A problem that occurs all too often is that someone will think of a particular threat and then not test it because it seems impossible. No one could possibly use the exploit to attack the system. The very idea of using a particular exploit is so remote that there isn't any need to consider it. Unfortunately, the impossible exploits have a tendency to become possible, so you need to check them, too. Anyone who works with applications long enough will eventually have a story about a user who did something so terribly stupid that it actually worked and caused the system to crash. Never assume that the chance of something occurring is so remote that it won't happen — if it can happen, then it can happen to you.

Checking the impossible often involves thinking outside the box. Of course, creative people who think outside the box may not even realize the box exists, so telling them about it is fruitless. Consequently, the best course of action is simply to let people try anything that comes to mind. If someone asks whether to try something, tell this person to go ahead and do it, no matter how brainless the act may seem at the time. Developers have learned all kinds of interesting lessons from people who haven't a clue as to what they're doing.

According to someone who shall go nameless, a particular application developer thought to create application security as a separate process. The use of a separate process in a completely different module would keep the application safe because the security module could monitor everything from the outside. Code inside the application couldn't access the security module directly. The scheme seemed to work just fine until a user came along and used Task Manager to end the security module. Due to a flaw in the application, the user now had full access to every application feature. Who would think that ending the security process would cancel out security? The most interesting part of this story is that the user wasn't trying to break anything, he was merely looking for processes he could remove from his Windows installation to improve performance. It's an example of the need to check the impossible.

Tales of the Simple Security Breach

Most security breaches are simple. For example, someone told me about a business where security experts circumvented the key-card security with incredible ease. All the security experts did was place a piece of paper under the door. A sensor on the other side of the door automatically opened the door when someone approached. Because this sensor was a little too close to the bottom of the door, the security experts were able to circumvent the key-card security with ease.

In another case, a college had installed fancy lever latches on the doors to classrooms and faculty offices. The doors were normally locked from the outside to keep intruders at bay. A student figured out a way to pull down the inside latches from the outside using a coat hanger. The college ended up developing a new solution that wouldn't allow entry via coat hanger. Remember to look for simple breaches.

Understanding the Art of Interactions

Computer security requires an understanding of interactions. A failure in one area will almost certainly cause a problem somewhere else. Many exploits rely on interactions that someone didn't anticipate. In fact, some exploits actually use a security hole in one application to provide an avenue for attack in another application. Consequently, you can't consider the security of your application without considering the environment in which that application runs and the interactions of your application with other applications (no matter how feeble the connection may seem).

One of the best ways to keep interactions minimal is to maintain a simple application environment. The fewer processes running while the application is running, the less chance that an interaction will cause a security issue. This principle works the same as reducing failure points to improve reliability.

However, make sure you look at processes, which can include background applications, services, and the like. Even these hidden bits of software can cause security issues for your application.

Interactions also concern how the application works with the outside world. Flawed data in a database can cause problems. Likewise, an unsecured network connection can help someone get into your application. In some cases, even natural events can cause a security failure. The same natural events, such as lightning, that can cause the application to perform unreliably can also cause your application to have security holes that you never suspected.

Updating Your Security Profile

A *security profile* is a document that describes the security environment for an entity. In this case, the entity is your application. However, you could possibly create a security profile for the users in your organization or the cars in the parking lot. The concept is the same in all cases. The goal is to provide a document that describes security needs and requirements. An organization can use this documentation to determine a course of action to overcome the security issues.

Applications have specific needs when it comes to a security profile. The following list describes some of the security requirements that your profile should include (this isn't complete — every organization will also have special requirements that you should include):

- ❑ Critical security needs to address in the next patch
- ❑ Noncritical security needs that require workarounds or other documentation
- ❑ New exploits to check
- ❑ Potential security issues that aren't fixed
- ❑ Changing security conditions that could cause problems
- ❑ User training requirements that the organization needs to address
- ❑ Potential configuration concerns
- ❑ Interoperability or interaction concerns that could cause security failures
- ❑ Results of any audits or other professional inspections of your application

Creating a security profile isn't a one-time event. Every time something changes in the security environment, you need to update the document to reflect the change. Make sure you use a consistent method for making updates to the security profile so it doesn't look like someone's notes, rather than a document used to improve application security.

Some security profiles actually include a change list so that people reviewing the document can locate the changes quickly. For example, if you fix an application error that leads to a security flaw, you should remove its requirement from the list, but add the fix to the change list. The change list makes it possible for others to see improvements in the security environment. Of course, you have to list the bad along with the good. Make sure you add new threats or flaws to the list as needed and add them to the change list as well. It's a good idea to provide a short description of each change in the change list.

Managing the Monitoring Process

In order to create a good working environment and still perform the required monitoring tasks in your organization, you must manage the process carefully. For example, you must notify users that you plan to monitor them. In fact, you should have them sign a statement that says that they know you're monitoring them and that they agree to monitoring as part of the employment agreement. Otherwise, you'll run into problems at some point. Someone will say there was no warning and cause you grief when it comes time to take action after this person has sold your entire customer database to your competitors.

It's important to realize that most states have no legal requirements for you to tell the user anything about the monitoring you perform. You can perform the monitoring covertly and not say anything to anyone about it. However, the work environment can become quite tense once users find out that you do use monitoring — an open approach to monitoring is usually better than trying to keep things hidden. Make sure you do check for any local ordinances regarding monitoring. Laws change every day and you don't want to find yourself on the wrong side of a privacy concern. Monitoring may be a fact of life today, but there isn't any good reason to make it a subject of discontent.

On the other hand, you don't want to become overly oppressive. Make sure that users realize monitoring is in place and reemphasize monitoring organization-wide at specific intervals, but don't go out of your way to hit users over the head with the facts of monitoring every day. No one likes to work in an environment where no trust is felt. In fact, you should probably go out of your way to let users know that you trust them; it's simply a requirement that you provide monitoring, you should say, and then state the reasons. Blaming the monitoring on the government is always useful because then it takes the pressure completely off your organization. You could also try to blame customer concerns. However, when all else fails, you need to state specific organizational reasons for the monitoring.

In some cases, monitoring actually protects users and you should also make them aware of this potential benefit. More than a few users have received blame for something they didn't do. Monitoring records tend to exonerate users who haven't done anything wrong. These records can prove especially helpful when the user has to work with cranky customers all day. Some customers will stoop to any means of making the user's life difficult after a disagreement, and the monitoring records can foil these attempts. It takes only one incidence of helpful monitoring records to make most users agree that they really are a good idea. The point is, if you can find a positive way to promote the monitoring, the user may focus on the positive, rather than the negative.

Users should know how you plan to use the monitoring records you create. You don't have to provide precise details, but telling users that you have no intention of posting their records on the Internet for everyone to see can be helpful. You can put privacy concerns to rest by telling users that only the administrator reviews these records unless a potential illegal activity surfaces.

It's also helpful to tell users about the consequences of illegal activities. Ensuring that users know that you plan to prosecute data theft is a good deterrent to sloppy use of organization data. Open treatment of this sore subject will receive some respect from the users who have to live with monitoring. Of course, once you make policies known, you need to stick by them so that users don't get the idea that the policies are merely words that no one follows.

Encrypting and Decrypting Data

The trade press has carried many stories of lost laptops with data on them. Unfortunately, most of these stories end the same way — the data on the laptop are in plain text, making it possible for anyone who happens to find the laptop to steal the data. Of course, the first question is why the data are on the laptop where anyone can grab them in the first place. It seems as if users with the smallest potential reason usually get their way and have a copy of the organization's data plopped in the very place where it's easiest to steal.

Users and management will ignore the argument to keep the data on the company network where such information is easier to protect in many cases. Therefore, you have to find another way to overcome the problem of data being simply too easy to access. Windows provides individual data encryption, of course. However, when users not only leave the laptop in the airport but also leave it turned on and logged in, Windows security isn't going to be much help. That's why you should consider encrypting the data separately, as part of the application. At least this approach makes it a little less likely that anyone walking through the airport will see sensitive organization data.

When you use encryption, you should also incorporate features into the application — features users can't override — that keep the data out of other people's hands. For example, you can ensure that the application logs the user out after so many minutes of inactivity. In fact, if you can close the application so that outsiders will have a harder time figuring out which application created the data, so much the better. Anything you can do to make that data unusable to an outsider, while making the same data accessible to the user, is helpful. Encryption is an imperfect solution, but it's better than simply watching other people walk off with the data.

Backups are essential when you perform data encryption. Someone who is determined to obtain your data and is cheated by your data encryption may choose to delete the data. The principle at work, here, is that if the nasty person can't have the data, then no one can. Consequently, when using data encryption, you must consider that your data are still vulnerable to erasure and especially vulnerable to damage. If you don't make consistent and timely backups, then you may as well tell management now that the data will disappear someday — probably the day the organization needs that data most.

One of the reasons that you want a separate password and encryption setup for the application is that many users will forget their usernames and passwords — no matter how often they enter them. Some users do a data dump every time they go on vacation and can hardly remember where they work when they get back, much less their names and passwords. Making it possible for an administrator to recover the data and restoring the username and password so the user can get in is important.

Some applications now include a feature that makes it possible to delete data files from a remote location. You can build this feature as a service that starts automatically every time someone boots the machine. The service can check for an Internet connection. When it finds such a location, it validates the user's machine. If the user's machine is stolen, the validation fails and the service automatically erases the hard drive (using a technique that writes 1s and 0s to the hard drive). You can discover how to write a Windows service using C++ at `http://www.devsource.com/c/a/Using-VS/Writing-a-Managed-Windows-Service-with-Visual-C/` — the process for working with C# is similar.

Anyone asking you about data encryption for laptops and even desktop machines should receive an emphatic *yes* because the consequences of not encrypting the data are dire. It's not just company secrets that are lost, but people's identities as well. However, the biggest loss that occurs with lost data is customer confidence. The money that lost confidence costs is incalculable because the word of mouth factor makes the effects far worse than anyone can imagine.

Using encryption (and therefore, decryption) isn't free. When working with an underpowered system, the speed consequences are quite noticeable. If you add encryption after an application is already in production, users will very likely notice and complain about the speed loss. The best policy when it comes to encryption is to assume you always need it and add it during the design phase, when no one will notice the speed decrease.

Making Your Application Reliable and Secure

This chapter has provided some insights on real-world security. If you take nothing else away from this chapter, always remember that security depends on vigilance and flexibility. Your fixed fortifications will help, but they're a small part of an overall strategy of keeping the bad person at bay. If nothing else, make it possible that when someone does steal your data they get nothing from this act. Data encryption is the one reality that you shouldn't discount. Any unauthorized access will normally mean accessing the data outside your application.

It's time to consider the real-world security requirements for your organization. Of course, you'll want to use development techniques that erect walls high enough to keep honest people honest. In addition, you'll want to keep your data safe by using encryption techniques that assume someone will break through your defenses. However, you need to perform two other important tasks. First, you must create a standard for managing and monitoring applications in such a way that users have the access they require, but you also make it easier to see unauthorized access. Second, it's essential to set time aside to monitor new threats and determine how they affect your application. When you find a new threat that you can't easily fix through an operating system or other patch, or circumvent through new security settings such as changing your firewall setup, you need to add application code to handle the new threat.

This part of the book has spent time with essentials, especially the importance of the performance triangle. Of course, applications are more than basics — they usually require some type of specialized programming to accomplish some goals. The next part of the book describes some special techniques you can try when creating your applications. You may not need these techniques with every application, but it's nice to know the techniques are available. Chapter 22 begins with one of the most commonly used special techniques — XML serialization.

Part IV: Special Coding Methodologies

22

Serializing XML

XML databases have become more popular for storing small amounts of data, hierarchically formatted data, or larger amounts of simple data. The data appear in your application as a series of hierarchical objects, objects within objects, that end with an `XMLDocument` object holding everything together. Of course, storing a host of objects on your hard drive isn't going to work. You need some way to place those documents on the hard drive so that they conform to standard storage methods and some way to retrieve them so that you can rebuild the object structure as needed. The storage process is *serialization*, while loading the document from disk relies on *deserialization*. The resulting disk on file is in XML format.

Fortunately, Visual Studio has a considerable number of storage technologies built into it. Often you can read and write XML data without worrying too much about the underlying structure because the XML file is truly data. However, you may want to store the data as structured settings or configuration information. Perhaps you want to provide custom handling of the data so that the application can interact with this data in a specific way. When you want to interact with XML in these specialized ways, you must create a customized class to perform the task. The class tells how to serialize and deserialize the data so your application can interact with them properly.

This chapter helps you understand the specialized techniques you can use to create applications that interact with XML in certain ways. Using XML files has significant advantages over other techniques you might have tried in the past. For example, when your application relies on XML files instead of using the registry, you can move the application to a different machine with significant ease. In addition, XML files are easier to fix than the registry. Because XML files don't use a customized storage technique, you can also view them from other applications, making data reuse extremely easy as well.

Many developers are viewing XML storage technology as a fix for many of the ills that accompany other techniques. Certainly, XML data storage is more straightforward than using the binary storage techniques employed by earlier computer applications. However, XML files aren't perfect — they come with problems of their own. One of the bigger issues is that XML files are huge compared to their binary counterparts. Everything appears in human-readable form, making the file two or three times as big in most cases. Of course, storage is cheap today, so the file size issue may not be much of a concern for your organization. A second concern is that the human-readable format of the data files also creates a security problem, since anyone can read the data — you don't even need a special application to do it. Solving this issue is considerably harder and you'll likely have to provide a creative application-specific solution.

The code listings in this chapter don't provide a full description of the sample application. To obtain a complete code listing for this sample, download the sample code from the publisher's Web site at `http://www.wrox.com/WileyCDA/WroxTitle/C-Design-and-Development-Expert-One-on-One.productCd-0470415967.html`.

Using XML as a Storage Methodology

You have many options for storing data on your system. In fact, one of the benefits of using computers is that they offer so many different ways to accomplish the same task. Only the human component of the computer places any limitations on what computers can do. Storage methods in the past have included binary files, standardized storage such as the registry, databases, plaintext files, and many other storage forms. XML is a relative newcomer to computer data storage, but it has many benefits that you should consider as part of your application design and development process:

- Structured storage akin to databases
- Plaintext format so you can view the file using just about any utility
- Easy to fix with a plaintext editor
- Extremely flexible — you define the storage structure
- Hierarchical structure so the records need not follow the relational model

The following sections view XML as a storage methodology. You'll see how XML can benefit you as a developer, your application, the administrator, and the end user.

Implementing an XCopy Application

As described in the "Using the XCopy Deployment" section of Chapter 16, an XCopy deployment is one in which the entire application appears within a single folder. The folder may have subfolders (hence the need for XCopy to copy or move the application from one location to another), but the application is essentially self-contained. Being self-contained means that the application settings also appear in the application folder — moving the application also moves the settings. However, the XCopy application has only the application settings in the folder, not the user settings.

When creating an XCopy application, you may actually create several XML serialization classes to handle data at specific levels. Only the application settings appear in the folder; the other files can appear in other locations on the system. The reason that these files appear in other places is that you must keep these settings separate from each other. User-specific settings that affect one user shouldn't affect every other user on the machine. Consequently, you often have to design the application such that it considers these levels of settings:

- **Organizational (optional):** Includes anything that affects the organization as a whole, such as the implementation of policies or the location of networked drives.

- **Machine (optional):** Affects machine-level configuration, such as the use of special drivers or the location of machine-level resources. These settings could also include Windows-specific features for a particular machine, such as networked drives. Machine-level settings affect the local machine and are tied to a specific machine. These settings move with the machine, not with the application.
- **Application (often included):** Modifies application-level behavior, such as the use of local application settings or data. Application settings affect everyone who uses the application, rather than just one user. If settings affect every application on the system, rather than the local application, you may consider implementing them as organizational-level settings to make changes easier (you have to look in only one place); however, using the application level for these settings also works.
- **Administrative (rare):** Defines administrator-level settings for the local machine. These settings differ from user-level settings in that the user only relies on them while acting as an administrator. In addition, every administrator uses the same settings. As with machine settings, administrator settings normally affect a single machine and move with that machine, rather than with the application.
- **User (normally included):** Configures the user's choices for the application. For example, if the user wants to use a particular color scheme, that choice would appear in this file. Each user has different settings to reflect that user's needs or wants. User-level settings move with the user, not with the application.

Each of these levels represents a change in scope. Every entry on this list provides a different way of viewing the data and the data are used in different ways. A user's data have no place in the application folder. Not only don't you want to move that data with the application but leaving the user's settings in plain view may also represent a security breach or privacy concern. The "Choosing a Data Location" section of the chapter describes how these files affect storage location as well.

At this point, you may be yelling, "Foul! It's obvious from the previous paragraph that the application isn't self-contained after all." A common point of confusion for developers is that when you create an XCopy application, the application is self-contained, but not necessarily all the application settings. In this case, the application and the application-level settings appear in a single folder. However, the user settings appear with the other user data, the machine settings appear with the other machine settings, and so on. The issue is one of organization. Many current application issues stem from a lack of organization — moving the application, the user, or the machine to a different location is too hard because the data used to configure the entities appear in a central location such as the registry and are too difficult to extract from the storage container. Using XML serialization helps free you from this concern and makes it considerably easier to move different application elements as needed without affecting any other application element.

Viewing the Sample XML Data

Some developers probably avoid using XML serialization because the very name of the technology sounds complex. However, the data need not be complex to let you perform a lot of work. In fact, as shown in Figure 22-1, the data are often quite simple. In this case, the sample application (described as the chapter progresses) stores both data and settings for individual users in the user's folder. A data folder for any other level of storage can follow a similar pattern — keep the data simple to make any needed repairs equally simple. Of course, you'll want to document the file as part of the design process so that everyone knows what it contains.

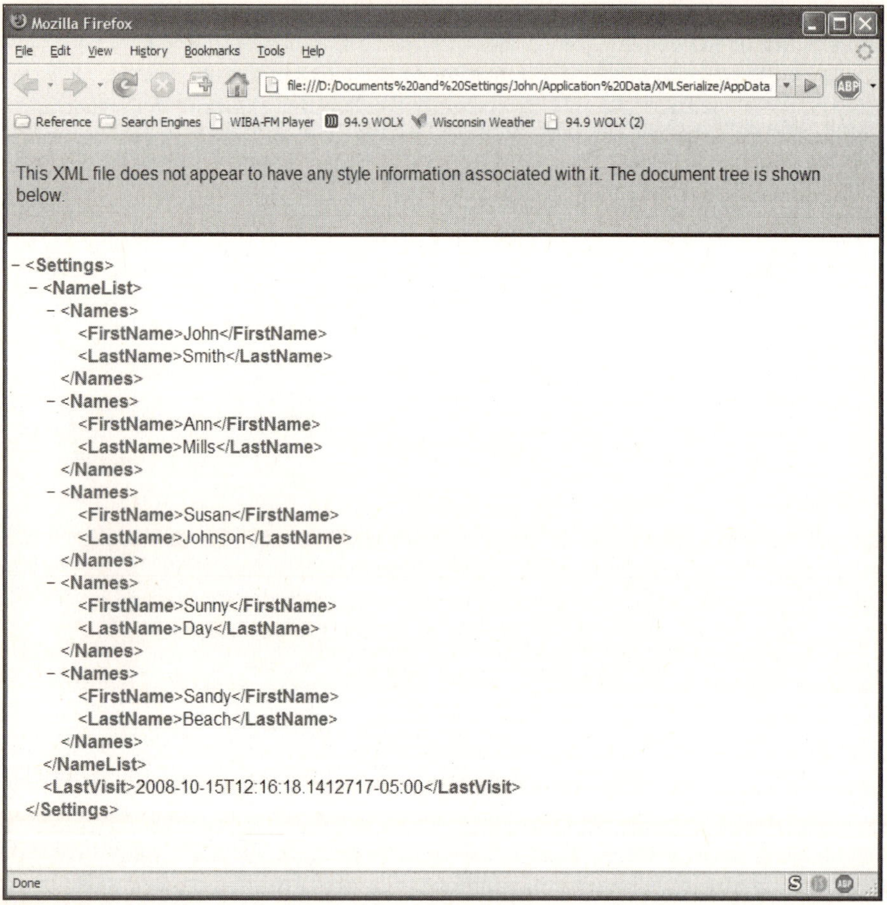

Figure 22-1: The sample application uses a simple XML file to store both data and settings.

It's helpful to use different applications for viewing and repairing XML data. You can view XML data using any browser, which means that if you simply want to see what the user is storing, you can do so without installing anything special. A browser provides a safe viewing environment. However, you should probably use a special product such as Microsoft's free XML Notepad 2007 (`http://www.microsoft.com/downloads/details.aspx?familyid=72d6aa49-787d-4118-ba5f-4f30fe913628`*) or Altova's XML Spy (*`http://www.altova.com/`*) to edit the data. The Altova product isn't free, but you can download a free trial copy to determine whether you like it. (See the "Editing XML Files Using XML Notepad 2007" section of Chapter 29 for a description of XML Notepad 2007.) Although you can edit any XML file using Notepad in an emergency, relying on a professional XML editor can help reduce the potential for edit-induced errors, such as a misplaced angle bracket. To reduce the potential for errors further, you should create an XML Schema Definition (XSD) file for the file and use it as you edit to prevent mistakes. You can learn more about using XSD at* `http://www.w3schools.com/Schema/default.asp`*.*

In this case, the XML file contains two pieces of data. The first, `<NameList>`, is an example of data entries. This list appears in the Name List field of the sample application as shown in Figure 22-2. The `<NameList>` element contains `<Names>` child elements — each of which describes one name entry. The `<Names>` elements, in turn, contain `<FirstName>` and `<LastName>` child elements that describe each `<Names>` entry. The `<LastVisit>` element shows an example of a property setting for the application. It simply tells the application the last time that the user started the application and used it. This information appears in the Last Visit Date field of the sample application. Of course, you can make properties mean anything, and a file can have as many properties as you need to make the application functional.

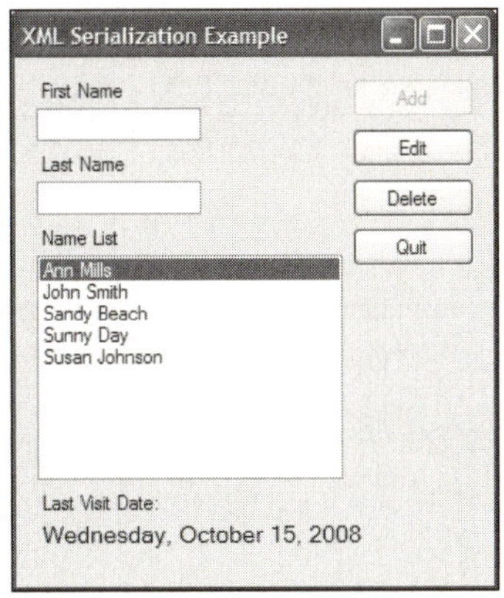

Figure 22-2: The sample application uses XML serialization to store both application data and settings.

The reason the sample application stores the data at the user level, rather than the application level, is that each user will have a different last visit date and a different set of names to store. In some cases, you might store data at the application or organizational levels, depending on how the application uses the data and whether others in the organization need to access that data. From a user perspective, storing the data this way means that it's relatively easy to move the data from one location to another — everything appears in one location. In fact, you could easily add an application feature to move data to another location for the user.

Using XML Data in Reports

The moment you create an XML file containing data, you have a potential data source for reports based on that data. In fact, it often helps to put the storage class you create (see the "Creating the XML Storage Class" section of this chapter for details) into a library so that you can use it with multiple projects. The storage class is your key to easy data manipulation, and the data file presents the information you want to see in the report. Using the XML serialization approach means that you spend considerably less time developing report applications because you already have the means to extract the necessary data — all you really have to do is display them in some way (whether on paper or on screen is up to you).

An important consideration when working with XML data in reports is that you often need to create a specific visualization for the user. For example, if your data record all the orders made by a particular customer, it may not include a totals field for each order because most theories of data storage say not to store calculated data. Not storing calculated data when using the XML serialization technique is even more important because the XML files tend to become large. Consequently, when working with reports, you may need to trade application speed for storage size and efficiency.

Creating the XML Storage Class

The XML storage class is the centerpiece of XML serialization. If you don't get this part of the application right, working with the XML data is going to be difficult. The storage class provides an interface between your application and the data on disk. In some respects, the storage class is a kind of a data provider. However, this data provider is smart in that it usually knows where to find the data you need, so all you really need to consider are the data themselves — what you plan to do with them, how you plan to present them.

The XML storage class can appear complicated at first, but if you break it down into pieces, creating one becomes considerably easier. The following sections describe the design elements of an XML storage class. You can use this pattern to create just about any XML storage class you'll ever need.

Defining the XML Data Elements

An XML storage class provides the code needed to manipulate the XML data file. The class requires three elements:

- Properties to describe the data elements
- A method to load the data
- A method to save the data

Listing 22-1 shows a skeleton of the code used to create the XML storage class for the sample application. Don't worry about the details for right now, the listing shows basic design concepts that you need to implement this technology.

Listing 22-1: A class structure for storing data in XML format

```
public class Settings
{
   // A list of names stored by the program.
   public Names[] NameList{get;set;}

   // The last date the user used the program.
   public DateTime LastVisit{get;set;}

   public static Settings LoadSettings()
   {
      ... Code Used to Load Settings ...
   }

   public static void SaveSettings(Settings Current)
   {
      ... Code Used to Save Settings ...
   }
}
```

Every entry in the XML file shown in Figure 22-1 appears as part of this class. The `<NameList>` element in Figure 22-1 is the `NameList` property in this listing. Likewise, the `<LastVisit>` element is the `LastVisit` property. The names you choose for your properties affect the application output, so you need to choose property names carefully. Use property names that work in both the data file and within the application.

Notice that `NameList` uses a custom data type, `Names[]`. The XML file reflects this requirement using the `<Names>` child elements. The "Creating the Customized Data Description" section of the chapter provides details on this custom type. The use of an array means that the XML file can have multiple copies of `<Names>`. Meanwhile, `LastVisit` relies on the `DateTime` data type, so you don't have to do anything special to store it. However, some developers miss one potential gotcha of working with data types that appear in the .NET Framework or as part of a third-party library. When you view the documentation for the `DateTime` data type (see `http://msdn.microsoft.com/en-us/library/system.datetime.aspx`), it shows this data type has the `Serializable` attribute. If you don't see the `Serializable` attribute, you can't use the data type for XML serialization — at least not without help.

The `LoadSettings()` and `SaveSettings()` methods aren't all that special. The `LoadSettings()` method loads the data and passes them to the caller as a `Settings` object. Notice that the data type matches the class name for your XML storage class. Likewise, the `SaveSettings()` method stores the data. The caller must provide the data as a `Settings` object — again, the name matches the XML storage class name. The "Obtaining the XML Data from Disk" section of the chapter describes the `LoadSettings()` method in detail, while the "Implementing a Save Routine" section of the chapter describes the `SaveSettings()` method in detail.

Creating the Customized Data Description

When you create custom data types for the XML storage class, you need to add one important piece of code — the `Serializable` attribute shown in Listing 22-2. If you leave out this attribute, the compiler will still compile the application for you. However, when you attempt to use the class to manipulate data for XML serialization, you'll see an error. You can discover more about this requirement at `http://msdn.microsoft.com/en-us/library/system.serializableattribute.aspx`.

Listing 22-2: Defining the data elements

```
[Serializable()]
public class Names
{
   public String FirstName{get;set;}
   public String LastName{get;set;}

   // The default constructor.
   public Names()
   {
   }

   // A constructor that accepts inputs.
   public Names (String NewFirstName, String NewLastName)
   {
      FirstName = NewFirstName;
      LastName = NewLastName;
   }
}
```

The Names class appears as the <Names> element in the XML file shown in Figure 22-1. This class contains two properties, FirstName and LastName, which receive entries in the XML file (the <FirstName> and <LastName> elements).

The code shown in Listing 22-2 is simple. All it contains are properties for each of the data values. In both cases, the properties use the String data type. If the application required another custom data type, you would define another class to describe it. This class would appear in the XML file with the appropriate child elements, just as the <Names> element appeared with the <FirstName> and <LastName> child elements. Using classes in this way, you can create any number of levels of data desired.

A final consideration is the kind of constructors that you need. In most cases, you need to define two constructors. The first constructor provides the default implementation and doesn't accept any arguments. You can assign default values to each of the properties; however, in many cases it isn't necessary to do so. The second constructor accepts values for each of the properties the class supports. Depending on how your class works, you probably won't want to create constructors that accept values for only some of the properties, because it leaves the data type in an uncertain state. It's better to force the developer to provide specific values for each of the parameters, even if the value is null.

Designing Bulletproof Properties

The sample application uses extremely simple property definitions for clarity. In a real-world application, you need to assume that some can (and probably will) provide inaccurate or non-useful data at every level of the XML file input. Consequently, you need to provide properties that check every datum that the XML file accepts. In most cases, you want to check for the following data properties in every property:

- Data type
- Data length
- Data content (relying on a RegEx expression whenever possible)
- Allowable entries (for data that provide specific values)

Theoretically, making these checks will prevent someone from using the property incorrectly. When a data input error does occur, make sure you don't change the data value — the default response should make no change at all, rather than use a default value. If you make a change, the change could be precisely what the caller wants in order to cause the application to behave in an unanticipated manner.

In addition, you'll probably throw more exceptions back to the caller. Attempting to handle all the exceptions locally is a wonderful idea from a reliability perspective, but it prevents the caller from knowing that something has gone wrong. This is one situation where an exception actually provides a level of communication with the person using your XML storage class. Failure to communicate will cause confusion on the part of the developer. Of course, this person won't be quite as thrilled about using your XML storage class the next time.

Exceptions describe special conditions, something not expected. Chapter 14 describes some ways of handling the errors described by exceptions. You can always handle an error locally, and then throw a custom exception that helps the caller understand the problem with his or her call. Whether you use a custom exception depends on the complexity of the error and whether any of the standard exceptions will fulfill the requirement. You can also choose to log errors as needed to understand the issues that developers using the XML storage class encounter. These log entries can help you create better classes in the future and could also make it possible for your class to handle a few additional errors locally.

Saving Data in XML Format

After you finish creating the XML storage class, you'll want to test it out, which means creating code to save the file to disk. The following sections describe issues you should consider before you build the save method and then show how to build such a routine for the sample application. Of course, the principles also work fine for your application.

> **Validating Your Data**
>
> It's essential that you verify the data the application writes to the hard drive under a number of conditions, including conditions that could incur data loss. If your data is simple enough, you can view it to look for potential problems using the technique described in the "Viewing the Sample XML Data" section of the chapter. However, sometimes you'll need to use automation to check the data content and look for potential problems. The point is that you need to validate the data or you can't be sure that the application will read them properly the next time it needs the data.
>
> When you validate your data, check first for the essentials. For example, XML files have specific requirements to ensure they are well formed. In addition, you should verify the XML file against your XSD file — the specification that defines the structural requirements for the XML file. Don't forget to review the output data for content problems. For example, you may see damaged data or truncated entries. In many cases, this final check requires the human touch because a human viewer can quickly see issues the computer can't easily see.

Choosing a Data Location

One of the most important concerns for the save routine is thinking about where you want to save the data. Choosing the wrong location can cause significant problems later. Here are some suggestions for various data storage techniques you may require (these settings rely on the data storage scenarios described in the "Implementing an XCopy Application" section of this chapter):

- **Organization:** Stores organizational settings on a network drive because they affect the organization as a whole. In addition, only a network administrator has permission to write to these files — a user can only read the settings as part of loading the application.
- **Machine:** Normally placed in the `\Windows\System32` folder where they can affect the machine as a whole. The local administrator can change these settings, but not every user who works with the machine.
- **Application:** Always appears within the application folder so that you can implement XCopy application solutions.

- **Administrative:** Normally appears in the local Administrator's folder or on a network folder depending on how the settings affect the application. Place administrator-specific application settings that affect the local system in the Administrator's folder on the local machine.
- **User:** Typically appears in the user's personal folder (but not necessarily in My Documents). Use the My Documents folder when you want the user to interact with the settings in some way (such as double-clicking them to start the application). Otherwise, hide the settings from view in the user's Application Data folder within a custom subfolder (see Listing 22-3 for details).

Implementing a Save Routine

The save routine performs a number of important tasks. As a minimum, your save routine should perform the following steps:

1. Locate the data path used to store the data.
2. Determine whether the data directory already exists — if not, create it.
3. Create the XML serializer used to serialize the data. You must tell the XML serializer what kind of data to write.
4. Create a `StreamWriter` object to perform the actual task of writing the data. This object contains the path to the data file and the data filename.
5. Serialize the data using the `XmlSerializer` object with the `StreamWriter` object.
6. Flush the data to disk from the Windows cache and then close the file.

Listing 22-3 shows the `SaveSettings()` method. This method accepts a `Settings` object, which contains the data to save, as input.

Listing 22-3: Saving the settings to disk

```
public static void SaveSettings(Settings Current)
{
   // Create a user-specific settings string.
   String UserPath =
      Environment.GetFolderPath(
         Environment.SpecialFolder.ApplicationData) +
      @"\XMLSerialize";

   // Determine whether the directory exists.
   if (!Directory.Exists(UserPath))
      Directory.CreateDirectory(UserPath);

   // Define an XML serializer.
   XmlSerializer DataWrite =
      new XmlSerializer(typeof(Settings));

   // Create a stream writer to output the data.
   StreamWriter Output =
      new StreamWriter(UserPath + @"\AppData.CONFIG");
```

```
        // Save the settings.
        DataWrite.Serialize(Output, Current);

        // Flush and close the output file.
        Output.Flush();
        Output.Close();
    }
```

As you can see, the example code implements all the requirements for saving the data. In this case, the method saves the data to the user's Application Data folder as defined by the `Environment.SpecialFolder.ApplicationData` enumeration in the `\XMLSerialize` folder (a custom folder for this application). The `Environment.GetFolderPath()` method is the best way to obtain the location of a special Windows folder on any machine. You can see a complete list of the folders you can access using the `Environment.SpecialFolder.ApplicationData` enumeration at `http://msdn.microsoft.com/en-us/library/system.environment.specialfolder.aspx`.

It's important to both flush and close the data file when you exit the routine. Otherwise, you can experience odd exceptions, none of which tells you about the actual problems. For example, if you forget to flush the file (empty the Windows cache) using the `Flush()` method, you can see the exception shown in Figure 22-3. If you forget to use the `Close()` method, you'll almost certainly see the exception. The exception seems to indicate that another application has the file open. However, the actual problem is that your application didn't close the file after you wrote to it the last time, so your application has the file open. The odd thing is that CLR will eventually close the file for you as part of disposing of the `StreamWriter` object — so you won't see the error consistently.

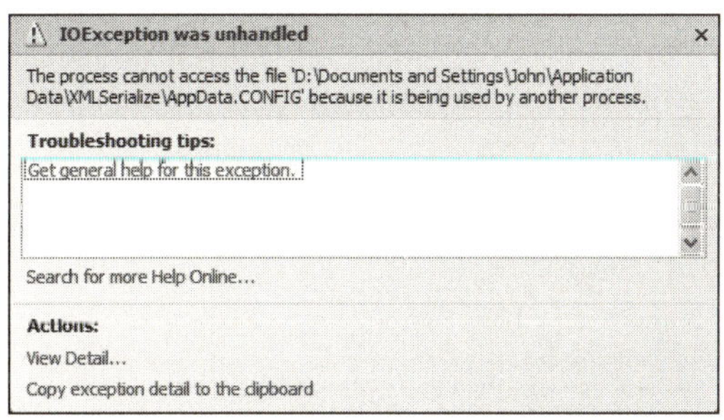

Figure 22-3: Examine errors carefully because they don't always point to the real cause of a problem.

You'll use the `SaveSettings()` method to save changes to the data whenever necessary. In most cases, it's a good idea to save the data whenever you make a change to ensure that the application doesn't lose anything. As a minimum, you'll add the `SaveSettings()` method to the `FormClosing` event handler as shown in the following code:

```
    private void frmMain_FormClosing(object sender, FormClosingEventArgs e)
    {
        // Save the date of the last visit.
        CurrentSettings.LastVisit = DateTime.Now;
        Settings.SaveSettings(CurrentSettings);
    }
```

The `frmMain_FormClosing()` method begins by saving the current date and time to the `CurrentSettings.LastVisit` property. The `CurrentSettings` object is a global variable that methods use whenever they need to access the application data or settings. The "Obtaining the XML Data from Disk" section of the chapter describes how the application creates this object. After the method updates the date, it calls `Settings.SaveSettings()`, which is a static method (so you don't need an object to access it), to save the data.

Loading Data in XML Format

Saving the data for your application is the first part of a two-part task. The next time you start the application, you need to load the XML data from disk. In addition, the code must interpret these data and put them into a form the application can understand. Deserializing the data isn't any more complex that serializing it. Both processes begin with a good XML storage class definition. The following sections describe the deserialization process in detail.

Obtaining the XML Data from Disk

At some point, you'll have an XML data source on disk. In order to use this XML data source in your application, you must load the file. Visual Studio provides a number of methods for loading XML data. For example, you can simply use the `XMLDocument.Load()` method to perform the task. However, when you use these techniques, you must work with the XML data as you would any other XML document. Because you serialized the data and have an XML storage class to use, you have a better option as shown in Listing 22-4.

Listing 22-4: Loading the settings from disk

```
public static Settings LoadSettings()
{
   // Create a user-specific settings string.
   String UserPath =
      Environment.GetFolderPath(
         Environment.SpecialFolder.ApplicationData) +
      @"\XMLSerialize";

   // Determine whether the application settings exist.
   if (!File.Exists(UserPath + @"\AppData.CONFIG"))
      return null;

   // Define an XML serializer.
   XmlSerializer DataRead =
      new XmlSerializer(typeof(Settings));

   // Create a stream writer to read the data.
   StreamReader Input =
      new StreamReader(UserPath + @"\AppData.CONFIG");

   // Load the settings.
   Settings Current;
```

```
        Current = (Settings)DataRead.Deserialize(Input);
        Input.Close();

        // Return the current settings.
        return Current;
    }
```

In this case, the code begins by creating a user path. This part of the code is very much the same as the `SaveSettings()` method shown in Listing 22-3, so you could possibly place this code in another function to make updates easier.

Before it can do anything else, the code must determine whether the data file exists. When the file doesn't exist, the method returns a `null` value. The `null` return value is a signal to the caller that the data don't exist yet and that the caller will need to create them.

When the file does exist, the code creates an `XmlSerializer` to read the data. Notice that you must tell the `XmlSerializer` how to read the data by providing the data type using `typeof(Settings)`. The code creates a `StreamReader` next. The `StreamReader` provides the connection between the disk and the application. At this point, the code can read the data.

Notice that you must perform type conversion on the output of the `DataRead.Deserialize()` method because the method returns an `object`. Of course, you must provide `Input` as the data source on disk. When the data read is finished, the code calls `Input.Close()` to close the data source. You don't need to flush the data cache in this case because you haven't written any data to disk.

Normally, you'll read application configuration data during the application initialization. Listing 22-5 shows a typical scenario. Notice that you must call `InitializeComponent()` before you read the data to ensure that any required controls are ready for use.

Listing 22-5: Loading and interpreting the data file

```
    // Holds the current settings.
    Settings CurrentSettings;

    public frmMain()
    {
        InitializeComponent();

        // Load the settings when available.
        CurrentSettings = Settings.LoadSettings();

        // Initialize CurrentSettings when the settings
        // aren't available on disk.
        if (CurrentSettings == null)
            CurrentSettings = new Settings();
        else
        {
            // Retrieve the stored values.
```

Continued

Listing 22-5: Loading and interpreting the data file *(continued)*

```
            foreach (Names ThisName in CurrentSettings.NameList)
               lstNameList.Items.Add(
                  ThisName.FirstName + " " + ThisName.LastName);

            // Show the date of the last visit.
            lblLastVisit.Text = CurrentSettings.LastVisit.ToLongDateString();
         }
      }
```

The code begins by creating a global variable, `CurrentSettings`, to hold the XML data stored on disk. Next, the code calls `Settings.LoadSettings()`, a static method call, to load the data from disk. If the return value is `null`, meaning the application hasn't stored any data on disk yet, the code creates a new instance of `Settings`. Otherwise, the code acts on the data in `CurrentSettings` to fill `lstNameList` and set the last visit date in `lblLastVisit`.

Using XML Data to Modify the Environment

It's important to realize that application settings can cover a lot of ground. The example described in this chapter loads some user data and settings from the user's folder on the hard drive. However, you have many more options than data and settings. Many applications require a special environment to run. For example, the application may require the addition of path information to locate data on disk or set a particular environment variable. You can perform many of these kinds of environmental changes using the `System.Environment` class (see `http://msdn.microsoft.com/en-us/library/system.environment_members.aspx` for details).

In many cases, the .NET Framework doesn't provide direct access to the Windows environment, so you must rely on P/Invoke to perform the task (see Chapter 27 for details on using P/Invoke). The `SystemParametersInfo()` function is one of the key calls to use for needs of this sort. You can learn more about this extremely useful function at `http://msdn.microsoft.com/en-us/library/ms724947.aspx`. You can use this function to modify the following types of environmental options:

- Accessibility
- Desktop
- Icon
- Input
- Menu
- Power
- Screen saver
- UI effect
- Window

As you can see, you can interact with many Windows features using this single call. In order to use this function, you must add the following line of code to the beginning of your code:

```
using System.Runtime.InteropServices;
```

The `SystemParametersInfo()` function may look intimidating at first, but it really isn't. Here's how the method definition looks:

```
[DllImport("User32.DLL", SetLastError=true)]
public static Boolean SystemParametersInfo(
   UInt32 uiAction,
   UInt32 uiParam,
   StringBuilder pvParam,
   UInt32 fWinIni);
```

When using this method, `uiAction` contains a constant value that defines the action to perform. The `uiParam` contains the size of the buffer used to hold data for the call. You use `uiParam` with `pvParam`, which contains the actual data you want to pass, such as the name of a file. The `fWinIni` argument contains the flags for performing the task, such as flags used to change wallpaper information. Finally, the return value is a Boolean indicating success or failure.

All the `uiAction` values come from a single header file, `WinUser.H`, which you can view at places such as `http://www.woodmann.com/fravia/sources/WINUSER.H`. Of course, if you have installed the C++ files on your system, you can simply load the file into Visual Studio and use it as you create your application. Here are some examples of `uiAction` values defined as constants:

```
// Defines actions for getting or setting the wallpaper.
const UInt32 SPI_SETDESKWALLPAPER = 0x14;
const UInt32 SPI_GETDESKWALLPAPER = 0x73;

// Update the user's information.
const UInt32 SPIF_UPDATEINIFILE = 0x1;

// Tell other applications about the change in status.
const UInt32 SPIF_SENDWININICHANGE = 0x2;
```

Notice that all the values appear as `UInt32` and you define them all as hexadecimal values, since that's what `WinUser.H` uses. Using hexadecimal values also makes it easier to perform certain tasks, such as creating flags because you see the data as the call will see them. Flags rely on bit positions, and decimal values make it difficult to work with bits.

Tread Softly in the User's Environment

You want to change the user's environment carefully. For the most part, users define their work environment carefully because they have to live in that environment. When you change the user's work environment, you can create conditions in which the user becomes less efficient — the user experiences an emotional reaction that can end in everything from depression to anger.

Unfortunately, environmental changes can have even more serious consequences. In some cases, a seemingly simple and innocuous change can cause significant problems. For example, changing the screen resolution on a system where someone uses low-vision software can make the computer unusable. Modifying the source capabilities or other functionality of the computer can prove equally troublesome, so change the environment with care.

Manipulating Serialized XML Data

You have some XML data you want to work with, a method for saving that data to disk, and a method for loading the data into the application each time it starts. At this point, you're ready to manipulate the data, which is the point of the sections that follow. In this case, the application modifies the user data in some way and presents those changes on screen.

Adding New Data

Before you can have a usable database, you need data to fill it. The data can come from any source. For example, you can choose to store environmental information or something as simple as the date. More than a few scientific applications retrieve data directly from sensors, and security systems use information from cameras or other sources. Applications often use Web services as a data source or even manipulate information already found in organizational data sources. Much of the data will come directly from the user, as is the case for the example application. Listing 22-6 shows the code used to add new data to the database for the sample application.

Listing 22-6: Creating a new data entry

```
private void btnAdd_Click(object sender, EventArgs e)
{
   // Add the first and last names to the list box.
   lstNameList.Items.Add(txtFirstName.Text + " " + txtLastName.Text);

   // Add the name to the settings.
   if (CurrentSettings.NameList == null)
   {
      // Create a new Names array.
      Names[] NewList = new Names[1];

      // Initialize the values.
      NewList[0] = new Names(txtFirstName.Text, txtLastName.Text);

      // Add the results to the current settings.
      CurrentSettings.NameList = NewList;
   }
   else
   {
      // Create a new list to hold the name.
      List<Names> NewList = CurrentSettings.NameList.ToList<Names>();

      // Add the new entry.
      NewList.Add(new Names(txtFirstName.Text, txtLastName.Text));

      // Add the results to the current settings.
      CurrentSettings.NameList = NewList.ToArray<Names>();
   }
```

```
        // Save the settings to disk.
        Settings.SaveSettings(CurrentSettings);

        // Remove the information from the text boxes.
        txtFirstName.Text = "";
        txtLastName.Text = "";
    }
```

As shown in the code, you must consider two cases when adding data to the XML data file. Either the data file already has entries, in which case you add a new entry to the list, or the data file is new, which means there aren't any existing entries.

The sample application uses a list box to display the list of names. The first task the code performs is to add the names using the same format as all the other names in the list. This is a friendly view for the data where the first name and last name appear separated by a space. Any applications you create will also need to provide a friendly view.

The next step is to determine how the application will add the data to `CurrentSettings`. If the user hasn't added any data in the past, the `CurrentSettings.NameList` property is `null`. In this case, the code creates a new `Names[]` array. Remember that `Names` is a custom data type created for this application. The example relies on the `Names` constructor that allows the first name and last name as input. It then adds the resulting array to the `CurrentSettings.NameList` property.

If the second case occurs, where the `CurrentSettings.NameList` property already has input, the code transforms the `CurrentSettings.NameList` property into a list using `CurrentSettings.NameList.ToList<Names>()`. It then simplifies the task of adding a name to the list using the `NewList.Add()` method. The code ends by converting the list to an array using `NewList.ToArray<Names>()` and adding the results to the `CurrentSettings.NameList` property.

No matter how the code adds data to the `CurrentSettings.NameList` property, it needs to save the data to disk using the `Settings.SaveSettings()` method. Any application you create should follow the same process — saving the data whenever there is a change. If your application experiences a catastrophic failure, the saving process will preserve most of the information intact.

Consider placing the save routine on a separate thread to improve performance for network drive saves. You may find that your application runs slowly if you have to save large data files over a network connection. Using a threaded application will make the apparent speed of the application greater. However, you're exchanging speed for reliability in this case. If the application fails before it completes the save, you could end up with a damaged data file. Consequently, you must weigh the risk against the need to provide acceptable speed.

Editing Existing Entries

In most cases, the second thing that happens to data the user adds to the XML data file is that it requires change. Perhaps the user made a mistake in data entry or the data have simply changed. Editing tasks become common as an application becomes older. Consequently, the second feature you normally add to your application is the ability to modify data as needed. Listing 22-7 shows the code used to perform this task in the example.

Listing 22-7: Changing a data entry

```
private void btnEdit_Click(object sender, EventArgs e)
{
   // Obtain the individual name values.
   String WholeName =
      (String)lstNameList.Items[lstNameList.SelectedIndex];
   String[] Values = WholeName.Split(' ');

   // Create the form and place the values in it.
   frmEdit ThisEdit = new frmEdit();
   ThisEdit.txtFirstName.Text = Values[0];
   ThisEdit.txtLastName.Text = Values[1];

   // Display the form.
   if (ThisEdit.ShowDialog() == DialogResult.OK)
   {

      // Update the data in the list box.
      lstNameList.Items[lstNameList.SelectedIndex] =
         ThisEdit.txtFirstName.Text + " " +
         ThisEdit.txtLastName.Text;

      // Modify the current settings.
      for (int i = 0; i < CurrentSettings.NameList.Length; i++)
         if ((CurrentSettings.NameList[i].FirstName == Values[0]) &&
             (CurrentSettings.NameList[i].LastName == Values[1]))
         {
            CurrentSettings.NameList[i].FirstName =
               ThisEdit.txtFirstName.Text;
            CurrentSettings.NameList[i].LastName =
               ThisEdit.txtLastName.Text;
         }

      // Save the settings.
      Settings.SaveSettings(CurrentSettings);
   }
}
```

The code begins by obtaining the data currently shown in the list box and modifying it for use by the application. The friendly view is nice for users, but not very useful for the application. In this case, the application uses the simple `WholeName.Split()` method to perform the task. How you manipulate the data for your application depends on how you change it to make it user friendly. In some cases, you must create a balance of sorts between the needs of the user and the need for the application to ensure you can keep the user interface and the data source in sync.

At this point, the application creates a new form called `frmEdit`. Figure 22-4 shows how this form appears to the user. When the application displays the form, it contains the first and last name of the user entry that the user selected for change. This form has all the usual features and one special change to make it friendlier to the application. The default `TextBox Modifiers` property setting is `Private`. The example sets this property to `Public` so that the data contained within the controls is easier to access. If you want to make the application more secure, you could also expose the data values through a property. Of course, using this approach would also means more setup before you could create the form for display.

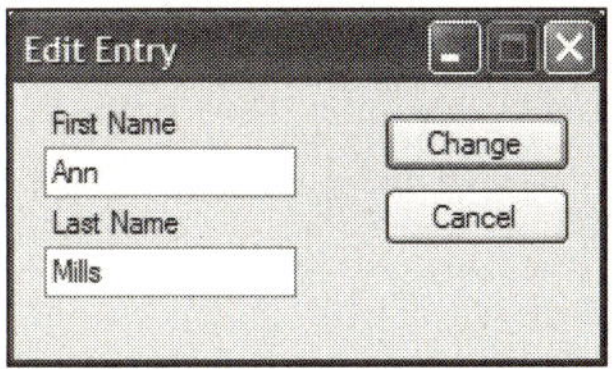

Figure 22-4: Modify the data as needed.

Now, the application must wait for the user to do something. When the user finally clicks either Change or Cancel, the form closes and returns a `DialogResult` value to the caller. When the value is `DialogResult.OK`, the code performs additional processing. In order for this technique to work, you must set the `DialogResult` property for each of the `Button` controls. Otherwise, the caller has no way of knowing which button the user clicked.

The first task the code performs is to update the information in `lstNameList`. Because this is an editing function, the code relies on the `lstNameList.SelectedIndex` value to locate the proper entry to change. The code then adds the user-friendly view of the data as normal.

The second task is to locate the entry to modify in the data. The example uses a simple `for` loop to perform the task. When both the `CurrentSettings.NameList[i].FirstName` and `CurrentSettings.NameList[i].LastName` properties match the selected value, then the code can make the required changes. In this case, all the code needs to do is replace the existing values. The code then saves the resulting changes using the `Settings.SaveSettings()` method. As always, saving the data after each change provides a certain level of reliability.

Considering XML File Search Times

It may seem as if XML data files are extremely inefficient when it comes to searches. You must search for a particular value without benefit of an index, as you would have in a database. Because the code doesn't know where the data appear in `CurrentSettings.NameList`, it must search through the list, one item at a time, until it locates the needed entry. The example data file is likely to contain just a few items, so search times are short.

Using an item-by-item search isn't so bad when you have a short list or if the item appears near the beginning of the list. However, when the needed entry is the last item of a rather lengthy list, the search time can become excessive — far longer than a user is willing to wait. The search time for edits is one of the limiting factors for using the serialized XML approach described in this chapter. Although you can put save routines on a separate thread, you may find working with searches a bit harder.

Because of the way this application works with the data, it could place the save routine on a separate thread. In fact, you could use this application as a pattern for your own application to make it possible to perform saves in the background.

Continued

An alternative that you could try is to sort the list and then use a binary search technique to reduce the time required to find the information. Of course, you also have another alternative. Microsoft now provides Language INtegrated Query (LINQ) with Visual Studio, and using this technology could significantly improve search times. Chapter 23 describes LINQ in detail.

The bottom line is that XML serialization has limits. At some point, you'll have to deal with a search that simply won't run very efficiently and users will complain. Keep this issue in mind as you design your application to use serialized XML techniques.

Deleting Data Entries

Adding data entries means that you'll eventually want to delete them as well. Deleting data is always dangerous because you never know when the user will delete something accidentally and want it back. Implementing an undo feature is outside the scope of this book, but you could consider adding undo if you feel that users are likely to make a lot of deletion mistakes and the data are hard to recreate. Listing 22-8 shows the simple deletion technique used for the example in this chapter.

Listing 22-8: Removing old data entries

```
private void btnDelete_Click(object sender, EventArgs e)
{
   // Obtain the selected value.
   String WholeName =
      (String)lstNameList.Items[lstNameList.SelectedIndex];
   String[] Values = WholeName.Split(' ');

   // Locate the right element.
   for (int i = 0; i < CurrentSettings.NameList.Length; i++)
      if ((CurrentSettings.NameList[i].FirstName == Values[0]) &&
          (CurrentSettings.NameList[i].LastName == Values[1]))
      {

         // Create a new list from which to remove the name.
         List<Names> NewList = CurrentSettings.NameList.ToList<Names>();

         // Remove the selected entry.
         NewList.RemoveAt(i);

         // Add the results to the current settings.
         CurrentSettings.NameList = NewList.ToArray<Names>();
      }

   // Save the settings.
   Settings.SaveSettings(CurrentSettings);

   // Delete the selected value from the list box.
   lstNameList.Items.RemoveAt(lstNameList.SelectedIndex);
}
```

The code begins by obtaining the selected entry in the list and modifying it so the application can use it. This technique is the same one used for editing entries as described in the "Editing Existing Entries" section of the chapter.

After the code determines what to search for, it uses a `for` loop to locate the information. In order to remove the entry using the simplest possible approach, the code transforms the `NameList[]` array into a `List` using a call to `CurrentSettings.NameList.ToList<Names>()`. Notice that you must provide the type of the data to the `ToList()` method or the call won't work. Now that the code has a `List` to work with, it can use the `RemoveAt()` method to remove the required entry. Finally, the code simply converts the `List` back into an array using the `NewList.ToArray<Names>()` method and stores the new array in `CurrentSettings.NameList`.

The code ends by saving the new `CurrentSettings` to disk. It then removes the entry from `lstNameList`. As with editing, deleting entries from a long list can take time. Theoretically, you can perform this task in a thread to make the application more responsive to user needs. However, there is always the risk of data corruption when you trade speed for reliability.

Sorting the Data Entries

Most users don't work well with random data — that is, data that appear in any random order. Users like to see data ordered in some way. Consequently, you need to sort the data entries at some time. You have the following options for sorting the data entries:

- Sort the data before the user sees it on screen.
- Maintain a sorted data list in the data file.

The first option, sorting the data before the user sees them on screen, is actually the faster approach and requires significantly less work on your part. It's the approach used by the application because there isn't a good reason to expend time and energy on sorting the data entries on disk. To implement this approach, you can choose a control that provides sorting, such as the `ListBox`. All you have to do to see the list in sorted order is to set the `Sorted` property to `True`. The code within the `ListBox` control takes care of all the details for you, so you don't really have to worry about sorting at all.

The second option, sorting the data in the data file involves some additional work on your part because now you have to create a method for sorting the data. The advantage to sorting the data file is that sorting the data can speed other tasks such as editing and deleting entries. Sorting isn't a quick solution that will fix every potential speed problem, but it can help significantly in some situations.

At one time, the code for performing this task (sorting the data entries) could become quite complex and many developers were less than enthusiastic about creating it. However, with the addition of LINQ to Visual Studio, sorting your data has become a lot easier. Look again at the `SaveSettings()` method shown in Listing 22-3. If you add the following code to the beginning of this method, the entries appear on disk in sorted order.

```
// Sort the Current data so it appears sorted on disk.
IEnumerable<Names> Sorted =
   Current.NameList.OrderBy(
      Names => Names.FirstName + Names.LastName);
Current.NameList = Sorted.ToArray<Names>();
```

You'll have to read Chapter 23 to get a full appreciation for the beauty of this technique. However, this LINQ technique begins by creating an `IEnumerable<Names>` object named `Sorted`. The addition of the source type, `Names`, is essential to make this technique work. The `Current.NameList.OrderBy()` method relies on a special expression, a *lambda expression*, to order the information in `Sorted`. In this case, the lambda expression is performing a comparison. It tells the method to compare each element in `Names` and sort them by using a combination of `Names.FirstName + Names.LastName`. As you'll discover later, LINQ focuses mainly on what you want the code to do, rather than how to do it. That's the case here — you tell the code how you want the data sorted and then the code determines how best to achieve the task. The result is a completely optimized sort routine that doesn't require much work on your part at all.

After the code sorts the data, it must place it back into `Current.NameList` for saving. Remember that `Sorted` is an `IEnumerable<Names>` type, so you can make a direct assignment. The way to perform this task is to call on the `Sorted.ToArray<Names>()` method. Notice again that you must provide a source type for the code to work. Otherwise, Visual Studio will claim that it doesn't know how to perform the task (and it doesn't, because you haven't told it everything you want it to do). After the `SaveSettings()` method ends, you can verify that the data on disk really are sorted (many developers find it amazing that such simple code actually does something). Figure 22-5 shows a typical example of the sorted data entries.

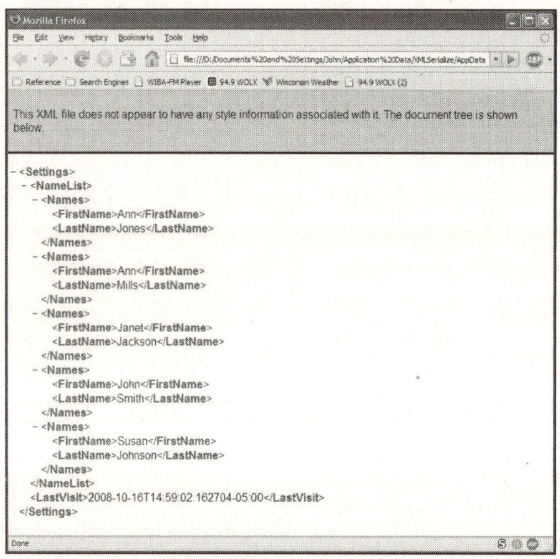

Figure 22-5: Storing the data in sorted order could help your application perform better.

This kind of coding is where the techniques in Chapter 19 come into play. You can use the various profiling techniques to determine whether sorting the entries on screen or sorting the data file on disk works best for your needs. The mistake that many developers make here is that they get false results because they don't fully end one method before they begin another. For example, if a developer is in a hurry when performing the profiling task, it would be quite easy to forget to set the `ListBox Sorted` property to `False`. If you make this mistake, your sorting data on-disk profile results will reflect the on-screen sorting as well.

Likewise, you can impair the quality of the profiling for the on-screen sorting by using a sorted data file. The user certainly won't enter the data in sorted order, so using a sorted file will give you false results by making the on-screen sorting appear faster. As you can see, you must exercise care when testing for this scenario.

In general, you'll find that on-screen sorting is faster when you perform simple loading and saving of the data file and the user adds data to a relatively short list most of the time. When the user begins working with a long list and performs mostly deletes and edits, using on-disk sorting will likely prove faster. Of course, the complexity of your application also affects the performance of these two techniques — on-screen sorting works better with less complex applications.

Displaying Data Entries on Screen

A final consideration for using the serialized XML data technique is that the user will still want to see data in a usable format on screen. Of course, you already know about the need to create calculated fields as required from the "Using XML Data in Reports" section of this chapter and the requirement to sort data from the "Sorting the Data Entries" section of the chapter. However, the user usually expects more than a few calculated fields and sorted data.

In most cases, you must fine-tune the presentation to reflect real-world requirements that the user has, and some users will have different needs than others do. The best way to achieve this goal is to add settings information to the user's data file that provides specific information on how the user wants to see the data displayed. You can categorize these settings as follows:

- Aesthetic (the appearance of the display)
- Data centric (the presentation of the data)
- User interface (such as the use of speed keys)
- Layout (the order of controls on the display)
- Filtering (the amount and type of data displayed)

The only way to fine-tune the data presentation is to perform extensive user testing. The user testing should include every group that will interact with the application. In addition, you should include someone from every skill level in each group as part of the testing team when possible. However, you need to balance the testing results with the requirements of the XML data file. Remember, you don't want to create an immense file that slows the application to a crawl. Consequently, you must consider the trade-offs of the design decisions you make. If the requirements for a particular data storage and presentation task become too intense, you may want to consider a robust storage technology such as a full database implementation. As mentioned earlier in the chapter, XML serialization is only one tool in what should be a full toolbox.

Implementing Your Design

This chapter has described an important technique you can add to your toolbox, serializing XML. Using serialized XML in place of other strategies, such as the registry, can significantly decrease support costs for your organization. In addition, the technique preserves data format, while making it easier to interact with the data in new ways. Of course, as with any tool, using serialized XML in the wrong place can also cost you in ways that older binary formats don't. The biggest issue for most organizations today is that XML is difficult to secure, making it a less useful candidate for sensitive information. The larger file size can also prove to be a problem on devices that have limited memory, making serialized XML a less helpful technique for mobile devices.

If you've used the registry, plaintext files, or databases to store configuration in the past, now is the time to give serialized XML a try. Even though you may initially think that using serialized XML is more difficult or time consuming than other techniques, you'll appreciate the way it helps you create flexible applications that have fewer problems locating and using needed data. Make sure you take the same time to define the schema of the data you must store as you would with a database storage technique, because the resulting XML file is a kind of database. Try various approaches to interacting with the data. You may find that this new technique offers flexibility in storing settings that makes it easier for you to slim down your code and make it faster.

Chapter 23 discusses another fascinating technology, Language INtegrated Query (LINQ). The most interesting part of LINQ is that you use the same query technique for nearly any data source, including a few sources that you normally can't query easily within C#. Of course, you can use LINQ to query your XML files. For example, by using LINQ, you can perform a query across the network that locates all the users who have a particular option selected. You can't perform the same kind of query using the registry or plaintext files (the plaintext files are theoretically doable, but creating the required code would be incredibly hard). Consequently, Chapter 23 builds on what you've discovered in this chapter and demonstrates a new way to query all structured data on your system.

23

Working with LINQ

Language INtegrated Query (LINQ, pronounced link) is potentially one of the best features that Microsoft has added to Visual Studio in a long time. It has the potential to change the way you write code and can help you create significantly faster code as well. The briefest way to describe LINQ is as a specialized query language that looks a little like Structured Query Language (SQL, pronounced sequel), yet works equally well on any data source for which you have a provider (the specialized code used to perform the LINQ query).

This short description really doesn't do LINQ justice. The "Sorting the Data Entries" section of Chapter 22 shows a use for LINQ that hardly falls into the usual category of a query. When you look at what the two lines of code in that example do, you begin to understand the vast scope of what LINQ can possibly do for you as a developer. This chapter builds your knowledge of what LINQ can do, but it can't show you everything. Consider this chapter that barest introduction to a much larger topic.

The copy of LINQ that comes with Visual Studio comes with four providers that supply access to standard data sources. These providers include:

- Objects
- DataSet
- SQL
- XML

This chapter provides very short examples of how to use each of the standard providers. It's important to know, though, that developers are writing LINQ by the gross and you can potentially use LINQ to access just about any data source imaginable (and a few things that most people don't consider data sources in the strictest sense). By the time you complete this chapter, you'll have the barest understanding of LINQ.

Understanding LINQ Support in Visual Studio 2008

Visual Studio 2008 comes with LINQ support built into it. Actually, the underlying functionality is part of the .NET Framework, but you'll find that Visual Studio 2008 augments this functionality from a coder's perspective as described in the rest of this chapter. However, it's important to understand that LINQ isn't a static feature. The functionality is dynamic — you can add or subtract from the LINQ features that come with Visual Studio. Of course, Visual Studio does come with a basic LINQ setup, which is what the majority of this chapter considers. The following sections consider some essential issues of LINQ support in Visual Studio.

Understanding LINQ and Providers

LINQ relies heavily on the concept of a provider. A *provider* is a special piece of interpreter code that accepts LINQ as input and outputs instructions that the data source can understand. In many respects, a LINQ provider is similar to the database provider counterpart. However, Microsoft has done a significantly better job of standardizing the support provided with LINQ than it has with the database providers used with Visual Studio.

Standard query syntax is an essential part of LINQ. The provider determines what data source you can access and which standard LINQ features you can use to access that data source, but the basic principles for creating a query remain constant from provider to provider. Consequently, if you know how to use the LINQ to XML provider, you also have a good basic knowledge of the LINQ to SQL provider. This similarity of query techniques extends to providers that aren't part of Visual Studio, such as LINQ to RDF (Resource Description Framework). LINQ standardization has led to a significant third-party following — see the "Using Third-Party Providers" section of this chapter for additional details.

Contrasting LINQ with SQL

Some developers confuse LINQ with Structured Query Language (SQL). The two query techniques do have similarities, so it's easy to understand how someone could make this error. For example, in both cases you tell the interpreter what you want done, not how to do it. A special optimization engine acts in both cases to create an execution plan that ensures the query provides the fastest possible performance.

LINQ and SQL really are different and you can't substitute one for the other. Many developers find that LINQ is easier to use (see the blog entry at `http://www.amazon.com/gp/blog/post/PLNK1NSFQ6IM27N1Z` as an example). However, other developers aren't quite sure where Microsoft is going with LINQ (see the blog entry at `http://sqlserver-qa.net/blogs/sql2008/archive/2007/06/17/783.aspx` as an example).

The actual syntax differs between LINQ and SQL as well. Listing 23-1 shows an example of a SQL query for the Northwind database. In this case, the query obtains the names of the customers who reside in London.

Listing 23-1: Obtaining data from SQL Server using SQL

```
private void btnSQL_Click(object sender, EventArgs e)
{
```

```
        // Create the connection.
        SqlConnection Conn = new SqlConnection(
           "Data Source=(local);Initial Catalog=Northwind;" +
           "Integrated Security=SSPI;");

        // Create the command.
        SqlCommand Cmd = new SqlCommand(
           "SELECT ContactName FROM Customers WHERE City = 'London'", Conn);

        // Open the connection.
        Conn.Open();

        // Execute the command.
        SqlDataReader Reader = Cmd.ExecuteReader();

        // Obtain the result.
        StringBuilder DisplayData = new StringBuilder();
        while (Reader.Read())
           DisplayData.Append(Reader.GetString(0) + "\r\n");

        // Display the result.
        MessageBox.Show(DisplayData.ToString());

        // Close the connection.
        Conn.Close();
    }
```

The code begins by creating a connection to the SQL Server. Notice that you must know how to create the connection. In this case, you must know the source of the data, the database you want to use, and the kind of security required.

The next step is to create a command for SQL Server to perform. To perform this task, you need to know SQL, a second language.

After the code creates the command, it opens the connection and reads the data from the connection based on the command. The result is a `SqlDataReader` object, `Reader`, that the application uses to read the information from the database one record at a time. The code places this data in a `StringBuilder` object, `DisplayData`. Finally, the application displays the data on screen as shown in Figure 23-1 and closes the connection.

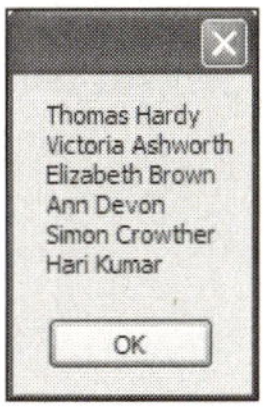

Figure 23-1: The output of this application is a simple list of names.

Listing 23-2 shows the code required to display the same output shown in Figure 23-1 using LINQ. The technique is considerably different. In order to use this approach, you do need to perform some preparatory work. The "Using LINQ to SQL" section of the chapter describes the work you must perform. The main focus now is on the actual LINQ code.

Listing 23-2: Obtaining data from SQL Server using LINQ

```
private void btnLINQ_Click(object sender, EventArgs e)
{
   //Define the XML mapping source.
   XmlMappingSource MS;
   MS = XmlMappingSource.FromUrl(
      @"..\..\NorthwindMap.XML");

   // Create the DataContext object.
   Northwind DB = new Northwind(
      @"Data Source=(local);Initial Catalog=Northwind;" +
      "Integrated Security=True", MS);

   // Create the query.
   var ThisCust = from Custs in DB.Customers
                  where Custs.City == "London"
                  select Custs.ContactName;

   // Obtain the result.
   StringBuilder DisplayData = new StringBuilder();
   foreach (String ThisName in ThisCust)
      DisplayData.Append(ThisName + "\r\n");

   // Display the result.
   MessageBox.Show(DisplayData.ToString());
}
```

The code begins by creating an `XmlMappingSource` object, `MS`. The easiest way to view an `XmlMappingSource` is as an agreement between the database and the provider on how to interact with the content of the database. Consequently, the `XmlMappingSource` contains specific information about the database such as the names of the tables and the columns within each table. The `XmlMappingSource` frees you from having to worry about the database structure as much, because IntelliSense can provide hints on working with the database. You have a number of options for defining an `XmlMappingSource`, but using an external XML file as shown in Listing 23-2 is the easiest way to perform the task. In this case, the code calls the `FromUrl()` method to load the file. The other methods include:

- `FromReader()`
- `FromStream()`
- `FromXml()`

Interestingly enough, Microsoft provides automation for generating the XML file automatically. The "Using LINQ to SQL" section of the chapter provides additional details about the SQLMetal utility used to perform this task. Figure 23-2 shows part of the XML mapping file used for this example, which was generated by SQLMetal.

If you use the SQLMetal tool, you'll find that you always use the `FromUrl()` *method to create the* `XmlMappingSource`. *The other methods shown in this section let you create customized XML mapping to the database. In short, you have considerable flexibility in telling the LINQ to SQL provider how to interact with your database. However, most developers will opt for the simpler method of working with SQLMetal to define the XML mapping.*

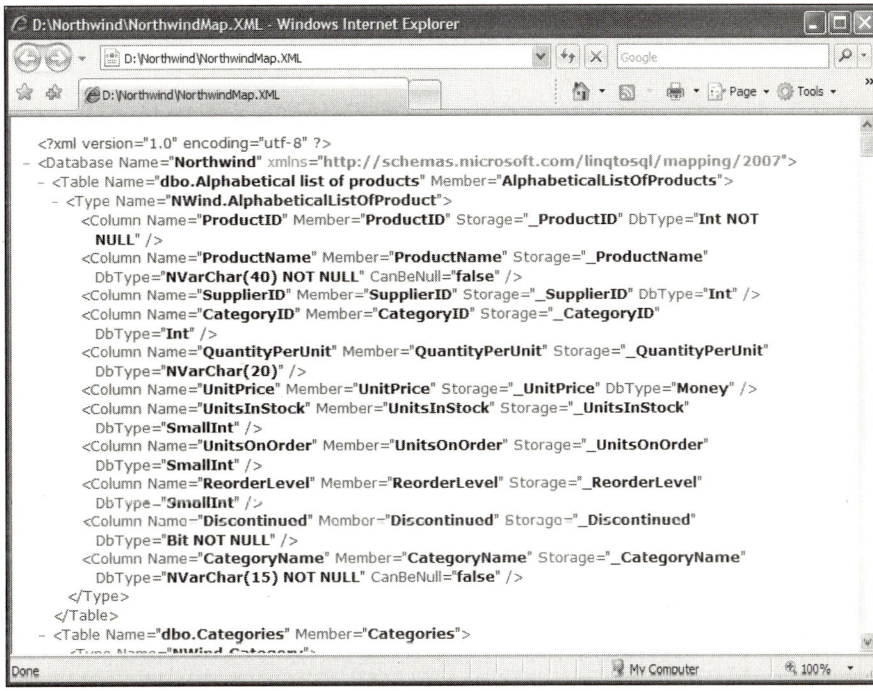

Figure 23-2: XML mapping is a special LINQ feature that makes interacting with SQL Server easier.

The next step is to create a connection to the database. The information you provide is similar to the information you supply when working with SQL. However, only the information is the same. You never use the object to open or close the connection — all of that code resides within the provider.

The query presents the greatest difference between the SQL and LINQ approaches. The query begins by creating an individual element object, `Custs`. Observe that you don't define a type for `Custs`; the provider determines what to use automatically. The next step is to define a source for the information, which is the `Customers` table located in the `DB` object. The next bit of code determines the conditions for retrieving records — the `Custs.City` field must contain the word *London* in it. Finally, the query tells what information to select from the table, which is `Custs.ContactName` in this case. The result is the same as the SQL query, but you perform less work to do it. When you create a `SqlCommand` object, you must know the SQL statement required to retrieve the data. On the other hand, when you create a LINQ query, the provider tells you what to type through IntelliSense.

The output from a LINQ query is actually a kind of query object. The `var` keyword tells the compiler that you have a variable of some undefined type that the provider will define later. LINQ providers perform a lot of the heavy lifting for you. The `ThisCust` variable does have a data type, as do all C#

variables, but you don't need to worry about the data type when working with `ThisCust`. Following each step of a LINQ query sequence in the debugger is enlightening because you see that `ThisCust` actually provides access to the previously defined query.

The example ends by building a `StringBuilder` object, just as the SQL example did. The approach is a little different, but the concept is the same. The code displays the data on screen and you see the same information shown in Figure 23-1. At this point, the code simply ends — you don't even have to close the connection because the provider addresses this task for you.

Using LINQ for Non-query Solutions

One of the important issues to think about when using LINQ is that you've probably used it and didn't think about it in the past. Microsoft has extensively integrated LINQ into C#, making it a natural part of the language for accomplishing some tasks. When working with other query languages, you must think about the query because it doesn't integrate well with C#. The two languages (C# and the query language) really are different. The "Sorting the Data Entries" section of Chapter 22 shows one case in which LINQ integration is invisible. The `OrderBy()` method used in that example is one of the operators described in this chapter.

Many of the queries you create using LINQ work with common objects or other nontraditional sources of data. Adding third-party providers to your Visual Studio setup makes it possible to use even more nontraditional data sources. It's no longer a matter of thinking of databases or Web services. With the right provider, any object, service, application, or file can become a source of information. Even when you don't use them as a data source, you can perform tasks such as filtering the information. In short, you'll find uses for LINQ that go beyond the simple queries offered by other query languages. When thinking about LINQ, also consider these non-query uses:

- Filtering
- Sorting
- Ordering (including grouping)
- Adding two sources together
- Analyzing
- Differentiating
- Mathematical computation

Defining the Basic Operators

No matter how you interact with LINQ, you use a set of operators to perform tasks. The most common use of these operators is to create queries, so that's what this chapter focuses on. However, it's important to remember that these same operators can perform other tasks, depending on the capabilities of the provider you use.

The LINQ keywords help you create queries. In some respects, these keywords work and act like the keywords in SQL (see the "Contrasting LINQ with SQL" section of the chapter). As previously mentioned, the keywords provide parameters that tell LINQ what to find. As a minimum, you must define a `from` keyword when creating a query (non-queries don't require the `from` keyword as shown in the example in the "Sorting the Data Entries" section of Chapter 22). The `where` and `orderby` keywords provide additional conditions. The following sections describe each of the simple LINQ keywords.

Working with the From and Select Operators

The `from` keyword is the only keyword that you must include as part of a LINQ query. The `from` keyword determines the data source used to select information. You add one `from` keyword for each data source you want to include in a query. Here's an example of the `from` keyword in use:

```
var ThisQuery =
    from StringValue
    in QueryString
    select StringValue;
```

The query actually requires four lines, each of which has a different purpose. Here is a quick summary of the purpose of each line.

- **var**: The `var` line is a variable that eventually holds the query. Even a simple query includes an `IEnumerator` object that you can use to select individual query values.
- **from**: The `from` line contains the `from` keyword and a variable used to hold the current enumerated value. For example, if you define an array like this one:

  ```
  String[] QueryString =
      { "One", "Two", "Three", "Four", "Five" };
  ```

- `StringValue` will contain, in turn, the values One, Two, Three, Four, and Five. It's important to note that we're using a simple string here. The variable can end up holding any kind of value depending on the kind of query you're making, so it's never safe to assume the variable has a specific value in it.
- **in**: The `in` line has the `in` keyword and defines where to find the data. In this case, you're querying `QueryString`. However, you can use any source that LINQ supports. All you need is a provider to access the data source.
- **select**: The `select` line has the `select` keyword, followed by a definition of what to select. In this case, the code selects the entire value. However, the selection can include just about anything. For example, you could add a carriage return and linefeed at the end of each value. It's possible to add constants to the values, analyze the values in specific ways, and perform other tasks using the selection. Using operators, you can manipulate the selection in other ways.

Working with the Where Operator

The `where` keyword performs filtering. Most queries will require filtering of some sort because you won't normally want to look at the entire dataset. The kind of filtering you perform depends on the data source you're using, but generally, you can work with the `where` keyword variable using the methods that you would when working with a variable of that type alone. For example, when working with a `String`, you can choose to filter the data by length, substring, or comparison as needed.

A `where` keyword can appear anywhere after the `from` keyword and before the `select` keyword when creating a query (non-queries may have just the filtering capabilities of the `where` operator). The placement of a `where` keyword can affect how it filters the query. LINQ processes each `where` keyword in turn and uses it to filter the current selection. You'll see how filtering works as the chapter progresses. For now, look at this simple example of a query with the `where` keyword:

```
var ThisQuery =
     from StringValue
     in QueryString
     where StringValue.Length > 3
     select StringValue;
```

As you can see, this query contains all the elements described in the "Working with the From and Select Operators" section of the chapter. The `where` keyword interacts with the `StringValue.Length` property. Any string longer than three characters appears as part of the selection. Consequently, if you use the same `ThisQuery` array as before to test this query, the values Three, Four, and Five appear in the output, but One and Two don't because they aren't longer than three characters.

In some cases, a developer will retrieve the entire dataset even when the application won't use the entire dataset under the assumption that using the entire dataset will reduce code complications later. In fact, retrieving the entire dataset has many undesirable side effects, such as making the application perform poorly and use resources inefficiently. Using resources inefficiently can also affect application reliability and having the entire dataset available can open potential security issues. In short, retrieve only what you need to ensure the application performs properly.

Working with the orderBy Operator

Data will often appear in an order other than the one you need to obtain useful output. The `orderby` keyword changes the order of the data to meet specific needs. As with the `where` keyword, you can use any of the native methods provided by a data type to perform the ordering. You can also use operators and other methods to order the data. The following example shows one way in which you can order a LINQ query.

```
var ThisQuery =
     from StringValue
     in QueryString
     orderby StringValue
     orderby StringValue.Length
     select StringValue;
```

In this case, the query uses two `orderby` keywords. The first `orderby` keyword sorts the entries alphabetically, while the second sorts them by length. The effects are cumulative, so order is important. Let's say you begin with an array containing the words one through six. The output of this query is One, Two, Five, Four, and Three. To see how order is important, you could try this query.

```
var ThisQuery =
     from StringValue
     in QueryString
     orderby StringValue.Length
     orderby StringValue
     select StringValue;
```

In this case, the output is Five, Four, One, Three, and Two. The alphabetical sort ends up overwriting the length sort, even though the two sorts are equal. Of course, this doesn't address the question of whether the sorts really are cumulative. When you try this query:

```
var ThisQuery =
    from StringValue
    in QueryString
    orderby StringValue.Length
    select StringValue;
```

the output is One, Two, Four, Five, and Three. This sort order reflects the original order of the data elements grouped by length. Consequently, the two-phase `orderby` shown initially really does change how LINQ orders the data.

You may also wonder whether you can combine the two-phase `orderby` into a single `orderby`. If you were working with two numeric values, LINQ would allow you to combine the two sorts using the `&&` operator. However, because this ordering relies on a `string` and an `int` value, you can't combine them.

Creating LINQ Queries

LINQ queries (as contrasted to non-queries) follow a specific format as described throughout this chapter. Like SQL queries, LINQ queries can use a single data source. Unlike SQL queries, you can perform useful work with a single data source in LINQ, depending on the kind of data with which you interact. However, like SQL queries, some LINQ queries do require multiple data sources. You can divide the use of single and multiple data sources into simple and complex queries.

Use of multiple data sources does allow you to create complex queries in LINQ. However, LINQ includes another feature — a sort of temporary variable that you create using the `let` operator. The addition of the `let` operator provides another level of complexity that helps you perform tasks such as data analysis as part of the query. In short, the `let` operator provides another way to view the data in such a way that you perform nontraditional tasks with it.

The `join` *and* `let` *operators are examples of two operators that increase complexity, but also improve functionality and flexibility of LINQ queries. Depending on the provider you use, you may find that the developer includes other operators or implements the functionality of the* `join` *and* `let` *operators in ways other than the standard providers do. Make sure you understand how third-party providers work before you implement them in code — not every vendor provides the same level of flexibility described in this section.*

The following sections consider the techniques for creating LINQ queries. You'll discover the uses of both simple and complex queries. In addition, you'll see how to use the all-important `let` keyword to create interesting queries that perform analysis in ways that you may not have thought possible.

Defining Simple Queries

Simple queries rely on a single data source, which may seem limiting at first, but you'd be amazed at the number of queries you can perform. Unlike using SQL, a LINQ query may include only one data source, such as an array or a `ListBox` control. Simple queries are normally short and easily optimized by the built-in query optimizer. Most simple queries rely on the following keywords:

- `var`
- `from`
- `in`
- `select`
- `where`
- `orderby`

Most stand-alone keywords have method counterparts. Look again at the first query shown in the "Working with the `OrderBy` Operator" section of the chapter. You can use the following method approach to duplicate this query.

```
var ThisQuery =
   QueryString.OrderBy(StringValue => StringValue).
   OrderBy(StringValue => StringValue.Length);
```

The method approach relies on lambda expressions. A lambda expression consists of three parts:

- Enumerated value (`StringValue` in this case)
- The => operator
- An expression (`StringValue` or `StringValue.Length` in this case)

Using the method approach as some advantages. For example, you can make the query code shorter. In addition, the precise order in which the LINQ provider accomplishes tasks is clearer in some cases. The method approach will accommodate a `join`. However, you can't use it for the type of analysis provided by the `let` keyword. The method approach does provide access to a number of additional features. You can perform any task that the object can normally perform as part of the query. The method approach also makes some analysis methods, such as `Min()` and `Max()`, available. Whether you choose the keyword or method approach depends on what you want to do and the level of support the provider includes for various tasks.

Using the method approach can make your code harder to debug because you can't follow the progress of the LINQ query as easily. Consequently, use the keyword form when learning new LINQ techniques to reduce the learning curve.

Performing Joins of Multiple Data Sources

The `join` keyword performs the same task as join does in SQL. It combines two data sources into a single data source using some criterion. A `join` can have all of the variations found in SQL, but the default is an inner join.

Rather than make `join` difficult to understand, consider the basics of using it with two arrays. Normally, you'll use two `from` queries to work with arrays. For example, the following query shows how to obtain matching values from two arrays no matter where those values appear.

```
var TwoFroms = from QueryA in ArrayA
               from QueryB in ArrayB
               where QueryA == QueryB
               select new { QueryA, QueryB };
```

The output of this query is a new value that contains the matching values from the two arrays. The array elements, `QueryA` and `QueryB`, both contain the same value because that's the requirement of the `where` clause of the query. If you use the following two arrays:

```
Int32[] ArrayA = { 1, 2, 3, 4, 8 };
Int32[] ArrayB = { 1, 3, 5, 7, 8 };
```

The output will contain three array elements. These array elements will contain two integers each and the output values will include 1, 3, and 8. The goal right now is to see how a `join` will compare to using two from parameters. The following query produces the same output as the first query, but it uses a `join` instead.

```
var Joined = from QueryA in ArrayA
             join QueryB in ArrayB
             on QueryA equals QueryB
             select new { QueryA, QueryB };
```

Notice that the `join` version of the query varies in three important ways. First, you use `join` instead of the second `from`. Second, you use the keyword `on`, in place of `where` because `join` creates a single physical element to replace the multiple elements. Third, `equals` replaces the `==` operator. This is your first example of an operator. The amazing thing is that IntelliSense tells you that you need to use `equals` in place of the == operator, so you can't make a mistake.

The output of this query is an array. IntelliSense even tells you the name of the array members. Consequently, you use the following code to display the combined output shown in Figure 23-3 (in this case, `Output` is a `StringBuilder` object).

```
// Obtain the combined output and display it.
foreach (var Value in Joined)
   Output.Append(Value + "\r\n");

MessageBox.Show(Output.ToString(), "Combined Output");
```

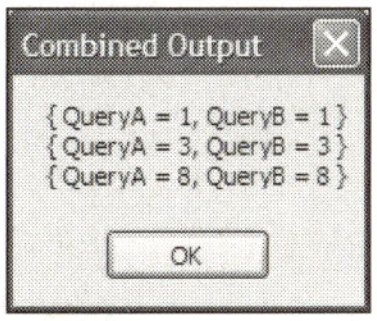

Figure 23-3: The joined output is actually an array.

When you want to interact with a specific part of the output, you need to access the required array member. Here is another version of the output that displays a particular array member as shown in Figure 23-4:

```
// Obtain the QueryA output and display it.
Output = new StringBuilder();
foreach (var Value in Joined)
   Output.Append(Value.QueryA + "\r\n");

MessageBox.Show(Output.ToString(), "QueryA Output");
```

Figure 23-4: Access a specific array member to obtain that particular piece of the output.

As you can see, the second output code accesses `Value.QueryA` directly. You can also perform a `join` using the method technique. Here is the same query using the `Join()` method. The results are the same as those shown in Figure 23-3:

```
// Perform the query using the method technique.
Output = new StringBuilder();
var Joined2 = ArrayA.Join(
   ArrayB,
   QueryA => QueryA,
   QueryB => QueryB,
   (QueryA, QueryB) => new { QueryA, QueryB} );

// Obtain the combined output and display it.
foreach (var Value in Joined2)
   Output.Append(Value + "\r\n");

MessageBox.Show(Output.ToString(), "Combined Method Output");
```

In this case, you begin with `ArrayA` and you join it to `ArrayB` using the `Join()` method where `ArrayB` appears as the first parameter. The second parameter is a lambda expression that describes how to interact with the outer key (what you want to do with `ArrayA`). The third parameter expression describes how to interact with the inner key (what you want to do with `ArrayB`). The forth parameter is the output you want to create given `QueryA == QueryB`. Needless to say, this is a case where the method approach is definitely less clear than using the keyword approach and you may want to avoid it whenever possible.

The examples in this section do point out an important feature of LINQ — you can usually perform a task using multiple approaches. The approach you use should reflect your personal coding style, the clearest query, and the best performance. In many cases, this means experimenting with several forms of the query to test it out. Experience will eventually show you which approach to use in a given situation.

Using the let Operator

Sometimes a query will involve a calculation or analysis that you must perform multiple times to obtain the desired information. Creating a query that performs the calculation multiple times wastes time and resources, so Microsoft has included the `let` keyword to provide a means of storing calculated values. In fact, you can even pass these calculated values outside the query to save additional time processing the data later. Here's an example of a query that uses the `let` keyword to create a calculated value:

```
var Squares =
   from QueryA in ArrayA
   from QueryB in ArrayB
   let TheSquare = QueryA * QueryB
   where QueryA == QueryB
   where TheSquare > 2
   select new { QueryA, QueryB, TheSquare };
```

In this case, the query creates a calculated value named `TheSquare`. We're looking for a square, so `QueryA` must equal `QueryB` (otherwise, it would be simple multiplication). The code then uses this value to perform a comparison of the calculated value to a constant to determine which values to include in the output (the output will contain values greater than two). Finally, `TheSquare` appears as part of the output so that the application doesn't have to compute the value again later. Given two arrays like this:

```
Int32[] ArrayA = { 1, 2, 3, 4 };
Int32[] ArrayB = { 1, 2, 3, 4 };
```

and output code like this:

```
foreach (var ThisEntry in Squares)
   Output.Append(
      ThisEntry.QueryA + " * " +
      ThisEntry.QueryB + " = " +
      ThisEntry.TheSquare + "\r\n");

MessageBox.Show(Output.ToString(), "List of Squares");
```

The output for this example will display the values shown in Figure 23-5.

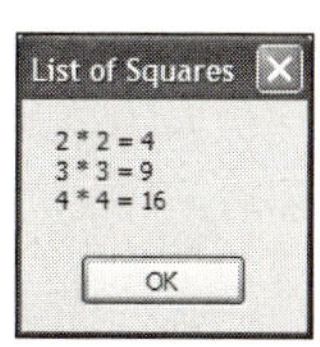

Figure 23-5: The output produces a list of squares.

As you can see, the query examines each of the possible square values, determines which ones are greater than two, and then outputs only those that exceed two. Using `let` as part of the query doesn't make the output any different — you can achieve the same effect using other means. However, using `let` does tend to improve application performance and make the query itself easier to understand.

Using LINQ to Interact with Any Data Source

LINQ can literally access any data source and you'll normally use the same approach every time. The fact that you can use a consistent approach makes LINQ incredibly easy to use. After you learn how to work with one provider, you can normally adapt to any other provider with very little extra learning time. Of course, the learning curve can prove a little steep for that first provider, because LINQ uses a different approach to access data as described in the "Contrasting LINQ with SQL" section of the chapter for the LINQ to SQL provider.

The following sections provide a very quick overview of the four providers that Visual Studio has as a default. In addition, you'll learn about the wealth of other providers available as of this writing (developers are creating new LINQ providers every day). The bit of information that you should take away from these sections is that LINQ can access a considerable number of data sources using a single flexible approach that makes your coding efforts less cumbersome.

Using the Built-In Providers

As previously mentioned, Visual Studio comes with a number of built-in LINQ providers. You can access these providers at any time and you may even find that they simply appear as part of IntelliSense when you need them. These four providers are:

- LINQ to Objects (lets you use any object, including some controls, as a data source)
- LINQ to DataSet (works with the `DataSet` control)
- LINQ to SQL (provides access to SQL Server)
- LINQ to XML (helps you interact with any XML data source)

Because all four of these providers come with Visual Studio, and Microsoft has created them for you, they provide the best way to learn about the full potential of LINQ. Many third-party providers don't include the full LINQ functionality because the full functionality isn't required to interact with the data source or the provider is a work in progress. In general, you want to begin working with LINQ using one of the built-in providers so that you have the best experience possible.

The built-in providers also offer considerable flexibility. The most flexible provider is LINQ to Object because you can use it to access any object. In fact, you could use LINQ to Object to access nearly any data source if desired because most data sources present themselves as objects. However, LINQ to Object is best suited to working with components and controls. For example, you could use LINQ to Object to query the content of a list box. The other three providers enhance basic LINQ to Object functionality to accommodate special needs of other data sources.

Always remember that a LINQ provider is a kind of translator. The provider reads your query and translates it into something that the data source understands. The better the provider understands the data source, the better it queries that data source and the less work you do to obtain the data you want. Think of the human equivalent of a translator. The better the translator speaks the other language, the better the translation. Consequently, you need providers for two purposes: to improve communication and to access data sources with unique requirements.

Using LINQ to Objects

The LINQ to Objects provider can literally access data in any kind of object, which means that this is your universal access provider. However, LINQ to Objects isn't always the best way to access data because it provides generic access, which means that you won't see specific features of a particular object. For example, you wouldn't get the XML mapping functionality that LINQ to SQL provides for accessing a SQL Server database when using LINQ to Objects. Consequently, you'll want to locate a specific provider whenever possible.

The example in this section is going to do something atypical. It uses LINQ to order the data in a combo box. As you type data into the combo box, LINQ will automatically reorder it for you. In addition, LINQ will eliminate any duplicate values and present the input in a consistent format — all without complex programming on your part. Listing 23-3 shows this simple example of working with a combo box control.

Listing 23-3: Using LINQ with controls

```
private void cbResult_KeyPress(object sender,
                               KeyPressEventArgs e)
{
   // Check for an Enter key press.
   if (e.KeyChar == (char)Keys.Return)
   {
      // Add the appropriate text to the list.
      cbResult.Items.Add(cbResult.Text);

      // Perform the required LINQ update.
      String[] CBQuery =
         cbResult.Items.Cast<String>().OrderBy(
         TheseItems => TheseItems).Select(
         TheseItems =>
            TheseItems.Substring(0, 1).ToUpper() +
            TheseItems.Substring(1,
               TheseItems.Length - 1).ToLower()).
                  ToArray();

      // Clear the current Items list.
      cbResult.Items.Clear();

      // Add the updated list to the Items property.
      foreach (String ThisString in CBQuery)
         cbResult.Items.Add(ThisString);
   }
}
```

A combo box doesn't include code for adding new entries, so you add it using the `KeyPress` event handler. Whenever the code detects that the user has pressed Enter, it adds the input, `cbResult.Text`, to the `cbResult.Items` property. At this point, you have an unordered list of items in `cbResult.Items`.

Now is the time that you have to think about the control update. At some point, you'll want to clear the control to add the ordered list to it. Otherwise, the control will actually display two lists — one ordered and another unordered. To make this query work, you must create the output in such a way that the result is non-deferred, because otherwise you'll end up with a blank output. The LINQ query in this example uses the lambda expression method to obtain a non-deferred array output. The query looks extremely complicated, but it really isn't if you take it apart one element at a time.

The Quick View of Deferred and Non-Deferred Evaluation

LINQ actually supports two kinds of evaluation: deferred and non-deferred. The essential difference between the two kinds of evaluation is that a deferred evaluation doesn't produce the query set until you begin to output the data to screen or manipulate it in other ways. A non-deferred evaluation creates the result set immediately when you define the query. Consequently, a deferred evaluation provides you with the most current output, while a non-deferred evaluation takes a snapshot of the data at a specific time.

Both deferred and non-deferred evaluations have a place in your toolbox. A discussion of the precise differences between the two and the coding techniques you use to produce them is outside the scope of this book. However, you can see a good discussion of this topic at `http://blogs.msdn.com/ericwhite/pages/deferred-execution.aspx` and `http://blogs.msdn.com/dancre/archive/2008/03/25/implications-of-the-just-in-time-nature-of-linq.aspx`.

The `cbResult.Items` property doesn't provide the required functionality, so you must cast it as a `String` array before you can work with it using the `Cast<String>()` template. If you try to use the property directly, you receive an error message telling you that the `System.Windows.Forms.ComboBox.ObjectCollection` doesn't include a definition for `OrderBy()`.

Now that you have access to `OrderBy()`, you can use the `OrderBy()` method to order the output with a lambda expression. In this case, you simply use `TheseItems` as the ordering mechanism, but you could use any expression desired. The ability to change the ordering by modifying a simple expression is one of the reasons you want to use LINQ to order the combo box output. You don't have to worry about any complex programming strategy to obtain the desired output.

Ordering the output is only the first step in the process. It's also important to define a specific selection criteria. In this case, the user can input the text in any form, but the combo box will display the text using initial uppercase. Consequently, the `Select()` method includes text manipulation code that ensures the output appears in the correct form.

The final bit of code is actually the most important. You use the `ToArray()` method to convert the output to a standard array. This is the non-deferred part of the query — the part that makes the rest of the query work. The next step clears the `cbResult.Items` property, so a deferred query will see an empty data source at this point and fail to produce any output. The final step uses a `foreach` loop to add the items back into the list in the order you specified. Figure 23-6 shows the output from this example.

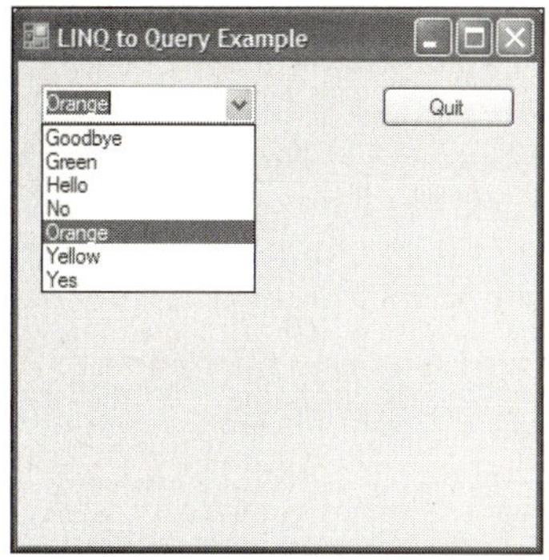

Figure 23-6: Controls can benefit from the features that LINQ provides.

This example also provides the means to delete entries. Unfortunately, the `KeyPress` event doesn't detect the Delete key, so the example adds the required code to the `KeyDown` event handler. Unlike adding entries, deleting entries doesn't require you to modify the order of the list. Consequently, you can still address this portion of the example using straight code, as shown here:

```
private void cbResult_KeyDown(object sender,
                              KeyEventArgs e)
{
   // Check for a Delete key press.
   if (e.KeyValue == (int)Keys.Delete)

      // Remove an item when no longer needed.
      cbResult.Items.Remove(cbResult.SelectedItem);
}
```

In this case, whenever the code detects the Delete key, it removes the selected item from the list. Notice that this portion of the code uses an `int` for detection, rather than a `char`. Otherwise, the code behaves as you'd expect.

Using LINQ to DataSet

You can use LINQ to DataSet to interact with the `DataSet` control. The `DataSet` control can help you access a number of data sources, including those found in databases. Consequently, use this provider when you can't find a specific provider for your database and you can get the data you want to manipulate into the `DataSet` control.

This example is going to examine an extremely simple scenario — accessing data within a `DataSet` that contains a single `DataTable`. The `DataTable` contains a number of records, and the query will extract those matching specific criteria. The project depends on a simple Windows Forms application.

Defining the Test Tables

The example will use a special class to create the `DataSet`. Begin by adding a class file to your application and calling it `CreateDataSet.CS`. The `DataSet` entries rely on the `WeatherEntry` structure shown here.

```
public struct WeatherEntry
{
   public String Name;
   public DateTime Day;
   public Int16 Temp;
   public Boolean Sunny;
   public Int16 WindSpeed;
   public Double Barometer;
}
```

In order to support the database nature of the example, you must provide a special using directive. Add the following directive to the top of the class file:

```
using System.Data;
```

Real weather entries likely contain far more data than shown here, but the example entry provides a number of data types and makes it possible to create a number of query types. Listing 23-4 shows how the example works with the `WeatherEntry` structure to create a data table. Notice the use of individual methods so that you can use as little or much of the sample data as required for an example.

Listing 23-4: Creating test tables

```
public static DataSet CreateDS(String DSName,
                               String DTName)
{
   // Create some test data.
   WeatherEntry[] Data = CreateDataSet.CreateQuickData();

   // Create the dataset.
   DataTable TestTable =
      CreateDataSet.CreateDT(Data, DTName);
   DataSet ThisDS = new DataSet(DSName);
   ThisDS.Tables.Add(TestTable);

   // Return the result.
   return ThisDS;
}

public static DataTable CreateDT(WeatherEntry[] Entries,
                                 String DTName)
{
   // Create the table.
   DataTable DT = new DataTable(DTName);

   // Add the columns.
   DT.Columns.Add("Name", typeof(String));
```

```
    DT.Columns.Add("Day", typeof(DateTime));
    DT.Columns.Add("Temp", typeof(Int16));
    DT.Columns.Add("Sunny", typeof(Boolean));
    DT.Columns.Add("Windspeed", typeof(Int16));
    DT.Columns.Add("Barometer", typeof(Double));

    // Add the data.
    foreach (WeatherEntry ThisEntry in Entries)
       DT.Rows.Add(ThisEntry.Name, ThisEntry.Day,
          ThisEntry.Temp, ThisEntry.Sunny,
          ThisEntry.WindSpeed, ThisEntry.Barometer);

    // Return the data table.
    return DT;
}

public static WeatherEntry[] CreateQuickData()
{
    // Create the weather data.
    WeatherEntry[] QuickData =
    {
       new WeatherEntry {Name = "Joe",
          Day = new DateTime(2008, 11, 01),
          Temp = 75, Sunny = true,
          WindSpeed = 10, Barometer=30.02},
       new WeatherEntry {Name = "Ann",
          Day = new DateTime(2008, 11, 02),
          Temp = 70, Sunny = false,
          WindSpeed = 25, Barometer=29.35},
       new WeatherEntry {Name = "Sally",
          Day = new DateTime(2008, 11, 03),
          Temp = 89, Sunny = true,
          WindSpeed = 0, Barometer=30.15},
       new WeatherEntry {Name = "Irvin",
          Day = new DateTime(2008, 11, 04),
          Temp = 84, Sunny = true,
          WindSpeed = 5, Barometer=29.98},
       new WeatherEntry {Name = "Nancy",
          Day = new DateTime(2008, 11, 05),
          Temp = 72, Sunny = false,
          WindSpeed = 30, Barometer=29.41},
       new WeatherEntry {Name = "Joe",
          Day = new DateTime(2008, 11, 06),
          Temp = 82, Sunny = false,
          WindSpeed = 10, Barometer=29.11}
    };

    // return the weather data.
    return QuickData;
}
```

All the methods in this class are static so that you can call them directly from the code. The `CreateQuickData()` method defines an array of type `WeatherEntry`. This code relies on the LINQ object initializers and collection initializers feature (read more about this topic at `http://msdn.microsoft.com/en-us/library/bb384062.aspx`). Older versions of C# don't have this feature, but you could easily create the array using the same methods you've employed in the past. When the `CreateQuickData()` method exits, it returns an array of test data — you can substitute your own data as desired to test specific LINQ features.

The `CreateDT()` method accepts an array of type `WeatherEntry`, along with the table name, as input. The code begins by adding columns of specific types to the table. It then uses a `foreach` loop to create the `DataTable` rows. Finally, the `CreateDT()` method returns a `DataTable` to the caller.

The `CreateDS()` method accepts the name of the `DataSet` and its associated `DataTable` as input. This code shows how to work with the other static methods in this class within your own test applications. The output is a `DataSet` that contains one table and is ready for use with your test applications. This class provides as much automation as is feasible for testing purposes in this chapter.

Outputting the Results

Now that the class used to create the `DataSet` is complete, it's time to look at the code for the application itself. The example relies on a `DataGridView` control for display, so you'll want to add this control to your application and name it `ThisDGV`. As a minimum, you must define columns for the `DataGridView` control before you can fill it with data. Here is the simple code that this example employs to create columns for each of the outputs:

```
public frmMain()
{
   InitializeComponent();

   // Add the columns.
   ThisDGV.Columns.Add("Name", "Name");
   ThisDGV.Columns.Add("Day", "Day");
   ThisDGV.Columns.Add("Temp", "Temperature");
   ThisDGV.Columns.Add("Sunny", "Sunny?");
   ThisDGV.Columns.Add("WindSpeed", "Wind Speed");
   ThisDGV.Columns.Add("Barometer", "Barometer Reading");
}
```

Exploring the Connection

If you've followed the previous sections about creating the test `DataSet`, you should have a basic application setup at this point. It's finally time to define the first LINQ query. A single table `DataSet` isn't completely out of the question for many application uses, but when working with a database, you'll probably use more tables than shown in Listing 23-5. This example simply provides the basics, using a simple `DataTable`.

Listing 23-5: Defining a simple LINQ to DataSet connection

```
private void btnTest_Click(object sender, EventArgs e)
{
   // Obtain a DataSet.
   DataSet TestMe = CreateDataSet.CreateDS("TestDS",
                                           "TestTable");
```

```
        // Perform a query.
        var DataOut =
           TestMe.Tables["TestTable"].Rows.Cast<DataRow>().
           Where(
              ThisEntry =>
                 ThisEntry.ItemArray[0].ToString() == "Joe");

        // Display the results.
        foreach (DataRow ThisRow in DataOut)
           ThisDGV.Rows.Add(ThisRow.ItemArray);
     }
```

The code creates a test `DataSet` using the `CreateDataSet` features. The "Defining the Test Tables" section of the chapter tells you how this class works.

Creating a LINQ query is only a little different from working with queries on arrays and other control types. As when you work with a control, you must begin with `Cast<DataRow>()` in the query or the `TestMe` `DataSet` won't provide the required functionality. After you perform the cast, you can begin using methods such as `Where()` to refine the query.

It's important to notice the difference in the lambda expression for this query. Look at how the lambda expression accesses a particular element of the `ItemArray` and converts it to a `String` from an object in order to perform the comparison. Another way to formulate this query is to perform the cast into a separate object and then work directly with that object, as shown here:

```
// Perform the cast.
IEnumerable<DataRow> Sequence =
   TestMe.Tables["TestTable"].AsEnumerable();

// Perform the query.
var DataOut = Sequence.Where(
   ThisEntry =>
      ThisEntry.ItemArray[0].ToString() == "Joe");
```

After the code makes the query, it takes the records returned as part of this query, showing them as a portion of a `foreach` loop and displaying them in `ThisDGV`. Notice that you must add the `ThisRow.ItemArray` property using the `dgResult.Rows.Add()` method. Figure 23-7 shows the output of this application.

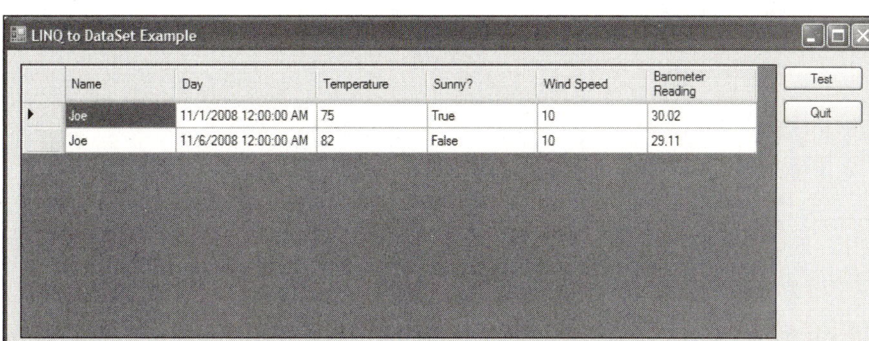

Figure 23-7: LINQ DataSet queries are quite small and fast.

Using LINQ to SQL

LINQ to SQL gives you access to SQL Server databases. Some developers will find using LINQ to SQL confusing because LINQ to SQL does have similarities to SQL (the language used by SQL Server). However, once you get used to the LINQ way of performing a task, you may find that you prefer it to SQL for many tasks.

LINQ to SQL isn't always the best option for accessing SQL Server. For example, you may find that some complex queries actually execute faster on the server, so you may choose to use a stored procedure (sproc) instead of LINQ to SQL. (Stored procedures are scripts you create for use with SQL Server directly on the server.) It's important to remember that LINQ to SQL is simply another tool at your disposal and that you shouldn't make it the only tool you rely on. You should also realize that the future of LINQ to SQL may be unclear. The article at `http://www.infoq.com/news/2008/11/DLINQ-Future` *tries to clear up some current confusion on the part of developers regarding LINQ to SQL.*

Working with LINQ to SQL is a little more complicated than working with LINQ to Object. That's because you need to create a map of the database data structure in order to access it using LINQ. Fortunately, Microsoft makes this part of the process easier by including a special tool for the task called SQLMetal. The following sections describe how to create a very basic LINQ to SQL connection and use it to perform a query. It's important to remember that this is the tip of the iceberg and LINQ to SQL provides significantly more functionality than shown in the example.

You may be wondering why I'm not using the AdventureWorks2008 database for the example. The AdventureWorks2008 database is relatively complex and doesn't lend itself to simple examples. In addition, the current version of SQLMetal isn't capable of creating the required entity classes when working with AdventureWorks2008.

Testing the Visual Studio Connection

Working with LINQ to SQL is a bit different than using a direct connection. Before you begin this example, install SQL Server on your system and then download the Northwind database from the Web site at `http://www.microsoft.com/downloads/details.aspx?FamilyID=06616212-0356-46A0-8DA2-EEBC53A68034`. Follow the installation instructions provided on the Web site to install your copy of Northwind on the test system. You may find that the Web site instructions are too terse to follow — Microsoft provides more detailed instructions as part of the `\SQL Server 2000 Sample Databases\ReadMe_SQL2000SampleDbScripts.htm` file on your hard drive. To ensure that everything is in place before you begin this example, you'll want to test the connection from Visual Studio. Open a copy of Visual Studio and use the following steps to test the database connection:

1. Choose View ➪ Server Explorer. You'll see the Server Explorer.
2. Right-click Data Connections and choose Add Connection from the context menu.
    a. If you haven't chosen a data source previously, you'll see the Choose Data Source dialog box. Select Microsoft SQL Server in the Data Source list and click Continue.
    b. Server Explorer will display the Connection Properties dialog box shown in Figure 23-8 (this one already has all of the information filled out).

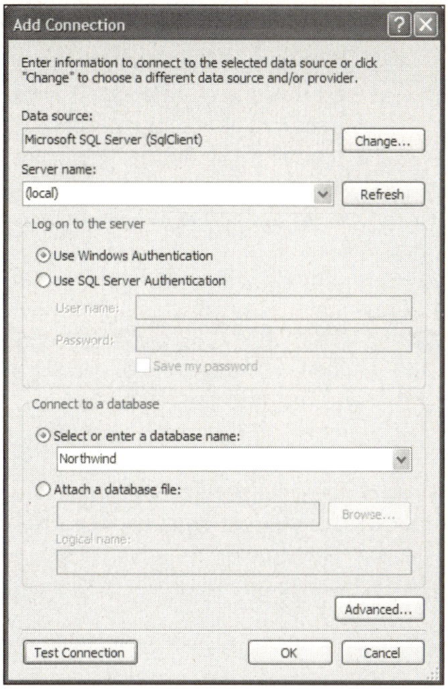

Figure 23-8: Use the Connection Properties dialog box to check for the example database.

3. Type the name of the remote server, your machine (local), or a period (.) in the Server Name field.
4. Click the down arrow in the Select or Enter a Database Name field. You should see the Northwind database, as shown in Figure 23-8. If you don't see this entry, it means that an error occurred. Try installing the database a second time. A second failure usually means that there's a problem with your SQL Server setup and you might need to reinstall the product. At this point, you need to make sure you can actually access the database.
5. Choose the Northwind database.
6. Click Test Connection. When the installation program installs the database properly and you can access Northwind, you'll see a success message.
7. Click OK to clear the success message and Cancel to clear the Database Connection dialog box.
8. You can close Visual Studio if desired.

Because you're the only one using SQL Server, you don't need to worry about assigning login permissions for the test database. If you want to test any applications created in this book with the full version of SQL Server, you probably will need to assign login permissions to the test database to ensure it works as anticipated.

Generating the Northwind Entity Classes and XML Mapping Files

Visual Studio 2008 includes a new tool called SQLMetal that helps you generate classes for your databases just as the designer does. The reason you need this tool is to create entity classes for the Northwind database. For the most part, you don't need to know anything about these entity classes to use them with the Northwind database. You can learn more about entity classes at `http://msdn.microsoft.com/en-us/library/bb425822.aspx`. If you have an older version of Visual Studio, you can download the SQLMetal tool from `http://msdn2.microsoft.com/en-us/library/bb386987.aspx`.

SQLMetal is a command line tool, so knowing how to work at the command line is a plus. However, some people find the command line a little daunting so someone came up with a user interface for SQLMetal. You can download this tool at `http://sourceforge.net/projects/sqlmetalbuilder/`. This chapter uses the command line version to make things easier to understand and a little faster. It pays to try both the command line and the Windowed version of SQLMetal, however, to see which version you like better.

In addition to the entity classes, you may also need XML mapping files to use the Northwind database in some cases. The basic examples in this chapter don't use the XML mapping file, so you can skip creating the XML mapping file if you only plan to work with the basic examples (simply omit the `/Map` command line switch).

The following steps show how to create the Northwind entity classes and XML mapping files without telling you much about how entity classes work. The procedure assumes that you don't have a lot of experience at the command line, but it's important to follow every step or you may end up with an unusable configuration. The procedure also assumes that you're working with Vista or Windows Server 2008 — some steps are overkill in Windows XP and Windows 2003 because these older versions of Windows lack the strict security of the newer versions.

1. Choose Start ➪ Programs ➪ Microsoft Visual Studio 2008 ➪ Visual Studio Tools. Right-click Visual Studio 2008 Command Prompt and choose Run As Administrator from the context menu. Windows opens an administrator command prompt that looks like the one shown in Figure 23-9. Unlike a standard command prompt, this command prompt has additional features for working with Visual Studio.

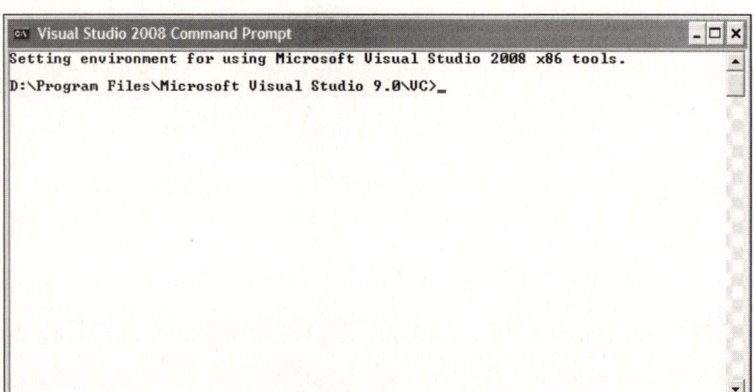

Figure 23-9: Open an administrator command prompt for working with Visual Studio commands.

2. Type **`MD \Northwind`** and press Enter. Windows creates a new folder named Northwind.
3. Type **`CD \Northwind`** and press Enter. You'll see the Northwind folder you just created. This folder will hold the files you need to work with the Northwind database. You'll add these files to your project and add a `using` statement to use the generated classes within your application.
4. Type **`SQLMetal /Server:<Server Name> /Database:Northwind /Namespace:NWind /Code:Northwind.CS /Map:NorthwindMap.XML /Pluralize /Functions /Sprocs /Views`** and press Enter. If you didn't install SQL Server using the Windows integrated security, you'll need to add the **`/User:<User Name>`** and **`/Password:<Password>`** command line switches to the command line to gain access to the server. In this case, your command line will be: **`SQLMetal /Server:<Server Name> /User:<User Name> /Password:<Password> /Database:Northwind /Namespace:NWind /Code:Northwind.CS /Map:NorthwindMap.XML /Pluralize /Functions /Sprocs /Views`**.
    - The `/Server` command line switch tells SQLMetal which SQL Server instance to use.
    - The `/Database` command line switch is the name of the database to use within SQL Server.
    - The optional `/User` and `/Password` command line switches provide your credentials for accessing the SQL Server instance.
    - The `/Namespace` command line switch determines the namespace for the C# code file specified using the `/Code` command line switch (always include the CS file extension).
    - The optional `/Map` command line switch (always include the XML file extension) creates a mapping file that maps data the database understands to a C# counterpart.
    - The `/Pluralize` command line switch tells SQLMetal to automatically pluralize or singularize class names based on their use in an object environment (such as Customer for a table or Orders for a collection).
    - The optional `/Functions`, `/Sprocs`, and `/Views` command line switches tell SQLMetal to extract the functions, stored procedures, and views from the database file, in addition to the database structure. SQLMetal provides a number of other command line switches that you'll find explained at `http://msdn2.microsoft.com/en-us/library/bb386987.aspx`.

Some earlier documentation for SQLMetal shows that you can generate the code and mapping files separately. SQLMetal no longer allows this option — you must use the `/Code` and `/Map` command line switches together. You also have the option of using the `/Code` command line switch by itself.

When you follow this procedure, SQLMetal connects to your SQL Server and opens the Northwind database for use. It then generates the files you need to work with the Northwind database, including all of the functions, stored procedures (sprocs), and views. All this code resides in the NWind namespace, so you need to add `using NWind;` to your code files to access the resulting classes. All of the code resides in the `Northwind.CS` file. The mapping information appears in the `NorthwindMap.XML` file. Your output should look like the output in Figure 23-10 when the utility runs without error.

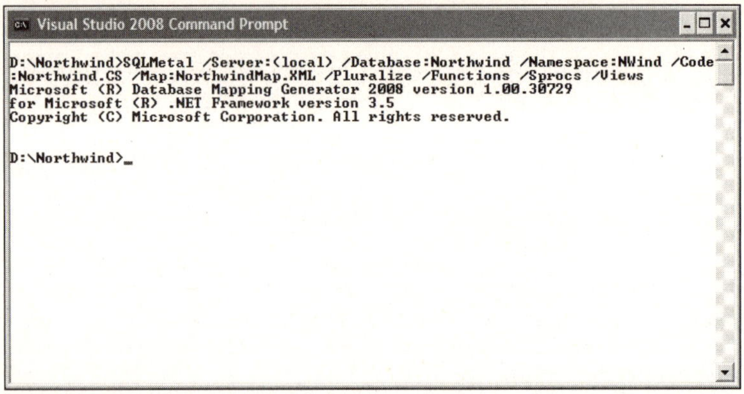

Figure 23-10: Create the entity classes you need when working with the sample applications.

Defining the Project

A typical LINQ to SQL project will require some additional configuration on your part. The following steps provide you with the basics you need to create a project:

1. Create the basic project as you normally do.
2. Right-click the project entry and choose Add ➪ Existing Item from the context menu. Visual Studio displays the Add Existing Item dialog box.
3. Select the All Files (*.*) option. Locate and highlight the `Northwind.CS` and `NorthwindMap.XML` files in the Northwind folder that you created earlier. Visual Studio will select both files, as shown in Figure 23-11.

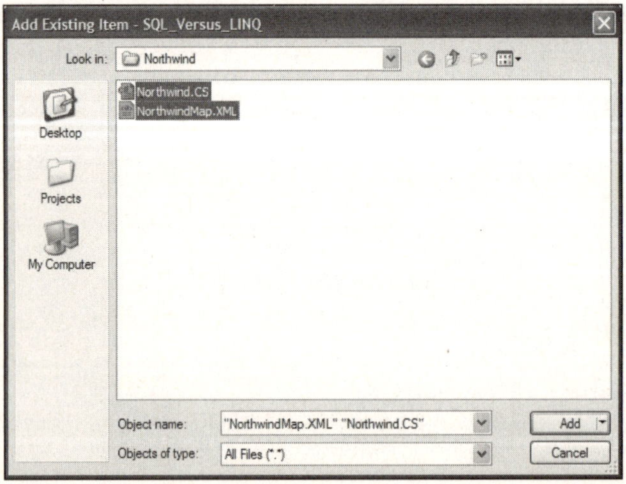

Figure 23-11: Select both the entity class and XML mapping files that you created earlier.

4. Click Add. Visual Studio adds both files to your project.

5. Right-click References and choose Add Reference from the context menu. Visual Studio displays the Add Reference dialog box shown in Figure 23-12.

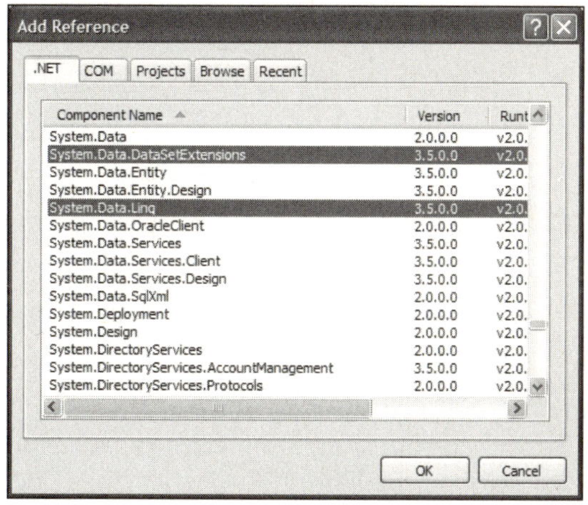

Figure 23-12: Add the required references to your project.

6. Highlight the `System.Data.DataSetExtensions`, `System.Data.Linq`, and `System.Xml.Linq` entries (as needed). Click OK. Solution Explorer now displays the files and references you need to create a project.

7. Type the following code in the main project file (adding these references provides access to the database and required mapping functionality).

```
using NWind;
using System.Data.Linq.Mapping;
```

Adding the Code

You can finally add some code to your project to interact with the Northwind database. This example relies on a connection string. You could also rely on an existing connection, but the technique shown here works reliably. Listing 23-2 (explained earlier in this chapter) shows the code for this example. The "Contrasting LINQ with SQL" section of the chapter describes how the code works and shows the output from this example.

Using LINQ to XML

You can use the LINQ to XML to manipulate any kind of XML data, even when that data doesn't appear in a file with an XML extension. For example, Microsoft places application configuration data in a CONFIG file, but that file is still in XML format, so you can use LINQ to XML to manipulate it.

Working with XML in memory will help you understand how XML works with LINQ to XML. Of course, you'll normally read XML data from a file or obtain it from a Web service. The principles are the same no matter where you obtain the XML data.

LINQ to XML differs from the other LINQ providers described in this chapter because it focuses on the formation of the data, rather than performing outright queries. In other words, this form of LINQ will help you create data with greater ease. Of course, you can also query the data by placing the data in a `DataSet` and using LINQ to DataSet to interact with them (see the "Using LINQ to DataSet" section for details). When working with LINQ to XML, you should consider the following tasks:

- Load XML documents into memory from files or streams.
- Serialize XML documents in memory to files or streams.
- Define your own XML documents using XML queries.
- Create simple XML queries that look like any other LINQ query.
- Create complex XML queries that use XPath-like axes to locate specific bits of data.
- Modify the in-memory presentation of an XML tree using methods such as `Add`, `Remove`, `ReplaceWith`, and `SetValue`.
- Validate the content of XML trees using XSD to eliminate potential database contamination.
- Transform data from one format to another using XML as the starting point, the end point, or as an intermediary between two dissimilar formats.

The example in this section begins discussing some practical elements, such as loading and saving XML as a file. You'll then see how to perform a query against XML data. Of course, this example only whets your appetite — the LINQ to XML provider can do considerably more than you see here.

Creating the Project

You create an XML manipulation program the same way you create any other program. Of course, you want to ensure all of the references you need are in place, including `System.Xml.Linq.DLL`. After you add the appropriate references, add the required using directives. This example requires that you provide the following using statements:

```
using System.Xml;
using System.Xml.Linq;
using System.IO;
```

Building an XML Document

Before you can work with the XML document, you need to create one. Listing 23-6 shows the XML document creation code used for this example.

Listing 23-6: Creating the XML document

```
// Holds the XML document.
XDocument ThisDoc;

private void btnCreate_Click(object sender, EventArgs e)
{
   // Define the new XML document.
   ThisDoc = new XDocument(
```

```
            // Add the declaration.
            new XDeclaration("1.0", "utf-8", "yes"),

            // Add a list of contacts.
            new XElement("Contacts",

               // Each contact has specific elements.
               new XElement("Contact",
                  new XElement("Name", "Jane Newton"),
                  new XElement("Address1", "123 First St."),
                  new XElement("Address2", "Suite 3"),
                  new XElement("City", "Anywhere"),
                  new XElement("State", "WI"),
                  new XElement("ZIP", "99999-9999")),

                // A second contact.
               new XElement("Contact",
                  new XElement("Name", "George Banes"),
                  new XElement("Address1", "99 North Rd."),
                  new XElement("Address2", "First Floor"),
                  new XElement("City", "Somewhere"),
                  new XElement("State", "CA"),
                  new XElement("ZIP", "88888-8888"))));

         // Display the result.
         wbResult.DocumentText =
            ThisDoc.Declaration.ToString() +
            ThisDoc.Document.ToString();

         // Enable the Save button.
         btnSave.Enabled = true;
      }
```

The interesting feature of this example is that it creates the whole XML document, `ThisDoc`, using a single line of code. In fact, you can create XML documents of any length and complexity using a single line of code. The problem with this approach is that it does make debugging a little more difficult. The debugger can't show you what is happening with the individual elements when they all appear in a single line of code.

After the code creates the XML document, it displays it on screen. This approach does work, but the results may not appear as you expected them to appear. Figure 23-13 shows that you see only the two contact entries and none of the tags supporting them.

The tags do exist. The application relies on a `WebBrowser` control to display the output, so you can right-click the control and choose View Source from the context menu. The application opens a copy of Notepad with the code-behind for the Web page, as shown in Figure 23-14. As you can see, all the tags are there and the application has even formatted them nicely.

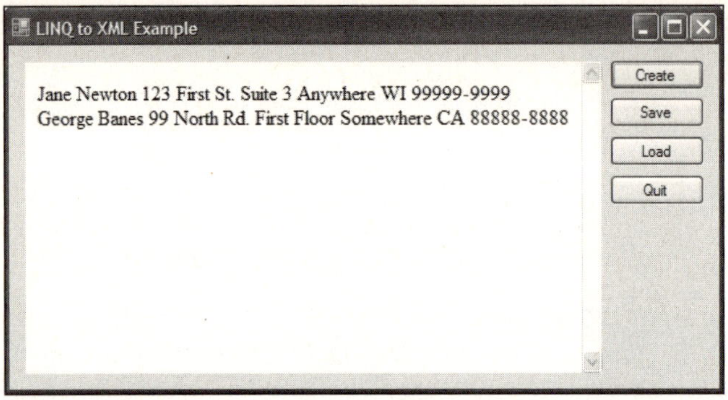

Figure 23-13: The output shows the names and addresses.

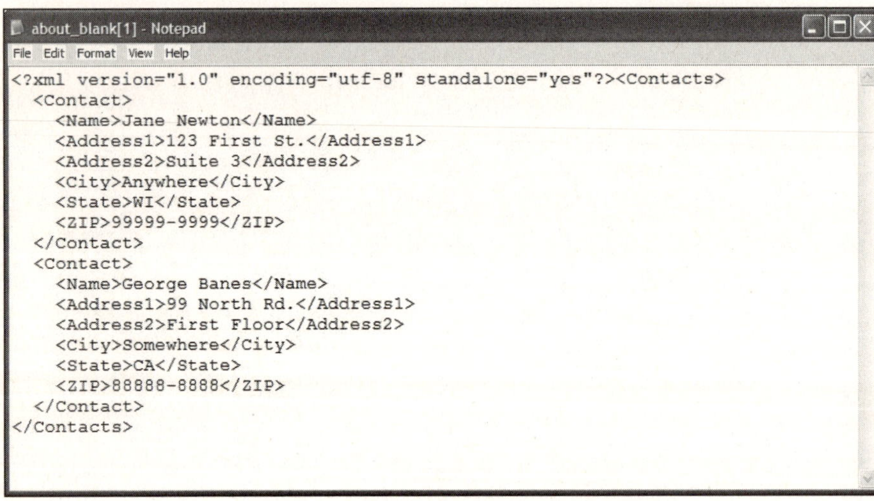

Figure 23-14: The source shows the true document information.

Saving an XML Document

The document created in the "Building an XML Document" section still resides in memory. It's time to put the XML file on disk. The application stores this file in the same folder as the application executable using the code shown here:

```
private void btnSave_Click(object sender, EventArgs e)
{
    // Save the document where you need it.
    ThisDoc.Save(Application.StartupPath +
        @"\Test.XML", SaveOptions.None);

    // Reload the document.
    wbResult.Navigate(
        Application.StartupPath + @"\Test.XML");
}
```

The `ThisDoc` object includes the `Save()` method, which lets you save the document to disk without writing a lot of code. All you need to supply is a string that includes the file path and filename. The `Save()` method also includes some special save options that appear as part of the `System.Xml.Linq.SaveOptions` enumeration.

The `System.Xml.Linq.SaveOptions` enumeration provides the means to save an XML document in a specific way. These options are mutually exclusive, which means you can combine them to achieve specific results. The following list describes each of these options:

- **None:** Causes the application to indent the XML while serializing it. This option makes the XML easily readable by humans, but also adds to the disk storage requirements because the document now contains additional white space.
- **DisableFormatting:** Saves the document with all insignificant white space intact, which means the resulting document contains all the formatting you provided while creating it.

After the code saves the file to disk, it can display the information correctly in the `WebBrowser` control. In this case, the code relies on the `Navigate()` method to reload the XML file. Figure 23-15 shows the results of the loading process. The result is an XML file that looks the same as if you had loaded it using Internet Explorer.

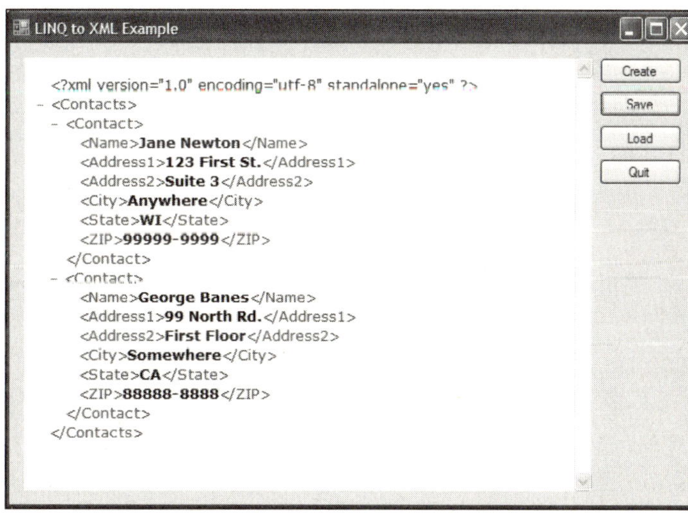

Figure 23-15: The XML looks closer to the anticipated output.

Loading an XML Document

The final task to perform in this example application is loading the XML document from disk. As before, `XDocument` makes this task relatively straightforward, as shown in Listing 23-7.

Listing 23-7: Loading an XML document from disk

```
private void btnLoad_Click(object sender, EventArgs e)
```

Continued

Listing 23-7: Loading an XML document from disk *(continued)*

```
{
   // Verify that the file exists.
   if (File.Exists(
      Application.StartupPath + @"\Test.XML"))
   {
      // Load the document.
      ThisDoc = XDocument.Load(
         Application.StartupPath + @"\Test.XML");

      // Display the document.
      wbResult.Navigate(
         Application.StartupPath + @"\Test.XML");
   }
   else
      // Display an error message.
      MessageBox.Show(
         "The Test.XML file doesn't exist. " +
         "Click Create!");
}
```

The code begins by checking for the existence of the file using the `File.Exists()` method. When the file doesn't exist, the example displays an error message and then exits the method.

When the file does exist, the code loads it using the static `XDocument.Load()` method. This method actually creates a new `XDocument` based on the content of the file. Notice that you don't have to do anything special to load the XML document and you don't have to worry about creating a `TextReader` to do it. Everything takes place in the background. As with the `Save()` method, you also have access to some special load options.

The `System.Xml.Linq.LoadOptions` enumeration provides the means to load an XML document in a specific way. These options are mutually exclusive, which means you can combine them to achieve specific results. The following list describes each of these options:

- None
- PreserveWhitespace
- SetBaseUri
- SetLineInfo

The example ends by displaying the file in `wbResult`. It relies on the `Navigate()` method to perform this task. You see output similar to Figure 23-15.

Using Third-Party Providers

With feature bloat running rampant and developer time in ever-limited quantity, you may wonder whether LINQ is the right choice for you. In most cases, you'd find a list of qualifiers where you'd need to decide whether a technology is the right one for you. The thing about LINQ is that it's actually a very good technology that can apply to anyone's needs. If you have to search for data, then LINQ is a good choice because it can search just about anything you can think of today. You won't have to wait until tomorrow to use it while you wait for drivers or additional software. In short, anyone who searches for data can use LINQ to meet that need.

Of course, now you're thinking that this chapter is offering you the fabled silver bullet solution. LINQ isn't a silver bullet, either. The other tools you have now for searching are still useful and you'll need to employ them. For example, even Microsoft admits that LINQ has performance problems, in some cases, when it comes to searching SQL Server databases. In fact, you can read the five-part blog series about performance issues at `http://blogs.msdn.com/ricom/archive/2007/06/22/dlinq-linq-to-sql-performance-part-1.aspx` to obtain a good overview of the problems (but not any significant solutions).

It's also important to understand that LINQ works with most data sources, but not all of them. For example, you can easily use LINQ with most public Web services and some private Web services as well. However, even though you can use LINQ quite easily with the Amazon, Google, or AOL Web services, you'll find that it doesn't work at all with the eBay Web services due to security concerns. In short, specific Web service requirements can prevent LINQ from working properly. You can find a complete list of LINQ providers (LINQ to solutions) at `http://blogs.msdn.com/charlie/archive/2006/10/05/Links-to-LINQ.aspx`. Table 23-1 shows the known providers as of this writing.

Table 23-1: A Listing of LINQ Providers

Name	Purpose	URL
LINQ Extender	Toolkit for building LINQ providers	`http://www.codeplex.com/LinqExtender`
LINQ over C# Project	General	`http://www.codeplex.com/LinqOverCSharp`
LINQ to Active Directory	General	`http://www.codeplex.com/LINQtoAD`
LINQ to Amazon	General	`http://weblogs.asp.net/fmarguerie/archive/2006/06/26/Introducing-Linq-to-Amazon.aspx`
LINQ to Bindable Sources	SyncLINQ — a kind of data binding	`http://www.paulstovell.com/blog/why-synclinq-should-matter-to-you`
LINQ to CRM	Customer Relationship Management (CRM)	`http://www.codeplex.com/LinqtoCRM`
LINQ to Excel	General	`http://www.codeplex.com/xlslinq`
LINQ to Expressions	MetaLinq	`http://www.codeplex.com/metalinq`
LINQ to Flickr	General	`http://www.codeplex.com/LINQFlickr`
LINQ To Geo	Geospatial data	`http://www.codeplex.com/LinqToGeo`
LINQ to Google	General	`http://www.codeplex.com/glinq`
LINQ to Indexes	General	`http://www.codeplex.com/i4o/Release/ProjectReleases.aspx?ReleaseId=3519`

Continued

Table 23-1: A Listing of LINQ Providers *(continued)*

Name	Purpose	URL
LINQ to IQueryable	Component Object Model (COM)	`http://blogs.msdn.com/mattwar/archive/2007/08/09/linq-building-an-iqueryable-provider-part-vi.aspx`
LINQ to JavaScript	General	`http://www.codeplex.com/JSLINQ`
LINQ to JSON	JavaScript Object Notation (JSON)	`http://james.newtonking.com/archive/2008/02/11/linq-to-json-beta.aspx`
LINQ to LDAP	Lightweight Directory Access Protocol (LDAP)	`http://community.bartdesmet.net/blogs/bart/archive/2007/04/05/the-iqueryable-tales-linq-to-ldap-part-0.aspx`
LINQ to Lucene	General	`http://www.codeplex.com/linqtolucene`
LINQ to Metaweb	Freebase (an open, shared database of the world's knowledge)	`http://www.codeplex.com/metawebToLinQ`
LINQ to MySQL, Oracle, and PostgreSql	General	`http://code2code.net/DB_Linq/`
LINQ to NHibernate	General	`http://www.ayende.com/Blog/archive/2007/03/17/Implementing-Linq-for-NHibernate-A-How-To-Guide-Part.aspx`
LINQ to RDF	Resource Description Framework (RDF) file access	`http://blogs.msdn.com/hartmutm/archive/2006/07/24/677200.aspx`
LINQ to SharePoint	General	`http://www.codeplex.com/LINQtoSharePoint`
LINQ to SimpleDB	General	`http://www.codeplex.com/LinqToSimpleDB`
LINQ to Streams	General	`http://www.codeplex.com/Slinq/`
LINQ to WebQueries	General	`http://blogs.msdn.com/hartmutm/archive/2006/06/12/628382.aspx`
LINQ to WMI	Windows Management Instrumentation (WMI)	`http://bloggingabout.net/blogs/emile/archive/2005/12/12/10514.aspx`, `http://tomasp.net/blog/linq-expand.aspx`, and `http://tomasp.net/blog/linq-expand-update.aspx`
LINQ to XtraGrid	General	`http://cs.rthand.com/blogs/blog_with_righthand/archive/2008/02/23/LINQ-to-XtraGrid.aspx`

Even with these few warts, however, LINQ is a good solution for many search needs and you should at least try it. You need LINQ because it has so much to offer and it doesn't require a lot of time to learn or use. LINQ provides the experimental platform that most developers crave. In those few situations where LINQ can't do a good job for you, experimentation can at least help you understand the data source better.

Implementing Your Design

This chapter has helped you discover how LINQ can make your coding experience better. Most developers will find that LINQ makes a fine query tool and stops there. Actually, that's okay. You don't necessarily have to become a LINQ guru to experience how this language helps you create better programs in better time. The one bit of information to take away from this chapter is that LINQ can help you query nearly any data source (and it gets closer to querying everything every day).

LINQ is one of those technologies that look like smoke and mirrors at first. You'll find yourself asking how the magician does the trick. The best way to see how LINQ works is to create some examples on your own and work through them with the debugger. Trace into the calls so that you can see how LINQ actually works. After you see a few examples, the technology will begin making sense. Fortunately, you're using C# as your language of choice. For some odd reason, the Visual Basic .NET debugger doesn't go into all of the details that the C# debugger does.

Chapter 24 shows you another new technology that Microsoft has provided as an addition to Visual Studio — F#. Besides adding yet another single letter language to the list, F# does have something very special to offer — it's a functional language. Just what is a functional language? You'll have to read Chapter 24 to find out. However, for the moment, consider that a functional language will complement, not replace, the functionality that C# provides. You'll find F# has some unique features to add to your toolbox and that those features will make tasks such as multiprocessing development easier.

24

Augmenting Applications Using F#

You may think you already have enough computer languages from which to choose. To a certain extent, you probably do. Theoretically, you could build any application desired using just machine code, but few people would argue that using machine code alone would provide a very productive environment. In fact, it has been at least 20 years since I worked with machine code. Computer languages came about because developers needed faster ways to work than machine code provided. The reason for newer languages is always the same. Sure, C is a great language, but C++ is better, and many developers would argue that C# is better still. Consequently, this chapter argues that Microsoft's F# is simply another in a long series of language updates designed to supplement your current language in a specific way.

At the time of this writing, F# is still essentially a beta product, which means that the results you obtain depend a lot on how the installation performs, your particular configuration, and the version of Visual Studio that you use. Don't let the term Community Technology Preview (CTP) *fool you — you're beta testing F# for Microsoft. F# is already stable enough for noncritical applications and you should definitely use it for experimentation. However, because Microsoft is still working on F#, you should probably avoid using it for critical applications. Remember that it's important to create reliable applications and beta language products tend not to be reliable. The example in this chapter relies on the September 2008 CTP.*

F# truly is a complementary language to other Visual Studio languages. Yes, you could probably build perfectly acceptable applications using F# alone, but F# requires a different way of viewing application development, as described in this chapter. For the C# developer, F# offers certain efficiencies and can make a significant difference in application performance (that's speed, reliability, and security).

The examples in this chapter aren't meant to teach you F#. You'd easily need an entire book to accomplish that task. Rather, view these examples as an introduction to F#. The examples simply show how F# differs from C# and demonstrate some concepts you need to consider as you move forward with learning more about F#. You'll find that F# is an exciting language with some interesting possibilities to make the development process easier.

Understanding F#

As previously mentioned, F# is a different kind of a language. If you've worked your entire career with procedural languages, be prepared for a shock. Development doesn't always follow a procedural form. In fact, many nonprocedural languages exist in the world and F# is just one of them. Nonprocedural languages exist to fulfill special needs. Often, it's important to view a problem from a different perspective. For example, when working with Language INtegrated Query (LINQ) (see Chapter 23 for details) or Structured Query Language (SQL), you tell the interpreter what to do, not how to do it. The interpreter looks at the problem and creates an optimized solution for you. F# is a functional language, which solves a different sort of problem. The following sections describe what a functional language is and how it can benefit you.

Some developers assign mystical properties to some languages. At the end of the day, the computer doesn't care about the language you use — all it sees is the machine code that all the layers of language eventually generate. In fact, if you really want to look at the raw form of language, a language simply specifies which switches to change in a circuit — nothing more. A language exists for the developer's benefit, so you should always use the language that serves your needs best.

Considering the Functional Language

Although I normally detest categorizing anything, it's important to categorize F# as part of analyzing it and determining how best to use it. There are many ways to categorize languages. The categories are there to help people decide which language is best for a particular use, but often they end up confusing more than helping. In this section, you categorize F# from the perspective of how it performs tasks — in short, you need to answer the question of how the way F# performs tasks differs from the way in which C# and Visual Basic.NET perform tasks.

F# is a *functional* language, contrasted to C# and Visual Basic.NET, which are *imperative* or *procedural* languages. A functional language is one that relies on equations to define a task. When you use a functional language, the code X = Y means that X and Y are equal. You aren't assigning the value of Y to X. In other words, there is no procedure as there is with C#. The code doesn't imply any form of steps.

An equation defines a specific relationship; there isn't any state to consider or mutable data to manage. Consequently, working with a functional language has certain advantages over an imperative language, because the contents of an identifier (the F# version of a variable) remain the same throughout the execution of the application. It doesn't matter which processor works with the identifier because the identifier always remains the same. F# applications don't suffer the concurrency problems that you must deal with when using an imperative language.

Chapter 25 discusses concurrency issues in more detail because they also affect multithreading. A concurrency issue is one in which the value of a variable is changed by two different entities. The first entity assigns a value to the variable, and then a second entity changes that same variable. When the first entity attempts to use the variable, the variable contains the wrong value — the value assigned by the second entity.

Functional languages also tend to produce succinct code. You create the application using equations and then supplying data to those equations. An equation can be a constant, a function, an object, or anything else that F# supports. Consequently, when you look at an identifier, you could possibly see anything. Some developers have a very hard time understanding this concept, but you've already worked with it to some extent if you've created an eXtensible Stylesheet Language Transformation (XSLT) application, because XSLT has a strong functional language bias.

At this point, you have enough information to start working with F#. I don't want you to become overwhelmed with all of the details just yet. In fact, this chapter tends to show you that F# really isn't that hard to begin using. Of course, functional languages are far more complex than I've indicated here. You can see some good write-ups about functional languages at `http://en.wikipedia.org/wiki/Functional_programming_language` and `http://www.cs.nott.ac.uk/~gmh//faq.html`.

Defining the Need for Functional Languages

Many of the functional languages of the world are used for academic purposes; you typically don't see them used in real-world development. The lack of a practical use is unfortunate because functional languages have a lot to offer. F# is an effort to make functional languages useful in the real world. Not only can you mix and match F# with C# or Visual Basic.NET, but you can use it to create scripts and perform other complex tasks on its own. It's important to remember the three strengths of F#, though, when you consider using it:

- List processing
- Pattern matching
- Concurrent programming strategies

The final use, concurrent programming strategies, is one of the most important considerations as developers begin writing applications for multi-core processors. While you can write perfectly acceptable thread-safe applications using C# (see Chapter 25 for details), using F# tends to enforce the requirements for concurrency and to make writing these applications considerably easier.

A valid criticism of multi-core processor use today is that applications can't make use of the additional processors because developers don't write applications to exploit them. In addition, because imperative languages include the concepts of state, the resulting code can't run across processors because each processor would need to share state information. As a result, many applications use just a single core and the remaining cores tend to remain idle or at least underused.

F# applications also enforce the atomic access requirements for concurrency that can prove difficult to provide with other languages. You get these benefits without extra work on your part because they are part of the F# language. In sum, you gain access to all the processors in a system because such concurrency is a natural part of working with F#. The Microsoft Web site at `http://research.microsoft.com/fsharp/fsharp.aspx` tells you more about the reasons that you'll want to add F# to your toolbox.

Obtaining F# Support for Visual Studio 2008

Visual Studio 2008 doesn't come with F# installed. F# is an add-on much like any other add-on you can obtain for Visual Studio 2008. After you install F#, you'll find that you have new templates that help you create F# applications. The following sections describe how to download and install F# on your system.

You don't necessarily need a copy of Visual Studio to work with F#. However, the examples in this chapter assume that you do have a copy of Visual Studio 2008 installed. This chapter doesn't assume that F# works with earlier versions of Visual Studio and none of the examples are tested for use with earlier versions of the product. That said, theoretically F# should also work with earlier versions of Visual Studio if you're willing to fiddle with your configuration.

Downloading the Product

You won't find F# at the command line or within Visual Studio; you must download and install it. The main prerequisite is that you must have some form of the .NET Framework installed on your system, which includes the use of Mono (`http://www.mono-project.com/Main_Page`).

The inclusion of Mono as part of the picture means that you can use F# on Linux/Macintosh. You can also use it with Windows Server 2008 Server Core version, which currently doesn't support the .NET Framework, interestingly enough. Check out this revelation at `http://technet.microsoft.com/en-us/cc730470.aspx`. According to Microsoft, they do plan to create a light version of the .NET Framework for Server Core in the future, but for now Mono does provide a good alternative.

Microsoft recommends that you have a copy of Visual Studio to work with F#. However, this isn't actually a requirement, just as it isn't a requirement to have a copy of Visual Studio to create C# applications. You can create perfectly acceptable F# applications using nothing more than Notepad and the command line tools that come with the F# installation. In fact, if you plan to use F# on Linux/Macintosh, you'll need a good text editor because Visual Studio doesn't work on Linux/Macintosh.

You can find the F# download at `http://research.microsoft.com/fsharp/release.aspx`. Download the latest version of F# in either MSI (Microsoft Installer) or ZIP form. Use the MSI version if you want to obtain full F# support for Visual Studio because the installer adds projects to the Visual Studio IDE for you.

Installing F#

This section assumes that you've downloaded the MSI file and plan to install Visual Studio 2008 support for F#. The following steps tell how to perform this task.

1. Right-click the MSI file and choose Install from the context menu. You'll see a Preparing to Install message for a few seconds, after which, you'll see the usual Welcome dialog box.
2. Click Next. You'll see the end user licensing agreement.
3. Read the end user licensing agreement. Check I Accept the Terms in the License Agreement and click Next. You may see an odd dialog box that tells you to wait until the installer computes the disk usage requirements. Wait until the dialog box disappears.
4. Click Next, if necessary, to display the Destination Folder dialog box where you can choose the location of the F# installation. The default setting uses the `\Program Files\FSharp-<Version>\` folder of your boot drive, which works fine in most cases.
5. Click Next. The installation program will tell you that it's ready to perform the installation.

6. Click Install. The installation program performs the installation tasks. Be patient, the Visual Studio portion of the installation can require up to a minute to complete. The progress indicator will show that the installation is complete, but you'll see a lot of hard drive activity, so don't cancel the installation at this point.
7. Click Finish. F# is ready for use.

Experimenting at the Command Line

Most .NET languages work just fine at the command prompt. What you really purchase with Visual Studio are development tools — templates, design aids, and other functionality. If you want to create a C# application, you can use nothing more than Notepad to do it. Consequently, it isn't too surprising that you can use F# at the command line and it's instructional to do so for your first application. The following sections show how to use the command line approach.

As with the F# compiler, you can use the C# compiler directly by accessing `CSC.EXE`*. Even if you don't have Visual Studio installed, you can obtain a copy of* `CSC.EXE` *by downloading the .NET Framework Software Development Kit (SDK) from* `http://www.microsoft.com/downloads/details.aspx?FamilyID=fe6f2099-b7b4-4f47-a244-c96d69c35dec`*. You can download the .NET Framework 3.5 SDK at* `http://www.microsoft.com/downloads/details.aspx?FamilyId=E6E1C3DF-A74F-4207-8586-711EBE331CDC` *as an alternative to using the .NET Framework 2.0 SDK. At least a few people use C# for scripting purposes without cracking open a copy of Visual Studio. You can read more about working with C# at the command line at* `http://www.charlespetzold.com/key/CommandLine.html`.

Modifying the Command Line Path to Accommodate F#

To begin working with F# at the command line, you'll want to add the commands to your path. Adding the commands to your path makes them easier to access. The following steps tell how to perform this task.

1. Right-click My Computer and choose Properties to display the System Properties dialog box.
2. Click the Advanced tab.

If you're working with Vista or Windows Server 2008, you'll right-click Computer, choose Properties, and then click the Advanced System Settings link within the System window to display the System Properties dialog box.

3. Click Environment Variables to display the Environment Variables dialog box.
4. Highlight the `Path` environment variable in the User Variables for `<User Name>` list and click Edit. You'll see the Edit User Variable dialog box.
5. Type **";"** (path elements are separated by a semicolon), and then add the path for the F# executables to the path. Using the current version, that means adding a path of `C:\Program Files\FSharp-1.9.6.2\bin` when you use the default installation (your installation folder may differ from the one shown in this step).
6. Click OK three times to complete the process.

Defining a Basic Script

Now that you have the correct path in place, let's open a copy of Notepad or another text editor. Type the following code:

```
let displayMsg = "Hello World!";;

printf "Message: %A" displayMsg
```

The first line defines an identifier named `displayMsg`. You use the `let` keyword to create new identifiers. The `displayMsg` identifier has a value of `"Hello World! "`. Notice that you haven't defined any type information; F# will infer the type from the output of the equation. All identifiers have an output in F#, even if that output is `null` (or void). Notice that you must end the `let` statement with a double semicolon.

The second line tells F# to print the value of `displayMsg`, whatever that value happens to be at the moment. The text within double quotes tells what to print. F# replaces the `%A` with the output of `displayMsg`.

Save the file you've created as `Test.FS`. All F# code files have an FS extension. Remember to choose the All Files option in the Save As Type field of the Save As dialog box when working with Notepad, or the file will have a TXT extension, rather than an FS extension.

Running the Application

It's time to run the test application. Open a command prompt and change directories to the location you saved the `Test.FS` file. F# has a number of command line utilities. For now, you need to consider two utilities.

- **FSC:** Compiles the example. You can then run the resulting executable anytime you want.
- **FSI:** Provides an interactive environment where you can try out commands before committing them to a code file.

It's time to try out the application code. The following steps show how easy it is to run an F# application:

1. Type **`FSC Test.FS`** and press Enter. FSC will compile `Test.FS`.
2. Type **`Test`** and press Enter to see the output shown in Figure 24-1.

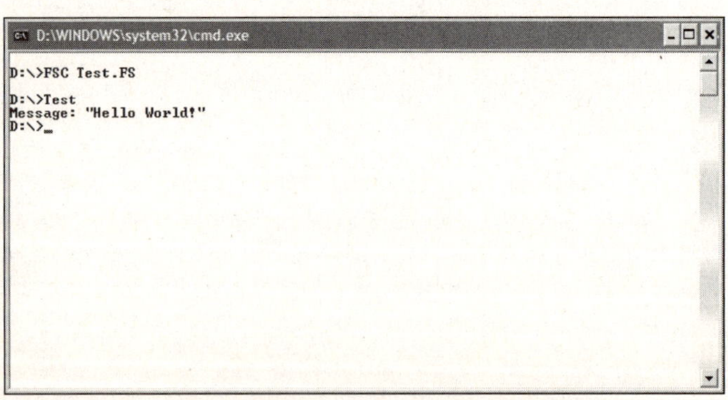

Figure 24-1: Output from the compiled F# application.

Depending on your configuration and the version of F# you download, you may see a warning message of: "`Test.FS(1,1): warning FS0058: The first non-comment text in an F# source file must be '#light' or '#light "off"'. A future release of F# will make '#light' the default. '#light "off"' is primarily for generated code and for writing code inthe subset of F# that cross-compiles with OCaml when you run the text code.`" *It's safe to ignore this warning.*

Interacting with F#

The FSI utility works a bit differently from the FSC utility described in the "Running the Application" section of the chapter. Type **`FSI Test.FS`** and press Enter. The FSI utility will load and execute the file. At this point, you should see output similar to Figure 24-1, but you can also modify the code as desired. Figure 24-2 shows the difference in the two environments.

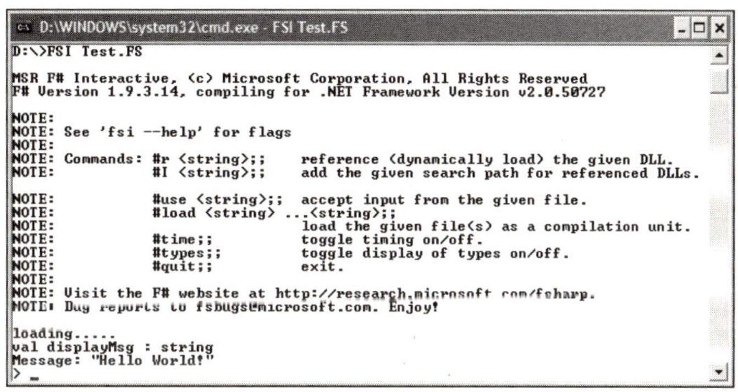

Figure 24-2: The FSI environment begins with the same output, but also displays interactive messages.

To test the interactive nature of FSI, try typing **`let displayMsg msg = msg;;`** and pressing Enter. This command creates a new `displayMsg` identifier that accepts a single variable, `msg`, as input and outputs that value unmodified. Now, you wouldn't actually create an identifier like this in the real world, but this command does demonstrate the interactivity of FSI in a simple manner. FSI responds with:

```
val displayMsg : 'a -> 'a
```

Notice how the output looks sort of like the lambda expressions used with LINQ. The two environments are different, but this similarity is interesting. The problem now is how to send the value you want to display to `displayMsg`.

F# uses a special pipeline operator (|>) to send information to identifiers. To try out the operator, type **`printf "Message: %A" "Hello World!" |> displayMsg;;`** and press Enter. You can send any message to `displayMsg` this way — try it out to see how the functions work in F#. For example, try substituting `Goodbye` for `Now!` as the message. When you finally finish working with the function, type **`#quit;;`** and press Enter to exit the interactive mode. Figure 24-3 shows the entire interactive sequence.

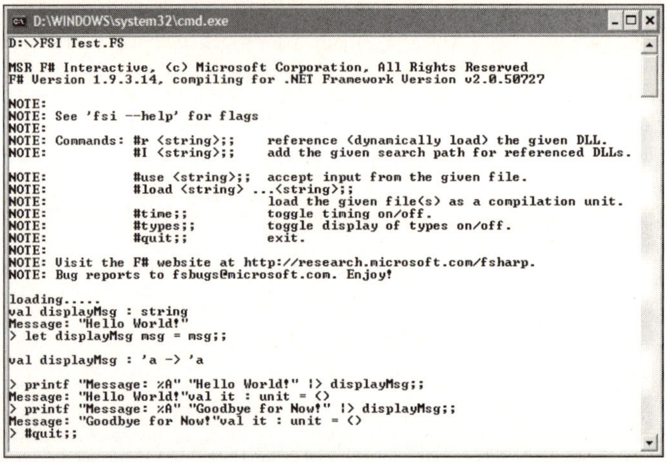

Figure 24-3: Interactive sessions let you discover how to work with F# with ease.

Creating an F# Application

Working at the command line is interesting, but most developers will use F# from within Visual Studio, so that's where this section creates the next example. When you install F# using the MSI file, you also get a new template for Visual Studio. The following steps help you create a new project:

1. Choose File ➪ New ➪ Project and you'll see the New Project dialog box shown in Figure 24-4. You'll find the F# project template in the `Other Project Types\F# Projects` folder. (Depending on your Visual Studio version and the version of F# you use, you may see the project in the `Project Types\F# Projects` folder.)

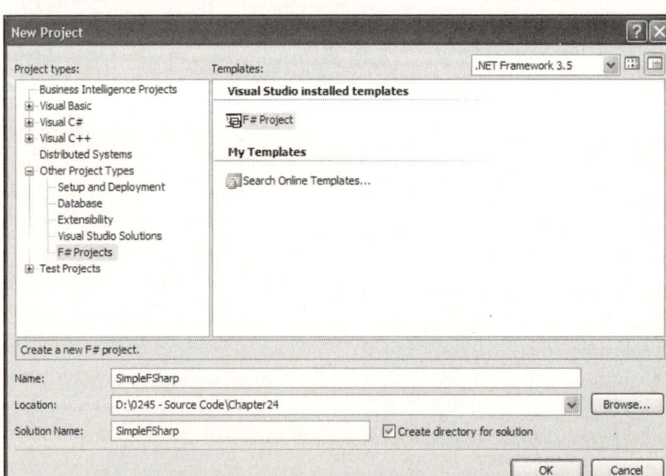

Figure 24-4: Visual Studio provides a new project template you can use to create F# applications.

2. Type a name for your new project (the example uses `SimpleFSharp`) and click OK to create it. What you'll see in Solution Explorer might be a little disappointing, but it's really quite flexible.

3. Right-click the project entry and choose Add ➪ New Item from the context menu. You'll see the list of F# items shown in Figure 24-5. I'm not going to discuss all of these items in this chapter, but as you can see, F# has a lot to offer.

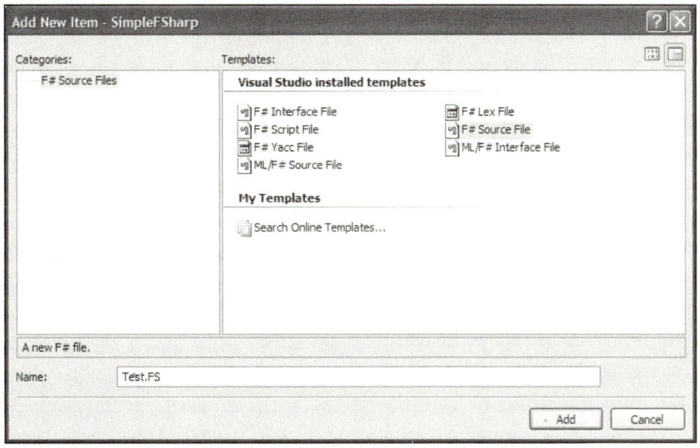

Figure 24-5: Use the F# item templates to create the kind of application you want.

4. Highlight the F# Source File entry, type a name for the new file (the example uses `Test.FS`), and click Add. Visual Studio automatically opens the file and you'll normally find a wealth of source code inside, as shown in Figure 24-6 (you could possibly see just the word `#light` in the file).

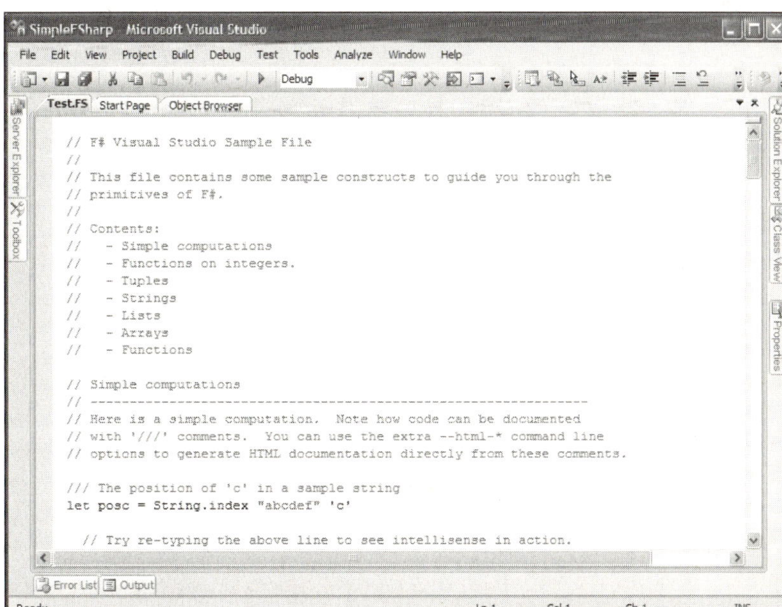

Figure 24-6: Try all the standard debugging features with the default F# example.

Working with this example can help you understand how F# works. More importantly, you can set breakpoints, check the value of variables, and perform other debugging tasks just as you would with any other .NET programming language. To use the application, simply click Start Debugging (the right-pointing arrow on the toolbar shown in Figure 24-6). If you want to simply see the output from the application, place a breakpoint on line 178, which is the line shown here:

```
let resT1 = eval envA expT1
```

Implementing Your Design

This chapter has given you a starting point for learning more about F#. Sometimes, a short chapter like this one is all a developer needs to find an exciting new tool that makes the development process considerably easier. F# fulfills some interesting needs in the new world of hardware in which developers find themselves. Although this chapter doesn't provide you with anything even approaching a tutorial, I hope that you've found the information valuable and will at least consider adding F# to your developer toolbox. Even if you end up using F# only in situations where you need to improve the multiprocessing capabilities of your applications, the effort of learning F# is certainly worth the performance gain your application will experience.

Try out the examples in this chapter — just to see how F# works. Take some time to trace through the code with a debugger so you can see how F# differs. After you complete this chapter, decide whether F# is a good fit for your next application. If it is, start learning F# now. Get yourself another book on the topic and go through the entire tutorial. Because of the way F# works, you'll likely find a use for it in a number of application scenarios.

Chapter 25 looks at another topic that developers commonly face — multithreading. Don't confuse multithreading with multiprocessing. A multithreaded application may not work across processors. In fact, multithreaded applications commonly use a single processor. The purpose behind multithreading is to use processing cycles more efficiently. A multithreaded application can perform high-priority tasks immediately (such as responding to user requests) and lower-priority tasks later (such as printing a document when the user is busy thinking about something). Chapter 25 helps you understand how multithreading can fit within your current application plans and how to use multithreading to gain a more responsive application. Even though your application is actually slower because it must use processing cycles to manage the multithreaded environment, the user will see it as faster because the user-specific code runs first and at a higher priority than background tasks.

25

Creating Multithreaded Applications

Multithreading, the ability of an application to spawn several concurrent tasks, is something that many developers associate with complex applications that perform mighty deeds. However, as you'll discover in this chapter, multithreading is a technique that can benefit nearly any application when used correctly. By using multithreading correctly, you can make an application more responsive to user requests and use system resources more efficiently. In addition, you can perform tasks in the background that actually anticipate user needs — making the application appear clairvoyant.

This chapter isn't going to make you a guru on creating multithreaded applications. In fact, you'll barely see any code in this chapter. The point of this chapter is to discuss the ramifications of multithreading on your application design. The technique used to create multiple threads is well understood and documented, but the question of when and how to use multithreading is neither well known nor standardized. Many developers misuse multithreading techniques in their code because they don't fully understand the ramifications or requirements of using it to achieve a desired result.

You will see a basic multithreaded application in this chapter. The technique is actually quite simple. Of course, any simple technique can become complex under the right circumstances. Some application designs have a wealth of obscure code to control multithreaded operations. In many cases, overuse of techniques such as semaphores indicate a poor application design. When working with multithreading, use the Keep It Simple, Stupid (KISS) acronym.

Talking about the KISS principle, Language INtegrated Query (LINQ) has the potential for letting you add multithreading to your application while reducing application complexity. This chapter also provides you with a quick overview of how LINQ can help you become better at adding reliable (simple) multithreading to your application.

Understanding Multithreading

Before you can use multithreading in your application, you must understand it. Many developers today have a hard time understanding multithreading because they have lost contact with the hardware. A developer has to understand the hardware at some level in order to truly understand the implications of multithreading. Of course, there is no reason for the developer to understand the innermost workings of the processor — a basic understanding is fine. The following sections examine multithreading from a number of perspectives, most of which involve some level of hardware understanding as well.

Defining Multithreading

The basic concept of multithreading is simple. Every application is a *process* — a kind of container that represents the entire executing application. A process can contain one or more threads of execution. Each *thread* is a series of instructions that you want the computer to perform. The thread is essentially the machine code instructions that the processor executes. A processor can only handle one thread at a time because there is only one set of registers that hold data the processor manipulates. There are all kinds of techniques, such as pipelining, to make the processor more efficient, but for the purpose of this discussion consider the processor capable of executing only one thread at a time.

The processor is incapable of understanding the concept of multithreading. All the processor knows is that the machine-level code tells it to move something from memory and place it in a register. The processor then adds something to this register or performs some other task with the data. The instructions never include any concept of multithreading. When thinking about the processor, think simple. If you're really interested in seeing the operations that a processor performs, check out the Web site at `http://home.comcast.net/~fbui/intel.html`. A quick scan will show that the processor's idea of work has nothing to do with multithreading — the multithreading the processor performs is simply another set of instructions. Multithreading exists within software, so something must write the instructions to perform multithreading — normally this task is a combination of your code and the output of the compiler.

A processor executes instructions using one or more clock cycles. Each clock cycle uses a fixed amount of real time based on the frequency of the clock used to drive the processor. Nothing short of changing the processor clock speed can make the processor go faster or slower during the execution of the program. It's unusual for a system to change the processor clock speed, so you can assume that the clock cycles require more or less a fixed interval. Consequently, you can't produce clock cycles out of thin air — they're a fixed resource.

When a process contains multiple threads, the process must manage those threads. The process decides when to create a thread and when to destroy it. Processes can pause and restart threads as well. A process must always contain at least one thread of execution or the process dies. The management the process performs is simply another set of instructions that the processor performs — one at a time. When the processor is performing these management tasks, it isn't executing any code from the user code threads within the process — management takes time in the form of processing cycles.

Thread management also occurs on other levels such as the Common Language Runtime (CLR). When these management tasks take place, the process doesn't receive any clock cycles, so it doesn't perform any useful work. The processor executes the tasks that CLR wants it to perform without any regard to the application process needs. The point of this discussion is that multithreading (and indeed, multitasking) uses processor cycles, so an application that relies on multithreading can't run faster than the application that relies on a single thread. Physically, the multithreaded application must run slower because there are only so many processor cycles available and some of those cycles are now used to address multithreading behaviors. Any idea a developer might have that applications suddenly run faster when multithreaded is simply false.

Many applications today use multithreading to give the application the appearance of greater speed through better responsiveness to user needs. The application only has the appearance of greater speed — it actually runs slower. The user thinks the application is running faster because the application is more responsive, but the overhead for running the application has actually increased because you must now have code that also monitors the threads. Consequently, any discussion of multithreading must include the idea that multithreading is a kind of magician's trick — smoke and mirrors that make the application appear to do something it isn't actually doing: running faster.

When you create a multithreaded application, you must do so with the idea that the application will run slower. The application gives the illusion of running faster because the user thread — the thread that interacts directly with the user — has a higher priority than other threads and always runs first. In short, to make multithreading viable in your application, you must carefully separate task lines and give the user tasks higher priority. In addition, because the user is single tasking, giving two user threads the same priority is an error. Only one user thread can run at a time because there is only one single-tasking user to interact with that thread.

Differentiating Multithreading and Multiprocessing

Some developers view multithreading and multiprocessing as about the same technology. After all, the process has multiple threads of execution in both cases. However, multiprocessing is a superset of multithreading. An application that can use multiple processors must start with all of the capabilities and coding features of a multithreaded application.

The application that can use multiprocessors must also consider issues of state and modality. When you create another thread on the current processor, often, the registers continue to include pointers to the current application state. In addition, the registers contain information about the process. When you move the thread to another processor, this information is lost. Consequently, applications with multiprocessing capability must consider additional maintenance issues that add to application overhead. The state and modality issues are one reason that languages such as F# can help when working with multiple processors — F# doesn't include the concept of state or modality.

It's possible to see a speed gain when using multiprocessing. That's because you're using two or more processors to do the work. Each processor works independently, so the process can perform multiple tasks simultaneously (rather than simply making it appear that the tasks are simultaneous as a process does with one processor). However, you won't see twice the performance due to the additional processing overhead and the fact that other applications are probably using the processor, too. Speed tests are uncertain when using multiple processors because you can't easily duplicate the load on each processor when the application runs. Consequently, speed is harder to gauge when using multiprocessing and any metrics you obtain during the testing phase are of dubious value.

Continued

> Applications that rely on multiprocessing are also harder to test than applications that rely on a single processor. The test environment can use the same processor to perform two tasks during one run and different processors to perform them on the next. As a result, you can't easily determine whether a fault you detect is due to the underlying code or the multiprocessing functionality. Generally speaking, you should test code libraries in a single processor environment first to get the code to an error-free state (or at least as close as possible) before you add the complexity of multiprocessing.

Considering the Benefits

At one time, operating systems for PCs were single tasking — that is, they ran one application at a time and that application had full access to the underlying hardware. When Windows and other operating systems first appeared, they added multitasking capabilities to the operating system. Now the user could run multiple applications at once. However, multitasking places some important restrictions on the application. For example, a multitasked application can't access the hardware directly — the operating system must control access to ensure all applications can use the hardware. Developers are willing to live with these restrictions because of the advantages of being able to perform more than one task as a time.

Developers are willing to live with restrictions posed by multithreading for much the same reason as they live with multitasking restrictions — multithreading provides a number of benefits that developers consider crucial to some kinds of application development. The following list provides an overview of the benefits afforded by multithreading:

- **Responsiveness:** It's important to remember that multithreaded applications are more responsive than single-threaded applications — not faster. However, responsiveness counts for a lot, especially when an application runs on a server and must respond to hundreds of users. A responsive application can often stop processes the user decides are unimportant or even fatal. In addition, responsive applications give the user the feeling of being the only one working with an application, even when there are hundreds of other users.
- **Efficiency:** Computers spend more than a little time waiting. At one time, the biggest culprit was the user. The computer would merrily waste millions of computing cycles waiting for the user to press the "Any Key." However, now computers also waste time waiting for networks, hard drives, Web services, and myriad other time wasters. Using multithreading lets an application continue working while waiting for something else to happen, making the entire application faster due to improved efficiency (versus computing speed).
- **Simplified coding:** Using multithreading can simplify coding by letting you compartmentalize certain application requirements. For example, you can make calls to a Web service a separate unit, which reduces overall application complexity. Because these threads appear as separate entities, you can even assign them to different areas of the team, making the team more efficient as well. Think about threads as being mini-applications within applications with regard to some coding practices.
- **Scalability:** The one overriding contribution of multithreading to application design is scalability. A multithreaded application scales better than a single-threaded application because the process can spawn as many threads as needed to handle the tasks at hand. By placing each task in an individual thread, the process can control application execution better, which means the application bogs down less.

Responsiveness also helps improve scalability. Developers know that frustrated users tend to keep pounding the keyboard to determine the status of their request — NOW! Every time the user hits the request key, the application generates yet another request. All those extra requests tend to make the application even less responsive and to bog down further. Adding multithreading, so that the application can provide status information to the user, reduces frustration and relieves the multiple request issue — making the application scale better.

- **Fewer required hardware resources:** A side effect of making the application more responsive, efficient, and scalable is that your organization can usually get by with less hardware. How much less hardware and the kind of hardware depend on the application you're creating.
- **Reliability:** Using multithreading can add a certain reliability factor. The simplified coding enjoyed by a multithreaded application is only part of the picture. When a particular thread fails, it doesn't matter why or how, the process can simply kill the errant thread and create a new one to take its place. The user doesn't see anything — everything occurs in the background. Except for a little additional pause, the application continues to work as if nothing happened.

The list isn't complete. Depending on your viewpoint, you may find additional reasons to use multithreading in your application. The application type, user needs, organizational requirements, and other factors also change the multithreading picture. One of the worst things you can do when designing your application is to decide to use multithreading without listing the benefits particular to your application. These benefits act as a list of goals that you hope to achieve with your application. Consequently, you should always go through the exercise of defining how multithreading will benefit your application, the users, and the organization before you decide to add multithreading.

Listing the benefits of multithreading answers the question of whether multithreading adds enough value to overcome the deficiencies described in the "Considering the Deficiencies" section of this chapter. Multithreading isn't the right choice for every application — you must consider the trade-offs before you add multithreading to your application design. Even some complex applications don't benefit enough from multithreading, while an incredible number of small applications can benefit. Never let application size or complexity be the determining factor.

Considering the Deficiencies

It's important to consider the problems with multithreading as well as the advantages — otherwise, you'll get a lopsided view of this programming strategy. Developers often decide to forgo multithreading because it does present some daunting deficiencies that make it a less than perfect development strategy. You shouldn't automatically decide against multithreading because of these issues, but you must consider them. Balancing your view is the best way to come to a good decision about multithreading. With this in mind, the following list presents some of the most common multithreading deficiencies:

- **Conceptual complexity:** Humans are single-tasking creatures, despite constant efforts to become otherwise. Even intense efforts to multitask produce flawed results and most studies show that humans who try to multitask do so inefficiently (see the article at `http://www.psychologymatters.org/multitask0306.html` as one example). It's little wonder then, that trying to conceptualize an application that performs more than one task at a time comes hard to developers. Many developers simply can't manage the task and end up botching any attempt to add multithreading to an application design. This is one area where experience really does play a big role. If your team has less experienced developers, you may want to save multithreading for another project.

- **Debugging complexity:** Multithreaded applications perform more than one task at a time. Following all of those threads while you debug your application can prove nightmarish. If you have a hard time conceptualizing the multithreaded design, you'll really have a hard time debugging the application later. Besides the conceptualization problems, debugging presents the issue of discovering which thread has a particular error or understanding why multiple threads have the same (or sometimes different) errors.
- **Testing complexity:** Timing is everything in some multithreaded applications. Because the application performs multiple tasks concurrently, you can't be sure when a testing error is due to a problem in the code, in the switching logic, or somewhere in the thread management code. In most cases, every time you run a test, you'll get slightly different results due to multithreading issues. Consequently, you'll often need to run test suites multiple times to ferret out interaction and timing issues that don't ever occur in single-threaded applications.
- **Security:** When writing your multithreaded application, you'll probably include code to help the application become more self-healing. This code can also hide security issues. If an attacker knows that your code is self-healing and doesn't report thread errors (or that no one monitors them when the application does report the errors), the attacker realizes that he or she has carte blanche to attack viciously and often — no one will notice.
- **Concurrency management:** Your application will need to include some form of concurrent management in most cases to keep various parts of the application synchronized. Writing this concurrent management code is an additional task and proves difficult unless you have experienced developers doing it.
- **Overhead:** As your multithreaded application runs, it wastes both processing cycles and resources due to multithreading overhead. If your system is already marginal when it comes to resources, making the application multithreaded will only make matters worse and could cause the application to become unreliable. Yes, multithreading does use resources more efficiently by using them during user think time, but the system must still have the baseline resources required to handle multithreading during surge conditions.
- **Porting issues:** Multithreaded applications tend to port to other systems less easily. Developers tend to make design decisions based on the target system, which means that the application becomes less flexible and less portable. Only a great design can mitigate this potential problem, and even then you may find that the resulting application is less portable. Of course, if you only intend to use the application on a specific set of systems, you won't need to consider this particular issue.

As with the benefits in the "Considering the Benefits" section of this chapter, this list isn't complete. You must consider the potential deficiencies of multithreading for your own application. It's harder to come up with deficiencies than it is to develop a list of advantages, but it's important that you do so or you won't get the whole picture. Multithreading is a great technology, but only when you use it correctly and in the right circumstances.

Looking at the Current State of Multithreading

Multitasking is the most mature technology when it comes to running more than one application at a time, but multithreading is a close second. You can find literally millions of articles about multithreading online. Microsoft and other vendors provide innumerable resources to help you implement multithreading and you'll find that many multithreading features are built into the .NET Framework in such a way that they require little effort on your part to use. In many respects, you'll find few surprises when it comes to multithreading, except in the areas of increased automation and language functionality. Therefore, multithreading is actually a relatively safe technology to use in the right circumstances.

Of course, figuring out when the circumstances are right is hard. Here are some best practices to consider.

- The benefits must outweigh the risks (see the "Considering the Benefits" and "Considering the Deficiencies" sections of the chapter for details).
- Your team must have the proper mix of experienced developers — people who have worked with multithreading projects in the past.
- The application design must include multithreading from the outset.
- The organization must have the required hardware to run multithreaded applications.
- You should create goals associated with the multithreading to keep the project on track.
- You should ensure that debugging and testing are both thorough, and performed more than once to locate potential conflicts.

It's essential not to assign multithreading tasks the application can't perform. For example, your application won't run faster and there is no reasonable expectation that multithreading can make it faster. However, multithreading can make your application more responsive. The current state of multithreading is that many developers don't understand it well, despite the fact that multithreading has been around for so long and is a mature technology. The bottom line is that if you don't understand multithreading or can't conceptualize how your application should work with it, don't use multithreading.

The technology to watch today is multiprocessing. Unlike multithreading, multiprocessing does offer the promise of additional application speed. Multiprocessing is a new, risky, evolving technology, so you must use it with care. In addition, you must realize that current tools don't support multiprocessing properly — multithreading, as the mature technology, is often the better choice. If you really must have multiprocessing today, check out the Parallel Computing resources at `http://msdn.microsoft.com/en-us/concurrency/default.aspx`.

Creating a Basic Multithreaded Application

A multithreaded application can work on several levels. You can place a monitor or application feature in the background as a thread, such as monitoring the system for a specific event or printing a document. A multithreaded application can also spawn multiple copies of the same thread to handle specific system events.

You'd probably never create an application like the example described in the following sections. The sole purpose of this application is to demonstrate how .NET multithreading capabilities work.

The example below shows both scenarios. The application creates a thread that monitors the system for specific events. The thread operates separately from the user interface. Whenever the background thread detects the target event, it creates a new thread to handle that event while continuing to monitor the system for new events. The following sections show how to create the multithreaded application example.

Defining the Project

The example begins with the standard Windows Forms Application template. To make the example work, you'll need several controls as shown in Figure 25-1. As you can see, there isn't anything very complicated about the layout. The display area is a `ListBox` control, rather than a `TextBox` control, to make displaying data easier.

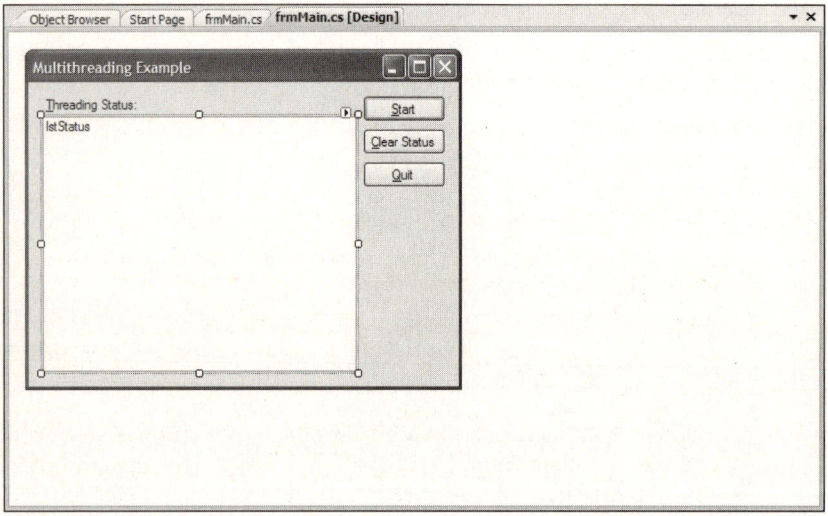

Figure 25-1: Create a basic Windows forms application and add the controls shown here.

After you create the basic layout, you can add some basic code for the Quit button. In addition, you'll need to add the following code to the beginning of the file.

```
using System.Threading;
using System.IO;
```

Adding the File Processing Thread Class

The example application actually includes two thread classes. The first thread class processes the individual files as shown in Listing 25-1. The second thread class appears in the "Adding the Monitor Thread Class" section of the chapter and it provides the monitoring functionality for the application.

Listing 25-1: Defining the file processing technique

```
// Contains the specifications for managing the file.
public struct ManageFile
{
   public object Sender;
   public String Filename;
   public String EventType;
}
```

```
// This class actually processes the file.
public class ProcessFile
{
   public void ProcessTheFile(object Data)
   {
      // Extract the data.
      ManageFile ThisFile = (ManageFile)Data;

      // Obtain a reference to the dialog box.
      frmMain ThisDialog = (frmMain)ThisFile.Sender;

      // Update the information in the list box.
      ThisDialog.DoCallback(ThisFile.EventType + " " + ThisFile.Filename);
   }
}
```

Begin by looking at the `ManageFile` structure. The `Sender` object is a reference to the dialog box application. You may wonder why you need this reference. A good many examples you see place the thread procedure as part of the application class, which doesn't reflect the reality that most developers will place the thread in its own class. Consequently, you don't have direct access to the dialog box should you need to change something in it, such as updating status information. The `Filename` and `EventType` entries are simply the data that the thread will display.

You may find a few of the features of this thread class odd. For example, the `ProcessTheFile()` method accepts an `object` as input, rather than the actual parameters used to process the file. This parameter setup is a requirement of the `ParameterizedThreadStart()` delegate used to actually create the thread. Of course, an `object` can be anything, so the example uses the `ManageFile` structure to pass the information that the `ProcessTheFile()` method really needs. You need to remember this trick when working with multithreading applications because Microsoft doesn't explain it very well. Because `Data` is an object, the code needs to coerce it to the right type.

After the code performs the conversion of `Data`, it can obtain a reference to the `Sender` object, which is of type `frmMain` in this case. The resulting object, `ThisDialog`, contains a reference to everything you make `public` in the dialog box. However, you can't directly change objects in `ThisDialog`. What you need to do instead is set up a callback. The "Developing the Application Code" section of the chapter describes the callback and tells what you need to do to create it. The bottom line is that every time you add, delete, or modify a file in the target directly, the change appears in the `ListBox` shown in Figure 25-1.

The file processing thread could perform any task desired. For example, you could choose to analyze or modify the file. Let your creativity run wild — this technique lets you encapsulate any file operation in such a way that it won't affect the rest of the application.

Adding the Monitor Thread Class

The file processing thread merely provides a way to process files one at a time. However, you need a way to detect the changes. The pattern for this part of the application is a monitor class that detects the change, creates a file processing thread to handle it, and then moves onto the next file (or waits for a change to occur). The reason you need a monitor thread is to free up the user interface portion of the application to respond to user requests. This thread simply hangs out in the background waiting for something to happen, and you don't even need to worry about it much. Listing 25-2 shows the basic code used to create the monitor thread.

Listing 25-2: Defining the monitoring technique

```
// Contains the specifications for creating the monitor.
public struct MonitorData
{
   public object Sender;
   public String Path;
   public String FileSpecification;
}

// This is the monitor thread class. It contains code for the monitor
// portion of the example.
public class MonitorDrive
{
   // Reference to the originator.
   object OriginalSender;

   // File system watcher object.
   FileSystemWatcher Watcher;

   public void DoMonitoring(object Specifications)
   {
      // Extract the data.
      MonitorData ThisData = (MonitorData)Specifications;

      // Set the originator reference.
      OriginalSender = ThisData.Sender;

      // Create a file system watcher.
      Watcher = new FileSystemWatcher(ThisData.Path);

      // Set the file system watcher filters.
      Watcher.NotifyFilter =
         NotifyFilters.Attributes |
         NotifyFilters.CreationTime |
         NotifyFilters.DirectoryName |
         NotifyFilters.FileName |
         NotifyFilters.LastAccess |
         NotifyFilters.LastWrite |
         NotifyFilters.Security |
         NotifyFilters.Size;

      // Set the file system watcher file type.
      Watcher.Filter = ThisData.FileSpecification;

      // Define the file system watcher event handlers.
      Watcher.Changed += new FileSystemEventHandler(Watcher_Changed);
      Watcher.Created += new FileSystemEventHandler(Watcher_Created);
      Watcher.Deleted += new FileSystemEventHandler(Watcher_Deleted);
   }
```

The code begins with another structure, `MonitorData`, and it has the same purpose as the `ManageFile` structure described in the "Adding the File Processing Thread Class" section of the chapter. The `Sender` `object` is the same `object` used with `ManageFile`. In fact, the `MonitorDrive` class actually passes this object onto `ProcessFile` when starting a new thread. The `Path` variable contains the location of the path to watch on the system, while the `FileSpecification` variable contains the file specification to monitor. `FileSpecification` can include wildcard characters. For example, if you want to watch for changes in any file, simply supply `*.*` as the `FileSpecification`. Likewise, you can watch all text files by supplying `*.TXT` as the `FileSpecification`.

The `MonitorDrive` class contains a number of global variables and methods. The `OriginalSender` `object` contains a reference to the current `frmMain` object. The class uses `Watcher` to monitor the file system for changes in the desired location.

The main method for this class is `DoMonitoring()`. This method starts the entire monitoring process. It begins by converting the incoming data from an `object` to a `MonitorData` structure. It then stores the reference to the dialog box (`frmMain`) in `OriginalSender`.

Never manipulate the components of the user interface directly. In most cases, you'll rely on callbacks or other techniques to modify the user interface elements indirectly. Even if it appears you can manipulate an element directly, you're usually doing so at some level of risk. You must always use a thread-safe technique to modify user interface elements from a thread class.

The next step is to create a `FileSystemWatcher` object, `Watcher`. The contractor accepts the location to watch as an input. The code sets the `NotifyFilter` property to the kinds of changes that `Watcher` should monitor. This property appears to affect only the `Changed` event handler, so you don't need to make this modification when monitoring for created or deleted files. The `Filter` property is mandatory and it contains the file specification you want to monitor. Careful use of wildcard characters can greatly improve application flexibility.

Make sure you create the folder you want to monitor before running the code. The example uses `C:\Temp`, *so you'll need to create a* `\Temp` *folder on your C drive when you run the code unmodified. Otherwise, modify the code to match the folder you want to monitor.*

Before `Watcher` can perform any useful work, you must define one or more event handlers for it. In this case, Watcher monitors the `Changed`, `Created`, and `Deleted` events. Some developers find the method of creating event handlers hard to remember. Microsoft makes the job easier by adding functionality to Visual Studio to create the required code automatically as shown in Figure 25-2. All you need to do is press Tab as shown in the IntelliSense prompt.

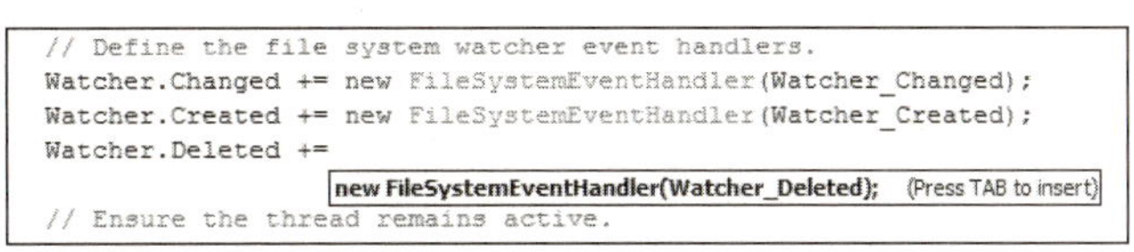

Figure 25-2: Visual Studio helps you create many of the features you need to handle thread events.

`Watcher` isn't active at this point — it's just sitting there. Look again at Figure 25-1 and you'll see that it includes a Start button. Click this button and the application begins monitoring the file system for changes. Clicking the button also changes the caption to Stop. This toggle calls two different methods in the `MonitorDrive` class as shown in Listing 25-3. All that these two methods do is set `Watcher.EnableRaisingEvents` to `true` to start monitoring and `false` to stop monitoring the file system.

Listing 25-3: Enabling and disabling the Watcher

```
public void EnableWatcher()
{
   // Enable the watcher.
   Watcher.EnableRaisingEvents = true;
}

public void DisableWatcher()
{
   // Disable the watcher.
   Watcher.EnableRaisingEvents = false;
}
```

The `MonitorDrive` class includes three event handlers — one each for every event that `Watcher` monitors. Listing 25-4 shows just one of these event handlers because the three event handlers are essentially the same in the example.

Listing 25-4: Handling file system Watcher events

```
   void Watcher_Deleted(object sender, FileSystemEventArgs e)
   {
      // Create the management data.
      ManageFile FileData = new ManageFile();
      FileData.EventType = "Deleted";
      FileData.Filename = e.FullPath;
      FileData.Sender = OriginalSender;

      // Create the thread delegate.
      ProcessFile ThisFile = new ProcessFile();

      // Create the thread.
      Thread CheckThisFile = new Thread(ThisFile.ProcessTheFile);

      // Set the thread up as a background task.
      CheckThisFile.IsBackground = true;

      // Start the thread.
      CheckThisFile.Start(FileData);
   }

   ... Other Event Handlers ...

}
```

This code begins by creating a new `ManageFile` structure. Notice that some of the input is literal, some comes from the `FileSystemEventArgs` object, `e`, and some comes from the user thread in the form of `OriginalSender`.

New threads consist of two parts: the delegate and the thread itself. The code creates the delegate first, which is of type `ProcessFile`. The resulting object, `ThisFile`, is an instance of `ProcessFile` that you can use to execute the `ProcessFile` instructions. Using a delegate may seem odd at first, but delegates are useful for letting you set object-specific properties before creating the thread.

After the code creates the delegate, it defines the thread. Threads rely on specific methods to start. When that method ends, so does the thread. Consequently, if you want to keep the thread alive, you must construct the method in such a way as to not exit until you want it to exit. In this case, the thread object, `CheckThisFile`, relies on the `ThisFile.ProcessTheFile()` method.

Creating the thread isn't enough to start it. If it were, execution would cease in the method that created the thread until the thread ended, making threads less than useful. Threads can execute in a number of ways. The example application relies on background worker threads. To create a thread that executes in the background and lets execution of the current thread continue immediately after starting the new thread, the code must set the `IsBackground` property to `true`.

At this point, you have a delegate and a thread object. The code uses the `CheckThisFile.Start()` method to start the thread. It passes the data the thread needs to execute as part of the method call. Now, for a few seconds anyway, you have two threads of type `MonitorData` and `ProcessFile` executing.

Developing the Application Code

If you've been following along in the chapter, you know that we now have a thread class designed to process individual files and another monitor class designed to check the file system for changes. The final part of the picture is the user interface. The application you build will probably have a more complex user interface than the example application does. The user interface is simple on purpose to help highlight the multithreading aspects of the application. In general, the user interface must perform these basic thread-related tasks.

- ❑ Create the delegate
- ❑ Create the thread
- ❑ Start the thread as a background task
- ❑ Manage the thread
- ❑ Provide thread access to user interface elements

The example shows how to perform all of these tasks. Listing 25-5 shows how to perform the first three tasks. You'll normally perform these tasks together.

Listing 25-5: Creating the file system monitor

```
// The monitor delegate.
MonitorDrive ThisMonitor;

// The monitor thread.
Thread Monitor;

public frmMain()
{
   InitializeComponent();

   // Create the monitor delegate.
   ThisMonitor = new MonitorDrive();

   // Create the monitor thread.
   Monitor = new Thread(
      new ParameterizedThreadStart(ThisMonitor.DoMonitoring));

   // Set the monitor thread for background operation.
   Monitor.IsBackground = true;

   // Create the monitor data.
   MonitorData MonitorInfo = new MonitorData();
   MonitorInfo.FileSpecification = "*.*";
   MonitorInfo.Path = @"C:\Temp";
   MonitorInfo.Sender = this;

   // Start the thread.
   Monitor.Start(MonitorInfo);
}
```

The application relies on two global variables, `ThisMonitor` and `Monitor`. As with the monitor code described in the "Adding the Monitor Thread Class" section of this chapter, `ThisMonitor` is the delegate, while `Monitor` is the thread. The `frmMain()` constructor instantiates the delegate first, and then creates the thread. Even though the `MonitorDrive` class code doesn't show it, both thread classes rely on the `ParameterizedThreadStart` class, rather than the `ThreadStart` class. You have the option of stating the correct thread creation class directly or letting the compiler choose the correct class for you. Normally, the compiler works just fine.

Because this is a background thread, the code sets `Monitor.IsBackground` to `true`. In addition, the code creates a `MonitorData` data structure and fills it with the appropriate data. Notice that since this is the root of `Sender`, the code uses `this` to indicate the current object. You can change the `MonitorInfo.FileSpecification` and `MonitorInfo.Path` property values to anything that works on your system.

The final step is to start the thread using `Monitor.Start()`. Notice that the code passes the data structure to the thread to provide startup values.

The next step is to manage the thread. The code in Listing 25-6 shows a toggle between start and stop conditions. You probably won't add code specifically like this to your application, but you'll likely use the same logic. In other words, rather than provide a user interface element to manage the thread directly, your application will probably include code to manage the thread indirectly based on application conditions.

Listing 25-6: Starting and stopping the monitoring process

```
private void btnStartStop_Click(object sender, EventArgs e)
{
   if (btnStartStop.Text == "&Start")
   {
      // Modify the button text.
      btnStartStop.Text = "&Stop";

      // Update the status.
      lstStatus.Items.Add("Monitor Thread Started");

      // Start the watcher.
      ThisMonitor.EnableWatcher();
   }
   else
   {
      // Modify the button text.
      btnStartStop.Text = "&Start";

      // Update the status.
      lstStatus.Items.Add("Monitor Thread Stopped");

      // Stop the watcher.
      ThisMonitor.DisableWatcher();
   }
}
```

The code performs tasks that you probably expect, such as changing the `btnStartStop.Text` property and adding status information to `lstStatus`. At one time, the Thread class included the `Suspend()` and `Resume()` methods that you used to pause and continue the thread. However, Microsoft has deprecated these methods. Instead, you must include logic within the thread class itself to start and stop the thread. The code for this thread class appears in Listing 25-3. It sets the `Watcher.EnableRaisingEvents` property to the appropriate value. Instead of starting and stopping the thread, you modify the thread behavior to start or pause the file system watching activity. That's why the example code uses the delegate, `ThisMonitor`, instead of the thread to start and stop file system monitoring activity.

The final step is to provide thread access to user interface elements. You have a number of choices to accomplish this task, but the easiest and most thread-safe method is to use a callback. Listing 25-7 shows the callback code for this example.

Although you have probably seen different terms used for the technique shown in Listing 25-7, it helps in this case to think of the code as an actual callback. The thread calls back to the user interface to update information. Thinking about the process this way makes the code easier to understand and recreate.

Listing 25-7: Providing an update route for the file processing thread

```
// Create a delegate for performing list box updates.
private delegate void UpdateCallback(String Information);

public void DoCallback(String Information)
{
   // Define an event handler for the update.
   UpdateCallback ThisUpdate = new UpdateCallback(UpdateStatus);

   // Perform the update.
   this.Invoke(ThisUpdate, new object[]{Information});
}

private void UpdateStatus(String Information)
{
   // Update the list box status.
   lstStatus.Items.Add(Information);
}
```

In this case, the code begins by creating a delegate, `UpdateCallback`. This delegate specifies that the caller must provide a `String` value as input. Notice that the delegate is `private` — you don't want someone outside the current class to access it.

The public face of the callback is `DoCallback()`. The `DoCallback()` method creates a new event, `ThisUpdate`. Notice that `ThisUpdate` is local to `DoCallback()` and not global. Every time a thread calls `DoCallback()`, the application creates a new instance of `ThisUpdate` that is local to the particular `DoCallback()` call, making the code thread safe.

After the code creates `ThisUpdate`, it uses the `this.Invoke()` method to call on the `UpdateStatus()` event handler. `UpdateStatus()` receives the update string that the thread sent to `DoCallback()` and uses it to update `lstStatus` using the `Items.Add()` method.

It's at this point that you begin understanding why multithreaded applications can be so hard to design, write, and test. This application contains quite a lot of code to perform such a seemingly simple task. However, as promised earlier in the chapter, the individual pieces of code are actually quite short. This example demonstrates the many trade-offs of multithreading originally discussed in the "Considering the Benefits" and "Considering the Deficiencies" sections of this chapter.

Testing the Multithreaded Application

Testing is significantly more difficult when working with a multithreaded application because there is a certain level of random behavior. The essential rule of testing for multithreaded application testing is to test more than once — more is better. This section isn't going to provide an in-depth tutorial on complete testing procedures for the example application, but it does give you a look at how the application works. Try the following steps with the application you just created:

1. Click Start to start the application. You'll see Monitor Thread Started.
2. Create a new file. You'll see Created `<New Text Document>`.
3. Change the filename. You'll see Changed `<Text Document>` with the new name.

4. Open the file, type something, and close it again. This time you see Changed <Text Document> twice. The first time tells you that the size of the file has changed, while the second tells you that the date of modification has changed.
5. Delete the file. You'll see Deleted <Text Document>.
6. Click Stop to stop the application. You'll see Monitor Thread Stopped.
7. Retry Steps 2 through 5. In this case, the application doesn't display any messages, showing you that the application does indeed stop monitoring the file system. You can track the progress of the application through the debugger by placing breakpoints directly in the various thread classes. It isn't possible to trace through threads directly.

Figure 25-3 shows the results you should see when performing the testing steps shown in the text. Of course, you can try dragging and dropping files to the folder and performing other tasks as well. In the end, you'll see that the multithreaded application works quite well for monitoring the file system, and you will probably use this code in applications of your own.

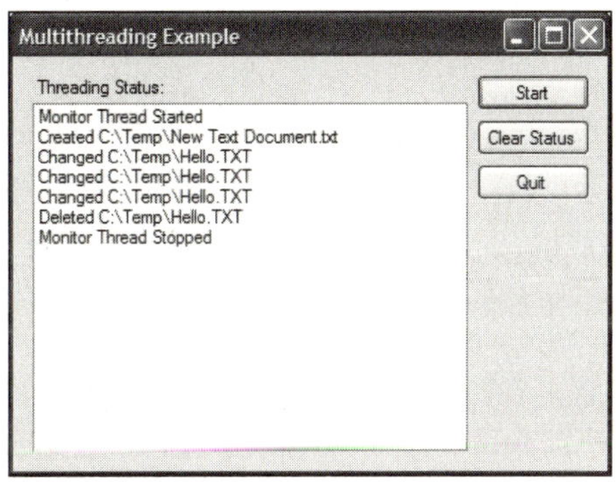

Figure 25-3: The example application shows each of the file events that occurs in the target directory.

One thing you should do is place a break point in one of the MonitorDrive class event handlers, such as Watcher_Created(). Now, to see how the threads work within the application, open the Threads window by choosing Debug ➪ Windows ➪ Threads. What you'll see is a display similar to the one shown in Figure 25-4.

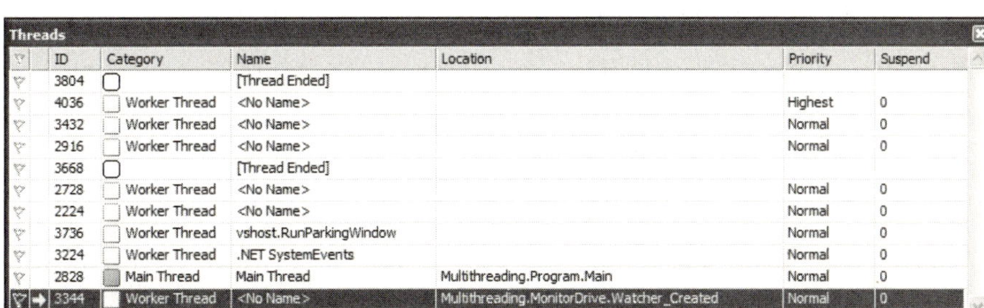

Figure 25-4: Every time the application calls an event handler, it creates a thread for the event handler.

Notice that you have a main thread and the worker thread. The worker thread is for the `Watcher_Created()` event handler. Now, place a break point in the `ProcessTheFile()` method and click Continue in the Visual Studio IDE. What you'll see now is the original `Watcher_Created()` event handler thread and a new thread for `ProcessTheFile()` as shown in Figure 25-5. For some reason, the IDE removes the thread name, but the ID is still there (3344 in this case — your number will differ from the one shown).

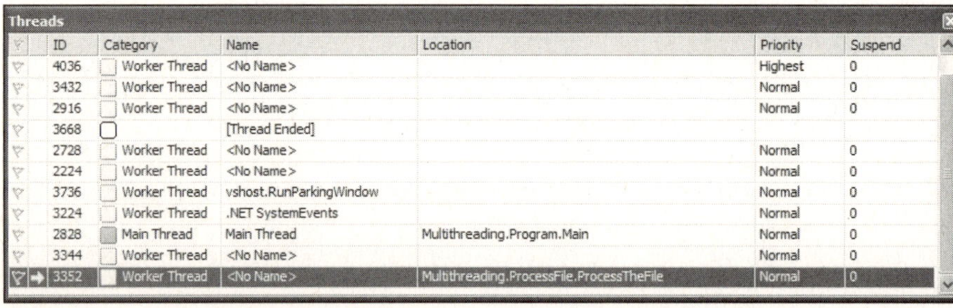

Figure 25-5: Once the event handler does its work, the application creates another thread to process the file.

Now, let's say you delete a couple of files at one time. What you might see in the Threads window is a listing of one event handler thread, `Watcher_Deleted()`, and several `ProcessTheFile()` threads as shown in Figure 25-6. This display shows the multithreading functionality at work. In order to understand multithreading well, it really does pay to spend some time playing in the debugger to see how the application reacts.

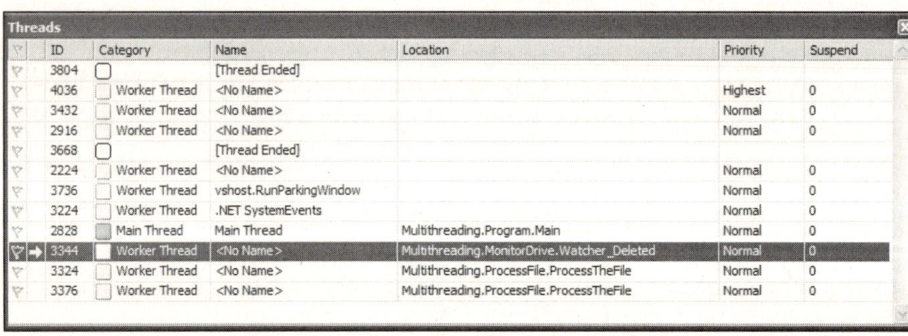

Figure 25-6: The application will show you the multithreading at work if you play with it enough.

It helps if you go through the various break points quickly, so that calls to `ProcessTheFile()` *can build up. Waiting too long between clicks will prevent you from really seeing the multithreading working. You can add some* `Thread.Sleep()` *calls to* `ProcessTheFile()` *to make it easier to see the multithreading at work.*

Using LINQ to Improve Multithreaded Application Performance

Microsoft is always working on new strategies to make its programming products better. One new technology that provides parallel processing for Language INtegrated Query (LINQ) is called Parallel LINQ (PLINQ). You can download your copy of PLINQ at `http://www.microsoft.com/downloads/details.aspx?FamilyId=348F73FD-593D-4B3C-B055-694C50D2B0F3`. The most important official place to find more information about PLINQ is at `http://blogs.microsoft.co.il/blogs/tamir/archive/tags/PLINQ/default.aspx`.

At the time of writing, this new technology is experimental and not in a released state. However, you'll want to keep your eye on this technology because using declarative syntax means you don't have to tell the application how to perform the task. Instead, you tell the application what task to perform. Chapter 23 tells you more about working with LINQ to create queries for various data sources such as SQL Server, XML, and even plain objects. When you combine LINQ with parallel processing, the technology becomes quite a bit more exciting than it already is.

You can read more about PLINQ at `http://www.bluebytesoftware.com/blog/PermaLink,guid,81ca9c00-b43e-4860-b96b-4fd2bd735c9f.aspx`. You can also find a good article on this topic at `http://www.informit.com/articles/article.aspx?p=1230070`. The blog at `http://channel9.msdn.com/forums/TechOff/259356-Multithreaded-Search-with-LINQ/` also has some interesting insights into working with LINQ and multithreaded applications. If you prefer a video format, check out the Web site at `http://channel9.msdn.com/posts/DanielMoth/Parallel-LINQ-PLINQ/`.

Implementing Your Design

This chapter has provided the answer to two important questions. The first is when you should use multithreading in an application. The second is how to apply multithreading to obtain a desired result. When you have the answer to these two questions, your applications:

- Run more efficiently
- Respond to user needs better
- Anticipate user needs to a degree

It's amazing to see how many application developers attempt to use multithreading for all kinds of purposes other than these three application modifications. By this point, you should know that other uses of multithreading are doomed to failure because the underlying hardware doesn't support anything else — multithreading isn't the same as multiprocessing.

The question you must ask yourself now is whether you can use multithreading to improve your application in some way. Remember that multithreading always reduces overall application speed, so if your application is already slow, it'll be slower when you're done adding multithreading. In most cases, the best way to discover the utility of multithreading is to try it out in an application. Run the application through both unit and performance testing to see the effects of multithreading. Don't be afraid to try methods that you're sure will fail. Doing so will help you see the effects of making the wrong choices on your application speed and reliability. The point of all the testing is to see what works and doesn't work with your particular application. Some developers have come up with amazing results by working with multithreading techniques in interesting situations that don't appear to fit the common wisdom.

Chapter 26 looks at another application need, reports. An application isn't very useful if it can't produce output of some type. A database isn't particularly helpful if it can only store data efficiently and correctly — the database manager must be able to output the data so that the user can see it in order to provide a useful level of functionality. Although many organizations are using printed reports less often, the concept of reports is the same in electronic format. The only real difference between printed and electronic reports is the level of flexibility you have in creating interesting output information. Chapter 26 looks less at the mechanics of printing than the definition of a good report — how you make reports useful to the end user while keeping sensitive data secure.

26

Creating Reports and Other Output

In some respects, reports and other forms of application output (other than the user interface itself) can be the most difficult part of the application. The problem is that many developers underestimate the difficulty of this particular component and end up seriously stressed trying to create it. It's important to realize from the outset that reports and other kinds of output are difficult to create for the following reasons (the list uses the word report to refer to all kinds of output):

- Reports are an emotional component of the application and not everyone reacts the same to them.
- User needs for report information vary by user, so a report that looks fine to one user won't meet the needs of another user (conceivably, you could be required to create one or more reports for every user).
- Device capabilities for outputting reports vary greatly, so writing code to address individual devices can be difficult.
- The .NET Framework doesn't provide the functionality required to produce truly useful reports without writing a lot of additional code — you must rely on a third-party product to perform the task if you want to get the reports done before you're old and gray. (Exporting content from a grid to Excel doesn't count as a report — that's a dump and a topic for another discussion.)
- It's probably impossible to get a complete list of reports at the outset of the application design process. However, you should get as many reports designed as possible during the design process and keep users from asking for a host of reports late in the development process.
- Many users have no clue as to what they really want in a report, so the result ends up containing everything and becoming the antithesis of everything it should be. Getting detailed requirements of what the report should contain as early as possible is essential. However, don't act surprised when the user changes his or her mind.

- ❑ Many developers create report code of mechanistic perfection, rather than artistic flexibility, which makes the report less useful to users.
- ❑ Managers often request reports that they think users need, but then no one uses.

This chapter doesn't attempt to tell you how to write code for building reports and other output. There are entire books on the topic and you'll find more than a few third-party products to help you with the mechanics of the task. Rather, the purpose of this chapter is to help you discover the design and development requirements for reports. Creating a good report hinges on more than simple coding technique or design fluency. When you create a report that truly works, the user, management, and you will all know it.

Because this chapter focuses more on art than science, you may find that you disagree with some or many of my recommendations. These recommendations come from personal experience and surveys of readers who have gone before you. Of course, it's your art — not mine, nor the other readers of this book. If you feel that reports printed on yellow 24-pound stock using purple ink is the height of fashion and your users agree, feel free to use the combination that works for you. Experimentation and a willingness to freely express your ideas are hallmarks of the good report.

Defining the Elements of a Good Report

I'm watching a woman study a report for a while. Then she brings the report closer. Not finding satisfaction, she breaks out reading glasses, and then tosses them aside. Finally, she throws the report down to the desk with a grand gesture of disgust. The report is dead — it has failed to enlighten the woman and is a failure overall because the print is simply too small to see. It's easy to find examples of bad reports because they abound everywhere. However, finding an example of a good report — now that's hard because the good report exists as much in your personal imagination as it does in the presentation of content. The following sections help you define the elements of a good report.

Defining the Players

Reports require an understanding of a number of players. Of course, the obvious player is the developer creating the report. In most cases, the developer is the one who initiates the process of defining and developing reports.

Managers are the group that defines company policies regarding reports. In some cases, a manager fulfills several roles, but the most important role is to guide the reporting process so it meets organizational, customer, and legal requirements (among other things).

Users define the report characteristics and content. The user is the developer's customer and will ask the developer to provide certain features. In many cases, the user's needs are as individual as users themselves.

Viewers are the people who see the content the user creates using the report software the developer provides. The viewer judges the appropriateness and effectiveness of the report. When viewers decide that the report really doesn't meet their requirements, the developer is often blamed for putting a bad reporting mechanism together. It behooves the smart developer to know the manager, user, and viewer when creating a report.

Starting with the Acceptable Report

The developer often finds it difficult to quantify the makings of a good report. Sometimes you have to start with an acceptable report before you can create a good report. In fact, developers would do well to focus attention on the acceptable report first and add the flourishes of a good report later. Even an acceptable report requires some level of creativity. However, you can quantify the elements of an acceptable report because it contains the following elements:

- Is easy to read, which means it uses the right font size and typeface.
- Contains only the information the viewer really needs.
- Organizes the content in a manner that emphasizes the most important content first.
- Reduces clutter by grouping related information.
- Diminishes complexity by keeping content succinct.
- Provides an overview when necessary.
- Defines terms the reader may not understand.
- Uses visual elements, such as rules, to divide contrasting information discretely (such as details and summaries).
- Includes sufficient white space to help the reader's eye follow individual entries across (or down) the page.
- Highlights targeted information, without detracting from the overall content of the report.
- Targets only one type of information for each report.

You could probably add items to this list that reflect the needs of your specific organization. This list contains only general features that you want to include in the acceptable report. Even so, you may be asking yourself whether any report can meet all these requirements. The short answer is that creating the acceptable report requires patience and practice, both of which seem in short supply in most organizations today.

Improving the Acceptable Report to the Good Level

If an acceptable report includes all the features in the previous list, it's hard to imagine what a good report will contain. Again, much of the focus of the good report is in the artistic expression of the content it contains. Consequently, you may find the items in the following list don't reflect your particular tastes. However, you may want to consider these features at least for your next report.

- Contains graphics only when required to express report content (such as icons for bullets) or organizational need (such as a logo).
- Imparts the correct emotional feel for the data in the report (such as the use of red print for negative numbers).
- Uses artistic elements in such a way that the viewer obtains the correct nonverbal input without being overwhelmed.

- ❑ Anticipates the needs of the hurried viewer who may look at the report for five seconds or less.
- ❑ Helps the viewer with tunnel vision to see the bigger picture.
- ❑ Uses color effectively and relies on color to express nonverbal messages.
- ❑ Designed with the needs of the viewer with special needs in mind (such as someone who is colorblind).
- ❑ Provides portrait (uses pages more efficiently) or landscape (shows more data on one line) orientation depending on the amount of data to display.

Good reports often include a flair that expresses the design style of a particular developer. In fact, you should choose someone on your team who already has the makings of a good artist to design and build your reports. It's important to express a willingness to let the developer have a free hand in the design, but you must also restrain the design to reflect the user's and viewer's requirements. In short, the report must express a balance that is extremely hard to achieve in some cases.

Beware of the manager with the red pen. In many cases, managers feel that they can design reports with greater impact than someone who has all the required qualifications and talents. In most cases, the manager ends up in an argument with the developer over such trifling matters as the width of a rule used to separate details from summary information in the report. These arguments never end well. As the team leader, you have to be willing to work with both management and the developer in creating the report to produce an environment that is conducive to getting the right report out as quickly as possible. In many cases, this means you have to argue with the manager with the red pen or be willing to go over his or her head to achieve the desired result. Good reports are always spoiled by too many cooks in the development kitchen — always stand by your master chef.

Testing the Report

Don't get the idea that the artistic nature of good reports precludes testing. As with every other part of your application, you must test reports completely to ensure they work as anticipated and provide the desired results. The more flexible you make a report, the more testing it requires. In fact, you'll probably find that report testing requires considerably more time than other areas of your application simply because everyone will have a different approach to presenting the data.

One of the essential keys to report testing is to create report mock-ups before you write a single line of code. Get the users, managers, and viewers to sign off on the design. Otherwise, you'll face constant turmoil during the development process. Avoid letting people change their minds once the report design is in place, unless the change will materially affect the report content. Again, you want to avoid the "flavor of the day" approach to reports, where stakeholders feel that they should be able to change the report design to match their mood. If you don't create a good design, the report will never be finished, and you'll never get to test it.

Use the mock-ups you create during the testing process. Make sure everyone tests to the mock-up, rather than their current view of the artistic elements of the report. Of course, you still want to encourage people to point out flaws — a summary that contains incorrect information is useless to everyone who relies on the report.

Understanding User Report Requirements

Developers are disadvantaged when it comes to reports. In most cases, developers never use the reports they create. In fact, it's fair to say that developers don't even understand the reports fully in some cases. When a developer looks at a financial report, it looks like a bunch of numbers — the user sees the health of the organization. The difference in perception and understanding between developer and user is important because it helps explain why so many reports end up not satisfying user needs. Unless the developer plans to get the same education and experience as the user has, there is little chance the developer will ever truly understand the report. There is a gulf between developer and user that is hard to ignore and even harder to overcome.

It isn't always possible for the developer to create a good or even an adequate report when the gulf between developer and user becomes too large. In this case, it's prudent to give the user a free hand in developing the report personally. The "Creating the Self-Modifying Report" section of this chapter provides insights on how to give the user the power to create the perfect report, without overwhelming the user with development details.

As with many development issues, it's important to build some level of understanding between developer and user in order to obtain useful results. The greater the level of understanding, the better the outcome of the report design process. Breaking the problem into manageable pieces is the best way to proceed. You can usually break report requirements, from a user perspective at least, into three pieces:

- Content requirements
- Formatting needs
- Organizational policies

The following sections discuss all three of these issues. In addition, you'll find information about how to build a better rapport between developer and user.

Considering the Content Requirement

Report content may seem straightforward, but the user almost certainly sees the content differently from the developer. As previously mentioned, the developer often sees a data type, numbers, or text, while the user sees the value of the content, such as the health of the organization. Because the numbers or text lack value to the developer, it's impossible for the developer to provide the same emphasis on the content that the user will place on it. Consider these issues when discussing content with the user:

- Content meaning (how the user will interact with it)
- Content emphasis (whether it needs a special font or other emphasis)
- Data formatting (adding a dollar sign, controlling the number of decimal places, and so on)
- Entry placement (its merit to the user and viewer)
- Caveats (the disclaimer used to emphasize proper use or the nature of content presented)

Content is the visual presentation of the user's view of data. The content has the user's stamp on it. A user controls content to make a particular point during a presentation to a viewer. The content isn't the same as the data. When working with content, the user filters the information, organizes it in a particular way, derives new data from existing data, and performs other manipulations of the data in order to present the material in a particular way that proves or disproves a particular assertion.

Even simple reports follow a pattern of filtering and reorientation of data to make a point. The content of an inventory may not include specialty items that the user wants to keep secret. The inventory may also place an emphasis on positive elements of inventory management and reduce or even eliminate potential inventory management failure points. The inventory is also filtered to exclude information that the viewer doesn't need to know and may contain summaries that the viewer can use to get an overview without reading the entire report. This overview is normally biased by the user's own perception of the data. Content presents the user's personal political view of the data.

Defining Formatting Needs

A report requires formatting for a number of reasons. The formatting isn't mere window dressing to the user or the viewer. In fact, formatting often conveys more than the actual content because formatting is often subliminal. Consider these issues when discussing formatting with the user:

- Organizational requirements to separate data of different types
- Nonverbal message requirements to convey content meaning
- Artistic elements used to convey the user's personal take on content and viewpoint
- Colors used to present report elements
- Specialized graphics or icons
- Standard or specialized bullets, numbering, shading, and other presentation elements

Formatting is the nonvisual presentation of the user's view of data. When a user formats a report, you often see personal biases in the choice of color, use of rules, addition of graphics and icons, and the use of other visual elements. As with body language, formatting presents a nonverbal message between user and viewer. This nonverbal message often says things that content can't and can prove more important to the user than the actual content of the report. This isn't a book on psychology, but some psychology major has probably studied how reports exemplify characteristics of the person who created them. The user relies on formatting to convey a sense of self.

In most cases, the formatting the user requests won't reflect your personal taste. However, you're not the one using the report — the user uses it. Consequently, even when a report looks hideous to you, it's still the user's expression of self and you need to honor it. Of course, most people will stop short of saying that the hideous report looks spectacular — a certain amount of tact is part of the job.

Including Organizational Policies

The one area where developers can do well is in implementing organizational policies, assuming management and users explain those policies in sufficient detail. In this case, the developer must place the input from management above the input from the user in importance because management generally controls organizational policy. However, the developer should actually start by reading written policy before talking with anyone, because sometimes organizational-level understanding of written policies is poor at best. Understanding the written policy will help the developer work out any differences between perceived organizational policy and the written policy for a report. Consider these issues when discussing organization policies with management and users:

- Placement and use of logos and icons
- Placement and use of legal messages and caveats
- Addition of the copyright (©), trademark (™), and registered trademark (®) symbols
- Restrictions of information dissemination to certain users and viewers
- Use of organization-sanctioned formatting, content appearance, and artistic elements
- Addition of sign-off and other management blocks to the report

Policies are the organization's method of controlling the presentation of data to meet organization needs and address legal requirements. The organization uses policies to control the user's free expression of information in a way that preserves the organization's public image. An organization may choose to limit the selection of graphic elements to keep certain ideas under control so that the organization's image isn't sullied through inappropriate graphic additions.

The legal requirements are generally more important to the organization than other policies, however; because we live in a litigious society. Addressing specific legal requirements is a must or someone outside the organization will sue for damages. In this particular case, the smart developer runs all reports through the legal department so that the lawyers can sign off on it. Nothing would be worse than forgetting to dot some legal i and finding that the organization now has to defend itself in court.

The formatting and legal requirements for internal reports is usually less intense because no one outside the organization will see them. However, developers are sometimes surprised to find that those internal reports see the light of day when least expected. Always consider organization requirements and make sure someone signs off on them before you make the report active on a production system.

Developing User Rapport for Reports

The scene is a conference room filled with caffeine-crazed individuals, each with a personal political agenda. The two alpha participants are sparring over report requirements as if the discussion requires a life-and-death struggle. Tension fills the air. The beta members of the team know that they have little chance of getting their requirements fulfilled. After an hour or more, the meeting breaks up and the developer leaves without really understanding anything more about the reports that the users require. A growing ache in the pit of the developer's stomach tells the tale of the conflict — no one has won anything, the reports will probably fail, all the beta participants will complain to someone else that no one addressed their needs, and the alpha participants will leave knowing the developer will never be able to oblige their contradictory requirements. This is exactly what happens in organizations throughout the world — the scene plays out repeatedly and is the reason your reports don't work.

Someone once said that one of the redeeming purposes of software is to avoid meetings. I'm sure this enlightened individual is happy that someone else, me, remembered this comment, because no one else seems to have taken the advice. The smart developer talks with every user who needs a report individually — possibly over coffee and doughnuts. Relaxing the individual and assuring him or her that the report will meet that person's needs is possibly the most important thing you can do. Take time to understand individuals. Ask about their families — put them at ease. If you don't take time to work with individuals when it comes to reports, you'll pay the price later in failed output. Every user has needs when it comes to reports and you must fulfill them all.

Separate needs from wants. All users also have wants for reports — things that they don't actually need to accomplish a given task. Address wants only as time permits and as a good-faith measure.

Use e-mail to work out as many report details as possible before you conduct any meetings. In fact, if possible, avoid meetings completely because meetings don't work when it comes to reports. When you have a meeting, you have a room (sometimes a virtual room) full of individuals who have different needs and a desire to struggle for the political power that seems so necessary to some people. Avoid all that by avoiding the meeting. You may end up having to create additional reports as a result of not having the meeting, but you'll also find that the level of user satisfaction is also considerably higher than if you take the meeting approach.

The most important thing you can remember about reports is that groups don't use reports — individual users use reports. One user takes a report and presents it to a group of viewers, often with other information and visual aids. Even if an administrative assistant simply sends a report to a boss, there is the user and viewer relationship. The administrative assistant filters the information and then presents that information to the boss — the presentation takes place, albeit on a small scale. Your job as a developer is to satisfy the administrative assistant, not the boss. The administrative assistant must satisfy the boss (consequently, don't try to satisfy the boss — you already have enough work to do).

Developing a rapport between the user and yourself doesn't have to be hard. In fact, if you do things right, it can be a pleasant experience and you might find it the most fulfilling part of designing and building an application. The problem with most development cycles today isn't that the developer has a problem creating good reports — it's that the developer places emphasis in the wrong place and tries to satisfy the wrong parties using an incorrect approach.

Creating the Self-Modifying Report

One of the hardest, yet most beneficial, report types to create is the self-modifying report. In this case, you place the requirement to define the report specifications in the hands of the user. Yes, your application still provides the means of accessing content, formatting the information, and placing it in a usable form for output. In addition, your application still provides the support for the various output formats (such as files or electronic media). However, the user decides what content should appear in the report and what color to make rules separating details from summary information.

The benefit to this kind of report is that the user can play "what if" and design the perfect report for a particular need without consuming developer time. If the user doesn't like the initial report, then it's possible to modify the parameters until the report is perfect. Many organizations follow this pattern now with good results, and users tend to produce better results using it. A developer may only need to modify the report when new content becomes available or the organization changes in some other way. In short, it seems as if everyone wins using this solution.

Unfortunately, appearances are deceiving. You can't simply give the user a copy of Crystal Reports (`http://www.businessobjects.com/`) and expect good results. Crystal Reports is a developer-type tool that provides the user with extreme control over the report output. Users need a little more hand-holding than a product such as Crystal Reports provides. (Crystal Reports is a great tool for the developer, so you shouldn't dismiss it completely. The full version of this product integrates directly into Visual Studio and Visual Studio comes with a downgraded version of Crystal Reports, so it's a very helpful addition to your toolbox.)

What most users will want is a way to specify content. The specification process should let the user control:

- Detail fields
- Summary fields
- Data groups
- Data ordering

In addition, unless your company has strict requirements, most users will want to control report appearance to some degree. For example, users commonly want to have access to the following appearance items as a minimum:

- Foreground colors (based on details, summary, and groups)
- Background colors
- Highlighting
- Icons or other graphical elements

The user will very likely want to control the form of output, within company policy, as well. For example, a user might need printed reports as handouts, slides to display on screen, a computer file for personal use, and other formats as needed to support viewers.

All these characteristics seem reasonable. However, the user interface for such a report is difficult to create. The developer must decide precisely how to present information in the least confusing manner possible, while providing the user with the desired level of flexibility. The entire process can quickly become mired in complexity and the user may still not like the result when the developer provides too much structure.

Devising Other Forms of Application Output

Whether you believe that the world may be moving away from paper or not doesn't always matter when it comes to output. Users commonly request other kinds of output from applications today, so you may not always work with paper output produced by a printer. Alternative output varies considerably today, so you may have to become very creative when trying to produce applications to support it. Here are just a few of the options you may need to consider when designing output choices for the application you create:

- Electronic media (including e-mail, word processing, spreadsheet, and database applications)
- Presentation media
- Mini-books (including PDFs)

- Audio presentation
- Webcasts
- Web media
- Mobile device formats

Many of the output forms in this list have subtypes that you may have to support. For example, electronic media comes in a wealth of formats, even though the reliable Portable Document Format (PDF) file seems to appear most often. However, don't be surprised if you end up supporting any of a number of open document specifications in the works. New formats such as OpenDocument (`http://en.wikipedia.org/wiki/List_of_applications_supporting_OpenDocument`) are becoming more popular. Expect users to want output in Microsoft's new DOCX format as well. Even Microsoft is starting to see the need to support additional formats in products such as Office (read more at `http://www.microsoft.com/Presspass/press/2008/may08/05-21ExpandedFormatsPR.mspx`).

Of course, supporting too many output formats can become cumbersome. If your organization is large, you'll probably find that users want you to support so many formats that you'll probably end up spending years writing the required code. Consequently, you must eventually define a policy stating the supported formats for an organization in order to keep applications supportable. When a user buys a new device, part of the specification for that device is that it support one or more of the official output standards. Some users will complain, quite loudly in fact, but format support is an area where you need to consider how many formats you can honestly support and then request that someone help you discover which formats are most common.

No matter how many formats you support, someone will complain — count on it. Consequently, the question is always how many formats can you support, not how many formats users want (or conceivably need). Requesting that someone outside your team discover the X number of most common formats also reduces the chance of users attempting to say that the formats the application supports are biased toward your own preferences. Anything you can do to keep complaints to a minimum is good.

Part of the problem with supporting alternative output is that most of these alternatives are electronic and rely on specific formatting. Obtaining a standard on which to base your output can prove difficult for proprietary formats, so open source formats — those supported by a standards organization — are the best choice for alternative application output. Using open source formats let you write code that outputs the required format directly, without having to rely on some intermediary to perform part of the translation.

When you must support a proprietary format, it might be easier to rely on the host application to perform part of the work for you. Most applications support common formats. If nothing else, you can always output the data as pure text and let the user reformat it, but this approach is bound to cause howls of anguish from disgruntled users who spent hours formatting their data just so within your application. For example, consider the case of exporting data to an older version of Word so that the user can manipulate it as part of a larger report. When working with Word 2003, you might consider the following alternatives:

- Outputting the report as text
- Creating a Rich Text Format (RTF) document using the specification at `http://msdn.microsoft.com/en-us/library/aa140277.aspx`

- Developing an HTML document that contains all of the required formatting
- Using XML to transmit the data and transforming the XML to match reporting criteria with XSLT
- Creating a DOCX file and adding the Microsoft Office Compatibility Pack for Office to the Word 2003 installation

There isn't any perfect way to output reports to alternative destinations in many cases. To obtain the output you want, you normally have to bend the rules a bit and get creative in your approach to the problem. Using third-party products can definitely reduce the drudgery of writing all the code from scratch. However, consider using an intermediary or an alternative-supported format when necessary to avoid causing the user additional work and to retain the investment you've made in researching the best report format.

Considering the DOCX Option

Getting output to the right location is hard. If you have Office installed on your network, however, the task may be easier than you originally thought. Office 2003 users can access Office 2007 documents, usually without loss of formatting, using the Microsoft Office Compatibility Pack. You can download this product at `http://www.microsoft.com/downloads/details.aspx?familyid=941b3470-3ae9-4aee-8f43-c6bb74cd1466`.

Once you install the Microsoft Office Compatibility Pack for an Office 2003 user, your application need only output Open Office XML (OOXML) formatted documents to support both Office 2003 and 2007 (OOXML is the basis for new Office 2007 file formats such as DOCX). Of course, there is always a worry about supporting new Office 2007 features in older applications. In most cases, the Office 2003 products will even warn you when you might lose some Office 2007 formatting when opening the document. This isn't a perfect option, but you'd be amazed at how detailed you can make the document formatting. You can discover more usage details about this option at `http://office.microsoft.com/en-us/products/HA101686761033.aspx` and `http://office.microsoft.com/en-us/word/HA100444731033.aspx`.

The DOCX option is valuable for developers because a DOCX file is really a ZIP file in disguise. Within the DOCX file are a number of folders that contain XML files that you can easily reproduce in code — giving you full access to the power of Word without worrying about proprietary format issues. Some people are even reading DOCX files directly in Internet Explorer (see the article at `http://www.labnol.org/software/tutorials/docx-reader-open-docx-files-internet-explorer/2637/` for details).

For the developer, Office 2007 offers advantages over older Office document formats because Microsoft has documented the format through ECMA (see the specification at `http://www.ecma-international.org/publications/standards/Ecma-376.htm`). You can read more about the whole OOXML file format at `http://msdn.microsoft.com/en-us/library/aa338205.aspx`.

Implementing Your Design

This chapter may not have satisfied your need to find the perfect guide to reports. In fact, it's quite likely that you're still searching. Until you conclude that the perfect report exists partially in your own imagination, you won't find the perfect report. The emphasis of this chapter is that reports are part art, part science, and part content. Creating the perfect report is difficult because many people lack the artistic ability to create them. Artists have a certain feel for what works that you can't put into words, and this chapter has pointed out that particular issue. You can create a perfectly acceptable report using the techniques found in this chapter, but it may not be a great report — one that grabs the attention and conveys information intensely enough to create change in an organization.

Just as organizations have team-building activities, they should also have artistic development activities — the kind of activities that tell the developer it's all right to have an imagination. A major problem with most schools today is that they teach mechanics alone — they're all substance, no philosophy. Nowhere does this problem become more apparent than when the developer attempts to create a useful report. One of the tasks you should perform right now is to build the artistic developer. Give people on your team permission to think strange thoughts, test the limits, and view the world in a different way. You may be amazed at what your "unleashed" team is capable of doing — some of it will be terrifying, but some of it will be quite exciting indeed.

Chapter 27 moves from the exotics found in this chapter to the intense. Writing low-level code is hard; writing it using .NET may completely fry your brain. Fortunately, using a little creativity (you developed it in this chapter, after all) and some detective skills, you can write low-level code with less difficulty than you might imagine. The material in Chapter 27 helps you discover the wonders of Platform Invoke (P/Invoke). Using P/Invoke, you can fathom the depths of Windows and work seeming miracles for which other developers will hold you in awe.

27

Designing Low-Level Application Elements

Sometimes you need a low-level function to perform a task. For example, you might need to monitor system messages and act on them by calling a Windows function that the .NET Framework doesn't support. Microsoft continually improves the support that .NET Framework provides for low-level Windows functionality, so the need to perform low-level tasks will decrease over time. However, there is always a need to perform them because Microsoft won't support every low-level Windows function as part of the .NET Framework, and you may need low-level calls to access third-party software or hardware. C# really excels when you need to perform low-level tasks because it supports functionality (such as unsafe pointers) not found in other languages such as Visual Basic. NET. You use the Platform Invoke (P/Invoke) functionality that the .NET Framework provides to perform low-level tasks.

This chapter can't provide you with everything you need to know about working with P/Invoke. In fact, I've written an entire book on the topic, *.NET Framework Solutions: In Search of the Lost Win32 API* (Sybex, 2002). However, this chapter does provide you with a good overview of the topic that you can use to extend your reach from managed applications into the world of native code.

> *Applications that contain function calls that rely on P/Invoke aren't platform independent. If you want to use your application on Linux or the Macintosh using Mono (*`http://www.mono-project.com/Main_Page`*), it can't contain any calls to P/Invoke. In fact, the application won't run on Windows Server 2008 Server Core either, since there isn't a full version of the .NET Framework available for that operating system. In short, P/Invoke incurs a cost in portability that you must consider before using it in a production environment.*

Defining P/Invoke

Microsoft defines P/Invoke as a method for accessing the Windows 32-bit Application Programming Interface (Win32 API). However, it would actually be more accurate to say that P/Invoke provides the means to access any native code from the managed environment of your application. A wall of sorts exists between the managed code of your application and the native code that makes up most of Windows and third-party applications. In order to breach this wall, you must write code that marshals function calls and data between the two environments. *Marshaling* means to make the data in one environment acceptable to a different environment — data flows both ways when working with P/Invoke. P/Invoke provides the method of marshaling the function calls and data.

This chapter assumes that you know something about the Win32 API. If you aren't familiar with the terms pointer *and* handle, *you probably shouldn't waste your time on this chapter because there isn't space to acquaint you with these ideas. If the idea of placing data on word boundaries is foreign to you, you may understand some material in this chapter, but some of it will go right over your head. This is an overview, not a complete discussion of P/Invoke.*

Using P/Invoke should be your last choice. Although P/Invoke is an extremely useful technique and you must use it in some situations, using P/Invoke also presents limitations that you should avoid whenever possible by relying on managed-code methodologies. Here are some issues to consider when working with P/Invoke:

- Your application will depend on a particular platform and may not even work with all versions of Windows (depending on which version of the Win32 API you use when writing the application).
- P/Invoke often relies on tricky marshaling techniques that aren't obvious in the Win32 API documentation.
- The developers on your team must have a good understanding of pointers, something that most native-code developers know little or nothing about.
- In many situations, the code must pack data structures in a certain way. *Packing* causes the data in the data structure to align on specific boundaries.
- Data types in the native-code environment differ from those found in managed applications. Your team must know how to translate one type to another.
- Windows often uses special techniques to provide results to the calling application, such as the use of messages. Your development team must know how to respond to these requirements.

P/Invoke can answer some hideously complex programming needs. For example, a customer once asked me to write code that would detect whenever a Word application started and modify the content of menus and dialog boxes as needed, regardless of document or template loaded by the user. This application had to detect the user login and modify Word uniquely for each user type. Unfortunately, you can't answer this requirement using Visual Studio Tools for Office (VSTO); this kind of modification requires P/Invoke, and the code is complex because you must use low-level Windows calls to directly manipulate the contents of dialog boxes — extreme coding here. You can get the overview of this technique by reading the series of articles in the following list:

- Working with Windows Messages in .NET (`http://www.devsource.com/c/a/Using-VS/Working-with-Windows-Messages-in-NET/`)
- Hooking Windows Messages in .NET (`http://www.devsource.com/c/a/Using-VS/Hooking-Windows-Messages-in-NET/`)

- Globally Hooking Windows Messages in .NET (`http://www.devsource.com/c/a/Using-VS/Globally-Hooking-Windows-Messages-in-NET/`)
- Special Windows Message Hooking Techniques for .NET (`http://www.devsource.com/c/a/Using-VS/Special-Windows-Message-Hooking-Techniques-for-NET/`)

Despite the problems with P/Invoke, you'll find it works extremely well once you understand the concepts. The Win32 API code has been around for a long time, and Microsoft constantly fixes errors in it, so the reality is that this code is relatively stable. Once you determine a certain technique works to access a particular Win32 API call, you can use the technique on any Windows system with the required software installed. The biggest concern you have is ensuring that the target system supports the same version of the Win32 API that you use in your applications — otherwise, your application can experience side effects. Error handling is also essential if you want to provide a reliable application.

The question you might have now is what you can do with P/Invoke. A more appropriate question is what you can't do. Using P/Invoke provides you with access to the entire Win32 API and any third-party product that has a native-code API. In addition, you regain access to all the libraries you wrote in C++ and thought you'd never be able to use again. You can find a listing of the Win32 API calls at `http://msdn.microsoft.com/en-us/library/aa383749(VS.85).aspx`.

Calling External Functions

This first example is very simple. In fact, you'd never actually perform this task using P/Invoke. However, the example provides you with the basics you need to understand what P/Invoke does and how to use it. In this case, the example shows how to display a dialog box that belongs to a host dialog box. You open the Windows dialog box in a modal fashion so the user must dismiss it to continue using the application. It's very easy to perform the same task using managed code, but the simplicity lets you compare P/Invoke against managed code.

To ensure your P/Invoke code works as anticipated, follow the same routine every time you work with it. Calling an external function requires a deceptively simple six-step process as shown here:

1. Add the directives required to access the external function and resources.
2. Create data structures, enumerations, and constants as needed to handle external function requirements based on Win32 API specifications.
3. Define the external function reference based on its entry in the Win32 API.
4. Create and fill any data structures or other variables needed to call the external function within the managed code.
5. Add calls to the external function and provide parameters as specified by the Win32 API.
6. Supplement P/Invoke functionality by adding error-handling code that detects Win32 API errors.

The reason this process is so deceptive is that interpreting the Win32 API in a managed way is an art. The Win32 API isn't always very clear about what an external function requires as input. In addition, translating Win32 API data structures, variables, and other needs into a form that works in a managed environment is hard. For example, the very act of creating a handle to a resource isn't always clear, and many Win32 API calls require handles (a handle is a pointer to the resource — a means of grabbing the resource and using it).

The following sections show how to perform the basic steps to make an external function call. This example doesn't rely on any data structures, but you do see how to work with some basic data types. The "Designing Data Structures" section of the chapter shows how to work with data structures as part of writing a P/Invoke application.

Adding the Required Directives

The directives you add to use P/Invoke are simple. All you need is the line of code shown below.

```
using System.Runtime.InteropServices;
```

However, you may find that you have to add other `using` directives, depending on the complexity of your code. For example, you may find that you need to use dynamic compilation techniques to compensate for differences between platforms. An application that executes without error in Windows XP may not work in Vista. You can read about dynamic compilation at `http://www.west-wind.com/presentations/dynamicCode/DynamicCode.htm`.

Working with P/Invoke often entails using what some developers consider exotic techniques to achieve a desired result. An open mind is your best tool when working with P/Invoke. Plan the method you'll use to work with external functions before you write a single line of code. Ensuring you know which directives to add before you begin coding will make the coding progress smoothly.

Providing Structures, Enumerations, and Constants

Enumerations are a good friend when it comes to P/Invoke. However, you probably won't see them used as often as you should with the examples currently found in some books and on the Internet because many of the developers who know how to use P/Invoke also know the Win32 API well enough to think they don't need the enumerations. Using enumerations as part of your P/Invoke strategy nets the following benefits:

- Developers can write code faster because they know which values to use through IntelliSense.
- The application will contain fewer errors because the developer has more support.
- The external call is better documented within the code, making it easier for other developers to modify it later.
- It's easier to match the values the developer is using with the Win32 API documentation.

The example requires the use of two enumerations. The first enumeration tells which button the user clicked, while the second enumeration provides input values that determine the appearance of the dialog box. The enumerations you create will depend on what kinds of input the external function requires and how far you want to automate the process of working with the external function. Listing 27-1 shows the first enumeration.

Listing 27-1: Creating a basic enumeration for return values

```
// Define the potential return values.
public enum ReturnValues
{
    IDOK      = 1,
    IDCANCEL  = 2,
    IDABORT   = 3,
    IDRETRY   = 4,
    IDIGNORE  = 5,
    IDYES     = 6,
    IDNO      = 7,
    IDCLOSE   = 8,
    IDHELP    = 9
}
```

The code in Listing 27-1 looks like a normal enumeration. However, you need to consider a few twists here. First, the name of the enumeration elements isn't random — each element name appears within the documentation for the `MessageBox()` function. You can see this list at `http://msdn.microsoft.com/en-us/library/ms645505(VS.85).aspx`.

The values are also specific to the `MessageBox()` function. Otherwise, the managed code wouldn't truly communicate with the Win32 API function. Unfortunately, the `MessageBox()` documentation doesn't tell you what these values are — it's as if Microsoft is saying the values are secret. Searching for these values can prove cumbersome, but a couple of techniques work quite well, and you should try them out. The first technique depends on having C++ installed on your system. Open a command line to the `\Program Files\Microsoft Visual Studio 9.0` directory (or other Visual Studio version directory). Type the following command and press Enter:

```
FindStr /M /I /S "IDOK" *.H
```

The FindStr utility helps you locate strings found in files. The `/M` command line switch tells FindStr to display only the filenames. The `/I` command line switch tells FindStr to perform a case-insensitive search. As with most command line utilities, the `/S` command line switch tells FindStr to look in the current directory and all subdirectories. You specific the search string next, followed by the file specification, which is always `*.H` for searches of this type. Figure 27-1 shows the output of this command on my system (your system will likely differ).

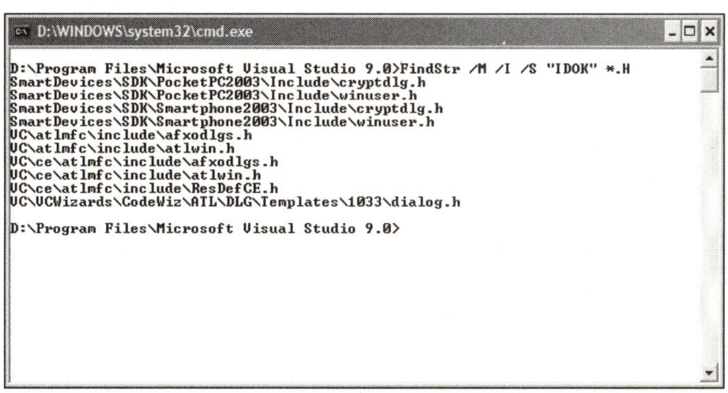

Figure 27-1: Use FindStr to locate the constants you need within the C++ header files.

The second technique for locating the values you need is to perform a standard Google search. Combine the constant you want to search for with `#define` (the keyword used to define a constant in C++) for best results. Unfortunately, Google usually provides less helpful results than the FindStr approach, so install C++ on your system if you plan to work with P/Invoke regularly. Even if you don't work with C++, ever, you'll still save time in the end.

As previously mentioned, the second enumeration provides the values used to change the appearance of the dialog box. For example, you use these values to control which icon the dialog box contains and which buttons it uses. Listing 27-2 shows the standard list of configuration options found in `WinUser.H`. These values are safe — they should work across all platforms.

Listing 27-2: Defining enumeration values of a specific type

```
// Define the type enumeration.
public enum MsgType : uint
{
   MB_OK                = 0x00000000,
   MB_OKCANCEL          = 0x00000001,
   MB_ABORTRETRYIGNORE = 0x00000002,
   MB_YESNOCANCEL       = 0x00000003,
   MB_YESNO             = 0x00000004,
   MB_RETRYCANCEL       = 0x00000005,
   MB_ICONHAND          = 0x00000010,
   MB_ICONQUESTION      = 0x00000020,
   MB_ICONEXCLAMATION   = 0x00000030,
   MB_ICONASTERISK      = 0x00000040,
   MB_ICONWARNING       = MB_ICONEXCLAMATION,
   MB_ICONERROR         = MB_ICONHAND,
   MB_ICONINFORMATION   = MB_ICONASTERISK,
   MB_ICONSTOP          = MB_ICONHAND,
   MB_DEFBUTTON1        = 0x00000000,
   MB_DEFBUTTON2        = 0x00000100,
   MB_DEFBUTTON3        = 0x00000200,
   MB_DEFBUTTON4        = 0x00000300,
   MB_APPLMODAL         = 0x00000000,
   MB_SETFOREGROUND     = 0x00010000,
   MB_TOPMOST           = 0x00040000
}
```

This enumeration contains a few differences from the previous enumeration (beside the obvious difference of the values). Notice that the enumeration is of type `uint`. If you don't add the `uint` type, you might find that the compiler treats some values as negative numbers and the call will fail. In fact, when you see `uint` defined for a particular function call, and you plan to handle that parameter using an enumeration, always declare the enumeration type as `uint`.

The Win32 API documentation will often define a host of values, but you'll see these values defined in terms of some other value in the C++ header file. For example, in Listing 27-2, `MB_ICONWARNING` is defined as equaling `MB_ICONEXCLAMATION`. Don't fall into the trap of assigning a numeric value to these enumerated values. Otherwise, changes in the Win32 API won't appear correctly in your code when you make an update.

When you look at the `MessageBox()` function documentation at `http://msdn.microsoft.com/en-us/library/ms645505(VS.85).aspx`, you'll notice that there are some values in the documentation that don't appear in the enumeration. For example, the `MessageBox()` function also supports a value of `MB_CANCELTRYCONTINUE` as one of the inputs. This value doesn't appear anywhere in the `WinUser.H` file. However, a search online tells you that the value does appear in `MessageBoxDialog.H` as a special value for Windows XP users. Sometimes these special values can cause problems for your code because they require use of a special function call — (`MessageBoxEx()` in this case) — or work only for a particular platform (Windows XP in this situation). It's a risk to include these other values in your enumeration, but sometimes you must for compatibility reasons. In this case, a search of the Microsoft Knowledge Base tells you that there is definitely a time to use the `MB_CANCELTRYCONTINUE` value (see `http://support.microsoft.com/kb/899175` for details).

Creating an External Function Reference

It's time to begin creating the external function call reference. The Win32 API version of the `MessageBox()` function looks like this:

```
int MessageBox(
    HWND hWnd,
    LPCTSTR lpText,
    LPCTSTR lpCaption,
    UINT uType
);
```

As you can see, the `MessageBox()` function requires four input arguments and returns an `int` value that tells you which button the user clicked. Obviously, you'll need to translate some of these inputs into something that the managed-code environment will understand. For example, managed code doesn't provide an equivalent of the `HWND` data type. In some examples, you see that the developer substitutes an `int` value for the `HWND` data type, but this is a mistake. Use an `IntPtr` instead to ensure that Windows receives the correct input.

Fortunately, you can use standard strings for the `lpText` and `lpCaption` parameters. The "Working with Function Call Data" section of this chapter tells how to ensure these parameters match the input that Windows expects. Again, the managed-code environment doesn't include anything that remotely matches the `LPCTSTR` data type.

The first three parameters don't require a specific input. You can provide any legal handle for `hWnd`, and `lpText` and `lpCaption` can contain any string. However, `uType` is different. You must provide a correct numeric value for this input or the call will fail. Theoretically, you can simply provide the right numeric value, but you really won't want to take time to figure out this value every time you write an application. Consequently, using an enumeration to represent this input only makes sense. Listing 27-3 shows the definition used to for the `MessageBox()` Win32 API function.

Listing 27-3: Defining the external message box call

```
// Define the function call.
[DllImport("User32.DLL",
           CharSet=CharSet.Unicode,
           SetLastError=true,
           EntryPoint="MessageBox")]
```

Continued

Listing 27-3: Defining the external message box call *(continued)*

```
    static extern ReturnValues ExternMessageBox(
        IntPtr hWnd,
        [MarshalAs(UnmanagedType.LPWStr)]
        String lpText,
        [MarshalAs(UnmanagedType.LPWStr)]
        String lpCaption,
        MsgType uType);
```

Every P/Invoke call begins with the `[DllImport]` attribute. What you include with that attribute as parameters depends on the call you want to make. The one mandatory parameter is the location of the function within the Windows DLLs. In this case, the `MessageBox()` function appears in the `User32.DLL` file. The `MessageBox()` function documentation shown at `http://msdn.microsoft.com/en-us/library/ms645505(VS.85).aspx` provides this information to you near the bottom of the page.

The example uses the Unicode character set, so you must include the `CharSet=CharSet.Unicode` argument. Not every function provides support for every character set, so you need to read the documentation before you decide on which character set to use. Every Windows function does support the Unicode character set.

If you want to provide error handling for the function, you must include the `SetLastError=true` argument. Otherwise, the managed environment doesn't monitor the Win32 API errors. Unlike an error in the managed environment, you may not even know that an error occurred until you perform the proper checks (see the "Providing Error Handling" section of the chapter for details). Consequently, you should probably consider this argument mandatory.

The `User32.DLL` file contains many functions (references to these functions are called entry points), so you have to tell your application which function to use. Normally, your application will use the name you assign to a function as the entry point name as well. However, in this case, `MessageBox()` is a common managed-code method that you don't want to hide by declaring the external function as `MessageBox()` as well. The code gets around this problem by supplying the `EntryPoint="MessageBox"` argument. It then declares the actual function name as used within the managed environment as `ExternMessageBox()`. When you call the external form of `MessageBox()` from your code, you'll actually use `ExternMessageBox()` to do it.

You declare all P/Invoke calls as `static extern`. The function return type in this case is the `ReturnValues` enumeration described in the "Providing Structures, Enumerations, and Constants" section of the chapter. You'll see how this works in the "Working with Return Values" section of the chapter. For now, all you need to know is that the return type is `ReturnValues`. The remainder of the function declaration includes the function name and the four arguments described earlier. Because the function is external, you end the declaration with a semicolon and don't include any implementation details.

Working with Function Call Data

It's important to remember that P/Invoke is an interface between managed and native code. While the .NET Framework knows all about the managed code, it knows next to nothing about the native code. In some cases, the compiler can figure out how to interact with the native code, but in other cases, you must provide the compiler with additional information using the `[MarshalAs]` attribute. This is another of those entries found in the `System.Runtime.InteropServices` namespace. You can apply this attribute to:

- Parameters
- Fields
- Return values

As described in the "Creating an External Function Reference" section of the chapter, the `MessageBox()` function requires a `LPCTSTR`, or a Long Pointer to a null-Terminated Constant STRing, as input for the `lpText` argument. Of course, the managed environment doesn't provide a variable of this type — the closest you can get is a `String`. It turns out that you actually need to define the variable type better than a `LPCTSTR`. The actual variable type you need to make a Unicode call is a Long Pointer to a Wide String (`LPWStr`). To tell the compiler you need a `String` of this type, you use the `[MarshalAs(UnmanagedType.LPWStr)]` attribute as shown here.

```
 [MarshalAs(UnmanagedType.LPWStr)]
String lpText
```

Notice how you use the `UnmanagedType` enumeration to determine which type to use for marshaling purposes. You can read more about the `UnmanagedType` enumeration at `http://msdn.microsoft.com/en-us/library/system.runtime.interopservices.unmanagedtype.aspx`. The `[MarshalAs]` attribute is useful for a wide range of interoperability tasks. For example, you also use it when creating an application that interacts with Component Object Model (COM) components in some low-level manner.

Using the External Function within Managed Code

After you define the enumerations, constants, structures, and variables, create the function, and add any required marshaling, you can finally begin using the external function. Of course, this all assumes that you've performed the required tasks correctly. Don't get discouraged if your first attempt fails — sometimes P/Invoke proves difficult even for someone with experience. The following sections show two phases of using the `ExternMessageBox()` function.

Creating a Basic Dialog Box

It's always best to test your new P/Invoke function simply. Use the least amount of code possible to test the function to ensure it works as anticipated — and then move to more complex testing. Otherwise, you'll quickly find that you can't figure out why something isn't working as it should. The `ExternMessageBox()` function does require the four basic inputs, but you can simplify things by not testing the output and by using a simple OK dialog box. Listing 27-4 shows an example of how you can perform this task.

Listing 27-4: Display the basic dialog box

```
private void btnTest_Click(object sender, EventArgs e)
{
   // Display a basic message box.
   ExternMessageBox(
      this.Handle,
      "Hello From Windows",
      "This is a Win32 API Call",
      MsgType.MB_ICONINFORMATION | MsgType.MB_OK);
}
```

The goal of this example is to create a modal dialog box that is attached to the application that creates it. In order to do this, you must pass the handle of the current application to Windows. The `this.Handle` property contains the required handle. If you had wanted to create a freestanding dialog box instead, you'd pass `IntPtr.Zero` in place of `this.Handle`. Because many developers do want a freestanding dialog box, they make the initial parameter an `int`, rather than an `IntPtr`, but that makes the resulting function considerably less flexible and is the wrong way to do things in the end.

The example passes two strings. The first is the text within the dialog box, while the second is the title bar text. Notice that you don't have to do anything special to make the strings acceptable to Windows. That's due to the use of the `[MarshalAs]` attribute in the function declaration.

The final parameter is the kind of dialog box you want to create. Notice that the example uses the `MsgType` enumeration to provide these values. In this case, `MsgType.MB_ICONINFORMATION` tells Windows to add an information icon, while `MsgType.MB_OK` tells Windows to add an OK button. You "OR" the values together to create a composite value. You can also do things like making the dialog box the topmost window and selecting a default button when the dialog box contains more than one button. Even using the enumeration, however, you can make mistakes. For example, your dialog box can't have more than one icon type or the call will fail. Figure 27-2 shows the output from this example.

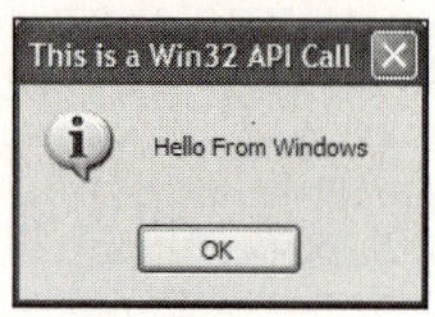

Figure 27-2: The example's output is a simple dialog box.

Working with Return Values

After you perform an initial test of the function, you must perform tests on other levels of functionality it provides. The second usage example interacts with the return value and ensures that the external function doesn't interfere with the normal functioning of the `MessageBox` class. Listing 27-5 shows the code you'll use to perform this task.

Listing 27-5: Demonstrating two-way data flow

```
private void btnTest2_Click(object sender, EventArgs e)
{
   // Display a message box and determine which button the user
   // clicked.
   ReturnValues ThisValue = ExternMessageBox(
      this.Handle,
      "Click Any Button",
      "Return Value Check",
      MsgType.MB_ICONQUESTION | MsgType.MB_YESNOCANCEL);

   // Display the result.
   MessageBox.Show("You Clicked: " + ThisValue.ToString(), "Result Value");
}
```

The overall `ExternMessageBox()` code is the same as before. However, in this case, the dialog box uses a different icon type (`MsgType.MB_ICONQUESTION`) and provides access to three buttons (`MsgType.MB_YESNOCANCEL`). Of course, the message and title bar text are also changed to match the function of the dialog box. When the code displays the dialog box, you see the output shown in Figure 27-3.

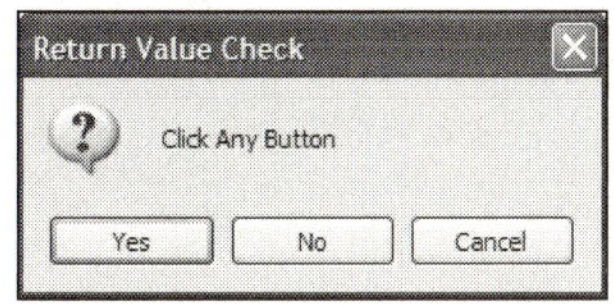

Figure 27-3: This example's output contains additional buttons.

After the user clicks a button, the call returns. The function places the value of the button that the user clicked in `ThisValue`, of type `ReturnValues` (the enumeration described in the "Providing Structures, Enumerations, and Constants" section of this chapter). You can now test the output of the dialog box using the same techniques you use with a managed dialog box that relies on `DialogResult`.

Don't use `DialogResult` *in place of* `ReturnValues` *when working with the external* `MessageBox()` *function. The return values are different, and you'll receive the wrong output. This rule generally applies to all external functions. Always create a custom enumeration to handle the output when the function produces a fixed set of return values.*

One of the most important tests is to ensure the external function doesn't interfere with the managed class. The example shows one way to perform this task and simultaneously test `ThisValue`. When you click Yes, you see the message box shown in Figure 27-4. The output is correct and you can verify that the `MessageBox.Show()` method still works fine.

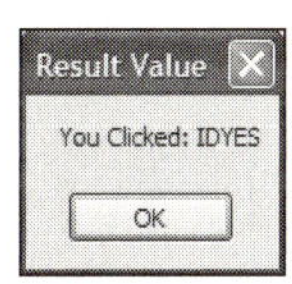

Figure 27-4: The final output shows that the function call works as expected.

Providing Error Handling

The `ExternMessageBox()` function is relatively well designed. It includes features that tend to reduce the ability of the developer to use the function incorrectly. Even when the developer does use the function incorrectly, it generally isn't fatal to the host application. The problem with working with Windows functions is that they often fail and don't tell you. For example, if you try to pass a nonexistent handle to `ExternMessageBox()`, Windows won't raise any kind of error — the call will apparently succeed.

However, the call will definitely fail when you pass a nonexistent handle. The following sections discuss various error handling needs and requirements.

Obtaining and Displaying the Error Number

You can provide error handling for Windows functions. In order to provide this feature, you must set the `SetLastError=true` parameter of the `[DllImport]` attribute. Otherwise, .NET doesn't maintain the error status either. Whenever you call on the external function, .NET will track the error information that Windows provides. In most cases, a return value of 0 tells you that the function call succeeded. However, you always want to verify this information using the Win32 API documentation.

Using the `SetLastError=true` *parameter always incurs a speed penalty. The penalty is small, but can become noticeable when you perform a number of function calls in a short time, such as within a loop. In most cases, the speed penalty is the price you pay for a reliable application. However, in some cases, the Windows function doesn't return a success or failure value, which means that adding the* `SetLastError=true` *parameter isn't beneficial. Always verify that the function actually returns a standard error output before you add any error handling for it to your application.*

Of course, simply adding an attribute to your application won't accomplish much. You must also add code to the managed environment to handle the error. Listing 27-6 shows how to perform this task using the simple example from before.

Listing 27-6: Detecting, handling, and displaying errors

```
private void btnTest3_Click(object sender, EventArgs e)
{
   // Create a dialog box with an error.
   ExternMessageBox(
      new IntPtr(5),
      "Hello From Windows",
      "This is a Win32 API Call",
      MsgType.MB_ICONINFORMATION | MsgType.MB_OK);

   // Windows won't display an error message; you must
   // retrieve it.
   if (Marshal.GetLastWin32Error() == 0)
      MessageBox.Show("There was no error!");
   else
      MessageBox.Show("Code Shows an Error of: " +
         Marshal.GetLastWin32Error().ToString());
}
```

In this example, the code contains an error. A window with a handle value of 5 probably doesn't exist on your system. Consequently, creating a new handle using `new IntPtr(5)` is an error. This example may seem contrived, but it's important that you see the error handling at work.

The code won't display a "Hello From Windows" dialog box this time. In fact, it will go directly to the error handling code. The key to this code is the call to `Marshal.GetLastWin32Error()`. When this return value is 0, the call succeeded. Any other value indicates an error. In this case, you see an error output as shown in Figure 27-5.

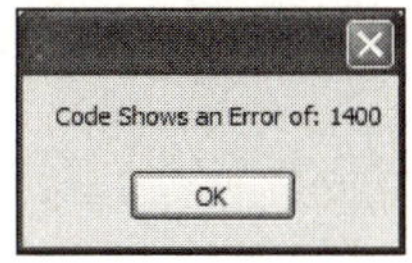

Figure 27-5: The application produces an error.

Interpreting the Error Number

Well, it's just fine that you know the error number is 1400. Unfortunately, the number doesn't tell you anything. You have a number of ways to handle this situation. The first method is to simply look up the number using a resource such as the one found at `http://msdn.microsoft.com/en-us/library/ms681381.aspx`. This technique works fine, but there is an easier way. When you install the C++ tools, you get a little utility called Error Lookup. In fact, you can start it by choosing Tools ⇨ Error Lookup in Visual Studio. Type the error number in the Value field and click Lookup. You'll see a result like the one shown in Figure 27-6 for this example.

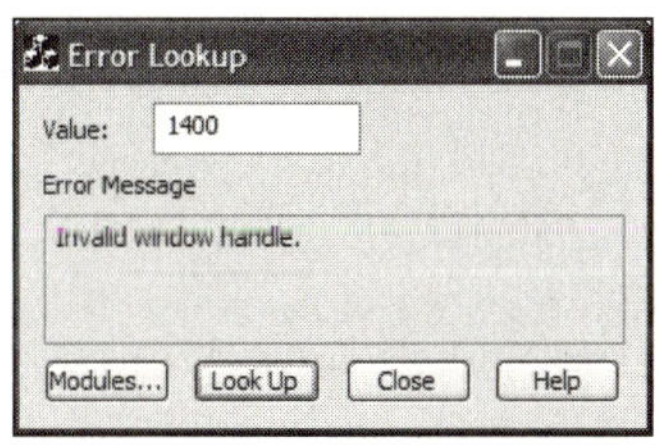

Figure 27-6: Error Lookup shows error numbers in human-readable form.

If Error Lookup can't seem to find the error value you need, click Modules. Type the name of the DLL file, such as `User32.DLL`*, in the Module Name field and click Add. Error Lookup will now look into that module to find error information.*

Using FormatMessage() to Translate the Error Number

The third method of translating an error number is to use the `FormatMessage()` function that is described at `http://msdn.microsoft.com/en-us/library/ms679351.aspx`. This function can prove a little more difficult to use than `MessageBox()`, partly because it has so many options associated with it. In general, when accessing an error message through a .NET application, you'll use the options shown in this example. Just so you can see constants at work, this example relies on constants, rather than an enumeration, for part of its output. Listing 27-7 shows the `FormatMessage()` declaration and its associated constants.

Listing 27-7: Defining the FormatMessage() function

```
// Declare the FormatMessage() function.
[DllImport("Kernel32.DLL")]
```

Continued

Listing 27-7: Defining the FormatMessage() function *(continued)*

```
public static extern Int32 FormatMessage(Int32 dwFlags,
                                         IntPtr lpSource,
                                         Int32 dwMessageID,
                                         Int32 dwLanguageID,
                                         out String lpBuffer,
                                         Int32 nSize,
                                         Int32 Arguments);

// Constants used to format the message.
public const Int32 FORMAT_MESSAGE_ALLOCATE_BUFFER = 0x00000100;
public const Int32 FORMAT_MESSAGE_IGNORE_INSERTS  = 0x00000200;
public const Int32 FORMAT_MESSAGE_FROM_STRING     = 0x00000400;
public const Int32 FORMAT_MESSAGE_FROM_HMODULE    = 0x00000800;
public const Int32 FORMAT_MESSAGE_FROM_SYSTEM     = 0x00001000;
public const Int32 FORMAT_MESSAGE_ARGUMENT_ARRAY  = 0x00002000;
public const Int32 FORMAT_MESSAGE_MAX_WIDTH_MASK  = 0x000000FF;
```

In this case, the function declaration provides only the required information. However, you could easily dress up this declaration using the same approach used in the `MessageBox()` function. This is one of the instances where the return value isn't a success value. The return value shows how many characters are in the output string. If this value is 0, then the call didn't succeed. In short, this is a case where 0 doesn't equal success as it does for the vast majority of Windows functions such as `MessageBox()`.

The `dwFlags` parameter tells `FormatMessage()` how to process the message. Microsoft provides a wealth of methods for performing this task. You'll see how the most commonly used flags work a little later in this section. A complete discussion of all the flags is outside of the scope of this book.

The `lpSource` parameter contains one of two values depending on how you use it. This parameter is the equivalent of adding a new module to the Error Lookup utility. In most cases, you'll load a library into memory using the `LoadLibraryEx()` function and then pass the handle to that library as the input for `lpSource`. A full discussion of this feature is outside the scope of this book.

The `dwMessageID` parameter is the error number you want to format. You obtain this value using the `Marshal.GetLastWin32Error()` method.

The `dwLanguageID` parameter defines the language you want to use when creating the string. This parameter normally contains a value of 0 because you normally want to format the message using the current language — whatever that language might be. In order to use this feature, the library containing the strings for the error number you want to format must have the string in the desired language. Most libraries don't contain strings in multiple languages, so normally you won't use this feature.

The `lpBuffer` parameter is the output from the `FormatMesage()` function. However, the .NET environment doesn't know that it's an output unless you tell it. That's why this argument contains the `out` keyword. Notice that the output is of type `String`. In some cases, you must use a `StringBuilder` instead because otherwise the call will fail. The key to this decision (in most cases) is whether the function can use the `LocalAlloc()` function to allocate memory for the output. Fortunately, P/Invoke takes care of all the details for you behind the scenes.

The `nSize` parameter contains the size of the buffer found in `lpBuffer`. This parameter assumes that you've allocated local memory to perform the call. However, the best approach when using this function is to let the function allocate the memory for you and then allow P/Invoke to handle the details in the background. Normally, you set this value to 0.

The `Arguments` parameter is special. It lets you insert information into the formatted message. However, it's far easier to perform any required formatting using managed code. Consequently, you normally set this argument to 0. If you were to use this parameter, you'd need to marshal an array to the native-code environment — a somewhat tricky task, but quite doable.

Now it's time to see the `FormatMessage()` function at work. Listing 27-8 shows a modified version of the code in Listing 27-6. In this case, the code uses the `FormatMessage()` function to translate the error number into human-readable form.

Listing 27-8: Using the FormatMessage() function

```
private void btnTest4_Click(object sender, EventArgs e)
{
   // Create a dialog box with an error.
   ExternMessageBox(
      new IntPtr(5),
      "Hello From Windows",
      "This is a Win32 API Call",
      MsgType.MB_ICONINFORMATION | MsgType.MB_OK);

   // Windows won't display an error message; you must
   // retrieve it.
   if (Marshal.GetLastWin32Error() == 0)
      MessageBox.Show("There was no error!");
   else
   {
      // Define a string to hold the output.
      String   ErrorString;

      // Call FormatMessage to change the number into
      // human-readable text.
      FormatMessage(
         FORMAT_MESSAGE_ALLOCATE_BUFFER |
         FORMAT_MESSAGE_FROM_SYSTEM |
         FORMAT_MESSAGE_IGNORE_INSERTS,
         IntPtr.Zero,
         Marshal.GetLastWin32Error(),
         0,
         out ErrorString,
         0,
         0);

      MessageBox.Show("Code Shows an Error of: " +
         ErrorString);
   }
}
```

Creating the error is the same as before, as is the basic error detection code. However, once the application detects an error, it works to translate the message into human-readable form. The `FormatMessage()` function relies on three constants in this case to define how to format the message. Here is what the three constants mean:

- `FORMAT_MESSAGE_ALLOCATE_BUFFER`: The `FormatMessage()` function creates a buffer for `lpBuffer` large enough to hold the string. Because you're using a managed `String` object, you don't have to worry about allocating or deallocating memory. However, this isn't always the case. In some odd cases, you must allocate the required memory and deallocate it as needed — you won't see any such examples in this book, and the need for memory handling isn't standard practice. If you find that you must allocate memory, use the `Marshal.AllocHGlobal()` method to do it. The `Marshal.FreeHGlobal()` lets you free the memory when you're done using it.
- `FORMAT_MESSAGE_FROM_SYSTEM`: This flag tells `FormatMessage()` to search the standard system message tables for the error number and provide the resulting text as output. Unless you're working with a third-party DLL, this is normally the best approach to take to finding the required message. If you find that you can't find the required string, then you'll need to load a DLL containing the messages and search through that module.
- `FORMAT_MESSAGE_IGNORE_INSERTS`: This flag tells `FormatMessage()` to ignore the `Arguments` parameter. As previously mentioned, you'll normally want to perform any formatting using managed code, rather than rely on the `FormatMessage()` function to perform the task for you.

The rest of the function call is straightforward. The function explanation earlier in this section explains what each of the other parameters is for and how you use it. Notice that when you call the function, you must supply the `out` keyword with `ErrorString`. A function with the `out` keyword in the declaration always requires the `out` keyword when you call it. After the code calls `FormatMessage()` it displays the result using `MessageBox.Show()`. Figure 27-7 shows the results.

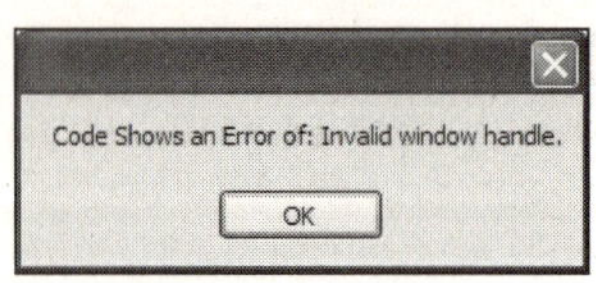

Figure 27-7: You now see the error message in human-readable form.

Designing Data Structures

Data structures can easily become quite complex when working with P/Invoke. This section provides you with the quickest of quick overviews of the topic. However, it's a useful bit of code that you'll probably want to put aside for future use. This example works at the command line. It demonstrates how to extend the functionality that .NET provides for working with the console. In this case, you discover a technique for erasing a certain portion of the display, without affecting any other portion. While you read through this example and try it out on your own machine, you'll discover some important principles of working with structures.

Enumerating the Standard Console Handles

You may eventually get tired of enumerating things when working with P/Invoke and even more tired of hearing about handles. Windows includes the concept of a standard handle — a handle whose number never changes. This example relies on three standard console handles:

- Input device
- Output device
- Error device

Listing 27-9 shows the enumeration for the standard handles. Notice that in this case, the enumeration relies on type `int`, and it contains negative values. These values match the values in the C++ header files precisely. You'll often find yourself switching between `int` and `uint` values for enumerations when working with P/Invoke.

Listing 27-9: Defining an enumeration of the standard console handles

```
// This is an enumeration of the standard console
// handles.
public enum StdHandleEnum
{
   STD_INPUT_HANDLE   = -10,
   STD_OUTPUT_HANDLE  = -11,
   STD_ERROR_HANDLE   = -12
};
```

Creating the Basic Data Structures

Before you can do anything with a display, you need some type of coordinate. Otherwise, you can't position the cursor to read or write anything. Normally, a coordinate appears as part of a structure and provides *X*- and *Y*-axis information. Listing 27-10 shows the coordinate structure, `COORD`, for this example.

Listing 27-10: Defining a screen coordinate

```
// This structure contains a screen coordinate.
[StructLayout(LayoutKind.Sequential, Pack=1)]
internal struct COORD
{
   public short X;
   public short Y;
}
```

In some respects, structures you use for P/Invoke are the same as any other structure you create. However, as with other P/Invoke features, you must add attributes to control the structure to make it usable. In this case, you rely on the `[StructLayout]` attribute. You can read more about this attribute at `http://msdn.microsoft.com/en-us/library/system.runtime.interopservices.structlayoutattribute.aspx`.

The [StructLayout] attribute doesn't have any required parameters. However, you'll likely use the same two parameters for most of your code. The most commonly used parameter is LayoutKind. In this case, the code tells P/Invoke to lay out the variables in the same order in which they appear in the data structure. In some cases, you must specify exact field positions to make the layout work properly, but this is a rarity.

The Pack parameter is actually more important in this case than LayoutKind. This parameter tells how to pack the data for transmission. In this case, the code tells P/Invoke to align the data on byte boundaries. You can choose other boundary values when working with P/Invoke. Read the Win32 API documentation carefully to determine what kind of alignment Windows requires. In some cases, you must fiddle with the Pack parameter to get Windows to accept the data.

Graphics routines also need to describe rectangular areas in most cases. The SMALL_RECT structure shown in Listing 27-11 performs this task.

Listing 27-11: Defining a rectangular area

```
// This structure contains coordinates for a
// rectangular area of the display.
[StructLayout(LayoutKind.Sequential, Pack=1)]
internal struct SMALL_RECT
{
  public short  Left;
  public short  Top;
  public short  Right;
  public short  Bottom;
}
```

This structure starts out with the same [StructLayout] attribute as COORD. The actual structure elements define the left, top, right, and bottom coordinates of the display. The Left and Top entries are normally set to 0, but don't count on it.

Now that the code has a method for accurately placing the cursor on screen and performing other tasks that require coordinates, and a method for describing rectangular areas, it's time to build a structure that holds data about the screen buffer. Without this data, you don't know the size of the screen buffer or understand how to work with it. Listing 27-12 shows the code used for the CONSOLE_SCREEN_BUFFER_INFO structure.

Listing 27-12: Using a COORD to define the screen buffer layout

```
// This structure defines the console screen buffer
// layout.
[StructLayout(LayoutKind.Sequential, Pack=1)]
internal struct CONSOLE_SCREEN_BUFFER_INFO
{
   public COORD      dwSize;
   public COORD      dwCursorPosition;
   public short      wAttributes;
   public SMALL_RECT srWindow;
   public COORD      dwMaximumWindowSize;
}
```

Notice that this structure uses the same [StructLayout] attribute parameters as the COORD data structure. You'll find that you use these two attributes more often than any other structure layout.

This structure embeds the COORD and SMALL_RECT structures. The Win32 API often uses embedding to create complex data layouts. Sometimes the layouts become so complicated, that you'll want to spend some time teasing them apart. Otherwise, you'll slowly drive yourself nuts.

The CONSOLE_SCREEN_BUFFER_INFO data structure provides information about the buffer size, current cursor position, attributes used to determine screen element colors, the size of the rectangle occupied by the screen buffer, and the maximum window size. You can find a complete description of the entries in this data structure at http://msdn.microsoft.com/en-us/library/ms682093.aspx.

Defining the Function Calls

Working with the console window requires four external functions as a minimum. Here is a quick overview of each function:

- GetStdHandle: Obtains a handle for a standard device (one of the three defined in the StdHandleEnum enumeration). The code uses this handle to perform tasks with the device in question.
- GetConsoleScreenBufferInfo: Obtains information about the console screen buffer using the handle you obtain using GetStdHandle(). The information in this data structure helps you manipulate the console screen.
- SetConsoleCursorPosition: Now that you know the size of the console screen buffer and its other characteristics, you can position a cursor in the rectangular area provided by the console screen buffer. Once the cursor is positioned, you can do something with that cursor position.
- FillConsoleOutputCharacter: Windows lets you do a host of things with a particular cursor position. The example uses the FillConsoleOutputCharacter() function to place a space at the current cursor position — effectively erasing the data.

Now that you have an idea of what tasks the various functions will perform, it's time to view their declaration. Listing 27-13 shows the declarations for the four external functions (all of which are in Kernel32.DLL).

Listing 27-13: Declaring the screen manipulation functions

```
// Returns a handle to any standard input or output.
[DllImport("Kernel32.DLL", SetLastError=true)]
public static extern IntPtr GetStdHandle(StdHandleEnum nStdHandle);

// Returns information about the console screen buffer
// to make it easier to clear.
[DllImport("Kernel32.DLL", SetLastError=true)]
public static extern bool GetConsoleScreenBufferInfo(
   IntPtr hConsoleOutput,
   out CONSOLE_SCREEN_BUFFER_INFO lpConsoleScreenBufferInfo);

// Positions the cursor on the console screen.
[DllImport("Kernel32.DLL", SetLastError=true)]
```

Continued

Listing 27-13: Declaring the screen manipulation functions *(continued)*

```
public static extern bool SetConsoleCursorPosition(
   IntPtr hConsoleOutput,
   COORD dwCursorPosition);

// Writes any character on the console screen. Using a space
// clears the display area.
[DllImport("Kernel32.DLL", SetLastError=true, CharSet=CharSet.Auto)]
public static extern bool FillConsoleOutputCharacter(
   IntPtr hConsoleOutput,
   short cCharacter,
   int nLength,
   COORD WriteCoord,
   out int lpNumberOfCharsWritten);
```

The `GetStdHandle()` function is relatively easy. It accepts one of the standard device options as input and provides an `IntPtr` to that handle as output. All three of the remaining calls use this handle to access the device. In this case, an output value of 0 indicates a failure, rather than success.

The `GetConsoleScreenBufferInfo()` function accepts a handle to a device as input and provides a completed `CONSOLE_SCREEN_BUFFER_INFO` as output. Notice that this function outputs a `bool` to indicate failure or success. Consequently, you can test the output using a simple `if` statement.

The `SetConsoleCursorPosition()` function accepts a handle to a device and a `COORD` structure as input. The `COORD` structure tells the function where to place the cursor on screen. As with the `GetConsoleScreenBufferInfo()` function, this function provides a `bool` as an indicator of success or failure.

Of the four functions, the `FillConsoleOutputCharacter()` is the hardest to understand. First, notice that the `[DllImport]` attribute contains `CharSet=CharSet.Auto`. This setting ensures that the output the function provides matches the user's display. Otherwise, you might find that the output isn't quite correct. The function accepts a device handle, character to write, the number of times to write the character, and the coordinates to use for writing the character as input. Notice that this function also relies on a `bool` to indicate success or failure. However, you can also check `lpNumberOfCharsWritten` to verify that the function has written all the characters you requested.

Using Data Structures within Managed Code

It's time to try out the data structures and functions in an application. Listing 27-14 shows the code used to work with the data structures and associated functions.

Listing 27-14: Erasing all or part of the display

```
static void Main(string[] args)
{
   // Contains the console screen buffer settings.
   CONSOLE_SCREEN_BUFFER_INFO CSBI;

   // Handle to the output device.
   IntPtr hOut;
```

```
      // Number of characters written to the screen.
      int CharOut;

      // Home cursor position.
      COORD Home;

      // Write some data to the screen.
      for (int i = 0; i < 23; i++)
         Console.Write("Some Text to Erase!\r\n");
      Console.Write("\r\nPress any key...");
      Console.ReadLine();

      // Clear the screen.
      // Begin by getting a handle to the console screen.
      hOut = GetStdHandle(StdHandleEnum.STD_OUTPUT_HANDLE);

      // Get the required console screen buffer information.
      GetConsoleScreenBufferInfo(hOut, out CSBI );

      // Set the home position for the cursor (upper left corner).
      Home.X = 0;
      Home.Y = 0;

      // Fill the console with spaces.
      FillConsoleOutputCharacter(hOut,
                                 (short) ' ',
                                 CSBI.Size.X * CSBI.Size.Y,
                                 Home,
                                 out CharOut);

      // Place the cursor in the upper left corner.
      SetConsoleCursorPosition(hOut, Home);

      // Show the screen is clear.
      Console.ReadLine();
   }
```

The code begins by creating an empty `CONSOLE_SCREEN_BUFFER_INFO` structure. You might wonder why the code doesn't initialize this structure. The `GetConsoleScreenBufferInfo()` performs this task automatically. In fact, initializing the structure could cause memory problems. P/Invoke often requires some level of interpretation on your part to get the calls right. The code also creates other variables needed to work with the functions as indicated by the comments.

At this point, the application writes some data to the console. Otherwise, you won't know whether the erasure works or not. You should see an entire display full of text if you're using a standard 80 × 25-character mode console screen.

Now begins the interesting part. The code obtains a standard handle using `GetStdHandle()`. In this case, because the code is writing data to screen, it requires a handle to the `StdHandleEnum.STD_OUTPUT_HANDLE`. This value appears in `hOut` and the code uses it in all subsequent function calls.

The next task is to fill `CSBI`, the `CONSOLE_SCREEN_BUFFER_INFO` structure, using `GetConsoleScreenBufferInfo()`. When this function returns, you can discover all kinds of interesting information about the console screen buffer.

The code has to define a starting position for erasing the screen next. Consequently, it initializes the `Home` data structure with zeros for the left and right position. The `FillConsoleOutputCharacter()` function uses this information and the information found in `CBSI` to erase the entire screen. Notice that the code doesn't actually use the `CharOut` variable for anything. In some cases, when working without parameters in P/Invoke, you must provide a dummy variable or the call will fail because Windows is expecting it.

The final task is to reposition the cursor to the upper left corner of the console screen. The `SetConsoleCursorPosition()` function performs this task using `Home` as the coordinates.

Implementing Your Design

This chapter has demonstrated techniques for working with P/Invoke. It's a fun chapter, in a way, because you get to work with managed applications in way that most people don't. However, don't let the fun aspect of P/Invoke cloud your thinking. Remember that P/Invoke is the option of last choice in most cases. Look for other alternatives when you can. When you must use P/Invoke, always remember that safe pointers are always better than using the unsafe pointer option. In fact, unsafe pointers are reserved for extreme cases where you must access functionality at all costs. Make sure you always test your P/Invoke code thoroughly and in multiple environments. Small differences between systems are amplified when you use P/Invoke.

Obviously, P/Invoke is a necessary solution to some problems. What you need to do is determine this requirement up front as part of the design process, rather than wait until you begin coding. Planning can save you considerable woe later. You may want to spend time looking at third-party solutions for the problem, rather than incur the problems of using P/Invoke yourself. Of course, you'll want to become familiar with P/Invoke should you need to use it in your application. The examples in this chapter provide a good starting point. Take time to work through the examples in the debugger so that you build an understanding of how P/Invoke works. Try creating a few applications of your own. Work especially with applications that rely on structures to pass data, because this requirement can prove to be the most daunting of all when building an application.

So far, this book has focused on what you can do for yourself — everything from designing the application to building a team to implement the design. However, in the real world, development teams seldom have time to do everything themselves. At some point, you have to be willing to say that you could probably perform a task given time, but you don't have the time. Chapter 28 begins a new part of the book that looks at third-party solutions to development problems. Third-party solutions cover everything from tools you use to create applications to libraries that contain precooked code you can use to enhance your application. As with most design and development decisions, working with a third party carries risks, and Chapter 28 helps you understand them.

Part V: Resources and Tools

28

Choosing Resources and Tools

Many developers put little, if any, time or thought into the resources (such as third-party libraries) and tools (such as an XML editor) they select. What normally happens is that someone suggests downloading this terrific new piece of software, and the eye candy dazzles the developer — at least for a while. However, it's not long before reality sets in. After a while, the resource or tool becomes part of the clutter on the developer's hard drive unless the developer is particularly careful about keeping the hard drive clean. Of course, not every resource or tool constitutes clutter. In fact, some resources and tools become lifelong friends (expressed in computer years). However, the valued resource or tool is more the exception than the rule.

Throughout this chapter, you'll see the term resource *used generically. A resource is any non-application software you use to assist you in creating applications. Of course, the most common resource is the third-party library containing routines you don't want to write yourself. However, a resource could be an icon or other graphics library. In fact, resources can include a host of things that don't happen to be tools (application software).*

The purpose of this chapter isn't to dissuade you from playing. I've spent more than a little time playing myself. Sometimes playing is even necessary for a developer's mental health — after all, you don't want to find yourself saying, "Bad user, kill, kill, kill." However, after you see just how bad a particular resource or tool is, you don't want it hanging around either. This chapter provides hints and tips on making that fateful decision of clearing out the resource or tool you really didn't need in the first place.

Creating a toolbox for your team is even harder than creating your own toolbox. Now you have to consider the needs of more than one developer, and developers tend to be individualistic. Developers argue over everything, it seems — especially what constitutes the best resource or tool. Unfortunately, if you're leading the team, you have to make the decision of what everyone will use despite the individualism you'll encounter. In order for the team to operate as a cohesive whole, everyone on the team must use the same resources or tools — to do otherwise invites a kind of chaos you really don't want to see in person.

Ending Time-Wasting Clutter

Many developers are pack rats. They accumulate resources and tools that they'll never use, yet refuse to remove them from their hard drive because they might need them tomorrow. The results are predictable. Whenever you ask them about a particular resource or tool, they must dig through the clutter on their hard drive to find it, assuming they can find it at all. In general, your hard drive should contain the resources and tools that you're using today for your current project. It doesn't take very much time to remove all of the extraneous accumulation of resources and tools that don't fit the current project, and you'll find that you work considerably faster when you do.

Now before anyone begins writing me hostile e-mails, it's important to remember that this discussion is about your hard drive. Most of us have archives of resources and tools that have proved helpful in past projects, and you'll probably want to maintain those archives — just don't maintain them on your hard drive. The resources and tools on your hard drive should focus on the current project. By maintaining a focus, you make it easier to locate precisely the resource or tool that you need now. If you find that one of those other resources or tools really is necessary to the current project, you can easily restore it to the hard drive from your archive.

Precisely what constitutes necessary is often in the eye of the beholder. To keep clutter at bay, the hard drive normally should contain just the resources and tools you're using now. However, some developers do have preferences for some resources or tools that they use often enough that they deserve a permanent place on the hard drive. Just how you decide what to keep for the current project and what to maintain for future use because you use it so often is up to you.

The following sections discuss some of the techniques you can use to create your own resource and tool archive. The archive is simply the place you put resources and tools that you aren't using for the current project. You might use them in the next project, but you're not using them today. You'll also find discussions of how and when to update resources and tools, and how to maintain a conversation with vendors over the direction of resource and tool changes. When you complete these sections, you should have a better idea of how to organize resources and tools on your system. These sections won't provide input on specific resources or tools.

Designing and Building Your Own Resources and Tools

The development world literally is filled with resources and tools, so it might seem odd that you can't find the specific resource or tool needed for your current project. However, the problem occurs more often than you might think, and developers often scratch their heads wondering what to do next. Obviously, using someone else's software is usually easier than building something on your own. In fact, it's usually less expensive, too. The problem is that trying to fit that square peg of a resource or tool in the round hole of your project won't work. You need resources and tools that match your project completely.

Designing and building custom resources and tools doesn't always equate to performing the work yourself. If you see a resource or tool on the market that almost-but-doesn't-quite fit your project requirements, you can often convince the vendor to produce a custom version that will fulfill the requirements. Of course, the cost will be higher than buying the off-the-shelf product, but the vendor can often produce what you need faster than you can and for less money. The vendor approach is the best solution to the problem in most cases.

Larger organizations often dismiss the usability and usefulness of shareware and freeware products. After all, no one would simply give away software that's useful. It may surprise you to know that shareware and freeware authors often do produce great products and then simply don't have the finances to market their product any other way. In some cases, these shareware and freeware products act as advertisements for the consulting services that the authors provide. Consequently, if you see a shareware or freeware product that almost meets your needs, you may want to try to set up a consulting arrangement with the author. This approach isn't going to be as fast as the shrink-wrap vendor approach, but you may actually save money in the end.

Finally, you might not find a resource or tool of any sort that comes close to meeting your requirements. When this situation occurs, you often have to develop the resource or tool yourself. However, you probably won't want to develop it exclusively as an in-house project. If your organization has run into this problem, you can bet that someone else is running into it, too. Consider developing your resource or tool in distributable form so that you can recoup some of the expenses by selling the product to someone else.

Creating the Archive

Every developer should have an archive of useful resources and tools. The archive isn't the place to put untested software — it contains resources or tools that you have fully tested and expect to use. In fact, you may want to have two archives — one that contains tested software and one that contains software used for a project. The archive should appear in a specific location. If you're an independent developer, you might place the archive on one or more DVDs to make it easy to search and work with. A team might place its archive on a network drive so that the software is accessible to anyone who needs it.

An archive is useless, however, if it isn't documented. You should document each piece of software to make it easier to identify later. In fact, the documentation should probably appear in a custom database set aside for the purpose. You can maintain any list of facts that your organization finds helpful. Here are a few items that you should definitely consider as part of the documentation.

- Software name
- Version number
- Release date
- Superseded (an indicator of whether the software has been superseded by a newer version)
- File size
- Development system requirements
- Development platform requirements
- Target system requirements
- Recommended by
- Description (a paragraph or two at least)
- Project where used
- Personal rating
- Types of projects where you think the software might be useful

- ❑ Where you found the software (for example, the URL where you downloaded it)
- ❑ Licensing requirements
- ❑ Type of software (one or two words used for grouping purposes)

It's just fine to put older software in your archive. In fact, you'll definitely want to keep those older versions. I have had many occasions to use an older version of a piece of software in a situation where a newer version provides too many features or simply wouldn't work. In some cases, you'll have data files that work with the older version and may need to resurrect the older version to read them. If you really don't have a place for the older versions, consider some type of offline or even offsite storage so that you have the product when you need it.

Going through the process of creating an archive helps you weed out the software you'll never use. The software may work just fine — it may do everything the vendor intends for it to do — it simply may not meet a particular need and you may not ever use it. In addition to weeding out software you don't need, you can also use this process to remove duplicate software. When you find yourself writing essentially the same description multiple times, you probably have too many kinds of that particular software. It doesn't take long for most developers to establish a favorite when working with multiple pieces of software that perform the same task. Again, it isn't that the other software doesn't work; it's simply that you prefer a particular vendor's version of it. Getting rid of the duplicates can avoid confusion later.

One of the reasons you want to include the file size as part of your database is so you know the disk requirements for a particular piece of software. Sometimes, it's helpful to have both a full and mini-version of the same type of software. The mini-version is easier to transport to another location and may actually appear on a disc of software you take with you when you visit a client site. Consequently, duplicate software isn't always a bad idea.

Recommendations are either helpful or useless in the software industry. You probably receive hundreds of recommendations in a given year. The problem is sorting out which recommendations to follow and which ones to ignore. By recording who recommended a particular piece of software that you find helpful, you begin building a picture of which recommendations work. After a while, you begin seeing patterns in the kind of software that a particular person is good at recommending as well. This could eventually lead you to working with that person in other ways — they may have hidden talents that you don't know about, and their recommendations will often reveal these talents.

Your archive could eventually become damaged. That's why you want to record where you obtained a particular piece of software. Vendors often keep older versions of their products online for years after they've released a newer version. Of course, the newer version appears on the home page — you need an URL to locate the older version. If you aren't working with shrink-wrap software, consider providing other details about where to locate another copy of the software should you need it. Even a person's name and telephone number can prove useful.

Because you're developing software, you need to know the licensing terms of every resource and tool you use. In many cases, you must pay an additional cost to use a particular resource or tool on a client system. Consequently, you want to find software with favorable licensing terms whenever possible. This is another situation where you might want to maintain duplicate software. Your system may have a professional-level version of a product, but the client system may receive a less capable version of a tool that works with the same data or performs the task that the client machine requires. In some cases, you need both a distributable and a development version of a resource — especially when working with libraries.

Updating Resources and Tools Effectively

When resources and tools become outdated, you begin to see them fail with the current development environment or fail to match pace with changes in data. If you have a larger resource and tool archive, you may find it difficult to track updates. Many vendors release their products on a two-year cycle. Of course, the precise update cycle usually depends on what Microsoft is doing at the time. Vendors aren't going to release an update for the current version of Visual Studio two months before Microsoft releases an entirely new version. Therefore, you have to keep track of changes in the industry.

It's important, though, to track the software updates, which is one reason you want to record the release date for each entry in your archive. By knowing the release date, you begin sorting your archive by those pieces of software most likely to require an update. Because you recorded the download location, you can begin looking for the newer version there or on the vendor's home page. Of course, you won't want to base your search on superseded software — the software that the vendor has replaced with a newer version.

With the proper entries in your database, it's possible that you could even automate the search to an extent by building an application to look for newer versions. Unfortunately, automation will prove less than 100 percent efficient because each vendor will have a different method of indicating that new software is available. Even so, you might be able to automate a large portion of the update search.

Don't forget that most vendors maintain an e-mail notice system for updates. Tools may also include an automated online search. Every time you start the tool, it looks online for a newer version. Not every resource or tool has these benefits, but it's worth the effort to check. The time you save is your own, so it's valuable.

No matter how you ensure that you update your resources and tools, you should do so regularly. The use of older resources and tools won't affect just you or your application. These older versions also affect the user and could affect the organization. When using older resources and tools, you may encounter the following issues.

- Compatibility issues
- Broken features
- Missing bug fixes (some of which could invite viruses)
- Development environment issues
- Data damage (when a resource or tool works with a newer data format incorrectly)
- System crashes

Developing a Rapport with Vendors

You won't get to know the vendor of every resource or tool that you use. In fact, doing so would be so time prohibitive that you probably wouldn't get anything else done. However, you should get to know vendors of resources and tools that you use regularly. If you really don't want to have to create your own resources and tools, then you need to work with the vendor to provide the resources and tools you want (understanding, of course, that there are probably thousands of other people working with the vendor, too).

Vendors usually provide a number of interaction methods. Of course, you can always provide feedback through direct e-mail or other contact. Sometimes calling a representative with questions and feedback will help. In many cases, a vendor will also provide surveys that you can fill out to express your preferences. Usually, these surveys provide entries that show how long you've been a customer and which products you actually own. A vendor will generally place greater emphasis on long-term customers with a number of products.

Participating in a product's beta cycle is also a good way to provide feedback. In this case, you get to shape the product before it even appears on the market. Of course, the vendor will have other considerations than your feedback — cost and timing concerns usually play a big role in determining which product features make it into the final product and which don't.

If you feel strongly enough about a product, you can also do things like feature it on your Web site and provide help to other users. These actions almost always attract the vendor's attention. Some vendors, such as Microsoft, have special programs for people who provide support of this sort. These people usually receive preferential treatment of some kind. Having someone with the vendor's ear on your team is always helpful because you can be assured of getting questions answered quicker.

In some cases, it's good to work with the vendor for one other reason. If a vendor knows that you'll be a longtime customer, you often get benefits that the casual customer doesn't get, such as reduced prices for products. The vendor is more likely to respond to your input as well because a longtime customer is worth quite a lot. Sometimes you get other preferential treatment such as better support and reduced support costs. Unfortunately, the vendor won't know that you're a longtime customer unless you make a bit of noise. Talking with the vendor is your best way to obtain better quality service.

Defining a Useful Resource

You're playing with a graphics library, and you wonder whether it might not add some pizzazz to your current application. After working with the library for a while, you find that the code is well written, it has good vendor support, the vendor has provided adequate examples, and even the help file is easy to follow. The question now is whether the graphics library is useful. The answer to that question depends on whether you have allocated time to add pizzazz to your current application. In many cases, you haven't allocated pizzazz time, and the library will simply add to the time required to get the application out the door. Consequently, even though the resource is well constructed and you might use it in a project sometime in the future, it isn't useful today.

Many of the decisions you have to make about resources are difficult because you can see how the resource will benefit the project. In fact, you wonder how you didn't think about the need that the resource addresses while designing the project. It's extremely easy to become infatuated with working with that resource to the detriment of your project. Several months down the road you find that your project is behind schedule and that the resource hasn't performed as expected because you never planned it as part of the project. Consequently, the first rule of useful resources is that you have planned to use them. Experimenting with new resources is always a good idea — otherwise, you'll never find those nuggets of useful ideas for future projects, but you also need to keep your eyes on the goal of finishing the current project on time and within budget.

The second rule of useful resources is that you need to understand them. If you obtain a new resource that no one understands, the learning curve will prove steep, and you could end up behind schedule again, even if you planned to use the resource as part of your design. A useful resource is one that you already know completely or know enough about to use with very little training time invested. Now, if you're between projects, you can spend as much time as desired learning how to use the new resource. The time you invest today will pay dividends tomorrow.

A third rule of useful resources is that they integrate well with your project. I've seen any number of applications that relied on a resource that felt bolted on. In one such case, the application actually opened a DOS prompt and called on the resource to generate an external file. The application then loaded the file and processed it. The actual process was longer, but it reminded me of a Keystone Cops comedy (see `http://en.wikipedia.org/wiki/Keystone_Cops` and `http://www.a-1video.com/sennett.htm` for a description of some of the movies in this very old series), where everyone is running around and no one is accomplishing anything. (Mack Sennett was the inspired director of this film series — learn more about him at `http://www.biographcompany.com/celebrity/sennett.html`.) Yes, the application finally obtained the correct result, but the application's author should have definitely chosen a different resource to perform the task.

Defining a Useful Tool

Obtaining a useful tool is less difficult than obtaining a useful resource in many cases. When the tool is for your personal use, it need only satisfy your tastes. If you feel comfortable with a particular XML editor, you shouldn't let anyone convince you to use something else unless you truly feel that the newer tool has some significant advantage or you're working as part of a team. However, if you're uncertain about a tool, the question is one of determining that the tool is useful.

> *The same pressures that affect any other application developer often motivate tool creators — the latest version of any tool contains the latest features, even if no one has requested or needs those features. The problem with this approach, especially when it comes to developer tools, is that the old version may actually work better for a particular project. Consequently, it's usually prudent to maintain those old versions somewhere — perhaps on a DVD devoted to the purpose. Yes, you normally use the latest version of the tool to ensure it works properly with your development environment, but sometimes using the older version of the tool can prove helpful. Tools usually consume very little space, so the software you save today may help you complete a project tomorrow.*

Most developers begin evaluating a tool based solely on the features it provides. It's true that any tool you obtain will have to have the features required to perform the task. However, in most cases, just about any tool you pick up will have most of the features you need. A mini-version of the tool might not possess them, but you can generally categorize tools that will meet the requirements.

After you review the tool's feature set, you might end up with a whole list of potential tools that fulfill your needs. The question now is how the tool feels. Developers aren't standard users, they can usually figure out even complex user interfaces with relative ease. The ease of use of a tool takes on a different meaning with the developers — you can usually state it quite simply using a single word, *fast*. A developer usually doesn't have a lot of time to putz around with a tool that has a less than helpful interface — more help is not necessarily better.

More developers need to pay attention to how a particular tool uses system resources. It's not hard to find a developer who has chosen a particular tool, only to find that it won't run on the client system when the developer needs to perform diagnostics. Choosing a tool that runs only on the developer's system is usually a recipe for disaster — the developer can't guarantee that the tool won't see use on the user's machine.

The last criterion you should use in choosing a tool is price. Sometimes a tool is simply too expensive for even the most ardent developer. However, this really should be the last product element you look at because developer tools are for the professional — they're part of the cost of doing business. Now, it's true, you can find a wealth of shareware and freeware tools out there that work just fine. In fact, I use more than a few of them myself. There isn't a good reason to throw money at an expensive alternative when you can find something useful for little or nothing. However, it's usually not a good idea to let cost be the determining factor in choosing a useful tool.

Creating a Team Toolbox

Some teams really don't work together. When you look at a professional team of any sort, everything from people in the army to players on the football field, the one striking feature is that they're all using the same gear. They wear the same clothes, use the same equipment — everything is the same. If you're creating a development team, the best way to ensure success is to make your group into a real team, not just some semblance of a team. Although you can probably forgo putting everyone into uniform (although successful teams often do), you want to make sure everyone is using the same equipment. Otherwise, chaos will reign. With this in mind, the following sections discuss team needs.

When creating a development team, you must consider the experiences of the individual team members. In some cases, getting someone with experience with a particular resource or tool is incredibly valuable. Even if the resource or tool isn't your first choice for the team toolbox, the experience provided by the team member will more than make up for deficiencies in the resource or tool in many cases. Be careful to weigh all your options, however, to ensure you really are getting a good deal for the team as a whole.

Understanding the Team Needs

People need to feel part of the team. If someone is singled out (gets special treatment), it takes away from the team. The greatest needs the team has are for everyone to feel part of it and for the team to become cohesive as a result. When you obtain resources and tools for your team, every member should receive the same materials — at least within reason. At a minimum, everyone should have the same IDE version and basic tool set. Everyone should have access to all the same resources on the network drive. Now, it may happen that your database developer has a special need for database work — getting the database developer this tool won't affect the other members of the team because they truly don't need the tool.

As part of developing a picture of the team needs, consider how the members of the team will use the resources and tools you provide. For example, it's quite possible that someone will work extensively with XML files. However, just about everyone will at least view those files. Getting a good XML editor is probably going to be a good idea. You never know when other team members will also have to edit or otherwise manage that file. When one person has a great tool and other team members struggle with something inadequate, it hurts the morale of the team as a whole. Make sure everyone gets a tool for a common use that will meet every potential need, even if you can't see that need at the outset of the development effort.

It's important to obtain input from the team members. You have a number of good reasons for asking for their input:

- The most important reason is that team members will grumble if they feel they haven't been heard. During the entire project, you'll hear people whispering about how the product they would have chosen would have worked better.
- You can't possibly know about every product out there, so sometimes a team member will make a suggestion for a product choice that actually works better than the one you intended to use.
- In some cases, you won't see a need for a product until you're well into the project. A team member might see this need at the outset.
- Team members may point out potential problems in using a particular product — issues that you may not have considered.

Defining Usage Requirements and Policies

Once you develop your team toolbox, you'll want to put some usage requirements and policies into writing. No matter how much you let people talk about their choices and all the reasons you present for making a particular choice, some people will simply ignore you and try to use their own resources and tools on the project. At some point, you'll notice that the application is creating inconsistent results, and the culprit will very likely be that alternative resource or tool. Everyone must use the same toolbox once you put it together.

You should actually create two documents: one that considers usage requirements and another that contains team policies. The first document will spell out when and how the team will use various resources and tools. If you don't put things into writing, team members may not truly understand how to use the various tools you've provided.

Make sure the usage document considers licensing details. For example, you may not purchase a copy of the XML editor for every team member, so you'll need to spell out when various people can access the tool. You'll also need to install metering software on the network to ensure that you don't have too many people using the tool at one time.

The second document will spell out the procedures for making toolbox changes. In addition, it will tell the developers what will happen if they don't use the required resources and tools. Obviously, you don't want to fire someone simply because they used a different XML editor, but you still need to have some policy in place that puts teeth into the requirement to use the toolbox.

Obtaining Resources and Tools

This chapter has helped you understand the need to obtain good resources and tools to create applications. Of course, getting those resources and tools requires some experimentation on your part, which is actually one of the fun aspects of being a developer. However, don't let the candy store mentality take over — evaluate resources and tools as they relate to the current project and put everything else aside. It's important not to clutter your hard drive and work area with resources and tools that won't help you achieve your goal, no matter how glitzy they might appear or how convincingly the salesperson talked.

When you talk with someone else about resources and tools, they often act as if they know the perfect product for your project, even though they have no idea of what your project is all about. The developer community regularly produces a wealth of resources and tools that can meet a need. These resources and tools often rely on the best design principles and complete the tasks the vendor intended them to perform quite well. However, the resource or tool may not accomplish the task you have in mind. When you turn down a particular resource or tool, consider that it may work for another project, but not this project — evaluate it again later when you're working on the next project. The hardest thing to do at this point is to remain focused on the current project and find the resources and tools you need to complete it. Always remember to write down what you want to do and then look at resources and tools based on that specific goal.

Microsoft produces a lot of resources and tools. In fact, someone could probably write a book that discusses nothing but Microsoft resources and tools. Chapter 29 discusses a few of these Microsoft-produced resources and tools. All these resources and tools relate in some way to a topic discussed in this book. Of course, only you know whether the resource or tool will meet a need for your current project. Consider Chapter 29 a guide to some of the tools that Microsoft provides and an overview of some of the other resources and tools that you'll find on the Microsoft Web site. Sometimes searching through Microsoft's bag of tricks can save you considerable time and effort, but remember to toss the junk aside.

29

Microsoft Resources and Tools

Microsoft provides a wealth of resources and tools for you to use. If you're an MSDN subscriber, you receive some of these resources and tools as part of your regular subscription updates. However, the subscription provides you with the tip of the iceberg — you have access to far more resources online. In fact, you have access to so many resources, it's truly hard to know where to begin — you could spend months checking it all out. Unfortunately, you'll just have to find ways to deal with all the goodies.

One of the problems that this chapter addresses is that Microsoft doesn't place its resources and tools in one place. You might end up looking in several places before you find the tool you need. Consequently, the first part of this chapter discusses some of the things you can do to find the resources and tools you need.

The remainder of the chapter describes some of the tools you might want to check out. I'm not making a recommendation that you use a particular tool to the exclusion of some other tool that you really like better. All that these sections provide is a basic overview of the tool so that you can make up your own mind as to the viability of using the tool to create your next application. In general, these sections describe tools that cost little or nothing, so they're a deal for what they accomplish, but you may find that you need to rely on a shrink-wrapped tool to obtain the level of functionality you require.

I'm always looking for new tools to use and discuss in my books. If you find a free or low-cost Microsoft tool that you really think I'd like to know about, write me at JMueller@mwt.net. Let me know why you think this particular tool is such a good deal.

Finding Microsoft Resources and Tools

Everyone knows that Microsoft produces a ton of software. Few people view Microsoft as innovative, and that reputation is partly deserved because Microsoft doesn't innovate very often. However, the one thing Microsoft has is resources and tools that come out of the process of creating Windows, Visual Studio, and other products their engineers design. In some cases, you're using precisely the same resources and tools as the Microsoft engineers do when you download a resource or tool from a Microsoft Web site. The only problem is finding those resources and tools. The purpose of the sections that follow is to help you locate Microsoft resources and tools with greater ease.

Considering MSDN

The first place that many developers go when they need a resource or tool is the Microsoft Developer Network (MSDN) Web site at `http://msdn.microsoft.com/`. Even if you don't have an MSDN subscription, you can find useful items and download them. Of course, the entire Web site is a resource. If you need to know about the `System.Runtime` namespace (see `http://msdn.microsoft.com/en-us/library/system.runtime.aspx`), you can find a full description here that matches the copy of MSDN on your hard drive in every way. It's even possible to locate the documentation for older versions of products so you can see a snapshot of the features that a product provides (versus the newest version that probably appears on your hard drive).

When you click the Downloads tab, you see only a few of the downloads available — the other downloads are lurking somewhere in the MSDN documentation. For example, the Downloads tab won't show sample code or tools that Microsoft makes available. However, clicking the Downloads tab will show you downloads for various versions of the .NET Framework, along with some other interesting resources you'll want to track.

To see some of the more interesting downloads, click Library. On the Library tab, you'll see entries for various MSDN features, such as the .NET Development. Drill down into this entry, and you see an entry for Beta Versions and Previews (`http://msdn.microsoft.com/en-us/library/aa338210.aspx`). At the time of this writing, you can discover Acropolis CTP 1 and Microsoft Project Code Named Velocity CTP2 on this Web page.

The main page to visit on MSDN if you're interested in downloads is the MSDN Download Center at `http://msdn.microsoft.com/en-us/aa570309.aspx`. Most of these links take you to another Web page where you can choose specifics of your download. For example, click the Windows SDK link and you'll see the Windows SDK Web page (`http://msdn.microsoft.com/en-us/windows/bb980924.aspx`), where you can choose a particular Windows SDK version to download. Microsoft even provides helpful advice on choosing a Windows SDK version that fits your needs.

Looking at TechNet

You might not initially think that TechNet has a lot to offer the developer. However, some of the most interesting tools that Microsoft has to offer appear on TechNet as part of its SysInternals Web site (`http://technet.microsoft.com/en-us/sysinternals/bb545027.aspx`). There are so many interesting tools on this one Web page that you might spend a month or so exploring them all (assuming that you also plan to do some work). For example, the ListDLLs tool has saved me more than a few hours of work. Another good tool to check out is Process Explorer, which can help you make sense of which processes are running and what they actually do. Make sure you check out the SysInternals home page (`http://technet.microsoft.com/en-us/sysinternals/default.aspx`) to get all the details on new additions to this massive library.

TechNet is also where you'll find the various Microsoft servers and associated downloads. The server information includes virtualization technology (`http://technet.microsoft.com/en-us/virtualization/default.aspx`). Many developers use virtualization now to keep their real machine in better shape. If you crash a virtual server with an errant program, it's no big deal — you can bring it back online in seconds. Crashing your physical machine can have dire results, including having to reformat and reinstall software.

Many developers use scripts for various purposes, especially now that Microsoft seems to use PowerShell considerably more often (such as with Exchange Server). TechNet does have the scripting links you'll need, but the actual material appears on Microsoft's main Web site. Check it out at `http://www.microsoft.com/technet/scriptcenter/default.mspx`*. Consequently, don't always assume that something will appear on TechNet, even if it's logical that it should appear there.*

One of the most important places for a developer to visit on TechNet is the Security TechCenter (`http://technet.microsoft.com/en-us/security/default.aspx`). The Web page contains some obvious developer aids, such as UrlScan, a tool that can help you identify potential holes in your security. When designing an application, you'll also want to check out the latest security bulletins to ensure you don't have any usable holes in your application design. A second check of security bulletins is helpful as you begin the testing phase of your application.

Interacting with Microsoft Download

Microsoft Download is probably where you expected to find all the downloads discussed so far, but don't worry, it contains more software than the typical developer can probably learn fully in four or five years at least. (Because the content constantly changes, give up any idea of ever catching up.) The Microsoft Download Center Web page at `http://www.microsoft.com/downloads/Search.aspx` provides full search capability. Unfortunately, the search engine isn't always as helpful as you might like it to be, so you'll also want to read the tips in the "Discovering Resources and Tools Online" section of this chapter.

To optimize your searching on the Microsoft Download Center Web page, choose a particular download category in the first Search field. In most cases, you'll probably start with the Developer Tools category. However, you might also want to try the System Tools category. After you choose a category, type a search term such as `XML Edit`, and click Go. This is a good technique for locating a copy of XML Notepad 2007 (described in the "Editing XML Files Using XML Notepad 2007" section of the chapter).

You can perform a detailed search when desired. Simply click the Advanced Search link to display the Advanced Search page at `http://www.microsoft.com/downloads/advancedsearch.aspx`*. This page lets you set a number of search criteria: keywords, product or technology, category, release date, method to sort the results, and the number of results per page.*

As with other parts of Microsoft's vast Web domain, you have other options when working with Microsoft Download. The search page also has a number of links in two groups:

- Popular Downloads
- New Downloads

These two groups may have the links you want most if you're looking for something new to try. In both cases, you can click a list to see more downloads.

Below these two groups on the search page is a list of categories. If you click one of these category links, you go to a Web page that shows the software downloads for that particular category. Unfortunately, the results don't appear in any particular order. Click one of the three column headings to sort the information in a particular order. You can choose from:

- Title
- Release Date
- Popularity

Using the Microsoft Knowledge Base

The Microsoft Knowledge Base is a series of short articles that tell you about various topics, such as fixes for errors in Microsoft products. However, the Microsoft Knowledge Base also includes how-to articles and a host of other useful items. The Microsoft Knowledge Base isn't a download source, strictly speaking, but still it's a resource you need to know about and consider using. Surprisingly, some developers never visit the Microsoft Knowledge Base (in part, because it's so hard to search efficiently).

You don't access the Microsoft Knowledge Base directly. Instead, you rely on Microsoft Help and Support to access it. The best idea is to use the Advanced Search page at `http://support.microsoft.com/search/?adv=1`. If you happen to have a Knowledge Base number, you can type it directly into the search field and access the Knowledge Base immediately. Otherwise, you'll need to fill the fields in as carefully as possible to obtain the results you want.

After you click Search, you'll see a list of Knowledge Base articles that match the criteria that you specified. Click a link and you go directly to that article. If you don't see the article you want, try making the "On what product do you want to search?" field less specific, or change the product altogether. Generally, it's easier to find what you want using the techniques describe in the "Discovering Resources and Tools Online" section of the chapter.

Exploring Microsoft Research

Microsoft Research (`http://research.microsoft.com/`) is perhaps my favorite place to visit for things Microsoft. This Web site is where you find all the ideas Microsoft is testing today, so this isn't even beta in most cases — you're seeing a glimmer of what Microsoft plans to do tomorrow. Of course, the first question is why you should even waste your time on software that isn't released yet. The answer is that Microsoft will never release many of these pieces of software in a packaged form, yet the software does interesting things that could help you create better applications.

As an example, at the time of this writing, you can find the C# Software Transactional Memory (STM) download at `http://research.microsoft.com/research/downloads/Details/6cfc842d-1c16-4739-afaf-edb35f544384/Details.aspx`. This software is extremely interesting because it provides a means to share data in multithreaded applications without the use of locks. The new technique borrows from database management — it relies on transactions where a change is either committed or aborted as needed. Because this technique relies on transactions, you won't experience coding problems such as deadlock. Consequently, this technology has the potential to significantly change how you write multithreaded applications — imagine the ease of writing a multithreaded application where you don't have to worry about deadlock.

You were probably expecting something a bit more exotic and less work related in this section. If that's the case, check out the article about WorldWide Telescope (WWT) at `http://research.microsoft.com/displayArticle.aspx?id=2002`. Using this technology, you can explore the universe — or at least the parts we know about today. This article is interesting because Microsoft is actually promoting someone else's idea. Who would have imagined that?

Microsoft also provides some amazing tools on the Microsoft Research Web site. For example, a more practical technology is one that permits you to add zoom to your Web site. You can begin with a high-resolution image, but only show a general view of it. The viewer can then zoom into an area of interest to see the details. The technology can work with any image — everything from detailed plans for your next device to the design of a new chip. Check out this product at `http://research.microsoft.com/IVM/HDView/`.

The Microsoft Research Web site is one location you have to explore, rather than search. Part of the problem is that you wouldn't know what to search for — the technology is new (or at least new to Microsoft). The only way to discover what's on this Web site is to spend some glorious hours looking through it without aid of a search engine. Microsoft provides two ways to look for technologies:

- **Name:** `http://research.microsoft.com/research/downloads/Browse.aspx?sortCriteria=shortName`
- **Date:** `http://research.microsoft.com/research/downloads/Browse.aspx?sortCriteria=shortDate`

Yes, you can probably use a search engine to locate specific technologies that you may have heard about on Microsoft Research, but you'll want to use a third-party search engine such as Google to do it. Check out the "Discovering Resources and Tools Online" section for details.

Discovering Resources and Tools Online

Trying to find something on a Microsoft Web site can be difficult, especially considering the fact that Microsoft constantly moves things around, seemingly to annoy the developers who use the site. Microsoft's own search engine usually produces dubious results. More than a few developers have complained about not finding resources or tools that they know exist on the Microsoft Web sites due to a failure of Microsoft's search engine. To make things worse, the MSDN materials typically appear at two domains: `msdn.microsoft.com` and `msdn2.microsoft.com`. Consequently, you must perform every MSDN search twice.

Fortunately, the Microsoft domains are well known. As a result, you can perform what is known as a site search with Google and locate information faster. Simply begin with your keywords at the main Google search site at `http://www.google.com/`, type the word `site`, followed by a colon, and then the domain you want to use:

- `msdn.microsoft.com`
- `msdn2.microsoft.com`

- technet.microsoft.com
- www.microsoft.com
- download.microsoft.com
- support.microsoft.com
- research.microsoft.com

Using the site search method is easy. For example, if you want to find everything Microsoft has to offer on its newer MSDN site for XML editors, you would type `XML edit site:msdn2.microsoft.com` in the Google Web page's search field. Likewise, if you want to find all the information available on a 2000 error for Internet Information Server (IIS), you'd type `Internet Information Server 2000 error site:support.microsoft.com` in the search field.

Site searches work well for a number of other Microsoft resources. For example, you may have spent hours looking for a download, only to find that Microsoft has moved it yet again. To find the download fast, type the filename, followed by `site:download.microsoft.com` in the Google Web page's search field. You'll be amazed at how fast you can find whatever you need.

Let's say that you do find an interesting link on Google, but Microsoft insists that the link no longer exists. Google usually provides a special link called Cached. You see it at the end of the link description. Simply click this link and you'll see the cached version that Google provides of the Microsoft Web page. Consequently, even when Microsoft says a resource is gone, it really isn't gone — Google usually has the copy you need.

If you're still stumped in finding that lost Microsoft Web page, you can rely on another resource. Go to the Internet Archive Wayback Machine site at `http://web.archive.org/collections/web/advanced.html`. Type the URL you want in the Find This URL field, choose the dates you want to see (optional), and click Go Wayback. The Web site shows you an archived copy of the Web page in question. In many cases, you can go back to Google with the title of the article or other MSDN resource you want and find the latest version of that Web page on MSDN.

Google sometimes provides less than stellar results. The hit you really want is there somewhere, but you can't find it without plenty of effort. The paid ads and other factors that affect Google's search engine get in the way. If you get too many hits, try enclosing your search terms in quotes. For example, if you want to find the support article entitled, "How to use structured exception handling in Visual C# .NET and in Visual C# 2005 or Visual C# 2008," you can type `"How to use structured exception handling" site:support.microsoft.com` in the Google Web page's search field. A test of this search term during the writing of this chapter returned only two results — making it very easy to find the desired result.

Editing XML Files Using XML Notepad 2007

Microsoft makes extensive use of XML in many of its products, and most developers today make extensive use of XML as well. In fact, it probably wouldn't be too inaccurate to say that the use of XML will increase to the point where knowledge of XML will become required for all developers and probably most administrators as well. It's no longer possible to manage some Microsoft applications, such as Exchange Server, without some knowledge of XML, and you'll find that XML is also good to know even when dealing with Visual Studio.

In many cases, XML files don't even have an XML extension any longer. Microsoft uses a wealth of file extensions for XML files today. Any configuration file (many have a CONFIG extension) is likely to use XML. Another example of hidden XML files is the CSPROJ files used with a C# project. In fact, you can find XML in many files on your hard drive, many of which won't have an XML extension. (As an experiment once, I opened a command prompt, typed `FindStr /M /I /S /C:"<?xml version="`, and pressed Enter — I was amazed at the number of file types that contain the traditional start of the XML processing instruction.)

You'll also find that many log files and even some lower-level operating system data files all rely on XML. With this change in mind, you really need a good XML utility to work at the command line, but many of the free products on the market come up lacking. The following sections describe XML Notepad 2007 — a free Microsoft utility that helps you manage XML files on your system.

Obtaining XML Notepad 2007

Microsoft has produced a number of versions of XML Notepad. Old versions of XML Notepad won't install on Vista or Windows Server 2008. You must download and install XML Notepad 2007 from the Web site provided in this section in order to obtain a working copy of XML Notepad. Even XML Notepad 2006 fails to install on newer versions of Windows. XML Notepad 2007 provides a decent level of XML support and you'll find that it works just fine for most, if not all, XML file administration needs. You can obtain this utility at `http://www.microsoft.com/downloads/details.aspx?familyid=72d6aa49-787d-4118-ba5f-4f30fe913628`.

For many developers, the need to work with XML extensively would give them good reason to purchase a product such as Altova's XML Spy (`http://www.altova.com/products/xmlspy/xml_editor.html`). XML Notepad 2007 doesn't have all the functionality of these high-end products, but it still provides sufficient functionality to meet most developer needs.

Using XML Notepad 2007 the First Time

After you install XML Notepad, the setup program automatically opens an HTML page containing information about XML Notepad. You'll typically find this file at `\Program Files\XML Notepad 2007\Readme.HTM` or `\Program Files (x86)\XML Notepad 2007\Readme.HTM`. One of the links opens a sample XML folder. In this folder, you'll find the `Basket.XML` file that appears in Figure 29-1. Right-click the file in Windows Explorer and choose Edit with XML Notepad to open the file. Figure 29-1 shows all the elements expanded so you can see how XML Notepad displays the information for you.

The XML Notepad display color codes entries by type and includes special icons to identify various types. For example, value entries appear with a special icon to differentiate them from elements. Notice that the first entry is the XML processing instruction, which normally appears in purple. You can use the same techniques that you normally use with Windows Explorer to access entries. Selecting an entry in the left pane highlights its content in the right pane.

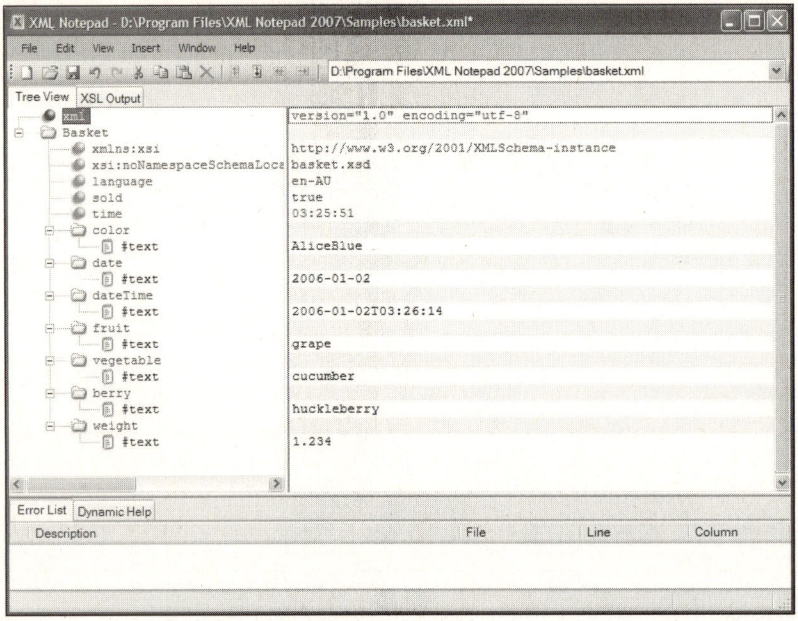

Figure 29-1: XML Notepad provides a safe editing environment for your XML files.

Making File Modifications

You add a new entry by selecting it from the Insert menu. As an alternative, you can add new entries by right-clicking an existing entry and choosing the entry type from the context menu. In both cases, the new entry appears as a child of the currently selected entry in the left pane.

You type a value for the new entry in the right pane. When you make a mistake in creating an entry, such as not adhering to a restriction in an XML Schema Definition (XSD) file, XML Notepad provides an entry in the bottom pane. Double-clicking the error entry takes you to that position in the file.

Using XSLT Files

If your file has an eXtensible Stylesheet Language Transformation (XSLT) processing instruction, you can view the output by clicking the XSL Output tab. The `RSS.XML` file provides a sample of this XML Notepad feature as shown in Figure 29-2. You can change XSL files by clicking the ellipsis button (…) and choosing another XSL file in the Open dialog box. Click Transform to display the transformed XML file.

Comparing XML Files

One of the more interesting features of XML Notepad is the ability to compare two XML files. You begin by loading the primary XML file into XML Notepad. Here are the steps you use to perform this task:

1. Load the source XML file — the one you want to compare against the target file.
2. Choose View ➪ Compare XML Files to display an Open dialog box.

3. Select the target XML file and click Open. You'll see an XmlDiff window open that has a complete comparison of the two files. This feature is helpful when you need to compare configuration settings or server events found in logs.

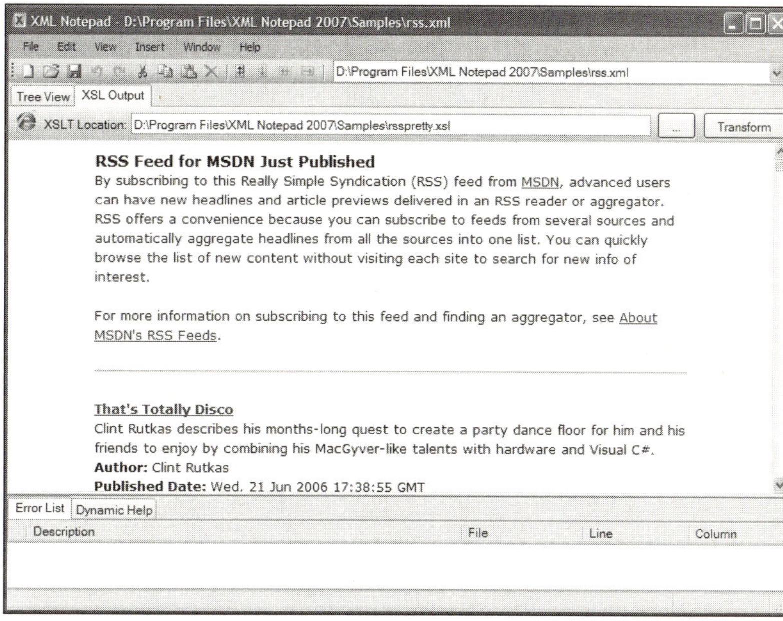

Figure 29-2: Use XSLT files to make XML files easier to read.

Enhancing Visual Studio 2008 Using Microsoft PowerCommands

Many developers wish they had better control over the Visual Studio IDE. For example, many developers would like to clear all the Output pane data with a single command, rather than using one command per Output pane. The Microsoft PowerCommands add-in helps you perform a number of tasks, such as clearing the Output panes, faster.

A number of the products you find on the Microsoft Web site have issues, just like any other tool or resource you might download. Make sure you select the Discussions tab from the main page and read all the comments from other developers. In addition, select the Issue Tracker tab from the main page so you can see which issues Microsoft is currently addressing. Microsoft is constantly fixing problems with these products, so the version of Microsoft PowerCommands that you use will likely contain fewer issues than the version presented in this chapter.

Discovering more about Microsoft PowerCommands is easy. The main Web site for Microsoft PowerCommands is `http://code.msdn.microsoft.com/PowerCommands`, where you can learn about new features and updated versions. You download the product at `http://code.msdn.microsoft.com/PowerCommands/Release/ProjectReleases.aspx`. After you download the product, double-click the `PowerCommandsSetup.MSI` to start the installation process.

The Microsoft PowerCommands appear as part of the Options dialog box. Choose Tools ➪ Options to display this dialog box and then select the PowerCommands folder. You'll see the options shown in Figure 29-3 when working with the General Subfolder. Here is how you use those options (Microsoft PowerCommands disables both options at the outset):

- **Format Document On Save**: This feature formats the files in your project every time you save the document so that the formatting is always correct. It's the same as choosing Edit ➪ Advanced ➪ Format Document, except that you don't have to perform the task manually.
- **Remove and Sort Usings On Save**: This feature removes unused `Using` statements during save. After removing the unused statements, it sorts the remaining statements so that you can see them with greater east. You can only use this feature when working with C# code.

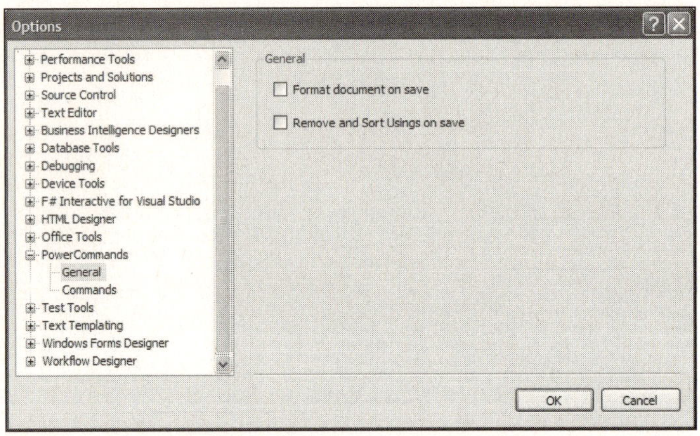

Figure 29-3: The General folder contains options that affect how you save a document.

Automatic document modifications during a save are only part of the picture. The Commands tab contains a list of commands that Microsoft PowerCommands supports. You can use the checkboxes in the Commands folder shown in Figure 29-4 to enable or disable the commands.

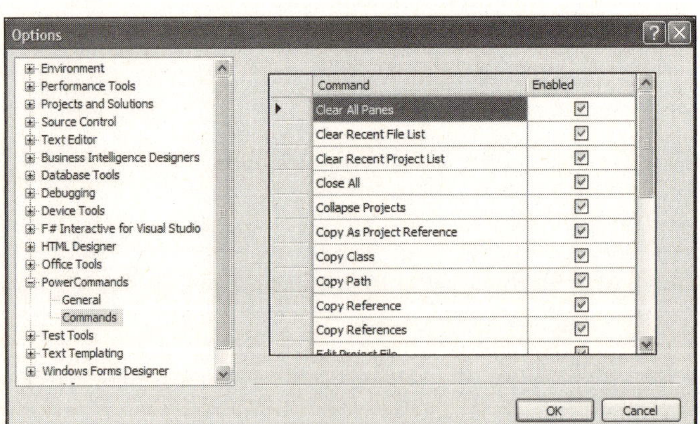

Figure 29-4: Enable or disable commands as necessary to keep Microsoft PowerCommands useful.

Here are the commands that the current version of Microsoft PowerCommands supports.

- **Clear All Panes**: Clears all the Output panes. You execute this command by clicking the Clear All button on the Output window.
- **Clear Recent File List:** Clears all or part of the Visual Studio recent file list. You execute this command by choosing File ➪ Recent Files ➪ Clear Recent File List. Microsoft PowerCommands displays a Clear List dialog box where you can choose individual files to clear from the list. Check Select All to select all the files in the list. Click Clear and Restart to clear the files from the list.
- **Clear Recent Project List:** Clears all or part of the Visual Studio recent project list. You execute this command by choosing File ➪ Recent Projects ➪ Clear Recent Project List. Microsoft PowerCommands displays a Clear List dialog box where you can choose individual projects to clear from the list. Check Select All to select all the projects in the list. Click Clear and Restart to clear the projects from the list.
- **Close All:** Closes all open documents. You execute this command by right-clicking any document tab and choosing Close All from the context menu.
- **Collapse Projects:** Collapses a project or projects in Solution Explorer starting with the root node that you select. This feature can reduce clutter within Solution Explorer, making it easier to locate the particular project with which you want to interact. You execute this command by right-clicking the node and choosing Collapse Project from the context menu. This command is available at the following nodes:
    - Solution
    - Solution folder
    - Project
- **Copy As Project Reference:** Copies a project as a project reference so that you can use it within another project. You execute this command by right-clicking the project node in Solution Explorer and choosing Copy As Project Reference from the context menu.
- **Copy Class:** Copies the entire selected class (all its code) to the clipboard. The command automatically renames the class for you when you click Paste Class to paste the class copy into the code editor. Renaming the class avoids potential class conflicts. This command works within a single project item or project with dependent subitems. You execute this command by right-clicking the file containing the class you wish to copy in Solution Explorer and choosing Copy Class from the context menu. When a file contains more than one class, this command becomes unavailable.
- **Copy Path**: Copies the full path of the currently selected item in Solution Explorer to the clipboard. You execute this command by right-clicking an item in Solution Explorer and choosing Copy Path from the context menu. This feature works with the solution, project, project item, and folder nodes.
- **Copy References:** Copies references used in one project to another project. This command lets you copy a single reference, a set of selected references, or the entire References node of a project. You execute this command by right-clicking in Solution Explorer the reference or references you want to copy and choosing Copy Reference from the context menu.
- **Edit Project File:** Opens the MSBuild project file (`CSPROJ` extension) for the selected project inside Visual Studio. Modifying this file controls how Visual Studio builds the project (an advanced developer task that you normally won't want to perform). This command combines the `Unload Project` and `Edit Project` commands. You execute this command by right-clicking the project entry in Solution Explorer and choosing Edit Project File from the context menu.

This command can fail when working with a C# project. You'll normally see a dialog box telling you that the `Unload Project` command is unavailable. Unfortunately, Microsoft doesn't appear to have a fix for this problem at the time of writing. The `Edit Project File` command only works with solutions that have multiple projects.

- **Email CodeSnippet:** Lets you e-mail a code snippet to anyone with ease. You execute this command by highlighting the code you want to e-mail, right-clicking the highlighted area, and choosing Email Code Snippet from the context menu.
- **Extract Constant:** Creates a constant definition for the text you choose (such as a numeric value). Using a constant can make your code easier to read. You execute this command using the following steps:
    1. Highlight the text you want to make into a constant.
    2. Right-click the highlighted text and choose Refactor ⇨ Extract Constant from the context menu. You'll see an Extract Constant dialog box.
    3. Choose the visibility of the constant in the Visibility field.
    4. Type the name of the constant in the Identifier field.
    5. Click OK to complete the process.
- **Insert Guid Attribute:** Adds the `[Guid]` attribute to your code. You execute this command by right-clicking anywhere within a class and choosing Insert Guid Attribute from the context menu. The GUID automatically supplied by this command is always unique.

A Globally Unique IDentifier (GUID) provides a unique way to identify parts of your application to an external client, such as a Component Object Model (COM) application. In order to add a GUID to managed code, you must supply the `[Guid]` attribute.

- **Open Command Prompt:** Opens a Visual Studio command prompt at the physical path of the selected item. The command prompt has all the standard environment variables required to interact successfully with Visual Studio commands. This command works with the solution, project, folder, and project item nodes. You execute this command by right-clicking the item of interest and choosing Open Command Prompt from the context menu.
- **Open Containing Folder:** Opens a copy of Windows Explorer with the physical path of the selected item opened. This command lets you see where an item in Solution Explorer is physically located on the hard drive and interact with it. You execute this command by right-clicking the item of interest and choosing Open Containing Folder from the context menu.
- **Paste Class:** Pastes a class that appears on the clipboard into the position selected in the Solution Explorer hierarchy. It's possible to paste classes into either a project or folder node. The new class has a different name to avoid naming problems. You execute this command by right-clicking a project or folder node in Solution Explorer and choosing Paste Class from the context menu.
- **Paste References:** Pastes one or more references from the clipboard to a project. Use the Copy References command to copy the references from the project to the clipboard. You execute this command (in C#) by right-clicking the References node in Solution Explorer and choosing Paste References from the context menu.
- **Reload Projects:** Reloads projects that you have unloaded from a solution. You execute this command by right-clicking the solution entry in Solution Explorer and choosing Reload Projects from the context menu. The solution entry is only available when a solution has multiple projects in it.

- **Remove and Sort Usings:** Removes all the `using` statements that a project file doesn't need and then sorts the remaining `using` statements. This command helps you remove unneeded `using` statements, making the code easier to understand. You execute this command by right-clicking a project entry and choosing Remove and Sort Usings from the context menu.
- **Show All Files:** Shows the hidden files in all the products displayed in Solution Explorer. Normally, when you click the Show All Files button, it only affects the selected project node. You execute this command by clicking the second Show All Files button in the Solution Explorer toolbar. (It would have been handy if the developer had used a different icon at least and had made the prompt read something like, "Show All Files in All Projects.")
- **Transform Templates:** Executes a custom tool associated with text templates. This command is available from either a Domain Specific Language (DSL) project node or a DSL folder node. You execute this command by right-clicking the item of interest in Solution Explorer and choosing Transform Templates from the context menu.
- **Undo Close:** Reopens the most recently closed file and returns the cursor to its previous position in that file. In short, it's as if you never closed the file. You execute this command by choosing Edit ➪ Undo Close or pressing Ctrl+Shift+Z.
- **Unload Projects:** Unloads all the projects in a solution. This command is helpful when you need to modify the MSBuild project file. You execute this command by right-clicking the solution entry in Solution Explorer and choosing Unload Projects from the context menu. The solution entry is only available when a solution has multiple projects in it.

Some of the commands have extended functionality, so you'll want to read about it in the `PowerCommands Readme.DOCX` file that you can download separately. For example, the `Undo Close` command lets you reopen any previously closed file out of order. Simply choose View ➪ Other Windows ➪ Undo Close Window to display the Undo Close window displayed in Figure 29-5. Double-click the window you want to reopen and you'll see it opened again.

Figure 29-5: Many commands have extended functionality.

Obtaining Resources and Tools

This chapter has provided you some insights into getting free (or essentially free) resources and tools from Microsoft. Of course, the world doesn't consist of Microsoft alone. However, getting resources and tools from Microsoft does have the advantage that you know the resources and tools should at least work in most cases, and that the vendor isn't going to abandon them immediately. Whether a resource or tool is useful depends on your particular tastes and needs. Don't forget the lessons in Chapter 28 — a cluttered toolbox isn't necessarily a happy toolbox.

It's time to look at what Microsoft has to offer for you. Use the material at the beginning of this chapter to decide how to search for what you need. Have some fun. Download a few of the resources and tools you find and try them. Sometimes developers get into a rut, and trying out new software gives you a different perspective. Because the Microsoft resources and tools are less likely to cause problems than third-party products, you should also find it easier to get them approved for use (or at least trial) in your organization than third-party products of uncertain origin.

Don't ever get involved with Microsoft's trial products except for experimentation. Some developers will try out a trial product, start developing something with it, and then find the trial period is over way too soon. Microsoft provides generous trial periods in most cases, but that only ensures you're completely hooked before the trial period is over. Unless you plan to invest in the product, never rely on a trial product for production use.

Chapter 30 looks at third-party products you may want to consider using with your C# setup. As with the Microsoft tools suggested in this chapter, you may find that while these tools are nice, they simply aren't useful for your current project. It truly is important to choose resources and tools that are useful, but look at these tools as potential ideas for your own toolbox. Chapter 30 also provides third-party guidelines you can use for getting better resources and tools.

30

Third-Party Resources and Tools

Microsoft products have spawned a huge third-party following. These third-party vendors make everything from user-level add-ons to administration utilities to developer resources and tools. In fact, the third-party vendors may create more software than Microsoft does when put together. It's unlikely that you'll see everything third-party vendors have to offer. Some of it will fade into obscurity before you even hear about it. Much of this software is high quality. Unfortunately, quality doesn't always guarantee that a significant number of developers will hear about the product — the vendor who yells the loudest often gets the attention of developers.

Although this chapter discusses developer tools, developers often need user- and administrator-level resources and tools as well. Developers actually have the opportunity to have more fun with computers than anyone else does. Not only do developers use more categories of software than anyone else, but they also have the knowledge and skills to use more software. It's important to have a bit of fun now and then, so check out the user- and administrator-level products, too.

This chapter begins with some tips and techniques you can use to locate useful third-party resources and tools. You'll then see reviews of a number of interesting third-party products. As with the Microsoft products in Chapter 29, there isn't any way to discuss all the products out there in a single chapter. In fact, it may very well be impossible for a single author to do justice to the topic. However, these products all stand out in some way, and you might want to try them out in your next project.

Finding Third-Party Resources and Tools

Third-party resources and tools come in all shapes and sizes. You can find a third-party product to meet nearly any need, and more products become available every day. Of course, this wealth of potential resources and tools causes a problem. The average developer could go quite crazy trying to figure out which product will serve a need best because there are so many to try. Reading reviews may not always help because the review author may not know which questions to answer for you (unless the author is very good at reading minds). Consequently, you need some method of finding the resource or tool that fulfills your requirements (understanding that several products may actually do the job and that you need to find just one).

Third-party resources and tools have a lot to offer. It would be a terrible idea for any developer to dismiss third-party products in favor of a pure Microsoft solution. In fact, here are some of the things that third-party vendors have to offer that you should consider when deciding on a third-party solution.

- **Greater flexibility:** Even if you have access to only one third-party product, you have doubled the number of options at your disposal (the Microsoft solution and the third-party solution). Every product you find increases your flexibility and will help you develop the best possible application.
- **Alternative perspective:** Third-party vendors want to differentiate their products in some way. In fact, the bullet points you see on the third-party vendor's Web site often illustrate these differences and give you a point of comparison. The alternative perspective offered by a third-party vendor may actually help you create a better application by helping you to see the problem from another angle.
- **Lower cost:** Microsoft does give away a lot of software. However, most of its products come with a price tag, and you can often find a third-party equivalent with little or no price tag. Of course, it's impossible to provide a direct comparison between the Microsoft product and the third-party product because they'll most definitely provide different functionality. Consequently, you must always weigh cost against the requirements of your project.
- **Improved reliability:** Some third-party products offer better reliability than their Microsoft counterparts do. A smaller company is often more agile than Microsoft is and can fix problems noted by developers faster than Microsoft can. The faster pace of fixes can spell better reliability for your applications because the application will suffer from fewer potential flaws introduced by external software.
- **Customized solutions:** A few third-party vendors will customize their product to meet your needs. The cost of this service can be quite high. However, when you can't find precisely what you need, using a customized third-party product often lets you obtain what you need at a lower cost than relying on a consultant.
- **Community support:** Microsoft does provide strong community support, but often that support provides a parroted version of Microsoft's dogma. Third-party vendors often provide more robust community support, and the support often views issues from more than one angle. As a result, the solution you obtain from community support is better balanced and more considered.
- **Availability of code:** Open source vendors, especially, offer you a peek at their code. In many cases, you can simply download the source code for a product and modify it to meet your needs (be sure to consider licensing requirements).

None of the vendors I have ever seen offers all these benefits. You usually get one or two of the benefits in this list from a particular vendor. The point is that you need to shop around for the third-party vendor who offers the best package and the greatest number of benefits that help you complete your project.

The other side of the coin is that third-party vendors often lack some of the benefits of working with Microsoft, in part because they don't have access to Microsoft's resources. Therefore, when you begin looking at third-party solutions, you must also consider these potential negatives.

- **Lost productivity:** Some third-party vendors promise everything and deliver nothing (or nearly nothing). Unfortunately, you won't usually find out about the less-than-stellar product until you have spent some of your own precious time. The bottom line is that third-party software often represents a certain level of risk. You must be willing to risk your time and resources to determine whether the product works as expected.
- **Widowed software:** Even the best third-party vendors end up out of business, bought by another company, or simply without the means to continue supporting specific software. In all cases, the result is that you end up with widowed software — a resource or tool that has no support whatsoever. So far, Microsoft has proven remarkably resilient, and most people would agree that they aren't going out of business anytime soon. In addition, even when they stop supporting their software, someone else usually will. Consequently, you usually don't have to worry about widowed software when working with Microsoft.
- **Uneven support (or no support at all):** Third-party vendor support is uneven — a vendor will usually do a good job in one area and not cover another. You might find, for example, that the help files are excellent, but that the vendor doesn't include useful examples. No matter how good the community support, most developers need some level of vendor support to successfully use a particular resource or tool. In the worst-case scenario, a third-party vendor will actually offer their software as is — without any support.
- **Hidden costs:** Sometimes a third-party resource or tool will rely on another resource or tool that isn't included as part of the software download. Consequently, when you attempt to install the resource or tool, you'll find that it requires you to install something else, and sometimes it doesn't even tell you where to find the required resource or tool. At a minimum, you'll spend additional time and effort locating the required resource or tool. In the worst-case scenario, the required resource or tool incurs additional fees that you must pay in addition to the cost of the resource or tool that you want for your application. Hidden costs can become a deal killer for third-party software.
- **Compatibility issues:** No one knows their software better than Microsoft. In fact, Microsoft has been accused of using hidden libraries and other tricks in the past. Third-party vendors usually can't overcome documentation problems with Microsoft's libraries either. Because of these and other issues, third-party software often suffers a penalty in the form of compatibility issues. The software simply doesn't interface correctly with Windows or some other piece of Microsoft software.

Locating a third-party resource or tool can be difficult. The problem isn't one of locating just any third-party resource or tool — a simple Google search will often satisfy this requirement. However, given the potential positives and negatives of working with a third-party vendor, you must go further than a simple search online. It's important to know that the third-party product will actually work as expected before you spend a lot of time testing it against your personal requirements. In addition, you need to consider the support and cost issues of working with a third-party vendor. Here are some of the techniques you can employ to find a good third-party product.

- **Word of mouth:** Your friends and acquaintances will talk to you about the products they use to solve problems. In most cases, this is the most trustworthy advice you can get. In addition, because the other person knows you and the way you work, the advice is usually more targeted than the information provided by other sources. However, the weakness of this source is that it's often uninformed. A professional reviewer may see a host of products, but your friend or acquaintance may see only one or two at most. Consequently, the friend or acquaintance can't provide the depth of knowledge found in other sources.

- **Online reviews:** Depending on the source of the review, the information may not be any better than provided by word of mouth. In addition, online reviews are often biased because people who are unhappy with the product are more likely to say something than those who are happy with it. However, online reviews, when taken with a huge grain of salt, can provide you with insights into the product that you might not get elsewhere because these people have likely used the product for a project. In addition, online reviews often provide a greater variety of opinions than other sources.
- **Group discussions:** Getting information through a list server, forum, or other group venue can prove useful because it's interactive and you can ask questions over time. The other participants have time to think about a good answer and can often correct erroneous information provided by other participants. However, the value of this information is only as good as the participant's level of knowledge, and you can't easily measure that knowledge. In addition, people both pro and con often plant information in these discussions that could lead you to the wrong conclusions.
- **Seminar and other endorsements:** Seminars and other professional venues often provide you with a knowledgeable perspective on a product. In addition, because seminars and other public venues are interactive, you can ask questions. However, the time allocated for these venues is extremely limited, and sometimes you get mistaken information from the rushed presenter. In addition, the presenter provides a single perspective, which means that the information may not reflect your needs at all.
- **Articles:** Articles and reviews written by a professional author provide you with a knowledgeable perspective on the product. Because the author has likely reviewed a number of products in the category, you obtain information that is based on a comparison of these other products. A professional author will likely research multiple opinions as part of writing the review. However, you're still seeing one person's view of the product — a view that may not match your own. In addition, articles offer static information — you can't easily ask questions. Consequently, you may make assumptions about the product that aren't true based on your perception of the article content.
- **Microsoft recommendations:** Microsoft realizes that it can't address every need and provides support to third-party vendors to meet these other needs. When a product proves exceptional (or the vendor belongs to the right program), Microsoft makes a recommendation of that product. In most cases, no one from Microsoft actually says anything about the product — you simply see it on a Microsoft Web site. Unfortunately, simply placing a product on a Web page doesn't tell you much, and you won't know whether the product will meet your needs until you test it yourself.

Nothing replaces your personal test of the third-party product. Unfortunately, the review that you read online tells you how that person views the third-party product — you may end up with an entirely different opinion (positive or negative) after testing. Even if a product won't meet today's need, your personal testing may prove that the product will meet a need in the future. Personal testing requires an investment from you. Here are some things to consider before you begin the testing process.

- Never test when you're tired.
- Avoid performing tests when you're pressed for time.

- Consider how you'll use the product, rather than becoming absorbed by the product's eye candy.
- Use checklists to help test products evenly.
- Ask others to test the product as well so that you obtain a trusted second or even third opinion.
- Always test vendor claims to determine whether they're true.
- Make your decision based on facts you gather, rather than emotions you feel.

Using Vischeck to Test Application Colors

One of the least asked questions when designing an application is whether other people can see it. The assumption is that everyone has the same vision as the developer, but this is a shortsighted perspective (pun intended). Some people will require a high contrast display, while others will require that you avoid certain color combinations.

You can easily check for the first issue by opening the Display applet (right-click the Desktop and choose Properties from the context menu). The Appearance tab contains the settings you need to change. Set the Windows and Buttons field to Windows Classic Style, the Color Scheme to any of the four High Contrast settings, and the Font Size to Extra Large as shown in Figure 30-1. If your application still has a usable presentation, try the other three color schemes one at a time.

Figure 30-1: Checking your application against a high-contrast display is essential.

Verifying that your application will work for someone with colorblindness is significantly harder. The problem is that there are six kinds of colorblindness, and Windows doesn't provide a means to simulate any of them. Consequently, most applications aren't checked for color problems, and a good many colorblind people have an insanely hard time working with applications that just happen to have the wrong color combinations. Fortunately, you can use the Vischeck site at `http://www.vischeck.com/` to determine how an image looks to people with colorblindness.

The Vischeck Web site isn't the only tool available for checking colorblindness, but Vischeck is free and it does a remarkable job of simulating the three major forms of colorblindness. Use the following steps to use this product to check either an application image (simply grab a screenshot of your application and upload it) or a Web site (supply a URL to the Web site):

1. Click the Vischeck link on the main Web page at `http://www.vischeck.com/`. You'll see an explanation of what Vischeck is all about and how it works. It's helpful to read the explanation.
2. Click Run Images if you plan to check screenshots of your application or Run Webpages if you plan to check your Web site. You'll see the Web page shown in Figure 30-2 when you select the Run Images option. When you use Vischeck on a Web site, you see essentially the same image as shown in Figure 30-2. However, instead of obtaining an image from your hard drive, you provide a URL. Go to Step 6 if you plan to check a Web site.

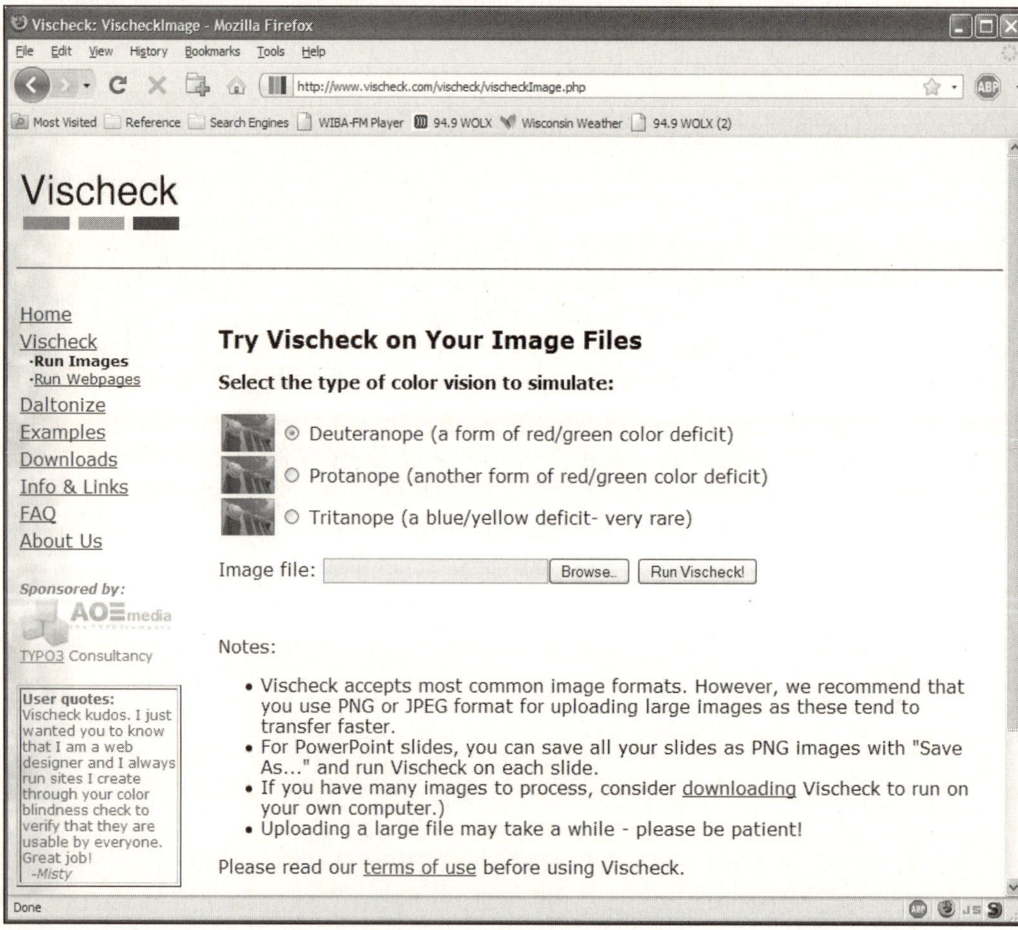

Figure 30-2: Provide an image to determine how it looks to someone with colorblindness.

3. Click Browse to locate a Portable Network Graphics (PNG) or Joint Photographic Experts Group (JPEG/JPG) file on your local hard drive. (I also tested Vischeck with a BMP file, and it worked

fine, but other file formats aren't officially supported.) You can't paste an image from the clipboard to the program online. It also appears that you can't specify a Web URL — the image must appear on your local hard drive.

4. Select a colorblindness option. You'll eventually want to run all three of the available tests on your image to ensure it looks acceptable with all forms of colorblindness.
5. Click Run Vischeck! Figure 30-3 shows typical output from this application when using the Deuteranope (a form of red/green color deficit) option. The left side of the screen shows the standard display, while the right side of the screen shows the modified display. Even in the black and white images of the book, you'll see there is a significant difference in this color blocks test. Some colors are significantly different — so different that you really can't imagine what it would look like. At this point, the check is completed.

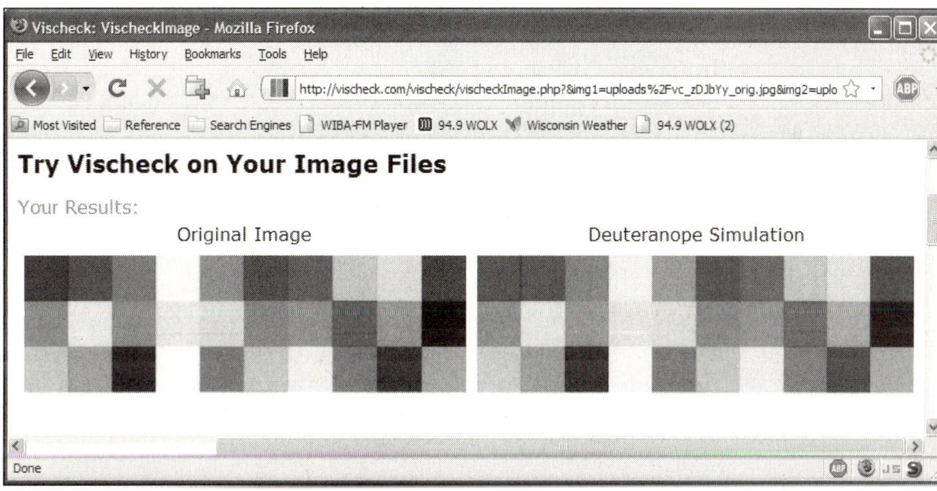

Figure 30-3: The output shows the difference between what you normally see and what a person with deuteranopia sees.

6. Type the URL of the Web page you want to check in the URL field. The example uses `http://www.vischeck.com/` as the URL.
7. Click Run Vischeck! It will appear at first that the check didn't work. However, you'll see two links at the top of the page.
8. Click the link associated with the simulation. For example, if you're running a deuteranope simulation, click the Deuteranope Simulation link. Figure 30-4 shows a deuteranope simulation view of the main Vischeck Web page as of this writing.

The Vischeck Web site actually hosts several useful applications. One of these applications demonstrates the process of Daltonization, correcting color for someone with colorblindness. Of course, you can't actually make people see the full spectrum of color if their eyes are unable to detect certain colors, but you can improve their ability to see an image despite the colorblindness. You can read about this process at `http://www.vischeck.com/daltonize/`. *Of course, it helps to see Daltonize at work, so you'll want to try out the online version at* `http://www.vischeck.com/daltonize/runDaltonize.php`.

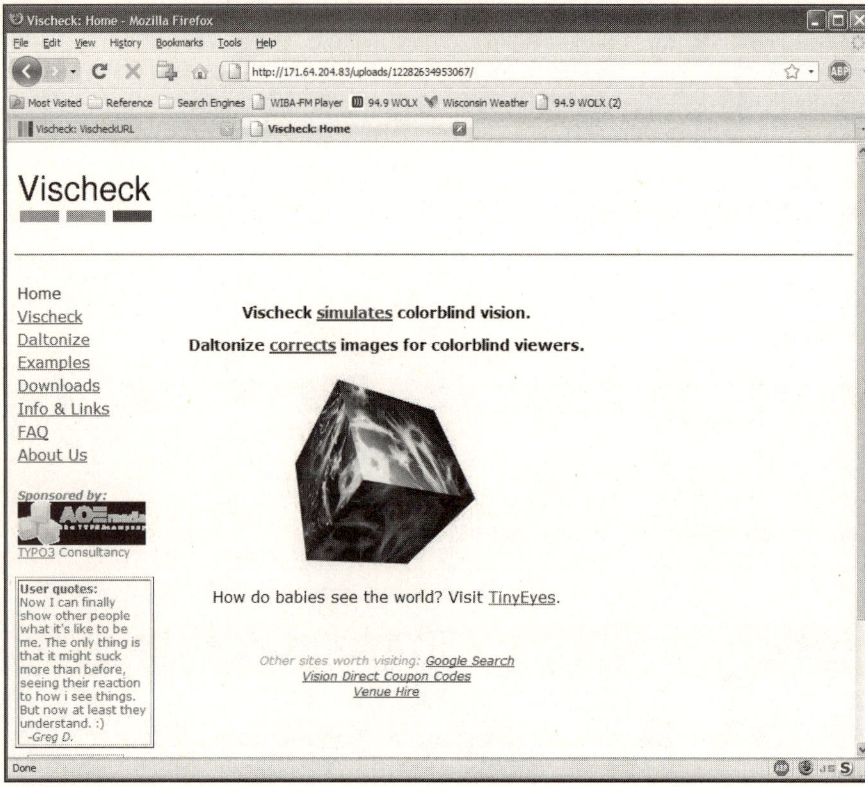

Figure 30-4: Vischeck can show Web sites as easily as images.

As you can see, this Web site is exceptionally useful if you only have a few images to check. Fortunately, you can download a version of Vischeck for Photoshop, PaintShop Pro, and other software at `http://www.vischeck.com/downloads/`. Using this local version will save you considerable time and effort.

Vischeck is a good place to start, but it isn't a complete solution. Using Vischeck on more than a few sites or to check more than the three common forms of colorblindness might prove difficult. The Web abounds with other colorblindness checkers, including IBM's aDesigner, which IBM has donated to the Eclipse Accessibility Tools Framework (ACTF) project (see the download page at `http://www.eclipse.org/actf/downloads/tools/aDesigner/index.php`). Many of these tools require that you install operating environments such as Java. I've been unable to find an equivalent to the IBM offering for the .NET environment — if you know of such a product contact me at JMueller@mwt.net.

Using FxCop to Improve Code Reliability and Consistency

This entire book has focused attention on the need to write applications that work reliably and securely, but still deliver an appropriate level of speed. You have many tools at your disposal for improving all three parts of the performance triangle in your application — many of these have appeared in this book. Of course, it's always nice to include some automation to make the attainment of your goal easier. FxCop is a utility that looks at your code and reports on any problems it finds. This check is in addition to the other checks that Visual Studio can perform for you (see the "Checking Your Code" section of Chapter 20 for details). The following sections tell you more about FxCop and how it can help you create better applications with less effort.

Obtaining a Copy of FxCop

The developers at Microsoft created FxCop to help developers meet best-practices requirements for application building. You can obtain the latest version of the product at `http://code.msdn.microsoft.com/codeanalysis/Release/ProjectReleases.aspx?ReleaseId=553`. The download link appears near the bottom of the Web page as `FxCopInstall.EXE`. When you click the link, you'll need to agree to the FxCop licensing terms before the download begins. The package includes both command line and GUI versions of FxCop that you can use in a variety of ways.

This chapter uses the 1.35 version of FxCop, which is the currently released version of the product. Microsoft is working on the 1.36 version of FxCop as of this writing and it probably includes features I don't discuss. If you prefer to use the beta of this version, you can download it at `http://www.microsoft.com/downloads/details.aspx?familyid=3389F7E4-0E55-4A4D-BC74-4AEABB17997B`.

After you download `FxCopInstall.EXE`, double-click the file to begin installation. The following steps describe the installation process.

1. Click Next to get past the Welcome screen.
2. Read and accept the licensing agreement by checking "I Accept the Terms in the License Agreement." Click Next. You'll see the Choose Setup Type dialog box shown in Figure 30-5. The FxCop installation doesn't require much disk space (7,185 KB), so the best idea is to perform a complete install to ensure you have everything you need. The rest of the sections in this chapter assume you have performed a complete install.
3. Click Complete. You'll see a Ready to Install dialog box.

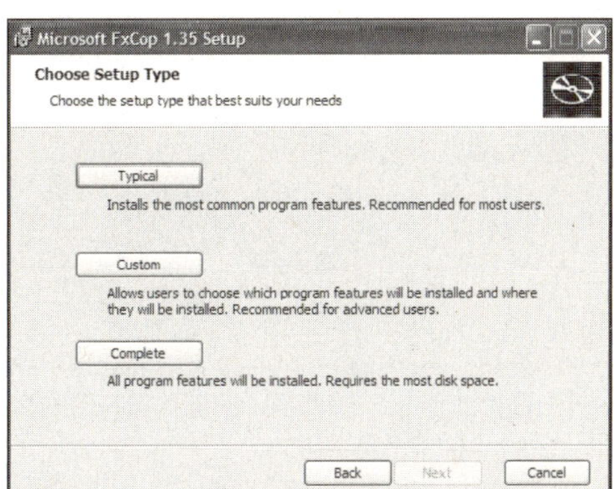

Figure 30-5: Perform a complete install to ensure you have everything you need.

4. Click Install. The installation program performs the required installation tasks.
5. Click Finish. The installation is complete.

Using the FxCop GUI

The easiest way to use FxCop is to create your application and then use the GUI to analyze the result. The following steps show you how to get started:

1. Choose Start ➪ Programs ➪ Microsoft FxCop 1.35 ➪ FxCop 1.35 to start the application.
2. Click the New Project button, and you'll see a new project.
3. Click Add Target for Analysis and select your application. You can choose any .NET executable (EXE or DLL). FxCop will load the application, and you can drill down to see its various components. Notice that FxCop works with the executable, not with the code, making it different from code analysis.
4. Click Analyze and see the result. Figure 30-6 shows the result of testing the ApplicationExit application from Chapter 12.

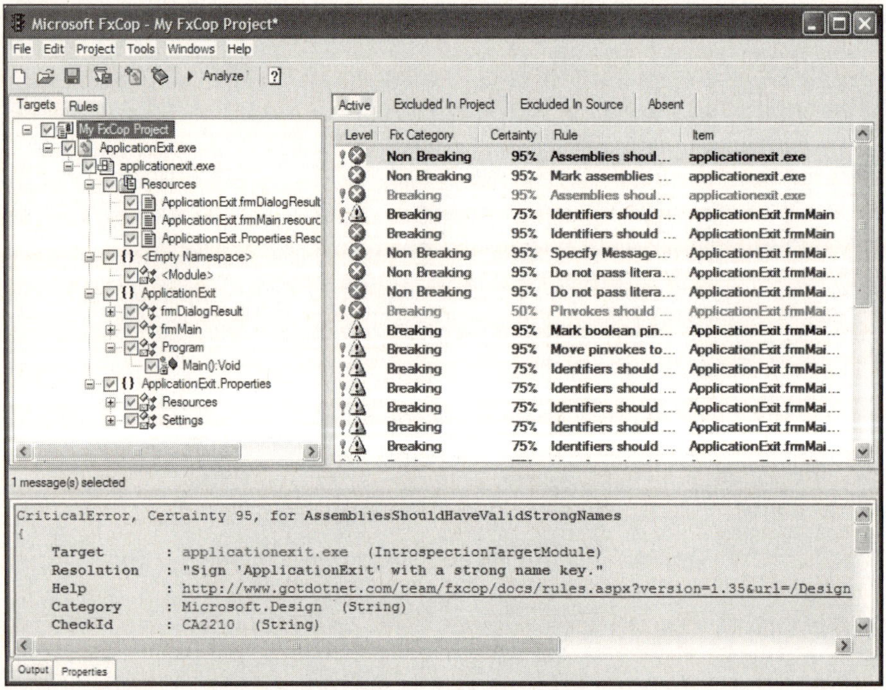

Figure 30-6: Most applications will break at least a few of the rules.

The left side of the display shows a breakdown of the application. Click a particular level and you'll see the problems with that portion of the application. In this case, Figure 30-6 has the application level selected, so you're seeing all the problems that FxCop found. When you select a particular problem in the right pane, you see additional information about it in the Output pane at the bottom of the display.

The Output pane isn't a very friendly way to view issues with your application. To read more about a particular problem, double-click it, and FxCop will display a dialog box like the one shown in Figure 30-7. It's probably a good idea to skip the Issues tab because it doesn't tell you much more than the Output pane does. The following list describes the other tabs.

- **Rule Details:** Shows the kind of information that FxCop provides. You're not expected to know how to fix the problem — FxCop provides guidance that really makes the process easy.
- **Message:** Provides a hierarchy showing the source of the problem. You can see precisely where an error occurs within your application, removing a lot of the guesswork from the repair process.
- **Rule Support:** Contains a link that takes you to a Web page where you can find out more about the basis for a particular rule. Reading the information on the Web page can help you understand the error better and make fixes significantly faster. Unfortunately, at the time of this writing, the links are for the old GotDotNet Web site, so they're broken. Someone will likely fix this issue in the next release (at least, I hope they do).
- **Notes:** Lets you create notes about a particular error. These notes are stored with the FxCop project for later reference. You can add, remove, and edit notes as needed.

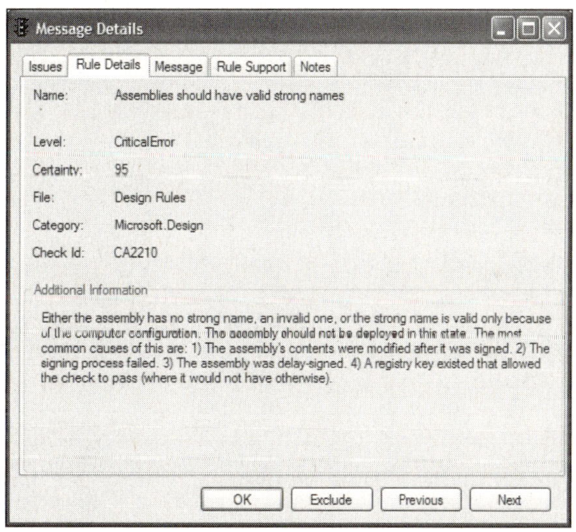

Figure 30-7: FxCop doesn't leave you wondering how to fix errors.

Notice that you can click Previous and Next to move from error to error in the list. If you decide that you don't want to handle a particular error, simply click Exclude to remove it. Whenever you exclude a rule, FxCop will ask you to provide a note explaining why you excluded it. Click OK when you want to close the dialog box.

Repairing the Errors

Let's look at a few of the issues the FxCop found. Beginning at the first error, FxCop notes that no one has signed the assembly — giving it a strong name. An assembly with a strong name is harder to tamper with and therefore harder to corrupt. The strong name doesn't protect the assembly from prying eyes — you need a product such as Dotfuscator to modify the code in such a way that others can't really understand what you're doing. You can sign the application using the features on the Signing tab application's Properties window.

The next error concerns Common Language Specification (CLS) compliance. The application doesn't indicate whether it's compliant. A CLS-compliant application only uses features that are available as part of CLS. For example, if your C# application uses a `UInt32` variable, it's not CLS compliant because the `UInt32` type is a language-specific feature. The purpose in marking an application CLS compliant is to indicate it can run in any environment that completely emulates CLS. Using a `UInt32` data type would mean that you could only run the application on a Windows system that allows access to unsigned integers. Because ApplicationExit relies on P/Invoke for one of its calls, you must mark it as non-CLS compliant as shown here.

```
// Define the assembly as non-CLS compliant.
[assembly:CLSCompliant(false)]
namespace ApplicationExit
{
   ... Other Code ...
}
```

Marking an assembly might not seem like a very big deal, but consider the changes that are happening with computing as a whole. The application you build today on a 32-bit machine might have to execute on a 64-bit machine tomorrow. Considering CLS issues today means you'll have less work to do to update the application tomorrow.

The example application uses `frmMain` for the name of the form. FxCop marked this as an error because the standard convention is to use Pascal case for class names. In addition, `frm` isn't a word, so FxCop suggests correcting the spelling of the word. Simply changing the name of the class to `FormMain` (initial capital letter and recognizable name) clears up this problem. More importantly, this change makes the class name easier to read and understand. However, the code executes much as it did before — nothing has really changed. Because this application has multiple forms, you must make the same change for all of the forms.

One error that you won't see fixed in this section is the use of string literals. If you're using an application with a single language and have no intention of ever using it with other languages, you can exclude this rule safely. FxCop will point out globalization issues unless you specifically tell it not to do so. In fact, you'll find that FxCop points out a host of globalization issues with the ApplicationExit example.

The original version of ApplicationExit has the `DllImport` calls marked as `public`. FxCop rightly points out that P/Invoke calls should appear as `private`. You can easily fix this problem by making the `public` to `private` change as shown here.

```
// Define the external function for posting a message.
[DllImport("User32.DLL", SetLastError = true)]
private static extern Boolean PostMessage(
   IntPtr hWnd, UInt32 Msg, Int32 wParam, Int32 lParam);
```

However, FxCop also points out that variables such as `hWnd` are misspelled. This is a case where you have to know to disobey the rules in the interest of making the application code easier to understand. Using the same variable naming as the C++ counterparts will make the `DllImport` calls easier to understand later. Consequently, you'd want to exclude this particular rule.

Another possible P/Invoke issue is how to marshal return values. For example, the Win32 API has several methods of defining a Boolean return value. Consequently, you should legitimately tell the compiler how to marshal the return value. For example, the `PostMessage()` function returns a Boolean, so you must add the `[return: MarshalAs]` attribute shown here.

```
// Define the external function for posting a message.
[DllImport("User32.DLL", SetLastError = true)]
[return: MarshalAs(UnmanagedType.Bool)]
private static extern Boolean PostMessage(
   IntPtr hWnd, UInt32 Msg, Int32 wParam, Int32 lParam);
```

Although there isn't any rule that says you must place P/Invoke calls in a separate class, Microsoft is trying to convince developers to do so. You can choose one of three class names based on the kind of P/Invoke calls you create as follows:

- `SafeNativeMethods`: The code is safe for anyone to call, even malicious code. You can use this code as you would any managed code. For example, a call that returns the time of day is considered safe.
- `NativeMethods`: This code is security neutral. Calling it doesn't present an overt risk. However, the system does check caller security and prevents unauthorized callers from using the external call. For example, closing the application isn't something you would want just anyone to do, but in general, it's security-neutral code.
- `UnsafeNativeMethods`: This code is dangerous when called by a malicious caller. For example, erasing a file on disk would be a problem if malicious code performed the task.

In this case of `PostMessage()`, you have a `NativeMethods` class entry. Consequently, you'd change the P/Invoke code for ApplicationExit as shown here.

```
internal static class NativeMethods
{
   // Define the external function for posting a message.
   [DllImport("User32.DLL", SetLastError = true)]
   [return: MarshalAs(UnmanagedType.Bool)]
   internal static extern Boolean PostMessage(
      IntPtr hWnd, UInt32 Msg, Int32 wParam, Int32 lParam);

   // Create a constant for WM_QUIT.
   internal const int WM_QUIT = 0x0012;

   //// Uncomment this call to use the PostQuitMessage() technique.
   //// Define the PostQuitMessage() function.
   //[DllImport("User32.DLL")]
   //public static extern void PostQuitMessage(Int32 nExitCode);
}
```

Notice that the `NativeMethods` class is defined as `internal` and `static`. The calls are also defined as `internal` and `static` now. In addition, only the calls that are actually in use are uncommented. Of course, this means changing the call as well. Consequently, you'd change the `btnPInvoke_Click()` method as shown here.

```
private void btnPInvoke_Click(object sender, EventArgs e)
{
   // Exit the application and post a WM_QUIT message.
   NativeMethods.PostMessage(this.Handle, NativeMethods.WM_QUIT, 1, 0);

   //// Uncomment this version to see PostQuitMesage() at work.
   //// Here is an alternative method to output a WM_QUIT message
   //// and exit the application.
   //// Note that the application handle is for CLR, not for the
   //// application.
   //NativeMethods.PostQuitMessage(1);
}
```

As you can see, the only real change is using the `NativeMethods` class. Otherwise, the code works as before. At this point, the code should clear all of the FxCop tests.

Considering the Rules

You can work directly with the FxCop rules. Simply choose Windows ➪ Rules and you'll see the display of rules shown in Figure 30-8. The checkmarks next to each of the rules in the left pane show that the rule is active. If you want to deactivate a particular set of rules, such as Globalization Rules, simply remove the checkmark next to that entry. When you perform the next analysis, FxCop won't use the inactive rules. The rules you select appear as part of the project file, so you don't need to worry about modifying the rules each time you restart the project.

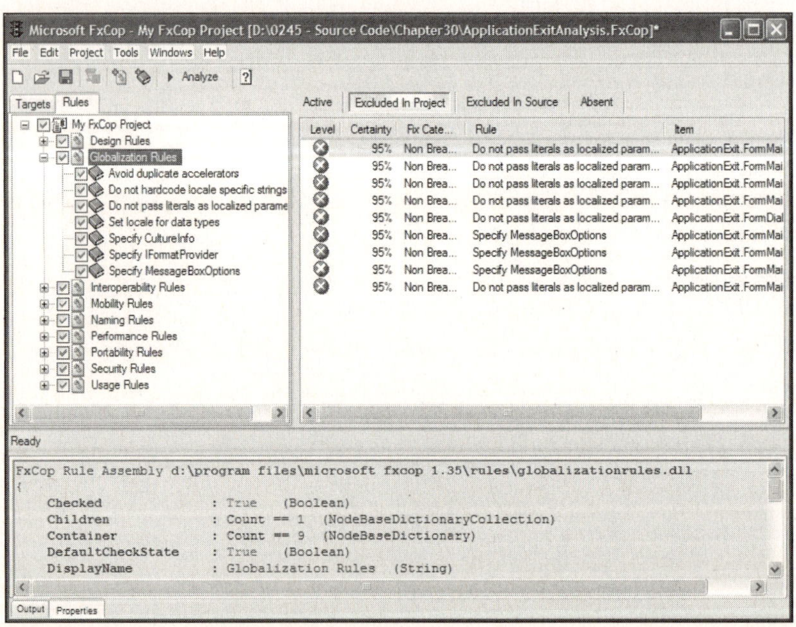

Figure 30-8: Make rules inactive as necessary to perform the analysis you need.

The right pane in Figure 30-8 serves another purpose. If you double-click one of these entries, you can make the rule active again by clicking Unexclude. Consequently, the rules you exclude are easy to reactivate if you make a mistake.

The Output pane tells you the details about any rules you select. For example, you can determine the location of the DLL that supports the rules. In fact, you can create your own custom rules for FxCop. The article at `http://www.thescarms.com/dotnet/fxcop1.aspx` explains how to perform this task.

Employing FxCop during a Build

Let's say that you don't want to have to build the project and then execute FxCop separately. It's possible to overcome this problem by adding FxCop directly to the application build process because FxCop comes in a command line version, too. The FxCop documentation shows how you can add FxCop as an external tool to the Visual Studio .NET interface, but this means you'll still have to execute it separately.

To make the process automatic, choose Project ➪ `<Application Name>` Properties to display the application Property Pages dialog box. Select the Common Properties ➪ Build Events entry and click Edit Post-build next to the Post-build Event Command Line property. You'll see a Post-build Event Command Line dialog box similar to the one shown in Figure 30-9.

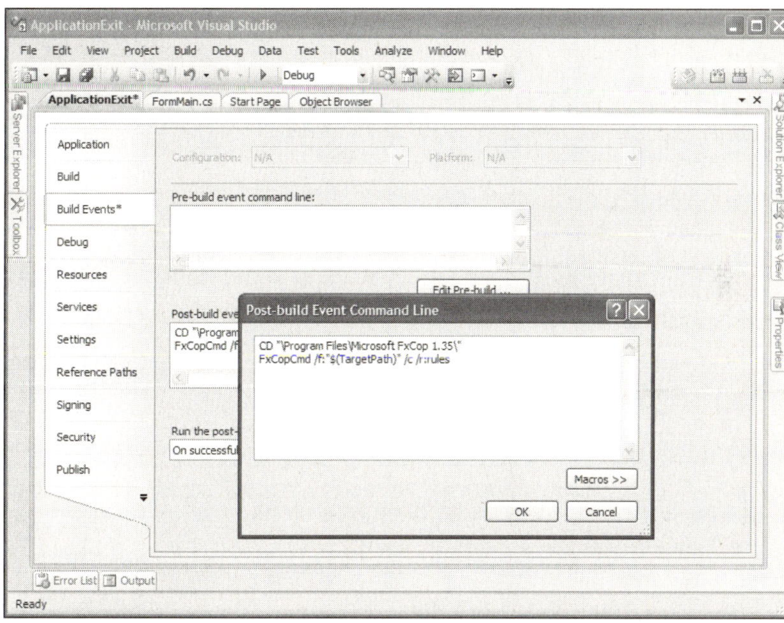

Figure 30-9: Add FxCop to the build process so it executes automatically.

All you need to do, at this point, is type instructions for using FxCop. Here are some basic instructions that work well with the current version:

```
CD "\Program Files\Microsoft FxCop 1.35\"
FxCopCmd /f:"$(TargetPath)" /c /r:rules
```

The first entry tells the compiler to change directories to the FxCop directory and then use the command line version of FxCop to check your application. Here is what the command line switches mean:

- `/f`: Tells the location of your application. You can substitute the `$(TargetPath)` macro in quotes as shown in the example to provide FxCop with the location of your code.
- `/c`: Tells FxCop to output messages to the console so they appear in the Output window of Visual Studio.
- `/r`: Tells FxCop to use the rules found in the `\rules` folder.

Now, every time you build the application, FxCop will also run and display any errors in your code. Figure 30-10 shows typical output in the Output window.

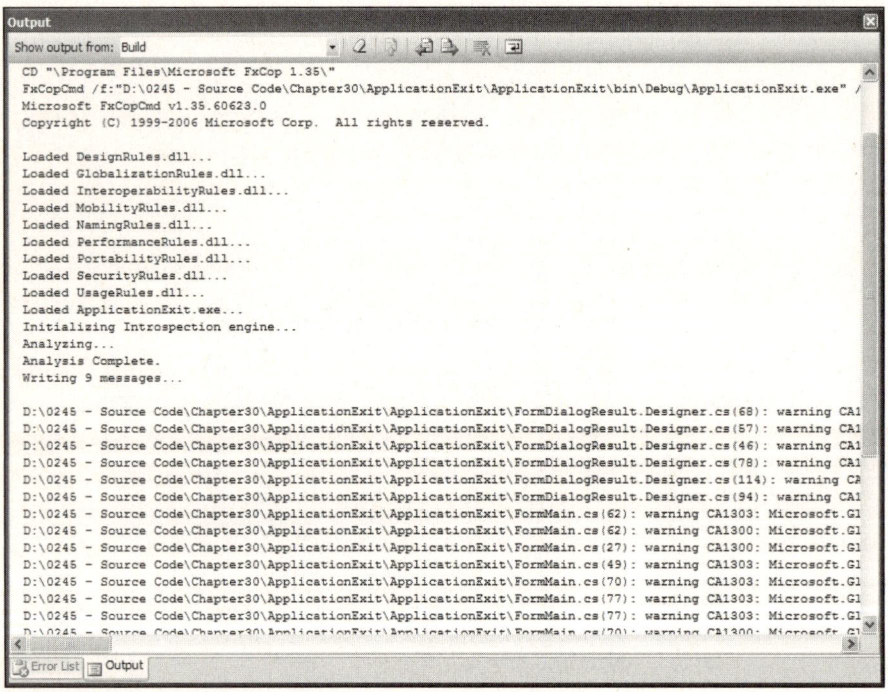

Figure 30-10: The Output window shows the FxCop results every time you build your application.

Using LINQPad to Create LINQ Queries

Sometimes you find a tool that makes it less necessary to remember everything required to perform a task. These tools, when well constructed, help the developer write code considerably faster and with fewer errors. If you found some of the logic in Chapter 23 a tad hard to follow, then you'll probably want to look at a product such as LINQPad (`http://www.linqpad.net/`) to help you create your Language INtegrated Query (LINQ) statements.

You must have the .NET Framework 3.5 installed on your system to use LINQPad. If you don't have it installed, LINQPad displays an error message when you try to start it. You can download the current version of the .NET Framework at `http://msdn.microsoft.com/en-us/netframework/default.aspx`.

After downloading LINQPad, you can use it immediately — it doesn't have an installation program of any sort. You can use LINQPad to create queries for any of the standard LINQ providers including:

- LINQ to Objects
- LINQ to SQL
- LINQ to XML

Using LINQPad is extremely easy. Simply double-click `LINQPad.EXE` and you'll see the LINQPad window where you can begin work. When you want to use LINQ to SQL, click the Add Connection link. You'll see a SQL Connection dialog box like the one shown in Figure 30-11. This dialog box looks and acts very much like the one in Visual Studio. Specify a server, define the database you want to use, set the logon details, and click Test to test the connection. The two big differences are the Options group and the "Remember this connection" option. The Options group contains options that control how LINQPad creates the LINQ statement. The "Remember this connection" option tells LINQPad to remember the connection for future use. The connection will appear in the connection pane every time you start LINQPad (you can easily delete connections you no longer need).

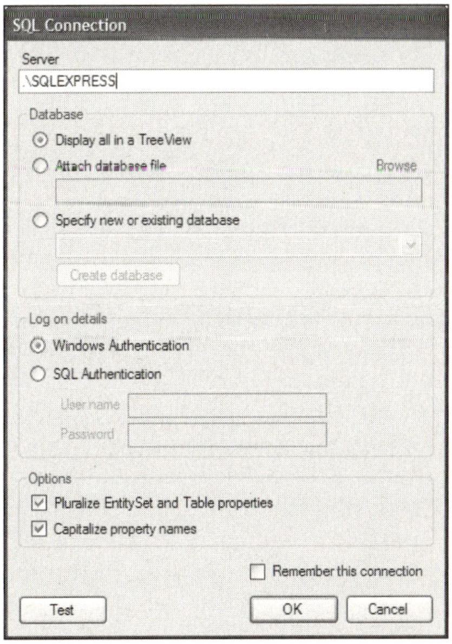

Figure 30-11: Create a connection to the database you want to use for the query.

You can begin creating your query immediately after you have the connection in place. The connection pane shows a complete hierarchy of the database you select. In this case, the example relies on the

Northwind database as shown in Figure 30-12. You can drill down to any level within the database. In addition, the application shows connections between tables. For example, the Products table relies on the Categories table, so you see a link for Products when you drill down into Categories as shown in the figure. Click the link and you automatically open Products so you can interact with it. As you see items you want to use in your query, you can drag and drop them into the query editor (the upper right pane).

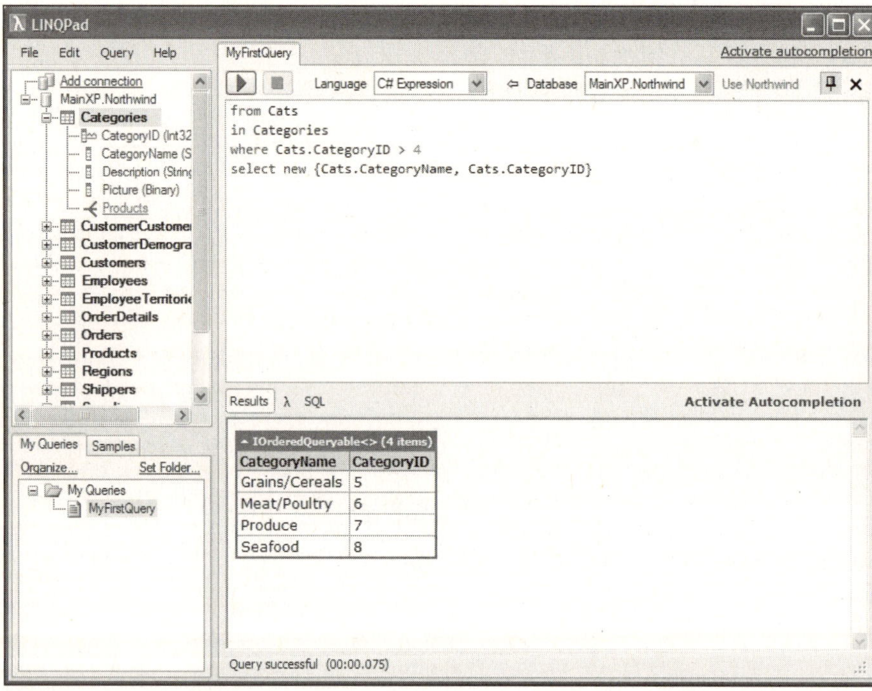

Figure 30-12: LINQPad lets you test queries fully and then save them for future use.

Figure 30-12 shows a quick query that demonstrates how LINQPad works. In this example, the query requests all categories with a `CategoryID` higher than 4. The output displays the `CategoryName` and `CategoryID` columns. When you complete a query, click Execute (the green right-pointing arrow) and you'll see the results in the lower right pane. If you want, you can save the query using the File ➪ Save command, and it will appear in the My Queries tab as shown in the figure. Click Set Folder if you want to change the location of the folder that LINQPad uses to store your queries. Click Organize when you want to remove old queries or perform other organizational tasks.

LINQPad includes a wealth of examples you can try. They appear in the Samples tab in the lower right pane. You can also choose to make queries in a number of ways including:

- C# Expression
- C# Statement(s) (actual code)
- VB Expression
- VB Statement(s)
- SQL

This is a very short overview of a more complex product. The thing is that LINQPad has the potential to save you considerable time and effort. Not only does it make creating queries faster, but you can save queries for future use, which means you don't have to go digging through your code every time you need a query that you used in the past. More importantly, LINQPad demonstrates that you can often find useful third-party tools that don't cost a penny, yet provide considerable value to you as a developer.

Obtaining Resources and Tools

This chapter has provided you with some insights into finding third-party resources and tools. It's important to remember that, overall, third-party products are normally no better or worse than a Microsoft offering. However, because there are so many third parties, what third parties have to offer is choice. If one third party doesn't provide the resource or tool that you need, then another third party probably will because third parties make money by differentiating their products. The most important concept you can take away from this chapter is that third parties offer the variety to answer an array of needs. You may use one third-party product for one project and another for a different project — always use the third-party product that fits your needs best.

Working with third-party products means taking time to test and rate them yourself. Relying on product reviews and other forms of documentation from other people is helpful, but only you know how a particular product will work for the project you're working on now and the projects you'll work on later. It isn't simply a matter of personal taste — each project is different and has unique requirements that you must address when selecting a third-party product. To make yourself more efficient, consider keeping a third-party vendor notebook. Make detailed notes about each of the products and refer to your notebook first when you need to locate a third-party product to fulfill a particular requirement. After you have worked on your notebook for several years, you'll begin noticing that you can answer many of your questions simply by referring to this single resource.

You're at the end of the book — congratulations! The final major entry in this book is a glossary that you should use to answer your questions about the meaning of terms that I use. The glossary is helpful because it defines the words as I use them. Because technology changes so much, it's important to have an unchanging resource you can use to determine how the book uses terms that may change in meaning tomorrow.

If you have any questions about this book, or feel you'd like to make a comment about it, always feel free to contact me at JMueller@mwt.net. I value your input and want you to know that I'll use it to improve my books in the future. You'll always receive a prompt, courteous response from me (unless I happen to be on vacation when you write, then the answer could take up to two weeks — please be patient). The most important question you can answer, now that you've finished the book, is whether you found it useful. Give me the details — I really want to know because knowing the details makes me a better author.

Glossary

This book includes a glossary so that you can find terms and acronyms easily. It has several important features you need to know about. First, every uncommon acronym in the entire book appears here (including some you know, such as LINQ and XML). I have left out common acronyms such as CPU because I expect you to know them, as well as units of measure and most file extensions. This way, there isn't any doubt that you'll always find everything you need to use the book properly.

Second, these definitions are specific to the book. In other words, when you look through this glossary, you're seeing the words defined in the context in which they're used in this book. This might or might not always coincide with current industry usage, since the computer industry changes the meaning of words so often.

Finally, I've used a conversational tone for the definitions in most cases. This means that the definitions might sacrifice a bit of accuracy for the sake of better understanding. The purpose of this glossary is to define the terms in such a way that there's less room for misunderstanding the intent of the book as a whole. In the following two sections, you discover what you should do if you don't find a term in this glossary and the list of special terms for this book.

What to Do If You Don't Find It Here

While this glossary is a relatively complete view of the words and acronyms in the book, you'll run into situations when you need to know more. No matter how closely I look at terms throughout the book, there's always a chance I'll miss the one acronym or term that you really need to know. In addition to the technical information found in the book, I've directed your attention to numerous online sources of information throughout the book and few of the terms the Web site owners use will appear here unless I also chose to use them in the book. Fortunately, many sites on the Internet provide partial or complete glossaries to fill in the gaps:

- Acronym Finder: `http://www.acronymfinder.com/`
- Free Online Dictionary Of Computing (FOLDOC): `http://nightflight.com/foldoc/`
- Microsoft Encarta: `http://encarta.msn.com/`
- Microsoft Security Glossary: `http://www.microsoft.com/security/portal/glossary.aspx`
- More Microsoft Glossaries: `http://www.winlexic.com/more_microsoft_glossaries.htm`
- TechEncyclopedia: `http://www.techweb.com/encyclopedia/defineterm.jhtml`
- Webopedia: `http://webopedia.internet.com/`
- yourDictionary.com: `http://www.yourdictionary.com/`

Some entries in this list are quite specialized. For example, the Microsoft Security Glossary discusses the Microsoft view of security terms. You can find other Microsoft Glossaries listed at `http://www.microsoft.com/resources/glossary/default.mspx`. If you still don't find what you need, try the Microsoft Search page at `http://search.microsoft.com/`, type the word `glossary`, add a specific area such as `network`, and click Submit Query.

The Word List

The following sections provide an alphabetical list of words for this glossary. The list includes both technical terms and acronyms. You won't find definitions for legal or other noncomputer terms. In addition, the list doesn't contain common acronyms such as CPU or units of measure, such as KB.

Accessibility A measure of a user's ability to interact with an application. For example, applications should provide both mouse and keyboard access to every control to ensure the user can reach the control for use. An application should support all devices without providing specialized support for a particular device unless necessary. A Braille input device should receive no special treatment beyond that required for a keyboard.

Activity Diagram A graphical presentation that models the dynamic activity of a system by showing the flow of control from activity to activity. For example, a user may need to configure the application to perform a print job, choose a particular printer and configure it, and then print the document. Activity diagrams model the workflow that occurs when working with a particular object so that you can better see how the object will have to react to the various activities that the user performs.

Adaptive Software Development (ASD) An agile programming methodology that comes out of the Rapid Application Development (RAD) model (adds to what RAD already provides). ASD replaces the elements of the waterfall model with a series of speculate, collaborate, and learn cycles. Each of these cycles helps move a particular component or other aspect of the application forward. Most developers rely on ASD when they require a mission-focused or feature-rich environment in which to create the application. In most cases, ASD relies on specific periods for each phase of a cycle, so ASD is time boxed. In addition, because of the way ASD works, it's extremely flexible and fault tolerant. You can discover more about ASD at `http://www.adaptivesd.com/` or `http://www.softwareplanner.com/se_sp_adaptive_software_mkt.asp`.

Add-in An external application designed to work with a host application, such as Visual Studio, and enhance its capabilities. In most cases, an add-in is a feature that didn't attract enough attention for the vendor to add it to the host application, but does provide enough functionality that a group of users wants it.

Agile Programming An application development methodology (versus a technique) that tends to focus on speed of development and stakeholder interaction. Agile doesn't come in just one form — you find many agile programming techniques discussed on the Internet. In fact, agile didn't arrive as a single technology. Many developers contributed toward making agile the programming technology you see today. Not every project is agile-programming friendly. The speed of development that agile promotes can result in a loss of application speed, which is an important factor in real-time and embedded application development. In addition, because agile tends to focus on code reuse and the use of off-the-shelf modules, you may find it difficult to customize an application as fully as the customer wants. The greater the level of customization, the more likely it is that your application doesn't fit the agile model.

Amazon Web Services (AWS) A set of methods and properties that enables a developer to access the Amazon database using technologies such as Simple Object Access Protocol (SOAP) and eXtensible Markup Language (XML) over HyperText Transfer Protocol (HTTP). Amazon publishes the services using the Amazon Web Services Kit and through programmatic interfaces such as Web Services Description Language (WSDL).

American Standard Code for Information Interchange (ASCII) A standard method of equating the numeric representations available in a computer to human-readable form. For example, the number 32 represents a space. The standard ASCII code contains 128 characters (7 bits). The extended ASCII code uses 8 bits for 256 characters. Unicode has largely replaced ASCII in most cases today because it supports a larger character set. The charts at `http://www.i18nguy.com/unicode/codepages.html` provide examples of various character sets.

API See Application Programming Interface (API)

Application Programming Interface (API) A method of defining a standard set of function or method calls and other interface elements. It usually defines the interface between a high-level language and the lower-level elements used by a device driver or operating system. The ultimate goal is to provide some type of service to an application that requires access to the operating system or device feature set.

ASCII See American Standard Code for Information Interchange (ASCII)

ASD See Adaptive Software Development (ASD)

AWS See Amazon Web Services (AWS)

BASIC Beginner's All-Purpose Symbolic Instruction Code (BASIC)

CA See Code Analysis (CA)

CAB See Cabinet File (CAB)

Cabinet File (CAB) A compressed-format file similar to ZIP files used to transfer code and data from one location to another. For example, many Web sites use the CAB file to download applications to a user system using a browser as the intermediary. Use the Compress utility to create the file and the Expand utility to decompress the file.

Camel Case A method of naming variables that relies on combining multiple words while retaining the original words. Camel case appears in a number of places in popular culture. For example, the surnames MacLean and VanDyke are both examples of camel case. In this case, the surnames reflect the original language's use of two words for the surname, but the English language's preference for a single word. You also see it for company names. RadioShack is an example of a company name that uses camel case. In some cases, technology uses camel case, such as VistaVision, which is a widescreen format for movies. It's little wonder that camel case appears in application code because everyone already knows how to use it.

CAPTCHA See Completely Automatic Public Turing Test to Tell Computers and Humans Apart (CAPTCHA)

Cascading Style Sheets (CSS) A method for defining a standard Web page appearance using formatting information. The formatting may include headings, standard icons, backgrounds, and other features that would tend to give each page at a particular Web site the same appearance. The reason for using CSS includes speed of creating a Web site (it takes less time if the developer doesn't have to create an overall design for each page) and consistency. Changing the overall appearance of a Web site also becomes as easy as changing the style sheet instead of each page alone. CSS is also a standards-supported technology, so it represents an easy method for developers to create Web pages that will work in standards-compliant browsers.

CD Compact Disc

CEO Chief Executive Officer

CLR See Common Language Runtime (CLR)

COBOL Common Business-Oriented Language

Code Analysis (CA) A number used to indicate the warning level of a particular code analysis fault. The CA numbers reflect specific rules that Microsoft has created for writing safe code. You can find these numbers described at `http://msdn.microsoft.com/en-us/library/ee1hzekz.aspx`.

Code Document Object Model (CodeDOM) A method of describing how to create assemblies on the fly within a .NET assembly. The CodeDOM describes how to create and compile the code, which the host assembly emits and runs. Creating code dynamically lets an application handle unforeseen situations and provides flexibility in application design.

Code Snippet A snippet is a short piece of code that you use regularly that isn't necessarily an entire function or method. For example, when creating a console application, you may rely on a particular piece of code to determine whether the application is in a release or debug state. Because the console window normally closes immediately, you can use code within a define block to add a pause to the screen. Now, when you debug the application, the screen stays in place so you can see how the screen looks. This kind of code is too short to place in a library. However, you use the short piece of code often enough that you do want to save it in some form. Consequently, it's a perfect candidate for a snippet.

CodeDOM See Code Document Object Model (CodeDOM)

Collaboration Diagram A graphical presentation that shows the interaction between objects as a sequence of numbered messages. When you look at a collaboration diagram, you see the static nature of the object hierarchy. Each object that interacts with another object has a connection called an association.

COM See Component Object Model (COM)

COM+ See Component Object Model Plus (COM+)

Common Language Runtime (CLR) The engine (pronounced clear) used to interpret managed application tokens within the .NET Framework. All Visual Studio .NET languages that produce managed applications can use the same runtime engine. Visual Studio .NET calls on the Just-In-Time (JIT) compiler to compile the source code into a special tokenized form called Intermediate Language (IL) and CLR interprets the IL. (It's also possible to access the JIT compiler outside of Visual Studio .NET at the command line.) The major advantages of this approach include extensibility (you can add other languages) and reduced code size (you don't need a separate runtime for each language).

Community Technology Preview (CTP) A type of public beta test of a product where the participants work with the pre-release software on a test system to determine how it will work in their current production environment. The CTP software is normally available for public download and the vendor provide caveats as to usability. Bug reporting isn't as formal as with a beta test and the vendor tends to provide less support for a CTP.

Completely Automatic Public Turing Test to Tell Computers and Humans Apart (CAPTCHA) One of several techniques for ensuring a visitor to a Web site is human, rather than some form of automation. You can read more about CAPTCHA at `http://www.captcha.net/`.

Component In programming, a nonvisual element, such as a tooltip or timer. The component is an object that includes properties, events, and methods. The user may not interact directly with a component. For example, a tooltip adds functionality to an existing control; the user doesn't interact with it directly.

Component Diagram A graphical presentation that models the behavior of a component using the black box approach. This diagram uses interfaces to describe a group of operations that a component uses or generates. For example, Windows uses the IUnknown interface to interrogate a component and discover more about it. The interfaces describe what you can do with the component and often represent standardized behaviors that the component implements in order to interact with the system in a particular way.

Component Object Model (COM) A Microsoft specification for a binary-based, object-oriented code and data encapsulation method and transference technique. It's the basis for technologies such as OLE (Object Linking and Embedding) and ActiveX (components and controls). COM is limited to local connections.

Component Object Model Plus (COM+) An updated version of both the Component Object Model (COM) and Distributed Component Object Model (DCOM) that includes features for modern remote and disconnected applications. COM+ applications are registered on the server and client machines using standard installation programs and specialized administrative tools. The technology can use both standard connected and queued communication. Later versions of COM+ can even act as Web services with the proper configuration.

Component-Oriented Programming (COP) A programming technique that relies heavily on components. In this approach, almost none of the application code resides within the application itself; every major aspect of the application appears as part of a component. Whether you find this methodology useful depends on the kind of application you create. You can find an interesting paper on this topic at `http://www.cs.jhu.edu/~phf/pub/thesis-uci-2003.pdf`.

Control In programming, a visual object, such as a button or checkbox. The control is an object that includes properties, events, and methods. Users generally interact directly with controls.

COP See Component-Oriented Programming (COP)

Counter An application designed to measure performance on a Windows system. The counter is part of a performance object. It's normally stored with other counters associated with the same performance object within a dynamic link library (DLL) on the host machine. A counter may allow monitoring of one or more instances of the same type of device or other object as individual performance statistics.

Crystal Clear An agile programming methodology that focuses on efficiency and habitability, rather than on processes and artifacts. Alistair Cockburn originally proposed Crystal Clear as part of his book, *Crystal Clear, A Human-Powered Methodology for Small Teams* (Addison-Wesley, 2004). The typical Crystal Clear team has no more than eight people because larger groups require more management to perform well. You can discover more about these seven properties in the article entitled, "Crystal Clear Applied: The Seven Properties of Running an Agile Project," by Alistair Cockburn at `http://www.informit.com/articles/article.aspx?p=345009`. You'll also want to read the material on Crystal Clear methods at `http://alistair.cockburn.us/index.php/Crystal_light_methods`.

CSS See Cascading Style Sheets (CSS)

CTP See Community Technology Preview (CTP)

Data Encryption A method of changing data from human-readable form into an encoded format, then back again to protect the data from security breaches. Some type of equation is used to encrypt the data that relies on either public or private keys to unlock the data later. The length of the key in bits and the type of equation used often determine the ability of the encrypted data to withstand decryption by unauthorized parties.

Data Encryption Standard (DES) An unsafe method of data encryption that relies on symmetric key encryption. This methodology was originally introduced in 1975 and standardized by ANSI in 1981. As computer technology has improved, the encryption technique has become easier to crack, making it an unreliable means of protecting data.

DataBase Administrator (DBA) The specialist in charge of one or more databases on server. The DBA makes configuration changes, performs management tasks such as backups, creates stored procedures, and generally cares for the database.

DBA See DataBase Administrator (DBA)

Deployment Diagram A graphical presentation that shows how the system interacts when deployed on a system. The diagram consists of nodes, components, and connections. A node is a physical resource that executes the code within components. The connection shows a physical relationship between two nodes. Nodes can contain any number of components. Consequently, a client application may have a component that requests data from a server. The deployment diagram would show the client and server machines as nodes. The Ethernet communication between the two nodes appears as a connection. Within each node are the components used to solve a particular problem.

DES See Data Encryption Standard (DES)

Deserialization The act of converting a serialized data stream into an object using the class description as a template. The application performing the conversion must have access to the class template and know the method of serialization.

Development Team The group of individuals engaged in creating an application. In most cases, the team members are mainly developers. However, the team could also contain artists and other individuals tasked with creating resources for the application. In addition, the team may have a technical writer and other experts who help build noncode portions of the application. The development team will also include management (which may or may not be a technical expert).

Digital Video Disc (DVD) A high capacity optical storage media with capacities of 4.7GB to 17GB (higher with newer technologies) and data transfer rates of 600KBps to 1.3GBps (faster with newer technologies). A single DVD can hold the contents of an entire movie or approximately 7.4 CD-ROMs. DVDs come in several formats including DVD-R, DVD-RW, DVD+R, DVD+RW, and DVD-RAM that allow read-only or read-write access. Newer dual-layer DVDs promise even greater storage capacities. All DVD drives include a second laser assembly used to read existing CD-ROMs. Some magazines will also use the term *digital versatile disk* for this storage media.

Disk Operating System (DOS) The underlying management software used by older PCs to provide basic system services and to allow the user to run application software. The operating system performs many low-level tasks through the Basic Input/Output System (BIOS). The revision number determines the specifics of the services that DOS offers; check your user manual for details.

DOD Department of Defense

DOS See Disk Operating System (DOS)

DVD See Digital Video Disc (DVD)

ECMA See European Computer Manufacturer's Association (ECMA)

Encryption See Data Encryption

Entity Relationship (ER) A modeling language feature that contains an entity description, such as a database table, and the relationships between this entity and all other entities in the model.

ER See Entity Relationship (ER)

European Computer Manufacturer's Association (ECMA) A standards committee originally founded in 1961. ECMA is dedicated to standardizing information and communication systems. For example, it created the ECMAScript standard used for many Web page designs today. You can also find ECMA standards for product safety, security, networks, and storage media.

Event Handler A special method or function that reacts to specific system or user events such as clicking a button on a form or the loss of focus for a textbox.

Evolutionary Model An application development technique that relies on software prototyping as the means for creating an application. In other words, you work intensely with the client by creating the forms and reports required for the application and then adding the glue code required to make those forms and reports functional as you go.

Exception An unforeseen event within an application, usually captured and addressed by specialized code called a handler. Exception handling gets its name from the concept that it only happens when an exceptional (extraordinary) event occurs. An exceptional event is one that the developer didn't anticipate happening. In fact, it's possible to say that it's impossible to anticipate the event occurring, so an exception is the only way to handle it.

Expression A combination of variables, database fields, relational operators, methods, and functions that evaluate to a value. An expression is normally an abstraction of a real-world concept or idea. For example, when a developer creates a math equation, the expression is an abstraction of some real-world concept (such as the flow of water in a pipe) in most cases.

eXtensible Markup Language (XML) 1. A method used to store information in an organized manner. The storage technique relies on hierarchical organization and uses special statements called tags to separate each storage element. Each tag defines a data attribute and can contain properties that further define each data element. 2. A standardized Web page design language used to incorporate data structuring within standard HTML documents. For example, you could use XML to display database information using something other than forms or tables. It's actually a lightweight version of Standard Generalized Markup language (SGML) and is supported by the SGML community. XML also supports tag extensions that allow various parts of a Web-based application to exchange information. For example, once a user makes a choice within a catalog, that information could be added to an order entry form with a minimum of effort on the part of the developer. Since XML is easy to extend, some developers look at it as more of a base specification for other languages, rather than a complete language.

eXtensible Stylesheet Language Transformation (XSLT) The language used within the eXtensible Style Language (XSL) to transform the content provided in an eXtensible Markup Language (XML) file into a form for display on screen or printing. An XSL processor combines XML content with the formatting instructions provided by XSLT and outputs a new document or document fragment. XSLT is a World Wide Web Consortium (W3C) standard.

eXtreme Programming (XP) An agile programming methodology that relies on programming methodologies taken to an extreme level in order to respond to stakeholder needs more reliably and promptly. In some respects, there's nothing new about XP because it relies on the same software engineering practices used for older development models. The basic premise behind XP is to introduce flexibility into the development process. XP seeks to introduce the flexibility, while maintaining the deliberate and disciplined approach used by earlier software models. In short, it's attempting to provide you with the best of both the waterfall model and agile programming techniques. You can obtain a better view of XP at `http://www.extremeprogramming.org/`.

FDD See Feature Driven Development (FDD)

Feature Driven Development (FDD) An agile programming methodology that focuses on the features in an application. Jeff De Luca initially created FDD to meet the specific needs of a 15-month, 50-person software development project at a large Singapore bank in 1997. One of the best places to obtain additional information about FDD is on Jeff De Luca's Web site at `http://www.nebulon.com/fdd/index.html`. You'll also want to visit the Feature Driven Development community Web site at `http://www.featuredrivendevelopment.com/`.

Firewall Hardware or software (or a combination of both) used to prevent unauthorized access to a private network. The firewall can use any of a number of techniques to detect unauthorized packets and deny access to them. Most firewalls not only check incoming packets, but outgoing packets as well. There are many types of firewalls including packet filter, application gateway, proxy server, and circuit-level gateway. For maximum protection, the proxy server normally works best in a hardware configuration.

FORTRAN Formula Translation (language)

Functional Language A functional language is one that relies on equations to define a task. F# is a functional language, contrasted to C# and Visual Basic.NET, which are imperative or procedural languages. When a developer uses a functional language, the code X = Y means that X and Y are equal. The developer isn't assigning the value of Y to X. In other words, there is no procedure as there is with C#. The code doesn't imply any form of steps.

Globally Unique Identifier (GUID) A 128-bit number originally used to identify a Component Object Model (COM) object within the Windows registry. Microsoft now uses the GUID wherever a system requires a unique identifier. When working in COM, the system uses the GUID to find the object definition and allow applications to create instances of that object. However, the system can use the GUID for other purposes as well. GUIDs can include any kind of object, even non-visual elements. In addition, some types of complex objects are actually aggregates of simple objects. For example, an object that implements a property page will normally have a minimum of two GUIDs: one for the property page and another for the object itself.

Graphical User Interface (GUI) 1. A method of displaying information that depends on both hardware capabilities and software instructions. A GUI uses the graphics capability of a display adapter to improve communication between the device and its user. Using a GUI involves a large investment in both programming and hardware resources, but reduces overall system complexity for the user. 2. A system of icons and graphic images that replace the character-mode menu system used by many older devices. The GUI can ride on top of another operating system (such as DOS, Linux, and UNIX) or reside as part of the operating system itself (such as the Macintosh and Windows). Advantages of a GUI are ease of use and high-resolution graphics. Disadvantages include cost, higher workstation hardware requirements, and lower performance over a similar system using a character mode interface.

GUI See Graphical User Interface (GUI)

GUID See Globally Unique Identifier (GUID)

Hash A technique for converting data into a unique numeric value. Unlike encryption, hashing data isn't reversible; the resulting number only represents the data, but doesn't actually contain data. If a sender and receiver can agree upon a protocol, they can use a hash to send common information, rather than rely on sending the data. This is the method that Windows uses to validate passwords. The server actually stores a hash of the password, rather than the password itself. When a user types the password into the logon dialog box, Windows converts it to a hash and sends the hash to the server. Because this number is unique and Windows requires that you provide a password, and not the hash, the password is considerably safer.

HTML See HyperText Markup Language (HTML)

Hungarian Notation A method of naming variables that relies on specific prefixes and postfixes to identify the variable type and usage. Charles Simonyi originally created Hungarian notation during the days of the Disk Operating System (DOS) to make the functional type of identifiers apparent. The naming convention grew from there to see use in Windows programming where, at one time, the purpose of an identifier was even harder to determine. You can see a write-up of the history of Hungarian notation at `http://msdn.microsoft.com/en-us/library/aa260976(VS.60).aspx`.

HyperText Markup Language (HTML) 1. A data presentation and description (markup) language for the Internet that depends on the use of tags (keywords within angle brackets <>) to display formatted information onscreen in a non-platform-specific manner. The non-platform-specific nature of this markup language makes it difficult to perform some basic tasks such as placement of a screen element at a specific location. However, the language does provide for the use of fonts, color, and various other enhancements onscreen. There are also tags for displaying graphic images. Scripting tags for using scripting languages such as VBScript and JavaScript are available, although not all browsers support this addition. The `<OBJECT>` tag addition allows the use of ActiveX controls. 2. One method of displaying text, graphics, and sound on the Internet. HTML provides an ASCII-formatted page of information read by a special application called a browser. Depending on the browser's capabilities, some keywords are translated into graphics elements, sounds, or text with special characteristics, such as color, font, or other attributes. Most browsers discard any keywords they don't understand, allowing browsers of various capabilities to explore the same page without problem. Obviously, there's a loss of capability if a browser doesn't support a specific keyword.

I/O Input/Output

IDE See Integrated Development Environment (IDE)

IIS See Internet Information Server (IIS)

IL See Intermediate Language (IL)

Incremental/Iterative Model An application development technique that creates an application by building it a small piece at a time. The design team breaks the application into functional pieces (called builds) at the outset of the project. The idea is to build each piece separately, test it, and then add it to the whole. This process is similar to the waterfall model. However, the incremental/iterative model also overcomes a considerable number of problems with the waterfall model.

Integrated Development Environment (IDE) The development tool used to write application code. An IDE provides all of the tools needed to write an application using one or more specialized editors. The IDE normally includes support for development language help, access to any tools required to support the language, a compiler, and a debugger. Some IDEs include support for advanced features such as automatic completion of language statements and balloon help showing the syntax for functions and other language elements. Many IDEs also use color or highlighting to emphasize specific language elements or constructs.

IntelliSense A special Visual Studio code editor feature that uses balloon windows to provide usage hints and acceptable values for coding elements such as methods and properties.

Intermediate Language (IL) The common tokenized language that all .NET compilers output. The Common Language Runtime (CLR) interprets the tokens that reside in the IL. The use of a tokenized output ensures that all languages can share the functionality provided by the .NET Framework. Because CLR understands this one common language, any compiler that produces it is compatible with .NET.

Internet Information Server (IIS) Microsoft's Web server that runs under the Windows operating system. IIS includes all of the standard Web server features including File Transfer Protocol (FTP) and HyperText Transfer Protocol (HTTP), along with both mail and news services in older versions of the product. The latest version of IIS concentrates on developer requirements and doesn't provide mail and news services. This newer version of IIS relies on a modular approach that depends on the .NET Framework, rather than the monolithic architecture used in older versions of IIS.

JavaScript A language with a C-like syntax. Most browsers support JavaScript and developers like to use it for local and remote applications alike. There are many versions of JavaScript, including Microsoft's JScript and the European Computer Manufacturer's Association (ECMA) ECMAScript.

Lambda Expression A technique for describing a function without actually creating the function code. The lambda expression is borrowed from functional programming languages and expresses what to do, rather than how to do it. In the .NET environment, a lambda expression is used in the same way that a delegate is used. The developer provides one or more target variables and the operations to perform on those targets. The lambda expression appears as part of a method call, which governs its use and the function created to address the expression components.

LAN See Local Area Network (LAN)

Language INtegrated Query (LINQ) A technique for querying data from any source that relies on a common structure. Special code called a provider interprets the query and translates it into a form that the data source can understand. Visual Studio comes with a number of standard providers: LINQ to Objects, LINQ to DataSet, LINQ to SQL, and LINQ to XML. Each provider enables access to a different kind of data. Third parties have created a number of additional providers, making it possible to obtain data from myriad data sources using a common query language.

LCID See Locale Identifier (LCID)

Lifecycle Model A method of creating a lifecycle (creation to retirement) for your application based on real-world goals and requirements. Using a lifecycle model helps you create a sequence of events for your application based on best practices that have evolved through years of trial and error by other developers.

LINQ See Language INtegrated Query (LINQ)

LISP LISt Processing

Local Area Network (LAN) Two or more devices located in a relatively small physical area connected together using a combination of hardware and software. The devices, normally computers and peripheral equipment such as printers, are called nodes. A Network Interface Card (NIC) provides the hardware communication between nodes through an appropriate medium (cable, wireless, infrared, microwave transmission, or other means). There are two common types of LANs (also called networks).

Peer-to-peer networks allow each node to connect to any other node on the network with shareable resources. This is a distributed method of files and peripheral devices. A client-server network uses one or more servers to share resources. This is a centralized method of sharing files and peripheral devices. A server provides resources to clients (usually workstations).

Locale Identifier (LCID) A number that uniquely identifies a country, language, or other nationalistic information. An application, online resource, or data manager uses the LCID to provide specific information, services, or resources in a form that the user can understand. For example, many applications support more than one language and the application would use the LCID to change the prompts to match the user's language.

Macro A series of recorded keystrokes and other information used to perform a repetitive task within the Visual Studio IDE. An example of a repetitive task using a macro is compiling an application and then placing it in the debugging state. A macro could reduce the time required to get the application ready for debugging or other kinds of testing.

MDI See Multiple Document Interface (MDI)

Mean Time Between Failures (MTBF) A reliability statistic that predicts the average life of an entity (such as a device or an application) based on the component structure of that entity and real-world testing. This number represents the amount of time that the average entity will run before it requires replacement. Obviously, some entities will run longer and others shorter than the number of hours specified using the MTBF. The MTBF is designed to allow companies to plan a component replacement strategy.

Microsoft Installer (MSI) 1. A technique for installing applications within Windows that allows later removal even if the system configuration has changed. This technique also provides support for additional vendor information, partial installations, multiple configurations, and installation recovery. 2. A file format containing instructions for installing Windows applications. The file is actually a database that contains specialized instructions and data in a specific format that is read by the Microsoft installer application.

Microsoft Management Console (MMC) An application that hosts specially constructed Component Object Model (COM) objects called snap-ins that help the user manage Windows, a device, or an application. MMC acts as an object container for Windows management objects such as Component Services and Computer Management. The management objects are actually special components that provide interfaces that allow the user to access them within MMC to maintain and control the operation of Windows. A developer can create special versions of these objects for application management or other tasks. Using a single application like MMC helps maintain the same user interface across all management applications. The combination of one or more snap-ins and the MMC host is called a console and the settings appear within Microsoft Console (MSC) files.

ML MetaLanguage

MMC See Microsoft Management Console (MMC)

MSC Microsoft Console File

MSDN Microsoft Developer Network

MSI See Microsoft Installer (MSI)

MTBF See Mean Time Between Failures (MTBF)

Multiple Document Interface (MDI) A method for displaying more than one document at a time within a parent window. The interface enables the user load more than one document at a time within a single application. In most cases, the user can display a single document using the full editing area, or display multiple documents using sections of the editing area. Many word processors and spreadsheets use the MDI to help the user create complex document associations and to enable editing between documents.

Multiprocessing An application execution method where a single application executes on multiple processors. Unlike multithreading, it's possible to execute multiple threads of execution simultaneously using this technique. Creating a multiprocessed application is incredibly complex because the individual threads can't rely on state information or assume anything about the processor register content. Most programming languages do not currently support multiprocessing directly.

Multitasking The ability of some processor and operating environment/system combinations to perform more than one task at a time. The applications appear to run simultaneously. For example, you could download messages from an online service, print from a word processor, and recalculate a spreadsheet at the same time. Each application receives a slice of time before the processor moves on to the next application. Because the time slices are fairly small, it appears to the user as if these actions occur simultaneously.

Multithreading An application development technique that breaks an application into two or more tasks that end up as multiple threads of execution. Each thread performs a different task, such as interacting with the user or printing a document. Using this technique allows the operating system to devote more resources to higher priority tasks; increasing perceived system performance.

NASA National Aeronautics and Space Administration

Object Model Map The visual representation of the object model associated with a particular application. You can see a number of examples of object models online. For example, look at the Word Application Object Model Map at `http://msdn.microsoft.com/en-us/library/bb288731.aspx`.

OCaml Objective Categorical Abstract Machine Language

OCX See OLE Custom eXtension (OCX)

OLE Custom eXtension (OCX) A component or control designed to make adding various capabilities to an application easier for the programmer. Essentially, an OCX is a DLL with added programmer and Component Object Model (COM) interfaces. Component technology has evolved to include a wide variety of uses including both client-side and server-side application elements. A component differs from a control in that a component is usually used for a processing task and lacks a user interface. Controls include application elements such as pushbuttons and textboxes.

OOXML See Open Office XML (OOXML)

Open Office XML (OOXML) A document format created by Microsoft that is the basis for new Office 2007 file formats such as DOCX. The DOCX file format is valuable for developers because a DOCX file is really a ZIP file in disguise. Within the DOCX file are a number of folders that contain XML files that a developer can easily reproduce in code; giving the developer full access to the power of Word without worrying about proprietary format issues.

Open Software Description (OSD) A type of file used to describe software components, component version, underlying structures, and dependencies on other files.

OSD See Open Software Description (OSD)

P/Invoke See Platform Invoke (P/Invoke)

Pascal Case A method of naming variables that relies on combining multiple words while retaining the original words. Microsoft uses Pascal case to differentiate between some types of naming conditions, such as class, enum type, enum values, event, exception class, read-only static field, interface, method, namespace, parameter, property, and public instance field. The difference between Pascal case and camel case from the Microsoft perspective is that camel case variables begin with a lowercase letter, while Pascal case variables begin with an uppercase letter.

PDF See Portable Document Format (PDF)

Performance Triangle The combination of speed, reliability, and security that address the performance characteristics of an application. Enhancing one element of the triangle normally adversely affects the other two elements. Speed is a measurement of how fast the application performs a task. Reliability is a measurement of the Mean Time Between Failure (MTBF) as well as the application's ability to perform its designated task. Security measures the application's ability to complete tasks without letting external forces affect it, as well as the ability to maintain the integrity of application data.

PHP See PHP Hypertext Processor (PHP)

PHP Hypertext Processor (PHP) A scripting language used mainly for Web page design. The PHP language strength lies with its compatibility with a wide range of Database Management Systems (DBMSs). As with ASP, the developer can switch easily between HTML and PHP, making it possible to create complex Web pages using script alone. Rasmus Lerdorf created PHP sometime in 1994. At that time, the original abbreviation meant Personal Home Page Hypertext Preprocessor, but it was later changed when the project became a public effort. Zeev Suraski and Andi Gutmans eventually rewrote the PHP parser from scratch to solve a number of issues in the PHP versions prior to PHP 3.

Platform Invoke (P/Invoke) The .NET technology used to access the Win32 Application Programming Interface (API). The process includes importing a function from a Windows Dynamic Link Library (DLL) and marshaling data such that the Windows function recognizes it as a native type. P/Invoke makes it possible to mix managed and native code in a single application.

Portable Document Format (PDF) A formatted, book-like, document format originally created by Adobe. This document format initially captured the output of desktop publishing applications. Many other applications, especially graphics applications, now output to the PDF format. Users can view PDF files using the free Acrobat Reader utility or other applications.

QA See Quality Assurance (QA)

Quality Assurance (QA) The group responsible for verifying an application meets all of its design goals, follows organizational policy, and works as anticipated. QA normally performs a strict level of testing according to a specific plan designed to verify every element of the application.

RAD Rapid Application Development (RAD)

RAD Model See Rapid Application Development (RAD) Model

Rapid Application Development (RAD) Model An application development technique that emphasizes the rapid construction of prototypes to model various processes and the use of iterative development to keep all stakeholders involved and constantly updated on changes to the application. Because RAD emphasizes the use of frameworks and automation, the resulting application generally performs less well than a hand-coded application and the user may see a slight loss of functionality. However, in exchange, the RAD model does provide faster application development and easier application maintenance. Most developers today use some form of RAD for their development, and Microsoft has based Visual Studio on RAD concepts. James Martin originally introduced the term *RAD* in 1991.

RDF See Resource Description Framework (RDF)

Reflection The technique used to read metadata within a .NET application. In general, reflection is used to read application attribute values. It's most common for developers to want to know the attributes that an assembly contains because the attributes describe assembly features. For example, a developer could use an attribute to describe the interface for a component or control.

Resource Description Framework (RDF) A standardized (through the World Wide Web Consortium, W3C) method for describing metadata. RDF is normally associated with Web site data, but could be used to model any metadata. The main benefit of RDF is that it provides interoperability between applications, even when those applications execute on different platforms. RDF relies on the eXtensible Markup Language (XML) to store data in a structured manner. You normally see RDF used to store information such as sitemaps, updates, and search terms. However, developers also use RDF to create other types of ontology, such as music data storage.

Rich Text Format (RTF) A file format originally introduced by Microsoft that allows an application to store formatting information in plain ASCII text. All commands begin with a backslash. For example, the `\cf` command tells an RTF capable editor which color to use from the color table when displaying a particular section of text.

ROM Read-Only Memory

RTF See Rich Text Format (RTF)

Scrum An agile programming methodology that originally appeared as part of a 1986 article entitled, "The New New Product Development Game" (see `http://harvardbusinessonline.hbsp.harvard.edu/b01/en/common/item_detail.jhtml?id=86116` for details) by Hirotaka Takeuchi and Ikujiro Nonaka. Other people added more to the original concept until Scrum came out as part of Ken Schwaber and Mike Beedle's *Agile Software Development with SCRUM* (Prentice Hall, 2001). The original intent of this programming strategy is software development project management. However, many developers have adapted Scrum for other uses.

SDI See Single Document Interface (SDI)

SDK See Software Development Kit (SDK)

Self-Documenting Code A theoretical technique for creating code in such a way that the purpose of that code is obvious without the use of comments. The term *self-documenting* is the lazy developer's way out of writing good comments; comments that everyone working with the code will find useful. The concept of self-documenting code is a myth. Yes, a developer can often see the purpose of a piece of code when he or she has sufficient programming skill and experience with the application, but it's important to consider the needs of the developer who lacks experience as well.

Sequence Diagram A graphical presentation that provides a more complicated form of a collaboration diagram with a time perspective instead of a structural perspective. The sequence diagram displays a series of events in the form of objects and the messages they exchange. This diagram shows what happens given a particular set of circumstances over time.

Serialization The act of converting an object or other complex data into a data stream (normally bytes) in preparation for transmission or offline storage. The method of serialization determines the ability of the application to convert the data stream back into an object later.

Service Level Agreement (SLA) A contract that specifies minimum levels of support or other services provided by a vendor to a client. See `http://www.service-level-agreement.net/` for guidelines on creating an SLA.

Simple Mail Transfer Protocol (SMTP) One of the most commonly used protocols to transfer text (commonly e-mail) messages between clients and servers. This is a stream-based protocol designed to allow query, retrieval, posting, and distribution of e-mail messages. Normally this protocol is used in conjunction with other e-mail retrieval protocols such as point of presence (POP). However, not all uses of SMTP involve email data transfer. Some Simple Object Access Protocol (SOAP) applications have also relied on SMTP to transfer application data.

Single Document Interface (SDI) A method of displaying information where each window is independent of the other. The application shows just one window at a time. If the user wants to display multiple documents, then the application forces them to open multiple application instances.

Skin A reference to the physical appearance of an application. Unlike most applications, skinned applications can have a fanciful appearance. The skin is a graphic representation of how the particular device will appear to the user. One of the most commonly skinned Windows applications is the Windows Media Player.

SLA See Service Level Agreement (SLA)

SMTP See Simple Mail Transfer Protocol (SMTP)

Snippet See Code Snippet

Software Development Kit (SDK) A special add-on for developers to an operating system or an application that describes how to access its internal features. For example, an SDK for Windows would show how to create a File Open dialog box. Programmers use an SDK to learn how to access special Windows components such as the Component Object Model (COM) or the Media Player.

Software Specification A document describing the plan for building software. The plan helps developers create the software without losing focus on non-application requirements. In addition, the development team uses the specification to sell the software idea to nontechnical individuals, such as management. In most cases, a software specification is a written document and usually appears in some type of hard copy format (including electronic derivatives such as the Portable Document Format, or PDF).

Spiral Model An application development technique that relies on incremental evolutionary prototyping to produce an application. According to a number of sources, Barry Boehm defined this model in his 1988 article entitled, "A Spiral Model of Software Development and Enhancement" (see the Web site at `http://portal.acm.org/citation.cfm?id=45797.45801` for details). Each spiral builds on the previous spiral to define a completed application.

Sproc See Stored Procedure (Sproc)

SQL See Structured Query Language (SQL)

Stakeholder Any individual with a vested interest in a project. The stakeholder could be anyone, technical or nontechnical, who must provide input to allow the project to succeed. In many cases, the stakeholder is a subject matter expert who may have no application or development experience. However, the term *stakeholder* encompasses every individual involved in the project, so developers and other technical people are also stakeholders.

Statechart Diagram A graphical presentation that models the dynamic behavior of a system in response to some type of external stimuli. For example, this kind of diagram can answer the question of what happens when a user clicks a button on a form. In practice, the statechart diagram focuses on the states and transitions of an object.

Static Structure Diagram A graphical presentation that provides a sort of structural blueprint of the objects within an application. It shows detailed information about the static state of the application. This diagram shows all the classes associated with the application.

Stored Procedure (sproc) A scripted query found as part of a SQL Server database. The sproc (one of the few lowercase acronyms) contains instructions for executing a single- or multi-step query against the database. A sproc provides one of several forms of automation offered by SQL Server.

Structured Query Language (SQL) Language used by most Database Management Systems (DBMSs) to exchange information; also used by DBMSs as their native language. SQL provides a method for manipulating data controlled by the DBMS. It defines which tables to use, determines what information to get from the table, and resolves how to sort the information. A typical request will include the name of the database, table, and columns needed for display or editing purposes. SQL can filter a request and limit the number of rows using special features. Developers also use SQL to manipulate database information by adding, deleting, modifying, or searching records. The IBM research center designed SQL between 1974 and 1975. Oracle introduced the first product to use SQL in 1979. SQL originally appeared on mainframe and minicomputers. Today it's a favorite language for most PC DBMSs as well. There are many versions of SQL.

Tabbed Interface A type of dialog box with multiple pages where each page serves a different purpose but contributes to the application as a whole. Developers use a tabbed interface for mini-applications that have too much configuration information to fit on a single dialog box. A developer normally groups related controls and places them on a single page. The page has a tab that the user relies on to select it, and the name on that tab reflects the functionality of the group of controls. One of the better examples of a tabbed interface is the Display Properties dialog box used with Windows. The tabs include Themes, Desktop, Screen Saver, Appearance, and Settings.

Test Result (TRx) The file used to store test result information within Visual Studio.

Text Templating A Visual Studio feature used to generate code automatically based on the content of a text file. The full name for this Visual Studio 2008 feature is the Text Template Transformation Toolkit (T4). The default installation provides just one setting for this feature, the ability to turn the security message on or off as needed. Microsoft provides a wealth of information about T4 at `http://msdn.microsoft.com/en-us/library/bb126445.aspx`.

Throwaway Model An application development technique (also known as the code-and-fix or build-and-fix model) that is essentially a placeholder for applications you design and build for yourself. You don't intend to keep the resulting application.

Transact Structured Query Language (T-SQL) A Microsoft variant of the Structured Query Language (SQL) designed for use with SQL Server.

Triple Data Encryption Standard (Triple DES) A variation of the Data Encryption Standard (DES) where an application encrypts the data three times, rather than once, using DES. The resulting encryption is significantly harder to crack, but also requires more time to decrypt.

Triple DES See Triple Data Encryption Standard (Triple DES)

TRx See Test Result (TRx)

T-SQL See Transact Structured Query Language (TSQL)

UAC See User Account Control (UAC)

UML See Unified Modeling Language (UML)

Unified Modeling Language (UML) A specialized form of presentation used to express the design of an application. A method of graphically presenting the object model. The output is an object map of the application.

Uniform Resource Locator (URL) A text representation of a specific location on the Internet. At one time URLs included the protocol (http:// for example), the target location (World Wide Web or www), the domain or server name (mycompany), and a domain type (com for commercial). Many URLs no longer include the older standardized components, such as `http://msdn.microsoft.com`, which skips the www portion found in older URLs. URLs can also include a hierarchical location within that Web site. The URL usually specifies a particular file on the Web server, although there are some situations when a Web server will use a default filename. For example, asking the browser to find `http://www.mycompany.com`, would probably display the `DEFAULT.HTM` or `INDEX.HTM` file at that location. The actual default filename depends on the Web server used. In some cases, the default filename is configurable and could be any of a number of files. For example, Internet Information Server (IIS) offers this feature, so the developer can use anything from an HTM, to an ASP, to an XML file as the default.

Universal Serial Bus (USB) A form of serial bus that allows multiple external devices to share a single port. This technique reduces the number of interrupts and port addresses required to service the needs of devices such as mice and modems. Most USB connections also provide enhanced performance and management capability over the serial and parallel port connections that they replace. The advantages are so great that many computers no longer support either serial or parallel connections.

URL See Uniform Resource Locator (URL)

USB See Universal Serial Bus (USB)

Use Case Diagram A graphical presentation that acts as the starting point for most Unified Modeling Language (UML) projects. The use case diagram provides a kind of script that describes a sequence of events that the user will perform. The use case diagram begins with one or more actors. An actor is simply a user in a specific role. It's typical that an application will have multiple use case diagrams, one for each method of using the application. A single use case diagram can also show multiple actors, one actor for each influence for a particular activity.

User Account Control (UAC) A Windows security feature that increases security by reducing the chance that an application can perform any act on the user's behalf, without the user's knowledge. This feature first appeared as part of Windows Vista. The operating system displays a dialog box asking permission to perform the required task. When the user answers yes, the system performs a privilege elevation that allows the task to progress.

VBA See Visual Basic for Applications (VBA)

Visual Basic for Applications (VBA) A true subset of the Visual Basic language. This form of Visual Basic is normally used within applications in place of a standard macro language. Normally you can't create stand-alone applications using this language in its native environment; however, you could move a VBA program to Visual Basic and compile it there.

Visual Studio test MetaData Information (VSMDI) The file used to hold test information within a Visual Studio solution.

Visual Studio Tools for Office (VSTO) A specialized Software Development Kit (SDK) designed to provide programmatic access to Office applications and documents. Developers use VSTO to create customized Office applications.

Visualizer A special debugging tool that helps the developer to see the data presented in Visual Studio in a human-readable form; as a user would see it. Visual Studio provides four default visualizers: text, eXtensible Markup Language (XML), HyperText Markup Language (HTML), and DataSet. Visualizers were a new addition to Visual Studio 2005. Since that initial release, developers have worked out a number of visualizers to meet specific needs.

VSMDI See Visual Studio test MetaData Information (VSMDI)

VSTO See Visual Studio Tools for Office (VSTO)

WAN See Wide Area Network (WAN)

WAP See Wireless Access Point (WAP)

Waterfall Model An application development technique that evokes a mental image of a waterfall (some developers also call it the sequential software development model). The application planning, design, and implementation flow from one level to the next, until you finally end up with a finished application. A number of versions of the waterfall model exist because many developers started using this model back in 1970. In fact, according to a number of sources, the originator of the model, Winston W. Royce, actually used the model as an example of a flawed development process. However, some developers saw promise in the model and modified it to overcome the flaws.

Web Service A specialized application normally accessed through a Web site that relies on formatted XML for communication purposes. Web services vary greatly in capability. However, the general process is that a client makes a request using one of several techniques such as Simple Object Access Protocol (SOAP) or REpresentational State Transfer (REST). After the server verifies the request, it responds by sending the requested data to the client using formatted XML.

Web Services Description Language (WSDL) A method of describing a Web-based application (Web service) that is accessible through an Internet or intranet connection. The file associated with this description contains the service description, port type, interface description, individual method names, and parameter types. A WSDL file relies on namespace support to provide descriptions of common elements such as data types. Most WSDL files include references to two or more resources maintained by standards organizations to ensure compatibility across implementations.

Wide Area Network (WAN) An extension of the local area network (LAN), a WAN connects two or more LANs together using a variety of methods. A WAN usually encompasses more than one physical site, such as a building. Most WANs rely on microwave communications, fiber optic connections, leased telephone lines, or Virtual Private Network (VPN) to provide the internetwork connections to keep all nodes in the network talking with each other.

Win32 API See Windows 32-bit Application Programming Interface (Win32 API)

Windows 32-bit Application Programming Interface (Win32 API) The set of low-level functions used by Windows to perform tasks. Every Windows application relies on these functions to interact with the operating system and associated device drivers.

Windows Management Instrumentation (WMI) A Windows service and interface that helps an administrator or developer remotely monitor, control, and configure workstations or servers through the WMI database. This particular technology falls into the agent category and is very common on many network operating systems. An agent (special files executing on the client machine) allows the server to gain access to client machine resources and configuration information. Obviously, only machines that have the agent installed are accessible to the requestor.

Windows Management Interface Command line (WMIC) A utility used to execute changes against the Windows Management Instrumentation (WMI) database.

Wireless Access Point (WAP) A network connection for a mobile device that relies on a wireless Network Interface Card (NIC). There are many different protocols for wireless, so it's important to match the WAP to the NIC for the mobile device.

WMI See Windows Management Instrumentation (WMI)

WMIC See Windows Management Interface Command line (WMIC)

WMSvc Web Management Service

WSDL See Web Services Description Language (WSDL)

XML See eXtensible Markup Language (XML)

XML Path (XPath) A language used to select nodes in an XML document. In addition, a developer can use XPath to compute values based on the content of an XML document. XPath is a World Wide Web Consortium (W3C) standardized XML technology.

XML Schema Definition (XSD) The portion of the eXtensible Markup Language (XML) specification that defines data types and other data elements. Most browsers and other applications use XSD to verify the XML document. XSD is also related to a Web site containing such information by use of XML parsers. A designer can create a custom XSD for use with a particular application.

XP See eXtreme Programming (XP)

XPath See XML Path (XPath)

XSD See XML Schema Definition (XSD)

XSLT See eXtensible Stylesheet Language Transformation (XSLT)

ZIP A file that acts as a container for other files. The ZIP normally provides some level of data compression to make the resulting package smaller than the individual files. Most versions of Windows (starting with Windows XP) provide built-in support for the ZIP file.

Index

A

C

D

E

G

H

I

J

K

L

M

N

P

U

V

X

Y

Z